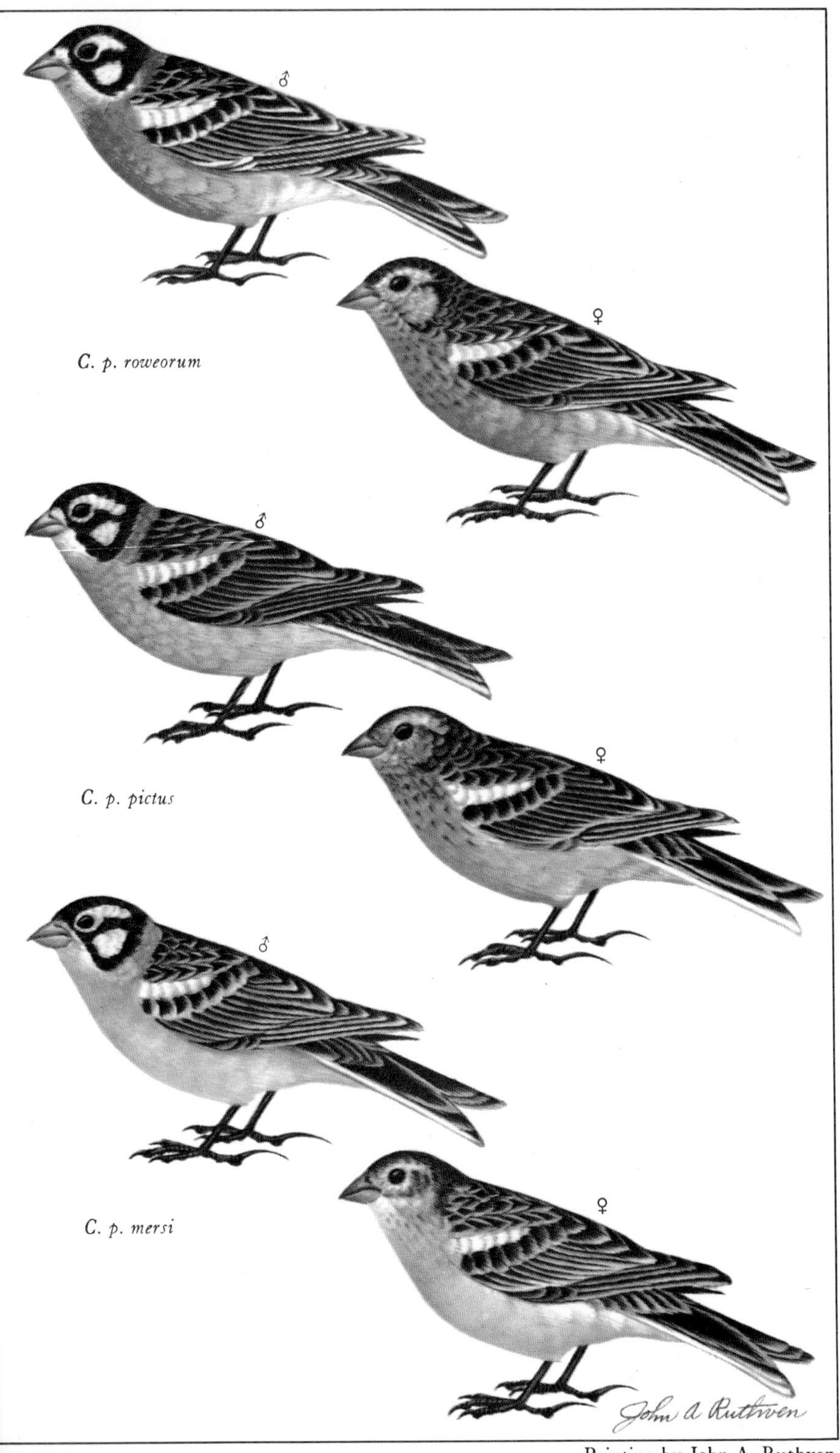

Painting by John A. Ruthven

Life Histories of North American Cardinals, Grosbeaks, Buntings, Towhees, Finches, Sparrows, and Allies

Order Passeriformes: Family Fringillidae

PART THREE

Genera Zonotrichia through Emberiza
Literature Cited and Index

ARTHUR CLEVELAND BENT and COLLABORATORS

Compiled and Edited by

OLIVER L. AUSTIN, JR.

Florida State Museum, University of Florida
Research Associate, Smithsonian Institution

DOVER PUBLICATIONS, INC., NEW YORK

Published in Canada by General Publishing Company, Ltd., 30 Lesmill Road, Don Mills, Toronto, Ontario.
Published in the United Kingdom by Constable and Company, Ltd., 10 Orange Street, London WC 2.

This Dover edition, first published in 1968, is an unabridged and unaltered republication of the work originally published in 1968 by the Smithsonian Institution Press as United States National Museum *Bulletin 237*.

International Standard Book Number: 0-486-21979-8
Library of Congress Catalog Card Number: 68-55072

Manufactured in the United States of America

DOVER PUBLICATIONS, INC.
180 Varick Street
New York, N. Y. 10014

Publication of the United States National Museum

The scientific publications of the United States National Museum include two series, *Proceedings of the United States National Museum* and *United States National Museum Bulletin.*

In these series are published original articles and monographs dealing with the collections and work of the Museum and setting forth newly acquired facts in the fields of Anthropology, Biology, Geology, History, and Technology. Copies of each publication are distributed to libraries and scientific organizations and to specialists and others interested in the different subjects.

The *Proceedings*, begun in 1878, are intended for the publication, in separate form, of shorter papers. These are gathered in volumes, octavo in size, with the publication of each paper recorded in the table of contents of the volume.

In the *Bulletin* series, the first of which was issued in 1875, appear longer, separate publications consisting of monographs (occasionally in several parts) and volumes in which are collected works on related subjects. *Bulletins* are either octavo or quarto in size, depending on the needs of the presentation. Since 1902 papers relating to the botanical collections of the Museum have been published in the *Bulletin* series under the heading *Contributions from the United States National Herbarium.* Since 1959, in *Bulletins* titled "Contributions from the Museum of History and Technology," have been gathered shorter papers relating to the collections and research of that museum.

This work forms number 237, parts 1–3, of the *Bulletin* series.

FRANK A. TAYLOR,
Director, United States National Museum.

NOTE ON THE FRONTISPIECE: The A.O.U. Check-List Committee has not as yet assessed the validity of the three races of Smith's longspur proposed in 1961. For further details of recent investigations see page 1634.—O.L.A.,Jr.

Publication of the United States National Museum

The scientific publications of the United States National Museum include two series, *Proceedings of the United States National Museum* and *United States National Museum Bulletin*.

In these series are published original articles and monographs dealing with the collections and work of the Museum and setting forth newly acquired facts in the fields of Anthropology, Biology, Geology, History, and Technology. Copies of each publication are distributed to libraries and scientific organizations and to specialists and others interested in the different subjects.

The *Proceedings*, begun in 1878, are intended for the publication, in separate form, of shorter papers. These are gathered in volumes, octavo in size, with the publication date of each paper recorded in the table of contents of the volume.

In the *Bulletin* series, the first of which was issued in 1875, appear longer, separate publications consisting of monographs (occasionally in several parts) and volumes in which are collected works on related subjects. *Bulletins* are either octavo or quarto in size, depending on the needs of the presentation. Since 1902 papers relating to the botanical collections of the Museum have been published in the *Bulletin* series under the heading *Contributions from the United States National Herbarium*. Since 1959, in *Bulletins* titled "Contributions from the Museum of History and Technology," have been gathered shorter papers relating to the collections and research of that Museum.

This work forms number [illegible] of the *Bulletin* series.

FRANK A. TAYLOR
Director, United States National Museum

Note on the [illegible] O.H. [illegible] the validity of the three names of Smith's [illegible] 1961. For further details [illegible] see [illegible]

Contents

PART THREE

List of Plates

PART THREE

ZONOTRICHIA QUERULA (Nuttall)

Harris' Sparrow

PLATE 68

Contributed by A. MARGUERITE BAUMGARTNER

HABITS

It was on a crisp June day in 1933 among the stunted spruces and the reindeer moss of the timberline at Churchill on Hudson Bay that I made the acquaintance of my first Harris' sparrow. I was captivated at once by the bold black hood and pink bill, the plaintive, melodious, two-toned whistle, and the shy, gentle ways of this large handsome sparrow of the middle west. A bird of mystery, I was in the heart of its breeding grounds where that veteran explorer, Edward A. Preble, had discovered young just out of the nest in 1900, and where George M. Sutton had found and described the eggs for the first time in 1930. By 1933 not a dozen men had seen the nest and beautiful speckled blue-green eggs of these elusive creatures.

It was a great satisfaction to renew their acquaintance in 1939 when we moved to the heart of their winter range in Oklahoma. Although they migrate through the plains states in enormous numbers and have been banded by the thousands in spring and fall, they are still birds of mystery. Only a handful have been studied through a winter, and none over a period of years. Perhaps it was a designing fate, certainly a happy coincidence, that led us after several years in town, to establish our permanent home on an acreage near Stillwater where Harris' sparrows shared our lawn and picnic place, our weedy chicken yard, and the brushy ravine that wound through our little pasture. These birds of mystery became our closest neighbors, constant guests at our winter feeding trays, and regular visitors to our banding traps.

From its earliest history Harris' Sparrow has been surrounded by an aura of excitement and drama. Because its distribution is restricted to the center of the continent, not until 1834 did the eager eyes of science view it for the first time. Harry Harris (1919) relates in fascinating detail how two separate parties of explorers discovered the species within two weeks and a few miles of one another. On an expedition headed westward across Missouri with John K. Townsend, Thomas Nuttall (1840) collected a bird on Apr. 28, 1834, that he subsequently named the "Mourning Finch," *Fringilla querula*. On May 13th the same year, Maximilian, Prince of Wied (1841), returning from an exploration of the upper Missouri River, likewise encountered the migrating flocks of these large handsome sparrows in southeastern

Nebraska. He collected specimens that he described in his account of the trip as *Fringilla comata*.

Each of these men delayed publishing his discoveries, Nuttall for 6 years, Maximilian for 7 years. Meanwhile John James Audubon completed the Elephant Folio of his epochal "Birds of America" without this interesting species. Traveling up the Missouri by steamship in 1843, Audubon and his companion, Edward Harris, saw the bird for the first time near Fort Leavenworth, Kans. Harris collected specimens and Audubon, unaware that it had already been discovered and named twice, described it in the octavo edition of his "Birds of America" (1843) as *Fringilla harrisii* in honor of his "excellent and constant friend." While the priority of Nuttall's specific name *querula* is clearly established, his singularly appropriate "mourning finch" was superceded through usage by Audubon's vernacular name.

Little was learned during the next 40 years of the distribution or the life history of these elusive birds. Believed originally to nest in the type area, it was soon realized that the birds found there were migrants. The careful work of Wells W. Cooke (1884) established the eastern limit of their range in the United States and its center roughly paralleling the 96th meridian, but its western and southern boundaries remained vague. The wealth of faunal and local studies of the ensuing three-quarters of a century have defined the normal winter range more precisely and showed stragglers dispersing widely into almost every state of the Union.

The summer home of the Harris' sparrow remained mere conjecture until Edward A. Preble (1902) found it breeding at Churchill. Preble (1908b) also found it in 1903 along the eastern shore of Great Bear Lake "in a habitat precisely similar to its chosen nesting ground on Hudson Bay. All indications therefore point to the conclusion that its principal breeding grounds are in the strip of stunted timber extending for 800 miles between Hudson Bay and Great Bear Lake, along the northern border of the transcontinental forest."

Ernest Thompson Seton (1908) verified Preble's conclusions when he found the species common from Great Slave Lake northward to the edge of the Barren Grounds, and discovered a nest with young almost ready to leave on August 5th. Other explorers in the North have added testimony, but without extending the birds' known breeding range.

Spring.—During spring migration Harris' sparrows spread out over a wide area that includes most of the central United States. The species then occurs regularly, though sparingly, from northern Illinois and southern Wisconsin to eastern Colorado, Montana, and eastern Alberta east of the Continental Divide. William Youngworth

Churchill, Manitoba J. R. Crittenden

NEST AND EGGS OF HARRIS' SPARROW

Churchill, Manitoba, June 25, 1947 A. S. Judd

NEST AND EGGS OF WHITE-CROWNED SPARROW

(1959) notes that these birds were found originally only in the upper Missouri River valley, but that during the past 60 years they have spread eastward and are now regular, though uncommon, migrants down the upper Mississippi River valley as well.

The northward movement begins in the southern parts of the winter range in late February and early March, surges into Nebraska and Iowa by mid-March, and into southeastern South Dakota by late March (Youngworth, 1959). Then occurs a pause first noted by Cooke (1913) before the birds move on into the Dakotas and Minnesota in late April and May (Swenk and Stevens, 1929). Thus no appreciable migration is evident beyond the winter range until May. As Orin A. Stevens (1957) notes: "In the spring Harris' Sparrows reach Fargo, North Dakota about May 7 * * * and are present about two weeks. It seems evident that both their arrival and length of stay are delayed by cold weather, and that their departure is hastened by a warm wave. They are restless and there are few repeat records of individual birds."

In their detailed study of the species, Myron H. Swenk and Orin A. Stevens (1929) note: "The vanguard arrives with remarkable uniformity during the first week in May or shortly thereafter at points over an area extending from the Dakotas to Minnesota and Manitoba. The passage of the vanguard across Saskatchewan, Alberta, and Northwest Territory to the breeding grounds of the species is made during the last half of May, though it is probably the middle of June before the migration of all the birds is completed."

Banding records show that some, at least, of the Harris' sparrows follow the same migration routes in spring and fall and in consecutive seasons, with occasionally the same stopovers. Other individuals, recovered from 25 to 100 miles on either side of their place of banding during a subsequent migration, manifestly shifted their migration path. Repeat records at banding stations (Swenk and Stevens, 1929) show that individuals may remain at given stopovers from 1 to 5 days during spring migration, averaging 1.5 days. In fall the periods are considerably longer, averaging 7 or 8 days, sometimes a month.

The speed at which Harris' sparrows migrate in spring is indicated by several recoveries in the Bird Banding files. A bird banded at Aberdeen, S. Dak., May 9, 1933, was recovered 325 miles away at Winnipeg, Man., 5 days later, having averaged 65 miles per day. Another banded at Ipswich, S. Dak., May 7, 1940, was taken 370 miles northward at Lake Manitoba 8 days later, having averaged 46 miles per day.

Nesting.—Almost a century after the discovery of Harris' sparrow on the Missouri prairies, the eggs of this handsome bird were still unknown to science. While a nest with young and fledglings just out of the nest had been collected and the breeding range roughly established, the region was virtually inaccessible during the nesting season. Completion of the railway to Fort Churchill opened a new world to ornithological exploration, and in 1930 Percy A. Taverner (Taverner and Sutton, 1934) found the birds common at the edge of timber a few miles south of the townsite. First noted on May 28, the birds became common by June 6. He found no eggs, but collected a nest with young on June 27. He last noted the species on September 5.

In 1931 two parties visited the Churchill area with the primary aim of finding the eggs of the Harris' sparrow. Most of the following information is summarized from the full and fascinating account by John B. Semple and George M. Sutton (1932) whose party discovered the first nest with eggs. On their way northward they observed Harris' sparrows in numbers at The Pas, Manitoba, 500 miles south of Churchill, on May 23. The train then preceded the migration and went from spring back to winter. On arrival at Churchill May 25 they found 2 feet of snow on the level and drifts 20 feet deep; temperatures ranged from 28° F. to about 60° F. during the day. They first observed Harris' sparrows there on May 27. Though the males were in full song, females collected showed unenlarged ovaries.

During late May and early June they saw numbers of birds daily on the barrens along the river, several miles from spruce timber; these they subsequently termed migrants on their way to more northwesterly regions. Of the nesting habitat at timberline they write: "We found the birds most common at the edges of the woodlands, in clearings near the railway track, and in the bushy margins of burned-over areas. As a rule but one pair of birds lived in a given patch of spruces or tamaracks; but sometimes two or three pairs inhabited the same narrow tongue of forest.

"By June 7, we had at least thirty pairs more or less definitely located in an area of five square miles; we had not, however, witnessed a single action indicative of nest building." In an atmosphere tense with keen but friendly competition, both between the two parties and the men within each group, the birds continued to act indecisively. The weather continued backward and the search continued fruitless. Semple and Sutton (1932) continue:

We watched certain pairs by the hour, and found them so amazingly noncommital about what we supposed to be their "territory" that we began to wonder whether we were anywhere near the actual nesting grounds. The birds would feed together for long periods in the morning, walking along among the moss and grass; kicking vigorously, like Fox Sparrows, through leaves and debris; then mount the low bushes, wipe their bills quickly, and fly to some far-distant part of the woodlands, where it was often impossible to find them. Sometimes, indeed, they became mildly excited at our presence; whereupon they would begin *weenking* loudly; but they usually soon lost interest, wiped their bills, shook themselves, and dashed off, leaving us to wonder where their nest could be. Frequently we found them feeding in tamarack trees; they appeared to be eating the buds. They were very graceful in their movements, climbing about on the slender, outermost twigs, and bowing this way and that like crossbills. Sometimes a single bird would fly suddenly from the ground under a bush, as if it had just come from a nest. Such a bird usually sought a rather high perch, often the top of a dead spruce near-by, where it would give itself over to a spasm of alarm notes, loud enough to summon all the yammering Lesser Yellow-legs from miles around; then it would dart away, to be seen no more. The habit of the birds, when frightened from the ground, of flying to rather high perches was characteristic.

By mid-June, all the birds we observed in the woodlands appeared to be mated. At this season the males so frequently sang in a chorus that it was sometimes difficult to separate a single song from the medley which sounded through the woods.

*   *   *   *   *   *

On June 15, a bird carrying a wisp of dry grass was observed to go to the ground somewhere near the base of a large spruce stump in a grove of live spruce trees which grew near a small lake and on rather high ground. Though a prolonged search was made, the nest was not found. We were torn, that evening, between high enthusiasm and frank exasperation, for we knew that there must be a nest somewhere in the vicinity and we also knew we had not found it!

To George Miksch Sutton of the Carnegie Museum-Cornell University party fell the honor and good fortune of discovering the first nest. He later describes (1936) in his inimitable style the personal feelings of an ornithologist at such a moment: "As I knelt to examine the nest a thrill the like of which I had never felt before passed through me. And I talked aloud! 'Here!' I said. 'Here in this beautiful place!' At my fingertips lay treasures that were beyond price. Mine was Man's first glimpse of the eggs of the Harris's Sparrow, in the lovely bird's wilderness home."

Returning to the Semple and Sutton (1932) account:

The circumstances of the finding were these: After watching a certain pair of birds for a time, the junior author started across a wet, open spruce woods, bound for an area a mile distant which the birds were known to frequent. Just as he entered a clump of comparatively tall spruce trees, he noticed a Harris's Sparrow picking at its belly with its beak, as if it had just come from a nest. He watched the bird for a time without moving, and then deliberately and quietly retraced his steps, marking the spot carefully. After about fifteen minutes he returned briskly, walked noisily through the water, the mossy mounds, and bushes, and, just as he was about to set foot upon the crest of one of the water-bound hummocks—he flushed the bird. The nest was less than twelve inches from his foot. The bird flew directly from the nest, without any attempt at feigning injury; it perched on a dead spruce bough about twenty yards away, where it wiped its bill. It gave no alarm note. The bird, a female, was collected at once, to make identification certain.

The nest, like that found by Ernest Thompson Seton (1908), was lined with grass, and in appearance and location resembled that of a White-throated Sparrow. It was placed a little to the southward of the top of a mossy, shrub-covered, water-girt mound in a cool, shadowy spot, about thirty yards from the edge of a clump of rather tall spruce trees. It was about thirteen inches above the brown water which surrounded the mound. The foundation material was largely moss, with a few leaves, slender weed stalks, and grasses; the lining was entirely of grass. The cup was 1¾ inches deep and 2¾ inches in diameter, as measured in the field. The walls were rather thin, for the moss into which the nest was built was very deep and soft. The eggs were sheltered from above by a few sprigs of Narrow-leaved Labrador Tea which were then in bud. The male bird was not seen. The clump of trees where this nest was found was in the forest about two miles back from the edge of the Barren Grounds; the woods were open, however, and the mossy, grassy spaces between the patches of trees had much the appearance of tundra.

During the next 3 weeks they found nine additional nests which they describe as follows: "The nests were built chiefly of grass, with a lining of finer grass (no hair, feathers, or plant down of any sort) and were situated usually in mossy hummocks among the stunted spruce trees, often on a small 'island,' under some sort of low shrub, and on a sheltered, southern exposure."

Frank L. Farley of Camrose, Alberta, who led the Canadian party and spent many subsequent summers in the Churchill region recorded similar observations. Quoting from a letter he wrote to Mr. Bent in July 1937:

"I found three good sets of Harris sparrows and got onto some of their secrets. I had formerly searched in the woods for their nests, but this year learned that they invariably nest in open growths, but *always* near enough a good-sized spruce tree so as to use it as a lookout for intruders. On the tops, or in the tops of these, they peer out at you as you approach, always thinking they are entirely hidden in the branches. We found the 3 nests all within 100 feet of good-sized lakes and all nests were under dwarf trees, one under a small tamarack 2 feet high, the second under a little spruce 2 feet high, and the third under a pretty little arctic willow shrub, not more than 2 feet high. We found one of the nests nearly a mile from any fair sized spruce woods. If one can find both birds, neither on the nest, it is a good bet that if one watches long enough you will see the bird drop to the ground from its look-out spruce, and then after waiting for 10 minutes, you may be able to flush it within 100 feet of the tree. The birds flush at very close quarters; my three all left hurriedly when I approached within 3 feet of the nests. The nest is always sunken into the ground and is bulky, made of coarse rootlets and last year's heavy grass stems for an outer covering, lined with fine grasses. I have never seen a feather used as lining as the Lapland Longspur and Horned Larks do. In some of the nests small pieces of moss are placed in the outer lining. After the birds know that the nest has been found, they both disappear not to return while you are near. They are the most secretive of any of the small birds I know and do not like the presence of humans near their summer homes."

Because of the secretive nature of these shy birds, neither these first parties nor subsequent visitors to the area were able to observe details of courtship, nest building, or length of incubation. Of birds collected as they flushed from the nest, all were females. In some cases only one bird was found near the nest; in other instances the male bird was on guard in the tip of a nearby spruce and gave the alarm. At Nest 4 with four eggs, (Semple and Sutton, 1932), a female flushed at 5 feet was found, upon dissection, to contain a fully formed egg in the oviduct, indicating a tendency to set before the full clutch is deposited. During early incubation the females flushed off at 3 to 10 feet, and refused to return as long as intruders remained in the area. Later the birds returned in half an hour or so.

Olin S. Pettingill (Semple and Sutton, 1932) describes ruefully the bird's behavior at another of the nests as follows:

> I set up my blind five feet away from the nest and attempted to make photographs. * * * The birds continued to *wink*, one *continuously*, during my presence. After 1½ hours one of the birds sang for a while a short distance away and returned suddenly to continue with the racket.
>
> For three hours I remained in the blind. I could see no indication throughout my stay that either parent would approach the nest. Both birds passed from one tree to another around the blind, making this circling a continuous performance. Not once did they drop to the ground nor come any nearer than this particular circle of trees. During the last hour I remained in the blind, the birds were as excited as they were the first hour. Had I been standing there without a blind they probably would have been no more alarmed. I feel sure that if I had left the blind near the nest the birds would have deserted.

Arthur A. Allen (1951) comments, "* * * the bird is so wary that photography is extremely difficult; our single picture of the bird on its nest gave us more trouble than any other. We spent nearly a week getting the bird accustomed to the blind, and then at the first click of the shutter she left and did not return until I gave up after two hours of waiting." In retrospect, I feel more fortunate than I realized at the time, to have "caught" a single photograph of another of Allen's nests in the summer of 1934. Possibly because the incubation period was well advanced, this bird returned to her nest within half an hour after the "go-way-ster" had departed and the neophyte photographer had endured the 10,000th mosquito. At any rate, it afforded an excellent opportunity to observe these handsome birds at close range, to compare the plumages of the male and his definitely duller mate, and to admire the artistry of their carefully concealed home among the gray-green lichens and sprigs of arctic crowberry.

Eggs.—The Harris' sparrow usually lays from 3 to 5 ovate eggs and they are slightly glossy. The ground may be white or greenish-white, heavily speckled, spotted, and blotched with "Natal brown," "Rood's brown," "Mar's brown," or "russet." One set in the

Museum of Comparative Zoology is very pale greenish white, heavily marked with spots, blotches, and a few scrawls that practically obscure the ground. Another set is dirty white with fine specklings over the entire egg. In markings and coloring, they are very similar to those of the white-crowned sparrow, but average slightly larger. The measurements of 46 eggs average 22.2 by 16.7 millimeter; the eggs showing the four extremes measure *24.7* by 16.4, 26.6 by *17.8*, *20.3* by 16.1, and 21.5 by *15.0* millimeter.

Of the 10 nests found in 1931 (Semple and Sutton, 1932), 6 contained four eggs or young, 2 contained five, and 2 had three. Farley (corres.) says: "I would say that four eggs is the usual number laid. Of 5 nests found in the last 3 years, 4 nests had 4 eggs and only 1 had 5." Only one brood is reared in this subarctic setting, though nests destroyed by untimely snow storms may be replaced as late as June 18.

Young.—The length of the incubation period has only recently been determined by Joseph R. Jehl, Jr., and D. J. T. Russell (1966) who state: "Minimum incubation period for one nest 13½ days, computed from laying of fourth to hatching of third egg; the fourth egg did not hatch." Little has been recorded of the development of young Harris' sparrows beyond descriptions of the plumage. The only observation on nest life that has been indicated is that both parents are in attendance. Perhaps when the life histories of our commoner and more easily-studied summer birds have all been put on record, some intrepid young student will elect to fill in the many remaining gaps in our knowledge of this bird of mystery.

Plumages.—Edward A. Preble (1902) first described the juvenal plumage of Harris' sparrow from those he collected at Fort Churchill on July 24, 1900, as follows: "Upper parts dusky black, the feathers edged with deep buffy and brown, the black predominating on crown, the brown on hind neck, and the black and brown about equally divided on back; outer wing quills edged with deep buffy, inner with brown; tail feathers edged and tipped with whitish; sides of head and lower parts buffy; chest and side streaked with black, which is most conspicuous on sides of chest and forms a prominent malar stripe; upper throat grayish white, with fine dusky markings."

Margaret M. Nice (1929) notes: "Among Preble's and Seton's specimens in the American Museum there are ten birds collected near Great Slave Lake in September. One, taken September 4, is a full grown bird in the nestling plumage. The others all have white chins and throats. Their crowns differ a good deal, but all have a more or less scaled appearance, for the feathers are black centrally, margined with pale grayish buffy; in the least mature birds the effect is predominantly buffy."

I recall the young birds I saw at Churchill during the summers of 1933 and 1934 as recognizably Harris' sparrows in a typical young fringillid pattern, streaky dark above, not radically different from the first winter plumage, and heavily streaked below on the throat, chest, sides, and flanks. The lower belly is white.

Winter plumages.—Three typical plumages occur in Harris' sparrows during their stay in the United States: (1) The white-throated, buffy immature with crown feathers broadly margined with buff and wide, buffy, superciliary stripe giving the bird an overall brownish cast. (2) The black-throated darker adult with crown wider and blacker, and the feathers less conspicuously margined with gray or buff, giving a sharper contrast above and below. (3) The full breeding plumage with complete black hood, gray cheeks, and dark postauricular spot acquired by a partial molt of all birds during March and April. (As characteristic of the genus and most of the family, the flight feathers and rectrices are replaced only in the complete postnuptial molt.)

Between these three typical plumages occurs a wide variety of intergradations, some almost impossible to catalogue as adult or immature. Crown feathers may be broadly margined over the entire crown, lightly margined, partially at forehead or rear, or almost solid black. White throats may be flecked, blotched, or patched with black; black throats may be flecked or patched with white until it is difficult to say which is the basic color. A number of birds have the black throat partially or broadly separated from the dark chest patch by a white band.

Considerable attention has been given these "intermediate" plumages. Robert Ridgway (1901) suggests that the birds with broadly margined crown feathers and a mixture of black and white in the throat and chin might be in their second winter, in a 3-year progression toward fully adult plumage. Swenk and Stevens (1929) elaborate on this theory, noting that about 80 percent of the migrating individuals in October and November exhibit these characteristics. Mrs. Nice (1929a) expresses surprise at the relatively small proportion of "black-hooded birds" in the wintering flocks at Norman, Okla. She raises the question as to the age at which this characteristic may be retained throughout the year and exhorts banders to solve the riddle. While operating banding stations near Stillwater, Okla., P. J. Park (1936), C. E. Harkins (1937), and G. M. Steelman and K. E. Herde (1937) consecutively made detailed observations of plumages and the prenuptial molt. They accept the 3-year age sequence theory, but while their work carefully details the progression of the plumages through a season, the few return records of birds from previous years are insufficient to substantiate any such conclusions.

My own studies at Stillwater, Okla., over an 18-year period indicate that much of this variation and intergradation in winter plumages is due to sheer individual variation, some to minor sex differences. Between February 1948 and May 1965, I banded at Stillwater a total of 1,722 Harris' sparrows, of which 121 individuals (50 banded as adults, 66 as immatures) returned a total of 204 times from 1 to 6 years after banding. Observations on their plumages may be summarized as follows:

Crown.—Adult birds (the 50 banded as adults and all returning birds) showed no consistent sequence from year to year in the amount of edging on the crown feathers or the amount of black, unveiled crown. Some birds banded as immatures returned the following winter (R–1) with crowns only lightly edged with gray and as much as half jet black. Others returned consistently year after year (R–1–2–3–4) with a heavy veiling over the crown and only a small black area on the forehead. Some varied from winter to winter from heavy to light and vice versa.

Superciliary stripe.—None of the returns had the broad, buffy "eyebrows" almost meeting on the forehead that characterize the first winter plumage.

Throat.—Birds whose throats were more than half white, with black flecks, blotches, or patches, usually showed the buffy "eyebrows" and were designated immatures. Adult birds with basically black throats displayed four throat patterns as follows: (1) Throat finely flecked black and white ("salt and pepper"). (2) Throat black with white blotches or patches. (3) Broad or partial white band separating black of throat and chest. (4) Typical adult all-black throat. These patterns occured indiscriminately in R–1 birds banded as immatures and in 6-year olds, in very small females (?) and very large males (?).

Lores.—Each fall I described in my records a number of birds as conspicuously big and black, or with lores, as well as throat and crown black, almost approximating the black hood of the breeding plumage. Of eight returns so described, all but one had been banded as adults and must have been in at least their third winter. Yet one banded in immature plumage showed the black hood early in the winter of his first return. In other cases I noted R–2 and R–3 birds with buffy lores, so that this appearance of the black hood cannot be associated consistently with old birds.

My records show that, far more often than not, individual birds retained their particular adult pattern from year to year, through one or more returns. They show no evidence whatever of a 3-year sequence of plumage patterns from first winter to full adult.

A single adult bird at Stillwater exhibited a reversal to its immature plumage in the second winter. Banded as an immature Dec. 2, 1962,

I described it on its R–1 return Feb. 13, 1964, as: "Typically immature plumage—crown heavily veiled, eye-line wide and buffy, throat white with only a few flecky lines radiating down from the dark chin, breast dark splotched, tail heavily frayed but white edging showing slightly." Victor Vacin has written me of a single similar "puzzler" among his 306 return records.

Molt.—Certain characteristics are acquired gradually through the winter. In immature birds the black fringe of the chin frequently appears during December and January, and Swenk and Stevens (1929) note it in some as early as October and November. In adults the buffy edges of the black loral feathers wear off and leave the bird dark-faced, not too unlike the black hood of the breeding plumage. Dark flecks may appear in the superciliary stripe by early February.

The prenuptial molt begins about the middle of March (earliest Mar. 3, 1951) and continues through most of April. By April 25 young and old are indistinguishable in velvet black hoods, gray cheeks, and fresh white feathers of chests and sides. The sequence of this molt is from chin and forehead (if not already black) to throat, crown, nape, and cheeks. New quills may appear in the chest and sides of some birds several weeks in advance of other areas. In first-year birds the superciliary stripe is frequently the last clue to immaturity, remaining a patchy buff and black until April or early May. Last to molt is the postauricular spot, which turns from brown to black.

An individual bird completes the molt in about a month. One individual I handled daily throughout the spring showed no quills until April 13; by May 9 this bird wore the full black hood, though still in heavy quills. Individuals traced by Mrs. Nice (1929a) at Norman, Okla., and a stray bird at Berkeley, Calif., by Russell H. Pray (1950) followed the same sequence. Young and old pass through the molt at the same time. First signs of molt in the spring have been observed some years in adult birds, in other years in immatures. While an occasional old return may be in full breeding plumage before the end of April, I also have notations on R–1s such as "molting head, chin, throat" on May 3, and "almost through molt" on May 14.

External sex differences.—Sex differences in plumage and measurements are slight and overlap considerably. In general the largest, stoutest, brightest birds are males and the smallest, most drab are females. The crown tends to be wider in males, narrower in females. A goodly number of intermediates cannot be sexed with certainty by external examination, though familiarity with the species increases awareness of minute differences. On my field cards I have hazarded guesses for as many as possible, resexing at each repeat or return. In some cases "immature females" have returned the next year as large, plump, glossy "adult males," but more frequently the guess has remained consistent. In birds killed by shrikes or found dead, dissection has proved the guess correct more often than not.

Male wing and tail measurements average slightly longer than female, and those of adults slightly longer than first-year birds of the same sex, but with too much overlap to be used for certain sex identification.

Weights.—During three winters at Stillwater, Okla., I weighed birds at the time of banding and at intervals throughout the season on scales accurate to .065 grams. The 754 weights recorded for 200 individuals between November and May reveal definite weight patterns for the species that can be correlated with age, migration, molt, and seasonal temperature.

Adult weights showed extremes of 28.4 to 48.8 grams and averaged 36.4 grams; immatures averaged 2 grams lighter at 34.4 grams, with extremes from 26.2 to 44.9. Weights of individual birds varied up to about 3 grams during the course of a day: lightest in the early morning, heaviest at dusk.

The seasonal trend was a rise from low weights on arrival in early November to comparative highs during the cold months of January and February, followed by a pronounced drop in March that lasted through April into early May. The May averages increased consistently and then soared sharply the last 2 or 3 days before departure. Monthly averages showed adults varying almost 4 grams from a low of 34.9 in March to a 38.8 gram high at departure in May; immature monthly averages varied almost 5 grams from an April low of 32.2 to a departure high of 37.0 grams.

Individuals not uncommonly varied as much as 8.0 to 8.5 grams during their stay, more than 20 percent of their average body weight. One small immature (presumably a female) that weighed 28.4 grams when banded Apr. 21, 1950, gained 7.3 grams to 35.7 grams by May 11. She returned the next fall, still classed as small at 32.3 grams. She gained only a gram during January and February, and dropped back to a normal 32.6 through April and the first fortnight of May. Between May 14 and 18 she shot up 5.2 grams to 37.8, a gain of 16 percent in less than a week. Converted into human terms these figures become spectacular—they compare to a woman of 120 pounds putting on another 20 pounds in the week preceding a vacation trip.

Food.—Food habits of the Harris' sparrows during their stay in the United States were thoroughly studied by Sylvester D. Judd (1901), who analyzed the contents of 100 stomachs for the U.S. Biological Survey. He reports that these birds subsist chiefly on vegetable matter, which constitutes 92 percent of the total food; 48 percent of the food is weed seeds including ragweed, smartweed, knotweed, black bindweed, pigweed, lambs'-quarters, gromwell, and sunflower; 25 percent of the food is the seeds of wild fruits and of various miscellaneous plants; 10 percent is grain, chiefly waste corn, but also including wheat and oats; and 9 percent is grass seed, mainly that of blue-grass, beard-grass, foxtail-grass, and Johnson-grass. The 8 percent of animal matter consists of insects, spiders, and snails, with a marked preference for leaf-hoppers among the insects constituting 2 percent of the total food. Additional animal foods quoted from various sources by Swenk and Stevens (1929) include grasshoppers, beetles, insect larvae, red ants, black carpenter ants, wire-worms, and moths.

Mrs. Nice (1929a) observes that in Oklahoma they feed on poison ivy berries and elm blossoms as well as weed seeds. We also noted this at Stillwater, and found that when the Chinese elm was in bud and bloom in late February, the birds spent considerable time in these trees. In Nebraska they are reported to take corn from the fallen ears in the fall.

At feeding stations they may be attracted by almost any small grain—canary and sunflower seed, hemp, millet, grain sorghum, chick-scratch, cracked corn, also occasional suet and crumbs. They have shown no interest whatsoever in wheat. A stray bird that wintered at Berkeley, Calif. (Pray, 1950) was found to nibble on suet, finely chopped meat, weed seed, breakfast cereal, both plain and baked with kitchen fat, but not sunflower seed. By far the greatest amount of feeding was done in the tops of the live oaks, where animal food appeared to be taken. Grass and pyracantha berries were also eaten occasionally.

In the summer a higher percentage of their food is animal matter, though they are still largely vegetarian. From Semple and Sutton (1932) comes the only information:

The Harris's Sparrow is primarily a ground feeder. It kicks and scratches energetically among the fallen leaves and dry weedstalks, and works its way through the grass and moss searching carefully for seeds and insects as it goes. We rarely saw the birds feeding for a very long period anywhere above the ground. They were sometimes seen in tamarack trees, however, where they appeared to be finding some sort of insect, or perhaps insect eggs, in the clusters of leaves.

We preserved the stomachs of several of the specimens collected, and six of these have been examined by the Bureau of the Biological Survey of the U.S. Department of Agriculture. According to the report given to us by Mr. Clarence Cottam of his identification of material found, the birds consume considerably more vegetable matter (about 66%) than animal matter. Among the vegetable matter found were seeds of various grasses, sedges and bulrushes; seeds of fruit-pulp of the curlew-berry, cranberry or an allied form, and the blueberry; seeds of birch, pigweed, and lamb's quarters; and a considerable quantity of oats which doubtless had been found by the birds along the railway tracks.

Among the animal matter found were remains of numerous insects, both in adult and larval stages—ground-beetles, leaf-eating beetles, wood-borers, click-beetles, leaf-miners, stink-bugs, small moths, horse-flies, ants, ichneumon-flies, crickets and other forms; several small spiders; and fragments of small snails and other mollusks.

The food of nestlings has not yet been studied. Presumably these birds follow the fringillid pattern, feeding their young on the insect life which abounds in their northern home, with increasing quantities of grass and weed seed and miscellaneous vegetable matter as the young birds develop.

Economic status.—During its sojourn in the United States the feeding habits of the Harris' sparrow are completely beneficial. The hordes that pass through the Prairie States consume great quantities of weed and grass seeds, and molest nothing of any value to man. In the summer they are beyond the reaches of civilization, where the insects and seeds they devour, however noxious, are of no concern. Thus the Middle West is blessed with a species both charming and blameless, to welcome and cherish without reservation.

Behavior.—Of their habits on the wintering grounds Mrs. Nice (1929a) writes:

Harris Sparrows are preeminently birds of underbrush; they frequent thick shrubbery along creeks and at the edge of woods, especially trees that are covered with vines. When alarmed, they, like Tree Sparrows, fly up, instead of diving into depths of cover as Song and Lincoln Sparrows do. They often perch high in trees, a characteristic not shown by any of our other wintering sparrows except Tree Sparrows and an occasional Fox Sparrow. Harris and Tree Sparrows and Juncos stay in flocks, mostly of their own species, all winter, while Song and Lincoln Sparrows are solitary.

* * * * * * *

In general we have found that *Zonotrichia querula* drove away smaller birds to some extent, but suffered, itself, from a special animosity from Cardinals. On April 29, I noted: "A Harris Sparrow is hopping about the kitchen door getting crumbs. He is a loquacious creature, chattering to himself, stopping every now and then to give a fragment of his sweet song. A young English Sparrow happens to come near—he flies at it viciously!"

* * * * * * *

January 19. Distinguished guests today—three Harris Sparrows arrive, all in the palest plumage. One is a tyrant, driving away the other birds; after he has eaten enough he settles down upon the water dish and rests, while five English Sparrows, the White-crown, the Plumbeous Chickadees and two of his own kind sit about in the bushes and wait.

* * * Number 9 had an amusing habit of sunning himself on the shelf, lying down stretched out to the left, even doing this while eating. Later O sunned himself, but the other birds never did. Sometimes O chased 5 away, but in general they were amicable. They both sang a great deal during the last five days of their stay.

At Stillwater an old Harris' sparrow, returned for his fourth season, discovered our weathervane feeder in the front yard and spent most of a cold, snowy month in it. After feeding, he would fluff up his feathers, close his eyes, and bask in the sun, safe within the glass enclosure, while the winds whipped the feeder around like a merry-go-round.

When feeding on the ground, the birds kick and scratch among the dead leaves and debris much like towhees and fox sparrows. When flushed, they fly out ahead of the intruder, lighting in the trees 50 to 100 feet ahead until he approaches again, passing and repassing one another, and finally circling back to their original weed patch. A flock frequently includes a mixture of Harris' and tree sparrows, juncos, goldfinches, a small number of song sparrows, and one or two cardinals.

At banding stations they are among the most charming and interesting of guests. Amiable, unsuspicious, easy to catch, quiet in the hand, they rarely struggle and never bite. When released, they often lie quietly in the outstretched hand, to the delight of visiting school children, and finally fly up to the nearest branch or bush.

Both in migration and on the wintering grounds, Harris' sparrows are proverbial repeaters. Swenk and Stevens (1929) and O. A. Stevens (1957) relate the frequency of their repeats to weather, their length of stay in the area, individual personality, and group habits. At Stillwater, birds whose territory lay near the traps repeated several times a day. Others repeated only occasionally in snowy weather, or not at all until another year, suggesting that they came from a greater distance and only when driven by food shortage.

Harris' sparrows appear to have personalities as variable as man himself. While some are quiet and meek, others are domineering and aggressive. Some are mild and easily handled, others become wild and difficult to catch in a trap. These latter I found became increasingly warier through the season, and developed characteristic patterns of evasion as recognizable as a color band or an albinistic feather. Eventually I caught the rest of the day's crop and let this one out the door on his own power. It is these wary individuals that escape the occasional shrike that gets into a trap. Their ability to dodge and dart, so exasperating when a cold, hungry bander is trying to empty his traps, means life and safety when the pursuer is a cold, hungry predator.

On the nesting grounds the birds become universally shy and wary, as previously discussed, so different from the innocent, unsuspicious behavior of many of their northern neighbors that one wonders what grizzly experience in migration may have altered their character.

Voice.—One of the pleasures of a home in rural Oklahoma is the flute-like chorus of the Harris' sparrows. Well named *querula,* the song has a tender, melancholy quality, and simplicity unique in my experience. Throughout the fall and winter an occasional plaintive, quavering, two-toned whistle can be heard from the weedy thicket beyond the garden, the underbrush along a roadside, fence row, or ravine. Fragmentary promise of spring, its ephemeral sweetness is broken by a hoarse chuckle or an imperious *cheenk!* During March the songs become more prolonged, with fewer of the grating notes, and by April the chorus is at its height, a source of delight throughout the migration period.

Mrs. Nice (1929) writes:

> Harris Sparrows have a wide repertoire in their winter home:
>
> 1. A gentle *tseep*, not often heard.
>
> 2. A loud staccato *tchip*, sometimes given singly, sometimes several in succession. This is the commonest call note. At night-fall a flock of Harris Sparrows will utter a great many of these notes, much like the bed-time hubbub of White-throats, but less loud and less prolonged. * * *
>
> 3. The querulous exclamation or "scold," a curious, grating, chuckling series, unlike any other bird note with which I am acquainted. It does not seem to indicate displeasure, but perhaps is conversational in nature. It is heard by itself and also during winter interspersed freely with the beautiful notes of the song. Nothing could be more incongruous than this mingling of serene beauty and absurd grumblings.
>
> 4. The song consists chiefly of clear minors of different pitches, besides which there is an occasional low husky note repeated three or four times. * * * In the following transcriptions of them h means high note; l, low note, i, intermediate in pitch; kee, husky note.
>
> hhhhh ll hhhh l ll hhhh lll hh ll ll hhhh ll hhh hhh lll hh ll l i hhh.
>
> hhhh ll ll h ll hhh ll i hh hhhh ll h lll kee kee kee kee scold scold hh ll ii hh i l.
>
> There was a very slight interval between phrases. High notes were given singly, in two's, three's, four's, and once five in succession. Low notes were given singly and in two's and three's.
>
> The most beautiful song of a Harris Sparrow in my experience was heard April 24, 1926 at 7 a.m., a mile from our grounds. I recorded a continuous song for about eight minutes, not, however, getting the beginning or end. * * * In this song there were only two pitches—high and low, and the husky note was absent; the general scheme seemed to be two or three high notes and then two low, but there were continual variations. There were never more than three high notes together; and only once, more than two low notes in a phrase. * * * Nothing could have been more perfect in its way. It was of exquisite sweetness, the very spirit of serenity and peace.

Aretas A. Saunders (corres.), who recorded five songs at Stillwater in 1955, states that "the notes of one song may be all on one pitch, or varied somewhat, from one-half tone to one and one-half tones. The pitch of songs varies from B5 to F6." (B in the second highest octave of the piano, F in the highest octave).

Swenk and Stevens (1929) who regard each phrase as a separate song, describe as follows several songs set to music by Mrs. Jane B. Swenk: "* * * one to five, usually two or three, whistled noted * * * all on the same high pitch (usually in the second octave above middle C) * * * followed after a very slight interval by one to four, commonly two or three, usually natural notes at a different pitch, at an interval of a half-step to a major third higher, but sometimes correspondingly lower * * *. In the spring this song is repeated over and over * * * for minutes at a time," producing what Mrs. Nice described above as "one continuous song."

On the nesting grounds, Semple and Sutton (1932) describe the summer song thus:

At this season the males so frequently sang in a chorus that it was sometimes difficult to separate a single song from the medley which sounded through the woods. The song most frequently heard was a single, whistled note, tenuous, fragile, a trifle quavering, and possessed of the plaintive character of the final *Peabody* phrases of the White-throated Sparrow's lay. Sometimes this note was repeated once, twice, even four or five times, the notes trailing into each other uncertainly. Other songs were more elaborate, and consisted of two notes at one pitch followed by two or three notes two steps higher, or two or three steps lower. Often the notes struck were not quite in key, this frequently being responsible, no doubt, for the minor effect the songs produced. The songs of several birds were sometimes so strikingly identical in pitch that a distant song sounded precisely like the echo of another song heard closer at hand.

In the morning, usually between eight and ten o'clock, and in the late afternoon or evening, when the weather was fine, all the birds sang together for long periods. Sometimes, indeed, the chorus continued practically all day long. During the regular song periods the performers often gave their songs with such regularity that two or three birds, singing at different pitches, sometimes produced simple tunes which were repeated again and again, unless some disturbance caused one of the singers to stop. One such tune, which the junior author heard and recognized instantly as part of the theme of a familiar classical composition [the first four measures of Schubert's *Minuet from the Sonata in G*, Opus 78, No. 3], was produced by at least two and possibly three birds. It was repeated, almost flawlessly, about twenty times.

The remarkable feature of this performance is, of course, that, though produced by two or three different birds, supposedly singing independently and at different pitches (liked belled horses at the circus), it kept so nearly true to a recognizable key note according to our diatonic scale.

Since we hesitated to collect birds whose nests we hoped to find later, we did not shoot any singing birds in an attempt to learn whether the female ever sings. Many times, however, we gained the impression that mated birds were singing to each other. One such case we noted on June 8. We were watching two birds which we assumed to be mates and which were feeding in a tamarack; one of them was smaller than the other, and the two seemed to be attached to each other. Suddenly feeding stopped and both began to sing, one in a lower, gentler voice than the other.

Harris's Sparrow has another, louder, and very striking song which we heard only occasionally. This song was so distinctly different from the usual whistle, and so suggestive of songs of some of the other species of sparrows, that for some time we could not place it. It began with a fine, swiftly descending, rather tuneless whistle or squeal, and closed with a series of from three to six rough, buzzing, drawled notes which decidedly resembled the usual song of the Clay-colored Sparrow (*Spizella pallida*). We wrote the song down thus: *Eeeeeeeeee, zhee, zhee, zhee, zhee, zhee.* We noticed that the bird usually gave this song from a high perch and that, after it had sung, it dropped to the ground stealthily or flew off hurriedly.

The alarm note was a loud *weenk*, or *wink*, readily distinguishable from the weaker *zheek* of Gambel's Sparrow and from the heavy *tchup* of the Fox Sparrow (*Passerella i. iliaca*). The call which accompanied mating was a fine, rolling chatter, similar to that given at such time by many other members of the sparrow tribe.

During late July and August (1934), when care of the young and the fall molt are sapping the vitality of most northern birds, we heard very little singing at Churchill. Seton (1908) notes that he "found the species in full song September 3" at Great Slave Lake. On migration during the fall they are generally silent. Thomas S. Roberts (1879) states that at Minneapolis, Minn., "I have never heard any song from them except on one occasion. That was in the fall, when a bird in the plumage of the year uttered a low, continuous warble as it sat on the top of a brush-pile. This was repeated many times, and reminded one somewhat of the subdued singing of the Tree Sparrow, often heard in the early spring."

Swenk and Stevens (1929) comment that when the southbound Harris' sparrows reach the region south of latitude 41°:

> * * * a region where the birds will linger in abundance from late September to late October, * * * their whole vocal behavior changes. The autumn is ordinarily a season when bird songs are conspicuous by their absence, but in the region mentioned the Harris's Sparrow sings as sweetly, if not as fully and volubly, in October as in May. It especially likes to sing in chorus in the evening, shortly before nightfall. At this season the song commonly consists of one or two drawling minor whistled notes, sometimes followed by a third note at a different pitch, all relatively slow and subdued as compared to the spring song, and very like the abbreviated songs of our other *Zonotrichias* at the same season. On bright days during the entire winter its more or less abbreviated song may be heard. As spring approaches the song becomes complete and more sustained.

Enemies.—Nothing has been recorded of actual predation on the nesting grounds. The North is blissfully free of many of our song-birds' worst enemies—snakes, house sparrows, starlings, cowbirds, the feral cat, small boys, agricultural practices, and that modern scourge, pesticides. A list of potential predators known within the breeding range of Harris' sparrow includes an occasional marsh hawk, peregrine falcon, pigeon hawk, sparrow hawk, horned owl, northern shrike, red fox, a few red squirrels, martens, and weasels. If the birds are as clever at concealing their nests from natural enemies as from visiting ornithologists, predation is slight indeed.

During the winter Harris' sparrows may suffer some losses to cats, boys with air guns, shrikes, and bird hawks of one kind or another. The greatest destructive force to the species, however, is undoubtedly weather. Storms during the migration and snow or ice that covers the food supply probably account for more fatalities than all other causes combined.

Life expectancy.—As the Harris' sparrow lays an average of 4 eggs for the single brood it raises each year and has comparatively few natural enemies, it may be assumed that when the birds leave the nesting grounds the ratio of young to adults is approximately 2 to 1, and the population is composed of roughly 66 percent immatures and 33 percent adults. An analysis of my banding records for 12 years at Stillwater, Okla., in the heart of the winter range, shows the proportion of young to adults fluctuating through the non-breeding season as follows:

Month	*Adults*	*Immatures*	*Totals*	*Percent adults*	*Percent immatures*
Oct.	4	7	11	36	64
Nov.	123	254	377	33	67
Dec.	106	172	278	38	62
Jan.	109	96	205	53	47
Feb.	90	97	187	48	52
Mar.	163	164	327	50	50
Apr.*	11	30	41	27	73
May*	2 R[1]	–	–	100	–
Totals	608	820	1, 426**	42	58

*By the end of April all birds are in adult plumage. Only birds of known age are included here.

**Total includes each return tabulated in month it returned.

Thus during the autumn the young of the year outnumber the adults by the anticipated two to one, and the ratio decreases only slightly in December. By January the effects of the higher mortality rate among the immatures begin to be evident; the proportion of young to old becomes nearly equal and apparently remains so through March. The April increase of immatures to 73 percent is based on a small sample of only 41 birds, which may well lack statistical significance. Far more likely, it suggests that the older birds tend to leave the wintering grounds for the north some weeks earlier than the first-year individuals. Also these ratios may be biased against the adults by the tendency of immature birds to enter the banding traps more readily in the spring as Stevens (*in* litt.) has suggested.

The higher mortality in the young birds is also demonstrated by shrike predation at the banding traps, which occurs at Stillwater almost entirely during mid-winter when the age ratio is approximately balanced. During the 18 years of banding there, shrikes killed in the traps a total of 36 immature Harris' sparrows and only 6 adults, one of which was somewhat crippled by a leg injury. The percentage of first year mortality cannot be determined from the data available, but it is probably in the neighborhood of 70 to 80 percent.

Annual mortality and longevity in the birds that survive the first year may be estimated from the numbers of wintering birds that return to the banding station in subsequent years. From the total of 1,361 birds banded at Stillwater between February 1948 and May 1960, 121 individuals returned one or more years for a total of 204 times through May 1965. Of these 66 were banded as immatures, 50 as adults, and 5 after April 25 when subadults could not be recognized. The survival of these birds permits the construction of the following table:

Age interval in years (x)	*Alive at start (lx)*	*Calculated deaths (dx)*	*Annual mortality (qx)*
1–2 (R–1)	121	57	47%
2–3 (R–2)	64	23	36%
3–4 (R–3)	41	19	46%
4–5 (R–4)	22	9	41%
5–6 (R–5)	13	6	46%
6–7 (R–6)	7	7	100%

These returns demonstrate a mean annual mortality from the first through the seventh years of 45 percent. The species' potential life span is thus slightly in excess of 10 years, but such advanced years are probably not attained by more than one bird in each thousand that survive the first year. Of my seven Return-6 birds, 4 were banded as adults, and hence were at least almost 8 years old the last spring they were taken, and could have been older.

The files of the Bird-Banding Office at Patuxent, covering a period of 25 years and representing thousands of Harris' sparrow records, contain only 13 Return-6 birds, including my 7. Of their three R-7 birds, the age at time of banding was not designated for two, but the third and a fourth bird also banded in Oklahoma City by Victor Vacin (correspondence) were immature when banded and therefore in their 8th year when last taken. The single R-8 bird that W. Wilkins banded as an immature in Chapman, Kans., Dec. 10, 1932, and recaptured Feb. 13, 1941, holds the all-time longevity record to date of 8½ years.

Fall.—After completing their late summer molt, the hordes of Harris' sparrows drift down from their northern home and swarm across the prairie provinces by mid-September. Swenk and Stevens (1929) point out: "A universal comment is that this sparrow is more common in the fall migration than in the spring. This seems to be connected with the fact that the fall movement is slower—requiring three months to pass from its breeding grounds to the southern extremity of its wintering range—the birds tarrying in attractive localities or wandering somewhat to one side until urged on by colder weather."

The few direct recoveries of fall-banded birds give some idea of the rate of the southward movement. One banded at Madison, Minn.,

Oct. 3, 1936, was taken at Woodward, Okla., November 21, having covered the 600 miles in 49 days, or 12.2 miles per day. A bird banded at Fargo, N. Dak., on October 2 was recovered at Yankton, S. Dak., 270 miles and 21 days later, having averaged 13 miles per day. Slightly better time was made by one banded at Tower City, N. Dak., October 21 and recovered at Le Mars, Iowa, 300 miles southward, November 10, an average of 15 miles per day. Two others banded at Fargo, N. Dak., October 23 and 24 were still tarrying in South Dakota, a scant 100 and 125 miles south, 7 weeks later in mid-December.

Swenk and Stevens (1929) write: "The results at Fargo indicate that the adults move southward more promptly than the immatures. About 90 per cent of the adults arrived by October 5, but only 50 to 60 per cent of the immatures (94 and 60 per cent in 1927, 88 and 48 per cent in 1928)." Stevens later (1957) comments that the individual length of stay, as judged by the capture of repeats, varied from 1 to 10 days, with an extreme of 24 days, and the average varied from year to year from 4.3 to 7.6 days.

Winter.—From their careful examination of a vast accumulation of records, Swenk and Stevens (1929) outline the species' normal winter range as extending primarily south of latitude 41° from southeastern Nebraska through Kansas and Oklahoma to central Texas, overlapping into western Missouri and northwestern Arkansas, a narrow strip some 200 by 900 miles between the 94th and 100th meridians, and north of the 28th parallel. A few birds often linger north of the 41st parallel well after the main migration has moved on. In his 32 years of observations in southern South Dakota and adjoining Iowa, William Youngworth (1959) has recorded the species 43 times in December, 6 times in January (including one flock of 20 birds), once in February and once in early March. He believes the birds are encouraged to remain by the urban development and the planting of trees and shrubs in these plains states, but that they probably move southward when the weather becomes bitter. In the Bird Banding files are records of three Harris' sparrows found frozen in haystacks at Northville and Ipswich, S. Dak., during January and February 1936.

The earliest fall record for the species at Stillwater, Okla., is October 24, but the species usually arrives here in the heart of the winter range during the first week of November. Graphs charting the daily arrivals of individuals at the Stillwater banding station show the period from early November through the first half of December as a series of peaks with new birds appearing almost daily. Most of these birds are migrants that repeat at the traps only a few times or perhaps remain a week or two before disappearing forever. At the same time many of the regular winter residents, both new and returns, are arriving.

The third week in December shows a sharp drop in new arrivals. The graphs now follow a long flat line through late December, January, February, and frequently into March, broken only by dips as a lone bird or two drifts in, and by occasional abrupt peaks during periods of heavy snow or extreme cold. The timing of these peaks is too irregular to indicate anything but local movements of birds in search of food. Most of the birds comprising them disappear as soon as the snow melts, perhaps to reappear during another storm in the same or a subsequent year, suggesting residence in a neighboring territory rather than migration. Meanwhile the traps are visited regularly by a small but constant number of repeaters, the birds that occupy the immediate trapping area throughout the season.

Field counts corroborate this pattern. Over a 6-year period 73 counts were made in a 20-acre tract surrounding the banding station. While the number of Harris' sparrows varied from year to year depending on weather and habitat changes, the proportions from month to month followed this same trend and showed a fairly stable population throughout late December, January, and February. Other groups could be anticipated regularly in favorable spots within a half mile of the station.

The size of the wintering territory of a Harris' sparrow flock appears to be quite limited under normal conditions. Restricted laterally by the brushy and weedy fringes of a particular hedgerow or timbered ravine, it may extend several hundred yards longitudinally and follow up side branches or tongues of suitable cover for shorter distances. Our regular repeaters remained roughly within the 20 acres adjoining our home, which included three banding traps 300 feet apart, a lawn with various feeding devices, and weedy borders of a garden, chicken yard, and brushy ravine. The birds visited two of the traps interchangeably and the third trap, nearer the house, less often, usually during severe weather.

During the winter of 1961–62 Donald D. Bridgwater (MS) operated banding traps at four other territories occupied by wintering flocks from ¼ mile to ¾ mile distant from my home station. Birds at each station were also marked by gluing differently colored chicken feathers to the tails with household cement, and trailed in scores of field censuses. Of the 254 banded, approximately half did not repeat at any station. His study revealed that more than half the repeaters banded at my home or the nearest substation, ¼ mile down the brushy ravine, traveled the intervening area fairly freely. Another station only ⅓ mile away but not linked with the ravine system showed only a 9 percent interchange, whereas a third station ½ mile distant at a well-landscaped home with a continuous feeding program revealed a

28 percent interchange with my station. Between the farthest distant stations, ¾ mile apart, there was only 2 percent interchange.

Similar studies by Charles E. Harkins (1937), P. J. Park (1936), and P. J. Steelman and K. E. Herde (1937) demonstrate the strong homing instinct in Harris' sparrows and the birds' fidelity to their winter territory. Birds caught at one station and released at another were never taken where freed—they either returned to the original station or disappeared. Individuals homed successfully to their territories from 2 miles away.

In March new birds surge in again, presumably migrants from farther south, which usually repeat a time or two and pass on. Some that come in with the March snows may linger into April or May and return another year, suggesting that they occupied nearby territories throughout the season. At this time many of the winter regulars make their last appearance.

April is generally a static period when the traps are visited primarily by the remaining repeaters. May brings a few more migrants and sees the departure of the last winter residents, which are usually the latest to leave. Though my last date for a new bird is May 11, the last repeats of the season are made characteristically by the all-winter residents, which have made the late records for Oklahoma of May 18, 19, and 26.

The many returns to the place of banding on the wintering grounds year after year indicate that attachment to the winter territory is strong and evidently established during the first year. Within their little circuits, and certainly on the wintering grounds, home is home to the Harris' sparrows throughout their brief and unpretentious little lives.

Distbibution

Harris' Sparrow

Range.—Mackenzie and southern Keewatin south to southern California, central Arizona, south central Texas, northwestern Louisiana, and Tennessee. Primarily mid-continental.

Breeding range.—The Harris' sparrow breeds from northwestern and central eastern Mackenzie (Mackenzie Delta, Kah-duonay and Crystal Islands) and southern Keewatin (Sandhill Lake) south to northern Manitoba (Cochrane River, Lac Du Brochet, Bird); casually east in summer to northwestern Ontario (Fort Severn).

Winter range.—Winters from southern British Columbia (Victoria, Comox, Lillooet, Vancouver, Okanagan Landing), southern Idaho (Nampa), Wyoming, Utah (Centerville, Linwood), northern Colorado (Fruita, Boulder, Longmont), east central and southeastern South Dakota (Huron, Yankton, Sioux Falls), and central Iowa (Woodbury and Polk counties) south to southern California (Encinitas; San Clemente Island), southern Nevada (mouth of El Dorado Canyon), southwestern Arizona (Tucson), south central Texas (Del Rio; Bee County), northwestern Louisiana (Shreveport), northwestern Mississippi (Hernando), and Tennessee (Memphis, Nashville); casually north to northwestern Montana (Libby), southeastern North Dakota (Fargo), Wisconsin (Polk and Shawano counties), southern Ontario (Neebing Township, Peterborough, Hamilton, Toronto), Michigan (Sault Ste. Marie, Midland), and Massachusetts (Greenfield, Warren, Bradford, Boxford, and Edgartown); and east to Pennsylvania (Bucks County), Maryland (Darnestown), Virginia (Ashburn), South Carolina (Gramling), Georgia (Atlanta), and Florida (Winter Park, Melbourne Beach).

Casual records.—Casual in migration north to south central Alaska (Cohoe), northern Alaska (Nikilik on Colville River delta), northern Mackenize (Bathurst Inlet), and New York (Ithaca, New York City, Fire Island), east to Massachusetts (Martha's Vineyard), Connecticut (Glastonbury), New Jersey (Troy Meadows), Maryland (Howard County), and south to Georgia (Athens), Florida (Leon and Brevard counties), Alabama (Birmingham) and Mississippi (Gulfport, Rosedale).

Migration.—Early dates of spring arrival are: Illinois—Chicago, May 3 (average of 8 years, May 12). Ohio—central Ohio, April 1. Iowa—Sioux City, average of 17 years, March 29. Minnesota—Minneapolis-St. Paul, April 27 (average of 7 years, May 7). Nebraska—Lincoln, average of 20 years, March 14. South Dakota—Sioux Falls, March 26 (average of 7 years, April 30). North Dakota—Jamestown, March 5; Cass County, April 27 (average, May 6). Manitoba—Treesbank, May 3 (average of 25 years, May 8). Wyoming—Torrington, April 19. Idaho—Lewiston, April 4.

Late dates of spring departure are: Tennessee—Nashville, April 11. Missouri—St. Louis, May 8 (median of 6 years, May 5). Illinois—Chicago, May 29 (average of 8 years, May 15). Ohio—central Ohio, May 14. Iowa—Sioux City, May 26 (average of 38 years, May 15); Winnebago, May 12. Wisconsin—northern counties, May 18. Minnesota—Minneapolis-St. Paul, May 24 (average of 5 years, May 20). Kansas—northeastern Kansas, May 19 (median of 19 years, May 10). Nebraska—Fairbury, June 4; Lincoln, average of 20 years, May 14. South Dakota—Sioux Falls, May 24 (average of 5 years, May 19). North Dakota—Cass County, May 29 (average, May 27); Jamestown, May 18. Wyoming—Torrington, May 14. Idaho—Potlatch, April 19.

Early dates of fall arrival are: Montana—Medicine Lake, September 30. Wyoming—Douglas, October 7. Saskatchewan—Saskatoon, September 22. Manitoba—Treesbank, September 10 (average of 22 years, September 19). North Dakota—Cass County, September 12 (average, September 16); Jamestown, September 14. South Dakota—Sioux Falls, September 18 (average of 5 years, September 25). Nebraska—Red Cloud, September 10. Kansas—northeastern Kansas, October 27. Texas—Sinton, November 9. Minnesota—Minneapolis-St. Paul, September 17 (average of 8 years, September 23). Iowa—Sioux City, September 23 (median of 38 years, October 8); Winnebago, September 26. Wisconsin—Stevens Point, September 27. Ohio—Buckeye Lake, October 20. Illinois—Chicago, September 19 (average of 14 years, September 27). Missouri—St. Louis, November 28 (median of 13 years, November 6). Louisiana—Baton Rouge, November 13.

Late dates of fall departures are: Washington—Opportunity, October 24. Montana—Missoula, October 28. Wyoming—Laramie, November 14. Saskatchewan—Saskatoon, November 5. Manitoba—Treesbank, October 20 (average of 22 years, October 9). North Dakota—Cass County, October 24 (average, October 21); Jamestown, October 23. South Dakota—Sioux Falls, November 7 (average of 4 years, November 3). Minnesota—Minneapolis-St. Paul, November 9 (average of 7 years, October 23). Wisconsin—October 27. Iowa—Sioux City, average of 17 years, November 11. Ohio—central Ohio, November 12. Illinois—Chicago, November 6 (average of 14 years, October 17).

Egg dates.—Manitoba: 21 records, June 11 to July 6; 7 records, June 26 to July 1.

ZONOTRICHIA LEUCOPHRYS LEUCOPHRYS (Forster)

Eastern White-crowned Sparrow

PLATE 68

Contributed by ROLAND C. CLEMENT

HABITS

The tremendous energy which drives small birds toward their breeding grounds in spring is well illustrated by the way in which some of them overshoot their destination. Witness the occurrence of the eastern race of the white-crowned sparrow on Fletcher's Ice Island (T–3) on June 16, 1957, when it was at 82°37′ N., 99°50′ W., only 150 miles from the North Pole and some 2,000 miles beyond the nearest nesting habitat of the species, as reported by Spencer Apollonio (1958).

Because unusual observational opportunities are required to recognize such events, we are less aware of them than the facts probably warrant. But it is this sort of random exploration of extralimital territory that helps account for the ability of so many species to colonize new territory as soon as it becomes suitable. We know, today, that the margin of the tundra which forms the northern limit of the white-crown's range has been both farther north and farther south during the last 10,000 years, and that the range and the population of this species have varied accordingly.

The eastern white-crown is best described as a subarctic and alpine zone bird, but so extensive is its range that only ecological characterization is really helpful. This has seldom been done and as a result "life zone" pigeon-holings are rampant with apparent contradictions. The only full awareness of the ecology of this bird in all the material before me is Harrison F. Lewis' excellent description, in a letter of July 1, 1963: "In coasting along the north shore of the Gulf of St. Lawrence from west to east, in latitude slightly north of 50°, one enters the breeding range of the white-crowned sparrow abruptly on passing Saint Genevieve Island, the easternmost of the Mingan Archipelago. The reason for the abruptness of this boundary is that the Mingan Islands, which border the coast for some 50 miles, are formed of limestone, as is, also, much of the adjacent coastal mainland. Eastward from Saint Genevieve, the mainland and the coastal islands are of acidic pre-Cambrian rocks, such as granite and gneiss. The vegetation of the limestone belt is much superior to that which grows on the adjacent pre-Cambrian rocks, and the bird life reflects this; for example, the ovenbird nests on the limestone of the Mingan region, but not beyond. West of Saint Genevieve I have only a few records of sporadic occurrence of the white-crown in the nesting season."

This Mingan region is an outlier of Paleozoic rocks. In his monumental photoreconnaisance of the vegetation and physiography of the Labrador-Ungava peninsula, F. Kenneth Hare (1959) marks it as the eastern terminus of the Laurentide massif and considers it an outlier of the coastal tundra that fringes the southeast coast of Labrador. Climatologists bring the 55° F. July isotherm, which transects the peninsula from west to east, to the coast just east of this region, and forms a rough boundary between the open subarctic woodland to the north, the closed-crown forest to the south and west, and the scrubby forest characteristic of the eastern tip of the peninsula at this latitude.

It is open, stunted tree growth and brush that attracts nesting white-crowned sparrows. At Goose Bay, Labrador, for example, I found them nesting only in the open, often burned, black spruce and dwarf birch on the high, sandy delta of the airport plateau. In better sites nearby, white-throated sparrows nested. An awareness of such temporary ecological changes in distribution allows me to view with interest the nesting reports of white-crowns at North Bay, Ontario, and at Baie Comeau and Godbout on the north shore of the St. Lawrence, as well as near Godthaab, Greenland, in 1824 (Salomonson, 1950); though I cannot credit them for lack of corroborative details on the ecology of the site.

Despite the fact that it was the first known and is the most widely distributed race, the eastern white-crown has been one of the least studied. No one has yet reported in any detail on the biology of the alpine populations of the Rocky Mountain massif, and the eastern group has only recently begun to attract the attention it deserves. In a study of geographic variation in the entire *leucophrys* group, Richard C. Banks (1964) reduces Harry C. Oberholser's (1932) Cordilleran race *oriantha* to synonymy with the eastern race, discounts W. E. Clyde Todd's (1953) proposal of the name *nigrilora* for the "ultratypical" Labrador peninsula population, and considers the slightly larger, reddish-backed and black-lored nominate *leucophrys* to be the ancestral population. "The species," he writes, "appears to be essentially a northern one which has extended southward only where summer conditions approximate those found in subarctic regions. Thus, in the western * * * United States, White-crowns are found only in high mountains and along the cool Pacific coast."

Spring.—The interaction between internal and external factors in the eastern population remains almost unreported. Only Marshall B. Eyster (1954) has shown that, compared to such congeners as the white-throated sparrow and the junco, the white-crown is much more prone to pre-migratory nocturnal unrest (*zugunruhe*).

Viewed from the central wintering grounds of the southern Great Plains, the spring migration involves a radiation northward. One population segment goes northwestward into the Rocky Mountain uplands, another more or less due north to the Cypress Hills of Saskatchewan and the Hudson's Bay country, but the largest segment trends far to the east of north, to summer in northern Quebec and western Newfoundland.

In an analysis of 198 recoveries and 9,107 returns from nearly 232,000 white-crowns banded between 1920 and 1963, Angelo J. Cortopassi and Richard L. Mewaldt (1965) show that migration is of a broad-front type and not oriented to landmarks—of 6,000 birds banded while on migration, not a single individual returned to the place of banding. Migration is by hops of at least 200 miles, with one 310-mile hop recorded in spring, and with a daily mean of about 50 miles. One bird banded by Ralph K. Bell at Clarksville, Pa.,

May 6, 1962, was recaptured 1,500 miles to the north at Battle Harbor, Labrador, on June 12, having averaged 40 miles per day.

The rapid northward surge of this species results in "a high fidelity of timing" as Cortopassi and Mewaldt put it—94 percent of the birds pass through 1,000 miles of the northeast's most populous countryside between May 2 and 18, with May 11 the median date for banding migrants in this region. Milton B. Trautman (1956) gives the principal movement at Buckeye Lake, Ohio, as May 8 to 20. In a letter to Ralph K, Bell, Gordon Wilson of Bowling Green, Ky., who has chronicled the birds of his region for 45 years, gives average departure as May 10, with May 28 as a late date.

The only evidence of physiographically-controlled spring migration I have seen is a letter from Clark S. Beardslee to Mr. Bent in 1951. reporting that in spring northbound white-crowns move eastward through Ontario, cross into New York State in the Buffalo-Niagara isthmus, then presumably circle eastward around the south side of Lake Ontario before moving northward into Quebec. Harold D. Mitchell has kindly confirmed these observations for me.

Dispersal into the subarctic breeding grounds on the interior Quebec-Labrador plateaus normally occurs during the last week of May, though late ice and snow may sometimes delay arrival a whole week. I was impressed by the influence of seasonal conditions when I arrived at Knob Lake in interior Quebec on May 18, 1957. A raging blizzard made it plain that winter's grip was still firm. Returning to within 15 miles of the St. Lawrence above Seven Islands, I found white-crowns abundant and obviously "dammed up" by weather, for they were occupying all sorts of habitats that are not usual for them. They sang softly while awaiting better conditions for concluding their migration. The first birds arrived at Knob Lake on May 23 that year, but even so, they had to spend several days feeding along plowed roadsides until the snow melted from the territories they were to occupy. Harrison F. Lewis' notes show that conditions were even more severe a decade earlier; his June 4, 1947 journal entry records that this "was an abnormally cold, late spring, with consequent heavy loss of life among small migrant passerines." He recorded 120 obviously delayed migrant white-crowns at Seven Islands, south and west of the breeding range.

Territory.—Territorial behavior has not yet been described for this race of the white-crown. I have twice seen fights in early June in the Knob Lake region, the birds facing each other breast to breast, then jumping, clawing, and flying at each other. Such jousts are usually short-lived.

The white-crown does best in "hybrid" habitats, where disturbance of the surface by fire or mechanical means has increased diversity and the shrub growth is still young. Under such conditions I have found two nests only 300 feet apart, and computed territory sizes as between .88 and 1.85 acres each. On the other hand, a breeding bird census of 18⅓ acres of open lichen woodland—the most extensive vegetative type of central Labrador—revealed a low density of two nests, or about 1 territory per 9 acres. This would be about 70 pairs per square mile, but Thomas H. Manning (1949) estimated that in western Ungava the population was between 10 and 30 pairs per square mile, the higher counts being in burnt areas.

Courtship.—The sexes being alike, it is difficult to follow territorial disputes and courtship until birds have been color-marked. No one has yet done this early enough in the season to unravel this phase of the life history of the eastern subspecies.

Within a week after arrival on the breeding grounds a good deal of territorial song is heard from about 5:00 a.m. to 10:00 a.m. and again in the evening. For a week or so thereafter the birds utter much high-pitched trilling with depressed crowns, either from the ground or from no more than 4 feet above it. This trill is quickly communicated to the whole nearby group, several other birds then repeating it. The trilling bird often attracts a companion who approaches with crest high and loud *pete* notes, as though alarmed, and they fly off together. Three-party nuptial chases are common at this season. More specifically, the bird that emits the high, trilling *dreeeee* note often crouches low, with head up, and flutters its wings as though rotated from the "wrist." I did not notice the tail-spreading and the spasmodic wing opening and closing that caught the attention of Francis Harper (1958) in this same area. As I proved by collecting, the female gives a loud chatter during these mating chases (this female contained oocytes up to 1 millimeter in diameter). Two weeks after the population arrived, while trilling was going on everywhere, I saw a female crouch and trill (I wrote whimper), and the male then mounted quickly three times. Soon afterward song fell off noticeably.

The male of the eastern white-crowned sparrow seems to share some notes and postures heretofore (Nice, 1943, and Blanchard, 1936) ascribed to the female only. On June 13, 1957, I collected a trilling, wing-flipping bird that turned out to be a male. Error is easy under the stress of collecting in close quarters, and a male that entered unobserved may have been the inadvertent victim of my search during the few seconds involved; but, again, on June 24, 1958, I saw a color-banded male, the mate of a female with eggs in the nest, rotate its wings "at the wrist," in the slow wing-flutter that the female gives while trilling in invitation to copulation (Blanchard, 1936).

Nesting.—Whereas Alfred O. Gross (1937) could write that "the height of the breeding season of the White-crowned Sparrow on the Labrador coast is during the first two weeks of July," for the Labrador peninsula as a whole, most eggs are laid by mid-June. This varies greatly from season to season, however, and from region to region; the season in the higher southern third of the vast peninsula, for example, is usually later than in the lower areas farther north.

In mid-morning on June 16, 1957, I surprised a bird forming a nest. It had pulled out mixed hairy-cap mosses and Cladonia lichens for a proper cup in the shade of a dwarf birch. From a total of some 30 nests examined *in situ*, it seems safe to consider my description (*in* Todd, 1963) as typical: "four inches in outside diameter and two and five-eighths inches inside. The inside depth was one and one-half inches. The main body of the nest is woven of fine grass stems, the outside is made up of mixed moss stems, and the bottom is lined with very fine root fibers, or in one case with white ptarmigan body-feathers." Harrison F. Lewis (*in* litt.) once found a nest lined with light gray hair, perhaps that of a dog. Most nests set into the moss-lichen or lichen-crowberry mat are partly concealed by overhanging branches of dwarf birch or Labrador tea; not infrequently a nest is neatly tucked into the lower side of a moss or crowberry (*Empetrum*) mound. Much less frequently, nests are built into moss hummocks on a string of heath shrubbery some distance out in a sphagnum bog. Although I have never seen an elevated nest, Arthur A. Allen wrote me that whereas all the nests he had found in the Churchill region were on the ground, on the Labrador Coast (North Shore) "the few nests I saw were in small firs." Earlier, Oliver L. Austin, Jr. (1932) had quoted Moravian missionary Perrett's notes from Makkovik, Labrador, concerning a nest "about three feet from the ground in bushes thrown over a boat to protect it from the sun."

On June 30, 1957, I found an otherwise typical white-crown nest in a "hybrid" habitat near the airport at Schefferville (Knob Lake), Quebec, which contained 8 eggs and had 3 birds in attendance. On July 2 the eggs and the two birds that came to incubate between 10:45 a.m. and 1:30 p.m. were collected by Don R. Oliver of the McGill University Subarctic Laboratory and shipped to me at Brown University, where William Montagna dissected them. Both birds were females in comparable stages of gonadal regression, with equally developed brood patches. One bird showed two clear follicles and what appeared to be two coalesced follicles; the other had three clear follicles and one questionable follicle. Although polygyny has been reported in Emberizines before (e.g., corn bunting) this appears to be the first American record and is unusual in that only one nest was involved.

Some pairs may mate a second time. On July 10, during their 7th day of caring for young, the banded pair I had under observation at Schefferville, Quebec, performed elements of the nuptial display. The female trilled and fluttered her wings as she left the nest; later I heard her trill while out of sight behind my blind and thought that the sounds indicated a mating chase; that same day the male twittered on crossing her in flight as they exchanged visits to feed the young. E. P. Wheeler, II (*in* litt.) once found a bird with unhatched eggs as late as July 30 on the Labrador coast.

Eggs.—The white-crowned sparrow lays three to five, and rarely six eggs. They are ovate, though some may tend toward either short or elongate ovate, and are slightly glossy. The ground is pale greenish or creamy white and is heavily marked with spots and blotches of reddish browns such as "Natal brown," "Mars brown," "chestnut," "Verona brown," or "russet." There is quite a range of variation; frequently the spottings obscure the entire ground, while in other cases considerable ground is showing with the markings concentrated toward the large end where they may become confluent. On eggs with much ground showing, undermarkings of "pale neutral gray" may be discernible. The measurements of 50 eggs of *Z.l.leucophrys* average 21.5 by 15.6 millimeter; the eggs showing the four extremes measure *24.1* by 16.5, 21.6 by *17.0*, *18.9* by 15.8, and 19.8 by *14.5* millimeters.

Of 29 sets recorded, 23 sets had four eggs, 5 had five eggs, and only one had six eggs. I therefore assume the three-egg clutches occasionally reported are probably incomplete.

A color-banded pair had four eggs on June 24, 1958, when discovered, and hatching occurred July 4, so incubation is at least 11 days. The female did all the brooding of the young, so it seems likely that she also did all the incubating of the eggs, as I found her on the nest after dark. Another bird was so bothered by the wind flapping my blind during a 3-hour watch that she was off the nest as much as she was on; she changed every 1½ minutes as a rule, and her longest periods on the eggs were 6 to 7 minutes.

Young.—I found that for the first and second days after hatching, the female turns the young, just as she turned the eggs earlier, at 10- to 20-minute intervals. Her brooding schedule is controlled by the male's visits, for she gets off the nest when he brings her food. He comes silently and directly to the nest, whereas she lands 10 to 15 feet away, always on the same side, then hops in slowly, nearly always using the same perches. On reaching the nest she gives a few alerting chips, to which the young make no vocal response until the

5th day, and the male responds to their trilling only after the 7th day. In 1957 I noted:

"It is surprising to see how well the pale lining of the female's feathering causes her to blend inobstrusively with the straw border of the nest as she broods. The young grow so quickly that on the third day they push up the female, beg, and gape without parental provocation. They nestle deeply into the nest when the sun dips in late afternoon. On the fourth day their eyes are open during shady intervals, and fully open the next day. They hug the nest when the female scolds and no longer gape at my touch. The tail feathers are now one quarter inch long."

"By the seventh day the female has trouble brooding since the young toss and turn. The next day they scratch and preen for the first time, and anticipate the parent's return by trilling."

Feeding and nest-sanitation are shared almost equally by the parents, the male making slightly more than half the feedings, and removing slightly more than half the fecal sacs. Usually the old birds carry the fecal sacs away, but they occasionally eat the small ones. On their 8th day the young receive feeding visits on an average of one every 10 minutes. On the 9th day they will leave the nest if disturbed, but probably stay on another day or two when not pressed.

Plumages.—One-day-old young are fluffy in mouse-gray natal down which covers capital, dorsal, alar, and femoral tracts, but not the ventral tract.

My Labrador notes contain a description of a fledgling about 2 days off the nest. It had dark brown eyes, the bill was brown, and the gape and most of the commissure corn-yellow, the tarsus lilac, and the toenails light horn gray. Francis Harper (1958) describes a young bird as having vermillion mouth linings, with commissure and tomia corn-yellow.

Richard R. Graber (1955) describes in detail the juvenal plumage on the basis of a bird from Colorado and another from Labrador:

"Forehead and crown streaked throughout with black. Crown and forehead white medially, brown laterally. Occiput dark, mottled brown and black. Nape mottled, white and black. Back streaked, black and buff. Rump and upper tail coverts rusty-buff, streaked with black. Rectrices and remiges black. Primaries edged with buff, secondaries and tertials with dull rust color. Uppermost (proximal) tertials edged and tipped with buffy white. Lesser coverts gray; medians black, edged with white; greater coverts black, edged with buff, tipped with white. Two white wing bars. Lores dark, brownish or gray. Narrow white supra-ocular stripe from eye to nape. Auriculars buff-tinged gray, post-auriculars like nape. Chin and throat white, flecked with black, and with black "mustache" marks. Under parts white, or lightly tinged with buff on chest, sides, and crissum. Chest, sides, and flanks heavily streaked with black. Belly and crissum immaculate. Leg feathers dark brown, edged with white."

Jonathan J. Dwight (1900) presumes that the first winter plumage is "acquired by partial postjuvenal moult, probably in August on its breeding grounds, which apparently involves the body plumage and the wing coverts partly but not the rest of the wings nor the tail." This is the "brown livery," the conspicuously more buffy immature plumage, in which the head is marked by broad reddish-brown stripes instead of the black and white of the adult.

Dwight also writes that first nuptial plumage is "acquired by a partial prenuptial moult beginning the end of March which involves chiefly the head and chin and a few scattering feathers elsewhere. The black and white crown is assumed, which soon shows nearly as much wear as the rest of the plumage. This becomes grayer and the stripes clearer. Old and young become practically indistinguishable" at this stage. Furthermore, "adult winter plumage [is] acquired by a complete postnuptial moult."

Robert A. Norris (1954) reports an extensive prenuptial molt during March and April, except for "the alulae, the primaries, secondaries and their greater (outer) coverts, the ten outside tailfeathers, and some of the feathers of the "wing lining." He felt it was "fairly certain that nonmolting birds such as my mid-March specimens would show * * * overlap between periods of molt and migration," assuming that completion of the molt requires 2 months.

Amelia R. Laskey of Nashville, Tenn., wrote Mr. Bent that she noticed unusually early beginning of crown molt during the first week of November 1932 and again in 1934. In the experience of both Mrs. Laskey and Ralph Bell, crown molt is normally complete by late April. Bell's notes show that crown molt takes at least 20 days.

Food.—Perhaps the most interesting item on the food of white-crowns is Francis Harper's (1958) discovery that in spring on the breeding grounds, these birds eat the green capsules of *Polytrichum juniperinum*, the hairy-cap moss. In 1957 I watched one bird pick and eat 120 capsules in exactly one minute. A female collected on June 8 had nothing but these capsules in her crop, and though all the white-crowns were utilizing this food at the time, some birds also picked up small brown seeds, a few sand grains, and black flies (*Simulium* sp.).

Like other terrestrial passerines, the white-crown is an opportunist. The hairy-cap moss capsules it consumes in late May and early June, when snows have just melted but before many insects emerge, are at that time the most available food. I have watched them eat the new green catkins of willows. The young are fed insects as nestlings, and themselves catch flies, mosquitoes, and spiders, as everyone who has studied them has noticed. In winter they are primarily seed eaters, and in spring or any other time these are available, they take fleshy fruits such as the red mulberry or the crowberry.

Behavior.—The white-crown has long had the reputation of being an aristocrat among the Emberizines. His neat attire, striking crown, and his habit of stretching his head upward to look around have probably combined to earn him this title.

But nobility should imply natural dominance. It was not until I saw white-crowns nesting adjacent to white-throated sparrows at Redmond Lake south of Schefferville, Quebec, that I realized that the white-crown is more mousy than regal in bearing, at least in summer. I found white-throats more deliberate, less upset by intrusion, their alarm notes a quiet announcement of awareness, and their flights shorter. White-crowns, on the other hand, were much more high-strung, always running while on the ground—even if they did this by hopping with both feet—and their alarm notes were more insistent, sharp, or nervous. These differences have an environmental basis, as the white-crowns occupy open country where they are more exposed to potential enemies and pressed by the wind, whereas the white-throats occupy the sheltered brushy borders of the closed-crown, Canadian-zone woodland that here reaches a northern limit.

This demeanor changes on the wintering grounds. Albert F. Ganier of Nashville, Tenn., who has studied their ways since the turn of the century, writes me that in his region the white-crowns remain in compact groups of 10 to 20 birds, hugging the same habitat week after week, either in a weed- and brush-grown fence row along some little-frequented road, or in an abandoned piece of farmland where plant succession is throwing up clumps and patches of herbacious and sapling growth. "Here," he writes, "they feed quietly on the ground, but when intruded upon rise to the top of the low growth and eye the intruder with apparent curiosity, rather than with fear. They crane their necks to get a better look and it would appear that they have not yet evolved a fear of man to the extent of most other birds." They are apparently not easily flushed out of these preferred coverts, as are the white-throats that fly ahead of the intruder.

Woodward H. Brown (1954) was impressed by the aerial feeding of white-crowns and saw them "occasionally spring 15–18 inches in the air, returning to former positions on grape vines, catching gnats or other small insects."

In Quebec-Labrador I was impressed by the fact that females when disturbed always sneaked off the nest for 10 or 20 feet in a sort of "mouse run," but without the wing-dragging display that shore birds and other species often add before sounding any alarm. On

July 3, 1958, while crossing a very wet sedge bog near Lake Matamace north of Schefferville, I watched a white-crown, which I took to be a male, catch insects by running in water up to its "knees," throwing up its tail, raising its white crest high, and "flashing" its wings much as a mockingbird does to flush out the insect life from the bog mat.

On July 10, 1944, at Goose Bay, Labrador, I flushed a pair of anxious adults and after 10 minutes of hunting finally drove out a close-sitting fledgling which a companion and I captured with difficulty. It was interesting that three adults drove at us frantically as we chased the young bird. They decoyed boldly with the "broken-wing" feint, and drew me 40 feet from the young one, returning to me each time I hesitated in following.

In 1958 at an elevation of 2,600 feet on Irony Mountain in central Quebec-Labrador, Henri Ouellet of the Canadian National Museum watched a white-crown feed a still-downy willow ptarmigan. E. P. Wheeler II, who has shared notes made during many years of patient field work in Labrador, noticed that white-crowns sometimes scratch for food very vigorously, using both feet at once as the fox sparrow does. This trait, and the tendency of white-crowns to take easily to man's newly created habitats in the northern wilderness, as song sparrows and their western congeners do farther south, raises interesting questions about the relationship of all these species. Raymond A. Paynter, Jr. (1964), in the course of a review of some North American Emberizinae, reaffirms the view that the basic differences between the song sparrows, the fox sparrows, and the crowned and white-throated sparrow groups are not clear-cut, and therefore urged that the genera *Melospiza*, *Passerella*, and *Zonotrichia* be merged. The existence of hybrids among the white-crowns (Miller, 1940), between the white-crown and the white-throat (Abbott, 1958), and between the white-crown and the song sparrow and the white-throat and the junco (Dickerman, 1961) lends impressive weight to the Paynter proposal.

Voice.—Often as I sat in the dusk in my tent or some miner's shack in the iron ore belt of interior Labrador in 1957, the song of the white-crown reminded me of that of a diminutive eastern meadowlark. "Especially is this so in chorus," I wrote, "and the first two notes are often like the black-capped chickadee's *sweet-ee* call." I syllabified one common version as, "*teu-dee * * * et tu aklavik*," a phrase which will mean more if pronounced in French. Everyone recognizes this song as like an imperfect white-throated sparrow song. To Ludlow Griscom it had the quality of a black-throated green warbler song, while Francis H. Allen wrote Mr. Bent that to him the song was "doleful rather than plaintive—the sweet expression of a state of utter boredom, as if the bird were saying, 'Oh, well, what's the use?' "

Harrison F. Lewis told Arthur A. Allen that he rendered the song as "Oh gee—it was the whiz-whiskey," to which the fox sparrow, so often a neighbor in the northland, would answer, "Well, my dear, why did you take it?"

The open, windy nature of the semibarrens that the white-crowns occupy in summer diminishes the impression their song makes on human visitors; so many songs are wafted away on the wind that only dominant phrases force themselves on the traveler's attention. The word renditions given above are the subjective efforts of pre-technological field ornithology. Today's field students use tape recorders and analyze their input from the visual record of a sound spectrograph that allows direct reading and comparison of duration and pitch. Donald J. Borror (1961) has analyzed a number of white-crown song recordings made by W. W. H. Gunn in northern Ontario and has provided the following objective description:

> The song usually begins with one to three clear whistled notes that are steady in pitch, and ends with three buzzy notes, the last lower in pitch than the two preceding. The first note is about 0.5 sec in length; if there are two or three similar introductory notes the second and third are a little shorter. The final buzzy notes are uttered at three to four per sec. Sometimes there are short clear notes or two-note phrases in the middle of the song and sometimes the second or third note of the song is slurred. One or two of the final buzzes (except the last) may begin with a short sharp note or be slightly up-slurred or both. Some songs end in a low trill rather than a low buzzy note. The songs of a given bird are usually very similar, but those of different birds often vary slightly.

The pitch of the white-crown's song is between 2,600 and 7,200 cycles per second.

Morning and evening song periods usually involve 15 to 20 minutes of uninterrupted song, and as each song is of 2-second duration and the interval between songs is 9 to 10 seconds, the total output during such a burst may be 100 or more songs. I have counted 194 consecutive songs.

Francis Harper (1958) writes the principal call note as "a *tsit*, which, when heard near at hand, seems to have a slight metallic rasp." Charles W. Townsend and Glover M. Allen (1907) distinguished a metallic *chink* call note from a sharper *chip* alarm note. In my field notes I described the call note as *pete*, identical by both sexes, and the alarm notes as higher pitched than the ordinary scold note.

Amelia R. Laskey (*in* litt.) mentions a ventriloquial song of the immature as follows: "At first the songs, coming at intervals, seemed to emanate from shrubs some 15 feet behind the bird, but as it came closer I could see its bill open and close. It was a lengthier song than the adults give in spring, and the bird erected its crown feathers as it sang."

Mortality.—It seems to me better to get away from the connotations of the word "enemy" and simply to point out that the white-crown is subject to the usual factors that cause attrition in animal populations, whether disease, the complex of factors engendering winter mortality, or direct predation by accipitrine hawks, shrikes, weasels, and the like.

It has its normal share of parasites, both external and internal. Oscar M. Root has kindly furnished a note on the identification of Hippoboscid louse-flies, *Ornithomyia fringillina,* found on immature birds by Gary C. Kuyava in Minnesota; Francis Harper (1958) has taken a mite of the genus *Lealaps* from a juvenile specimen in Quebec; and Robert A. Norris (1954) found biting lice (Mallophaga) on dried skins and also found that four out of nine specimens examined in Georgia had protozoan infections of the blood (Leucocytozoon), and one of these, a smallish individual which had not begun its prenuptial molt on March 17, was doubly infected with the malarial parasite, Plasmodium. One adult was heavily infected with abdominal helminths, the filarid nematode *Diplotriaena.* The individual infected with Plasmodium also had foot tumors caused by the virus *Epithelioma contagiosm.* Alfred O. Gross (1937) reports the mallophagan *Philopterus subflavescens* (Geof.) from young on the Labrador coast, and Herbert Friedmann (1938) reports parasitism by the cowbird at Okotoks, Alberta.

Of greater population significance, probably, is the loss of young birds during the first migration. For the Quebec-Labrador segment, especially, this must be a significant decimating factor because the young of the year are often wind-drifted out to sea, where they perish unless they are fortunate enough to reach an island from whence they can return. I have been particularly impressed with this problem in their lives at Block Island, R.I., where hundreds of white-crowns appear in autumn, when cold fronts pass out to sea, all of them immatures.

Fall and winter.—Young were on the wing as early as July 11, 1945, at Indian House Lake in northern Labrador, and Austin (1932) saw young flying on July 16, 1928 on the coast, although late July is a more normal date there. In August at Indian House Lake they were in loose family groups, feeding and playing in the alder strand that fringes the George River, and by mid-September when they leave the region, they are usually restricted to dwarf birch thickets in timberline areas on the slopes. On July 31 and again on August 3, 1957, at Scheffeville, Henri Ouellet noted a goodly number of both adults and young in the open, "feeding very little, and seemingly on the move." E. P. Wheeler's last date for Kutsertakh on the Atlantic slope of Labrador is Oct. 5, 1934.

At Buckeye Lake, Ohio, Milton B. Trautman (1940) records first arrival as October 1 to 8, with the peak of migration October 10 to 27, and the last departure November 3. White-crowns first wintered there in 1953. The ratio of immatures to adults, M. B. Trautman reports, was usually 2 to 1, though in some years there were 97 immatures to 3 adults. As earlier mentioned, on Block Island, 10 miles off the Rhode Island shore, immature birds are almost or quite alone, which suggests that adults are too experienced to allow themselves to be wind-drifted out to sea during migration. Robert A. Norris (1954) reports a wintering flock of 30 immatures to 1 adult in Georgia; he considered the sex ratio balanced.

Concerning autumn habitats, Milton B. Trautman (1940) writes, "As in spring, the birds were found in brushy situations, but many were also present in dense patches of high weeds, and in weedy uncut cornfields. Autumn sparrows were somewhat more secretive than were spring birds, and it was only by remaining quiet in a dense weed patch or brushy thicket and giving a Screech Owl whistle that a true indication of numbers could be obtained."

Robert A. Norris (1954) writes that white-crowns do not flock with other species and that on the Georgia wintering grounds he studied, the birds are "found in more open country with less cover and also farther from water than is typically the case with White-throated Sparrows." The March-April weights of his Georgia birds ranged from 23.7 grams for the smallest female to 31.2 grams for the largest male, the 13-bird sample averaging 30.05 grams. In a larger sample, however, Paul A. Stewart (1937) found that 21 adults ranged from 19.9 to 37.1 grams, with a mean of 31.26 grams; 31 immature birds ranged from 23.5 to 32 grams, with a mean of 27.56 grams.

Cortopassi and Mewaldt's (1965) plot of the distribution of this species from the Christmas Bird Counts of *Audubon Field Notes* shows that the wintering population has two centers of concentration, one in western Texas and southeastern New Mexico and the other in the Appalachian plateau and its western extension, the interior low plateaus and Ozark plateaus. In these two broad belts the bird-watcher may expect to see from 1 to 10 birds per hour afield during a full day's quest. They warn, however, that the Texas-New Mexico area of concentration may be the result of the oasis-like nature of suitable habitat, and the special attention this receives from the bird-counters. According to their analysis of banded bird data, only the eastern race of the white-crown is regular east of the 90° parallel. Between 90° and 105° (the Great Plains region) the eastern and Gambel's races migrate and winter together. Intergrades from the west side of Hudson Bay winter mostly in the Dakotas.

The eastern white-crown has apparently been extending its winter range both eastward and northward since about 1950. A very few now winter fairly regularly as far northeast as the New York City region (John Bull, 1964), where winter reports were hardly credible 20 years earlier (Cruickshank, 1942), and quite unknown when Ludlow Griscom (1923) summed up the status of that region's bird life. The climatic amelioration of the first half of the century may have facilitated this range expansion, but such new land-use practices as the planting of multiflora (*Rosa multiflora*) hedges and the great number of bird-feeding stations that have come into vogue during this period have unquestionably helped tide over individual birds.

Distribution

Eastern White-crowned Sparrow

Range.—Montana, northern Ontario, and Labrador south to central Mexico.

Breeding range.—The eastern white-crowned sparrow breeds from north central and northeastern Manitoba (Churchill, Cape Tatnam, intergrades with *Z. l. gambelii*), northern Ontario (Fort Severn), northern Quebec (Richmond Gulf, Fort Chimo), and northern Labrador (Port Burwell) south to central northern Ontario (Fort Albany), central and southeastern Quebec (Lake Mistassini, Godbout, Blanc Sablon), and northern Newfoundland (Flower Cove, St. Anthony).

Winter range.—Winters from Kansas, central Missouri (Kansas City, St. Charles County), central Kentucky (Louisville), West Virginia (Charleston), and western North Carolina (Asheville) south to Sinaloa (Elota), Aguascalientes, Nuevo León (Monterrey), northern Tamaulipas (Matamoros), Louisiana (Natchitoches, Houma), and south central Georgia (Tifton, Savannah); casually north to southern Michigan (Jackson) and southern Ontario (Toronto); south rarely to southern Mississippi (Saucier), northwestern Florida (Pensacola), and Cuba.

Casual records.—Casual in north central Alaska (Togulak Lake), northern Franklin (Fletcher's Ice Island at 82°37′ N., 99°50′ W.), Baffin Island (Taverner Bay, Lake Harbour) Greenland (Godthaab, Fiskenaes), and in Bermuda.

Migration.—The data deal with the species as a whole. Early dates of spring arrival are: North Carolina—Raleigh, April 14. West Virginia—Morgantown, May 3. District of Columbia—March 26 (average of 14 years, April 26). Maryland—Anne Arundel County, April 10; Montgomery County, April 20; Laurel, May 2. Pennsylvania—Renovo, April 22; Meadville, April 23; Beaver, average of 14 years, May 7. New York—Brooklyn, April 10; Yates County,

April 23. Connecticut—West Hartford, April 15; New Haven, May 4. Rhode Island—Jamestown, May 7. Massachusetts—Martha's Vineyard, April 2. Vermont—Peacham, April 5; St. Johnsbury, April 14. New Hampshire—Tamworth, April 18; Monroe, April 21. Maine—Portland, May 9; Lake Umbagog, May 12. Quebec—Quebec City, April 21; Montreal area, April 30 (median of 7 years, May 6). New Brunswick—Andover, May 8. Nova Scotia—Shelburne, May 6; Wolfville, May 13. Prince Edward Island—Canoe Cove, May 27. Newfoundland—Stephenville Crossing, May 21; St. Anthony, June 1. Illinois—Urbana, April 1 (median of 20 years, April 30); Chicago, April 26 (average of 16 years, April 29). Indiana—Lafayette and Indianapolis, March 31. Ohio—Oberlin, April 21 (median of 19 years, May 2); Buckeye Lake, April 23 (median of 40 years for central Ohio, April 28). Michigan—Detroit area, April 20 (mean of 10 years, April 25); Battle Creek, April 28. Ontario—Leeds County, April 22; Ottawa, April 30 (average of 24 years, May 7). Iowa—Sac County, April 26; Sioux City, April 30 (average of 32 years, May 5). Wisconsin—Grantsburg, April 6. Minnesota—Pipestone, March 30 (average of 34 years for southern Minnesota, May 4). Oklahoma—Payne County, March 3. Nebraska—Hastings, March 31; Holstein, April 10; Red Cloud, April 19 (average of 20 years, April 30). South Dakota—Faulkton, April 3; Sioux Falls, April 13 (average of 6 years, May 4). North Dakota—Lower Souris Refuge, April 23; Cass County, April 29 (average, May 4). Manitoba—Treesbank, April 29 (average of 17 years, May 8). Mackenzie—Great Slave Lake, May 13. New Mexico—Los Alamos, March 15 (median of 5 years, March 24). Colorado—Derby, March 30. Utah—St. George, April 28. Wyoming—Careyhurst, March 11; Laramie, March 29 (average of 7 years, April 20); Cheyenne, April 18 (average of 9 years, April 27). Montana—Libby, March 24 (median of 10 years, April 24); Terry, April 21 (average of 5 years, May 5). Alberta—Warner, April 21. Oregon—Rickreall, March 9. Washington—Shelton, March 20; Potholes, April 10. British Columbia—Milner, March 25. Yukon—Macmillan River, April 28. Alaska—College, May 4; Kenai, May 14; Kobuk, May 21.

Late dates of spring departure are: Florida—southern peninsula, April 27. Alabama—Marysville, May 14; Montgomery, April 28. Georgia—Macon, May 5. South Carolina—Charleston, May 5. North Carolina—Asheville, May 10; Wilkes County, May 3. Virginia—Blacksburg, May 17; Cape Henry, May 15. District of Columbia—May 22 (average of 16 years, May 15). Maryland—Baltimore County, May 26; Prince Georges County, May 22. Pennsylvania—Wilkinsburg, June 5; State College, May 25. New Jersey—West Milford and Morristown, May 27; Cape May, May 7. New

York—Westchester County, June 14. Connecticut—East Windsor Hills, May 30; Portland, May 22. Massachusette—Nantucket, May 26; Martha's Vineyard, May 23. Vermont—Topsham, May 24. New Hampshire—Hanover, May 26. Maine—Lisbon, May 23. Quebec—Arvida, May 31. Nova Scotia, May 24. Louisiana—Baton Rouge, April 27. Mississippi—Rosedale, June 2 (mean of 19 years, May 12). Arkansas—Fayetteville, May 16. Tennessee—Knox County, May 21; Nashville, May 20 (median of 20 years, May 11). Kentucky—Bowling Green, May 11. Missouri—St. Louis, May 30 (median of 15 years, May 10). Illinois—Chicago, May 31 (average of 16 years, May 25); Urbana, May 29 (median of 20 years, May 17). Indiana—Wayne County, May 24 (median of 16 years, May 11). Ohio—central Ohio, May 29 (median of 40 years, May 20); Oberlin, April 22 (median of 19 years, May 19). Michigan—Detroit area, June 4 (mean of 10 years, May 24). Ontario—Point Pelee and Whitby, May 29. Iowa—Floyd County, May 21; Sioux City, May 19. Wisconsin—Wausau and Viroqua, May 30. Minnesota—Cloquet, May 25 (average of 6 years for southern Minnesota, May 19). Texas—Sinton, May 7 (mean of 5 years, April 22); Austin, April 29. Oklahoma—Oklahoma City, May 26; Tulsa, May 17. Kansas—northeastern Kansas, May 30 (median of 18 years, May 9). Nebraska—Holstein, May 24. South Dakota—Faulkton, June 14; Sioux Falls, May 16. North Dakota—Cass County, May 25 (average, May 22); Jamestown, May 18. Saskatchewan—Kinloch, June 6. New Mexico—Los Alamos, May 29 (median of 6 years, May 13). Arizona—Tucson, June 6. Colorado—Colorado Springs, June 17. Utah—Kanab, May 14. Idaho—Moscow, May 28 (median of 11 years, May 16). Montana—Libby, June 2 (median of 10 years, May 12); Choteau, May 22. California—Orange County, May 22. Nevada—Mercury, April 28. Oregon—Linn County, May 28; Baker County, May 24; Lake County, May 20. Washington—Spokane, May 22.

Early dates of fall arrival are: Washington—Shelton, August 21; Hidden Lakes, August 30; Potholes, September 14. Oregon—Baker County, September 6 Wheeler County, September 13. Nevada—Clark County, September 13; Mercury, September 21. California—Lafayette, September 3. Montana—Libby, August 27 (median of 10 years, September 9). Idaho—Moscow, August 27 (median of 11 years, August 29). Utah—Uinta Basin, September 10; La Sal Mountains, September 13. Arizona—Wagner, September 9. New Mexico—Los Alamos, September 5 (median of 6 years, September 10). Saskatchewan—Sovereign, September 5. Manitoba—Treesbank, September 10 (average of 9 years, September 22). North Dakota—Jamestown, September 15; Cass County, September 18 (average,

September 22). South Dakota—Rapid City, September 11; Faulkton, September 13. Nebraska—Neligh, September 22; Lincoln, September 28. Kansas—northeastern Kansas, September 28 (median of 10 years, October 12). Oklahoma—Copan, October 6. Texas—Sinton, October 19 (median of 5 years, November 4). Minnesota—Minneapolis-St. Paul, September 18 (average of 14 years for southern Minnesota, September 29). Wisconsin—Chippewa County, September 3; Wausau, September 9. Iowa—Sioux City, September 24 (average of 32 years, October 15). Ontario—North Bay, September 7; Peel County, September 8. Michigan—Detroit area, September 17 (mean of 10 years, September 23). Ohio—central Ohio, September 27 (median of 40 years, October 6). Indiana—Chesterton, September 16; Wayne County, September 30 (median of 15 years, October 9). Illinois—Chicago, September 12 (average of 16 years, September 22). Missouri—St. Louis, September 25 (median of 15 years, October 3). Kentucky—Glasgow, October 3. Tennessee—Nashville, September 28 (median of 20 years, October 15); Knox County, October 18, Arkansas—Arkansas County, September 20; Fayetteville, October 8. Mississippi—Rosedale, October 2 (mean of 31 years, October 18); Saucier, October 12. Louisiana—Baton Rouge, October 28. Nova Scotia—Louisbourg, September 22. Prince Edward Island—Ellerslie, September 22. Quebec—Highmore, September 11. Maine—Lake Umbagog, September 23; Cumberland Mills, September 26; Portland, October 1. New Hampshire—Tamworth, September 20. Vermont—Hartland, September 10; Wells River, September 26. Massachusetts—Nantucket, September 19. Rhode Island—Newport County, September 27. Connecticut—Hartford, September 24. New York—Essex County, September 20; Long Island, September 23. New Jersey—Cape May, September 30. Pennsylvania—Erie, September 19; Renovo, September 23. Maryland—Baltimore County, September 27; Laurel, October 2 (median of 5 years, October 9). District of Columbia—October 1 (average of 7 years, October 13). Virginia—Blacksburg, September 14; Cape Henry, October 8. North Carolina—Mills River Valley, October 6. South Carolina—Berkeley County, October 9; Charleston, median of 5 years, October 20. Georgia—Athens, October 25. Alabama—Dauphin Island, October 7; Birmingham, October 17. Florida—Tallahassee, October 4; Pensacola, October 9.

Late dates of fall departure are: Alaska—Chena Hot Springs, October 18; Cohoe, October 5. Yukon—Macmillan Pass, September 4. British Columbia—Okanagan Landing, October 30. Washington—Wawawai, November 9. Oregon—Coos Bay, October 18. Alberta—Glenevis, October 10. Montana—Libby, October 20 (median of 10 years, September 30). Wyoming—Laramie, October 30 (average of 8 years, October 22); Cheyenne, October 14 (average of 6 years, October 4). Utah—Spectacle Lake, October 26. Colorado—Colorado Springs, November 12. Arizona—Parker Dam, October 30. New Mexico—Los Alamos, December 1 (median of 6 years October 28). Saskatchewan—Regina, November 5. Manitoba—Treesbank, October 27 (average of 8 years, October 2). North Dakota—Grafton, October 14; Cass County, October 9 (average, October 7). South Dakota—Faulkton, November 10. Nebraska—Neligh, November 1. Oklahoma—Payne County, November 14. Minnesota—Minneapolis-St. Paul, November 2 (average of 6 years for southern Minnesota, October 18). Wisconsin—Milwaukee, October 28. Iowa—Sioux City, October 30. Ontario—Ottawa, November 4 (average of 15 years, October 8). Michigan—Detroit area, mean of 10 years, November 11; Battle Creek, October 26. Ohio—central Ohio, November 30 (median of 40 years, October 29). Indiana—Indianapolis, November 23. Illinois—Chicago, November 9 (average of 16 years, October 23). Mississippi—Saucier, October 31. Newfoundland—St. Anthony, October 5. Nova Scotia—Shelburne, November 6; Yarmouth County, October 14. New Brunswick—Scotch Lake, October 30; Grand Manan, October 5. Quebec—Montreal area, October 29 (median of 7 years, October 17); Kamouraska, October 27. Maine—Falmouth, October 28; Lake Umbagog, October 13. New Hampshire—Ossipie, November 9; Concord, October 24; New Hampton, median of 21 years, October 22. Vermont—Woodstock, October 29; Wells River, October 26. Rhode Island—Newport County, November 24. Connecticut—Bristol, November 2; New Haven, October 26. New Jersey—West Milford, November 14. New York—Suffolk County, November 17; Saratoga County, October 31. Pennsylvania—Wilkinsburg and Indiana, October 30. Maryland—Baltimore County December 6; Laurel, December 4 (median of 4 years, November 11). District of Columbia—November 28. Virginia—Cape Henry, November 2.

Egg dates.—Alaska: 213 records, April 1 to July 11; 110 records, June 6 to June 16.

Labrador: 38 records, June 3 to July 11; 24 records, June 20 to June 30.

Ontario: 5 records, June 17 to June 28.

ZONOTRICHIA LEUCOPHRYS NUTTALLI Ridgway

Nuttall's White-crowned Sparrow*

PLATE 69

Contributed by BARBARA BLANCHARD DEWOLFE**

HABITS

White-crowned sparrows are among the best known and most widely distributed passerine birds of North America. They live close to man, and their original range may well have been extended as a result of man's activities, for the combination of bare ground, grass, and dense shrubbery they prefer is often concomitant to road-building, lumbering, farming, or burning. White-crowned sparrows are easily trapped in migration and on the wintering grounds, and large numbers are banded each year.

The breeding range of the species' western populations extends from sea level to over 11,000 feet and spans some 3,000 miles both north to south and east to west, from latitude 70°N. on the Arctic slope of the Brooks Range to latitude 34°N. at Gaviota, Calif. and from longitude 105°W. in central Colorado to longitude 168°W. on the Seward Peninsula in Alaska. Within this large geographic area the species is divided into four races which differ only slightly in color pattern, shade of plumage, and other morphological characters, but which vary markedly as to strength of migratory instinct and the timing of the breeding cycle. Nuttall's sparrow (*Z. l. nuttalli*) is permanently resident in the fog belt of California, and begins to nest in March or April, depending on the year. The Puget Sound spar-

---

*This account also contains material on *Zonotrichia leucophrys gambelii*, *Z. l. oriantha*, and *Z. l. pugetensis*.

**The author acknowledges with thanks Grant number 2804 from the Penrose Fund of the American Philosophical Society, which made possible the literature search for data on range, migration, and nesting cycle. Thanks are due F. S. L. Williamson, who contributed unpublished data on clutch size in *Z. l. gambelii* from the Terrestrial Avifauna Study, Project Chariot of the Atomic Energy Commission, and L. H. Walkinshaw, who contributed data on behavior, nesting, and clutch size in this race. Richard C. Banks contributed data on distribution.

The author also wishes to thank Barbara Lilley Mooney, who carried out the literature search, Priscilla Phillips, whose banding records and observations made possible the writing of the sections on fall and winter for *Z. l. gambelii*, and Anne Hinshaw Wing, whose analysis of Gambel's sparrow song appears in the text. Many ornithologists contributed unpublished data through personal communications, which are acknowledged in the text.

The original field data supplied by the author were obtained under grants from the National Science Foundation, Society of the Sigma Xi, American Philosophical Society, and from the Committee on Research, University of California, Santa Barbara.

Berkeley, Calif., May 3, 1946 J. E. Patterson

NEST OF WHITE-CROWNED (NUTTALL'S) SPARROW

Uinta Mountains, Utah A. D. Cruickshank

WHITE-CROWNED SPARROW FEEDING YOUNG

row (*Z. l. pugetensis*) comprises populations with every degree of migratory instinct, from those in northern California that forsake their territories in winter to flock only a few hundred yards away, to those of the Canadian border that fly a thousand miles each year between wintering and breeding grounds. This race begins nesting in early to late April, depending upon the latitude of the breeding population in question. Gambel's sparrow (*Z. l. gambelii*) is a strongly migratory race. It starts to nest in late May and early June in Alaska, and in the provinces and the Northwest Territories of Canada. The mountain white-crowned sparrow (*Z. l. oriantha*) is also migratory, and begins to breed from late May to early July in Alberta and the western United States, depending upon when the high mountain meadows become sufficiently free of snow to permit nesting.

Beneath this variability in migratory instinct and in the timing of the breeding cycle lie patterns of behavior common to all four races—the themes on which the variations are based. During territory establishment and defense, courtship, nest-building, incubation, and care of the young, the behavior is similar in all races. Therefore the accounts in the section on "Habits" based on my observations of Nuttall's sparrow at Berkeley apply also to the Puget Sound sparrow and Gambel's sparrow during comparable phases, and also to the mountain white-crowned sparrow insofar as my limited field work on this race permits comparisons. In fact, so similar is the behavior in all populations of white-crowned sparrows I have studied during the breeding season, that as I watched them I felt as if I were seeing the same birds, whether in central California, at the Canadian border, or in Alaska. Such racial variations as do exist lie not in the behavior patterns themselves but in the time of year the patterns emerge, and in the duration of the successive phases of the nesting cycle. These variations will be described in the sections under each race, which follow the general account for the species.

Where the observations are neither my own nor quoted from published accounts cited in the bibliography, I refer in the text to the observer who, through personal communication, supplied me with the data. If no citation is made, the statements are based on my field work done in the following localities for the periods stated:

Z. l. nuttalli.	California:	Berkeley (five years).
Z. l. pugetensis.	California:	Berkeley (five winter seasons); Eureka (one winter and one spring).
	Oregon:	Tillamook (one spring).
	Washington:	Friday Harbor (one spring and summer).

Z. l. gambelii.	California:	Davis (one winter season); Santa Barbara, (ten winter seasons).
	Alaska:	Mountain Village (one spring and summer); College (one spring, summer, and fall).
Z. l. oriantha.	California:	Sierra Nevadas and Lassen National Park (one summer).

Spring.—Spring is the time of transition from flocking to paired isolation on mutually exclusive areas. Territorial jealousy and sexual interest, which have been at low ebb during winter, emerge and rise to maximum intensity. The male sings with increasing frequency and vigor; he pursues and fights rival males, and the female trills and postures. At first these elements of territoriality and sexual interest may appear separately, unorganized into any integrated behavior. Later they are woven into a characteristic pattern. The end result is that pairs space out in orderly fashion and stay on their territories at least until the young of the last brood become independent.

In early, mid, or late January, depending on the weather, the male Nuttall's sparrow begins to sing more forcefully than in winter, more frequently, and from a more conspicuous perch. The adult male becomes less and less tolerant of the immature or mateless birds that have spent the winter in his area. When their song also increases in force and frequency, he pursues and attacks them until, about 3 weeks after the beginning of this phase, he regains sole possession of all or part of the territory he patrolled the year before. With this achievement, if he is already mated, he stops singing except for rare, weak songs. Boundary disputes or pursuits are also rare. Settlement is now complete, some 7½ weeks before incubation starts.

The immature or mateless males usually find mates during the period of singing, pursuits, and fighting. If they do not, they continue to sing after the mated males are silent. If a male loses his mate, he resumes loud singing and continues it until another female joins him.

Color-banding reveals that, except in instances of polygamy, territorial jealousy is not expressed by the female Nuttall's sparrow. Her weak song, which continues until nesting time, is not used for advertisement or warning. I have never seen her join in a fight and only rarely in a chase in which her mate was involved. In polygamy, on the other hand, all elements of territorial jealousy appear. The development of the territorial sense in the female independently of the male is illustrated in the behavior, in 1935, of females I and III, simultaneous mates of male I. The description is taken from Barbara D. Blanchard (1941):

> With the approach of reproduction * * * each female created for herself a subdivision of the main territory which she defended against the other female by loud singing and fighting, and in which she finally chose her nest site. From February 1 until late March, by which time both had nests, each female sang frequently from a favorite perch within her section. * * * Twice, when female III followed the male toward the section which belonged to female I, a fight ensued between the two females. They locked feet and jabbed each other on the breast. * * * Had they not been banded, I should have thought I was watching a boundary dispute between two males.

Territory.—Just as the behavior involved in territory establishment is nearly identical in the four races, so is the nature of the site chosen for the territory. Despite the variety of climatic and vegetational zones in which the four races nest, all the territories I have observed are strikingly similar in their appearance. So marked is the similarity that I think it must reflect deep seated preferences common to the western portion of the species—a conservative psychological theme with minor racial variations.

The similarity in appearance of the white-crowned sparrow territories at different latitudes and altitudes lies not in the presence of any one common element—such as a particular species of plant—or in any one topographic feature, but in a subtle yet definite combination of three elements: grass, bare ground, and shrubbery. These invariably exist in each male's territory. Two other elements are usually present near each territory but not necessarily within it: water, either salt or fresh, and tall trees.

The nature of the grass, bare ground, and shrubbery vary with climate and topography. The grass may be pure or mixed with lichens or mosses or sedges and small flowering plants. The bare ground may be a sandy beach or the rocky shore of a lake or river. It may be a road or a pack trail, a ploughed field or a clearing in the forest. The shrubbery may consist of any species of plant, native or exotic, that grows thick enough to shelter a nest or to provide a roost. Bracken fern, scrub conifers and alders and willows, salal, Labrador tea, lupine or rose or *Artemesia* bushes, and many exotic ornamental shrubs are examples of plants that make up this common element.

To list the three elements and the forms they take in different climates is not, however, to define a white-crowned sparrow's territory. Rather it must be understood in terms of the bird's temperament and habits. It seems to me that the essential feature is the mixture of grass, bare ground, and shrubbery in just the right proportions to permit ground foraging with quick escape to shelter. The areas of bare ground and grass must be large enough to facilitate foraging, but not so large as to require the birds to move more than a few wing-beats away from cover. The shrubbery must be extensive enough to conceal a nest and the devious route the female takes to and from it, but not so unbroken in extent as to require a long flight to reach open ground. Extensive areas of grass, bare ground, and shrubbery existing side by side in solid masses with abrupt linear interfaces do not constitute typical white-crowned sparrow country. What is most typical of a territory is its patchy appearance, because of the interstitial invasion of the open ground by shrubbery.

Such subtle characteristics of a landscape are easy to sense, but hard to describe. Yet, owing to the presence of the same characteristic elements with, of course, almost infinite local variations, the territories of white-crowned sparrows throughout western North America look much alike. An example of this is the similarity in appearance, or perhaps in "mood," of the landscapes at Desolation Lake in the high Sierras and at Point Lobos on the Monterey peninsula, both of which support breeding populations of white-crowned sparrows. In June of 1960 I found male white-crowned sparrows of the race *oriantha* spaced out and singing regularly along the edge of Desolation Lake in the Wilderness Area above and west of Lake Tahoe. I assume they were either nesting or about to nest there. At Point Lobos on the shore of the Pacific Ocean near Monterey, Calif., Nuttall's sparrows nest abundantly.

In spite of the obvious differences in the details of the two landscapes, the elements characteristic of white-crowned sparrow territories are present in both and confer on the two localities a common stamp. The high mountain lake is bordered by masses of bare granite with gnarled juniper trees and dwarfed pines. Pack trails meander along the edge of the lake, and tufts of grass and patches of alpine flowers grow in the lee of granite boulders. The same elements of a large body of water, bare ground, shrubbery, and grass comprise the landscape at Point Lobos. Here a similar scene is produced by the juxtaposition of ocean, steep granite cliffs, and wind-racked Monterey cypress. The grass is more extensive and the flowers more conspicuous, but the impression conveyed to me by both landscapes is essentially the same, that of a wind-swept barren land with warped trees, and a lee with sheltered spots where grass and flowers grow.

A second example of the similarity of white-crowned sparrow territories in widely separated areas is found in Nuttall's sparrow country near coastal farm lands of California and in Gambel's sparrow country on the outskirts of Fairbanks, Alaska. In the summer of 1956 I found Nuttall's sparrows breeding on the seaward edge of a farm in San Luis Obispo County. Their territories included both cultivated and wild land. They foraged in a pasture, used the fence posts for singing perches, and the native shrubbery beyond the pasture for shelter and nest sites. In the same pasture cattle grazed, dogs dug for pocket gophers, and domestic ducks waddled at the edge of the swampy patches.

In the summer of 1957 I found a similar landscape in Alaska near the cultivated fields of the University of Alaska's Agricultural Experiment Station. Gambel's sparrows had incorporated the cultivated land into their nesting territories. They foraged in the fields, roosted in the willow and rose tangles at the edge, and nested in the tall thick grass. Even the details of the scene reminded me forcibly of Nuttall's sparrow country 3,000 miles to the south: I found tracks of cloven-hoofed mammals at the edge of the field, in the distance I saw a pair of small carnivores hunting mice, and ducks moved along in the stubble at the far edge of the cultivated plots. It took considerable effort to realize that this was an Alaskan scene, not a California one, that the hoof-prints were those of moose, not cattle, that the carnivores were native red foxes, and that the ducks were wild.

This second example brings out another characteristic of many, if not most, white-crowned sparrow territories—their close connection with human habitation or with country altered by man. This is a feature not only of territories in the densely populated areas of California, but also of those in many parts of Alaska as well. In 1950 I went to Mountain Village, an Eskimo trading post on the lower Yukon, to watch the arrival of Gambel's sparrows. One boundary of the village is the river. Above the village scrub alder and willow merged into upland tundra. There were no roads or cultivated fields. I found arriving Gambel's sparrows carving out territories in the village, beside fish camps, even by the schoolhouse and trading post, and including in their areas the river's edge, which was used by the villagers as a thoroughfare to and from the trading post and as a place to tie their dogs. The undisturbed ground above the village was apparently also suitable for white-crowned sparrows, as a few pairs settled there, but only after all suitable areas in the village had been preempted.

I persisted in my search for Gambel's sparrows nesting on land in its natural state, and one day I found what appeared to be just such a spot about 6 miles upriver from the trading post. There I found open grassy knolls with bare ground grooved by tiny streams and surrounded by dense scrub alder. Gambel's sparrows were breeding there, and I found no trace of human beings, not even a rusty knife or a fragment of sawed wood. Imagine my dismay when, on describing the spot to the trader that evening, I found that this clearing was all that remained of a once-thriving Eskimo village that had been abandoned about 40 years before!

Courtship.—Courtship behavior includes both pairing and copulation. The two processes may be separated by several weeks. Like territory establishment, the elements of behavior involved in courtship are the same for all races. Such variations as occur involve the duration of courtship behavior, its relation to the stage of the reproductive cycle, and the length of time elapsing between pairing and copulation. Except in Nuttall's sparrow, I have little or no evidence of the permanence of the bond between mates.

As with few exceptions the Nuttall's sparrows I watched at Berkeley remained paired for life, only the immature and bereft adults sought mates in the spring. The rising intensity of the male's song and of the female's trilling and posturing thus may serve two different purposes in courtship: either they bring together two unmated birds and result in pairing, or they intensify the permanent bond between members of a pair that bred together the previous year. In either case the elements of behavior are the same. I shall describe them in adults already paired.

In January the female's interest in her mate gradually intensifies, expressed by low metallic trills and wing fluttering. At first her trilling is sporadic and seems to be called forth only by the loud song of a male (not necessarily her mate) or by a chase or fight in which the mate is involved; it may or may not be accompanied by fluttering of the wings. As the season advances, trilling and posturing are almost invariably linked, and more and more often occur independently of any apparent external stimulus. Both actions increase in intensity and frequency until the peak is reached some 6 to 8 weeks later, just before copulation, in early to late March, depending upon the year. As the female becomes engaged in nesting, both trilling and posturing cease, to be resumed in lesser degree prior to copulation for the second brood.

The intensification of the male's interest in his mate, insofar as I can judge from his behavior, is much more sudden. During January and February he seems indifferent to her trilling and posturing. He pays no special attention to her other than to forage with her and to utter location notes as he has done throughout the fall and winter. From early March, however, he punctuates long periods of indifference by "attacks" upon the female. Suddenly, with no warning that I can detect, his indifference changes to aggression. He chases the female and jabs her with his beak. Such "attacks" take place as much as 18 days before, and also a few days after, the first observed copulation. Another change that precedes coition by from 1 to 3 weeks is the beginning of evening song. During the half-hour before dark the male intersperses periods of foraging with faint singing, which seems directed at his mate rather than at neighboring males.

Such song gains in force and frequency until on the evenings when copulation occurs he follows his mate about, singing loudly before and after he mounts her.

Copulation occurs most often during the half-hour before dark, but may take place also during the day. The female follows her mate about and trills persistently, fluttering her wings and raising her tail. Suddenly she flies straight away from her mate, and lands either on the ground or in a tree some yards distant. Her mate follows and lands near her. He hops toward her, crown raised and tail lowered and spread, flutters above her a few seconds, then flies to a nearby perch and sings. I have seen the same pair copulate as many as 11 times in one evening. The average for 21 pairs is 5 times. The period during which the pair copulate lasts 3 to 6 days.

Since immature birds begin their courtship at the same time as the adults, they may pair as early as January, and the interval between pairing and copulation may last 6 weeks or more. The long courtship period characteristic of Nuttall's sparrow is a consequence of the fact that courtship begins when both sexes are in the early phases of the reproductive cycle, with immature gonads only a small fraction of their breeding size. This is not true for the migratory races.

In Nuttall's sparrow polygamy is not uncommon. In 5 years of observation of color-banded birds at Berkeley, I found three cases of a male with two mates.

Nesting.—The typical nest site is similar in the four races. The nest is usually placed either on the ground or a few feet above the ground, under or within dense but not necessarily extensive vegetation of whatever kind affords adequate concealment. Some of the species of plants in which nests have been found are conifers, especially young pines and spruce (Bolander, 1906; Farner, 1952; Jewett, 1916; Johnston, 1943; Kobbé, 1900; McHugh, 1948; Ray, 1906; Warren, 1912); scrub oak, willow and alder (Farner, 1958; Grinnell, 1900; Macoun, 1909; Ray, 1912); dwarf birch (Dice, 1920); bushes of wild rose, lupine, sage, thimble berry (Jewett, 1916; Ray, 1906); composite perennials such as *Ericameria* and *Eriophyllum* (Grinnell and Linsdale, 1936); many species of ornamental exotic shrubs; and, rarely, an annual plant (Grinnell and Linsdale, 1936, found a Nuttall's sparrow nest at Point Lobos in a 4-foot radish plant). Nests on the ground may be placed in a tussock of grass, in densely matted perennials such as Labrador tea, or, rarely, in a patch of moss (Grinnell, 1900). They are often built at the base of scrub willows or conifers (Grinnell, 1900; Macoun, 1909; Ray, 1912). Occasionally the nests are placed in exposed situations, as for example the Gambel's sparrow nest Edward A. Preble (1908) found in a tuft of short grass beside a much-frequented path in a field. Some atypical sites include one reported by Louis Bolander (1906) of a nest built 35 feet above the ground in a cypress, another in the outer drooping branches of a tall acacia tree, and a third in an ivy vine on a building (Blanchard, 1941).

The extremes of height of nests reported in the literature range from flush with the ground to 35 feet above it. The average height above the ground for 31 *nuttalli* nests at Berkeley was 3.5 feet with a range of 1.5 to 11 feet, for 16 *nuttalli* nests at Point Lobos 1.8 feet with a range of 1 to 4 feet. H. W. Carriger (pers. comm.) states that he occasionally found *nuttalli* nests on the ground. The Friday Harbor Puget Sound sparrows tended to nest on the ground with greater frequency than did the Berkeley *nuttalli*. Of the 45 nests I found at Friday Harbor, 14 were built on the ground in masses of dense scrubby salal (*Gaultheria shallon*) or in dead bracken fern or grass. I also found nests in native and exotic trees and shrubs. As nest-building started at this locality before the trees and shrubs were fully leafed, many of the nests in process of construction could be seen from a distance of several yards. The foliage grew so rapidly, however, that before the eggs were laid the nests were well concealed.

The eight *gambelii* nests I found at Mountain Village in 1950 were all built on the ground. When nesting began there, the only vegetation thick enough for concealment was either dead grass recently exposed by the melting snow or dense mats of dwarf perennials. At College, Alaska, in 1957 I found 13 nests on the ground and only one nest in dead twigs a few inches above the sloping ground of a railroad embankment.

The four *oriantha* nests I found in the Sierras were all on the ground, one at the center of an *Artemesia* bush, the others under scrub lodgepole pine. Records of *oriantha* nests in the literature include several on the ground in grass, on slanting willow stems or under scrub conifers, and several a few inches above the ground in spruce or pine. The highest on record is a nest Milton S. Ray (1912) found in the Tahoe region 4 feet above the ground in a lodgepole pine sapling.

In the matter of nest material the birds show great catholicity of taste and use whatever suitable material is available. If the nest is built on the ground, it may lack a platform; if it is placed above the ground it may have a bulky platform of twigs (Bolander, 1906). Materials used in the nest are: fine twigs and rootlets (Barlow, 1901), grasses, both green and dry, dead fern leaves, weed stems, shreds of bark and pine needles (Burleigh, 1930). Materials used for lining include fine grasses, feathers, and whatever mammal hair is available such as deer, cow, horse, and dog (Burleigh, 1930; Grinnell, 1900; Nelson, 1887; Ray, 1912).

In the three races I have seen, nest building is solely by the female. The following description for Nuttall's sparrow applies to Puget Sound and Gambel's sparrows as well. Such racial differences as exist involve the length of time the female takes to finish the nest and the interval between fledging the first brood and starting the second nest.

In Nuttall's sparrow the first hints of nesting are the male's "sseep" note, which may precede nest building by as much as 8 days, and the interest the female shows in nest material. For a week before she begins to build she may pick up straws and then drop them. During this period she may also utter the characteristic "eep" location note which she subsequently uses during nest building and incubation. She may protest if one approaches the future site of the nest. Several days or a week after these behavior elements have appeared separately, they merge and intensify into coordinated activity, and she begins continuous work on the nest. Her mate perches nearby and utters the "ssseep call note, which may stimulate her to build. The details of a single morning's work of one Nuttall's sparrow female are as follows:

On March 11, which was the second or third day she had worked on the nest, I watched her from 8:00 to 11:30 a.m. At 8:15 she carried material to the nest, and from then until 11:30 built almost continuously, making 135 trips with material, stopping only three times and then only for a moment to feed. Almost all the material was gathered within a few yards of the nest; it consisted of dead twigs and leaves, strands of dry grass, pine needles, small green plants, and fresh grass stems. Dead leaves and dry grass were brought most often. She brought only three twigs, all within the first hour. After every few trips she could be heard fluttering in the nest, probably molding the cup. This female spent parts of the next three days in building, but never worked as continuously as on March 11. By March 15 the nest appeared complete.

Nest-building in Nuttall's sparrow begins a few days before copulation, when trilling and posturing are reaching the climax. The number of days spent in building the first nest of the season was from 7 to 8 or 9 for the five nests found just as the female was starting work. Three were worked on during parts of 7 days, one during parts of 8 days, and one 8 or 9 days. If a clutch or a brood of nestlings is destroyed, the female starts a new nest within a few days and may complete it in 5 or 6 days.

Eggs.—The color of the eggs has been described variously as "pale greenish-blue, spotted and splashed with liver-brown" (Davie, 1883) or "a handsome light green or bluish-green shade, * * * heavily dotted, spotted, blotched or clouded with reddish-brown" (Dawson,

1923) or "* * * pale greenish blue, varying to brownish, spotted with cinnamon or reddish brown" (Gabrielson and Lincoln, 1959). The first description is for a clutch taken at Alameda, California, and hence *nuttalli*, the second of one collected in Humboldt County and therefore *pugetensis*, the third of eggs of Gambel's sparrow. Davie (1883) comments on a clutch assignable to *oriantha* collected at Hancock, Colorado: "* * * the markings are much heavier and thicker near the larger ends."

Some egg measurements are as follows: For *nuttalli*, a clutch of four eggs measured by Davie were .94 x .68 inch, .88 x .65 inch, and two .88 x .64 inch. Dawson gives the average measurements of 70 eggs of *pugetensis* as 20.7 x 16 millimeters, the extremes being 18.5–22.4 millimeters by 14.7–16.5 millimeters. For *oriantha* W. G. F. Harris gives the average of 40 eggs as 21.1 by 15.8 millimeters, the eggs showing the low extremes measuring *22.9* by *16.3*, *19.8* by 16.3, and 20.3 by *14.7* millimeters. For *gambelii* Harris gives the average for 40 eggs as 21.5 by 15.5 millimeters, the eggs showing the four extremes measuring *24.1* by *17.0*, *18.5* by 14.7, and 22.4 by *14.2* millimeters.

The limits of the egg-laying period for the four races are from early March to late July, and the date when the first clutch of the season is laid depends upon race and latitude. The number of eggs per clutch varies from 2 to 6, with two exceptional cases of 7 eggs per clutch. The average clutch size varies with race, latitude, the month in the breeding season the clutch is laid, and the age of the female. The eggs of one clutch are laid one each morning on successive days until the clutch is complete.

The rest of this section presents the data on eggs of Nuttall's sparrow. The respects in which egg-laying in the other races differ from *nuttalli* is discussed elsewhere.

The first egg is laid from 1 to 7 days after the nest is completed (an average of 3.6 days for 12 records), and from 4 to 9 days after the first observed copulation. The egg-laying season in *nuttalli* begins in most years in mid-March and finishes by late June. Extreme dates for clutches are Mar. 3, 1936, for a clutch I found at Berkeley, and July 24, 1898, for one M. S. Ray found in the San Francisco Bay Region. Median dates for first egg of first clutch laid at Berkeley for 5 years are as follows: Mar. 22–23, 1934 for six clutches, Apr. 4, 1935 for six clutches, Mar. 11, 1936 for seven clutches, Apr. 13, 1937 for nine clutches, and Apr. 7, 1938 for five clutches. The contrast in the median dates for the Berkeley population between 1936 and 1937 shows how weather conditions (chiefly mean temperature) can influence the time nesting starts in this race. This marked annual variation for the same locality is characteristic of the resident Nuttall's sparrows, which must adjust to the capricious winter and spring climate of California. The migratory races that nest in the far north where the country becomes suitable for nesting close to the same date each year do not show such wide annual fluctuations in the date of first egg laid.

The number of eggs per clutch varies from 2 to 5. The average for 215 sets is 3.27 eggs per completed clutch. The most frequent clutch size is 3 eggs. The percentages are as follows: 2 eggs per clutch 4.2 percent; 3 eggs per clutch 65.6 percent, 4 eggs per clutch 29.8 percent, 5 eggs (one clutch only) 0.4 percent. The average number of eggs per clutch increases from March through May, after which it declines: for March the average for 15 clutches was 3.00, for April 3.22 for 122 clutches, for May 3.48 for 50 clutches. In June the average of 21 clutches declined to 3.24, and in July, the average for 7 clutches was only 3.14.

The average for 24 first clutches was 3.04 eggs, whereas 10 second clutches averaged 3.60, 5 third clutches 3.00, and 3 fourth clutches also 3.00. I have records of all the clutches laid by one female for 2 years. In 1934 when she bred for the first time she laid four clutches of 3, 2, 2, and 3 eggs respectively; in 1935 she laid four clutches of 2, 4, 4, and 3 eggs.

Incubation.—Incubation is by the female alone. She sits on the eggs with her back flush with or below the nest rim, her tail raised at a sharp angle and her chin resting on the edge. She incubates for periods averaging about 20 minutes each, then leaves the nest to forage, uttering the same strident "eep" note she used while building the nest. Hopping about on the ground hurriedly, she covers a large area in a few minutes: This rapidity of movement is so characteristic that I have often identified an incubating female by this behavior. When the female returns to the nest she again utters a series of "eeps."

At the start of incubation the male achieves the highest development of territorial behavior. He guards his area by loud, almost continuous singing and patrol. Often, but not invariably, he appears to call the female off the nest. At such times he approaches the nest and sings, whereupon the female leaves and the pair forage together. The male therefore does not guard the nest in the absence of his mate, but he may be involved to some degree in her return. Often he flies to a perch near the nest and sings, whereupon the female gradually moves nearer and nearer and finally resumes incubation. At other times the female is the first to stop foraging and to fly toward the nest, followed by her mate.

In Nuttall's sparrow the beginning of incubation in relation to egg-laying varies; 5 females began on the day before the last egg was laid, 5 on the day the last egg was laid, and 1 the day after. Of 5 females with sets of three eggs, 3 started on the day the second was laid, 1 on the day the third was laid, and 1 the day after the set was completed. Of 3 females with sets of four eggs, 2 started on the day the third egg was laid, and 1 on the day the set was completed; 3 females with sets of only two eggs all started the day they laid the second.

The average time of hatching for 10 sets of eggs was 12 to 12½ days after the first day of continuous incubation. One set hatched in 11 or 12 days, two in 14 days, the remainder at the average time.

As might be expected from the individual variation in the beginning of incubation, the eggs of one set may hatch all on the same day or on two successive days. The longest intervals between first and last hatchings of eggs in one set were somewhere between 7 and 15 hours for a set of three eggs, and between 16 and 17 hours for a set of four. The eggs in any one set do not necessarily hatch in the order in which they were laid.

Young.—The following account of Nuttall's sparrow applies also to those populations of *pugetensis* and *gambelii* I have watched during this phase of the breeding cycle. Where racial differences occur, these are noted under the race in question.

On the day the young hatch, the adults follow essentially the same routine as during incubation. The female now alternates between brooding the young and gathering food for herself and for them. The behavior of the male is definitely affected and reflects awareness of the event. He continues his patrol but spends more time near the nest. He responds at once to the alarm notes of the female by flying straight toward the nest and scolding.

For at least the first 3 or 4 days the female bears almost the whole burden of feeding the nestlings. I have seen her start to gather insects within 2 hours after the young hatched, but have never seen the male visit the nest until the 2nd or 3rd day after, and then relatively rarely. At such times he never went directly to the nest, but carried the food to a nearby perch and held it in his beak for as much as an hour before feeding it to the young.

The 6th day after hatching is the last on which I have found a female brooding her young during the day; only rarely have I found one sitting on the nest in the daytime after her young were 4 days old. One female brooded her nestlings each night until the 8th day after they hatched.

Blanchard (1941) describes the nestling on the day of hatching as follows:

> The young bird just after hatching weighs a little over 2 grams. It has down on the head, dorsum, wings and thighs; this dries in about two hours and stands straight out from the body. The remnant of the yolk stalk is still visible, and the viscera can be seen through the transparent skin of the abdomen. The bird

breaths spasmodically, the entire body throbbing. It responds to jarring of the nest by raising its head and waving it about unsteadily, the mouth wide open. At first it holds this position only for a moment before its head drops forward and the "egg position" is resumed. I can hear no sound even when the beak is wide open.

The following description of the development of behavior of the nestling is based upon my observations and those of Richard C. Banks (1959): On the day after hatching I could hear the nestling squeak faintly. The earliest the bird can right itself is 2 days after hatching. The eyes begin to open 3 days after hatching and by the 5th day they are wide open. Reflexive grasping of the nest lining by the feet begins about 4 days after hatching. On the 5th day after hatching a new posture, crouching, is assumed. By the 7th day after hatching a large number of nestlings give protest notes when handled. The first concerted escape attempt occurs at 8½ days after hatching.

Banks (1959) describes the growth of the feathers in nestling Nuttall's sparrows as follows:

At hatching, dark spots representing feather papillae are visible beneath the skin surface on the alar, humeral, dorsal, and coronal tracts of White-crowns. External feather sheaths first appear when the birds are 2½ to 3 days of age. The first rupture of these sheaths occurs at age 5½ or 6 days. At 7 days of age, the tips of the primary sheaths begin to break. Feathers of the anal circlet appear without visible external sheaths.

After an initial slow start, feather growth is rapid and constant. Primaries grew at a maximum rate of 3.9 mm. per day; rectrices grew as much as 9 mm. in 3 days. Although weight increases occurred only during daylight hours, feather growth continued throughout the day.

The young normally leave the nest when about 10 days old. For 23 nestlings the time spent in the nest varied from 9 to 11 days, or an average of 10.1 days. Blanchard (1941) describes the subsequent life of the fledglings as follows:

The first few days after fledging, the young perch in the shrubbery near the nest. They are usually so well concealed and respond so quickly to the warning *tit* of the parents that it is impossible to see them. The male now shares about equally with his mate the work of feeding the young. When the parents bring food or come near them in foraging. the fledglings utter *teez* and flutter their wings.

By the third to seventh day after fledging, the young of seven broods which I followed had moved to clumps of shrubbery some distance away from the nest. This must have involved crossing several yards of open grass—whether by hopping or flying I do not know. I suspect by the former method, since my earliest records of flight are for birds which had been out of the nest from seven to ten days.

When the young of the first brood are about twenty days old, the male takes over most of the task of feeding them. By this time the female has usually begun to work on her second nest. When from twenty-five to thirty-one days old, the fledglings forage for themselves but still beg food from the parents. The adults continue to feed them a little longer but soon ignore their persistent *teez* and may even chase or fight them. The oldest fledgling I have seen fed by a female was thirty-two days old, the oldest fed by a male, thirty-five days. Once I saw a female fight with her thirty-five-day-old fledgling; the next year I saw this female chase away another of the same age.

At about this time the young start to wander outside their parents' territory. At least by the time they are forty-eight days old they leave it forever. None, not even those which spent the winter only a few hundred yards away, has ever been seen again in its parents' area.

Food.—The food of the Pacific coast races of *Zonotrichia leucophrys* is known chiefly from stomach content analyses made in the early 1900s by the Bureau of Biological Survey, Washington, D.C. Data were made available through the courtesy of Clarence Cottam, formerly in charge of Food Habits, Division of Wildlife Research, and by John L. Buckley, Director of Patuxent Wildlife Research Center. These and numerous references to food habits in the literature cited here show the catholicity of taste in this species.

Analyses of the stomach contents of birds taken in California and designated as "*nuttalli*" indicate that the predominant food is vegetable material, mostly seeds. (As most of the data are for specimens collected before 1928, the fall and winter specimens undoubtedly included migratory Puget Sound sparrows as well as resident Nuttall's sparrows.) For 90 individuals collected, some from every month of the year, the stomach contents of 52, or 58 percent, were reported as containing only dry vegetable matter. Seeds of *Amaranthus, Calendrina, Erodium, Polygonum, Stellaria,* and various grasses are among those listed. The stomachs of the remaining 38 specimens were classified as follows: 19 had vegetable matter plus insect material making up 10 percent or less of the contents; 13 had only fresh vegetable material (flowers, immature fruit buds, fruit pulp); 3 had partly fresh and partly dry vegetable material but no insects, and 3 had vegetable material plus insect material constituting 11 percent or more of the stomach contents. The small number of specimens with insect matter in the stomachs, only 22 out of 90, or 24 percent, is surprising, especially as most of the specimens (58, or 64 percent) were collected during the nesting season.

References in the literature include many observations on seed eating. Sylvester D. Judd (1898) lists Nuttall's sparrow as the most important gregarious sparrow that destroys weeds. He reports finding in a Nuttall's sparrow stomach 300 seeds of amaranth, and in another 300 seeds of lamb's quarters (*Chenopodium album*). He found the following seeds eaten by Gambel's sparrows: *Polygonum aviculare* (knotweed), *Alsine media* (chickweed), *Chaetocloa glauca* and *C. viridis* (pigeon grass). John McB. Robertson (1931) observed Gambel's sparrows and Puget Sound sparrows eating the small black seeds of the blue gum (*Eucalyptus globulus*), a tree in which they roost. John & James M. Macoun (1909) record Puget Sound sparrows at Huntingdon, B.C. on Sept. 9, 1901, feeding on thistle seed.

Joseph Mailliard (1927) also saw Gambel's sparrows eating the seeds of pigweed (*Amaranthus*), which they preferred to the bait he used for his traps.

White-crowned sparrows also eat fresh blossoms and leaves. Robert S. Woods (1932) claims that the races of white-crowned sparrow rank next to the linnet in destructiveness to vegetable crops. He states they have a special fondness for young plants of the cabbage family and for young beets and peas. Carrots seem to be immune. Fortunately for vegetable growers, the large winter flocks that forage over the farm lands in California's inland valleys leave for the north in April.

Unusual items of vegetable matter eaten are reported by several observers. Lyndon L. Hargrave (1939) saw Gambel's sparrows at Roosevelt Lake, Ariz., feeding daily on exposed seed pulp of fully ripened pomegranates still hanging on the bush. In March 1963 I watched Gambel's sparrows on the University of California campus at Goleta feeding on ripened olives that had fallen to the ground. Charles G. Danforth (1938) saw a Nuttall's sparrow fly up and appear to drink the sap overflowing from poplars (*Populus nigra*), which was extremely sweet and suggested sugar water. Nuttall's sparrows I collected west of Guadalupe, Calif., in February 1957 had the feathers about the base of the bill bright yellow with willow pollen. At College, Alaska, I saw Gambel's sparrows eating staminate willow catkins and the new leaf buds of willow, as well as the tiny green stalks of *Equisetum* and the capsules of mosses.

On several occasions I have seen white-crowned sparrows fly out to catch insects in mid-air. Joseph Mailliard (1919) reports seeing Nuttall's sparrows take insects by jumping into the air after them. The birds usually catch insects by hopping quickly about on lawns or other grassy areas and either picking up the insects from the grass or catching them as they rise from it. The summer of 1950 I watched Gambel's sparrows feeding on mosquitoes at the water's edge on the Lower Yukon at Mountain Village, Alaska. To get an approximate idea of the number of pairs with young, one had only to move slowly up the Yukon in a small boat close to shore and count the pairs gathering mosquitoes and other insects by the water's edge. Even those Gambel's sparrows whose territories did not abut on the river flew down there to forage. W. J. Maher (1959) observed young and adult Gambel's sparrows on the Upper Kaolak River in northern Alaska eating bread scraps and foraging actively for mosquitoes near the base of his tent. They were the only species of bird that fed about the tent.

Stomach analyses of 30 Nuttall's sparrows taken from September through February reveal a complete absence of insect material.

In March and April 17 out of 55 birds had some insect matter in their stomachs. A wide variety of insects has been recorded: "Hymenoptera," ants, caterpillars, beetles, and weevils. Joseph Grinnell and Tracy I. Storer (1924) state that an adult male mountain white-crowned sparrow taken at Tenaya Lake on July 3, 1915, had nothing but beetles in its stomach. G. F. Knowlton (pers. comm.) collected a female Gambel's sparrow whose stomach was "well filled with five mud-dauber wasps, two ants, six additional Hymenoptera and insect fragments."

Data on stomach contents of migratory white-crowned sparrows indicate that a shift to insects in the diet may start on the wintering grounds. Of 80 specimens taken in January, February, and March, only 12, or 15 percent, had any insect matter in the stomach, and in only one bird did the insect matter comprise more than 10 percent of the contents. In April 7 out of 21, or 33 percent of birds taken on the wintering grounds had insect matter in the stomach, and in all seven it made up more than 10 percent of the stomach contents. Of 12 Gambel's sparrows taken in migration in April on Saturnia Island, B.C., 11 had stomachs containing between 15 percent and 100 percent insect material, with the average percentage of insect matter totalling 73.6 percent. The 12th specimen of this group had only green vegetable matter in its stomach. Thus the shift to insects as a major component of the diet may occur a month or more before nesting begins.

Clarence Cottam (pers. comm.) makes the general statement for all species of birds whose stomachs have been analyzed by the Biological Survey, that races of the same species show little difference in their choice of food unless they occupy distinctly different habitats. The data available on food habits of white-crowned sparrows seem to substantiate this statement, although no detailed study of the food of races occupying the same area in winter has been made. As individuals of two or more races commonly forage together, it seems unlikely that any racial differences in food preference exist.

Voice.—The call notes of the Pacific Coast races are identical, and are used under identical circumstances. The location note, "eep," is used by members of winter flocks and by mated pairs as they forage, move through shrubbery, or fly from one place to another. The same note, uttered more stridently, is given by the female when buidling her nest and when she leaves or returns to her nest during incubation. A modification of this note, which sounds like "ssseep," has already been described as the note uttered by the male prior to and during nest-building. A scolding note, which to my ears sounds like "ip" but which William L. Dawson (1923) writes as "zink" or "dzink," is used to protest intrusion by a person or animal. It is also uttered when there is no obvious cause for alarm or excitement. Lone migrants frequently utter this note over and over again when they arrive on the wintering grounds in early fall. Flock members utter it as they go to roost when the note may be repeated with ever-increasing frequency, followed by a burst of song. A squabbling note that defies syllabification may be used by two birds as they dispute a morsel of food, or by a lone bird as it forages. One other call note is more restricted in its use: a warning "tit" given by parents with nestlings or young fledglings makes the young stop their food cries and stay quiet. As this note is not used until after the young hatch, one can be sure that a pair using it has young rather than eggs.

The habit of this species of singing at night is so characteristic that it is one of the best ways to identify the bird to the layman. Song in Nuttall's sparrow may express by itself or accompany other expressions of at least six unmistakable purposes or attitudes of mind: defiance or warning to territorial rivals, the search for a mate, sexual excitement, announcement of territorial boundaries (as when used on patrol during the incubation period), interest in the female's return to her eggs, and fright or physical shock. Examples of the first five have been given. I have two examples of the sixth (fright or shock). In the first, a male foraging with its mate dove into a clump of juniper; when I suddenly shook the bush into which he had disappeared, he burst into song. The second is furnished by Thomas L. Rodgers (pers. comm.). While transporting Nuttall sparrows in darkened cages by car through several miles of city traffic, he noticed that each time he put on the brakes suddenly, the sparrows would just as suddenly burst into song.

The song of the white-crowned sparrow is best described as a theme common to the species, with an almost infinite number of variations—racial, populational, and individual. The musical elements common to the song of the Pacific Coast races consist of one or two initial notes held for nearly half a second each, followed by two or more rapidly sung notes or by a trill or both. On this simple theme are built a wide variety of melodies, from robust simple tunes like those of Berkeley Nuttall's sparrows to the more delicate and complex melodies of Friday Harbor Puget Sound sparrows. So similar is the quality of voice in all members of the species that a white-crowned sparrow song, once learned, is unmistakable, no matter what the dialect. The racial and populational variations are like different melodies sung by the same voice. The individual variations are like the same melody sung with different accents.

Nuttall's sparrows and mountain white-crowned sparrows use rhythmic patterns closely related to each other. Gambel's sparrow uses a markedly different pattern described here in detail, and the

Puget Sound sparrow uses patterns reminiscent of the more complex Nuttall's sparrow patterns, but pitched higher. Some of the racial patterns are diagrammed in Peterson (1941); and Blanchard (1941) shows diagrams for populational variations in Nuttall's sparrow and the Puget Sound sparrow.

Anne H. Wing, a trained musician with a keen sense of pitch, studied the song of Gambel's sparrows at Johnson's Crossing, Yukon Territory, in June and July of 1948 (in a Report on a Study of Arctic Birds and Mammals, by Leonard Wing, 1948, manuscript for the Research Report of the Arctic Institute of North America). Her comments and interpretations are those of a musician rather than a biologist, and I include them along with her excellent musical description for, although I do not necessarily agree with all of them, they represent a fresh and provocative approach to the study of song in this species. Mrs. Wing (pers. comm., 1960) writes, in part:

I found that the Gambel's sparrow sang melodious, high-pitched songs of four beats in rapid march time. Stepping upward through the first three beats, downward with the fourth, these decidedly rhythmic songs were clearly whistled on the first two beats, burred on the third and fourth beats. Each song encompassed a range of pitch no greater than a "perfect fifth" interval, e.g., C to G (do–sol).

In its simplest form, the song contained four single notes. Any of the first three beats, and most often the third, might contain not one note but two or three shorter notes on the same pitch. The first beat, whether it contained one note only or two or three notes of shorter duration, was on one pitch. Occasionally in the third beat the short notes were successively a half-step higher. The fourth beat was always a single note, and this was lower in pitch than the last and highest pitch of the third beat. To put it simply, the melody marched quickly up a little musical hill, then stepped down.

In terms of the beats of the song, four beats of song were followed by ten beats of rest or silence. During the rest period, another bird could and often did fit its songs so as to achieve antiphony. Duetting was always in good musical taste, both in rhythm and in melody. If one altered its song in detail, the other was likely to do so as well, keeping the two songs in harmony.

Responsive singing took place most commonly in the hours of singing at dawn, when many birds seemed to congregate at different locations for the purpose of singing. One of my favorite listening places was the shore of the Teslin River. Wakened by the singing soon after midnight or at least by half-past twelve, I would walk down the bank, notebook in hand. Sometimes several birds would be singing the same tune in different keys, the songs overlapping in great confusion. This would soon resolve, perhaps as more birds arrived, into question and answer singing. Around three or three-thirty most of the birds had dropped out, their voices heard, perhaps, on the hillside where there were nests.

Musical replies to musical questions were definitely melodious by the highest standards of human musicians. The duets might be arbitrarily classified as, first, variations on a theme, and, second, mutually complementary songs, one the more obviously a completion of the other. To illustrate, (using letter names of scale tones and recalling that the songs rose through three beats, falling on the last) the singing of the song 'B flat, C, D–D, B flat' in alternation with the song

'D, E flat, E–F, B flat' settles nothing, and is an endless musical argument . . . variations on a theme. But the singing of the song 'G, C–C–C, D–D, B' and its response 'B, D, E flat—E natural, C' completes a musical sentence ending with a cadence (a return to the tonic). Even so, the birds go on singing it over and over again, a characteristic of birds but not of human musicians.

Twilight singing, especially morning twilight, with its greater proportion of duets and of unusual versions of the songs, was very interesting. If any originality of melody or any creative singing was possible, I believe that it occurred then. But if the birds were drawing upon a set of traditional tunes, they made aesthetic choices of rhythmic and melodic details within their songs, particularly when two birds were singing together in antiphonal duet.

Behavior.—As all the sections under "Habits" fall properly under the heading of "Behavior" in the broadest sense of the term, only a few mannerisms that distinguish white-crowned sparrows from other species likely to be found in the same habitat are mentioned here. One of the habits of winter flocks of white-crowns is to forage on the ground by roadsides. When disturbed, they fly or hop up and plunge over the embankment into the nearest cover. If the flock is large, the individuals may move almost as one bird. The essential feature of this escape reaction is the force with which they make a dash for the nearest cover. So characteristic is this behavior that one can use it as a diagnostic field character when traveling at high speed. Grinnell and Storer (1924) describe the ensuing behavior as follows: "If a flock of white-crowns is come upon while it is foraging on the ground, the birds get up quickly and dart into the shelter of some nearby thicket, each pursuing a separate course. There they remain for a short time, silent and motionless, but peering furtively at the intruder. After a short period of quiet, if there be no further cause for fright, they become active again, giving voice to faint *seeps* and, individually, they begin to hop up in the brush where they can see about before venturing into the open again."

Ralph Hoffman (1927) describes another trait of winter flocks: "When individuals of the flock disagree about a resting place they utter little confused squabbling notes, and just at dusk, when birds settle in thick trees for the night, and at dawn, they repeat for several minutes the alarm note, a metallic *pink.*"

Field marks.—Adult white-crowned sparrows are distinguished by the high, puffy crown, broadly striped with black and white, and by the clear pearly-gray breast. The sexes are alike, but females usually look somewhat duller, that is, the contrast between black and white stripes is not so striking as in the male. Immature birds are buffier than adults, with head stripings of dark red-brown and light buffy-brown instead of black and white. Ralph Hoffman (1927) writes:

"No other bird can be confused with an adult sparrow of the White-crowned group, if the markings of the head are seen. Immature birds might be mistaken by a beginner for several other birds with reddish brown on the crown. * * * When there are adults with the immature birds, the resemblance in the pattern of the head markings is obvious." Hoffman mentions the rufous-crowned and chipping sparrows as species with which immature white-crowned sparrows could be confused. The rufous-crowned sparrow lacks the pale stripe through the center of the crown, and the reddish crown of the chipping sparrow is set off sharply from the sides of the head by a white or whitish stripe and a black line below it."

Although one can easily identify the species, one cannot always distinguish between races of white-crowned sparrow on the basis of morphological characters alone. With practice one can, however, assign most individuals to one of two groups: *nuttalli-pugetensis* or *gambelii-oriantha-leucophrys*. For adults, the differentiating characters are the hue of the feathers on back and rump and the color of the bill. If an adult has brownish back and rump feathers and a yellowish bill, it belongs to the *nuttalli-pugetensis* group. If it has back feathers with reddish centers and grayish margins, grayish rump feathers and a cinnamon brown or reddish bill, it belongs to the *gambelii-oriantha-leucophrys* group. To distinguish between immatures of these two groups, bill color, but not color of back or rump feathers, is a reliable criterion. A different grouping, based on the color of the lores in the adult, places those with white or grayish lores in one group (*nuttalli*, *pugetensis* and *gambelii*) and those with a black lores (*oriantha* and *leucophrys*) in another. This distinction does not hold in all cases, however. Walter E. C. Todd (1953) reports "white-browed individuals" from the offshore islands and mainland of Hudson and James Bays in the midst of the *leucophrys* breeding range.

To distinguish between the races within each group is still more difficult. *Nuttalli* and *pugetensis* cannot be told apart by morphological characters alone. So similar are the members of these two races that separation requires comparison with large series of study skins, and then only the individuals at the extremes of the range of variation can be identified with certainty. Song pattern, on the other hand, is a reliable criterion for distinguishing between the two races. In localities where both winter together, the best way to distinguish the song patterns is to follow the advice of Peterson (1941) and "learn the song pattern of the local breeding birds thoroughly, and when the migrants * * * arrive * * * proceed to memorize carefully their respective song patterns." In the San Francisco Bay Region this system works particularly well, for the local populations of Nuttall's sparrows sing short simple songs quite different from the longer and more embellished ones of wintering *pugetensis*. At Carmel and Guadalupe, Calif. the distinction is more difficult to make, for the Nuttall's sparrows use a more complex pattern. With practice, however, one can use the same system here too. Behavior of the adults also gives valuable clues. Nuttall's sparrows tend to stay paired on their territories, are bold, and sing with considerable force in fall and winter. Puget Sound sparrows winter in large flocks, are more easily frightened, and sing with less force. In short, the adult Nuttall's sparrows behave like the permanent landowners they are, whereas the Puget Sound sparrows behave like visitors without attachment to a specific piece of ground. Distinctions of behavior do not apply to the immatures, for those of both races flock in fall and winter. With experience, however, one can usually distinguish between the song fragments uttered by Nuttall's and Puget Sound young of the year.

Trained observers can make the previous distinctions at close range and in a good light even with the naked eye. An additional character can be used with trapped birds—the color of the bend of the wing. It is bright yellow in adults and immatures of *nuttalli-pugetensis*, and whitish or only faintly yellowish in *gambelii-oriantha-leucophrys*. The point to emphasize is that whenever feasible, the individual should be examined for all these characters. In most cases the yellow bill and bend of wing and the brown back and rump feathers will occur together; likewise the cinnamon-brown bill and the reddish and gray back feathers and grayish rump will coexist in the same individual. In exceptional cases, however, one of these characters may be combined with those of the other group. I trapped one adult in early spring at Berkeley that had the bright yellow wing bend characteristic of *nuttalli-pugetensis* and the cinnamon-brown bill and reddish and gray back feathers and grayish rump of the second group.

As has been said, lore color can be used to separate typical Gambel's sparrows from the two other races of the second group, but the difference does not hold for all individuals. A number of museum specimens I have examined have loral areas partly white and partly black. Obviously the race to which such individuals belong cannot be determined by this character. As with *nuttalli* and *pugetensis*, the morphological distinctions between *oriantha* and *leucophrys* are slight, and identification requires comparison with large series of museum skins. Here again song pattern may be a more reliable criterion where two or three races winter together. I have no first-hand knowledge of the song patterns of *leucophrys*, but Otto Widmann (1911) states: "To one accustomed to the song of the species in the East the song of this Rocky Mountain bird is a great surprise, for it has no resemblance at all, only one note at the beginning to the monotonous ditty reminding one of the much more powerful and melodious song which we hear every May in the Mississippi Valley."

To my ear the song patterns of the California populations of mountain white-crowned sparrow are quite distinct from those of Gambel's sparrows wintering in California or breeding in the parts of Alaska where I have studied them. This correlates with Anne H. Wing's statement (pers. comm.): "The fact that the range of individual Gambel's sparrow songs heard at Johnson's Crossing, Yukon Territory, did not exceed a major fifth interval is interesting in the light of the fact that similar songs heard from white-crowned sparrows in the Rocky Mountain National Park (*oriantha*) containing the same note-names often ranged through more than an octave."

As one illustration of how color characters normally confined to one group of races may crop up in the other, Austin L. Rand (1948) describes an adult female collected in fall migration at Shoal Lake in southern Manitoba that had a pink bill, pale gray breast and belly, white bend of the wing and black lores combined with an olive brown rump, olive-toned edgings to the feathers of the upper parts, and heavily pigmented flanks. The black lores is referable to *Z. l. leucophrys*, the general color of the upper-parts and flanks is "very similar to those of *pugetensis* from the British Columbia coast," and the bill color and bend of wing is referable to either *Z. l. leucophrys* or *Z. l. gambelii*.

To sum up, racial differences in morphology are slight, and in many cases cannot be used as sole criteria to differentiate between races. Differences in behavior and song pattern are more marked, and therefore whenever possible should be used in addition to the morphological characters. Physiological differences, such as extent of prenuptial molt, amount of subcutaneous fat, and date of recrudescence of the gonads, are even more reliable criteria, but only in spring. Discussion of these lies outside the scope of this article. The locality of observation or collection, while important, gives only a partial clue to the identity of a given individual, for the winter ranges of several races overlap, and the breeding ranges of some are contiguous. Therefore the more characters one can scrutinize—morphologic, behavioristic, physiologic—the more reliable will be the identification. Intermediate individuals should be given no racial designation.

While the vagueness of the differentiating characters and their fluidity of distribution may be disconcerting to persons accustomed to less plastic species, they are the most fascinating properties of this interesting bird. The lack of trenchant racial differences and the abundance of intermediate individuals indicates the close relationship of all members of the species and, presumably, the recency of the evolutionary development of the present races.

Enemies.—I interpret the term "enemies" in its broadest sense, to include both native and introduced predators, parasites, and man in those rare cases where death of white-crowned sparrows results from his activities.

There is direct evidence that snakes, hawks, and owls prey on white-crowned sparrows. I have indirect evidence that shrikes, jays, and crows are also enemies. Grinnell and Linsdale (1936) found a 4-foot gopher snake in a bush with a nest of Nuttall's sparrows and almost touching one of the two remaining young birds. The same authors state that at Point Lobos Reserve sharp-shinned hawks make frequent captures. Their account of one such capture states that a hawk appeared from the pine woods, dashed down into the radish patch where white-crowned sparrows were feeding, and captured a bird apparently of this species. Winsor M. Tyler (1923) observed prairie falcons in the San Joaquin Valley and in the arid hills along the western rim of this valley. "From the time the falcons return to their nest cliffs in early spring through egglaying and incubation periods the Gambel sparrows (*Zonotrichia leucophrys gambelii*) are very abundant in the regions where falcons abound and a very heavy toll of these sparrows is taken." F. C. Evans and J. T. Emlen, Jr. (1947) found the remains of crowned sparrows (*Z. leucophrys* and/or *Z. coronata*) in barn owl pellets at Davis, Calif. Albert C. Hawbecker (1945) found six white-crowned sparrow remains in barn owl pellets at Struve Ranch near Watsonville, Calif. Herbert Brandt (1951) mentions the northwestern shrike as being a predator on Gambel's sparrows, and I have occasionally found a shrike perched on a trap where I was banding sparrows. I have seen jays and crows watch me intently as I made trips to nests. At Friday Harbor crows appeared to be chiefly to blame for destruction of the nests I was watching that did not last through to the fledging of young.

At Mountain Village weasels would undoubtedly have constituted a danger to the ground-nesting Gambel's sparrows had not Eskimo trapping kept their numbers to a minimum. In the 3 months I spent at Mountain Village in 1950 I saw a weasel only once. I watched it walk boldly along a path in full view to a point where two male Gambel's sparrows were perched near the ground facing each other at a territorial boundary. They were preoccupied with each other and hence unaware of the weasel, which gazed intently at them and stayed ready to spring as long as the birds remained near enough to the ground to be almost within striking distance. As soon as the birds flew off the weasel disappeared. At this locality jaegers that flew over the tundra above the village seemed to watch me as I looked for nests. As most of the Gambel's sparrows nested close to the village where the jaegers came only rarely, these probably did not constitute a great threat. At College most of the Gambel's sparrow nests I found were at the edges of farmland, and I never saw an actual raid by a predator. I saw red foxes nearby, however, and noticed the strong scent of fox near one Gambel's sparrow nest from which nestlings disappeared several days before they were due to be fledged.

As white-crowned sparrows live near human habitation, cats must be considered as enemies. They often interfere with banding operations by developing the habit of visiting the traps. One such case is interesting because of the reaction of the victim. As I was inspecting my traps I came upon a cat crouched beside one of them. It had badly mauled a Gambel's sparrow inside the trap. The bird was bleeding, some of its feathers were scattered on the ground, and it gave every sign of terror. I chased the cat away, banded and released the bird, and reset the trap. Less than 20 minutes later the same bird reentered the trap.

There are two records of white-crowned sparrow nests parasitized by cowbirds. Henry J. Rust (1917) found a nest with five eggs, including one egg of a cowbird, along Little Dry Creek in Fremont County, Idaho. Friedmann (1938) describes a nest in the Royal Ontario Museum at Toronto collected at Okotoks, Alberta, that contains one white-crowned sparrow egg and two eggs of the cowbird.

I have frequently found nematode worms in the body cavity of sparrows collected in or near Santa Barbara. Rarely I have found parasitic flies of the genus *Ornithoica* clinging to the feathers of trapped birds. Otto E. Plath (1919) found 36 full-grown larvae of *Protocalliphora azurea* (Fallen), (now placed in the genus *Phormia*) in the nest of a Nuttall's sparrow in the San Francisco Bay Region. They were determined to be sucking the blood of nestlings; some died as the result, others were retarded in growth. C. M. Herman, H. A. Jankiewicz and R. W. Saarni (1942) found protozoan parasites of the genus *Isospora* in one Gambel's sparrow.

In the category of accidents should be mentioned the occasional sparrow that kills itself by flying against a window. Alfred B. Howell (1914) reports seven Gambel's sparrows destroyed in an orange grove in Covina, Calif., when the trees were fumigated with hydrocyanic acid gas. Frank S. Daggett (1902) reported three Gambel's sparrows found dead on the surface of cyanide tanks at a gold mining camp in the Cargo Murchacho Mountains west of Yuma on the Colorado desert. On the whole, however, the effects of man's activities are usually beneficial to white-crowned sparrows. Roadbuilding and clearing allows them to extend their range into areas formerly too densely wooded for them.

The mortality rates for nestlings I followed are highest for Berkeley Nuttall's sparrows, lower for Friday Harbor Puget Sound sparrows, and lowest for Alaska Gambel's sparrows. Of 30 broods of Nuttall's sparrows I watched, only 12, or 40 percent, were successfully fledged.

Of 32 broods of Puget Sound sparrows followed in 1936, 19, or 59 percent were fledged. Of 8 broods of Gambel's sparrows at Mountain Village and 12 broods at College, 6 and 9 or 75 percent were successfully fledged. This suggests the interesting possibility that the northern breeding grounds may actually be safer than coastal California for raising young. The very fact that Gambel's sparrows maintain their numbers by raising only one brood is also indicative of the relatively lower nestling mortality.

Fall and Winter.—An arbitrary division between fall and winter does not accord either with the climate of coastal California or with the phases of the annual cycle in Nuttall's sparrow. A more meaningful designation of the time between breeding seasons would be the "base level," when territorial and sexual behavior decline to a low level but do not quite disappear. This period begins with the postnuptial molt in late July or early August and ends with the surge of territorial and sexual activities the following January.

The quotations that follow from Blanchard (1941) describe the behavior of Nuttall's sparrows on the University of California campus at Berkeley, Calif.

My banded pairs (of adults) remained on their breeding areas through the fall and winter. Mates foraged and perched together and followed each other about, uttering the *eep* which serves as the location note. Both sexes sang sporadically, and an occasional territorial dispute involved forceful singing and chasing. The instinct to patrol the area was absent or nearly so, however, and several of the pairs were joined by flocks of immatures and, rarely, by mateless adults. These newcomers were treated with such complete tolerance that only the most careful observation could detect a certain aloofness as well as a certain dominance in the established pair.

When the adults begin their postnuptial molt in late July and early August, they become so secretive and silent that it is nearly impossible to find even those banded birds whose forage routes one knows well. Trilling and posturing, chasing and fighting cease. Singing usually stops also, although I have one record of a loud and complete song from a heavily molting male.

Even though external signs of territorialism are suspended during the molt, a definite interest in the breeding area must persist in both male and female, as the following accounts show:

On August 14, 1935, I trapped an adult male about a mile north of the campus. Its tail was barely an inch long and its wings were still in the process of molting. I put the bird in a darkened cage and took it by car to the campus, where I banded and released it in an area at that time unoccupied by Nuttalls; the area was later taken over by a pair and therefore must have been suitable. On August 31 I found the male back on the spot where I had trapped it. Three days later I retrapped it and found that the tail had not yet reached full length and the feathers of the pileum were still in sheaths.

On September 3 of the same year I tried an identical experiment with an adult female which was just starting to molt. I trapped and released her at the same points as I had the male, and nine days later found her back where I had trapped her. By this time she was molting heavily on the wings, breast, and belly. Her tail feathers had been renewed but were just beginning to grow out.

The significant point of these experiments is not that the birds returned to their breeding areas, but that they did so at a time when activity is normally reduced to the minimum and when the pairs into whose area they may have wandered would almost certainly have made no effort to drive them out.

Banding data for the young birds indicate that during most of fall and winter they too are probably limited to a restricted area, within a few hundred yards of which they attempt to establish territories the next spring. Such wandering as they do probably occurs before they undergo the postjuvenile molt. Depending on when they are fledged, therefore, the period of wandering could last from May through most of August for young of a first brood, or about a month for young fledged in July.

On August 26, 1934, I trapped within 400 yards of its birthplace, a young bird beginning its postjuvenile molt; it had been banded as a nestling the previous May. Through the following winter this bird (male xi) stayed with a flock of unbanded immatures within an area of 1.7 acres which included the spot where I trapped him and at the edge of which he settled the next spring. In October and November of 1935 I banded three immatures, two of which stayed near by the rest of the winter and bred the next spring within 50 yards of where trapped. One of these was retaken the following July less than 200 yards away. These histories, together with the fact that I had seen groups of immatures foraging day after day in the same spots, made me suspect that they, like the adults, might limit themselves to small areas in fall and winter.

To substantiate this, I color-banded fourteen immatures in August and September of 1936. All but one were seen again that winter: twelve, from one to fifteen times within 200 yards of where trapped, and one, once, within 400 yards. Eight settled the next spring on territories from 100 to 400 yards from the trap sites. None was ever found farther than 400 yards away.

* * * The young birds begin to sing, though rarely, in mid-July, while still in juvenile plumage. This song may take the form of either a weak or abbreviated version of the immature song or a prolonged trill. As in most passerine birds, the immature song is much more variable than that of the adult. The young bird sings weakly, hesitatingly, often repeating notes of the first phrase before uttering the trill, which is sung so slowly that the separate notes can be heard. Every conceivable variation is used: the first three notes may be sung and the trill omitted, or one or more of the first three notes may be left out, and there are innumerable variations in the trill itself.

By mid-September—when most individuals have finished the molt—song and other evidences of renewed territorial interest may recur. One male I watched in 1936 on the Berkeley campus sang from a conspicuous perch in early September and throughout October. Twice in the first week of October he sang loudly every few seconds; his song was indistinguishable in force and frequency from that of breeding time. On rare occasions I even found two birds perched conspicuously, alternating in loud singing. Although females do not usually show signs of territorial jealousy, I have one case of a banded adult female which not only sang forcefully but engaged in a dispute with another adult. The immediate cause seemed to be the desire of both birds to feed on the same pyracantha berries.

During early September female III had frequented a certain bush on the edge of her territory until, we may imagine, habit verged upon necessity and the spot was unseasonably invested with the power to stimulate possessive jealousy. On September 9 and 15 I saw her sing there several times. Her song was complete but weaker than that of her mate. On the morning of September 17 I found her there on the ground, singing as forcefully as any male in breeding time. Then an unbanded adult in the same patch of shrubbery sang, somewhat less vigorously. This was male VIII, the neighbor on the east. They sang at one another for four or five minutes, shifting over the ground about six feet apart. Then the male chased female III around the edge of the shrubbery. She lit on the ground and both sang again. Another chase took place, then more singing. The next morning this was all repeated, but female III sang less forcefully. The same afternoon I found both feeding silently on the same berries two feet apart, and so for the next four mornings. Both sang occasionally, but I saw no more pursuits.

Territorial and sexual displays by adults in the fall are known for many species of birds (Marshall 1952).

"Pursuit is common among immatures in fall and winter. It is usually momentary, involving flock mates which may resume peaceful foraging a minute or so later. Sometimes, however, pursuit has been accompanied by loud singing and fighting, suggestive of a territorial dispute."

The data cited point to "* * * a more or less passive limitation of pairs to their breeding areas in winter, with almost complete tolerance of sojourning strangers and only rare flare-ups of jealousy between established neighbors. Restriction in winter is obviously not the product of conflicts between neighboring pairs; chasing, fighting, and patrol are almost completely absent. The attitude of the male toward immature and mateless birds gives us little reason to suppose that he would resent invasions of adjoining pairs if such occurred."

Banding.—White-crowned sparrows live close to man, trap easily, and forage and perch with the lower part of the leg exposed so that color bands are plainly visible. Many banded birds re-enter the same traps again and again. Each year thousands of white-crowned sparrows are banded, and hundreds previously banded are recaptured. In the April issue of the "Western Bird-Bander," the Western Bird-Banding Association publishes annually the numbers of birds reported banded by its members in western North America. In 1959, 6,616 white-crowned sparrows were banded. This is 5.9 percent of all birds reported banded that year, and is the largest total for any non-game species. Corresponding figures for 1960 are 5,338, or 4.3 percent of all birds banded, and for 1961, 5,418 or 4.2 percent of all birds banded. The number of banders reporting to this Association increased from 167 in 1959 to 185 in 1961 (Stoner et al, 1960, 1961 and 1962).

Because so many white-crowned sparrows are trapped each year, the data from banding would fill a large volume. No attempt is made here to summarize all the facts. Instead, I have chosen two long term studies to discuss in detail: one, a project conducted for 18 years under conditions as stable and as close to primitive as are ever likely to be achieved today in California, and the other, an experimental study begun in 1961 and still in progress as this article goes to press. Both projects illustrate the unique contributions of banding to our knowledge of *Zonotrichia leucophrys*.

The first is a study of survival of banded birds conducted by Jean and Mary Linsdale and co-workers in the winter seasons of 1937 through 1955 at the Hastings Reservation in the Santa Lucia Mountains, Monterey County, Calif. During the 18 seasons the study was made, the Linsdales banded 13,366 individuals of 46 species of native birds. Of these, 2,299 were wintering white-crowned sparrows, probably chiefly *pugetensis*, although the race is not specified. The results of the study are reported by Linsdale (1949) and by Linsdale and Linsdale (1956). Of special interest are the age profiles for each year for the population (Table 4, p. 94 of Linsdale, 1949). In 1942–43, for example, a total of 189 individuals were trapped. Of these, 113 were birds with immature plumage which were therefore less than 1 year old, and 16 were adults trapped for the first time. The rest were recaptures of birds banded in previous years; 51 were banded as immatures and hence their approximate age was known. Of these, 25 were between 1 and 2 years old, 9 were between 2 and 3 years old, 8 were between 3 and 4 years old, 7 were between 4 and 5 years old, and 2 were between 5 and 6 years old. The remaining 9 of the 189 birds trapped that season were banded as adults, and 2 of them were at least 6 to 7 years old.

Table 4 also gives data on the yearly decline in percentage of recaptures for a given batch of birds banded as immatures. Of the 122 birds banded as immatures in 1941–42, 25 or 20.5 percent were re-trapped in 1942–43; 10 of these, or 8.2 percent of the original 122 birds, were recaptured in 1943–44, 6, or 4.9 percent returned in 1944–45, 5, or 4.1 percent were taken in 1945–46, and 2, or 1.6 percent of the original total survived to re-enter the traps in 1946–47. As would be expected, the corresponding percentages of survivors are not quite the same if a different year is used as the starting point, but all the curves are similar in showing that the heaviest drop-off in captures of individuals surviving to their first winter comes between then and the next winter season. From then on, the decline in retrapped survivors is much more gradual.

The Linsdales' study reveals wide annual variations in the ratio of immatures to adults trapped. In 5 out of 10 seasons the ratio of immatures to adults was about 1 to 1. As a corollary, the average percentage of immatures per year for the 10-year period from 1938–39 through 1947–48 was 52.6. Yet in 1943–44, the ratio was about one immature to three adults, whereas the next season the ratio was reversed. This indicates the false impression that can be gained from sampling of atypical years.

The work just discussed is one of the most exhaustive banding operations involving white-crowned sparrows ever carried out. Yet the investigators state:

> In reviewing these observations, attention is directed to the small size of the area concerned in these winter studies. A long strip of 20 acres would include every trapping station as well as the ranges on the Reservation of nearly all the individual birds concerned. When this is compared with the long line of travel, over a thousand miles for the migrant species, the remarkable effectiveness of the controls over the birds which come and stay and return repeatedly between the two homes is given special emphasis. The rigidity of these controls is further demonstrated when we realize how small a part of the whole population of each species is represented on our minute area. If 4,000 crowned sparrows [here Linsdale refers to both golden-crowned and white-crowned sparrows] have wintered on our 20 acres in the last 11 years, how many have come to the 100 million acres of California? How was each of them able to find and stay in its particular home area? Before we make guesses pertaining to these questions we need to know more about what the birds really do.

One answer to some of these questions may be forthcoming from an experimental study of homing in *Zonotrichia leucophrys* and *atricapilla* begun in 1961 at San Jose, Calif., by Richard Mewaldt and his students. Mewaldt is attempting to find out, not what the birds do under natural conditions, but what they can do under extraordinary conditions they would not meet in nature (Mewaldt, 1962a, 1962b, and 1963; Roadcap, 1962). The results to date on displacement of white-crowned sparrows are briefly summarized here. He and his co-workers displaced 65 white-crowned sparrows of the races *pugetensis* and *gambelii* distances of between 9 and 164 miles from the banding station at San Jose. The most significant return was made from Visalia, Calif., 164 miles away, by a first-year *pugetensis* in only 7½ days. This bird had to cross the interior coast ranges to make its return.

Experiments with releases at much greater distances from the banding station are in progress. During the 1961–62 winter season, Mewaldt shipped 233 Puget Sound and 79 Gambel's sparrows by commercial aircraft from San Jose to Baton Rouge, La.; 67 of the displaced *pugetensis* and 2 of the *gambelii* individuals were proved "homers," for they had already been trapped at San Jose in at least 2 successive winter seasons. Releases at Baton Rouge were made on Oct. 28 and Dec. 5, 1961, and on Feb. 2 and Apr. 14, 1962. On June 24, 1962, one Puget Sound sparrow of the April 14 release was trapped at the banding station at San Jose. This individual, a male, had been banded as an immature at San Jose in March of 1957, and recaptured each season for the five intervening winters until he was shipped to Baton Rouge in 1961, so he was 6 years old when he made the trip back from Louisiana.

> This was the first *Zonotrichia* to appear in June at the station in its eight summers of operation * * * He was not seen after 24 June until again retrapped on 27 October, 1962. * * * Because he appeared to be in migratory condition in June, and because he was not detected between 24 June and 27 October, I suspect he spent July and August in his nesting territory somewhere in the Pacific Northwest.
>
> It is most reasonable to assume that this bird returned directly to San Jose, his winter home, from the release area at Baton Rouge, Louisiana, an airline distance of approximately 1,800 miles. The effective rate of return was at more than 25 miles per day over terrain not frequented by the race *pugetensis*. It seems inescable that this sparrow "homed" to his winter range from a remote and unknown release point. Bi-coordinate navigation of a very effective nature seems possessed by this bird. * * * As of 31 December 1962, 21 of the Baton Rouge releases have been retrapped at the banding station in San Jose. Although the numbers are not large, certain trends are appearing in the data. Thus far 7 *pugetensis*, 8 *gambelii* and 6 *atricapilla* have returned. It is perhaps significant that a greater percent (10%) of the strongly migratory race *gambelii* have returned than of either *pugetensis* (3%) or *atricapilla* (6%). Also of importance is the observation that 8% of adults have returned compared to but 3% of birds less than one year old at the time of displacement.

A brief review of earlier experiments with displacement of *Zonotrichia* winter visitants in California is given in R. Roadcap (1962).

Other important data contributed by banding are recoveries in the north of white-crowns banded on the wintering grounds, longevity records, and descriptions of the rate and sequence of prenuptial molt. In spite of the thousands of white-crowned sparrows banded each year, records of recoveries on the migration route and within the breeding range are still rare. Especially valuable, therefore, are the recoveries of Puget Sound sparrows mentioned by Mewaldt (1962b). In a personal communication he furnishes the following details of these recaptures:

> 25-11892 banded Nov. 23, 1957 as Im at San Jose; returned Oct. 25, 1958; returned Oct. 9, 1959; recovered Apr. 6, 1960 at Blaine, Wash. by Mrs. Lucille Kline . . . returned Oct. 15, 1960 to San Jose; returned Dec. 2, 1961.
>
> 22-136419 banded Aug. 26, 1959 at Vancouver, B.C., taken at San Jose Dec. 31, 1961.

27–169514 banded Sept. 18, 1959 as Im at Blaine, Wash. by Mrs. Kline; taken at San Jose Nov. 7, 1959 at our banding station and released
27–104107 banded Nov. 11, 1959 as Im at San Jose; found dead at Cassidy, Vancouver Island, B.C., letter Aug. 22, 1960.
31–138666 banded Jan. 28, 1962 as Ad at Alviso (8 miles from banding station at San Jose) was killed by a cat on August 19, 1962 at Bellingham, Wash.
31–188552 banded March 26, 1962 as Ad at Coyote (19 miles from band-station) was shot May 12, 1962 at Port Angeles, Washington.

Most of these birds were recovered in the north on dates marginal to the breeding season, so we cannot say with certainty that they had bred or been hatched where they were taken. The last individual listed is an especially valuable record, for May 12 falls within the nesting season. Hence we can say that this bird wintered at least as far south as latitude 37° N. and bred at latitude 48° N., an air distance of about 750 miles. This checks with the record of the Puget Sound sparrow banded at Berkeley, Calif. that was found the next summer at Victoria, B. C., also an air distance of about 750 miles (Clabaugh, 1929).

A wealth of data on longevity in white-crowned sparrows is accumulating through banding records. Linsdale (1949) gives the following records for white-crowned sparrows banded at the Hastings Reservation: "18 white-crowned sparrows have returned after 5 years, while 5 have been captured after 7 years, and 2 lived at least 8 years." C. G. Thompson (1960) reports capturing a Gambel's sparrow known to be 7 years old, a Nuttall's sparrow 6 years old, and four Puget Sound sparrows known to be 5, 6, 7, and 8 years old, respectively. The most complete individual record I know of is that for a Gambel's sparrow banded as an immature by Franklin G. Crawford in Altadena, Calif. Nov. 22, 1942. It was recaptured 11 times, at least once each year, through March 1950. On March 5 of that year it was taken for the last time when it was nearly 8 years old. Crawford (1950) states that this is the only individual, out of 848 birds he banded between 1941 and 1946, with a proved life or more than 5 years.

No list of the types of information yielded by banding would be complete without mention of the study conducted at Pasadena, Calif. by Harold and Josephine R. Michener (1943) on the rate and sequence of prenuptial molt in *Z. l. gambelii.* Repeated observations of the same individuals obviously played an important role in this thorough analysis. Banding and retrapping made this possible, and at the same time permitted the subjects of the study to live under natural conditions.

Distribution

Range.—Nuttall's white-crowned sparrow is resident along a narrow coastal strip of central California from Mendocino County south to Gaviota Beach, Santa Barbara County. (Two breeding records at Goleta Flat, Santa Barbara County.)

Egg dates.—California: 215 records, March 3 to July 24; 112 records, April 4 to April 27; 28 records, May 2 to May 15; 7 records, June 12 to July 24.

ZONOTRICHIA LEUCOPHRYS GAMBELII (Nuttall)

Gambel's White-crowned Sparrow*

PLATES 68 AND 69

Contributed by BARBARA BLANCHARD DEWOLFE

HABITS

The populations of Gambel's white-crowned sparrow discussed in this section are those wintering at Davis, Calif., and those breeding at Mountain Village and College, Alaska. As none of the thousands of Gambel's sparrows banded on the wintering grounds has been recaptured on the breeding grounds, we do not know where the birds of a given wintering population breed or vice versa.

Gambel's sparrows nesting in Alaska compress their breeding cycle into an even shorter period than the Puget Sound sparrows at Friday Harbor. They establish territories, nest, and care for the single brood of young until they become independent in about 2½ months. The greater part of the time saved lies in the fledging of only one brood, but compression of several other intervals is necessary to make fullest use of the short time between arrival on the breeding grounds and gonad regression. Males arrive first and in almost full breeding condition. They immediately establish their territories, so that no time is lost after the females arrive either in achieving physiological readiness to mate or in finding and defending nesting areas. The females are ready to mate and to begin work on the nest within a few days. The interval between completion of the nest and laying the first egg also averages shorter than in *pugetensis*.

Spring.—In spring the members of flocks wintering at Davis showed some slight hostility toward one another about 10 days before the first individuals departed. They squabbled over food and, less frequently, fought or pursued one another. Otherwise the behavior prior to migration was identical to that described for the Puget Sound sparrow. In 1943 the Gambel's sparrow flocks at Davis began to decrease in numbers on April 13, the last banded bird was seen April 20, the last unbanded one on April 30.

---

*Additional material on this race is included in the account of Nuttall's white-crowned sparrow, pp. 1292–1324.

My observations of Gambel's sparrows in migration were chiefly from April 21 to 26, 1936, when I watched a few transients at Friday Harbor. In marked contrast to the noisy breeding Puget Sound sparrows, the Gambel's sparrows sang so softly that it was hard to locate them even when they perched no more than 10 feet away. The few I saw were either solitary or in the company of migrating golden-crowned sparrows. Twice I found an individual perched in semidarkness high on a rafter inside a barn, with some golden-crowns. T. T. McCabe (personal communication) states that migrants may arrive in mountainous country in British Columbia long before they can live on the breeding grounds and may spend a month in valleys directly below suitable breeding areas.

The arrival of Gambel's sparrows on breeding grounds at Mountain Village and College, Alaska, differed from that of the Friday Harbor sparrows in two respects: The Gambel's sparrow males arrived more than a week ahead of the females, and they did not come in a body, but filtered in gradually over periods of 2 or 3 weeks. The influx of Gambel's sparrows destined to breed at Mountain Village in 1950 lasted at least 19 days. Two males came on May 9. I color-banded one and followed it through the nesting cycle. From then until May 25 males continued to come in. The average arrival date for 17 males was May 15. The females arrived between May 17 and 28, and the average date for 11 females was May 23. These data accord closely with those of Henry C. Kyllingstad (personal communication) for the same locality from 1942 to 1948. I assume his records of early arrivals are for males. His earliest record is for May 7, 1943, and his average date for "first Gambel's sparrow seen" is May 10. His average date when the species becomes common falls between May 14 and 15.

At College, Alaska, in 1957 the influx of males lasted at least 15 days. Gambel's sparrows were first reported in the area May 4, and migrating flocks were seen May 6. My observations provide the average arrival date of May 8 for 19 males I saw in places where the day before there had been none. By May 11 the numbers of males in the areas I was watching began to stabilize. The last male I suspected of being newly arrived came May 19. On May 16 I first saw a female. The average date of arrival for 12 females was May 17.

The Gambel's sparrows at both Mountain Village and College were less vigorous in their territorial displays than were the Friday Harbor Puget Sound sparrows, in spite of the fact that the Gambel's sparrows arrived with gonads much larger and closer to breeding condition than did the Puget Sound birds. On the margin of the range at Mountain Village territorial behavior was so weak as to scarcely deserve the name. At College the males displayed more forcefully, but still not so vigorously as had the Puget Sound males. The sparseness of the breeding population and the cold and inclement weather at Mountain Village could conceivably explain the lack of territorial display there, but at College, where Gambel's sparrows were abundant and the weather more favorable, other factors must have been responsible, the most likely one being the absence of females during this phase.

At Mountain Village newly arrived Gambel's sparrows sang weakly and showed no attachment to any piece of ground. If I approached them they flew straight away for distances up to a mile. Unlike the Nuttall's or Puget Sound sparrows in comparable stages of development, they showed no tendency to face me and sing, or even to seek shelter nearby. Some days after arrival, however, each male had established a headquarters where he spent the greater part of each day. The area still did not merit the term "territory" in the strict sense, for the males sometimes left their headquarters for hours. I saw some pursuits, but also cases of complete tolerance of one male by another. When the females arrived, each pair restricted their activities to an area, including the male's headquarters, but, with one notable exception discussed in the next section, neighboring males never had violent disputes such as I saw commonly at Friday Harbor.

One unique feature of behavior I observed at Mountain Village was that a few pairs nested where only one element of the typical breeding territory, dense shrubbery, was present. To reach the other two essential elements, namely grass and open ground, these pairs regularly flew from their nesting areas above the village a mile or so down to the river's edge. There they foraged, and if they had young they carried food back to the nest. To make these trips they had to pass directly through the nesting areas of other Gambel's sparrows, which did not appear to resent the intrusion. This is the only case I know where the three essential elements of the breeding territory were not contained in an area inhabited exclusively by a pair.

At College the settlement of the ground followed a more conventional pattern. Except for the fact that the males arrived first, territory establishment contained all the behavior elements of the Friday Harbor-Puget Sound sparrow population. Each male became attached soon after arrival to an area where he sang loudly and regularly. I saw frequent pursuits and fights, but they were neither so common nor so intense as those at Friday Harbor.

Courtship.—Courtship in Gambel's sparrow begins just as the males are achieving full breeding condition. Therefore the courtship period is shorter than those in the Nuttall's and Puget Sound sparrows, which begin this phase in a less advanced stage of gonad development. As in the Puget Sound sparrows wintering at Berkeley, there was no evidence of sexual interest between flockmates in the Gambel's sparrows wintering at Davis or at Santa Barbara. Indirect evidence from collecting records suggests that members of a given breeding pair may winter not only in separate flocks but at different latitudes. John T. Emlen, Jr. (1943) found from examination of Gambel's sparrow specimens at the Museum of Vertebrate Zoology and from his own collecting records that the sex ratios are unequal. At Davis, males outnumber females by more than 5 to 1. Emlen's findings are in accord with my own less-exact figures for the proportion of males to females in *gambelii* collected at Davis and in *pugetensis* taken at Berkeley. I, too, recorded the preponderance of males to females by about 5 to 1. That this is not entirely due to accidents of collecting the bolder and more conspicuous males is indicated by the fact that Emlen found Gambel's sparrow females outnumber males by almost 2 to 1 in the collections from the southern and eastern portion of the winter range. As we have no evidence of disparity in numbers of males and females on the breeding grounds of either race, at least some of the breeding pairs must break up and repair to different localities in winter.

At Mountain Village in 1950 the females must have gone directly to the males' territories on arrival. I never found any wandering free. Hence the day of arrival must also have been the day the bond between the pair started to form or to re-form between mates of the previous year. The interval between the day of arrival of the female and the first observed copulation varied from 1 to 10 days for three pairs. The same behavorial elements of singing, trilling, and posturing were present as in the other two races.

At College, on the other hand, the first females I found were not followed by or following a male, and did not appear to be attached to any particular area. They flew long distances, trilled, and postured without any external stimulus that I could detect, and as they foraged they poked into crevices and peered under tufts of dry grass. A few days later all females I saw were paired. Each was followed closely by a male, and she trilled and postured vigorously when he sang or came near her. She continued to peer into crannies and under grass tufts. Four days after I first saw a female I saw two pairs copulate and watched others go through all the characteristic behavior preliminary to coition. Also at this time the females were building nests.

I have no evidence of polygamy in the Gambel's sparrow, but color-banding adjacent pairs at Mountain Village revealed one case where a male tried unsuccessfully for 3 days to steal the mate of a neighboring male while his own female was completing her first clutch and starting to incubate. The facts were as follows (Oakeson, 1954):

On May 23, Male 1 acquired a mate. She built one nest, deserted it, and was finishing another when on May 28 copulation occurred. Female 1 must have begun incubation May 31, judging by the date her eggs hatched. Meanwhile the neighbor on the east, Male 7, had acquired a mate. She started her nest May 30. That same evening, Male 1 'attacked' her. * * * Male 7, which until then had been singing regularly but not forcefully, chased Male 1, then began to sing loudly from conspicious perches, patrolling his area as do males during incubation. The next evening, Female 7 was attacked again by Male 1. Then each time she flew, she was pursued by both males. Finally Male 7 began to chase the intruder, but could not drive him back to his own area. At 9:10 p.m., over one and one-half hours after the dispute had begun that evening, Male 7 began to patrol his territory, which now, owing to his intensified behavior, merited the term in all its connotations, and incorporated into his patrol a high aerial pole, from which he sang loudly. (Since there are no tall trees at Mountain Village the aerial poles near the Trading Post were favorite singing perches.) There followed a 'singing contest' between the two males. This lasted until 9:45 p.m., some time after other birds had quieted down for the night. During the contest, Female 7 trilled and postured vigorously but her mate was too preoccupied to pay any attention to her. The next evening, June 1, the performance was repeated, and Male 1 flew at Pair 7 whenever they attempted copulation, preventing the mating not only psychologically but also physically, at least as long as I watched. By the next day the situation had returned to normal: each male sang from his respective territory. Pair 7 must have succeeded in copulating, for the female finished her nest June 1, laid her first egg June 3, and all eggs hatched June 19.

Nesting.—At Mountain Village I first saw nest building 11 days after the average date for arrival of the males and only 3 days after the average day date for arrival of the females. The intervals between arrival and nest building at College are closely comparable: I first saw a female building on May 20, 12 days after the average date of arrival for males and 3 days after average arrival date of the females. At both localities the interval between arrival of the female and the start of nest building lasted only 2 or 3 days, as contrasted with the corresponding interval of 1 to 2 weeks for Puget Sound sparrows at Friday Harbor. The time spent in building is also shorter. At Mountain Village four Gambel's sparrow females spent 2 to 4 days in building. At College one female was first seen building on May 21, and again on May 24. She laid her first egg May 26. It will be remembered that both Nuttall's and Puget Sound sparrows spend from 7 to 9 days building the first nest of the season.

Eggs.—Gambel's sparrows lay the first egg from 0 to 3 days after the nest is finished. I have two records of females that worked on their nests the same day they laid the first egg of their clutch. For seven females seen while building, the average interval between the date they were last seen building and the date they laid their first egg was 1 day. The corresponding interval for *nuttalli* is 3.6 days, for *pugetensis*, 2.6 days.

Egg laying extends from late May through mid-July in this race. The earliest date for eggs is May 21 for two clutches I found at College in 1957. The median date for the same locality for 13 clutches I found was May 23. At Mountain Village in 1950 the median date was later, between June 2 and 3 for six clutches.

Clutch size averages greater in the Gambel's sparrow than in either *nuttalli* or *pugetensis*. The number of eggs per clutch ranges from 3 to 6, with one record of 7 eggs in one nest. The average of 76 clutches is 4.58. The most common number of eggs per clutch is 5. The percentages are as follows: three eggs per clutch 9.21 percent, four eggs per clutch 32.9 percent, five eggs per clutch 50.0 percent, six eggs per clutch 6.6 percent, and seven eggs per clutch (one record only) 1.3 percent. The average clutch size by month is: May 4.71, June 4.65, July 3.40 for 14, 57, and 5 clutches, respectively. I have no evidence that Gambel's sparrows lay more than one clutch per season if they successfully fledge one brood.

As in *pugetensis*, clutch size in the Gambel's sparrow appears to increase with latitude. Five sets of eggs taken between latitudes 51° and 55° N. average 4.20 eggs; 4 clutches collected between 56° N. and 60° N. average 4.50; 32 clutches between 61° N. and 66° N. average 4.56 eggs, and 27 clutches taken between 67° N. and 69° N. average 4.74 eggs per clutch.

Incubation.—I know the length of the incubation period for three females of this race. Two at Mountain Village hatched their eggs 12 days after they started incubating. One at College hatched her eggs 11 days after she began incubating. This is the only case in any of the races I found where the incubation period was less than 12 days. One of these females began sitting the day she laid the fifth and last egg of the clutch. The other two began sitting the day they laid the fourth of five eggs.

Young.—The nestling period in *gambelii* averages shorter than in *nuttalli* or *pugetensis*. For 13 nestlings watched at Mountain Village, the time spent in the nest ranged from 8 to 11 days, or an average of 9.6 days. For 15 nestlings watched at College, the time spent in the nest ranged from 7 to 9 days, or an average of 8.4 days.

Gambel's sparrow young become independent of their parents at least by the time they are 28 days old. I trapped three young of a pair at this age. In this, they do not differ significantly from the Puget Sound sparrow young at Friday Harbor.

Fall.—In 1957 I watched Gambel's sparrows before and during fall migration at College, Alaska (lat. 64°49′ N.). That same year, Mrs. Priscilla Phillips (personal communication) watched the arrival of Gambel's sparrows at Santa Barbara, Calif., some 2,400 air miles away. Though observations at these two localities complement each other in several respects, no identity of the two populations is implied, for despite the thousands of Gambel's sparrows banded each year, none has been taken on both breeding and wintering grounds, and we do not know how far a given individual travels. By analogy with the Puget Sound sparrow, we should expect birds nesting in the northern part of the breeding range to migrate to the southern part of the wintering range. Thus it is possible that Gambel's sparrows breeding at the latitude of College may winter in southern California. In this connection it is interesting that a singing male in breeding condition collected at College on May 6 was using a song pattern identical with one of the song patterns heard in winter at Santa Barbara.

Excerpts from my field notes outline the start and progress of migration as I recorded it at College in 1957.

"August 6. Kallio, Superintendent of the University of Alaska Experiment Station, reports Gambel's sparrows gathering in the strawberry patch at the Experiment Station. He interprets this as a sign the birds are getting ready to migrate.

"August 10. Gambel's sparrows appear to be definitely in migration. They utter *eep's* rapidly, and occasionally sing weak, fragmentary songs.

"August 13. After hunting along roadsides where breeding birds had been common I observed that the birds behave as a winter flock. They appear to be migrating. Two adults were seen in a flock of about ten birds. All were furtive, shy, keeping foliage between them and me. Other birds suspected of being in migration: Myrtle warblers, Ruby-crowned kinglets, Savannah sparrows.

"August 14. For the past week or so I have noticed that trapped birds utter call notes when I hold them in a darkened cage. They fight to escape and squirm more vigorously in my hand than they did before.

"August 15. Mr. Kallio reports that the numbers of Gambel's are now markedly fewer. About a week or ten days ago he saw the greatest number.

"August 17. There are definitely fewer Gambel's sparrows than on August 6 and 8. Other species flocking this a.m.: Juncos, Savannah sparrows.

"August 18. Heard only a few Gambel's sparrows.

"August 19. At meadow between 8- and 9-mile on road to Nenana, saw a flock of 18 Gambel's sparrows. No singing or uttering of location or alarm notes. They perched close together.

"August 25. 8:30 a.m. For the first time I do not see a sizable group of Gambel's at the trap sites.

"August 26. At meadow between 8- and 9-mile, found only three immatures. Heard no song. Saw no adults. I listened and looked at spots where found Gambel's sparrows last week. None there. Did not see any large migrating flocks anywhere this a.m.

"August 27. At junction of railroad tracks and road to Nenana, no Gambel's sparrows seen or heard. Saw one immature Gambel's in meadow between 8- and 9-mile. Heard two Gambel's songs in rapid succession.

"August 30. Drove slowly along Chena Pump Road to North Star Ranch. Stopped to look and listen. No birds of any species except fox sparrows seen or heard. Stopped back of trap site 3 and listened. Heard geese and a fox sparrow but no Gambel's sparrows."

To fill in the details of the picture of fall activity in the Gambel's sparrow at College, I operated 9 Potter traps at four stations around a field near the territories of about 11 nesting pairs, banded and released 256 adults and young, and collected specimens for analysis of molt, fat, gonad size, thyroid activity, and body weight. The data from banding and collecting during the period from June 26 to August 27 substantiate the impression, given by the field notes on behavior just quoted, that by early August migration was in full swing. The local breeding birds probably left the trapping area at least by late July, and from then on until late August successive waves of Gambel's sparrows passed through the area, staying on the average only a few days before moving on.

The data reveal a major difference between fall departure at College and spring departure at Davis and Santa Barbara: in the north the residents at the trapping area left very early in the migration period, and were replaced by successive influxes of birds, presumably from farther north, whereas in the south the winter residents gradually decreased in numbers until all had gone, and they were not replaced by others. One similarity between spring and fall departure has been noted: in both fall and spring, the birds may start their migration before the molt is finished, and while still accumulating fat.

Mrs. Priscilla Phillips (personal communication) made daily observations on the arrival of white-crowned sparrows at her home in Hope Ranch for five consecutive years, from 1957 through 1961. In addition, during the first three years she trapped and banded 399 Gambel's sparrows at her feeding station, where the combination of a nearby lemon orchard, brushy hillsides, and a well-watered lawn provided optimum conditions for attracting and observing the flocks, some adults of which had doubtless fed there the previous winter.

One point of particular interest is the near identity of dates for the first white-crowned sparrow seen by Mrs. Phillips at Hope Ranch in five consecutive years. Another is that the arrival consists of a series of discrete influxes, often several days apart. The numbers observed may even decrease between successive influxes, suggesting that not all the birds coming to Santa Barbara in the fall actually winter there. A third point is that the arrival period lasts at least 6 to 7 weeks. A fourth is that in the early part of the arrival period the birds come either singly or in small inconspicuous groups and are trap-shy, so it would be easy to miss the first arrivals. Fifth, the earliest Gambel's sparrows to appear are accompanied by Puget Sound sparrows, which do not tarry long in the area. By early to mid-October of 1957, 1958, and 1959, all of the birds entering the traps were Gambel's sparrows. All these observations are substantiated by Mrs. Phillips' banding records. One point on which observation and banding are not entirely in agreement is the proportion of young-of-the-year to adults. On this point, the data from observation tend to be more variable than those from banding.

Except for the sight record of one white-crowned sparrow on September 3, 1957, the dates for the first individual seen by Mrs. Phillips at Hope Ranch (either *gambelii* or *pugetensis*, race not determined) are Sept. 20, 1957, 1958, and 1959, Sept. 18, 1960, and Sept. 19, 1961. The earliest date when birds identified with certainty as *gambelii* were seen at Hope Ranch are also almost identical: Sept. 20, 1957, 1958, and 1960, Sept. 21, 1961 and Sept. 22, 1959.

Both observations and banding indicate that the arrival consists of separate influxes, with many or most members of the early ones probably continuing their flight south. Each influx is accompanied by much commotion: choruses of song, often weak and fragmentary, the uttering of call notes and squabbling notes, restlessness characterized by almost continuous movement in the trees or brush, and the frequent sudden flight or dive for cover of the whole foraging flock. On the basis of these characteristics of behavior, Mrs. Phillips estimates that in 1957 at least eight influxes occurred between September 20 and October 31. Others may have occurred in November, but by then the numbers coming to the feeding station were too large and too stable to reveal with certainty any new arrivals. In 1958 she again observed at least eight influxes, between September 20 and November 7, and in 1959 at least six influxes between September 20 and October 16, when she ended her daily observations.

Banding records indirectly substantiate Mrs. Phillips' impression that many members of each influx move on. Only 3 out of 60 Gambel's sparrows she banded between Sept. 20 and Oct. 17, 1957, were retaken the following winter.

The intervals between observed influxes for the 3 years at Hope Ranch varied from 2 to 15 days, with the shorter intervals tending to be in the early part of the arrival period. The average of 19 intervals between influxes is 6.0 days. The most commonly occurring interval (6 of the 19) is 5 days.

The period elapsing between the date the first white-crowned sparrow identified as a Gambel's sparrow was seen in Hope Ranch in 1957 (September 20) and the end of the arrival period, judged by stability of numbers trapped and observed and the general quieting down of the flocks (November 1 at the earliest) is at least 42 days. The comparable period for 1958 is at least 48 days. The fall arrival at Santa Barbara over a period of 6 to 7 weeks agrees with the data gained from banding and watching the birds at College, Alaska, in the fall of 1957, which showed the birds continued to pass through the trapping area from at least late July through August 27 or later.

To the question of whether immatures or adults arrive first in the Santa Barbara region, the data available give no consistent answer. Mrs. Phillips' observations at Hope Ranch agree with those of Henry Kyllingstad at Mountain Village as to the varying proportions of immatures and adults in successive influxes of migrants. The ratios also varied during the years Mrs. Phillips watched.

Although, as was stated at the beginning of this section, no identity of populations is implied, the observations and banding data from College and from Santa Barbara agree in the following respects. First, the periods of time the birds are on the move, passing through College and arriving at and passing through Santa Barbara, are comparable. Each is 6 to 7 weeks or more. Second, both at College and at Santa Barbara, the migration consists of a series of influxes. There is strong evidence that the members of a given influx did not stay long in the College area, and only slightly less conclusive evidence that many of the arrivals at Santa Barbara did not stay long there either. Third, neither at College nor at Santa Barbara was there a consistent pattern of arrival according to age group. Fourth, the ratios of immatures to adults trapped at College from mid-July through late August varied between approximately the same limits as did the sight estimates made of relative numbers of immatures and adults for the fall arrival at Hope Ranch the same year, and as did the trapping records at Hope Ranch for November of two years. Whatever the hazards of the flight south, the immatures appear to fare about as well as the adults.

The observations from College, Alaska, and from Santa Barbara, Calif., furnish data for estimates of the length of time spent in the southward migration. Assuming that birds of the latitude of College may fly as far south as Santa Barbara to winter, we know that the interval between the time the local breeding population left College (at least by July 22) and the earliest data of arrival of Gambel's sparrows that same year at Hope Ranch (September 20) is at least 60 days. This estimated migration period is over 1⅓ times as long as that estimated for the flight north in spring. Oakeson (1954) estimated that it requires approximately 35 days for the flight north from the latitudes of southern California to those of Mountain Village, Alaska, an air distance of about 2,700 miles.

An individual bird flying in about 60 days from the latitude of College to that of Santa Barbara, a distance of about 2,450 air miles, would average about 41 miles per day, which a white-crown flying at 20 miles per hour (Pearson 1961) could cover in about 2 hours. The birds should be able to fly twice as long, and twice as far daily, and still have ample time each day to forage and rest.

Winter.—In winter the Gambel's sparrow, like the Puget Sound sparrow, forms flocks that are homogeneous assemblages, with no hint of the tendency of flock members to pair off. Also like *pugetensis*, the *gambelii* flocks observed at Davis were approximately stable as to size and tended to restrict their daily movements to a limited area. The following quotation from Blanchard and Erickson (1949) refers to flocks whose members were color-banded at Davis in 1942–1943.

Throughout the winter the birds flock in groups of 30 to 50. Each flock is restricted to a given area, though there may be a substantial overlapping of areas. Of the 48 individuals either retrapped or identified by sight at Davis, 29 were found at the same spot where they had been banded, 12 were found not more than 500 yards away, which is not over the normal maximum distance traveled by any one flock in the course of a day. The remaining few were seen up to a maximum of 976 yards away. General localization of each flock to a specific area is further indicated by many hours of observation of individual flocks throughout the winter. Each flock had its headquarters, within a few yards of which it spent the greater part of each day.

Once the birds were established, behavior during the ensuing five months until mid-March showed little change. No fights and few pursuits were seen. Singing continued sporadically but was lacking in force, and the individuals which sang always did so as integral parts of the flock.

Not only may individuals stay in a restricted area one winter, but they may also return to the same place year after year. Bird-banders have furnished a wealth of data on returns of white-crowned sparrows Blanchard and Erickson (1949) note: "In Santa Barbara between 1943 and 1947, 282 Gambel sparrows were banded at stations where traps were operated at least occasionally throughout the months from September to May. One hundred, or 35 percent of the 282, were taken again. Of these 100, 47 were retaken in two succeeding winters, two in three, and one in four winters." Of 223 Gambel's sparrows Mrs. Phillips banded at Hope Ranch in 1957–1958, 14 returned the following fall. Of 129 birds banded there in 1958–1959, 8 were recaptured in the fall of 1959. F. G. Crawford (personal communication) states that "in preparing return records for Gambel sparrows, the similarity of calendar dates for original capture and return seemed to occur too frequently to be purely coincidental." Of 121 banded Gambel's sparrows recaptured by Crawford in succeeding years, 50 percent were taken within 30 days of calendar date of original capture.

The waves of migrants arriving at a given place on the wintering grounds do not stop with the onset of winter. Elliott McClure (personal communication), who banded nearly 3,000 white-crowned sparrows (presumably all or nearly all *gambelii*) at Bakersfield during four winters, states: "A wave of birds appeared to enter the area in October, increase in November, and decrease in December. This was followed by another increased flow through January and February which then decreased in March and April." After presenting several possible explanations for the wave-like movements of white-crowned sparrows suggested by the banding records, McClure concludes, "The wave action of these birds seems inescapable, both going south and returning north, and the mass of birds moving was great enough that unmarked ones were constantly entering the vicinity of the traps. Jean M. Linsdale (1949), working with White-crowns at Hastings Reservation about 150 miles north of Bakersfield and in the coastal range, found a similar wave action but with different distribution during the winter months." Although, as Mewaldt's data discussed in the following paragraph indicate, one cannot assume that the mid-winter waves observed by McClure came from any particular compass direction, the interesting point is that influxes of birds appeared during months when migration proper does not occur.

That white-crowned sparrows are potentially mobile in winter is indicated by the trapping records of L. R. Mewaldt (1963) who trapped and banded white-crowned sparrows (*Z. l. pugetensis* and *Z. l. gambelii*) at San Jose, Calif., for 8 consecutive seasons. From 1954–55 through 1960–61, the total numbers of both races trapped ranged from 181 to 292 per season, or an average of 227.1 for these 7 seasons. In 1961–1962 Mewaldt removed large numbers of banded white-crowns and shipped them by air to Baton Rouge, La. One of the many interesting results of this work was the increase in numbers of white-crowns trapped at San Jose that season—a total of 670 unbanded individuals. Mewaldt (1962) removed 430 birds for his homing experiment. He states: "Repeated removal of the 'hard core' of dominant birds coming to bait at the banding station probably permitted population pressure to fill the vacuum thus created." While the situation created by removal of many wintering white-crowns is obviously an unnatural one, the fact that so many birds came to Mewaldt's station shows the inherent mobility of winter flocks, and also that no assumption can be made as to the direction from which mid-winter influxes come, such as those reported by McClure.

In summary, the data presented in this section indicate flexibility, as well as stability, of the location of winter flocks. Apparently movement may occur during mid-winter as well as during the migration periods proper. We must think of wintering Gambel's sparrows as geographically stable, in that some individuals return to the same place winter after winter, but also as flexible, in that some may move about during mid-winter. Perhaps the relatively low recapture percentage of banded white-crowned sparrows in any wintering population reflects something more than mortality rates, or the low statistical probability of retrapping a given banded individual. It is conceivable that, during winter, some individuals may stay close to the continuous food supply that a banding station provides, while others may move about. In a species that shows high individual and racial variability in every physiological character so far studied, there is no reason to exclude the possibility of differences in individual behavior in winter. As an example of an individual that moved about during winter, T. E. Balch (personal communication) reports banding a Gambel's sparrow at Glenn, Calif., Jan. 24, 1960; on March 1 the same year the bird was taken 25 miles away at Chico, Calif.

Gambel's White-crowned Sparrow

Distribution

Range.—Central and western Canada and Alaska to Baja California and central Mexico.

Breeding range.—This race intergrades with *Z. l. leucophrys* on the south shore of Hudson Bay from Churchill to James Bay. The breeding range of the Gambel's white-crowned sparrow extends from northern Ontario (Weenusk, Fort Severn) to northern Manitoba (York Factory, Ilford, Hershmer, Churchill) into the Northwest Territories, (South Henick Lake, Artillery Lake, Coronation Gulf, Fort Good Hope, Mackenzie River Delta) west to the Yukon Territory (Lapierre House, Old Crow River) west to Alaska (Sheenjek River, Colville River Delta, Koalak River, Pitmegea River, Cape Lisburne) south in western Alaska (Kotzebue Sound, Wales, Nome, Norton Sound, Mountain Village) to southwestern Alaska and the Alaskan peninsula (Kanakanak, Nushagak, Egekik River, Port Moller, Izembek Bay) northeast to the Kenai Peninsula, the Knik Arm of Cook Inlet, to Copper Center, the Chitina River, into southern Yukon Territory (Burwash Landing, Slims River mouth) into British Columbia (Mile 85 on Haines Road, Bennett, Atlin, Telegraph Creek, Chezacut Lake) to northern Washington (Hart's Pass) east to

Field, British Columbia, intergrades with *Z. l. oriantha* near the United States-Canada border; north in Alberta (Banff Park, Jasper and Grimshaw) northeast to Saskatchewan (Fond-du-lac and Reindeer Lake).

Winter range.—Winters from southern British Columbia (Comox, Okanagan Landing), southeastern Washington (Cheney, Pullman, Snake River Canyon), southern Idaho (Heyburn), central Wyoming (Thermopolis), north central and southern Colorado (Mesa County, Boulder County, Pueblo County), northern and eastern Kansas (Wallace, Manhattan, Lawrence), western Oklahoma (Roger Mills County, Comanche County); west to the coast; south to southern Baja California (San José del Cabo), to the islands of Las Tres Marías, east of Nayarit (Las Varas), Aquascalientes (6 miles southwest of Aquascalientes), San Luis Potosí (San Luis Potosí), north to northern Tamaulipas (Nuevo Laredo, Matamoros), and to southern and central Texas (Brownsville, Böerne, Concho County).

Casual records.—Casual in migration or in winter in southern Ontario (Toronto), southern Wisconsin (Madison), Michigan (Jackson County; Huron Mountain, Marquette County; Whitefish Point), New York (Ithaca), Illinois (Waukegan; Newton, Jasper County), Ohio (Leetonia, Columbiana County; Waterville Township, Lucas County; Fairfield County), Maryland (Patuxent Research Refuge near Bowie), Virginia (Blacks; Lexington) Tennessee (Nashville), South Carolina (Mount Pleasant), Georgia (Tipton), and Alaska (Barrow), and British Columbia (Okanagan Landing).

Accidental in Alaska on Pribilof Islands (St. Paul Island), and Little Diomede Island (Ignalook Village); on Bank's Island (Sach's Harbour); District of Franklin; and in Japan (Honshu).

Migration.—Early dates of spring arrival are: Alberta—60 miles north of Edmonton, May 4. British Columbia—Pentincton, Lake Okanagan, April 23. Manitoba—Churchill, June 8. Mackenzie—Fort Enterprise, approximately 150 miles north of Great Slave Lake, May 26: Fort Providence on Great Slave Lake, May 9. Yukon—Forty-mile (lat. 64), May 10; La Pierre House, May 25. Alaska—Kodiak Island, before May 23; Mountain Village, May 7; Nome, May 29; Kowak delta, May 21; College, May 4 (2 years record).

Late dates of spring departure are: Aguascalientes—6 miles southwest of Aguascalientes, March 1. Durango—12 miles west of Lerdo, one specimen, March 1. Baja California—San Fernando; islands offshore: Los Coronados, Cedros, San Benito, April 29. Sonora—Guaymas, April 24. Coahuila—Boquillas wash in the Sierra del Carmen, April 27. Texas—Marathon, Brewster County, May 6; Pine Springs Camp in the Guadalupe Mountains, May 3. Oklahoma—Cheyenne, May 13; Indiahoma, May 8. Arizona—Tucson valley area, May 13;

Baboquivari Mountains, May 12; Fort Verde, May 11. Colorado—Mack, Mesa County, May 29; Clear Creek district, June 12. California—Twenty-nine Palms, May 6; Polvadero Gap, Kettleman Hills area, May 17. Nevada—Meadow Valley, Lincoln County, May 24; Eldorado Mountains, May 3. Oregon—Lake County, May 20. Washington—Cheney, April 27.

Early dates of fall arrival are: Washington—Prescott, September 2. Oregon—Wheeler County, September 13; Warner Valley, August 30. Nevada—Indian Springs, September 10; Boulder Beach, September 17. California—Eagleville, Modoc County, September 2; Los Angeles, September 20. Utah—St. George area, numerous by October 1. Colorado—Denver area, mid-September; Colorado Springs, September 8. Arizona—Pima County, September 23. Kansas—Manhattan, October 9; Wallace, October 12. Texas—Guadalupe Peak (10 miles east), October 6; Chisos Mountains, Green Gulch, November 14. Sonora—Cajon Bonito Creek, September 8. Baja California and offshore islands Los Coronados, Todos Santos, San Benito, Cedros, October 7. Tamaulipas—Matamoros, November 25. Las Tres Marias—Maris Madre, December 28.

Late dates of fall departure are: Alaska—Kowak River (now Kobuk) opposite the mouth of Hunt River, September 2; Nushagak, September 18; Fairbanks (70 miles southeast), October 20; Juneau, October 1. Mackenzie—Great Bear Lake, September 5. Ontario—Shagamu River, August 10. British Columbia—Alberta—Edmonton, September 26. Washington—Monument 83 on U.S. and Canada boundary at long. 120°38½′, September 3; Harts Pass, during the second week of August.

Egg Dates.—Alaska: 52 records, May 21 to July 13; 42 records, May 23 to June 15.

Alberta: 3 records, June 13, June 21, June 28.

British Columbia: 6 records, June 7 to June 22.

Mackenzie: 3 records, June 15, June 30, July 15.

Yukon Territory: 11 records, June 1 to June 17.

ZONOTRICHIA LEUCOPHRYS ORIANTHA Oberholser

Mountain White-crowned Sparrow*

Contributed by BARBARA BLANCHARD DEWOLFE

HABITS

This race consists of a group of western populations of white-crowned sparrows that breed chiefly at high altitudes in the Canadian

*Additional material on this race is included in the account of Nuttall's white-crowned sparrow, pp. 1292–1324.

and Hudsonian life zones and winter in the lowlands. Until they were designated as a separate race in 1930 by Harry C. Oberholser, they were included in the race *leucophrys*, although their breeding range is separated from the main portion of the *leucophrys* range by several hundred miles. In this article I include under *oriantha* those records for *leucophrys* prior to 1930 that pertain to the western populations.

One of the most interesting aspects of this race in California, where I observed it, is the fact that the breeding population consists of a series of isolated colonies highly variable in the time they begin nesting. Because the date when the snow melts enough to permit birds to nest on or near the ground varies considerably from one breeding locality to another, even in the same year, some populations of this race begin nesting in early June, whereas others have to wait until July. In fact many *oriantha* populations begin nesting later than do Gambel's sparrows in northern Alaska.

Another characteristic of *oriantha* in California is the small size of many of the breeding populations. Some of the high mountain meadows it inhabits are too small to support more than four or five nesting pairs. Also in marginal areas minor vegetative changes, such as those brought about by a series of unusually dry or wet years or by the interference of man, may render a suitable locality unsuitable for nesting white-crowns, or vice versa. This may explain discrepancies in the literature regarding the occurrence of this race, such as the early reports (Merrill, 1888, E. A. Preble, MS) of white-crowned sparrows breeding in the Mount Shasta and Crater Lake regions, where recent attempts to find them (Farner, 1952; Banks, personal communication; DeWolfe and DeWolfe, 1962) have failed.

A third interesting fact is that, although the latitudinal range of *oriantha* in California is approximately the same as that of *nuttalli*, its average clutch is significantly larger than that of the coastal form.

Data on clutch size and egg dates for *oriantha* are plentiful, but the literature contains almost nothing on its behavior. My own observations of this race in the Sierras and Cascades during the summer of 1960 include brief glimpses of territory establishment, incubation, and care of nestlings, none of which show obvious differences from those of the other races. I have no firsthand knowledge of behavior in this form during fall and winter. Owing to the paucity of information on the annual cycle, I present the data on habits in a continuous account rather than under the subheadings used for the other races.

Records of its movements in spring and fall suggest that not only does *oriantha* leave its wintering and breeding grounds later than does *gambelii*, but also that, depending on local weather conditions, *oriantha* may tarry *en route* between the two. Stephen S. Visher (1910) states that *leucophrys* (now *oriantha*) is an abundant winter visitor in Pima County, Arizona and that "they remain several weeks longer than *Z. gambeli* feeding on the blackberry-like fruits of the mulberry. Last seen June 8." Laurence M. Huey (1926) observed a flock of fifty white-crowns (which I assume were *oriantha*) on May 22 at El Rosario in Baja California. The following day only two were seen and one collected, indicating that most had departed the previous night. Joseph Grinnell and T. I. Storer (1924) state that what is now called the mountain white-crowned sparrow is a summer visitant to the Hudsonian Zone in the Yosemite region and that it passes through the lower levels on both sides of the mountains during spring migration.

The earliest definite records of the arrival of the Hudsonian white-crown in the Yosemite region are for May 10 (1916) * * * and for May 8 (1917) * * *. Migration was still in progress on May 22 (1919), as a male bird in Yosemite Valley on that date tarried only a short time before moving on. * * * Some individuals continue in their summer haunts until the end of September, several having been noted by us at Tuolumne Meadows on Sept. 29, 1915, but none anywhere later than that date.

Our highest record for the Hudsonian white-crowned sparrow was close to 11,000 feet altitude, in a patch of stunted willows in a draw between Mount Gibbs and Mount Dana, July 29, 1915.

Joseph Grinnell, Joseph Dixon and Jean M. Linsdale (1930) collected white-crowned sparrows thought to be still on their breeding grounds at Warner Creek in the Lassen Peak Region on Sept. 16, 1923 (elevation 8,000 feet).

Eustace L. Sumner and Joseph S. Dixon (1953) give many records of *oriantha* in Sequoia National Park. In 1942 the first spring arrival in the park was on May 12 after a snowstorm at Lewis Creek. In 1934 three white-crowned sparrows were seen (one was taken) in a willow thicket at 9,700 feet near Gallats Lake on the Kern-Kaweah River, June 7. That same year six were seen at Kaweah Gap, at 10,700 feet elevation, on June 16; one of these (a female parent, no. 9090 in the Dixon collection) and a nest with four fresh eggs were collected. The fall records are as follows: On Sept. 20, 1933, when the willows were turning yellow at Heather Lake, just one bird, an immature, was present; the adults apparently had left on their fall migration. In 1940, one was found in Deadman Canyon on September 22 (they were no longer common in the vicinity); on September 24 one was seen at Scaffold Meadow. Two white-crowned sparrows noted at Giant Forest on Oct. 3, 1934, were evidently fall migrants from higher regions, as this species had not been there during the summer; two immatures were seen just below Tharp's Rock on October 5; one adult and one immature at Willow Meadow and three adults at Cahoon Meadow on October 13.

For other states we have the following records: Percy M. Silloway (1907) states that the first white-crowned sparrow was heard singing at Flathead Woods, Mont. on June 5, 1906. Elliott Coues (1874) quotes Trippe as saying that this race appears in the lower valleys of Clear Creek County, Colo., the first or second week of May. As the snow disappears, the race ascends the mountain, reaching timberline by the middle of June. It commences building in July and young are hatched about the 20th of this month. In September it begins to descend; by October it is abundant at Idaho, and by November has disappeared. William L. Slater (1912) states that white-crowns arrive at Colorado Springs the last week of April, gradually move up the mountains, reaching timberline the middle of June. After nesting they descend in September and October to lower levels and linger until early in November. The species is common on the western slopes during migration.

At Mineral, Calif., a few miles from the south entrance to Lassen Volcanic National Park, Ranger Naturalist and Mrs. Merle Stitt (pers. comm.) reported seeing white-crowned sparrows in migration, both in spring and fall. The last date for spring of 1960 was May 24, two days after the last snowstorm of the season. On June 25 of that same year my husband and I found *oriantha* males starting to establish territories at King's Creek Meadows inside the Park, (elevation 7,400 feet) but no females had yet arrived. By July 4, Park Superintendent and Mrs. Dixon Freeland reported pairs of white-crowned sparrows common at that location. Where the birds had been between May and July is a mystery, but if they kept a schedule comparable to those described above by Trippe and Slater they probably stayed in the vicinity below the nesting-grounds and moved up as the snow melted and the high country became habitable.

When we arrived at King's Creek Meadows on June 25, 1960, we found several male mountain white-crowned sparrows already spaced out, singing frequently but weakly. We saw no females. The males showed about the same level of territorial jealousy as did newly arrived Gambel's sparrow males at College, Alaska. They perched conspicuously, alternating in song with their neighbors, and occasionally pursued each other, but we saw no noisy conflicts, such as I have described for the newly arrived Puget Sound sparrows at Friday Harbor. By the next day the volume and frequency of song had increased, but there were still no females. On July 4 other observers (Beatrice Freeland, pers. comm.) found these meadows "alive with song," with white-crowns of both sexes present in numbers. Whether the males arrive ahead of the females in all localities is not certain.

The eggs are laid from late May through early August. William L. Dawson (1923) states that this race may raise one or two broods. I have found no records, however, of a pair with young out of the nest and with a second nest of eggs or young such as was the rule in the Puget Sound sparrows at Friday Harbor. When all the available egg dates are arranged chronologically, they show no hint of a gap in the series that would suggest a second brood. My observations in 1960 provide one illustration of the wide variation between populations as to the time nesting may start. On June 19, 1960, my husband and I found a pair of mountain white-crowned sparrows at Tuolumne Meadows with young about four days old. If we assume that the incubation period was the same length as in the Nuttall's sparrow, the female would have laid the first egg of this clutch on June 1. At King's Creek Meadows, on the other hand, the females had not even arrived by June 26. Even assuming they came the next day and began work on their nests at once, they could hardly have started laying before June 29 at the very earliest, some four weeks later than the pair at Tuolumne Meadows.

The average number of eggs per clutch for 164 clutches is 4.03. If only those clutches of *oriantha* from localities within the same latitudinal range as *nuttalli* are averaged, the mean is almost identical,—4.04 for 145 clutches. This is significantly larger than the average clutch size for *nuttalli* (3.27 for 215 clutches). The number of eggs per clutch in *oriantha* is usually four whereas in *nuttalli* it is usually three. Percentages for *oriantha* are as follows: 3 eggs 5.0 percent; 4 eggs 87.6 percent; 5 eggs 6.8 percent; 6 eggs (one record only) 0.6 percent. Two extreme records of two and seven eggs each were not included in the averages; it is not certain that the set of two was complete and we have no evidence that the clutch of seven was laid by a single female.

As clutch size varies with month of laying in *nuttalli*, I calculated the average clutch size for *oriantha* for June and July separately: for June 122 *oriantha* sets average 4.08 eggs per clutch, 21 *nuttalli* sets average 3.24; for July 37 *oriantha* clutches average 3.89 eggs per clutch, 7 *nuttalli* sets average 3.14 per set.

These comparisons show that some factor or factors other than latitude and month of laying must be responsible for the difference in average clutch size between *oriantha* and *nuttalli*. The most obvious environmental difference is that of altitude and the resulting differences in the climates of the breeding grounds. A scatter diagram we constructed of the number of recorded *oriantha* eggs per clutch in relation to elevation, which ranges from 4,000 feet to 11,000 feet, shows no obvious correlation, either positive or negative, with altitude.

As the sets of *oriantha* eggs were taken over many years at many different latitudes, other variables may mask the altitudinal effect.

Distribution

Range.—Southern Saskatchewan and Alberta to Baja California and central Mexico.

Breeding range.—This race intergrades with *gambelii* from northwestern Alberta in the Canadian Rockies to Glacier Park, Montana. An isolated population breeds in the Cypress Hills region of southwestern Saskatchewan and southeastern Alberta. The Mountain White-Crowned Sparrow breeds from western Alberta (Gorge Creek, Bragg's Creek, Banff National Park) to northern Idaho (Continental Mountain) south to eastern Oregon (Wallowa Mountains), southwest through central and southern Oregon (Harney, Hart Mountain, Adel) to northeastern California (Warner Mountains). Isolated populations occur in the Cascades of west central Oregon (Three Sisters, Tumalo Creek, Crescent Lake) and of California (Bray, King's Creek Meadows in Lassen National Park). From the Warner Mountains the range in California extends southward through the Sierra Nevadas (Mohawk, Plumas County to Horse Meadow, Tulare County). Isolated colonies breed in southern California (San Bernardino Mountains) and in eastern California in the White and Sweetwater Mountains, and on peaks in Nevada (Ruby Mountains and Jarbridge Mountains). The boundary of the range continues through southern Utah (Cedar City, Kanab area, Bluff) to northern New Mexico (Pecos Baldy, Wheeler Peak) through central Colorado (Mount Ptarmigan, Colorado Springs, Boulder County, and Northgate) to Wyoming (Sierra Madre Mountains, Albany County, Fort Steele, Muddy Creek, Beartooth Plateau) and north through central Montana (Shriver) and on isolated mountain ranges (Crazy Mountains, Big Snowy Mountains, Little Belt Mountains, Big Belt Mountains) to Saint Mary's Lake.

Winter range.—Winters from southern California (casually to Los Angeles area, and Twenty-nine Palms; Coachella, Holtville), east to southern Arizona (Gila Bend; Pinal County), east to southern New Mexico (Silver City), and western and Central Texas (Frijole in Culberson County; Concho County; Kerr County); south to southern Baja California (San José del Cabo); south and east through Sonora, Sinaloa, Coahuila (Sabinas; Hipolito), Nuevo Leon (Monterrey), Aguascalientes (Aguascalientes), San Luis Potosí (Rio Verde), Guanajuato, Querétaro (San Juan del Rio); south to Jalisco (Atoyac; Ocotlan), and Michoacan (Pátzcuaro).

Migration.—Early dates of spring arrival are: Colorado—Salida, April 19; Sulphur Springs, May 2. Montana—Gallatin County near Bozeman, early in May; Bitterroot Mountains 7000 ft., June 11; Flathead Woods, June 5. Saskatchewan—Southern edge of Cypress Hills, May 21. Alberta—Waterton Lakes, May 21. California—Florence Lake, near Fresno in Sierra Nevada, April 20; Kings Canyon Park, May 12; Yosemite Valley, April 17. Oregon—Fort Klamath, April 26.

Late dates of spring departure are: Michoacan—Pátzcuaro, April 26. Baja California—Cape district, May 23. Sonora—Magdalena, May 15. Sinaloa—El Fuerte, May 13. Jalisco—Ojuelos, May 15. Texas—Tom Green and Concho Counties, until May. New Mexico—Apache, southwestern Grant County, April 30. Arizona—Pima County, June 8; Baboquivari Mountains, 3500 ft., May 22; Huachuca Mountains, May 13. California—Buena Park, May 1; Twenty-nine Palms, May 14; Palm Springs, April 26.

Early dates of fall arrival are: Arizona—San Francisco Mountain region, September 21. Texas—Concho County, mid October. Baja California—La Grulla, September 28. Sonora—Cajon Bonito Creek, September 8.

Late dates of fall departure are: Oregon—Southern Willamette Valley, early October. California–Eagleville, September 18; Panther Creek and Shasta River, late September; Florence Lake, September 1; Charlotte and Bullfrog Lakes, Kings Canyon, September 5. Saskatchewan—Cypress Hills, July 11. Montana—Upper Holland Lake, Missoula County, September 10; Gallatin County near Bozeman, mid October. Idaho—St. Joe National Forest, October. Utah—Uinta Basin, (October 5–25, date not specified); southern Utah, October. Colorado—descends to lower levels September–October, lingers until early November. Rocky Mountain National Park, October 26.

Egg Dates.—California: 155 records, May 30—August 7; 125 records, June 10—July 5. Nevada: 7 records for June 22. Oregon: 1 record for July 13. Alberta: 2 records for July 4 and July 6.

ZONOTRICHIA LEUCOPHRYS PUGETENSIS Grinnell

Puget Sound White-crowned Sparrow*

Contributed by Barbara Blanchard DeWolfe

Habits

The Puget Sound sparrows that compose the subject of this section are those that winter at Berkeley on the same ground with the resident

*Additional material on this race will be found in the account of Nuttall's white-crowned sparrow, pp. 1292–1324.

Nuttall's sparrows and those that breed at Friday Harbor, Wash. Identity of these populations is not implied, although Ernest D Clabaugh (1930) reports the capture in summer at Victoria, B.C., of a Puget Sound sparrow he banded in Berkeley the previous winter.

In addition to these variations, Puget Sound sparrows differ from Nuttall's sparrows in the timing and duration of the phases of the breeding cycle, in the average clutch size, and in the age when the young become independent of their parents. The strongly migratory populations of *pugetensis* nesting at the Canadian border compress the active part of their reproductive cycle into less than two-thirds the time consumed by the Nuttall's sparrows of central California. In 1936 the Puget Sound sparrows at Friday Harbor paired, established territories and fledged three broods in less than 4 months, whereas from 1935 through 1938 the Berkeley Nuttall's sparrows consumed from 6 to 6½ months each year to achieve the same fraction of the cycle. The compression is accomplished by the omission of one and the shortening of three other more or less sharply delimited phases. In *pugetensis*, territorial establishment requires about three weeks and is not complete until the first day of incubation. In *nuttalli* the same process is begun much earlier, and also requires about three weeks, so that territory establishment is finished some six and one-half to eight and one-half weeks before the first day of incubation. The ensuing period of relatively settled conditions, when chasing and fighting have either decreased or disappeared, does not occur in *pugetensis*. The three phases that are shortened are: the period of temporary abeyance of song (14 days in *pugetensis* in contrast to 46 to 59 days in *nuttalli*, depending upon the year) the interval between completion of the first nest and laying of the first egg (an average of 2.6 days for seven records in *pugetensis* compared with 3.6 days for 12 records in *nuttalli*) and the interval between fledging of one brood and laying of the first egg for the next (an average of 8.9 days for five records of *pugetensis* in contrast to 20 days for six records in *nuttalli*).

Spring.—The same behavior elements as those described for *nuttalli* appear in spring in *pugetensis:* increased force and frequency of singing, pursuits and fights, and trilling and posturing. Only the first element is manifested on the wintering grounds. The others are delayed, either until migration or more probably until arrival on the breeding grounds. Then both sexes of Puget Sound sparrows regularly engage in chasing and fighting and in trilling and posturing, with much greater intensity than occurs in *nuttalli*.

In late Feburary, about four weeks before migration, a few Puget Sound sparrows begin to sing with greater vigor and more frequently than in winter. From then on until late March and early April an increasing number of birds in a given flock participate in the singing until, on the eve of departure, one hears a chorus of song from each flock headquarters. This group singing is not an act of defiance, and provokes no hostile response either from other Puget Sound sparrows or from the by now highly territorial Nuttall's sparrows in whose areas the migrants live. I never saw either chasing, fighting, or trilling and posturing in the flocks of Puget Sound sparrows wintering at Berkeley.

Daily trapping of banded birds reveals that it takes about as long for the individuals of any one flock to depart as it does the entire local wintering population. The departure is spread over about two weeks. Adults tend to depart earlier than young of the year. The last members of a given flock to disappear are usually first-year females. From departure and arrival dates for this race at the extremes of the range, I believe that the longest spring migration is accomplished in not more than two weeks. I know nothing of the behavior during this period.

In the spring of 1936 I went to Friday Harbor, Wash., to watch the arrival of birds destined to breed there. The largest influx occurred between the evening of April 9 and the next morning. On April 10 I found almost every piece of suitable ground, which only the day before had been empty and silent, occupied by a male perched conspicuously and singing with full volume every few seconds. Close to him I often saw another, silent bird, the female. The shift from the unassorted gregariousness of the wintering grounds to paired isolation must have taken place either during migration or immediately upon arrival, for no flocks or fragments of flocks were in evidence. Observations on color-banded birds by Mrs. Forrest Fuller at Friday Harbor indicate that on the day of arrival the birds go directly to the areas where they subsequently breed, and that they return to the same spot in successive years.

From the day after arrival both chasing and fighting were common and continued unabated until the beginning of incubation about three weeks later. Territorial boundaries were so fluid as to scarcely deserve the name. Both sexes seemed more excited and restless than Nuttall's sparrows in the corresponding stage. During a boundary dispute neighboring males trilled vigorously and fluttered one wing, and females frequently took part in pursuits. The whole scene was one of confusion and unsettledness, in sharp contrast to the orderly and law-abiding Nuttall's on their mutually exclusive areas during the seven weeks before the start of incubation. Eventually, however, the same result was achieved. By the first day of incubation in late April and early May the fighting subsided and the pairs settled down to a routine identical with that of Nuttall's sparrow.

The behavior, then, of *pugetensis* in spring differs from that of *nuttalli*, in the interpolation of a migratory flight between the beginning and the end of the transition from flocking to paired isolation, in the time the three behavior elements appear relative to the start of breeding, and in the intensity with which they are manifested. The relative disorder among the migrants during the "shake-down" period is not unnatural and may represent merely the result of circumstances rather than an intrinsic variation in habit or temperament. The migrants must establish themselves on ground unseen for seven months and perhaps wholly unfamiliar to some of the adult birds. The first-year birds must seek and seize at once what the young Nuttalls drift into or seek at leisure. The sudden change from a gregarious to an isolated habit perhaps creates a deeper psychological disturbance and contributes to the violence of the process of spatial arrangement.

Courtship.—The Puget Sound sparrows arrived at Friday Harbor apparently already paired. On Apr. 12, 1936, two days after the main influx, I saw a female trill and posture. From this time on, both actions increased in force and frequency until April 21, when I first saw a pair copulate. By April 27 trilling and posturing ceased temporarily, to be resumed prior to the start of the second brood.

We have evidence that, as in *nuttalli*, the members of a breeding pair of Puget Sound sparrows may remate the following season. Mrs. Forrest Fuller (pers. comm.) observed the same color-banded pair nesting in the same hedge in her garden in 1936 and 1937.

Nesting.—At Friday Harbor in 1936, the females started to build the nest one or two weeks after their arrival. Behavior during nest-building and the time it took to finish the nest were the same as in the Nuttall's sparrow, but the interval between fledging the first brood and starting work on the second nest was shorter than in *nuttalli*. Six Puget Sound sparrow females that I followed started work on their second nests only two to four days after the first brood was fledged.

The female alternates between feeding her young and building the new nest. That this may result in confusion is illustrated by the behavior of one female I observed on the morning of May 28 (Blanchard, 1941):

> * * * I saw her disappear with material into the hedge a few feet to one side of the first nest site. There I subsequently found a new nest with the walls partly formed. * * * Between half-past eight and half-past nine she made seven trips to the hedge to feed the fledglings, then stayed away for half an hour. She returned at ten, carrying straws in her beak, flew to the abandoned nest,

hesitated a little, flew to the hedge where a nestling was perched, and emerged without the straw. I sought out the fledgling, which was crying for food, and found she had laid the straws at its feet!

About fifteen minutes later, female X brought food to the fledgling * * *. Five minutes later she again flew to the hedge with straws in her beak and this time went straight to the new site. When I looked at the nest that evening, its walls were complete, and a few pine needles and a little fine grass were heaped in the cup. On May 31, just six days after the first brood had left the nest, this female laid the first egg of her second clutch.

Eggs.—The interval between completion of the nest and the date the first egg is laid is shorter for *pugetensis* than for *nuttalli*. For seven records the interval ranged from one to four days and averaged 2.6 days, as compared with 3.6 days with a range of one to seven days for 12 records for *nuttalli*.

In *pugetensis* the eggs are laid between late April and late July. The earliest date recorded is April 23 at Eureka, Calif.; the latest date, July 23 at the same locality. (One clutch in the Museum of Comparative Oology collection at Santa Barbara is labeled "Oct. 31, 1908" but the condition of the eggs is not given.) At Friday Harbor in 1936 the earliest date for the first egg of a clutch was April 24, the latest, July 4. For first clutches of the season, the median date for 22 females at this locality was Apr. 29–30, 1936. That year one color-banded female laid her first egg on May 1, only one or two days from the median date for the population. The next year she laid her first egg on May 7. If she again came as close to the median date for the population, then in 1937 the median date would have fallen between May 5 and 9. This annual difference, if accurately estimated, would be less than a third as great as the difference in median dates for Nuttall's sparrows the same two years at Berkeley.

The clutch size in *pugetensis* averages greater than in *nuttalli*. The number ranges from three to five, and the average of 90 clutches is 3.87, compared with the average of 3.27 for 215 *nuttalli* clutches. The most common number of eggs per clutch is four, as compared with three in *nuttalli*. About two-thirds of the clutches in *pugetensis* had four eggs each, whereas in *nuttalli* about two-thirds of the clutches had three eggs each. The percentages for *pugetensis* are as follows: 3 eggs per clutch 23.3 percent, 4 eggs per clutch 66.7 percent, 5 eggs per clutch 10.0 percent. The average clutch size for all records, by month, is as follows: April 3.77, May 3.98, June 3.82, and July 3.25 for 22, 47, 17 and 4 clutches, respectively.

The second clutch averages larger than the first. Among 22 first clutches of eggs found at Friday Harbor in 1936, 3 had three eggs each, and 19 had four eggs. The average was 3.8. Of 7 second clutches, 4 had four eggs each and 3 had five eggs. The average was 4.4. A single third clutch had five eggs.

Clutch size varies with latitude in *pugetensis*. 32 clutches collected at latitude 41°N. average 3.56 eggs per clutch, whereas 48 clutches taken at latitude 49°N. average 4.04 eggs per clutch.

Incubation.—The start of incubation in relation to egg laying shows about the same variation as in *nuttalli*. The length of the incubation period is the same, and the eggs of any one set show about the same variability in hatching time as do those of *nuttalli*. I marked the eggs of three sets at Friday Harbor. They did not hatch in the order laid. One set of three hatched in the sequence 2, 1, 3, another 3, 2, 1, and a set of four in the order 2, 1, 3, 4.

Young.—The behavior of the parents up to the time the young leave the nest is identical with that of Nuttall's. For about the first week after the young are fledged the female alternates between feeding them and building the second nest. Thereafter the male takes over all care of the fledglings. On an average of 11 days after one brood has been fledged, the female has begun to sit on her second clutch. The male then performs the duties of feeding the fledglings and guarding the territory and the second nest. He makes short excursions with his young outside the territory, but never for more than a few minutes at a time. Once I found three males from contiguous areas foraging with their young in the same 50-yard-square raspberry patch. None appeared to resent the presence of the others.

As the time for the hatching of the second brood drew near, the males spent more and more time near the nest and less in feeding and watching the fledglings. The young birds left their parents' territories at an earlier age than did the young Nuttall's. One young bird was found alone across the border from its parents' territory when only 25 days old. Out of seven broods that I watched almost daily, the oldest fledgling fed by the male was 27 days old.

Owing to the compression of several phases of the cycle, particularly of the interval between broods, the Puget Sound sparrows, although they began to breed more than 6 weeks later than the Nuttall's, had time to raise three broods before the regression of the testes in late July. Unfortunately I was obliged to leave Friday Harbor before recording the fledging of the third brood. Two females that had fledged two broods each were sitting on their third clutches when I left. All but 2 of the remaining 11 pairs of the group I watched would have had ample time for a third brood before gonad regression as recorded at other stations of like latitude. The general average of success with the broods was not high. Before I left, only 3 out of 13 pairs raised two broods successfully, whereas each of the remaining 10 had raised one brood and made one or more further unsuccessful attempts.

Fall and Winter.—Most of the Puget Sound sparrow populations leave their nesting grounds in the fall and form large flocks which persist for 6 or 7 months. I have no first hand knowledge of their behavior in early fall before migration, nor during the flight south. This account begins with the arrival in California of the populations that winter at Berkeley on the same ground with *nuttalli*. The quotations below are from Blanchard (1941).

In late September and early October flocks of from twenty to fifty birds reach Berkeley, announcing their arrival by a chorus of song which is unmistakably distinct from that of the Berkeley Nuttalls.

Arrival dates are not identical for successive years, nor do all birds come on the same day in any one year. From 1934 to 1937 I saw the first Puget Sound sparrows on the campus on September 27, 30, 13, and 23, respectively. In 1935 a few birds came September 30, but it was not until October 5 that the first large flock arrived. In 1936 I heard a Puget Sound sparrow sing on September 13, and another observer heard one on the sixteenth, but I saw no large flocks until the twenty-sixth. In 1937 the period of arrival extended from September 23 to October 5.

In spite of the fact that one pair, at least, remated for two or more years on the same territory at Friday Harbor, I have detected no tendency to remain paired on the wintering grounds, no hint of such persistent mutual awareness as might reveal, within the winter flock, mates or nest mates of the past season. The flock is a homogeneous assemblage, without visible subdivision. It is more coherent than the smaller groups of immature Nuttalls. The latter are loose aggregates—individuals foraging on commom ground, unified only by fright. The flocks of Puget Sound sparrows show a continuous simultaneity, a commom responsiveness, producing true flock reactions.

Once on the wintering grounds the migrants show almost as strong a tendency to localization as do the residents. Year after year four flocks of Puget Sound sparrows have settled, each on a different area on the campus, and from the day of their arrival to that of their departure six months later have never left it but have foraged and roosted regularly at the same spots. Restriction to mutually exclusive areas is the rule, as has been proven at Palo Alto by the banding records of Price (1931). In February, 1928, by banding and by painting the tail feathers of Puget Sound sparrows on the Stanford campus, Price worked out the areas of three flocks and found almost complete mutual exclusiveness.

The adult Nuttalls are perfectly tolerant of the Puget Sound sparrows for the whole winter season. Even in spring, when the resident males are ready to fight and drive out other male Nuttalls, they allow the *pugetensis* flocks to wander unmolested through their territories and may even forage peacefully in the midst of the flock, set off from the rest by distinctions which can hardly be based on physical appearance. Differences in individual and flock behavior and in degree of aggressiveness undoubtedly account for the perfect cleavage between the groups. The larger flock of silent birds, obviously with no interest in the ground besides the food they are seeking, suggest no threat, rouse no jealousy. When a Nuttall landowner chances to hop or to fly straight at them, the Puget Sound sparrows always give ground, even to the extent of relinquishing a morsel of food too large to carry off.

* * * Up to the day of departure, the behavior of the wintering flocks suffers no radical change except for the increased frequency of song, beginning some four weeks before migration.

* * * Neither chasing nor fighting, other than occasional momentary disputes over food, occurs on the wintering grounds. There is no stimulation of trilling and posturing in the female. Neither territorial jealousy nor sexual excitement have yet come to the surface. The coherence of the flock is maintained up to the moment of departure.

Distribution

Range.—Southwestern British Columbia to extreme southwestern California.

Breeding Range.—The Puget Sound White-crowned sparrow breeds from the east coast of Vancouver Island (Quinsam River) and from the southwest mainland of British Columbia (Vancouver, Mission City) south, west of the Cascade Range through Washington (Nooksack Valley, North Bend, Chehalis, Cathlamet) and Oregon (Logan, 50 miles inland along the North Santiam River, Corvallis) southwest into extreme northwestern California (Smith River, east of Eureka) south to Weott and west to Cape Mendocino.

Winter range.—Winters from southwestern British Columbia (casually to Comox and Victoria); but more commonly from Oregon (southern Willamette Valley; Coquille) west to the coast; east to Dudley, Mariposa County; south to southwestern California (San Nicolas Island; La Jolla).

Casual records.—Casual in winter in Oregon (Crater Lake National Park—east entrance), Washington (Puyallup Valley in Pierce County) and California (Dudley, Mariposa County).

Migration.—Early dates of spring arrival are: Oregon—Tillamook, March 18. Washington—Seattle area, March 24; Friday Harbor, April 4; Bellingham, March 26. British Columbia—Colwood, Vancouver Island, last week of March; Vancouver, April 2.

Late dates of spring departure are: California—Sebastopol, May 1; Berkeley, April 21.

Early dates of fall arrival are: California—Sebastopol, September 3; Woodacre, September 21; San Nicolas Island, September 24.

Late dates of fall departure are: British Columbia—Alta Lake region, September 17; Colwood, Vancouver Island, first week of October; Vancouver, October 15. Washington—Friday Harbor, September 21 (2 years record); Seattle area, October 3. Oregon—northwestern Oregon, October 1; Netarts, September 10.

Egg dates.—British Columbia: 6 records, May 4–June 26.

California: 31 records, April 23—July 23; 9 records, April 28–May 8; 12 records, May 11–May 31; 8 records, June 6–June 26.

Oregon: 5 records, May 5–June 6.

Washington: 46 records, April 24–July 22; 22 records, April 27–May 6; 7 records, May 27–June 9; 3 records, June 24–July 22.

ZONOTRICHIA ATRICAPILLA (Gmelin)

Golden-crowned Sparrow

PLATE 70

Contributed by Junea W. Kelly

Habits

The strikingly handsome golden-crowned sparrow, the largest of the so-called "crowned" sparrows, is a bird of extreme western North America and many of the offshore islands. From its summer home just south of the Arctic Circle to its casual occurrences in winter just north of the Tropic of Cancer in southern Baja California, it ranges through more than 40 degrees of latitude. A common and familiar species, it winters plentifully from Vancouver Island south to northern Baja California, with central and southern California its winter metropolis. Announcing its arrival in autumn with its plaintive song of three descending minor notes, it spends 8 months of the year in this region.

On its California wintering grounds Joseph Grinnell and Alden H. Miller (1944) say it inhabits "An interrupted type of brushland, such as constituted by streamside thickets, chaparral where broken up by patches of open ground, and garden shrubbery. The cover sought is somewhat shadier and cooler on the average than that frequented by Gambel white-crowned sparrows, although commonly the two kinds of sparrows are members of the same flock."

Spring.—The movement northward from the wintering grounds apparently starts in April. The spring migration is largely along the coast and through the coastal lowlands and valleys. That individuals occasionally stray to higher elevations is attested by birds in spring plumage found frozen at 14,350 feet on Mt. Shasta (Chamberlain, 1916) and at 14,403 on Mt. Rainier (Brockman, 1941). Most birds have left California by the end of the first week of May. Ira N. Gabrielson and Stanley G. Jewett (1940) report the species most plentiful in Oregon in April and early May, with a latest day of May 25 in Lane County. Stanley G. Jewett et al. (1953) state that in Washington:

> The golden-crowned sparrow is a very common spring migrant west of the Cascade Mountains, where it begins appearing in some numbers the last week in April. According to Lien (Brown) the main body of the birds arrives at the Destruction Island Lighthouse between May 1 and 10. It is said to be impossible for the light-keepers to raise any garden truck while the flight is on, as the birds

come in immense flocks, much larger, apparently, than any appearing on the mainland. Some of the birds come to grief against the light; Lien counted 29 golden-crowns killed in this way between April 24 and May 26, 1916. Between April 28 and May 7, 1918, Bailey found golden-crowned sparrows common about Port Angeles and all through the valleys of the Elwha, Soleduck, Bogachiel, and Hoh rivers, often in considerable flocks wherever grain was to be found by the roadside or weed seeds in the open. Their cheery songs, he writes, were generally the loudest of the morning chorus.

Eastern Washington is evidently off the main path of migration of the golden-crown, though there are a few scattered records for that part of the state.

The birds reach their Alaska breeding grounds in May, according to Ira N. Gabrielson and Frederick C. Lincoln (1959), "early dates being Kiglauik Mountains, May 18; Hooper Bay, May 22; Nushagak, May 10; Chignik, May 14; and False Pass, May 5." George Willett (1920) reports from Forrester Island, "Golden-crowned Sparrows were usually plentiful from May 8 to 19." Brinda Kessel writes in a letter from College, Alaska, of observing birds there between May 2 and May 20, 1956. Joseph Grinnell (1900) first noted one May 23 in the Kotzebue Sound region, where he did not consider the species common. Harry S. Swarth (1934) collected one at Sitkalidak Island May 15, and Charles Sheldon (1909) reports seeing one May 26 on the upper Toklat River near Mount McKinley.

At the west end of the Alaska Peninsula Olaus J. Murie (1959) writes:

"May 22, near Moffet Cove on Izembek Bay, I heard the first golden-crowned sparrow. Next day there were many * * *. They were common among the alders, as far as these bushes grow up the valley toward Aghileem Pinnacles. They were noted in the alder patches at the base of Frosty Peak, at False Pass, and Ikatan. While not as numerous as some other sparrows, the golden-crown nests commonly throughout the region covered, though local range is naturally governed by the boundaries of the alder patches, which are by no means universally distributed."

Nesting.—In its Alaskan summer home the golden-crown occupies the high Hudsonian and Alpine-Arctic zones of the coastal regions rather than of the interior. Francis S. L. Williamson sent me the following unpublished notes from Anchorage in October, 1956:

"The species arrives at this latitude around the middle of May when there is frequently deep snow on its mountain nesting grounds. Nesting commences fairly promptly, toward the end of May, and reaches a peak in mid or late June. The birds are found on all the local mountains, primarily in the deep stream-carved canyons above timber line. They are abundant in both alder thickets and in the extremely dense herbaceous vegetation between timber line and the more alpine, heath-covered slopes of the higher country. They also occur locally in several places at sea level, usually where brush-covered slopes extend abruptly down to the shore as at Potter and Hope on Turnagain Arm. Farther down the Kenai Peninsula they are found along Cook Inlet at several low localities as at Deep Creek. During the last two nesting seasons on the Kuskokwim River near Bethel I saw only one bird, but the Eskimos tell me they are common in the dense alder and willow thickets bordering the numerous sloughs farther down the river toward the coast at Kwinhok."

No studies of the nesting habits of this species have ever been made, and little is known of its courtship, territoriality, incubation, or natal care. Donald D. McLean wrote me in a letter from Sacramento, Calif. "Courtship just barely begins before they leave for the north and I doubt if any actual choice of mates takes place. I have seldom heard their song in California sung at what I would consider full power." Persons familiar with the species in Alaska during June comment often on the continuous singing of males perched on the top of low bushes or matted birches, alders, and balsams.

Sidney B. Peyton wrote me: "A number of nests were found on June 18, 1955 in the Little Susitna Canyon about 60 miles north of Anchorage. The nests were quite bulky and well made of dry fern leaves and stems, dry grass, and willow leaves. Some were lined with grass alone, others with mixed grass and moose hair. The only nest above the ground was on the horizontal branch of a small willow tree and well hidden under last year's dry ferns. The others were sunk in the ground at the base of small willows and were very well hidden. * * * The nests contained equal numbers of four and five eggs, and all were about the same stage of incubation of about a week. * * * The same territory was covered June 23, 1956 and only one nest was located and only one other pair was seen. The time of the melting snow seems to govern their nesting in this locality." The average dimensions of several nests were: inside depth 2 inches, inside diameter 2¾ inches, walls 2 inches.

Harry S. Swarth (1934) writes: "A nest was found on Kodiak Island on June 11, containing three heavily incubated eggs. It was placed in a depression in the ground on a steep bank and was fairly well concealed by overhanging grass. On Nunivak, July 3, a nest was found containing young a week old. This was in a willow thicket on the top of a mound, the nest on the ground, almost entirely hidden by a dense network of tangled willow branches. Both parents were feeding the young." Alfred M. Bailey (1943) collected a nest at the end of the Seward Peninsula June 9, 1940 "in the moss on the ground along the foundation of an abandoned igloo."

In British Columbia Louis B. Bishop (1900) writes, "Osgood found an almost finished nest in a conifer at Summit Lake June 12. It was

Santa Ana, Calif. A. D. Cruickshank

GOLDEN-CROWNED SPARROW

Sault Sainte Marie, Mich., May 30, 1925 K. Christofferson

NEST AND EGGS OF WHITE-THROATED SPARROW

Maine, June 28, 1939 E. Porter

WHITE-THROATED SPARROW FEEDING YOUNG

composed of sticks and moss, lined with grass, and placed about 2½ feet from the ground." From the Atlin region Harry S. Swarth (1926) describes his search for this species' nests at the summit of Monarch Mountain at some 4,500 feet altitude June 19, 1924. After a fruitless examination of the balsams, a nest was found in a mat of birch.

A ledge of rock protruded a few inches from the ground in the center of the thicket, and the nest was sunk against this shelter, fairly well concealed by the vegetation above. There were five eggs, incubated about one-half. Within a few hundred yards a second nest was found in a similar situation, on the ground under some trailing birch, with four eggs incubated as the first lot were.

The first nest was built externally of gray plant fiber, a few balsam twigs, bits of dried flakes of bark, and a very little green moss; the lining was of dry grass, with several white ptarmigan feathers interwoven. External diameter, 120 mm.; internal diameter, 65 mm.; outside depth, 55 mm.; inside depth, 35 mm.

* * * Several hours after our first two discoveries, Brooks found a third nest, this one in a low thicket of balsam, a thicket about twenty feet square but with the sprawling branches rising not more than knee high above the ground. The nest was in the branches, about ten inches up, and was much bulkier than those on the ground. * * * The whole nest was about 180 mm. in diameter, and 90 mm. deep. The nest cavity was 76 mm. across. It contained four fresh eggs. * * *

On June 22 a fourth nest was found on the same mountain, in much the same situation as the first two.

On August 5 a nest was found on Spruce Mountain "containing naked young, probably about a week old."

Eggs.—The golden-crowned sparrow usually lays from 3 to 5 slightly glossy eggs. They are ovate although some tend to elongate ovate. The ground is creamy or pale bluish white and heavily speckled, spotted, and blotched with reddish browns such as "natal brown," "Verona brown," "Mars brown," "russet," or "chestnut." Some eggs have a few undermarkings of "pale neutral gray." There is considerable variation; often the bluish white ground color is entirely obscured either with very fine speckles or large clouded blotches which give it the appearance of being soft brown. These eggs are practically indistinguishable from those of the white-crowned sparrow, except that they average slightly larger. The measurements of 42 eggs average 22.7 by 16.4 mm; the eggs showing the four extremes measure *24.0* by 16.7, 22.9 by *17.2*, *21.2* by 16.3, and 21.5 by *15.2* millimeters.—WGFH

Young.—Nothing is known of incubation in this species. Probably, as in other *Zonotrichias*, it is by the female alone, but its duration has never been determined. Ian McT. Cowan writes me in a letter that a female nesting at Emigrants Peak, Jasper Park, on June 22, 1946 "stayed on the nest constantly and was repeatedly fed on the nest by her mate. The feeding was accompanied by a begging display similar to that of fledged young. The weather was cold with sleet and snow."

Nor has anything ever been published on the nest life and development of the young birds. Harry S. Swarth (1924) describes reaching the species' breeding grounds above timber line in the northern British Columbia mountains on July 22 to find "the young were out of the nest and flying about; the old birds could be seen singing from perches above the thickets in which they dwelt." He found the young so exceptionally wary he had great difficulty collecting three juvenile specimens:

At the first sign of danger a loud *chip* from the parent sends every youngster within hearing scuttling for the nearest tangle of prostrate balsam, but not to remain there. A prompt retreat is made to the far side of the bush, followed quickly by flight to another thicket perhaps a hundred yards away. Pursuit is heralded by warning alarm notes from the parent, and the youngster again flees to another refuge. Further pursuit is generally useless. In fact, young birds were seen to go five hundred yards or more in one flight when followed up. Meanwhile, the old bird, perhaps joined by others, remains nearby, giving warning from some conspicuous perch, utterly indifferent to approach within a few yards. * * *

The extreme wariness of the young golden-crowned sparrow is a trait that receives emphasis from the fact that, when the first winter plumage is attained a few weeks later, these same young birds are peculiarly tame and unsuspicious. Then they will permit of close approach, will in fact come themselves to inspect the stranger in the woods.

Plumages and Molts.—The natal down of the golden-crowned sparrow has never been described. Richard R. Graber (1955) describes the juvenal plumage as follows:

"No obvious sexual dimorphism. Feathers above nostrils light brown. Forehead and crown brown laterally, light buff medially. Light median area expands posteriorly. Entire crown streaked with black, least heavily on occiput. (A suggestion of light crown spot of adult.) Occiput and nape tinged with rusty brown, laterally. Back streaked with black and shades of buffy brown. Rump and upper tail coverts light brown obscurely marked with dark. Rectrices dull brown. Remiges dark gray (upper tertials black); primaries edged with buffy white, tertials with rust tipped with buffy white. Lesser coverts light brown, middle coverts blackish tipped with white. Greater coverts edged with rust, tipped with white. Two rather narrow wing-bars. Lores gray. Eye-ring buff above, whitish below. Auriculars mottled with gray, buff, and brown. Post-auriculars whitish, streaked with brown or black. Chin and throat whitish, flecked with black. Sides of chin and throat heavily marked with black. Underparts cream colored, not white as in other *Zonotrichia*. Chest, sides, and flanks heavily streaked with black. Belly and crissum sparsely spotted with black. Leg feathers brown and cream."

In his report on the Atlin region of British Columbia, Swarth (1926) states that this plumage in the golden-crown

> * * * is generally similar to the same stage in the three species of white-crowned sparrows. *Coronata* lacks the decided head markings that are seen in the juvenal white-crowns and it has a suggestion of yellowish upon the forehead. Compared with the grayish *leucophrys*, young *coronata* is generally darker colored and the ventral streaks are darker, heavier, and more extensive. Compared with *gambelii*, young *coronata* is generally browner. Young *coronata* and young *nuttalli* are closely similar in body coloration, but the former is slightly darker colored as a rule. *Coronata* has a heavier bill than the white-crowned sparrows, and this character is apparent in the young birds.
>
> The accompanying illustration (pl. 4) was made [by Major Allan Brooks] from studies of the freshly killed bird. The yellowish tinge to the lower parts, as there shown, is an evanescent color that soon disappears from the study skin. * * *
>
> On July 18 young were taken in juvenal plumage throughout and with full-grown rectrices. Others molting into first winter plumage were collected July 27 and August 5. One young bird still mostly in juvenal plumage was taken August 24.

Robert Ridgway (1901) describes the young in first winter plumage as "Similar to adult female, but without any lateral black stripe on pileum or well-defined median stripe, the whole forehead and anterior portion of crown yellowish olive, more or less flecked with dusky (sometimes with more or less indication of a black lateral stripe), the posterior portion of the pileum light grayish olive-brown, streaked with dusky." This dress is apparently assumed by a partial molt of the juvenal plumage before the birds leave the nesting ground.

The adult breeding plumage with its prominent yellow and grey median crown stripe is attained by a spring molt that starts in late winter and involves most of the head and body feathers, the tertiaries, the secondary coverts, and the central pair of tail feathers. In his excellent description of the process J. E. Law (1929b) notes:

> In individuals, the progress of molt seems to vary. One tract or another may be relatively further along in different birds, * * *. The time of molt is more erratic. On any day, in March and April, one may take birds of the same species which appear to be a month apart in progress of molt. Individuals with feathers still growing may be caught even in early May when all but a few members of the flocks of *Z. coronata* and *Z. gambelii* have departed from southern California, but most of the last to go have completed their molt before they depart. * * *
>
> I have not detected regular spring molt in any of the following tract series: Primary and secondary remiges, alula, upper and under primary coverts, outer five pairs of rectrices, dorsal saddle, and rump. It is significant that when wings and tail are folded, as they are much of the time that the bird is not flying, all of the above series are covered. The tertiaries cover the primaries and secondaries, the greater secondary coverts cover the alula and primary coverts, the under secondary coverts cover the under primary coverts, the wing covers the dorsal saddle and rump, and the deck [central] rectrices cover the remaining pairs of tail feathers. It appears, therefore, that only the tracts of the body directly exposed to abrasion and sunlight are renewed in the spring molt. * * *

When the spring molt is completed these western representatives of the *Zonotrichiae* are resplendent in a new plumage with very little difference if any between the sexes. No one who has noticed the frayed ragamuffins of late February and March and the stunning beauties of late April can doubt that the exposed contour plumage has been entirely renewed.

Before leaving the breeding grounds the adult birds undergo a complete postnuptial molt in which the bright head pattern is generally replaced by a considerably duller one. As Joseph Mailliard (1932), Emerson A. Stoner (1955), and Anna M. Smith (1958) have all noted, the crown stripes of adults in winter vary greatly, and at least five distinct types are recognizable. Whether these reflect sex or, more likely, age or vigor of the individual has not yet been determined satisfactorily.

Food.—On its California wintering grounds the golden-crowned sparrow subsists almost entirely on vegetable matter. Foster E. Beal (1910) reports: "For the determination of its food 184 stomachs were available, taken from October to April, inclusive. The animal food amounts to 0.9 percent, vegetable to 99.1.

" * * * It is evident that the golden-crown does not search for insects, and takes only those that come in its way. * * *

"Remains of buds and flowers were found in stomachs taken in every month of the bird's stay in the State, except October and November, when buds are very small. They were found in 56 stomachs; the average for the season is 29.5 percent, and in March it rises to nearly 78 percent."

Their fondness for buds and flowers does not make them welcome in the garden. They take a heavy toll of annuals, especially in California where many are planted in the autumn. They are particularly hard on ranunculus, stocks, primulas, pansies, and even eat such bitter leaves as those of calendulas. In the fall they do not hesitate to eat chrysanthemum flowers, and they also take buds of ornamental fruit trees and wistaria. They sometimes make serious inroads in truck gardens in the path of their spring migration (see Spring), and Edward W. Nelson (1881) notes they "claim their share of attention as they levy their tax upon the garden" in the settlement at St. Michael's, Alaska.

Grinnell and Storer (1924) observe: "In foraging, these sparrows, in scattered formation, advance out from the margins of the brush patches onto open ground where they hop here and there seeking their food, which is chiefly of a vegetable nature. They feed in particular upon green seedlings of various 'weeds.' When the birds chop up between the edges of their mandibles the sprouting succulent seedlings, the exuding juice soils their faces and not infrequently even the plumage of their breasts. After the first rains have started the new growth of annuals, the bills of the birds are quite characteristically gummed up with dried green stuff."

Joseph Maillard (1926) found the golden-crowns greatly preferred newly-sprouted weed seeds, up after a heavy October rain, to the grain bait spread before a trap. R. P. Parsons writes me in a letter from Carmel, Calif., "They have a most notable and special preference for newly planted lawns. They did not bother the seeds, but when it had sprouted and was 2 to 3 days above the surface, they descended on the new lawn in hordes."

Harold W. Clark (1930) found them feeding on small, black, bitter olives fallen from the trees in his yard after a heavy February frost. John McB. Robertson (1931) says they eat the plentiful seeds of *Eucalyptus globulus*. Robert S. Woods (1932) noted they are especially fond of young plants of the cabbage family and of beets and peas, but ignore carrots; also that they eat seeds of the naturalized tree tobacco (*Nicotiana glauca*).

Amelia S. Allen (1943) noted them in Berkeley, Calif., among the birds coming from the shrubbery to feed on swarms of winged termites that dropped to the pavement and shed their wings in early November. Peyton wrote me that on their nesting ground in Sustina Canyon the birds were eating mosquitoes. While there is little in the literature on their food habits in the north in summer, it is highly probable that, like the other *Zonotrichias*, they consume fair quantities of insects during the nesting season, and also feed them to their young. Gabrielson and Lincoln (1959) write that in Alaska "Gabrielson has seen them in company with other sparrows feeding on weed seeds about the edges of cultivated fields and in villages. He has also seen them in the tundra country feeding close to the alder patches on crowberries and other small fruits found in this habitat. On one or two occasions he has noted birds with insects in their bills obviously carrying food to their young, and it is probable that they regularly take such insect life as is available in the vicinity of their nests."

Voice.—The golden-crown's characteristic song is composed of three clearly whistled notes descending in a minor key and suggesting the words "Oh, dear me." To the miners carrying their packs along the Alaska gold trails the constantly repeated plaintive notes seemed to say "I'm so weary," and they nicknamed the singer "Weary Willy." Its habit of repeating its notes over and over again on dark days preceding rain has also earned it the name of "rain bird."

Frank N. Bassett (1920) gives the following musician's notation of the song: "There seems to be one song which is typical of the species, but occasionally it is transposed into other keys, and less frequently there are variations in it. * * * the most frequently heard song, outnumbering all the variations together. It begins on F [in the third octave above middle C] and with a gradual slur amounting to a *glissando* it descends one tone to E flat where there is a slight break and the E flat is struck again with a decided accent, passing a minor third lower to C without any special marks of expression. This last interval naturally pitches the song in C minor." He heard the typical song given in five different keys ranging from a whole tone higher (D minor) to a whole tone lower (B-flat minor), and noted three variations. He adds: "The *tempo* is the same for all songs, about 120 whole notes to the minute, although this may vary somewhat. The quality of tone is that of harmonics on the violin."

The birds usually sing from the top of a bush or, if lower down, from its periphery. In California they sing frequently from their arrival in September through October. Although singing diminishes during the winter, it does not stop entirely, and it picks up again quickly when the days start to lengthen in early spring. Often in the slack season one hears only the first two of the usual three minor descending notes. A common variation in April has the third and final note rising slightly instead of falling. Olaus J. Murie (1959) writes from Alaska: "On one occasion I heard a distinct variation of the song. Instead of three notes in descending scale, the usual second and third notes were reversed. It was the normal song for this bird, as I heard it day after day in the same clump of alder near camp.'

D. D. McLean says in a letter to me: "The typical *Zonotrichia* "chink" in the golden-crown is hard, insistent, and louder than in most other species, and the "tizeet" note is sharper and not so slurred. When feeding or loafing, the birds use much small talk of "chips," "churrs," and a "plear, plear, plear, plear" used as a scold-like greeting." Howard L. Cogswell writes me of hearing the three minor notes followed by a soft trill, once in November at Sunland, Calif., and twice in October near Pasadena. Peterson (1941) also remarks "sometimes a faint final trill." Grinnell and Storer (1924) state: "On occasion the Golden-crown is heard to indulge in a whisper song which is so faint as to be heard only at a very few yards' range."

Behavior.—On the wintering grounds the golden-crowned sparrows are usually found in mixed flocks with white-crowned sparrows. Often while watching white-crowns feeding on a lawn, one will notice a few golden-crowns coming out of adjacent shrubbery, usually staying close to the shrubbery and disappearing into it quickly when one approaches. John B. Price (1931) notes "Although easier to trap than the white-crowns, the golden-crowns are harder to observe in the field as they keep more in the bushes."

D. D. McLean writes me: "When feeding, this species is relatively quarrelsome toward others of the same species and genus. * * *

When loafing, they are more tolerant of their own kind and other species. Mixed flocks of *Zonotrichias* spend much of their time perched in or near the tops of bushes whisper-singing, preening, and carrying on twittering small talk. When such flocks are disturbed, they rarely fly en masse to new cover, but string along in singles and small groups. One thing I have particularly noted of interest to me is the fact that they rarely climb very high in trees during the winter, and about 25 feet would be near the maximum. However, in the spring during or just prior to the general move, they often go up to 60 or 70 feet. It has also been noted that most flights from these heights have been northward unless startled or forced in some other direction."

When they are excited, and sometimes when they are about to take flight or move to another perch, birds raise the feathers of the crown.

Gabrielson and Lincoln (1959) write "* * * this bird does not normally fly long distances but, when pressed closely, moves from one bush to another. It is adept at flying close to the ground from one patch of cover to gain access to another before becoming visible to an observer and is conspicuous only when it is in song during the breeding season and as an element of the feeding hordes of migrant sparrows in the fall."

Through observations on banded and color-stained birds, John B. Price (1931) found that golden crowns wintering on the Stanford campus, instead of establishing individual territories, formed distinct flocks that stayed within definite circumscribed areas of about 15 or 20 acres. Individuals from one flock seldom intermingled with those of other flocks on adjoining territories. He also found that individual birds returning to Stanford in successive winters tended strongly to return to the same flock territory. Eustace L. Sumner, Sr. (1933) discusses the species' homing instincts and flocking proclivities at Berkeley where he found similar fidelity to wintering territories and adds "The birds may desert the dry hillsides for the bottom of the canyon because in the latter location more green food is to be had; or they may leave because they do not like hot weather."

Field marks.—The golden-crown is the largest of the "crowned" sparrows and is darker brown than most of them. Peterson (1941) calls the adult "Like a White-crowned Sparrow with *no white line over the eye* and a *golden yellow,* instead of white, stripe through the center of the crown. Immature White-crowns (Gambel's, etc.) have the center of the crown buffy and resemble the Golden-crown, but have broad buffy lines over the eyes, which the latter species lacks. Immature Golden-crowns look like large female House Sparrows, but are browner and sometimes have a dull yellowish suffusion on the crown. Often they lack this yellow suffusion and are very plain.

These birds have little distinctive about them, unless it be the fine streaking on the otherwise unpatterned crown."

Enemies.—D. D. McLean says in a letter, "Enemies include the feral house cat, sharp-shinned hawk, pigeon hawk, boreal shrike, pigmy owl, screech owl, marsh hawk, and occasionally the Cooper's hawk. Among the major killers on their winter ranges in and around cities are picture windows and windows in patios where the birds can see through to other yards or shrubbery. During the first fall at my present residence in San Jose, as many as four golden-crowns and white-crowns were killed or badly injured in my neighborhood in one day after the birds first arrived in the area. Our subdivision was built up among the trees of a former prune and walnut orchard that apparently had been a regular wintering area for *Zonotrichia.* Most of us with patio windows now have split-bamboo drops to help prevent bird losses. Automobiles kill many along our highways as the birds fly across in front of speeding vehicles."

In this connection light-houses should be mentioned for, being night-migrants, many golden-crowns come to grief against them in thick weather, as noted (Spring) at Destruction Island, and duplicated at Triple Island light-house according to G. C. Odlum (*in* litt.).

Charles N. Richardson, Jr. (1908) watched a loggerhead shrike pursue a golden-crown in the open and finally kill it after it had sought protection in a thick bush. Ian McT. Cowan writes me of four newly-hatched young in a nest he found July 13, 1930 in Tonquin Valley, Jasper Park, being killed by a Columbian ground squirrel.

Fall and winter.—F. S. L. Williamson wrote me from Anchorage, Alaska, "The bulk of the birds leave this region in late July and early August, but I have seen juveniles until mid-September." Willett (1914) calls it an abundant migrant near Sitka "noticed from shoreline to above timberline on the mountains," arriving September 1 and still present in some numbers a month later. For the same area he wrote some years later (1928), "Most plentiful in fall migration between September 28 and October 12," with extreme dates of September 8 and October 21.

Concerning the southward flight Jewett et al. (1953) state:

"In the fall the mountain route is evidently popular with the golden-crowns, and the coast route nearly deserted. Our first records are for the alpine parks of Mt. Rainier, not far from timber line, September 2, 1919. After this date the species became more and more plentiful, occurring in scores or even hundreds in the moist subalpine meadows and greatly outnumbering the Gambel and Lincoln sparrows which also were common. * * * The main body of the migrating golden-crowns in the fall seems to cross the Columbia in the vicinity of Carson and Skamania, just where the river cuts through the Cascade

Mountains. The birds were noted migrating at Carson on September 10, 1918, after which date they became the most abundant sparrow, and they were still numerous at Skamania, September 29."

In California Grinnell and Storer (1924) report "Our earliest seasonal record for Golden-crowned Sparrow was made on October 2, (1915) when at least 7 adult and immature birds were seen in a coffee-berry thicket in Yosemite Valley. Thereafter, for a month or so, the species was noted in a number of places in the higher country * * *."

For the San Francisco Bay region Grinnell and Wythe (1927) report, "Arrives in the fall earlier and stays later in the spring than most other winter visiting birds. Has been observed as early as August 31 and is generally common by the last week of September." The species is becoming even commoner of late in the Bay area as suburban housing developments are being built on dry hillsides and other sites that in the past were unfavorable habitat. Feeding trays and bird baths in the suburban gardens supply ample food and water. On one patio in the Oakland Hills 60 golden-crowns were counted at one time recently.

Grinnell and Miller (1944) write: "Metropolis of wintering ground, the lower western and southern portions of California lying west of the Sierran divides and below the 4,000-foot contour of altitude. Winters regularly north to head of Sacramento Valley and on coast north at least to Humboldt County and south to San Diego County. * * * recorded from most of the islands. At times of migration reaches probably nearly all parts of the State."

Distribution

Range.—Alaska, Yukon, and western Alberta south to Baja California, northern Sonora, and Arizona.

Breeding range.—The golden-crowned sparrow breeds from western coastal Alaska (Cape Prince of Wales, Kobuk River Delta, Nunivak and Kodiak islands) and south-central Yukon (Rose River) south to southeastern Alaska (Lynn Canal), southern British Columbia (Alta Lake, Moose Pass), southwestern Alberta (Banff), and in the Cascade Mountains to extreme northern Washington (Okanogan County); casual in summer north to northern Alaska (Barrow).

Winter range.—Winters from southern British Columbia (Victoria, Okanagan Landing) southward, principally west of the Cascade Range and the Sierra Nevada, to northern Baja California (lat. 30° N.), casually south to southern Baja California (Cedros and Guadalupe islands, Cape San Lucas), Arizona (Ajo Mountains), and northern Sonora (Caborca) and east to Utah (Zion National Park), Colorado (Wray), and New Mexico (upper Gila River).

Casual records.—Casual east to Saskatchewan (Saskatoon, Regina, Indian Head), Colorado (Two Buttes Reservoir), Wisconsin (Racine), Illinois (Waukegan), Massachusetts (Bedford, Quincy), Pennsylvania (Easton), New Jersey (Cape May), Alabama (Dauphin Island), Louisiana (Grand Isle), and Texas (Orange County, Palo Duro, Canutillo).

Accidental in Japan (Honshu).

Migration.—Early dates of spring arrival are: Illinois—Chicago, April 29. Saskatchewan—Saskatoon, May 18. Colorado—Salida, April 19. Utah—Shunes Creek, April 22. Nevada—Overton, March 31; Churchill, April 30. Oregon—Malheur Refuge, April 29. Washington—Lake Crescent, April 18; Everson, April 21 (median of 8 years, April 28). Yukon—Sheldon Lake, May 19. Alaska—Mt. McKinley, May 26. Late dates of spring departure are: Arizona—Springerville, April 25. California—San Diego County, May 23. Oregon—Malheur Refuge, May 30. Washington—Tacoma, May 25. Early dates of fall arrival are: Washington—Mt. Rainier, September 2. Oregon—Klamath County, September 10. California—Santa Clara County, August 31. Idaho—Moscow, September 7. Arizona—Grand Canyon, October 8. Late dates of fall departure are: Alaska—Wrangell, October 21. Washington—Tenino, November 26. Idaho—Potlatch, October 6. Illinois—Waukegan, November 28. Pennsylvania—Tinicum, November 12. Alabama—Dauphin Island, November 9.

Egg dates.—Alaska: 31 records, May 27 to June 28; 18 records, June 8 to June 18.

British Columbia: 2 records, June 19 and July 28.

ZONOTRICHIA ALBICOLLIS (Gmelin)

White-throated Sparrow

PLATE 71

Contributed by JAMES K. LOWTHER * and J. BRUCE FALLS **

HABITS

The white-throated sparrow is a familiar bird in many parts of North America, particularly in the northeastern United States and the Canadian northland. It exhibits no subspecific variation, although it is distributed widely over most of North America east of the Rocky Mountains. The breeding range extends from Newfoundland west to northern British Columbia, and from West Virginia, northern New

*Dept. of Biology, Bishop's University, Lennoxville, Quebec.

**Dept. of Zoology, University of Toronto, Toronto, Ontario.

England, central Wisconsin and central Alberta north to the limit of trees in northern Canada. It winters over most of the eastern United States, with a westerly extension into southern Arizona, Nevada, and throughout California.

The first description of the white-throated sparrow was published in G. Edward's "Gleanings" (1760), and was based on a specimen from "Pensilvania." Edward's description formed the basis for the scientific name *Fringilla albicollis* Gmelin, which appears in Linnaeus' "System Naturae" (1789).

Perhaps the most familiar characteristic of the white-throated sparrow is its song, from which many vernacular names have arisen. A number of these names are listed by W. L. McAtee (1957)—Canada bird, Canada whitethroat, Canadian song sparrow, Hard-times Canada bird, Kennedy bird, Nightingale, Night-singer, Old Sam Peabody, Old Tom Peabody, Paddy-wack, Peabiddy bird, Peabody, Peabody bird, Poor Kennedy bird, Poor Sam Peabody, Sweet pinkey, Sweet sweet Canada bird, Tom Peabody, Whistle bird, Whistling sparrow, and Widow bird. French Canadians know the white-throat by such names as Frédéric, Petit Frédéric, Linotte, Rossignol, and Siffleur. The only names based on plumage characteristics are striped-head, white-throat, and, in French Canada, le Pinson à Gorge Blanche.

Until recently most published literature on the white-throated sparrow was concerned mainly with physiological studies, or with different aspects of migration and wintering habits. Comparatively little was known of the species on its breeding grounds. Since 1958 James K. Lowther, J. Bruce Falls, and others have been conducting researches on nesting habitat, nesting cycle, plumages, song, and behavior in the southern portion of Algonquin Provincial Park, Ontario. Unless otherwise noted, information reported here is drawn from these studies.

The white-throated sparrow is a brushland bird in both its breeding and wintering ranges. In Algonquin Park it nests most frequently in clearings in semiopen stands of balsam fir (*Abies balsamea*) and spruces (*Picea* spp.), and to a lesser extent in semiopen mixed stands of birch (*Betula papyrifera*), poplars (*Populus* spp.), balsam fir, and spruces. In general, the nest is located on the ground in areas of small trees between which are clumps of beaked hazel (*Corylus cornuta*) and a ground vegetation of blueberry (*Vaccinum* spp.) and various grasses and herbs.

Harold S. Peters and Thomas D. Burleigh (1951) reported that in Newfoundland some white-throats were present in the "high ptarmigan barrens where clumps of dwarf spruce and tamarack furnish shelter." At Goose Bay, Labrador, W. W. Judd (1951) found that white-throated sparrows occupied areas similar to ptarmigan barrens on the upper plateau, but on the lower plateau they "were seen in black spruce trees around borders of open areas in sphagnum bogs." In Maine, the white-throat "probably [reaches] its densest population at elevations on the mountains where thin soils support only a stunted and openly-spaced growth of trees" (Palmer, 1949). At Churchill, Manitoba, near the tree-line Falls found white-throats fairly common in very local sites where the spruce forest reached its maximum density and trees grew to 35 feet in height. Openings were present, however, including roadsides and a railway line. In this area the more open habitats with smaller trees were occupied by Harris' sparrows and white-crowned sparrows. In Saskatchewan, Alberta, and northern British Columbia, this species breeds in some areas of the aspen parkland, as well as in the boreal forest of the northern portions of these provinces. The parklands are characterized by "the dominance of mature aspen growing in semiopen stands with occasional dense groves of smaller aspens, scattered white spruce, white birch, and, in the depressions along seepage courses, groves of willows" (Munro and Cowan, 1947). Throughout most of the range, it appears that white-throats nest in areas similar to those reported for Algonquin Park.

Territory.—Males begin to sing and chase intruders from their territories soon after arriving on the breeding grounds. On May 19, 1959, most birds in Algonquin Park were paired and territorial boundaries were well established. Chases and fights between males occur frequently at the beginning of the breeding season but are seldom seen in late June and July. Advertising song is given chiefly from a few singing posts (see *Voice*). White-striped females occasionally sing (see *Voice*) but otherwise females appear to take no part in advertising or defending the territory. All the activities of the pair take place in the territory until about the middle of July when most of the young are becoming independent. After that males appear to be less aggressive and territorial boundaries are disregarded.

N. D. Martin (1960) censused a number of plots in Algonquin Park several times each year. He found that densities of white-throats varied from none in bog and hardwood forest to 56 territorial males per 100 acres in a stand of balsam fir and white spruce. Areas of 110 territories varied from 0.05 to 2.7 acres with an average of 0.52 acres. As these values are based on only a few observations of each bird, they must be regarded as minimum estimates. Maire Lainevool (unpublished data) carried out an intensive study of the territories of 20 mated and 3 unmated males in an open coniferous stand where the population density was about 25 territorial males per 100 acres. Each bird was watched for 1 to 4 hours in the morning several times during the breeding season. Territory size tended to decrease over the period from the arrival of the females until the young left the nest. Total areas occupied over the whole period averaged 1.9 (0.9 to 3.2) acres for mated birds and 2.5 (1.5 to 2.8) acres for unmated males.

J. K. Lowther banded 47 males and 30 females on breeding territories in 1959; 19 males and 3 females were retrapped on the same sites in 1960 and a careful search failed to reveal other banded birds. It thus appears that males have a greater tendency than females to return to the same territory from year to year.

Courtship.—As will be described later, the white-throated sparrow is a polymorphic species. For both males and females in winter and nuptial plumages, two color types, based on the color of the median crown stripe, were described—the white-striped and tan-striped types.* Among breeding birds, there is assortative mating of opposite types, a situation which is apparently unique among birds. Of 213 pairs caught and banded in Algonquin Park, 136 were of white-striped males and tan-striped females, 70 of tan-striped males and white-striped females, 6 of tan-striped males and females, and only 1 of a white-striped males and females. Therefore, white-striped birds mate selectively with tan-striped birds.

Investigations were made of behavioral differences between breeding adults of both types in Algonquin Park in order to determine at least some of the factors governing the assortative mating (Lowther, MS., and see also *Voice*). Experiments with tape recordings showed that white-striped males are more aggressive than tan-striped males toward singing individuals. Furthermore white-striped females sing, tan-striped females do not, and white-striped males act aggressively toward singing females, while tan-striped males do not. Finally, the trill note of a female elicits a copulatory excitation in males of both types, but when the trills are accompanied by songs of either males or females, this excitation of white-striped males is suppressed and is replaced by aggressive behavior. This is not true for tan-striped males, which were seen to copulate with their white-striped females, even when a tape recording of a strange male was being played.

From these data, Lowther suggested a mechanism that might govern the assortative mating in this species. As white-striped males act aggressively toward any singing white-throat and white-striped females sing, then these males drive off any white-striped female and thus mate only with tan-striped females. Alternatively, as songs of male birds are supposed to attract females, which they do in the white-

*The word "type" is substituted throughout this account for the author's technically more accurate "morph" (see Lowther, 1961) which may not be familiar to some readers.—Ed.

throated sparrow, the higher rate of singing of white-striped males attracts more females of either type. Thus white-striped males would have a greater choice of females from which to select their mates. By driving off the singing white-striped females, they monopolize the available tan-striped females and leave the white-striped females to mate with the tan-striped males.

As already mentioned (see also *Voice*), the trill of the female appears to be a precopulatory note which incites the male. When trilling, the female crouches on the branch, holds her tail level with or slightly above the line of the back, and flutters her wings. The male approaches with a relatively slow fluttering flight. Upon his approach, the female increases the intensity of trilling and wing-fluttering. The male mounts the female, and copulation occurs. Both partners preen for a few seconds following copulation.

Nesting.—Only the female white-throated sparrow builds the nest. In 1959 and 1960 in Algonquin Park, Ontario, eight banded female white-throats were observed carrying nesting material. In both years several male birds were under close observation, but none was ever seen carrying nesting material. As the female builds the nest without help from the male, she probably also selects the nest site.

Little is known about the process of nest building. During the Algonquin Park studies, it was estimated that nest-site selection and nest building took place between May 14 and May 22. Birds were seen carrying nesting materials only in the morning activity periods. The area over which the birds seek nesting material, the number of trips made to and from the nest, and the total time involved in nest building are not known.

If the nest suffers predation, or if the bird renests in the same general area in subsequent years, it builds a new nest a considerable distance from the first. Of the six renests noted in Algonquin Park, each was more than 100 feet from the first.

Lowther analyzed 39 nests for nesting materials. Each nest was divided into the outer portion and the inner lining, and each portion was analyzed separately. The other portions were made of coarse grasses in 36 nests, wood chips in 30 nests, twigs in 14 nests, pine needles in 10 nests, roots in 7 nests, and small quantities of deer hair, moss, and fine grasses in 4 nests. The linings were composed of fine grasses and rootlets in 38 nests, deer hair in 36 nests, pine needles in 8 nests, and small quantities of wood chips, twigs, roots, and mosses in 2 nests.

With few exceptions the nest is built on the ground at the edge of a clearing, and is usually well concealed by the ground vegetation. There are seven records of nests built off the ground. Macoun (1904) reported four of these—in the roots of an upturned stump, in a small thick bush on rocky ground, 3 feet up in a raspberry bush, and in a brush heap some distance above the ground. Walter B. Barrows (1912) records a nest 3 feet from the ground in a small balsam fir. Harrington (unpubl. notes) found a nest built 10 feet from the ground in a leaning cedar tree. A. F. Ganier and F. W. Buchanan (1953) found a nest 18 inches from the ground in a bog. All 42 of the nests found during the study in Algonquin Park were on the ground.

Of the nesting habitat in Newfoundland, Peters and Burleigh (1951) write: "They nest in cut-over land, second growth, open woods, brushy thickets and upon hillsides. They choose wet thickets as well as dry ones and may be found anywhere except the thick spruce woods." A similar nesting habitat in eastern United States and Canada was described by Forbush and May (1939): "Normally this bird breeds in the glades of coniferous woods, preferring northern firs and spruces, but on the hills from which most of the spruce has been cut, it often remains to breed in the waste left by the lumberman." Toward the southern limit of the breeding range in Ontario, white-throats nest in isolated patches of conifers, particularly cedar swamps and spruce bogs (Macoun, 1904). In the prairie provinces white-throats are abundant in the boreal forest to the north, and also occur to the south in the forested valleys of the Saskatchewan River and its tributaries. These valleys are forested with aspens (*Populus tremuloides*), balsam poplar (*P. balsaminifera*) and spruce (*Picea* spp.) (Houston and Street, 1959). In British Columbia, the species breeds in the parkland deciduous forests in the Peace River and Vanderhoof regions (Munro and Cowan, 1947). The forests in these regions are similar to those along the Saskatchewan River.

Of the 42 nests Lowther found in Algonquin Park, 36 were built under blueberry, the remaining 6 under mountain rice grass, sweet fern, beaked hazel, or haircap moss. Of the 36 nests built under blueberry, 28 were under plants 6 to 12 inches high. Two others were under cover less than 6 inches in height, and 13 were under cover greater than 12 inches high. Of the 42 nests 36 were on level ground; of the 6 on sloping ground 2 were placed in the middle of 10-foot embankments.

Structural canopies were present over 34 of the 42 nests. In all cases the canopy was a natural feature of the nesting cover—29 nests were each under a mat of dead fronds of bracken fern (*Pteridium aquilinum*) from the previous year, 4 were under clumps of dried mountain rice grass, and 1 was under the tip of a lower branch of a 30-foot white spruce tree. The remaining 8 nests that did not possess a canopy were divided into two groups—those located in cover greater than 12 inches in height, and those built later in the season in cover lacking an overstory of live bracken fern.

Although a canopy of dead bracken was a feature of many nests, in no case was the nest begun under an overstory of live mature bracken. At the time when many early nests were found, however, young growing bracken fronds were evident. As the season progressed and this bracken matured, new nests were restricted to patches of blueberry that did not contain bracken. Thus these later nests had no canopies of dead bracken.

Four characteristics of the larger vegetation within a 50-foot radius of the nest sites were notable. First, there was usually one large object or group of objects, a tree, shrub, stump, or log, close to each nest, and a positive correlation between the height of this object and its distance from the nest. In other words, the nest is positioned on the ground at a definite angle from the top of the nearest large object, which may provide a lookout point for the bird before it flies down to the nest.

The other three characteristics refer to the amount of cover afforded by the objects about the nest site, and the number of feet of edge around them. To measure those, a circle of 50-foot radius centered about the nest was divided into five annular rings, each 10 feet wide. The percent of cover, the number of feet of edge per square foot of total area, and the number of feet of edge per square foot of cover were measured separately for each of the five concentric areas. Measurements within a 10-foot radius about random points were made to show conditions in the general habitat for comparison with nest sites. Comparisons were also made between these same characteristics surrounding the nest sites of white-throats, song sparrows, and slate-colored juncos, all of which nested in the same general area.

The data showed that the average amount of cover within the 10-foot radius about sites of white-throat nests is similar to that within the general habitat in which the species nests, but the variation in the cover values about the nest sites is much less than that within the rest of the habitat. Also, the values for sites is intermediate between values for the open sites of song sparrow nests and the dense sites of slate-colored junco nests.

The amount of edge about objects within the 10-foot radius of nest sites of white-throats is significantly greater than the amounts of edge in the general nesting habitat of this species. Furthermore, it was found to be greater than that about sites of song sparrow and slate-colored junco nests.

Finally, measurements of the number of feet of edge per unit area of cover (which is a measure of the dispersion or arrangement of objects) showed that although the dispersion of objects within the 10-foot radius did not differ from the average dispersion in the rest of the nesting habitat, there was much less variation than that existing in the rest of the habitat. Comparison of this character for nest sites of the three species of sparrows studied showed that white-throats tend to select nest sites in areas exhibiting a degree of clumping of objects intermediate between the singly arranged objects about song sparrow nests and the dense clumping about junco nests.

Thus white-throated sparrows apparently select their nest sites in relation to the amount and dispersion of the nearby cover. As the species chooses conditions intermediate between the open areas in which song sparrows nest and the dense woodland in which juncos nest, the nesting habitat may be described as forest edge.

Eggs.—The white-throated sparrow lays from 4 to 6 slightly glossy eggs. They are ovate with some tending toward elongate ovate. The ground is creamy, bluish, or greenish white, and heavily marked with speckles, spots, and blotches of reddish browns such as "natal brown," "Verona brown," "Mars brown," "russet," and "chestnut." They vary considerably, often the ground is entirely obscured giving the egg the appearance of being light brown with cloudings and spottings of the darker browns; others may show a considerable amount of the greenish ground with bold blotches of the dark browns, and on these, undermarkings of "pale neutral gray" may be seen. The eggs are practically indistinguishable from those of the white-crowned sparrow except that they average slightly smaller. The measurements of 50 eggs average 21.0 by 15.4 millimeters. The eggs showing the four extremes measure *23.3* by 15.1, 21.6 by *16.8*, *18.8* by 14.7, and 21.3 by *14.2* millimeters.

The average of 41 clutches found over a two-year period in Algonquin Park was 4.1 with a range of 3 to 5 eggs. Houston and Street (1959) report an exceptional clutch of 7 eggs from Cumberland House, Saskatchewan. A few observations on renests in Algonquin Park showed no change in clutch size with time of year. Two observations of females carrying nesting material after the first eggs were laid suggest that egg-laying starts before the nest is completed.

Incubation.—Only the female white-throated sparrow incubates, as many authors (e.g. Knight, 1908; Forbush and May, 1939) have reported, and which our observations on color-banded birds in Algonquin Park confirmed. One egg is laid per day until the clutch is complete, but it is not known when incubation begins. Five observations of nests in Algonquin Park suggest that the eggs are laid early in the morning.

Once incubation has started, it is possible to approach to within a few feet—in some cases 2 or 3 feet—of the incubating bird, before she takes flight. Unless the observer stops or vigorously disturbs the vegetation, the female may remain on the nest. Once flushed she either flies directly to the nearest clump of bushes, or runs along the ground before flying. Usually she remains quiet for about 30 seconds, and then begins scolding with very fine, high-pitched chips, which are gradually replaced with louder, metallic ones. The louder notes attract the attention of the male, if he has not already been alerted, and he begins chipping. During most of this performance, the birds remain concealed in the vegetation.

The reactions of the parent birds become more intense as incubation progresses. The female is less inclined to leave the nest when a storm or rain shower approaches and if flushed, she returns almost the moment the intruder leaves the immediate area. Similar behavior has been observed late in the evening.

It is not known whether the male white-throat feeds the female when she is on the nest. Observations at two nests suggest that he may join the female at the nest on the day the eggs hatch. The significance of this is not understood.

The incubation period for the white-throated sparrow has been given by Knight (1908), Burns (1915), Forbush and May (1939) and Peters and Burleigh (1951) as 12 to 14 days. In the Algonquin Park study Lowther estimated the incubation period to be 11 to 13 days.

Young.—The young hatch almost naked, with only small tufts of clove brown down on the dorsal tract of the head, body, and wings. The eyes are sealed shut and open 3 or 4 days later. There is no information on the development of feathers in the various tracts. By the time the young leave the nest, the body and wings are fairly well feathered, and the tail feathers are about one quarter to one third erupted from their sheaths. Tufts of down remain on the ends of some of the head and back feathers for as long as a week after the birds have left the nest.

By the fifth day after hatching, the young birds begin to show signs of fear toward humans, suggesting that at this time they are totally imprinted on the parent birds. Usually the female bird broods the nestlings. Only once was a male seen brooding the young at Algonquin; he was flushed from the nest just before a thunderstorm broke.

Observations on 12 nests in Algonquin Park in 1959 and 1960 indicate that the nestlings leave the nest between 7 and 12 days after hatching, with 8 or 9 days being most common, and that they are able to fly within 2 or 3 days after leaving the nest. The exact time they become independent of parental feeding is not known. Both parents feed the young in the nest, and continue to do so after they have left it. When eventually the brood moves beyond the territorial boundaries, only the female accompanies them, the male remaining on his territory.

Of the 28 nests Lowther found in Algonquin Park prior to June 8 in 1959 and 1960, 22 survived to hatching. The eggs in all 22 nests hatched on either June 7 or June 8 in both years. Ten of these 22 nests were lost through predation, but fledged young left the remaining 12 nests between June 15 and June 20.

Although white-throats commonly renest after the loss of the first nest, they rarely rear more than one brood per season. Observations on some 50 pairs showed at least 16 that lost their first brood renested, and one pair renested after two failures. Yet some evidence suggests that occasionally white-throats do attempt a second brood. Lainevool (field notes) saw a color-banded female carrying nesting material after the first brood had been out of the nest about 10 days, but the second nest was never located. During this interval, the first brood remained with the male. L. de K. Lawrence (*in* litt.) reports a known second brood at Rutherglen, Ontario.

Plumages and molts.—Jonathan Dwight, Jr., (1900) calls the natal down "pale clove-brown" and describes the juvenal plumage as "Above, chestnut-brown, darkest on the head, streaked with dull black, median line and superciliary line olive gray buff tinged, the feathers of the back edged with buff. Wings and tail deep olive brown, the coverts and tertiaries chestnut edged and buff tipped, the secondaries and rectrices edged with paler brown, the primaries with brownish white; edge of wing white. Below, dull white, washed with buff on throat and sides and thickly streaked with clove brown, the whiter chin merely flecked, the abdomen and crissum unmarked. Bill slaty brown, feet pinkish buff, both darker when older."

The first winter plumage is acquired by a partial postjuvenal molt. In Algonquin Park in 1959, this molt started on some individuals during the last week of July, and most birds were in molt between August 15 and August 20. By the end of this month, most of the young birds were indistinguishable from adults. According to Dwight, and from our observations on banded birds in Algonquin Park, the body feathers and wing coverts are replaced, but not the wing and tail feathers.

In the first winter plumage the arrangement of black and brown on the lateral crown areas changes to black anteriorly grading into a mixture of brown and black toward the neck. The median crown stripe may remain the same olive gray as in the juvenal plumage, but usually it becomes lighter tan. A small percentage of young birds in winter plumage have the median crown stripe white (11 of 209 museum specimens examined). The superciliary line is yellow in front of the eye and light tan behind. Pale yellow appears on the edge of the wing. The throat patch is white or dull white edged with black, and within the patch two black malar lines extend posteriorly from the lower edge of each side of the lower mandible. Dwight describes the lower throat and breast as "ashy gray obscurely vermiculated with clove-brown, * * * Abdomen white, the flanks and crissum washed with wood-brown and duskily streaked." Some individuals acquire a central breast spot.

The nuptial plumage is acquired by a partial prenuptial molt that begins in late March or early April while the birds are still on the wintering grounds. Most birds complete the molt by late April, although a few birds caught in Algonquin Park early in May 1960 were in the last stages of the molt. The extent of the prenuptial molt varies among individuals, but it generally involves feathers of the head, throat, breast, and flanks; also the middle two rectrices and inner three secondaries are sometimes replaced.

From studies of 706 museum specimens and of 342 live birds breeding in Algonquin Park and sexed by cloacal protuberance (Wolfson, 1952), Lowther (1961, 1962) has shown that the white-throated sparrow is a polymorphic species. The two basic types differ essentially in the color of the median crown stripe, being either white-striped or tan-striped, and both types occur in both sexes. Associated with this dimorphism of the median crown stripe are other color variants. Although the plumage patterns of both types are similar to those of young birds in the first winter plumage, color intensities differ on different parts of the body. Regardless of sex, the white-striped birds are generally brighter colored and less streaked; they have more black on the lateral crown areas, less streaking on a wider and grayer chest band, less intense black on the malar markings of the white throat patch, and brighter yellow on the superciliary stripe; also they tend to have longer wing chords than do tan-striped individuals. A central breast spot occurs more frequently in the tan-striped birds.

Tan-striped adults are indistinguishable from the majority of immature birds in the first winter plumage.

Every one of 45 immature birds kept in captivity during the winter of 1961–62, including individuals of both types, underwent a prenuptial molt during the spring, particularly of the head and anterior body regions. Two additional birds banded as juveniles in 1959 were retrapped as adults in 1960; one was then a white-striped female, the other a tan-striped female. These observations indicate that the white-striped plumage may be attained in the first prenuptial molt.

Of the birds banded as adults in Algonquin Park in 1959, 1960, and 1961, 46 individuals of both types were recaptured in subsequent years for a total of 56 recaptures. Each of these birds showed the same color in later years as when it was first banded, most notably a tan-striped male banded in 1959 and recaptured in 1962. Similarly Forbush (1929), Hervey Brackbill (1954), and J. T. Nichols (1954, 1957) report banded individuals that retained their dull (tan) coloration after 2, 2 and 3, and 6½ years. Thus the two color types are permanent and do not change from one nuptial plumage to the next.

Adult white-throats undergo a complete postnuptial molt. The data from banded birds in Algonquin Park suggest that a few birds begin molting in late July, but the majority start in early August. Most adult birds undergo their postnuptial molt at the same time the young go through their postjuvenal molt. As the adult molt is more extensive than that of the immature birds, it extends over a longer period.

The winter plumage of adult birds differs little from the nuptial plumage except in the head pattern. Some birds retain the white-striped coloration into the winter plumage, but most white-striped individuals tend to have the median crown stripe and posterior superciliary line tinged with buff. The plumage in other regions is not changed appreciably. The tan-striped birds show no apparent change in plumages.

Comparisons of plumages of the white-throated sparrow with those of other related species of *Zonotrichia* give some insight into the nature of the color polymorphism of the white-throat (Lowther, MS.). Within each of the white-crowned, golden-crowned, and Harris' sparrow groups, the first winter plumages are uniformly colored and characterized by the presence of brown and tan (or gray and tan) and the absence of black and white (or gray) in the head pattern. This is unlike the first winter plumage of the white-throat, which has black as well as tan and brown in the head pattern. Adults of species of *Zonotrichia* other than the white-throat, and including races of the South American *Z. capensis*, are typified by a black and white or black and gray head pattern similar to that of the white-striped type of the white-throated sparrow.

Thus the white-striped color type of the white-throat represents the typical adult nuptial plumage of the species, and the tan-striped type represents the first winter plumage. The coloration of the plumage is unusual for the genus in that it combines the black of the adult with the brown and tan of the typical first winter plumage. The tan-striped adult plumage is, therefore, a retention of the first winter plumage through subsequent molts.

Food.—White-throated sparrows feed on both plant and animal matter. Sylvester Judd (1901) examined the contents of 217 stomachs collected during every month except June. From these he reported:

> The food for the year, as a whole * * * consists of 19 percent animal matter and 81 percent vegetable matter. Of the vegetable food, 3 percent is grain, 50 percent weed seed, and the remainder chiefly wild fruit * * *.
>
> Some grass seed is consumed, particularly seeds of such troublesome species as pigeon-grass, crab-grass and other panicums, and Johnson grass. This element forms about 5 percent of the total food and is taken chiefly during Septem-

ber, when it amounts to 24 percent of the food of the month. A little amaranth and lamb's quarters are eaten; and gromwell, chickweed, wood sorrel, sedge, violet and sheep sorrel are all represented in the diet. But the principal weed seeds found in the stomachs are those of ragweed and different polygonums. * * * The two weeds form 25 percent of the food for the year, of which ragweed furnishes 9 percent, and the polygonums 16 percent. During October, ragweed alone constitutes 45 percent of the month's food. * * *

The insect food resembles that of many other species in general character, but some interesting differences appear when it is reviewed in detail. Hymenoptera constitute 6 percent of the year's food; Coleoptera, 5 percent; Heteroptera and Diptera, taken together, 3 percent; and Lepidoptera, 3 percent, the customary quota of spiders, millipedes, and snails supply the remaining 2 percent of the animal food.

The following items may be added to Judd's list: fruits of dogwood, sumach, wild grapes, persimmon, smilax, cedar, and privet (Skinner, 1928); elder, mountain ash, blueberry, blackberry, wild cherry and high bush cranberry fruits (Roberts, 1932); and greenbriar, spice bush, wild sarsaparilla, and strawberry fruits (Howell, 1932). Lowther noted that raspberries and bunchberries were important food sources during August in Algonquin Park. White-throats in captivity feed readily on various cereal grains, oranges, tangarines, lettuce, cabbage, and leaves of geraniums.

The foods consumed appear to change with the season. During the winter the birds feed mainly upon weed seeds, small fruits, and occasionally insects which are picked up from the ground. Arthur T. Wayne (1910) reports that "with the approach of spring * * * [the white-throat] resorts to the tops of the tallest oaks and maples to feed upon their buds." Benjamin Warren (1890) records that in April and May the buds and blossoms of apple, maple, and beech trees are eaten. Milton B. Trautman (1940) reports that "during late April and May, the species ate great quantities of newly formed seeds of such trees as white elm, slippery elm, silver maple and red maple" which the birds obtained directly from the trees.

During the spring and early summer the white-throat becomes more carnivorous, and larval and adult forms of many insects constitute the bulk of the food. In Algonquin Park white-throats were observed feeding on Hymenoptera and Lepidoptera larvae which they gathered from the leaves and branches of trees and shrubs. The young apparently are fed entirely on animal matter. That this change to a carnivorous diet is not totally governed by the abundance of insects and lack of seeds and fruits is evidenced by the failure of white-throats to feed on bread crumbs and grain seeds put out at feeding stations during the summer. Lowther has observed white-throats bypass grain in favor of insect larvae in late May, June, and early July.

After the young have left the nest and are for the most part independent, vegetable matter becomes the major source of food once again.

The manner in which white-throats feed varies to some extent. Of the method of feeding on the ground, Skinner (1928) writes, "White-throats depend largely upon scratching to uncover food. * * * they give a triple scuffle with spread feet, and a quick jump backward to throw out the dirt behind them. At times these birds will scratch for as much as an hour without a pause beyond that necessary to pick up the food." When searching for insects in trees, the birds hop along a branch picking up insects, then move to another limb to repeat the performance. In Algonquin Park Mrs. Lainevool saw an adult white-throat chase and capture an adult dragonfly. Lowther also noted aerial feeding during the spruce budworm outbreak in New Brunswick in 1953 and 1954. At the time the adult moths were emerging from their chrysalises, white-throats were often seen chasing and capturing them in flight.

The birds eat only the pulpy parts of such fruits as grapes, blueberries, and bunchberries and do not swallow the skins and large seeds. The bird picks up the fruit with its bill, squashes it and manipulates the skin back and forth between the mandibles until all the contents are squeezed out before dropping it. The coarse husks of grains are also rejected, as are the hard parts of some adult insects, such as the wings of beetles and dragonflies. Large insect larvae are handled in a similar manner, probably to soften the outer cuticle, but the food is swallowed whole.

Field marks.—The white-throat is a rather large sparrow, with its back striped in reddish and dark brown; crown striped either black and white or black, brown and tan; throat patch white or dirty white, well defined from the gray or gray-tan of the throat and upper breast. The two most distinguishing features of this sparrow are the white throat patch and the yellow superciliary line in front of the eye. Young birds are usually, but not always, somewhat duller than the adults.

Voice.—The song of the white-throated sparrow is not likely to be confused with that of any other bird in its range. It consists of pure whistled notes, generally steady in pitch, and arranged in a definite pattern. As Elon H. Eaton (1914) states, "In New England, it has been likened to the words 'Old Sam Peabody, Peabody, Peabody' or 'Sow wheat Peeverly, Peeverly, Peeverly,' but farther north he is supposed to say, 'Oh sweet Canada, Canada, Canada.'" These paraphrases, repeated in so many books, indicate one pattern of the song which, as we shall see, is no longer the commonest one.

Donald J. Borror and William W. Gunn (1965) studied songs of 711 white-throated sparrows, 433 of which were recorded. Most of the birds were on their breeding territories from Massachusetts and New Brunswick to Minnesota and British Columbia, but 59 were on migration in New York, North Carolina, and Ohio. Most recordings were analysed with a Vibralyzer sound spectrograph; others were studied by listening to them at reduced speed. These songs were composed of the following types of notes: notes lasting more than a fifth of a second and relatively steady in pitch, similar notes beginning with a shorter upslur (rarely, a downslur), triplets (occasionally couplets) about as long as the preceding notes but more or less divided into three short notes usually of about equal length, and occasionally other types including short distinct notes less than a tenth of a second in duration. The pitch of steady notes in the whole sample ranged from 2,150 to 6,500 cycles per second (cps) and from 1,500 to 6,600 cps including upslurs and downslurs. Lowther and Falls recorded a bird with notes ranging from 7,000 to 10,000 cps but this bird also gave unusually high-pitched calls and was doubtless abnormal. Borror and Gunn found that the spread in pitch between notes in a single song might be as great as an octave, but averaged less than half this range.

A white-throat's song nearly always has at least one change of pitch, and there may be as many as three. Owing no doubt to the quality of the notes and the repetition of the melody, many authors have described the song as musical and A. V. Arlton (1949) uses musical symbols to depict the pattern. Borror and Gunn state, "Songs of the white-throated sparrow are relatively musical, but the birds do not stay on key very well, and the pitch changes in their songs do not follow our musical scale."

Most songs begin with one or more steady notes and end with a series of similar triplets. Aretas A. Saunders (MS.) provided information on the number of triplets and the length of songs based on notations of 106 songs. His data are bracketed after those of Borror and Gunn (1965), who found from 0 to 7 [0 to 10] triplets with an average of 1.8 [4.4]; song length varied from 1.2 to 6.1 [1.6 to 7.0] seconds and averaged 2.9 [3.7] seconds. Thus, the length of the song is quite variable and this is true even of songs of an individual. If a bird is disturbed it may omit some or all of the final triplets.

Songs of white-throats vary in a number of respects. Borror and Gunn describe 15 patterns based on the types of notes present and pitch changes through the song. Some patterns were much commoner than others and the proportionate representation of the different patterns varied geographically. The four patterns making up over 96 percent of the songs they studied are described here. The commonest type, accounting for 62 percent of the songs, begins with a long steady note followed by a triplet, another steady note usually upslurred at the beginning, and a few more triplets; the second and third notes are on about the same pitch and distinctly higher than the first note; the remaining notes are on the same pitch or slightly lower than the third note. The usual form of this song could be paraphrased "Poor Peabody, Sam, Peabody, Peabody, Peabody," using the familiar phrases. Songs of this type were abundant throughout the range of the species. A similar song in which the upslur of the third note in the foregoing pattern is replaced by a very short but separate note, accounted for 7 percent of the sample. It was found mainly east of Ontario, where it accounted for between a quarter and a third of the songs. Another common pattern, making up 10 percent of the sample, also resembles the first one except that the third and remaining notes are pitched distinctly lower than the second note but higher than the first note. Like the first pattern, it was widely distributed. The fourth common pattern is rather different from the others, beginning with two steady notes at about the same pitch, then dropping to a third steady note considerably lower in pitch, followed by a series of triplets at about the same or a slightly lower pitch than the third. This song accounted for 19 percent of the sample and was uncommon east of Ontario.

Most of the 11 rarer patterns are somewhat similar to those already described. Seven birds in Riding Mountain National Park, Manitoba, began their songs with a series of 7 to 10 short discrete notes followed by longer notes like those in the other songs. L. L. Snyder (1928b) reported a pattern of this sort as common in the Lake Nipigon region of Ontario in the summers of 1923 and 1924. W. W. Gunn did not find it in Ontario west of Lake Superior in 1956 and 1960. There is some indication that this pattern may be disappearing as Gunn found it to be much rarer in Riding Mountain Park in 1960 than in 1956.

It appears that the relative abundance of the different song types in an area may change over a period of years. This might account for the scarcity of the pattern referred to as the common one in many of the older books—the song that begins with two steady notes followed by a series of triplets. Borror and Gunn found only three songs like this, whereas about a quarter of those A. A. Saunders noted (Borror and Gunn) in the Adirondacks in 1925 and 1926 were of this type. W. W. Gunn however did not find it in the Adirondacks in 1960. In view of the many careful observers such as Saunders who have described this pattern and the extensive recent samples of Borror and Gunn, it seems reasonable to conclude that what was once a common song, at least in the Northeast, has almost disappeared.

The principal form of geographic variation in white-throat songs lies in the relative incidence of the various song patterns just described. It is usually easy to assign songs of individual birds to one of these patterns, but differences are recognizable among songs of the same pattern. Borror and Gunn (1965) state that, "songs of each pattern varied in the types of notes in the songs, the pitch of the first note, the amount of pitch change between notes, the length of the various notes, the length of the song and the number of notes it contained, and the relative loudness of different notes in the song." As already mentioned, songs of a given individual may vary considerably in length, but in other respects they vary much less than the songs of different birds. Thus songs of individual birds can often be recognized even from others of the same pattern, and the characteristic features appear to be retained from year to year. D. J. Borror was able to recognize seven of nine birds occupying a 30-acre point at Hog Island, Maine, by their songs, and the songs of the other two proved to be different when studied with the sound spectrograph. Several birds occupying the same general area from year to year had songs of the same pattern and pitch characteristics each year. Although not individually marked, they were probably the same birds. The experience of Falls and his students with songs of individual birds has been similar.

To determine whether white-throats were capable of recognizing different individuals by song, Ronald Brooks (unpublished data) played recorded songs of neighboring and distant individuals to males in their territories. Reactions were stronger to the strange songs, even if they were of the same pattern as the neighbor's song.

About three percent of the birds Borror and Gunn studied had two songs usually of different patterns. Harold Axtell noted the same phenomenon and writes (*in* litt.), "Usually the two songs are very different and one is given much less frequently than the other." Though an observer is apt to assume that the occasional quite different song comes from another bird, close observation might show this to be a more common situation than the above percentage indicates.

In order to determine which characteristics of the white-throat's song were important in species recognition, Falls (1963) played 15 artificial songs, generated by means of an audio-oscillator, to a large sample of males on their breeding territories. The test songs varied in the character of the notes, pitch, pattern of pitch change, and the length of the notes and intervals between them. Birds responded to a normal song by giving songs and calls and approaching the speaker. The importance of the different characteristics was judged by comparing the responses to test songs with responses to normal songs and to those of other species. As a song consisting only of continuous notes elicited normal responses, it was concluded that other types of sounds were not essential for species recognition. Similarly, variations in loudness between notes were shown to be unimportant, but songs that fell partly or wholly above or below the range of pitch Borror and Gunn (1965) found in their sample elicited very weak responses. Falls summarized the results of his experiments as follows: "To be effective, a white-throated sparrow's song must consist of unvarying pure tones within a certain range of pitch. Less important is the presence of notes of different pitch arranged in a certain pattern. The notes should be of a certain minimum length, and the intervals between notes should not exceed a certain maximum." This study dealt only with reactions of territorial males to song, and properties of song that appeared to be unimportant in this context may serve other functions.

To determine which characteristics of song are important for individual recognition, Brooks and Falls (unpublished data) played altered neighbor's songs to territorial males. The birds responded normally (see above) to songs altered in length, but strongly to songs altered in pitch, which they apparently no longer recognized as neighbors' songs. Thus pitch appears to be more important than timing for individual recognition.

Regarding inheritance of song, Borror and Gunn (1965) state, "Certain general features are common to all the White-throat song patterns we found (clear, whistled notes steady in pitch or nearly so, uually one or two pitch changes through the song, and the song ending in triplets), so it may be assumed that these features are hereditary." They suggest further that the different patterns are learned, and that the 11 uncommon patterns may be inaccurate copies of the four more common patterns.

Bruce Thorneycroft (unpublished data) raised a sample of nestling white-throats in isolation where they could not hear songs of adults. In the songs these birds developed none of the characteristics Borror and Gunn list was invariably present, and none of the songs contained triplets. This experimental evidence implies that the inherited basis of song in this species may be less than Borror and Gunn suggest.

In view of the unusual plumage variation in this species (see *Plumages*), it is of interest to consider the singing behavior of the various color types. No differences were noted between songs of white-striped and tan-striped males, and a recording of each elicited similar responses from both sexes. White-striped males, however, sing more often than tan-striped males both spontaneously and in response to recorded songs. In five-minute counts of spontaneous singing early in the morning, Lowther (MS.) found an average of 5.27 songs for 55 white-striped males compared with 1.34 for 44 tan-striped males. White-striped females occasionally sing early in the breeding season before nest building begins. Tan-striped females were not heard singing in the field, but Thorneycroft reports that, in a sample of hand-raised birds in the laboratory, three tan-striped females sang occasionally, but not so much as white-striped females. Lowther observed the responses to recorded songs by females of both types, which had been sexed by cloacal protuberance and color banded. He found that all of 33 white-striped females responded by singing, but none of 37 tan-striped females sang. Songs of females were of the patterns already described, but the pitch of the notes tended to waver and the songs were often cut short. Territorial males responded less strongly to a single recording of a female's song than to recorded songs of males.

White-throated sparrows usually sing from coniferous trees. While studying territorial behavior in Algonquin, Maire Lainevool (unpublished data) noted that each male sang mainly from two to four song posts, usually 20 to 40 feet above ground in the outer branches of a white spruce. White pines were used occasionally, but birches and aspens seemed to be avoided. A bird might give a few songs from other places, but often sang up to 50 times in rapid succession from a regular song post. Birds occasionally sang from a stump or small tree, but were never observed singing on the ground. However, Knight (1908) states that "the singer perches in the bushes or on the ground." During migration Falls has heard songs that seemed to originate on or near the ground.

A white-throat may sing in a variety of positions but usually perches on a branch with its back and tail in line and at an angle of about 45 degrees from the horizontal. When singing loudly, the bird throws its head back and its tail quivers noticeably in the rhythm of the song.

Early in the breeding season the white-throated sparrow may be heard singing at any time of the day or night, though much less frequently at night than during the day. Lowther noted that a bird in New Brunswick sang two or three times an hour when the moon was full but only three or four times a night when the sky was overcast.

J. B. Falls counted songs in 5-minute periods during the day, once a week from mid-May to the end of August 1955. From May 14th until June 25th, white-throats began to sing steadily about 3:30 a.m., E.S.T. They were often the first passerines to be heard. The number of songs increased to a maximum about 4:00 a.m. and then decreased. A second peak of singing sometimes occurred about 6:30 a.m. after which singing was much less frequent. These peaks resulted mainly from more birds singing rather than from a shortening of the intervals between the songs of individual birds, which were usually about 15 seconds. Birds sang occasionally in the afternoon, and a short burst of singing about 8:00 p.m. was followed by a rapid decrease. Regular singing began in the morning and ended in the evening at a light intensity of about 10 foot-candles. In mid-July singing was more general throughout the day but by mid-August only a few songs were heard at 4:30 a.m. and 7:00 p.m. On August 25th no birds sang. The increase in song in mid-July already mentioned was also observed by Dayton Stoner (1932) in the Oneida Lake region of New York and by Lainevool, who noted that mated birds sang more when their young became independent. She also observed that unmated males defending territories sang more than mated males during the breeding season.

Lainevool (unpublished data) investigated the effects of weather on singing by counting songs for 10 minutes at 7:30 a.m. in an area where 12 birds could be heard. Between June 2 and July 27, 1959 she made 37 counts. Although the results were not conclusive, they showed the birds tend to sing more on sunny than on cloudy days, on warm rather than cold days, and during high rather than low atmospheric pressures. There was very little song when the temperature was below 50° F.

A number of authors have reported hearing the primary song of this species during migration and on the wintering grounds. A. A. Saunders (1948) noted fall singing in southern Connecticut on the average from October 6th to November 6th with the extreme dates from September 26th to November 29th. He states that "Fall songs are not commonly perfect and full. They are shortened or the pitch of the last notes is badly flatted." George H. Lowery, Jr. (1955) reports that the song is often heard in Louisiana in mid-winter and describes patterns similar to those heard on the breeding grounds. A. A. Saunders (1947) describing the onset of spring song, reports hearing a white-throat as early as January 10th. The average date when he first heard regular singing was March 26th, the earliest February 18th, and the latest April 23rd.

Thus far we have discussed the territorial or advertising song of the white-throat. A good imitation or recording of this song will cause a territorial male to become quite excited and to approach the source of the sound. This suggests that the song functions as a threat to other males. As females often respond by giving the precopulatory trill, the song may also be a sexual stimulant to the female (Lowther, MS.).

Bruce Thorneycroft (unpublished data) took young white-throats from the nest and raised several groups in sound isolation. Their vocalizations were recorded at intervals beginning in July of the first year. During the fall and winter these birds tended to give a series of whistling sounds falling and then rising in pitch sometimes ranging over two octaves. The individual sounds were shorter than those in normal songs, quite variable in pitch, and often included upslurs and downslurs. Some were pure and others were made up of two tones a few hundred cycles apart. Various call notes accompanied these warblings. Subsongs of this type are heard preceding and, to a lesser extent, following the breeding season.

Carl Helms writes (*in* litt.) that he has heard subsongs given by young and adults during extreme fright. It is not clear whether this refers to the type of subsong described above. He also states that low intensity singing occurs at all periods of the annual cycle and at all times of day. Again it is not clear whether this refers to subsong or to a quiet version of territorial song. We have heard the latter from males responding to recorded songs near the boundaries of their territories.

The white-throated sparrow has several distinct call notes. Some of these are high pitched notes lasting half a second or more. Most commonly heard is the "tseet" (about 8,000 cps) which both sexes give when resting or feeding in migration or on the breeding grounds. It is usually heard when the birds are visually isolated from one another on or near the ground, and appears to be a contact note although it is hard to locate. As it is often heard when the birds are disturbed, it may also serve as a mild warning.

Carl Helms (*in* litt.) reports hearing similar notes from captive birds. One of these was a "peep" or "tsee" uttered softly by a female after the male's songs. Jack Hailman (*in* litt.) describes two other high pitched notes as "eeek" and "eeeee." He refers to them as "fear notes," the latter sound being an extreme alarm note or warning of the presence of a predator.

Another sort of note given by white-throats is shorter with the initial consonant hardened. Notes of this type vary from a quiet "tip," which includes a narrow range of frequencies near 8,000 cps and is difficult to locate, through a series of chipping sounds to a loud "pink" which covers a wider range of frequencies and is easily located. The authors have heard the "tip" from both sexes when perched in dense cover and when there was reason to believe that young were in the vicinity. On two occasions blue jays were disturbing the birds. This note may be given alternately with the "pink" note.

The louder chipping or "pink" notes are also given by both sexes and appear to serve as contact notes, or to express various kinds of excitement or alarm, for they vary considerably in intensity. "Pink" notes are often given when a flock is disturbed or going to roost in dense cover. The most intense notes of this type are heard during agonistic encounters or from the parents when young are disturbed or giving distress calls. These sounds are often accompanied by crest raising and vertical tail flicking.

Finally, the white-throat gives several kinds of repetitive calls. One type is the "Chu-chatter" (Helms) or "Chup-up-up-up," a series of low-pitched notes (2,000 to 3,000 cps) given by both sexes. This is evidently a threat note and according to Jack P. Hailman may be accompanied by a head-forward threat as when caged birds have an encounter while feeding. It may be given by the male in answer to the song of another male. Lowther has also heard it following the "eeek" note.

A variety of repetitive calls given by both sexes may be described as trills. One type consists of a rapidly uttered series of notes similar to the "tip" note already described. Another type consists of a series of short notes covering a wide range of frequencies (4,000 to 8,000 cps). Trills are occasionally heard when birds are disturbed or in agonistic encounters. Most commonly they are given by the female in answer to the male's song and may induce approach and mounting by the male (see *Courtship*). When given intensely by either sex these notes may be accompanied by wing fluttering or vibrations of the tail.

An adult caught in a mist net or held upside down may give a "distress call," which is a scream of rapidly uttered notes covering a wide range of frequencies sometimes including "pink" notes or snatches of song. Lowther heard this call from a caged white-throat that a snake had seized by the feet. Somewhat similar sounds, although fainter and higher in pitch, are given by young birds if they are handled after 5 or 6 days of age. Distress calls are a powerful stimulant and may attract several pairs of white-throats. The birds typically dash about in the vicinity and eventually settle down a short distance away, uttering "pink" notes. If young birds are giving the distress calls, "pink" notes from the adults tend to quiet them. Occasionally other species will also react to distress calls of white-throats.

Young birds also give other repetitive calls. Shortly after hatching, nestlings give "gaping notes" that consist of a faint, high-pitched buzzing trill. Fledged young, when out of sight of their parents, give short calls that resemble short distress calls but are of lower intensity.

Thorneycroft (unpublished data) found that birds taken from the nest and raised in sound isolation developed notes similar to those already described as "tseet, pink, chup-up, and trills."

Enemies.—Herbert Friedmann (1963) states:

The white-throated sparrow is generally an infrequent host of the brown-headed cowbird, but in southern Quebec it appears to be a regular and not uncommon victim. In the course of nearly 60 years of field observation, Terrill (1961) found the astonishing number of 507 nests of this sparrow within a limited area of southern Quebec; of these, 20, or 4 percent, had been parasitized by the cowbird. * * *

All in all, some 36 records have come to my notice. Apart from southern Quebec, the white-throated sparrow has been found to be victimized in Itaska

County, Minnesota, [and] in Michigan, by Alvin R. Cahn (1920, p. 116; 1918, p. 497), and in Wisconsin, by Robbins (1949). Rowan (1922, p. 229) found this sparrow rearing a young cowbird at Indian Bay, Manitoba. Snyder and Logier (1930, pp. 194–195) found a parasitized nest in York County, Ontario. Harrington and Beaupré collected other parasitized nests in Ontario, which are now in the Royal Ontario Museum. J. D. Carter (1906, p. 32) reported a nest in Monroe County, Pennsylvania. Hooper and Hooper (1954) noted a fledgling cowbird being fed by a white-throated sparrow in the Somme district, Saskatchewan. T. E. Randall and A. D. Henderson wrote me of at least seven parasitized nests in Alberta.

Reports of the predation of white-throats by raptors do not appear commonly in the literature. A. C. Bent (1938) described the capture of a white-throat by an eastern pigeon hawk, and the white-throat may well be included in Mr. Bent's term "various other sparrows" which he lists as food of the peregrine falcon, sparrow hawk, and great horned, screech, barred, long-eared, short-eared, Richardson's, and saw-whet owls. Lowther watched a short-eared owl chase a white-throated sparrow unsuccessfully at Mills Lake, District of Mackenzie, Sept. 5, 1957.

Some mammals are known to raid the nests of small birds. The only mammal suspected of disrupting white-throated sparrow nests in the Algonquin Park study was the red fox, inferred from the condition of two nests found destroyed and the response of a fox to a recording of a white-throat's distress call.

A number of types of external parasites have been found on white-throated sparrows. Joseph C. Bequaert (1956) lists three genera of louse flies: *Ornithoica vicina*, *Ornithomyia fringillina* and *Lynchia americana*. Only one tick, *Ixodes brunneus* was reported by R. A. Cooley and G. M. Kohls (1945) as occurring on this species. G. F. Bennett (MS.) reported the larvae of the botfly, *Protocalliphora metallica* on nestling birds. Bennett (1961) collected a number of black flies, *Simulium aureum*, *S. "latipes," S. croxtoni*, *S. rugglesi*, and *Prosimulium decemarticulatum*, five sandflies, *Culicoides crepuscularis*, *C. sphagnumensis*, *C. stilobezzioides*, *C. obsoletus* and *C. haematopotus*, and one mosquito, *Aedes canadensis* from white-throated sparrows in Algonquin Park.

The internal parasites found in the white-throat can be divided into two major groups—visceral parasites and blood parasites. Three of the visceral parasites are trematodes. E. E. Byrd and J. E. Denton (1950) list *Tanaisia zarudryi* in the white-throat, and Denton and Byrd (1951) add *Zonorchis alveyi* and *Brachylecithum nanum*. R. C. Anderson (1957, 1959) reports two nematodes, *Aproctella stoddardi* and *Diplotriaena thomasi* from the body cavity. The blood parasites found in this bird include the nematode *Aproctella stoddardi* and the protozoa, *Haemoproteus fringilla* and *Trypanosoma avium* (Bennett and Fallis, 1960).

Winter.—The main winter range of the white-throated sparrow is in the southern United States from Missouri and Massachusetts to Florida and southern Texas. It occurs casually south to northern Mexico, west to California, north to British Columbia and Newfoundland, and regularly winters in small numbers as far north as southern Ontario.

As most recoveries of banded birds are from North and South Carolina, R. B. Fischer and G. Gill (1946) conclude that "the bulk of the eastern white-throated sparrows winter in these two states. Progressively smaller numbers of wintering birds are encountered as one travels north or south." However, Lowery (1955) speaks of them as among the commonest winter birds in Louisiana. E. P. Odum (1958) reports on sex and age ratios and fat content of white-throats killed at a TV tower near Tallahassee, Fla. On the basis of these and similar data gathered on the campus of the University of Georgia, he suggests that "immature or first-year females probably tend to winter farther south than adults in general and males in particular."

Everywhere on the wintering grounds white-throats are reported to frequent sheltered locations. For example, Lowery (1955) states "They occur in all places where there is shrubbery or other woody vegetation but do not like to venture far into the open. Where there is one of them, there are usually a dozen or more." In Ontario they are often found singly or in small groups in shrubby ravines or cat-tail marshes, where they apparently do not sing in winter, but often make their presence known by the "tseet" call. However, in the southern part of the winter range, singing is reported by Good and Adkins (1927) and others (see *Voice*).

In different regions white-throats are found in company with a variety of other species. In Ontario, they occur with song sparrows and other finches. On the Pacific coast Ralph N. Hoffman (1927) reports that they are generally found with golden-crowned or Gambel sparrows. In Alabama Good and Adkins (1927) list many species with which they associate in winter. These authors mention the towhee as roosting with white-throats in underbrush. They found the following species with the white-throat at night in heaps of cut pine branches: chipping sparrow, vesper sparrow, slate-colored junco, and American pipit.

Distribution

Range.—Southern Yukon, Mackenzie, northern Ontario, central Quebec, southern Labrador, and Newfoundland, south to southern California, southern Texas, the Gulf coast, and northern Florida.

Breeding range.—The white-throated sparrow breeds from southern Yukon (Watson Lake), central Mackenzie (Fort Norman, Sifton Lake), northern Manitoba (Churchill), northern Ontario (Fort Sutton, Severn River), central western and southeastern Quebec (Fort George, St. Pauls River), southern Labrador (Goose Bay), and northern Newfoundland (St. Anthony) south to central British Columbia (Kispiox Valley, Nulki Lake, Charlie Lake), central Alberta (North Edmonton, Battle River area), southern Saskatchewan (Conquest, McLean), central northern North Dakota (Turtle Mountains), central Minnesota (Cambridge), northern Wisconsin (Oconto County), central Michigan (Clare and Lapeer Counties), northern Ohio (Ottawa and Ashtabula counties), northern West Virginia (Terra Alta), northeastern Pennsylvania (Pocono Lake), southeastern New York (Tannerville), northwestern Connecticut (Litchfield), southern New Hampshire (Mount Monadnock), Massachusetts (Weston, Milton, Raynham), and Rhode Island (West Greenwich); non-breeding birds summer casually south to Arkansas, Maryland, and New Jersey.

Winter range.—Winters from northern California (sparsely; Del Norte County southward), southern Arizona (sparsely; Tucson), central Colorado (Denver), southeastern Nebraska (Lincoln), eastern Iowa (Muscatine, Davenport, Clinton), southern Wisconsin (Madison, Milwaukee), southern Michigan (Kalamazoo, Marshall, Ann Arbor, Detroit), southern Ontario (London, Toronto), central New York (Buffalo, Rochester, Syracuse, Schenectady), southern Vermont (Bennington, Brattleboro), coastal New Hampshire, and southern Maine (Mount Desert Island) south to southern New Mexico (Rio Grande Bird Reserve), southern Texas (Brownsville, Houston), the Gulf coast, and northern Florida (Gainesville, Enterprise); north casually to British Columbia (Grindrod, Vernon), North Dakota (Fargo), Manitoba (Winnipeg), western and eastern Ontario (Port Arthur, Ottawa), Quebec (Montreal, Lennoxville, Quebec), New Brunswick (Scotch Lake), Nova Scotia (Cole Harbour, Wolfville), and Newfoundland (St. John's) and south to Nuevo León (Linares), northern Tamaulipas (Matamoros), and southern Florida (Cape Sable), and Bermuda. In migration, west rarely to western Washington (Bellevue, Yakima), and coastal California.

Casual records.—Accidental on Baffin Island (West Foxe Islands), Guadalupe Island, Outer Hebrides, and in England.

Migration.—Early dates of spring arrival are: District of Columbia—March 11. Maryland—Baltimore county, March 5; Laurel, March 16. Pennsylvania—State College, April 2 (average, April 24); Beaver, April 10; Renovo, April 13 (average of 26 years, April 22). New York—New York City, April 7. Connecticut—New

Haven, April 12; Portland, April 13. Rhode Island—South Auburn, April 15. Massachusetts—Essex County, April 11. Vermont—Shaftsbury, April 15. New Hampshire—New Hampton, April 13 (median of 21 years, April 19); Concord, April 23. Maine—Bangor, April 6; Lake Umbagog, May 10. Quebec—Montreal area, April 15 (median of 7 years, April 19). New Brunswick—Fredericton, April 13. Nova Scotia—Windsor, April 16. Prince Edward Island—Mount Herbert, April 18. Newfoundland—Gander, May 7. Tennessee—Nashville, April 22. Illinois—Urbana, median of 20 years, March 19; Murphysboro, March 20; Chicago, March 25 (average of 16 years, April 15). Indiana—Wayne County, April 3 (median of 17 years, April 17). Ohio—central Ohio, March 17 (median of 40 years, April 1); Oberlin, March 21 (median of 19 years, April 16). Michigan—Detroit area, April 2 (mean of 10 years, April 12); Battle Creek, April 19 (median of 35 years, April 25). Ontario—Southmag, April 18. Iowa—Davenport, March 17. Wisconsin—Dane County, March 31. Minnesota—Minneapolis-St. Paul, March 20 (average of 15 years, April 19). Oklahoma—Payne County, March 14; Cleveland County, April 4. Nebraska—Stapleton, March 21; Red Cloud, April 20 (average of 11 years, May 1). South Dakota—Yankton, March 22; Union County, April 11; Sioux Falls, April 18 (average of 5 years, April 26). North Dakota—Brandon, April 5; Cass County, April 22 (average, April 26); Lower Souris Refuge, April 25; Jamestown, April 28. Manitoba—East Kildonan, March 22; Treesbank, April 18 (average of 22 years, April 28). Saskatchewan—McLean, April 20. Mackenzie—Kennicott, May 14. Wyoming—Torrington, May 13. Montana—Billings, May 1. Alberta—Lake Mamawi, April 25. Oregon—Benton County, March 14; Salem, April 22. British Columbia—Tupper Creek, May 7; Bowron, May 11.

Late dates of spring departure are: Florida—Tallahassee, May 16; Pensacola, May 3; Gainesville, April 30. Georgia—Atlanta, May 29; Spring Hill, May 20. South Carolina—Charleston, May 17 (median of 7 years, May 14). North Carolina—Wilmington, May 31; Raleigh, May 19 (average of 9 years, May 12). Virginia—Lexington, May 25. District of Columbia—June 14 (average of 32 years, May 22). Maryland—Anne Arundel County, June 15; Laurel, June 10 (median of 6 years, May 27). Pennsylvania—Hartstown, May 29. New Jersey—Englewood, May 24. New York—Long Island, May 27. Connecticut—New Haven, May 25. Rhode Island—Kingston, May 16. Massachusetts—Concord, May 30. New Hampshire—Concord, May 25. Louisiana—Baton Rouge, May 6. Mississippi—Rosedale, May 24 (mean of 37 years, May 12). Arkansas—Benton County, June 12; Fayetteville, May 16. Tennessee—Nashville,

May 31 (median of 30 years, May 13); Knox County, May 14; Athens, May 10 (average of 7 years, May 4). Kentucky—Bowling Green, May 17. Missouri—St. Louis, May 30 (median of 15 years, May 12). Illinois—Chicago, June 1 (average of 16 years, May 26); Urbana, May 26 (median of 20 years, May 19). Indiana—Wayne County, May 30 (median of 17 years, May 17). Ohio—central Ohio, June 11 (median of 40 years, May 24); Oberlin, May 22 (median of 19 years, May 18). Michigan—Detroit area, May 29 (mean of 10 years, May 24); Battle Creek, May 24 (median of 10 years, May 10). Iowa—Sioux City, May 27. Texas—Austin, May 2; Sinton, April 29 (median of 7 years, April 9). Oklahoma—Cleveland County, May 5. Kansas—northeastern Kansas, May 20 (median of 11 years, May 9). Nebraska—Dakota County, May 27. South Dakota—Faulkton, May 30; Sioux Falls, May 26. North Dakota—Cass County, May 26 (average, May 23). New Mexico—Los Alamos, May 10. Arizona—Tempe, April 21. Colorado—Yuma, May 3. Wyoming—Torrington, May 13. California—Inverness, May 22; Santa Barbara, May 1. Oregon—Clackamas County, April 27. Washington—Seattle, May 9.

Early dates of fall arrival are: Washington—Seattle, October 7. Oregon—Central Point, October 6. California—Sebastopol, September 25; Fair Oaks, October 6. Montana—Fortine, August 23. Idaho—Moscow, October 7. Wyoming—Green River, September 23; Sheridan, September 26. Colorado—Fort Morgan, September 19; Denver, October 5. Arizona—mouth of Verde River, October 29. New Mexico—Los Alamos, October 29. North Dakota—Jamestown, September 4; Cass County, September 5 (average, September 10). South Dakota—Aberdeen, September 9; Sioux Falls, September 24. Nebraska—Lincoln, September 27 (average of 13 years, October 8). Kansas—northeastern Kansas, September 27 (median of 9 years, October 19). Oklahoma—Payne County, October 7. Texas—Austin, October 21; Sinton, October 30 (median of 5 years, November 11). Minnesota—Minneapolis-St. Paul, August 27 (average of 11 years, September 19). Wisconsin—Wausau, August 15; Forest and Langlade Counties, August 28. Iowa—Sigourney, September 28; Sioux City, average of 11 years, September 30. Michigan—Detroit area, September 3 (mean of 10 years, September 13); Battle Creek, September 20 (median of 16 years, September 29). Ohio—central Ohio, September 12 (median of 40 years, September 25). Indiana—Wayne County, September 20 (median of 16 years, September 28). Illinois—Chicago, August 30 (average of 16 years, September 8). Missouri—St. Louis, September 10 (median of 15 years, September 28). Kentucky—Bowling Green, September 23. Tennessee—Nashville, September 16; Knox County, October 3. Arkansas—Little Rock, October 10; Fayetteville, October 12. Mississippi—Rosedale, October 13 (mean of 35 years, November 3). Louisiana—Baton Rouge, September 28. New Hampshire—Concord, September 18. Vermont—Shaftsbury, September 11. Massachusetts—Martha's Vineyard, September 5 (median of 7 years, September 24); Belmont, September 6. Rhode Island—Jamestown, September 12. Connecticut—New Haven, September 13; Portland, September 15. New York—New York City, August 15 and September 9. New Jersey—Cape May, September 22. Pennsylvania—State College, September 10; Renovo, September 10. Maryland—Worcester County, September 13; Laurel, September 20 (median of 6 years, September 23). District of Columbia—September 14 (average of 36 years, October 8). North Carolina—Chapel Hill, September 29; Raleigh, October 4 (average of 19 years, October 16). South Carolina—Charleston, October 2 (median of 8 years, October 11). Georgia—Atlanta October 5. Alabama—Talladega, October 2; Auburn, October 3. Florida—northwestern Florida, October 10; Leon County, October 17.

Late dates of fall departure are: British Columbia—Saanich, October 21. Washington—Yakima, November 18. Oregon—Blaine, October 25. Alberta—Glenevis, October 2. Montana—Fortine, October 18. Saskatchewan—Eastend, October 14. Manitoba—Killarney, November 4; Treesbank, October 30 (average of 23 years, October 11). North Dakota—Cass County, October 21 (average, October 17). South Dakota—Aberdeen, November 7; Dunbar, November 16. Nebraska—Lincoln, average of 11 years, October 31. Oklahoma—Cleveland County, November 21. Minnesota—Minneapolis-St. Paul, November 15 (average of 6 years, October 28). Iowa—Sigourney, November 3; Sioux City, average of 14 years, October 25. Ontario—Port Dover, October 30. Michigan—Battle Creek, November 19 (median of 29 years, October 22). Ohio—central Ohio, November 18 (median of 40 years, November 8). Indiana—Wayne County, November 25 (median of 13 years, November 14). Illinois—Chicago, December 4 (average of 16 years, November 4). Tennessee—Nashville, October 23 (median of 29 years, October 8). Newfoundland—Gander, October 10. Prince Edward Island—North River, October 16. Nova Scotia—Yarmouth, October 25. New Brunswick—Scotch Lake, November 20. Quebec—Montreal area, November 11. Maine—Bangor, November 20; Lake Umbagog, October 30. New Hampshire—New Hampton, November 30 (median of 21 years, October 28). Vermont—Woodstock, November 15. Massachusetts—Essex County, November 14. Rhode Island—Providence, November 3. Connecticut—Portland, November 28; New Haven, November 20. New York—Tiana, October 31; Saratoga County, October 30. Pennsylvania—State

College, November 19; Pittsburgh, November 16. Maryland—Laurel, December 20. District of Columbia—December 13.

Egg dates.—Alberta: 21 records, June 1 to June 19.

Maine: 42 records, May 27 to July 12; 25 records, June 5 to June 16.

New Brunswick: 83 records, May 25 to July 20; 40 records, June 9 to June 26.

Nova Scotia: 26 records, May 18 to July 22; 18 records, May 26 to June 10.

Ontario: 83 records, May 23 to August 5; 42 records, May 31 to June 12.

Quebec: 68 records, May 27 to July 23; 36 records, June 2 to June 24.

PASSERELLA ILIACA (Merrem)

Fox Sparrow

PLATE 72

Contributed by OLIVER L. AUSTIN, JR.

In his classic "Revision of the avian genus *Passerella*," Harry S. Swarth (1920) brought the first semblance of unity and order to the bewildering array of forms making up the fox sparrow complex. Later, as more breeding ground material became available, subsequent students of the group have been able to redefine some of the ranges more exactly and to describe a few new forms, so that the current A.O.U. Check-List (1957) recognizes 18 subspecies as against Swarth's 16. Otherwise our concepts of the group's distribution, variation, and taxonomy remain essentially unchanged, and the recognized races fall conveniently into the three major divisions he delineated as follows:

1. The eastern and northern forms. Breeding across the continent from Newfoundland and Labrador westward to interior Alaska and British Columbia, these birds have the back reddish to gray, the tail and spots foxy red, the tail shorter than the wing, and a bill of medium size. They include the races *iliaca*, *zaboria*, and *altivagans*.

2. The northwestern coastal races. Breeding along the Pacific Coast from the eastern Aleutians southeastward to northwestern Washington, these birds have dull sooty-brown backs and spots becoming darker from north to south, the tail shorter than the wing, and medium-sized bills diminishing in size from north to south. They include the races *unalaschcensis*, *insularis*, *sinuosa*, *annectens*, *townsendi*, and *fuliginosa*.

3. The southwestern group. Breeding from the mountains of southern British Columbia and Alberta southward to central Utah,

Nevada, and south central California, in these birds the grays predominate, especially toward the south, the tail is equal to or usually longer than the wing, and the large, swollen bill increases in size to the westward and southward. Included are the races *schistacea, olivacea, swarthi, canescens, fulva, megarhyncha, brevicauda, monoensis,* and *stephensi*.

Many of these races are rather weakly differentiated. Allan R. Phillips et al. (1964), for instance, consider *canescens* and *swarthi* indistinguishable from *schistacea*, and call the California races "generously oversplit." However Swarth (1920) claims: "I believe it to be possible, at the present state of our knowledge, to arrive at a solution of the fox sparrow problem that will enable anyone to identify accurately perhaps ninety per cent of the specimens taken," but he warns in the same breath "it is to be doubted if diagnoses can be prepared enabling anyone positively to identify *all* specimens of *Passerella* secured. * * * Intergrades between two forms may resemble a third and, taken in their winter home, may have their characters wrongly interpreted. Also immatures of one form may bear some resemblance to adults of another * * *. Intergradation of characters apparently occurs wherever two races come together. Thus * * * there are intergrades to be found between any two contiguous forms."

The morphological variation in the species, though extensive, is almost entirely geographical in nature. As Swarth (1920) points out:

> In this species variation due to age, sex and season of the year is extremely slight. The juvenal plumage is essentially the same as in the following stages, with regard to color and markings, the distinguishing features of the first mentioned being mainly due to the different texture of the feathers. Where color differences are concerned as of subspecific value, the young birds show these differences just as do the adults. As regards the later stages, I am unable to distinguish any differences between immatures in first winter plumage and adults a year or more old. As to sexual differences, males average slightly larger than females, but in color and markings there is no discernible variation. Seasonal differences are shown solely as the result of wear and fading of the feathers. There is but one annual molt, after the juvenal stage is passed, occurring in the late summer and including the entire feather covering, with no assumption of a special breeding dress such as is seen in so many species of birds. Consequently, a study of variation in this group is narrowed down quite closely to a consideration of but one category of differences, namely, geographic variation.

Swarth's analysis of the species' external morphology encouraged Jean M. Linsdale to examine its internal structure. During the next decade he completed an exhaustive study of the species' osteology, based on a comparison of 465 skeletons representing 14 of the 16 subspecies Swarth recognized. From this Linsdale (1928) claims: "Significant geographic variation was found in every part of the skeleton that was examined. The various geographic populations do not vary uniformly with respect to all features of internal structure. Some characters, however, are evidently closely correlated geographically with other characters of internal structure." His most striking osteological finding was that: "In every case the samples with large bones in the wings and pectoral girdle belong to races which have long migration routes and the samples with those bones weakly developed belong to relatively sedentary races."

As a part of this study Linsdale also analyzed many aspects of the life history of the various forms, based on the published literature, available museum material, and his own experiences with the bird afield. From this analysis he concludes: "A consideration of the available material bearing on the natural history of the fox sparrow shows several well marked tendencies to vary geographically in habits and in responses to the environment. These tendencies to vary follow a definite order and parallels may be pointed out between them and tendencies to vary in features of structure." Nevertheless the only variations in "life history" features he enumerates are the following:

Under the head of summer habitat it seems reasonable to expect some expression of differential choice which may be correlated with change in geography. It is evident that not only is there a differential habitat choice through the range of the species but that, in general, the areas of uniform habitat correspond to the ranges of various subspecies. For example, in the schistacea group of subspecies the three smallest forms, in the Great Basin mountain ranges, are rather closely limited in summer to the narrow fringes of willow, aspen, and birch which grow along the streams on dry mountain sides. Farther west, in the California mountains, the birds are found scattered through the dense growths of chaparral on the high slopes. In the north where the climate is more moist the birds are found in various types of brushy vegetation in different localities, but everywhere the habitat is different from those of the southern races.

* * *

The songs of fox sparrows, considered from a geographic point of view, show tendencies to vary that may be correlated with differential choice of habitat and with structural differentiation. The species, as a whole, is especially noted for its highly developed vocal powers. There is, however, an easily distinguished gradation of volume and quality among the races of at least the *schistacea* group. The song of the smaller races in the Great Basin resemble that of some song sparrows more than that of some of the closely related fox sparrows in the territory to the west.

The rather bulky nests of this bird are usually so well hidden as to be found with difficulty. They are placed in numerous types of situations although usually near the ground. There appears, from incomplete information, to be a tendency for birds in the northern parts of the range to place their nests higher than do those to the southward. This might be partly due to necessity since in the south most of the available nest sites are within a few inches of the ground. A great variety of material is used in the construction of the nests.

There is a considerable amount of individual variation in respect to color in the eggs of this species. The eggs are, in every way, strikingly similar to those of the song sparrow. Records are sufficiently numerous to show that in the northern part of the species' range four is the usual number of eggs and five are

Uinta Mountains, Utah — A. D. Cruickshank

FOX SPARROW TENDING YOUNG

Tulare County, Calif., May 27, 1939 — J. S. Rowley

NEST OF STEPHENS' FOX SPARROW

not uncommonly found. In the southern portion of the range three is the number most frequently found, and two are often recorded. There is considerable evidence that at least some of the northern races regularly rear two broods in a season while those farther south rear but one.

All other features of the species' habits Linsdale was able to compare showed little or no observed variation between the different populations. He was hampered by the fact that, as he expressed it, "* * * many phases of its life-history are too little known. Especially desirable is more recorded information concerning the behavior of the birds through the breeding season." And he pleads "It is hoped that this summary of the available literature may serve as a basis for a more thorough investigation of the natural history of *Passerella iliaca*."

Despite Linsdale's plea, we know little more about the species' biology and ethology today than we did 30 years ago. In defense of this continued ignorance, it must be admitted that the species' innate shyness, a dominant trait in all its populations, makes it a most difficult subject to work with in the field. It is doubtless mainly for this reason that no intensive, detailed life history or behavioral study of any of the fox sparrows has ever been made. As the following accounts bear witness, nowhere in the literature is the courtship described, or the species' territoriality, or the sexes' sharing of the various natal chores, to name only a few features badly in need of further investigation.

PASSERELLA ILIACA ILIACA (Merrem)

Eastern Fox Sparrow

Contributed by Lewis McIver Terrill

Habits

The fox sparrow was first described by the German zoologist, Blasius Merrem, under the name *Fringilla iliaca* in 1786. In 1837 William Swainson erected for it the genus *Passerella* (Italian diminutive of *Passer*, sparrow), to which it is still assigned. The genus contains only this single species, which is endemic to North America and occurs at one season or another from the Atlantic to the Pacific and from the southern border of the United States northward to the limit of tree growth. Over this extensive range the current A.O.U. Check-List (1957) recognizes a total of 18 subspecies, and the fox sparrow's marked geographical variation is thus exceeded by only two other North American bird species, the horned lark and the song sparrow.

Merrem's type specimen from "North America" no longer exists, but Oberholser (1946) restricted the type locality to the Province of Quebec, in the heart of the breeding range of the eastern race. Merrem seemingly derived the name *iliaca* from an earlier (1766) Linnaean name for the redwing, in reference to the fox sparrow's superficial resemblance to a thrush. Various other specific names that have been given the bird, such as the Latin *ferruginea* and *rufa* and the English ferruginous, fox-colored, and fox, all emphasize a single feature, the rufous or reddish-brown color of the red fox in summer pelage that characterizes the eastern fox sparrow.

Spring.—The eastern fox sparrows leave their winter haunts in the southeastern states in late February or early March. Although numbers follow the Mississippi Valley and some move northward through the mideastern states, their best defined migratory route appears to lie along the Atlantic Coast. From birds banded in Massachusetts, New Jersey, New York, and Pennsylvania from 1924 through 1956 the banding office at Patuxent, Maryland, has had 53 recoveries, 13 of them in North Carolina, and 13 in Newfoundland and adjacent St. Pierre et Miquelon (Robbins, MS.) Thus about half the total recoveries were divided almost equally between Newfoundland and nearby islands, known to support an exceptionally large summer population of fox sparrows, and North Carolina where banding returns indicate large concentrations winter.

In the southern part, the winter range migration is leisurely with frequent halts. From February to the end of April the birds move gradually toward their summer haunts, feeding among the ground litter as they go. Shy by nature, in their usual breeding and wintering grounds they prefer thick cover where danger of discovery is least and they can quickly fade from view if disturbed. During migration, however, they often scratch for food among the dead leaves littering the ground in rather open hardwoods where there is little or no ground cover. Here they habitually seek safety by flying up to a high perch where they may remain immobile until the intruder has passed. You may have excellent if brief views of them in their tree perches, but once on the wing again they quickly disappear in steady flight.

John T. Nichols (1925) mentions the tendency of wintering fox sparrows to remain aloof in family parties or neighborly groups and notes: "The habits of the fox sparrow are such that there is little chance of confusing early migrants with wintering birds, the latter stick so closely to their particular bit of cover." Charles L. Whittle (1926) observes that in New Hampshire the birds "arrive in spring migration in little groups, usually of eight to twelve birds, which apparently remain together until migration is resumed."

In western Pennsylvania, however, W. E. C. Todd (1940) states:

Single birds are the rule in our region and seldom are more than a few seen together. * * *

This hardy sparrow is one of the earlier spring migrants. Usually it appears in March, before all the snow is gone, and terminates its stay before the end of April * * *. [It] is a bird of the thicket and underbrush rather than of the deep forest; it is fond of briery areas on the outskirts of woods, and of dense willow and weedy growths along streams. The latter habitat is strikingly reminescent of its usual haunts in the north country. Actually the bird is a sort of sublimated Song Sparrow; it is often found associated with that species and with the Towhee, the Junco, and the Tree Sparrow—birds of kindred tastes.

Many writers stress the migrating fox sparrows' fondness for swampy tangles or weedy stream borders. Witmer Stone (1908) states it frequents the edges of swampy thickets in New Jersey, where it is a common migrant with extreme dates of March 1 to April 10, "Though common every year during their passage, they seem, some years, to reach us all together, as it were, and for a short time the thickets simply swarm with them. I noticed such a flight in March, 1906, near Tuckerton."

Their preference for wet cover is, I think, more applicable to the southern part of their range. When the northbound fox sparrows reach Massachusetts, William Brewster (1906) notes that

"Fox Sparrows, like Juncos, prefer upland to swampy places, although they are sometimes seen along the banks of brooks in thickets of alders and other bushes. Their favorite haunts in the Cambridge Region are dense second-growth woods, where the trees are largely pines, hemlocks, or other evergreens; rocky pastures plentifully sprinkled with Virginia junipers; and clusters or belts of bushes bordering roadsides and neglected weed-grown fields. They often appear in apple orchards and among ornamental evergreens in cultivated grounds. We see them very regularly in our garden, although they visit it less frequently and numerously now than they did twenty-five or thirty years ago, when it was by no means uncommon to hear half a dozen males singing at once in the Norway spruces close to the house. No one who has listened to such a chorus is likely ever to forget the sudden outburst of wild, exquisitely modulated voices rising above the rushing sound of the boisterous March wind. Strange to say, the birds sing most freely and with the greatest spirit during stormy weather, especially when snow is falling."

They are not greatly inconvenienced by moderate snowfalls during the northward flight. In their search for food they make the snow fly as well as the leaves. Only when the snowfall is prolonged or when freezing rain forms a crust do they suffer. Then they are forced to leave the shelter of the thickets in search of food. Many such instances are on record when fox sparrows lose their customary timidity and are found about dooryards.

Francis B. White (1937) writes that at Concord, N.H., "You may expect to see these birds for nearly three weeks in the spring * * *. We make more intimate acquaintance with them in large numbers if they are caught in an April blizzard, when the deep snow in the forest forces them to feed in the beds of brooks, and drives some to visit barnyards and feeding stations, and to accustom themselves to human beings."

A study of *Audubon Field Notes* (1951–1957) indicates that many of the big influxes of fox sparrows reported, especially in coastal states, were associated with severe snowstorms. The spring of 1956 was a notable example. Following a severe winter, the Middle Atlantic Coast Region experienced "a heavy snowfall just as spring arrived. * * * A deluge of Fox Sparrows hit the area about Philadelphia, March 22–26. Unprecedented numbers reported from Maryland also; 25 were trapped at Wenonah, N.J. in one day, March 24." In the Northeastern Maritime Region: "From mid-March on, feeders were swamped with unprecedented numbers of Fox and Song Sparrows, etc., as these birds, having arrived in numbers, struggled to survive three feet of snow followed by freezing rain."

Harrison F. Lewis informs me by letter dated Apr. 9, 1956, that similar conditions prevailed near his home at West Middle Sable on the Nova Scotian coast: "This spring we are having an extraordinary visitation of fox sparrows. They were first seen yesterday during a snowstorm. Today they were conspicuous visitors to our feeding station where we provided hayseed and rolled oats for them. I counted a maximum of 11 there at one time. Many more were scattered in thickets all along our road. And how they sang! Single songs at first, but eventually a full chorus of clear and joyous music."

Winsor M. Tyler (1922) mentions two similar concentrations in the Boston region: "No such flight of Fox Sparrows as occurred this year [1922] has taken place since the remarkable flight in April, 1907. This year, as was the case fifteen years ago, a heavy snowfall came in April and prevented the birds from advancing northward. The Fox Sparrows were singing everywhere and collected in such numbers about our dooryards that they attracted the interest and admiration of many people who never saw, or heard, or heard of, a Fox Sparrow." Later he (1924) considers that such storms do not delay migration materially: "The Fox Sparrow appears to be an exception to the rule that favorable weather hastens migration in a marked degree. My records of migration dates of this bird during the past fifteen years show a remarkably slight range, in spite of extremes of weather. The *numbers* of Fox Sparrows which visit us from year to year vary enormously, but their *dates* of arrival and departure [at Boston] come respectively very near March 15 and April 15."

As the fox sparrows approach their summer homes they move more rapidly. Ralph S. Palmer (1949) says that in Maine "the peak population may be present within a very few days after the first birds are reported. * * * At any one place numbers are generally present for only about two weeks." In Ontario James H. Fleming (1907) calls it a regular migrant at Toronto between Apr. 5 and 29, but of local occurrence and usually not common. In the opinion of J. Hughes-Samuel (J. Macoun, 1909): "This species passes through Toronto so rapidly in its spring migration that it is quite easy to overlook it entirely, hence the idea, I think, that it is scarce."

In New Brunswick William A. Squires (1952) states the fox sparrow is a common to uncommon transient, with extreme dates in spring from March 20 to May 8. Apart from an occasional wintering individual, it is also a transient in Nova Scotia. Harrison F. Lewis (MS.) suggests the probability that all the Newfoundland birds and possibly part of the Labrador population pass through Nova Scotia. He adds: "Nevertheless fox sparrows are usually uncommon in migration in southwestern Nova Scotia. I generally see a few each spring and fall, but in the spring of 1955 I did not see any. It appears that, though these birds must regularly cross Cabot Strait between Cape Breton Island and Newfoundland, they prefer not to cross the broader waters of the Gulf of Maine, but either cross the Bay of Fundy towards its head or travel via the Isthmus of Chignecto."

Two recoveries of banded fox sparrows support this thesis: One banded at Philadelphia Mar. 28, 1940 was recovered at Rochdale, Cape Breton, Apr. 30, 1940; the other, banded at Concord, New Hampshire Apr. 17, 1933, was recovered at Port aux Basques, Newfoundland, just across Cabot Strait, May 13, 1933.

Although this would appear to be the easiest and most favorable route for fox sparrows or other passerines bound "down the coast" for Newfoundland, the records of James Bouteiller (1905–1909) from Sable Island, 100 miles off the Nova Scotian mainland, suggest that some of them cross broader stretches of water fairly regularly. He reports most fox sparrows on Sable Island, where the species does not breed, between April 14 and 17 and October 7 and 20, the chief migratory periods of the species in this latitude.

Fox sparrows migrate at night and usually arrive at their summer home in the dark of early morning. Roger T. Peterson (1955) records some arriving at Gander Airport, Newfoundland, Apr. 11, 1955: "A plane droned in the pre-dawn sky, * * * stray wisps of fog were beginning to blow in * * * . From overhead came the incisive lisps of unseen fox sparrows, the first migrants of the season."

Nesting habitat.—The one outstanding requirement for the fox sparrow's breeding habitat is dense, bushy cover where the birds can nest and scratch for food while well screened from view. This appears indispensable throughout the species' wide range. Southwestern races find excellent cover among the thorny tangles of mountain misery (*Ceanothus*) so abundant on many California mountain slopes. Farther north and east the nesting cover is commonly coniferous, or again it may be wholly deciduous alders and willows.

Newfoundland probably has more suitable cover than any other part of *iliaca's* summer range. There Peters and Burleigh (1951) claim: "It is a bird of the thicket and the forest, and it does not come regularly into towns and settlements. It prefers a brushy wood edge, grown up field, cut-over woodland or scrubby woods." At St. Anthony D. B. O. Savile (MS.) found it the dominant bird from May 25 to Sept. 3, 1951. He writes: "No area except open marsh or bog and a few bare hillsides is without this species. About town they invaded shrubby areas that would be utilized by song sparrows where that species occurs. As many as six territories were noted in 300 yards of road in mixed farm and waste land at the edge of town." William J. Brown (1912) also refers to fox sparrows nesting near dwellings: "A small area of evergreen fenced in is called a 'garden' by the Newfoundlander, and in such places fox and white-throated sparrows, ruby-crowned kinglets and several other species were nesting commonly."

On the south shore of the St. Lawrence fox sparrows are relatively scarce in the nesting season. A few have been found at Percé and nearby Bonaventure Island in Gaspé County. Farther west in Matane County I have seen a few in June at Leggatt's Point, 6 miles west of Metis Beach during the years 1917–1922, with a peak of five in full song on the evening of June 7, 1921. They were frequenting almost impenetrable stands of low, shrubby spruce bordering boglands. Several blackpoll warblers were singing in the same spot. When I revisited the same area June 18, 1957, neither species was noted. The low spruce growth had become a forest in which Swainson's thrushes, winter wrens, ruby-crowned kinglets, yellow-bellied flycatchers, Blackburnian and several other warblers were in full song.

Fox sparrows seem to have a penchant for islands, particularly those with steep, rocky shores where the growth is apt to be stunted and gnarled and more or less impenetrable. Here they find safer cover than on the adjacent mainland, because foxes and other predators, including man, are often absent. I believe the most southerly nesting haunts for this race along the lower St. Lawrence are a number of small islands in Rivière du Loup and Kamouraska counties, including Basque Island off Trois Pistoles where I heard 12 singing and found 2 nests June 12, 1929, Garden (Pilgrim's) Island off St. André, Brandy Pots, and Cacouna, on each of which my wife and I heard one or more singing.

On the Magdalen Islands Philip B. Philipp (1925) found the species common everywhere "in the bogs, in the stunted spruces along the beaches, and on the wooded hills." William Brewster (1883) also found it on the Magdalens and adds: "It was particularly abundant at Fox Bay, Anticosti, where its favorite haunts were impenetrable thickets of stunted firs and spruces near the coast. It also occurred plentifully in the heavier forests of the interior, especially about openings." When Frank W. Braund and E. Perry McCullagh (1940) visited Fox Bay in 1937, upwards of 50 years after Brewster's visit, they saw only six fox sparrows in the same area during their two-week stay from June 16 to July 1. While the dwarfing of vegetation under subarctic conditions ensures a degree of permanence to fox sparrow habitats, ecological changes are probably partly responsible for local population fluctuations.

In Labrador Leslie M. Tuck (MS.) states the fox sparrow "seems to prefer scrub spruce and rather thin spruce-fir forests, but also occupies the pockets of black spruce on the barrens, or caribou range, the fringes of swamps, and even deciduous forests in the river valleys." T. H. Manning and A. H. Macpherson (1952) observed the species most often on the eastern coast of James Bay from June 28 to Aug. 28, 1950, where alder patches and open or stunted spruce were mixed together on dry, rocky ground. Farther north near Great Whale River on the east coast of Hudson Bay, Douglas B. Savile (1950) found the fox sparrow "abundant, especially in slightly wet areas with Labrador tea (*Ledum*) and other low shrubs and a few spruces."

Nesting.—John J. Audubon (1834) was the first ornithologist to find the fox sparrow on its breeding ground. He describes its nest on the southern Labrador coast as built on the ground among the mosses and tall grass, and says that the eggs are laid from the middle of June to the fifth of July. "When one approaches the nest, the female affects lameness, and employs all the usual arts to decoy him from it."

While the nest is most commonly on the ground, it may also be built above it in a bush or tree, and it is always well screened from view. The male indicates its general location by his singing, and the loud alarm *tchek* from one or both birds usually tells one the nest is close by. Ground nests in thickets may be in plain view when one reaches them, as behind the tangle of interlaced branches that thwart one's advance into the thicket, there is no need of elaborate concealment under a tuft of grasses in the manner of the song sparrow, and usually little or no grass grows beneath such dense cover. One such nest with two fresh eggs I found in Saguenay County July 1, 1925, in a slight ground cavity under a stunted white spruce tangle was composed of plant stems and moss and lined with withered grasses. It was much less bulky and contained none of the twigs that normally compose the walls of tree nests.

A nest I found near Betchouane on June 24 was built on a dead branch leaning against a spruce bush. Well hidden by overhanging foliage, it was 2 feet from the ground, compactly built with many twigs and chips of punky wood in the outer walls, and held three fresh eggs. Two rather peculiar nests I found on Basque Island June 12, 1929, were in elbows of deformed white spruce trees 5 feet from the ground. Both were slight affairs of twigs and dead grass wholly embedded in the mass of twigs and spruce needles that had accumulated in the hollows of the elbows, and were indistinguishable as nests except from above. One contained two fresh eggs, the other three partly incubated eggs.

P. B. Philipp (1925) describes two distinct types of nests on the Magdalens: "One, and that most commonly adopted, is on the ground, either in a wet bog or on a dry hillside, under a thick mossy spruce root or brush pile and usually in a very thick place. The other situation is in a spruce bush, usually at a low elevation, though I have seen nests fifteen feet from the ground. This latter type is, of course, the easiest to find. The year 1923 was particularly favorable for tracking down nesting pairs. It was a late, cold Spring, and even in the first week in June the snow lay deep in the bogs and woods, and this drove the birds off the ground and into the spruces * * *." He describes a typical nest, presumably a bush nest, as having an outer wall of spruce twigs and sphagnum moss with a considerable amount of dead wood chips and coarse grass, and plentifully lined with cow hair.

Most of the nests William J. Brown (1911–1912) found in southwestern Newfoundland were in stunted spruces 2 to 8 feet from the ground. One, however, was at the exceptional height of 20 feet from the ground and held three large young on June 10. In 1911 he found a few nests on the ground, but in 1912—a late season when snow conditions made ground nesting impractical—all were in trees. Mosses and rootlets were the principal materials used, with the addition of spruce twigs in tree nests, and a lining of caribou hair. An unusual nest wedged, creeper-fashion, between the loose bark and trunk of a large pine, held the exceptional number of five young June 8, 1912.

Although the species prefers conifers for nesting sites, it sometimes uses deciduous trees. Harold S. Peters and Thomas D. Burleigh (1951) describe a nest at Tompkins, Newfoundland, May 16, 1947 "built in a crotch of a lower limb in a large yellow birch, and about seven feet above the ground. The deeply cupped nest was constructed of shreds of bark, grasses and weed stems, and lined with fine black rootlets."

L. M. Tuck (MS.) says that all the nests he found in Newfoundland were on the ground, and adds "perhaps it is easier to come across ground nests." This suggests that acceptable cover is sometimes less dense in Newfoundland than I found it in Saguenay County and Philip B. Philipp (1925) did in the Magdalens. Most nests L. M. Tuck found were under small spruces and composed of green mosses lined with dried grasses and sometimes a few feathers. The earliest he found at Cornerbrook May 18, 1951, with three eggs was under an alder bush not yet in leaf, and built of dry alder leaves lined with grass and two white feathers. The latest nest with three eggs on Gull Island July 1, 1950 was under a black currant bush and built entirely of grasses.

Eggs.—The fox sparrow usually lays from 3 to 5 ovate and slightly glossy eggs. The ground color of freshly laid eggs is "pale Niagara green," but upon exposure this fades to a greenish white. They are boldly marked with spots, blotches, and cloudings of reddish browns such as "natal brown," "brownish olive," "Mars brown," "warm sepia," or "Brussels brown." The markings are generally heavier toward the large end, but there is considerable variation both in pattern and in intensity of coloring. They range from eggs with very small spots covering the entire surface to eggs showing considerable ground with large confluent blotches at the larger end. The measurements of 50 eggs of the nominate race average 22.7 by 16.3 millimeters; the eggs showing the four extremes measure *25.5* by *17.4*, *20.3* by 15.5, and 22.3 by *15.2* millimeters.

Young.—The incubation period has never been measured accurately; Edward H. Forbush (1929) gives it as "probably 12 to 14 days," and Oliver L. Austin, Jr. (1932) suggests "about 13 days."

From his observations in the Magdalen Islands, P. B. Philipp (1925) says the female does most of the incubating and that the young are fed by both parents, who keep the nest "scrupulously clean." He adds: "* * * by the time they leave the nest [they] are well feathered with the family russet-brown. * * * they stay around in a family party till they are quite well grown. I think many * * * raise two broods, as I have found nearly fresh eggs late in June, in situations where I am certain the first nesting was undisturbed."

In southwestern Newfoundland W. J. Brown (1911) found many young on the wing by the first of June, also several nests with young in various stages. The presence of several other nests toward the end of June with three to four eggs he thought suggested two broods.

Young seem to leave the nest somewhat later on the west coast of James Bay, where Thomas H. Manning and Andrew H. Macpherson (1952) saw the first juveniles on July 22. After that date about half the fox sparrows they recorded were young of the year. Between June 22 and July 3, 1925, F. Napier Smith and I saw many young at several points between Baie Johan Beetz and Havre St. Pierre on the north shore of the Gulf of St. Lawrence. All were out of the nest, some being fed by adults, others apparently no longer under parental care. The fact that many adult males were still in full song and that the only occupied nests we found contained fresh or nearly fresh eggs suggested that two broods are reared annually in this region. Nevertheless proof of fox sparrows rearing more than one brood annually is still lacking.

Plumages and molts.—The natal down of the fox sparrow apparently has never been described. Richard R. Graber (1955) describes the juvenal plumage as:

"Forehead, crown and nape uniform chestnut. Back rusty buff, streaked with dark chestnut. Rump and upper tail coverts hazel. Tail rich chestnut. Remiges blackish, edged with chestnut (tertials and coverts broadly edged). Median and greater coverts lightly tipped with buff. Lores and eye-ring buffy white. Side of head concolor with crown, but with small whitish patch behind auriculars. Chin whitish, just behind mandible, otherwise dusky red-brown. Throat white, spotted and streaked with dusky-tinged chestnut. Chest, sides, and flanks (less so) heavily streaked with dusky-tinged chestnut. Belly white, only sparsely marked. Crissum buffy white, obscurely streaked with rusty. Leg feathers uniform chestnut."

According to Dwight (1900) the first winter plumage is "acquired by a partial postjuvenal moult which involves the body plumage and wing coverts but not the rest of the wings nor the tail." He states the first nuptial plumage is "acquired by wear which produces slight changes. A few new feathers are usually acquired about the chin in March, * * * Adult winter plumage acquired by a complete postnuptial moult. Practically indistinguishable from first winter dress. Adult nuptial plumage acquired by wear as in the young bird. * * * The sexes are alike and the moults correspond although the females may average duller in colors."

Food.—Fox sparrows are essentially terrestrial feeders and scratch lustily for their food amongst fallen leaves. Using both feet in unison, they display such remarkable balance that Charles W. Townsend (1905) wonders "why they do not pitch forward on their heads when they spring back." Amelia S. Allen (1915) comments on species at her feeding tray in California: "The habit of scratching for its food seems to be so firmly fixed that it usually scratches among the crumbs before picking them up."

When not on the breeding grounds the fox sparrow is essentially a vegetarian. According to Sylvester D. Judd (1901) the stomachs from 127 birds taken principally in the eastern U.S. in every month except June, July, and August contained 86 percent vegetable and 14 percent animal matter. Judd adds "The vegetable food differs from that of most other sparrows in that it contains less grass seed (only 1 percent), less grain, and more fruit, ragweed, and *Polygonum.*

Half the food consists of ragweed and *Polygonum*." The birds do little if any damage to cultivated fruits, for most of the fruit seeds found, of blueberries, elderberries, blackberries, grapes, came from birds collected in March, April, and May, and were obviously from withered fruits of the previous year the birds picked up from the ground.

Many observers list the seeds of smartweed and other *Polygonums*, ragweed and other noxious weeds as a particular source of winter food. Judd found that they habitally cracked open the larger seeds before swallowing the kernels, thus destroying any possibility of future germination. When scratching for fallen seeds in the spring the birds naturally turn up numerous ground beetles (Carabidae) and the small, many-legged millipeds of the *Julus* group. Judd lists these two invertebrates as the most important animal food eaten in April, when they total about 30 percent of the food of migrants. The stomachs of two birds taken at Ottawa Apr. 24, 1908 (C. W. G. Eifrig, 1910) contained a preponderance of insects, mostly beetles, also remains of spiders and millipeds and some seeds of gromwell (*Lithospermum*). October birds George E. Atkinson (1894) shot in witch hazel thickets at Toronto had eaten witch hazel buds, beetles, firefly (Lampyridae) and cranefly (Tipulidae) larvae, spiders, millipeds, and seeds of hound's tongue (*Cynoglossum*); many had also ingested particles of sand, gravel, and slate. W. B. Barrows (1912) records a fox sparrow in Wisconsin that had eaten 50 chinch bugs (Lygaeidae).

Very little information is available on the food of the eastern fox sparrows in their summer haunts, but it is thought to be mostly insects. Certainly the young are fed almost entirely on animal food. J. J. Audubon (1841) says that in Newfoundland and southern Labrador "I have frequently seen them searching along the shores for minute shellfish on which they feed abundantly." Ludlow Griscom (1926) observed a different type of beachcombing on the west coast of Newfoundland: "Along the Straits of Belle Isle family parties hunt along the beach, and occasionally nibble the dead and drying fish that strew the ground around the villages."

Voice.—The music of the fox sparrow inspired William Brewster (1883) to write one of the first and best appreciations of it:

What the Mockingbird is to the South, the Meadow Lark to the plains of the West, the Robin and Song Sparrow to Massachusetts, and the White-throated Sparrow to northern New England, the Fox Sparrow is to the bleak regions bordering the Gulf of St. Lawrence. At all hours of the day, in every kind of weather late into the brief summer, its voice rises among the evergreen woods filling the air with quivering, delicious melody, which at length dies softly, mingling with the soughing of the wind in the spruces, or drowned by the muffled roar of the surf beating against neighboring cliffs. To my ear the prominent characteristic of its voice is richness. It expresses careless joy and exultant masculine vigor, rather than delicate shades of sentiment, and on this account is perhaps of a lower order than the pure, passionless hymn of the Hermit Thrush; but it is such a fervent, sensuous, and withal perfectly-rounded carol that it affects the ear much as sweetmeats do the palate, and for the moment renders all other bird music dull and uninteresting by comparison.

Contemporaneously C. J. Maynard (1882) describes the song as he heard it on the Magdalen Islands as follows: "Its magnificent song filled the clear still air with melody. These fine strains consist at first of three clear rather rapid notes, given with increasing emphasis, then a short pause ensues, and the remainder of the lay is poured forth more deliberately, terminating with a well rounded note giving finish to a sweet song, which for sweetness and clearness of tone is seldom surpassed even by our best performers."

S. D. Judd (1901) characterizes its singing as "utterly unsparrow-like, a unique performance that seems not in the least akin to bird music, but more like the soft tinkling of silver bells." Perhaps it is its human quality that makes it so appealing, for as Robert T. Moore (1913) notes, the fox sparrow "does not sing a note which a human being cannot whistle." Moore made a special trip to the Magdalen Islands in June and July of 1911 to hear the species sing on its nesting grounds, and the following excerpts are from his musicianly account of his experiences there:

To me the Fox Sparrow stands out as the singer of joy. Many birds are of this kind, but few are to such a degree as this inhabitant of the stunted woodlands of the North. The musical construction indicates it, for instance the dancing rhythm, the major keys, and the speed with which it fairly shoots through the central phrase. But deeper than these are certain qualities in his physical being and character, which make for happiness: his robustness and virility, his excessive activity in all his waking hours.

The song-sites of the Fox Sparrow are conditioned by his habitat. Wherever there are low evergreens massed in dense clumps * * * there he will be found. * * * out along their edges these sturdy finches are bound to be and will be heard at all times of the day, be it sunlit or foggy. Each individual has his own particular clump and one or more song-sites in that clump, so that it is possible to go out day after day and find the same songster and hear the same song. Sometimes his favorite tree is five feet high and sometimes twenty, ordinarily it is ten, and whatever its height, it is usually a spruce and is always on the edge of the clump * * *. His favorite song-position on the tree is its tip. A point a foot below may be chosen, but never the lower branches and by no means the ground.

The last place is the region of his nest and from there no sounds are issued except call-notes. These consist of two kinds quite different from each other and neither musical. The most common is an explosive aspirate, which may be indicated by the syllable "chech" and is as loud as the call of the Hermit Thrush. The second is a fine, high-pitched note, which closely resembles the call of the Savannah Sparrow. The former is heard much more frequently and in conjunction with the latter is employed to protest against intrusion near the nest.

* * * unlike the Song Sparrow, [each] Fox seems to have but one [song] and is content to repeat it over and over, making slight additions at the height of the

season or reducing it at the end note by note to its melodic skeleton. The song has certain fundamental characteristics which never change. First, the quality of tone is always round and full, like the sound of a clear flute-note. It is not rendered ambiguous by what Mr. Schuyler Matthews calls "blurred tones," on the other hand it is not enriched by those overtones, which make the notes of the Wood Thrush so ethereal. It is decidedly human without touch of heavenly rapture, just a clear full tone, which is precisely the best medium for a message of joy and the most invigorating imaginable.

Townsend and Allen (1907) give the following version of the species' songs and calls in Labrador:

The song seemed richer and fuller than the best song given by this species during the spring migration in Massachusetts. Its clear flute-like notes are somewhat ventriloquial in character, and as the bird sings generally from a concealed perch inside of a spruce or fir tree a foot or two from the top, it is often difficult to find the performer. We have written down the song very inadequately in words thus: *cher-ee, hear-her, hear-her, tellit.* Or *to-whip, to-whee, oh-whee buzz tellit,* the last note short and faint and the main stress on the second and third bars.

The long drawn call note *stssp* so commonly heard in Massachusetts during the migrations, was rarely heard in Labrador. A sharp *chip chip* was occasionally emitted, and the bird when disturbed sometimes gave the usual alarm note, a loud *smack,* richer than that of the Junco and more like that of the Brown Thrasher. One individual who was *smacking* in a fir tree emitted faint sneezy notes with motions of swallowing between the *smacks.*

As with most birds, time of day has a bearing on the quality of the song. During spring migration the fox sparrow is always in better voice towards evening. I sometimes hear the low-voiced "whisper" song from the shelter of the thick brush at midday, and from the same quarter towards sundown almost the full-throated nuptial song. The undertones of the whisper song are easily recognizable, vastly different from the whisper songs of the catbird and song sparrow, and with a plaintive quality reminiscent of the songs of the white-crowned and vesper sparrows.

Occasionally there are short periods of song-revival in the autumn after the postnuptial molt. Aretas A. Saunders (1948b) writes of the fox sparrow in southern Connecticut: "I have records of fall singing in this species for ten years, but usually only on one or two days in each year; and of intervening years in which the bird was often common but no song was to be heard." His earliest record was October 30, the latest November 23, and the average about November 13.

The two types of call mentioned by Robert T. Moore (above) are quite distinct. The first, a loud "tchek," suggests a little the alarm notes of the junco, but more nearly perhaps the loud "tchack" of the brown thrasher. Commonly used to express distress or alarm, it is heard when the bird is disturbed near the nest. It may also be heard in migration when the birds are disturbed in dense cover, and may be repeated several times when the birds are cornered beneath a canopy of low branches with no chance of escape to a higher perch.

When migrants are disturbed on the ground, they usually seek a higher perch 25 to 50 feet from the ground. There they utter the other call, a fine, high-pitched "tseep," a very feeble note indeed for such a robust and dignified-looking sparrow, which apparently acts as a rallying or location note.

A modified form of the alarm "tchek" serves as a communal call when migrating fox sparrows are going to roost, which they usually do in young, shrubby evergreens or sometimes in a deciduous hedge. At dusk on Nov. 2, 1947, we watched a small group fly into a shrubby pine on the edge of a wood. As the birds mounted slowly from branch to branch in the manner of white-thoats going to roost, one after another uttered a single modified "tchek," recalling again certain notes of the junco and the hermit thrush. Usually fox sparrows roost at night only a few feet above the ground in heavy cover.

Behavior.—Although the fox sparrow is generally regarded as a robust, vigorous bird that often sings best in stormy weather, most writers stress its inherent shyness. In southwestern Pennsylvania Thomas D. Burleigh (1923) considers it usually "wary and hard to approach and as it likes dense underbrush it would often be overlooked were it not for the disturbance it makes as it scratches vigorously in the dead leaves."

Fox sparrows get along amicably with one another as a rule, but occasionally become quarrelsome. Francis B. White (1937) writes of fox sparrows caught in an April blizzard in New Hampshire and feeding in the beds of brooks: "Though mingling amicably with other species then, they fight furiously among themselves, towering up several feet, emitting a peculiar note, shrill, prolonged—a kind of squeal. * * * On one occasion, two were watched facing each other on the snow and singing defiantly in alternating strains."

They are also inclined to be pugnacious when other species invade their territory. The first fox sparrow to come to our garden at Ulverton, Quebec, appeared late the afternoon of Apr. 26, 1956, and set up a temporary feeding territory in a leaf-covered wildflower patch adjoining a thick spruce hedge. At first it was rather diffident as it sortied from the shelter of the hedge to scratch among the dead leaves for millet seed fallen from a food tray, and doubtless some insect food. As it fed there intermittently the next few days, it lost much of its timidity. Whenever a newly-arrived white-throated sparrow tried to feed in the same area, the fox sparrow crouched low, slimmed its body, darted at the white-throat with lowered head and opened bill and forced it to retreat. It sang the "whisper" song many times in sunshine and rain from concealed perches in the hedge.

The only instances of anting behavior by the fox sparrow I can find were reported by H. R. Ivor (1941, 1943), who watched them do so in his aviary.

Field marks.—The fox sparrow is ruddier and considerably larger than any other sparrow in eastern North America, even the white-crowned, from which its heavily streaked breast, foxy red upperparts and bright rufous red tail distinguish it at a glance. When, as so frequently happens, one obtains only a fleeting glimpse of the bird disappearing in the forest undergrowth, he cannot be sure whether he has seen a fox sparrow or a hermit thrush. The hermit's tail is a similar foxy red, but seen well the olive-brown back, thinner bill, and spotted rather than streaked breast are readily diagnostic.

Enemies.—Thanks largely to the density of its nesting cover, the fox sparrow apparently does not suffer greatly from predation during the breeding season. Weasels and other mustelids probably get a few eggs and nestlings, though there are no records of nesting failures in the eastern race, within whose breeding range the cowbird does not occur.

Perhaps the greatest single factor inimical to fox sparrows is inclement weather during migration or on the wintering grounds. Freezing rain that forms a crust on the snow is particularly disastrous. Arthur T. Wayne (1910) gives the following graphic description of such a disaster in South Carolina:

> The great cold wave of February 13 and 14, 1899, destroyed millions of these birds. There was a tremendous migration of Fox Sparrows on Monday, the 13th, following the coast line of the mainland. They apparently came from the northeast, migrating in a southwesterly direction. Thousands tarried in my yard all day long and swarmed in the piazza, fowl-yard, and every place that would afford protection. They would scratch away the snow in order to find a bare place, singing—that is the stronger birds—the whole time, while their companions were freezing by the hundreds. When they were benumbed by the intense cold, Boat-tailed Grackles * * * and Red-winged Blackbirds * * * would peck them at the base of the skull, killing them and eating them. The stronger Fox Sparrows would also eat their dead companions. It was a most pathetic sight.

Sprunt and Chamberlain (1949) add: "There have been similar though smaller invasions of Charleston. A remarkable one occurred between January 13 and 18, 1912. Sprunt's notes for March, 1914, read: 'Hundreds forced into the city by this cold wave. Scores seen along the Battery all day of the 14th.' Astonished at the numbers of the birds, people attacked them with sticks and small boys had a field day. A smaller concentration was noted on January 25, 1922, during a sleet storm in Charleston."

William Brewster (1906) comments that in Cambridge, Mass., "They were exceptionally scarce for five or six years following the winter of 1894–95 when they perished by thousands, from cold and starvation, in the South Atlantic States, but they have increased rapidly during the past three or four seasons and are now nearly back to their normal numbers."

Ira N. Gabrielson (1952) notes the loss of birds on the north shore of the St. Lawrence in Saguenay County, Quebec, of which H. F. Lewis (MS.) also writes: "The spring of 1947 was notably backward, cold, and late. Great numbers of passerine migrants from the south, including many fox sparrows, perished on the north shore during April and May because they could not obtain sufficient food. I was not there during those months, but in June, after my arrival, the loss of small land birds was described to me by many residents, and the great reduction in the regional breeding population of such birds was impressive."

L. M. Tuck (MS.) describes losses during a heavy late fall of snow on the Avalon Peninsula in Newfoundland. "On April 14, 1955, fox sparrows were fairly numerous. The following day there was a heavy snowfall with strong easterly winds. We put out chicken feed near our camp and attracted hundreds. * * * We could not feed all of them, however, and a large number perished. Several days later we found similar evidence of high mortality between St. Brides and Cape St. Mary's, where we found 16 dead fox sparrows while walking at random some nine miles. It would seem that the snowstorm coincided with the peak arrival of the fox sparrows while they were still on the coast, and consequently there was a rather heavy mortality."

External parasites recorded from fox sparrows in the eastern United States include four species of lice (Mallophaga), two of mites, and two of ticks (Peters, 1936).

Fall and winter.—The fox sparrows start to leave their northern breeding grounds in late August or early September, and most have left Canada by mid-November, though a few occasionally winter in sheltered places, particularly near the coast. The literature shows plainly that the Mississippi Valley and the Atlantic coastal states are the principal flyways in fall as they are in spring, and the birds are less plentiful in the more central states. As W. E. C. Todd (1940) notes: "It does not range southward along the Appalachian Highlands as do many Canadian zone species."

The autumn flocks frequent much the same habitats as in spring, except that they feed more often in open weedy places instead of within thick cover. In the vicinity of New York Eugene P. Bicknell (*in* Chapman, 1912) writes: "On its return in the autumn it again becomes a common denizen of hedgerows and thickets, and also invades the weedy grainfields, rarely, however, straying far from some thickety cover. Sometimes large numbers congregate among withered growths of tall weeds, whence they emerge with a loud whirring of wings as their retreat is invaded, and hie away in tawny clouds, flock after flock."

Norman A. Wood (1911) records an unusual feeding place on the Charity Islands in Saginaw Bay, Mich.: "This bird was first seen on September 25, and on this date numbers were seen about the pond, where they were feeding on the mud flats exposed by the low water. When alarmed, they flew into the thick willow and rose bushes at the edge of the pond. This was a favorite resort, and most of the birds seen at this time were near this habitat, although it was later seen nearly everywhere on the island, except on the open beaches. It was last seen on October 6, when a single bird was observed. The species appeared to migrate alone."

The eastern fox sparrow normally winters southward to central Georgia and northern Alabama and Mississippi, though unusually cold winters sporadically force it farther south. T. D. Burleigh (1942) relates how the species suddenly appeared in coastal Mississippi in unusual numbers during an unprecedented cold wave in January, 1940. The birds were first seen there January 4 and within a few days were actually plentiful. As no snow fell along the coast, the birds were able to obtain their normal food without trouble, and appeared to escape entirely the mortality experienced in more northerly sections where prolonged cold was followed by snow and freezing rain.

Distribution

Range.—Northeastern Manitoba, Ontario, Quebec, and northern Labrador south to southern Mississippi, Alabama, and central Florida.

Breeding range.—The eastern fox sparrow breeds from northeastern Manitoba (York Factory), northern Ontario (Fort Severn), northern Quebec (Richmond Gulf), and northern Labrador (Nachvak) south to north-central Ontario (Favourable Lake, Moose Factory), southeastern Quebec (Basque Island; Magdalen Islands), northwestern New Brunswick (Summit Depot), and southern Newfoundland.

Winter range.—Winters from southern Wisconsin (Hartland), southern Michigan (Ann Arbor; rarely Manistique in northern Michigan), southern Ontario (rarely; Reaboro, Ottawa), northern Vermont, Maine (York and Cumberland counties), and southern New Brunswick (Fredericton) south to southern Mississippi (Deer Island), Alabama (Montgomery County), and central Florida (Pensacola, Kissimmee); casually to Colorado (Denver) and southern Florida (Punta Rassa).

Casual records.—Accidental in Bermuda, Greenland (Sukkertoppen), Iceland, Germany (Mellum Island), and Italy (Genoa).

Migration.—The data deal with the species as a whole. Early date of spring arrival are: District of Columbia—average of 33 years, March 3. Maryland—Laurel, January 23 (median of 6 years, February 15); Baltimore County, January 26. Pennsylvania—Pittsburgh, February 29; State College, March 1 (average, March 25). New Jersey—Cape May, March 5. New York—New York City, February 18; Chatauqua County, March 20. Connecticut—New Haven. February 25. Massachusetts—Martha's Vineyard, March 4. New Hampshire—New Hampton, March 11 (median of 21 years, March 30). Maine—Bangor, April 1. Quebec—Montreal area, March 24 (median of 37 years, April 14). New Brunswick—Fredericton, March 21; Kent Island, March 24. Newfoundland, March 10–April 8. Kentucky—Bowling Green, February 12. Illinois—Urbana, February 13 (median of 20 years, March 1); Chicago, March 11 (average of 16 years, March 24). Indiana—Wayne County, March 10 (median of 11 years, March 21). Ohio—central Ohio—March 1 (median of 40 years, March 13). Michigan—Detroit area, March 18 (mean of 10 years, March 22); Battle Creek, March 24 (median of 18 years, April 7). Ontario—London, March 24. Iowa—Scott County, March 12; Sioux City, March 22. Wisconsin—Racine, March 17. Minnesota—Minneapolis–St. Paul, March 12 (average of 10 years, March 25). Nebraska—Dunbar, March 4. South Dakota—Sioux Falls, April 11. North Dakota—Berlin and Harwood Township, March 25; Cass County, March 25 (average, April 2). Manitoba—Treesbank, April 9 (average of 21 years, April 19). Saskatchewan—Indian Head, March 29. Mackenzie—Fort Simpson, May 1. Colorado—Durango, April 24. Wyoming—Fort Bridger, April 14. Idaho—Moscow, March 8 (median of 11 years, March 31). Montana—Great Falls, March 7; Libby, March 16 (median of 10 years, April 1). Oregon—Malheur Refuge, April 1. Washington—Bellingham, March 1; Seabeck, March 24. British Columbia—Sumas, April 22; Atlin, April 27. Yukon—Sheldon Lake, May 4. Alaska—Wrangell Island, April 22.

Late dates of spring departure are: Florida—Tallahassee, March 16; Pensacola, February 17. Alabama—Wheeler Refuge, April 7; Gadsden, April 6; Jackson, March 29. Georgia—Atlanta, April 2. South Carolina—Clemson, March 29 (median of 6 years, March 12). North Carolina—Chapel Hill, April 7; Raleigh, April 6 (average of 9 years, March 15). Virginia—Shenandoah National Park, April 16. District of Columbia—May 11 (average of 27 years, April 6). Maryland—Montgomery County, May 8; Frederick County, May 6. Pennsylvania—Renovo, May 16; State College, April 25 (average, April 15). New Jersey—Troy Meadows, May 11. New York—Madison County, May 10; Long Island, May 9. Connecticut—Portland, April 26; Concord, May 4. Massachusetts—Martha's

Vineyard (median of 3 years, April 4). New Hampshire—New Hampton, May 2 (median of 21 years, April 20); Concord, April 28. Maine—Bangor, May 2. Quebec—Montreal, May 19 (average of 37 years, April 29). New Brunswick—Scotch Lake, May 8. Louisiana—Baton Rouge, March 19. Mississippi—Rosedale, March 25; Gulfport, February 24. Arkansas—Fayetteville, April 9. Tennessee—Athens, April 18; Knox County, March 21 (median of 11 years, March 25). Kentucky—Bowling Green, April 15. Missouri—St. Louis, May 10 (median of 12 years, April 20). Illinois—Chicago, May 25 (average of 16 years, April 22); Urbana, April 29 (median of 20 years, April 15). Indiana—Wayne County, April 22 (median of 11 years, March 16). Ohio—central Ohio, May 20 (median of 40 years, April 23). Michigan—Detroit area, May 15 (median of 10 years, May 10). Ontario—Toronto, May 10. Iowa—Sioux City, April 24; Scott County, April 23. Wisconsin—Green Bay, May 22. Minnesota—Minneapolis-St. Paul, May 19 (average of 5 years, April 23). Texas—Austin, March 27; Sinton, February 16. Oklahoma—Payne County, April 4; Woods County, March 30. Kansas—northeastern Kansas, April 19. South Dakota—Sioux Falls, May 7. North Dakota—Berlin and Harwood Township, May 2. Manitoba—Treesbank, April 27. Saskatchewan—Indian Head, April 4. Arizona—Kofa Mountain, May 15. Wyoming—Albany County, May 6. Idaho—Moscow, May 28. California—Mt. Hamilton, May 4; Nicasio, April 29. Nevada—Lahontan Valley, April 23. Oregon—Willamette Valley, April 30. Washington—Everson, April 27. British Columbia—Westport, May 7.

Early dates of fall arrival are: Washington—Point Chehalis, September 8; Glacier, September 11. Oregon—Willamette Valley, September 23. Nevada—Carson City, August 12. California—Berkeley, September 8; Death Valley, September 9; Palo Alto, September 16. Montana—Fort Custer, October 8. Wyoming—Laramie, September 30. Arizona—Hoover Dam, August 29. New Mexico—Clayton, October 8. Saskatchewan—Davidson, September 15. Manitoba—Treesbank, September 12 (average of 11 years, September 23); Winnipeg, September 14. North Dakota—Bismarck, September 11; Berlin and Harwood Township, September 16. South Dakota—Sioux Falls, September 24; Milbank, October 1. Kansas—Kansas City, September 29. Oklahoma—Cleveland County and Norman, October 18. Texas—Dallas, October 6; Tyler, October 18. Minnesota—Hennepin County, September 14; Minneapolis-St. Paul, September 16 (average of 9 years, September 25). Wisconsin—Mishicot, September 18; Chippewa County, September 19. Iowa—Dubuque, September 18; Scott County, September 25. Ontario—North Bay, September 13. Michigan—Detroit area, September 19 (mean of 10 years, September 26). Ohio—Painesville, September 3; central Ohio, September 21 (median of 40 years, October 12). Indiana—Chesterton, September 26; Wayne County, October 10 (median of 12 years, October 22). Illinois—Chicago Region, September 9 (average of 16 years for Chicago, September 23). Missouri—St. Louis, September 26. Kentucky—Bowling Green, October 13. Tennessee—Nashville, October 14; Chattanooga, October 20. Arkansas—Fayetteville, October 18. Mississippi—Rosedale, October 11 (mean of 12 years, October 17). Louisiana—Baton Rouge, November 14. New Brunswick—St. John, September 20. Quebec—Saint-Bruno, September 20; Montreal, September 23 (average of 37 years, October 14). Maine—Lake Umbagog, September 30. New Hampshire—New Hampton, October 5 (median of 21 years, October 20); Concord, October 12. Vermont—Topsham, October 13. Massachusetts—Cambridge, October 1; Martha's Vineyard, October 4 (median of 7 years, October 6). Rhode Island—Newport, October 13. Connecticut—New Haven, September 16; Terryville, October 2. New York—Essex County, September 10; Bronx County, September 30. New Jersey—Brielle, October 10. Pennsylvania—Unity, September 7; Carnegie, September 28. Maryland—Denton, October 7; Laurel, October 8 (median of 7 years, October 19). District of Columbia—October 3 (average of 23 years, October 28). Virginia—Shenandoah National Park, Octoberl 8. North Carolina—Raleigh, October 17 (average of 11 years, November 15); Asheville, October 26. South Carolina—Eastover, November 8. Georgia—Athens, October 22. Alabama—Huntsville, October 24; Gadsden, October 31. Florida—Amelia Island, November 13; Gainesville, November 30.

Late dates of fall departure are: Alaska—Nushagak, October 22. Yukon—Macmillan Pass, September 7. British Columbia—Chilliwack, October 5; Sicamous, September 25. Washington—Ridgefield, October 11. Montana—Choteau, October 29. Idaho—Moscow, October 8 (median of 11 years, September 30). Colorado—Clear Creek district, November 11. Mackenzie—Fort Simpson, September 17. Saskatchewan—Indian Head, October 15. Manitoba—Winnipeg, November 6; Treesbank, November 3 (average of 8 years, October 9). North Dakota—Cass County, October 28 (average, October 18); Berlin and Harwood Townships, October 18. Minnesota—Bloomington, November 25; Minneapolis-St. Paul, November 20 (average of 10 years, November 9). Wisconsin—Dane County, November 24. Iowa—Scott County, November 25; Sioux City, November 5. Ontario—Ottawa, November 17. Michigan—Detroit area, December 21 (mean of 10 years, November 21); Battle Creek, November 12 (median of 13 years, October 26). Ohio—

central Ohio, November 28 (median of 40 years, November 14). Indiana—Lafayette, November 27; Wayne County, November 21 (median of 9 years, November 15). Illinois—Chicago, November 20 (average of 16 years, November 5). Kentucky—Bowling Green, November 10. Tennessee—Nashville, November 26 (median of 11 years, October 27). Mississippi—Rosedale, November 17. Prince Edward Island—Murray Harbour, October 5. New Brunswick—Fredericton, November 25. Maine—York County, December 8; Brewer, December 5. Quebec—Quebec, November 4; Montreal, November 30 (average of 37 years, October 29). New Hampshire—New Hampton, December 12 (median of 21 years, November 14); Concord, December 2. Massachusetts—Springfield, December 13. Connecticut—Danbury, December 5; New Haven, November 30. New York—Madison County, December 3; Cayuga and Oneida Lake Basins, November 30 (average of 18 years, November 3). New Jersey—Cape May, December 2. Pennsylvania—Pittsburgh and State College, November 23 (average, November 20). Maryland—Baltimore County, December 16; Allegany County, December 8. District of Columbia—average of 15 years, November 21.

Egg dates—Newfoundland: 117 records, May 8 to July 12; 94 records May 18 to June 12.

Ontario: 1 record, July 17.

Quebec: 9 records, June 2 to June 4.

PASSERELLA ILIACA ZABORIA Oberholser

Yukon Fox Sparrow

Contributed by OLIVER L. AUSTIN, JR.

HABITS

This subspecies differs from the nominate eastern race, from which it was split less than 20 years ago, mainly in being somewhat grayer, particularly on the head, and in having the streakings of the underparts less rufous and more sooty. Gabrielson and Lincoln (1959) state "This race never appears to be abundant, although it is a widely distributed summer resident * * * from Kotzebue Sound and the Colville River south to the Alaska Range. In this great region it is found as a brush bird which is adept at getting away from an observer."

Lee R. Dice (1920) gives its habitat in Alaska as "chiefly in the white spruces, paper birches, and willows along the streams, though one was noted in song in black spruces several hundred yards from other types of forest." Edward W. Nelson (1887) found the species near St. Michael's "sharing with the Tree-sparrows the bushy shelter of the alder thickets on hillsides and sheltered ravines" and noted it could be found "wherever a fair-sized alder patch occurs." John Q. Hines (1963) also noted "Fox Sparrows were commonly associated with alders and willows within the spruce forest" on the Noatak River. Joseph Grinnell (1900) in the same area found them "quite common up to the 23rd of August, when they abruptly disappeared. Until the day of their departure, their clear ringing songs were to be heard almost every hour of the day." Alfred M. Bailey (1948) states that in the Kotzebue Sound area they "wander far out on the tundra."

In the Mackenzie region Edward A. Preble (1908) writes: "its sweet song may be heard from the alder and willow thickets from the time of the bird's coming, though often a late snowstorm whitens its haunts." Thomas H. Manning (1948) notes that in northern Manitoba fox sparrows "favored the same habitats as Harris' sparrows, but differed greatly in behaviour. The latter are bold and perky and delight in showing off, while the fox sparrow quietly glides from one hidden perch to another."

Herbert Brandt (1943) describes a nest found on the slopes of the Askinuk Range: "The structure was supported by a much-divided willow crotch about a foot above the ground, and entirely lacked the concealment of the nests of many of the other bush-loving species which so tantalizes the ornithologist. The nest was strong and somewhat bulky, and had for its foundation numerous small twigs, but its real structure was composed mainly of ripe grass with some reindeer moss; while the well-molded interior was lined with finer grass and a little true moss." A nest J. W. Bee (1958) found near Umiat June 30, 1952, "the top of which was flush with the ground in a clearing among willows and alders, both bare of leaves, had four young approximately five days old." Preble (1908) found a nest on the Mackenzie June 23 that " * * * contained three eggs almost ready to hatch. It was built on dry ground on the border of a swamp and outwardly was composed of grass, moss, and strips of bark, and was lined with fine grass and dog's hair."

Gabrielson and Lincoln (1959) venture: "The period of incubation is the 12 to 14 days that is common among sparrows of this type, and the young usually remain in the nest a somewhat shorter period."

The same authors say: "The song—one of the most beautiful of sparrow songs—is a clear, loud, canary-like warble, which is difficult to describe but is easily remembered when once heard. As a songster it is conspicuous, usually choosing as a singing perch a twig that is well up in the bushes, the topmost part of a small tree, or on a conspicuous dead branch." Nelson (1887) states the males sing "*pew-e-e-dudy-jew*" from the roof of the highest building. Dice (1920) transliterates the song as "a trilled *Ee-chee weer-r-r-a-chr-r-r-ree.* The call note is a sharp *tchip.*" John Q. Hines (1963) comments: "Fledglings were observed in early July when males were still singing, although at a reduced level."

Gabrielson and Lincoln (1959) continue:

In their natural habitat, Fox Sparrows are seldom seen in long flights, usually ducking from one brush patch to another when disturbed and flying close to the ground vegetation. They fly with a nervous, jerky, fliting [sic] of the tail although this is not as marked as it is among the Song Sparrows.

Since it is a bird of the thickets, it is not surprising to find that such animal food as it takes consists of millipeds, beetles, and other insects found in such habitat. Otherwise its food consists largely of weed seeds and fruits. Although little is known about its feeding habits in Alaska, it can be expected that the usual berries and seeds of plants found in and close to the alder and willow thickets will furnish a large part of the food.

Grinnell and Miller (1944) state that on its wintering ground in California this race inhabits "Chaparral and tangles of low vegetation along stream courses; not known to differ importantly from habitat of other winter-visitant Fox Sparrows in the State."

Distribution

Range.—Northwestern Alaksa, northern Yukon, Mackenzie and northern Manitoba south to southern Texas, the Gulf coast, and northern Georgia.

Breeding range.—The Yukon fox sparrow breeds from northwestern and central northern Alaska (Utukok, Colville, and Porcupine rivers), northern Yukon (Old Crow, La Pierre House), northwestern and central eastern Mackenzie (Mackenzie Delta, Artillery Lake), and northern Manitoba (Churchill) south to northern British Columbia (Atlin, Tupper Creek), central Alberta (Red Deer), central Saskatchewan (Nipawin), and southern Manitoba (Duck Mountain).

Winter range.—Winters chiefly east of the Great Plains from eastern Kansas (Manhattan; Douglas County) and southern Iowa (Polk County) south to southern Texas (Laredo, San Antonio, Cove), Louisiana (Natchitoches, New Orleans), Mississippi (Gulfport, Biloxi), Alabama (Woodville), and northern Georgia (Roswell, Athens); rarely east to Virginia (Mt. Vernon, Alexandria), and west to Washington (Renton, Whitman County), central and southern California (San Geronimo, Pasadena), southern Arizona (Huachuca Mountains), and Colorado (Denver).

Casual records.—Casual on the Arctic coast of Alaska (Wainwright, Barrow area).

Egg dates.—Alaska: 40 records, May 3 to July 11; 22 records, May 27 to June 11.

Mackenzie: 10 records, June 1 to June 22.

PASSERELLA ILIACA ALTIVAGANS Riley

Alberta Fox Sparrow

Contributed by Oliver L. Austin, Jr.

Habits

The Alberta fox sparrow is not quite so red as the Yukon fox sparrow, with which it intergrades where their ranges meet, and it has the back practically unstreaked.

According to Joseph H. Riley (1912) this bird is found in summer "around the small dense clumps of stunted spruces that grow in the protected hollows above timber line." Harry S. Swarth (1924) found it associating with golden-crowned sparrows in tangles of alder and veratrum a little above timber line on Nine-mile Mountain, British Columbia, where, though it was "constantly heard singing," it was "so shy generally as to avoid observation." He found young birds "in process of change from juvenal to first winter plumage" flying about in the Skeena River region from July 22 to August 13. Writing from the Alta Lake region of British Columbia, Kenneth Racey (1926) notes: "The wonderful song of these birds is extremely sweet and in the mornings we could hear it regularly from the clumps of stunted fir trees in every direction."

On its California wintering grounds Joseph Grinnell and Alden H. Miller (1944) call it "Fairly common" and describe its habitat as "Chaparral-covered slopes, typically those of interior, semiarid areas; in winter stays below levels of heavy snow, where ground foraging activity may be carried on in the leaf litter."

Distribution

Range.—Central British Columbia and southwestern Alberta to northwestern Baja California.

Breeding range.—The Alberta fox sparrow breeds from interior central British Columbia (Thutade Lake) southeast to mountains of southeastern British Columbia (Mosher Creek, Mount Revelstoke) and Southwestern Alberta (head of Smoky River; Banff, intergrades with *P. i. schistacea*).

Winter range.—Winters chiefly in foothills of Cascade Mountains and Sierra Nevada in California (Paine Creek, El Portal), in coastal southern California (Yucaipa, Flinn Springs, San Clemente Island), and in northwestern Baja California (Santo Domingo, La Grulla); occasionally north to northwestern Oregon (Government Island) and east to southeastern Arizona (Huachuca Mountains).

Casual record.—Casual in Manitoba (Deer Lodge).

Egg dates.—British Columbia: 9 records, May 14 to June 26.

PASSERELLA ILIACA (Merrem)

Fox Sparrow: Northwestern Coastal Subspecies*

Contributed by OLIVER L. AUSTIN, JR.

HABITS

The six northwestern coastal subspecies are readily told from the other fox sparrow races by their sooty coloration and uniformly brown backs and tails. Their bills decrease in size and their coloring darkens from northwest to southeast in an almost perfect cline. Adjoining races intergrade wherever their ranges meet, and the differences between some forms are so slight that the practicality of such fine splitting is sometimes questioned. For instance George Willett (1933) states his "personal feeling is that we are attempting to recognize too many races of *Passerella* and that the situation might be greatly clarified by uniting some of the most closely allied forms." He suggests that uniting *insularis* and *sinuosa* with *unalaschcensis* "would greatly simplify the classification of the group."

In the same vein Gabrielson and Lincoln (1959) state: "It is not possible, however, to accurately identify [the Alaskan subspecies] in the field except as Fox Sparrows. All are large sparrows with dark brown or grayish brown backs with very heavily streaked underparts. * * * none of them save the bird of the interior [*P. i. zaboria*] can be named subspecifically on the basis of field identification. This one, however, is so distinctly colored that it can be identified in the field."

The same authors continue:

> During the breeding season in southeastern Alaska, it is one of the rather difficult birds to see because, in the heavy brush, it is a master at hiding except when occupying the song perch which it quickly leaves when disturbed. Unless a bird desires to leave a patch of brush, it is almost impossible to drive it out, as it runs about on the ground or through the lower branches almost like a mouse. The same is largely true of the Fox Sparrows found at Yakutat Bay. Farther to the west, however, the birds are more easily observed, due partly to the fact that there is less brush in which they may hide. Fox Sparrows are exceedingly common on the islands in Prince William Sound and they are not too difficult to find in the more heavily wooded sections of the Kenai Peninsula which is a major part of their breeding range. On Kodiak and west of that island, they are relatively easy to observe. In fact, Gabrielson has never found Fox Sparrows as easily seen or collected as those on Kodiak and the smaller islands to the west.

T. H. Bean (1882) found *unalaschcensis* on Little Kornushi Island in company with snow buntings and pipits on top of a ridge 1,200 feet above sea level. Grinnell (1910) records *sinuosa* as the most

*The following subspecies are discussed in this section: *Passerella iliaca unalaschcensis* (Gmelin), *P. i. insularis* Ridgway, *P. i. sinuosa* Grinnell, *P. i. annectens* Ridgway, *P. i. townsendi* (Audubon), and *P. i. fuliginosa* Ridgway.

abundant and widely distributed land bird at Knight Island, Prince William Sound, found from the beach to the timberline, but mostly in deciduous thickets. R. Rausch (1958) says that on Middleton Island in the same area,

> Next to the Savannah Sparrow, the Fox Sparrow was the most numerous passeriform bird on the island. It was closely restricted to the zone of high shrubs and its borders. Although generally shy, the birds often could be called in. The males sang from the tops of the higher willows, or from the high stalks of *Rubus spectabilis* along the upper bluff. * * * Fox Sparrows were often observed * * * along the edge of the bluff where the vegetation was contiguous with the dense growth on the side of the bluff. Farther south, near the beginning of the sea cliff, Fox Sparrows were common in a relatively wide zone of vegetation. Foraging and singing were observed here, but there was no evidence of nesting.

George Willett (1914) noted that *townsendi* was partial to the smaller grass and brush-covered islands in the vicinity of Sitka. He (1915) characterizes it as the most abundant land bird on Forrester Island, found "in wooded localities everywhere. Seemingly at least two broods are raised in a season. The location of the nests noted varied greatly, some being ten or twelve feet up in trees, some in brush thickets and on fallen logs and others on the ground. A brood of young left a nest near camp May 24 and fresh eggs were found as late as June 22." Here Harold Heath (1915) states: "This species of sparrow was the most abundant land bird in the region, being found from one end of Forrester Island to the other as well as on Lawrie and South islands. It was especially numerous in the vicinity of the camp where it fed at the boxes several of the fishermen provided for their feathered friends. Nests were also plentiful, principally in the roots of stumps and in crevices of the rocky cliffs. Judging from three pairs close to the tent, two broods are raised each year."

A. M. Bailey (1927) encountered the first ones in Hooniah Sound May 7 to 24,

> when from one to ten were seen daily. They were especially fond of the little mountain streams, where they fed in the dense tangle of undergrowth. They had become common at Juneau by May 26, and June 12 to 20, they were seen along the wooded mainland shores of Glacier Bay and on the beach of the outer Beardslee Island. * * * We found a nest on July 10 with four eggs apparently well incubated; another nest with four small young was seen July 19. They nest somewhat as do the Juncos, hiding their nest in the moss on some little slope, or under a log, or along a boulder; their nests are neatly made, and usually well concealed, the parent bird taking pains to slip away without attractng attention.

Grinnell (1909) describes a nest of *townsendi* from Admiralty Island as "a bulky structure 120 mm. high by 160 mm. across, the walls being very thick. The inner cavity is 70 mm. across by 50 deep. The main part of the nest is a matted mass of dead twigs, leaves, moss, and weathered grasses, and the lining is of finely frayed-out grasses mixed with duck feathers." He (1910) describes a nest of *sinuosa* found on Montague Island as "composed externally of a mixture of green moss, skeletonized leaves and coarse grasses, while in strong contrast there is internally a thick lining of fine, round grass stems."

Swarth (1912b) found *fuliginosa* on Vancouver Island on bush-covered slopes and in willow thickets along the creek bottoms, but not in the dense forests below. "They were very shy, and clung to the thickets of dense underbrush, so that is was difficult to get sight of one. Singing birds were usually perched on a projecting branch, about the center of an impenetrable thicket of salmonberry or alder into which they plunged at the first intimation of danger."

The migration of this group of birds has interesting aspects. As Swarth (1920) points out, they "* * * move directly southward along the Pacific coast, each [subspecies] into a more or less definitely circumscribed winter habitat. * * * The subspecies breeding at the northern extreme, *unalaschcensis*, *insularis*, and *sinuosa*, move the farthest south in winter, passing completely over both summer and winter habitats of *annectens*, *townsendi*, and *fuliginosa*, and reaching the extreme southern limits of California."

In his review of Swarth's 1920 opus, Percy A. Taverner (1921) comments:

Another important point brought out is that the birds breeding in the most humid climates are not the darkest or the largest of the species. *Unalaschcensis*, summering in the extremely moist Alaskan Peninsula, does not reach the extreme development of size or depth of color that is attained by *fuliginosa*, resident on the comparatively dry Vancouver Island region. This perplexing fact that would otherwise seriously shake one of our most cherished ecological principles * is explained by the fact that the northern race spends its winter in arid southern California, and probably experiences a much lower annual average moisture than does the darker and larger race. It is thus brought forcibly to our notice that, in studying the relationship between the bird and its environment, winter ranges and probably migrational routes should also be taken into consideration.

Grinnell and Miller (1944) describe the winter habitats of these subspecies in California as follows:

P. i. unalaschcensis: Chaparral, principally of "hard" or arid type. The ground litter beneath the screening cover of the chaparral plants is searched over and scratched through in foraging in a fashion typical of all winter visitant races of Fox Sparrows.

P. i. insularis: Chaparral areas, but apparently on the average of somewhat less arid type than those frequented by the races *P. i. altivagans* and *P. i. unalaschcensis*.

---

*Gloger's Rule, that dark pigments increase with environmental humidity.

P. i. sinuosa: A wide variety of chaparral cover or underbrush of forest and woodland is occupied, but preference is shown for inland areas and hence the majority of the birds occupy semi-arid chaparral of lower mountain slopes.

P. i. meruloides [*annectens*]*:* Chaparral and underbrush of forest and woodland, normally, in view of concentration of population near coast, of fairly moist character. Thimble-berry, poison oak, nine-bark, ceanothus and baccharis are frequent components of the plant cover. The forage beat is accordingly well shaded and the leaf litter in which the birds forage is wet and soft through much of the winter season when the birds are present.

P. i. townsendi: Typically, heavy forest undergrowth and tall dense chaparral in burned-over forest areas. The ground where activity centers is usually heavily shaded, moist, and well covered with soft leaf litter. Illumination of twilight intensity prevails throughout most of the day in the winter season in the habitat of this Fox Sparrow.

P. i. fuliginosa: Heavy coastal chaparral and forest undergrowth, typified by moist, weakly insulated thickets of thimble-berry, ceanothus, and salal. Through the damp, poorly-lighted alleyways beneath the bushes these birds move in search for food by the characteristic scratching method of this species. Concentration of birds in the bush tops at a source of disturbance suggests flocking, but merely because of close spacing of individuals; actually each Fox Sparrow moves independently along its forage beat on the ground and to some degree defends it against competing members of the species.

Distribution

Shumagin Fox Sparrow (*P. i. unalaschcensis*)

Range.—Eastern Aleutian Islands and Alaska Peninsula to coastal California.

Breeding range.—The Shumagin fox sparrow breeds on the eastern Aleutian Islands (west to Unalaska), the Shumagin and Semidi islands, and the Alaska Peninsula (east to the Katmai area).

Winter range.—Winters from southwestern British Columbia (Departure Bay, Vancouver) south through western Washington and western Oregon to California (Helena, Paine Creek, Escondido; Santa Catalina and San Clemente islands); rarely to northwestern Baja California (La Grulla).

Casual records.—Casual north to Pribilof Islands (St. Paul), Nunivak Island, and Point Barrow, Alaska. Accidental (apparently this race) in eastern Siberia (on Tshukotka, north of Anadyr).

Kodiak Fox Sparrow (*P. i. insularis*)

Range.—Kodiak Islands. Alaska, to coastal California.

Breeding range.—The Kodiak fox sparrow breeds in the Kodiak Island group, southern Alaska.

Winter range.—Winters chiefly in coastal districts of central and southern California (Lakeport, San Geronimo, Santa Monica Mountains, Catalina Island); less commonly from southwestern British

Columbia (Vancouver) south to interior California (Alta, Volcan Mountains).

Casual records.—Accidental in Japan (Honshu).

Valdez Fox Sparrow (*P. i. sinuosa*)

Range.—Kenai Peninsula and Prince William Sound, Alaska, to northwestern Baja California.

Breeding range.—The Valdez fox sparrow breeds in the Kenai Peninsula (Seldovia, Kenai Lake) and Prince William Sound districts (25 miles north of Valdez, Cordova) and on Middleton Island, south-central Alaska.

Winter range.—Winters from southwestern British Columbia (Departure Bay, Chilliwack) south through western Washington, western Oregon, and California (Cascade Range and Sierra Nevada westward; Santa Cruz, Santa Barbara, and Santa Catalina islands) to northwestern Baja California (10 miles south of Alamo).

Casual records.—Casual on the Pribilof Islands (St. Paul) and in Idaho (Moscow).

Yakutat Fox Sparrow (*P. i. annectens*)

Range.—Yakutat Bay, southern Alaska, to coastal California.

Breeding range.—The Yakutat fox sparrow breeds in the vicinity of Yakutat Bay (north shore of Yakutat Bay, Cross Sound), southern Alaska.

Winter range.—Winters chiefly in central coastal California; less commonly from southwestern British Columbia (Comox, Vancouver) to central interior and southern California (Pasadena, Upland).

Townsend's Fox Sparrow (*P. i. townsendi*)

Range.—Southeastern Alaska (chiefly on islands) to central coastal California.

Breeding range.—The Townsend's fox sparrow breeds in southeastern Alaska from Glacier Bay and Lynn Canal south through the Alexander Archipelago to the Queen Charlotte Islands, British Columbia; also on the adjoining Alaskan mainland north of the Stikine River.

Winter range.—Winters from southeastern Alaska (Craig, irregularly) and southern coastal British Columbia (Comox, Victoria, Chilliwack) south through western Washington and western Oregon to coastal northern and central California (Willow Creek, Somersville, Santa Cruz).

Casual records.—Casual in southeastern Arizona (Chiricahua Mountains).

Sooty Fox Sparrow (*P. i. fuliginosa*)

Range.—Southeastern Alaska (mainland) to central coastal California.

Breeding range.—The sooty fox sparrow breeds from the mainland coast of southeastern Alaska (south from the mouth of the Stikine River) and the coastal districts of British Columbia, exclusive of the Queen Charlotte Islands, south to northwestern Washington (Destruction Island, Lopez Island).

Winter range.—Winters from southeastern British Columbia (Comox, Vancouver) south in coastal areas to central coastal California (Palo Colorado Creek, Morro); casually to interior and southern California (Manzanita Lake, Los Angeles, San Antonio Canyon).

PASSERELLA ILIACA (Merrem)

Fox Sparrow: Western Mountain Subspecies*

Contributed by Oliver L. Austin, Jr.

Habits

In these nine races the tail is at least (rarely) equal to and usually longer than the wing. Grays predominate in their coloration, increasingly so from north to south, and the rather pale uniform gray head and back contrasts with the dull reddish-brown wings and tail. The spots and streaks of the underparts are dull. The bill is large and somewhat swollen, increasingly so from east to west in the California forms. As noted elsewhere, many of these subspecies are weakly differentiated from one another, and identifying specimens taken away from the breeding grounds is a task for the expert with good series of breeding material at hand for comparison.

In Oregon Charles E. Bendire (1889) found that *schistacea* seems "to prefer the willows and rose thickets along the streams in the more open country, but is generally most abundant close to the foot-hills of the mountains." In Montana Aretas A. Saunders (1911) found the same race prefers "the thickest and most impenetrable" willow thickets in the valleys. In northern Nevada Walter P. Taylor (1912) reports them common in the Transition life zone, especially on "rocky slopes, covered with chinquapin and quaking aspen thickets, with a sparse intersprinkling of mountain mahogany and timber pine." He also found them with white-crowned sparrows and

---

*The following subspecies are discussed in this section: *Passerella iliaca schistacea* Baird, *P. i. olivacea* Aldrich, *P. i. swarthi* Behle and Selander, *P. i. canescens* Swarth, *P. i. fulva* Swarth, *P. i. megarhyncha* Baird, *P. i. brevicauda* Mailliard, *P. i. monoensis* Grinnell and Storer, and *P. i. stephensi* Anthony.

Macgillivray warblers in the vegetation about springs in the mountain meadows.

Stanley G. Jewett et al. (1953) state that in Washington the race *olivacea* "occurs commonly in spring in the hawthorn copses of the Palouse country, as well as the wild rose and willow thickets of the Big Bend and lower east Cascades. As the summer advances most individuals evidently seek higher altitudes, and the species may be observed all the way to the scrubby conifers at timber line. Others, however, probably remain and breed in the lowlands, as summer records for several localities are at hand."

In Esmerelda County, Nevada, and Mono County, California, Jean M. Linsdale (1928) found *canescens*—

present in small numbers along the streams above the 8,000-foot contour line. They were always near water and were usually found at the edges of springy places where there were thickets of aspens and birches with dense ground covers of rose, gooseberry, or alder. The birds were found near snow-drifts where there was sufficient moisture and vegetation for their needs. Not a single individual was seen of heard on the nearby, dry, mountain sides which were covered with sage brushes and piñons. Tolmie warblers frequented the underbrush in the same places as the fox sparrows. The green-tailed towhee, often recorded as occurring in the same habitat as the fox sparrow, was numerous in this region in all the drier situations but only a few individuals were noted in surroundings favored by fox sparrows and those individuals were not limited in their ranges so closely to the stream sides as were the fox sparrows.

Grinnell and Miller (1944) describe the summer habitat of *fulva* as "large bushes and small conifers, and willow and aspen thickets, usually near water courses or meadows. Ceanothus patches in openings in the forest, streamside tangles, and artemisia brush near meadows or where mixed with other denser cover are typical situations occupied by this race. In each of these places, low, fairly dense, protective cover and leaf litter on the ground are afforded. Water or somewhat damp ground may also be a requirement."

They state the race *megarhynchus* inhabits:

In summer, most typically, tracts of *Ceanothus cordulatus* and manzanita, either in the form of large brush fields or in large clumps scattered in broken forest. To less extent other low cover providing similar dense protecting foliage; aspen thickets and streamside willow and alder tangles in the mountains may be inhabited. The brush in which these birds live, owing to temperature conditions in the zones occupied, provides at ground level, cool and somewhat moist places—refuges during the day from the high temperature and insolation of the bush tops. A requirement of all Fox Sparrows—leaf litter in which to forage—is amply supplied, although it is drier and harsher than in the breeding ranges of more northern forms. Nest locations are either above ground in the rugged, thorny bushes or sunk in the ground at their bases. In singing, as from bush tops or young conifers, the birds do not venture far from the shelter of the bushes and in moving about over the nesting domain covered alleyways are used perhaps more than flight lines over the brush.

Of the habitat *brevicauda* occupies in summer they say: "brushland consisting of *Ceanothus cordulatus*, *Prunus emarginata* and manzanitas, often intermingled with young conifers, especially firs. The infrequent meadowland in the range of this race may be occupied also if alder thickets or growths of false hellebore provide protecting cover. The brushland may exist in large tracts or in clumps in the open Canadian-zone forest. Burned-over forest land in recovery stages with heavy growth of brush is particularly favorable terrain."

They say *monoensis* prefers "brush composed of manzanita and ceanothus, and, commonly, streamside thickets of willows and wild rose and low aspen scrub with associated forbs about springs and wet meadows. Thus habitats characteristic for both *P. i. megarhynchus* and *P. i. canescens* are occupied."

The same authors note that *stephensi* occupies "in summer, chinquapin and ceanothus brush; less commonly brakes, willow thickets, and gooseberry brushes about mountain streams and springs. Although the brushland provides the same essential protecting cover and the somewhat moist ground-forage beat as in the ranges of more northern races of Fox Sparrows breeding in California, it is on the average drier and warmer. Presumably the leaf litter is prevailingly harsher. Less often are moist seeps available, although they are sought out by the birds when present. Nest sites and song posts are available much as in the ranges of *P. i. megarhynchus* and *P. i. brevicauda*."

Nesting.—Bendire (1889) writes of *schistacea:*

The Slate-colored Sparrow, according to my observations, prefers to nest in willow thickets, next in dense wild rose bushes, and occasionally in a bunch of tall rye grass, but always close to water. The nests are generally placed some little distance from the ground, rarely at a greater height than three feet, and are invariably well hidden. But a single instance came under my observation where the nest was placed directly on the ground; in this case it was hidden by an overhanging bunch of some species of swamp grass.

The nests of this form are bulky, but exceedingly well constructed affairs. The material composing the outer body is used at least in a very damp, if not in a positively wet state. It is thoroughly welded together in this condition, forming when dry a compact, solid structure which will retain its shape perfectly. They are rather deep for the small size of the bird, and cup-shaped. The finer finishing touches are attended to by the female, which fits the material used as the inner lining of the nest carefully in its place. As a rule two or three days are consumed in the construction of a nest, but I have positive evidence, in one instance at least, that a pair of these birds built an entirely new nest, and did it well too, between sunrise and sunset of the same day, and an egg was deposited in it that evening.

A typical nest Bendire describes as "outwardly constructed of various coarse plant fibers, willow bark, and marsh grass, and lined with fine grass tops taken from a species of rye grass. The outside of the nest is four and a half inches across by four inches deep; the inner diameter is two and a half incbes, the depth two inches. About one-third of the nests examined by me (some fifty in number), were lined inside with more or less horse-hair, and a couple, in addition, with feathers."

The nests of *fulva* he found in south-central Oregon Bendire (1889) states "are placed in various situations, *Kalmia* thickets, service-berry and willow bushes, as well as thick, scrubby evergreens, being preferred. They are always well hidden, and may be found from a few inches to six feet from the ground; none were found by me directly on the ground. Eggs may be looked for about June 12, and as late as July 15. The usual number laid is three or four, and but one brood, I think, is reared in a season." He describes a nest as "composed externally of coarse plant fibres * * * and a few horse-hairs. It is not as compactly built as nests of Townsend's or Slate-colored Sparrows. Its exterior is five inches wide by two and one half inches deep; inner diameter, three inches; depth, one and a quarter inches. It was evidently deeper originally, and has been much compressed and flattened in packing."

Of 14 nests of *megarhyncha* John W. Maillard (1921) found near Lake Tahoe, California, 6 were on the ground. Three of those above ground were in *Ceanothus* bushes, either near the edge of a thicket or well within it. One nest was 2 feet up in a crotch formed by a 2-inch branch and a willow. Another was 2 feet off the ground on a mass of dead branches and debris under a willow clump. One was on a dead aspen branch 3 feet above a small stream. He comments that all the nests followed a well-established form of construction, which he describes as follows:

In all instances the nest proper was composed of combinations of shreds of old bark, small dead twigs, old chips and small chunks of wood and dead leaves. All of this material, more or less decayed and very light in weight, was used in varying proportions in the different nests, sometimes one or two of these constituents being omitted. The wall of one nest contained several chips of wood, the largest of which was five and a half inches long by one and a quarter wide, and very thin, possibly a piece of berry basket. The lining of the nests was of finely shredded bark, dead rootlets, old dry grasses and sometimes horsehair.

* * *

Owing to the great shyness of this species but few opportunities for observing the actual nest building presented themselves. In one instance a bird was watched as it dragged a twig, at least eight inches in length, along the ground and up through and over the mass of dead branches and debris upon which, at a height of two feet from the ground, the nest was placed. Previously, the same bird had been seen carrying a small twig to its nest by direct flight. In another instance, where a nest was four feet and a half from the ground in a gooseberry tangle, the bird picked up twigs but a few yards from the nesting site and carried them to it by direct flight. These twigs varied greatly in length, the longest being estimated at ten inches, and several were dropped on the way. In a heroic effort to maintain a proper balance with a coveted twig while striving to reach its destination, the bird's body was almost perpendicular, its attitude and rapid wing movement reminding one of a hummingbird at a long-necked flower.

The continual song of the male, from his favorite perch near the nest site, and the fact that the sitting bird, while feeding nearby, is not replaced by its mate, leads to the belief that the female alone attends to the duties of nest construction and incubation. Sometimes, while near the nest, the male breaks into song, not only when standing on the ground but when he is scratching or hopping about in the brush as well.

In spite of the startling amount of general destruction of eggs, young and nests of birds, presumably by chipmunks, predatory birds, snakes, etc., prevalent in the Lake Tahoe region, no nests of this fox sparrow were molested before the eggs were hatched. This was probably due to the facts (established by careful observation) that incubation commences with the laying of the first egg, and that the sitting bird never goes far from the nest.

Wright M. Pierce (1921) says that eight nests of *stephensi* he found in the San Bernardino Mountains

are all very similar * * *. In size they average, outside depth, 4.5 inches; inside depth, 1.75; outside diameter, 6; inside, 3. Nests are composed of coarse sticks and pine needles, with some fine twigs and weed bark, lined with grass, weed bark, and, at times, mammal fur. The nests on the ground were usually less well made, with more pine needles and leaves, rather than coarse sticks.

* * * The birds nest, so far as we have found, either on the ground or up in buckthorn bushes. I believe they build more often on the ground, where the nests are very hard to locate, especially, if they are placed under a thick mat of tangled buckthorn. At times they seem to choose the most open sort of location. They just seem to be where they are! My experience indicates that the birds are very close sitters, and three seems to be the usual clutch of eggs.

Bendire (1889) writes that in *schistacea:* "Incubation, as nearly as I was able to determine, lasts from twelve to fourteen days; both sexes assist." Apparently nobody has ever measured the incubation period in this species accurately, and considerable disagreement is manifest in the literature on the roles the two parents play in various aspects of the reproductive cycle. It seems unlikely that such basic and ingrained behavior traits should vary between populations of the same species. In the absence of a definitive study, it appears most probable that nest building and incubation are almost entirely if not entirely by the female alone, and that the male remains close by and helps his mate feed the young after they hatch.

Young.—Linsdale (*in* Grinnell, Dixon, and Linsdale, 1930) made the following observations at a nest of *megarhyncha* which, when found on June 16,

* * * contained two young thought to be about three days old, helpless and downy rather than feathery. The female showed much concern and came within two meters of the observers. The male was indifferent and sang as soon as the observers withdrew. On June 17 the happenings at this nest were watched for most of the day. The female did most of the feeding of young, making trips at

intervals of from two to five minutes. Twice the male brought food for the young. When the nest was in the sunshine the panting female shaded it with spread wings. All the feces were eaten by the parent.

This female was watched caring for the young on June 21. It worked about the person seated close by, continually picking up small objects and uttering a faint *seet*. The wing ends were drooped and the tail was raised free of the ground; often it was turned somewhat at an angle sideways from the axis of the body. The male hopped about farther away, at a three-meter radius, and uttered a much louder metallic *klink*—then broke into full song. All the food was gathered within a radius of three meters of the nest.

Another nest containing nearly grown young birds was watched on June 21, 1925. The female foraged within eight meters of the nest, but the male went farther, sometimes twice that distance, to get food. The male was seen to gather insects and carry them to the female which took them in her bill and then carried them to the young birds. Although some of the food was obtained from among the leaves on the ground, most of it was picked off the growing vegetation. Twice the female picked off bits of green leaves of miner's lettuce (*Montia*) and fed them to the young. The remainder of the food was made up of insects. It looked to the observer as though the birds saw the insects best when they were between 15 and 30 centimeters distant.

A fox sparrow's nest that was found June 19, 1925, contained two half-fledged young which left when the nest was looked into. They were tolled out by the frantic actions and voicings of the two parents, which flopped along the ground under and through the bushes, giving their *klinks* in rapid succession. Other sympathetic fox sparrows came near.

How long after hatching the young remain in the nest is unknown, but as Grinnell (MS. *in* Linsdale, 1928) observes: "When young are nearly ready to leave the nest they will jump out and begin hopping away at even a slight disturbance. They go in different directions and are sometimes led away by the parents independently. After the birds have once jumped out of the nest they will not stay in it even if they are replaced."

How long the young remain with the parents after leaving the nest is likewise unknown. Wright M. Pierce (1921) tells how, while hunting for nests of *stephensi*, "We had not gone far until we kicked out a rather young fox sparrow from the brush, and then another. The parents were near at hand and played the broken-wing trick to perfection in their attempts to coax us away, all the while uttering their metallic 'chip.'" Jewett et al. (1953) write that in Washington "In the higher mountains, companies of 2 to 4 fox sparrows, usually family groups of adults and immatures still together, were commonly seen at least until the latter part of August, and often fully fledged young birds were observed teasing for attention. At this time of year the full song was no longer heard, and the birds remain silent, or utter merely a *chek* or *chirp* call note."

Voice.—The same authors comment of *olivacea*: "Few bird songs possess the attractive clear ringing quality of that of the fox sparrow. One noted June 5 at Cheney was 40 feet up in a dead alder singing with enthusiasm: *too-wheet-whoo—tsweek-tsuck-tseeka tsew!* The *wheet, tsweet* and *tseeka* notes were high and emphatic, while the others were pitched lower, the *tsuck* being an unstressed connective. An excellent rendition of the song by William L. Dawson (1909) is *ooree, rickit, loopiteer!* Few mountain birds, during July days, are better known for the beauty, strength, and vivacity of their song in the high mountains of the Mt. Baker country than the males of this species as they revel in the sunny landscape of the subalpine parks, and it is not unusual to find 4 males singing each within sound of one another's voice, although widely distributed along the climbing moraines (Shaw)."

On the other hand Bendire (1889) was not so highly impressed by the singing of *schistacea:* "While the female is covering her eggs, the male may frequently be heard giving vent to his nuptial song, in the early morning and just before sundown. His lay, however, is rather weak and of small compass, very much resembling that of *Melospiza fasciata* [*melodia*] *montana.* He delivers it while perched on some small twig, overlooking the thicket in which the nest is placed and generally close to it. Their usual call note is a repeated *tzip tzip.*"

Aretas A. Saunders (1910) made the following surprising observations of a pair he watched in a willow thicket near Bozeman, Montana in mid-April: "At first I believed, from their actions, that the birds were mating, but later, when I notist that both birds sang alternately, I decided that they must be rival males. The songs were very similar in every way except that one was somewhat weaker than the other. I finally secured the bird with the weaker song and was much surprised when, on later examination, it proved to be a female."

Enemies.—A. M. Ingersoll (1913) gives the following dismal account of his experiences while collecting eggs near Cisco, Placer County, Calif., in June and July, 1912: "Sixteen nests of Thick-billed Fox Sparrow (*Passerella i. megarhyncha*). Two nests and sets of eggs were taken by myself. Two nests were emptied of eggs by children. One with two eggs was abandoned before incubation commenced. One with four eggs was destroyed by sheep feeding on foliage of bush. Five nests with dead nestlings were examined after the snow. Four nests were emptied by jays. One nest containing two pipped eggs was discovered through the actions of a jay that had its feast interrupted." He attributes the "principal havoc" to fox sparrow nesting success, and to that of many other passerines there, to the activities of Steller's jays and an unseasonable fall of heavy snow that fell June 23.

Herbert Friedmann (1963) sums up the available information on cowbird parasitism in the species as follows:

The fox sparrow is an infrequent victim of the brown-headed cowbird. Only in one place has anyone considered it a common host; Saunders (1911, p. 40) wrote that in Gallatin County, Montana, "Mr. Thomas found the eggs and young quite commonly in the nests of the Slate-colored Sparrow." Ridgway (1887, p. 501) recorded a parasitized nest at Parley's Park, Wasatch Mountains, Utah, on July 23, 1869. The late H. J. Bowles wrote me years ago that a friend of his collected several sets of fox sparrow eggs with cowbird eggs near Spokane, Washington. Bendire (1889, p. 113) noted a cowbird's egg in a fox sparrow's nest at Palouse Falls, southeastern Washington, on June 18, 1878. Street (Houston and Street, 1959, p. 176) found another parasitized nest at Nipawin, Saskatchewan. H.B. Hurley (in litt.) found a nest with 2 eggs of the sparrow and 1 of the cowbird, five miles southeast of Sesters, Deschutes County, Oregon, on May 16, 1960. In the collections of the Santa Barbara Museum of Natural History there is a parasitized set of eggs collected on June 9, 1922, at Mammoth Lakes, Mono County, California.

These few records are all that I have noted. They refer to the northwestern race of the cowbird, *M. a. artemisiae*, and to the following races of the fox sparrow: *zaboria* in Saskatchewan; *olivacea* in Washington; *schistacea* in Gallatin County, Montana; *swarthi* in the Wasatch Mountains, Utah; *fulva* in Oregon; and *monoensis* in Mono County, California.

Winter.—Grinnell and Miller (1944) describe the California winter habitats of these races as follows:

schistacea (and *olivacea*): "inland chaparral, prevailingly of somewhat arid character, as with other races that winter in the interior."

fulva: "chaparral, as with other winter visitant races."

megarhyncha: "chaparral of semi-arid type is occupied."

brevicauda: "fairly dry chaparral, especially on ridges and on canyon slopes near the coast."

Distribution

Slate-colored Fox Sparrow (*P. i. schistacea*)

Range.—Southeastern British Columbia and southwestern Alberta south to northern Baja California, southern Arizona, and western Texas.

Breeding range.—The slate-colored fox sparrow breeds from southeastern British Columbia (Crowsnest Pass) and southwestern Alberta (Waterton Lakes Park) south through the mountains of northern Idaho (Glidden Lakes), north-central and eastern Oregon (Cascade Mountains south to Warm Springs; Howard; Wallowa Mountains), and western Montana (Judith River, Red Lodge), to north-central and northeastern Nevada (Pine Forest Mountains; 10 miles northeast of San Jacinto), southwestern Wyoming (Fort Bridger), and central Colorado (Cochetopa Creek).

Winter range.—Winters from northern interior California (Paine Creek), central Arizona (Hualpai Mountains, Natanes Plateau), and northern New Mexico (Manzano Mountains, Las Vegas) south through southern California (rarely to coastal districts; Alameda, San Nicolas

Island) to northern Baja California (Concepción; 20 miles southwest of Pilot Knob), southern Arizona (Ajo, Chiricahua Mountains), and western Texas (El Paso).

Casual records.—Casual in migration to western Nebraska.

Egg dates.—Oregon, 7 records, June 10 to July 5.

Washington Fox Sparrow (*P. i. olivacea*)

Range.—Mountains from southern British Columbia to northern Baja California.

Breeding range.—The Washington fox sparrow breeds in the mountains from southwestern and south-central British Columbia (Mount McLean, Nelson) south through central and eastern Washington (10 miles north of Grand Dalles; Blue Mountains).

Winter range.—Winters in interior California (Tehama County; Piute Mountains) and northern Baja California (Sierra Juárez).

Egg dates.—Washington 9 records, May 1 to June 13.

Utah Fox Sparrow (*P. i. swarthi*)

Breeding range.—The Utah fox sparrow breeds in mountains of southeastern Idaho (Bannock and Bear Lake counties) and of northwestern and north-central Utah (Raft River Mountains; Deep Creek Mountains; Wasatch Mountains south to Sanpete County).

Winter range.—Unknown.

Inyo Fox Sparrow (*P. i. canescens*)

Range.—Central Nevada to northern Baja California and southern Arizona.

Breeding range.—The Inyo fox sparrow breeds in central Nevada (Shoshone, Toiyabe, and Monitor mountains) and extreme central eastern California (White Mountains).

Winter range.—Winters in southern California (Santa Barbara, San Antonio Canyon, Blythe), northern Baja California (Laguna Hanson; 10 miles southeast of Álamo), and southern Arizona (Big Sandy Creek, Oracle).

Warner Mountains Fox Sparrow (*P. i. fulva*)

Range.—Central Oregon to northern Baja California.

Breeding range.—The Warner Mountains fox sparrow breeds from central and southern Oregon on the east side of the Cascade Range (Sisters, Keno, Steens Mountains) south to the Modoc Plateau of of California (Butte Lake, Warner Mountains).

Winter range.—Winters in southwestern California (Santa Barbara,

Cucamonga Canyon, Volcan Mountains) and northern Baja California (Laguna Hanson).

Casual records.—Casual in migration to northeastern Nevada (Secret Pass).

Thick-billed Fox Sparrow (*P. i. megarhyncha*)

Range.—Southwestern Oregon to northwestern Baja California.

Breeding range.—The thick-billed fox sparrow breeds in the mountains from southwestern Oregon (Onion Mountain, Robinson's Butte) south through central northern California (Siskiyou Mountains at Del Norte County line; Mount Orr; head of Dog Creek) and the Sierra Nevada of California (exclusive of the Mono Lake district) to lat. 37° N. (Kearsarge Pass); locally to west-central Nevada in the Tahoe district.

Winter range.—Winters in lowlands of central and southern California (Tower House, Inskip Hill, Nicasio, Santa Cruz and Santa Catalina islands, Witch Creek) and northwestern Baja California (La Grulla).

Egg dates.—(The data refer to all California forms.) California: 189 records, May 21 to July 8; 93 records, June 1 to June 15.

Trinity Fox Sparrow (*P. i. brevicauda*)

Range.—Coast ranges, central and coastal California.

Breeding range.—The Trinity fox sparrow breeds in the northern and inner coast ranges of California south of the Trinity River (Horse Mountain and Hayfork Baldy south to Mount Sanhedrin and Snow Mountain).

Winter range.—Winters in central and southern coastal California (Howell Mountain, Nicasio, Santa Monica Mountains, Santa Catalina Island).

Mono Fox Sparrow (*P. i. monoensis*)

Range.—Mono district of California and Mineral County, Nevada to northwestern Baja California.

Breeding range.—The Mono fox sparrow breeds in the Mono district on the east flank of the central Sierra Nevada in California (Woodfords, Mammoth, Benton); locally in adjoining Mineral County, Nevada (Walker River Range).

Winter range.—Winters in central interior and southern coastal California (Coulterville; Mount Wilson; Santa Catalina and San Clemente Islands) and northwestern Baja California (20 miles east of Ensenada; La Grulla).

Stephens' Fox Sparrow (*P. i. stephensi*)

Range.—Southern California.

Breeding range.—The Stephens' fox sparrow breeds in the southern Sierra Nevada of California (from Kings River southward) and in the high mountains of southern California (Mount Pinos, San Gabriel, San Bernardino, and San Jacinto mountains).

Winter range.—Winters at lower elevations in southern California (Santa Barbara, Hollywood, Claremont).

MELOSPIZA LINCOLNII LINCOLNII (Audubon)

Lincoln's Sparrow

PLATE 73

Contributed by J. MURRAY SPEIRS AND DORIS HUESTIS SPEIRS

HABITS

Those who know the Lincoln's sparrow no doubt think of it as the little bird that is "afraid of its own shadow," or perhaps as the sparrow that sings like a house wren, or again perhaps, as the bird that looks so like an immature swamp sparrow that experts often hesitate to identify it. If you have not yet met the elusive Lincoln's sparrow this will serve as an introduction to some of its most noteworthy characteristics.

Audubon (1834) tells how this species came by its name.

> We had been in Labrador nearly three weeks before this Finch was discovered. One morning while the sun was doing his best to enliven the gloomy aspect of the country, I chanced to enter one of those singular small valleys here and there to be seen. The beautiful verdure of the vegetation, the numerous flowers that grew sprinkled over the ground, the half-smothered pipings of some frogs, and the multitudes of mosquitoes and flies of various sorts, seemed to belong to a region very different from any that I had previously explored. But if the view of this favoured spot was pleasing to my eye, how much more to my ear were the sweet notes of this bird as they came thrilling on my sense, surpassing in vigour those of any American Finch with which I am acquainted, and forming a song which seemed a compound of those of the Canary and Wood-Lark of Europe. I immediately shouted to my companions, who were not far distant. They came, and we all followed the songster as it flitted from one bush to another to evade our pursuit. No sooner would it alight than it renewed its song; but we found more wildness in this species than in any other inhabiting the same country, and it was with difficulty that we at last procured it. Chance placed my young companion, THOMAS LINCOLN, in a situation where he saw it alight within shot, and with his usual unerring aim, he cut short its career. On seizing it, I found it to be a species which I had not previously seen; and supposing it to be new, I named it *Tom's Finch*, in honour of our friend LINCOLN, who was a great favourite among us.

By the time that Audubon came to write the original description of this bird, which was indeed new to science—although he found specimens already existed undescribed in the collection of William Cooper of New York—he used the more formal name "Lincoln's Finch, *Fringilla Lincolnii.*" It has since become customary to call the typical American Emberizinae "sparrows," and we now know this bird as Lincoln's sparrow.

During the summers of 1955, 1956, and 1957 we investigated the life history of Lincoln's sparrow in the vicinity of Dorion, a scattered community in Stirling Township, Thunder Bay District, about 50 miles northeast of Port Arthur, Ontario near the north shore of Lake Superior. Incidental observations were made at various other points along the north shore. Most of the literature dealing with this bird has to do with its occurrence and behavior on migration and with its song. A few accounts of nests and their contents have been published, but there is no study of the activities of the birds during the nesting cycle. Our studies were undertaken to fill in this gap in their life history. A good deal yet remains to be learned, particularly of the birds' relationships with other species and with the later stages of the nesting cycle. We have no personal observations of this species on its winter range. Reports of its winter activities in Central America suggest that its behavior and apparent abundance there are very different from our general concept of a secretive, uncommon species.

Lincoln's sparrow is found over a wide range, from its wintering area in Mexico and Guatemala to the limit of trees in northern Canada during the breeding season, and from the Atlantic to the Pacific. Throughout this range, it is largely a bird of shrublands. It occupies the scrub growth after a forest has been cut over, also the natural brush strips around the edges of bogs and along water courses, the new growth following forest fires, and the "permanent" scrub zones of the western mountains.

An essential feature of Lincoln's sparrow habitat appears to be the presence of low bush growth, usually from 4 to 8 feet high, and with openings in which tufts of grasses or sedges occur. It is often swampy or definitely wet underfoot, though this is not always the case. Lester L. Snyder told us that in the Abitibi region of northern Ontario he frequently found Lincoln's sparrow in dry, upland openings in the forest. In the Nipigon region he found the species in raspberry patches; farther south in the province, in wet places with swamp sparrows. At Grandview in the Thunder Bay District of Ontario the bird lives on generally dry and rocky hillsides with low shrub growth of dogwood, alder, willow and birch, occasional taller aspens and birches, and with openings where clumps of grasses and sedges grow around temporary rock pools.

We found Lincoln s sparrows in the Dorion region generally in recently cutover areas full of brush piles and stumps, fallen logs and new growth interspersed with grassy openings and rain pools. Marsh marigolds were a conspicuous feature of many territories in early June. Other plants frequently found were Labrador tea, sweet coltsfoot (*Petasites*), wood anemone, and young wild cherry shrubs. Small spruces, alders, willows, dogwoods, and saplings of birch and aspen were features of most of the territories. Many were adjacent to stands of larger trees of aspen, birch, and spruce, and the birds some-sometimes retired into these forests when disturbed. Many territories included isolated large trees of these same species left by the loggers because of imperfections, and which the bird occasionally used as song perches.

Lincoln's sparrows now appear to be invading the sort of manmade "forest edge" found along roadsides and after cuttings in forest country, but originally they must have depended for edge on fires and water, the edges of lakes, streams, and bogs. Many of the recorded nests have been in open sphagnum bogs in spruce forest.

Spring.—Lincoln's sparrows move northward in spring to their breeding territories from the wintering grounds. These lie as far south as El Salvador, Guatemala, Baja California, and Florida, and so the little birds move over most of the United States and much of Canada as they journey northward for nesting. Of their occurrence in New York, Ludlow Griscom (1923) writes:

> While uncommon it is a regular transient in our area, but will never be seen, except by a lucky "fluke," unless specially looked for. In spring it is particularly fond of water courses, the banks of which are grown with bushes, where it remains down among the roots and disappears at the slightest noise. By going as rapidly and noisily as possible through such a tract, a *trim, small, grayish-brown* Song Sparrow will sometimes flash into view for a second as it dives headlong into the bushes a few feet ahead. Making every possible effort to be quiet, the student should next make a wide detour and return to the bank *ahead* of where the bird was seen to enter. In this way I have had the bird come to me within six feet. * * * Lincoln's Sparrow will occur, however, in dense shrubbery almost everywhere, and I see it every spring in Central Park. It is exceptional to see more than one or two a season, and then it will occur on the big waves only.

At Toronto, migrating white-crowned sparrows and Lincoln's sparrows usually arrive at the same time. As the former is more conspicuous and noticed first, keen bird students in the area immediately become alert to the possibility of Lincoln's lurking in the underbrush. Considering the apparent rarity of the species, a surprising number of these tiny sparrows are caught in banding traps in spring. Thus the trap reveals a species ever-watchful eyes may have missed.

San Bernardino Mountains, Calif. W. M. Pierce

NEST AND EGGS OF LINCOLN'S SPARROW

Uinta Mountains, Utah A. D. Cruickshank

LINCOLN'S SPARROW AT NEST

William Brewster (1936) made some interesting notes on the appearance of six different Lincoln's sparrows in May 1899 at his October Farm, near Concord, Mass. One bird was of particular interest to him:

It appeared * * * on the 15th and remained until the forenoon of the 22nd, spending its whole time within or on the outskirts of the thicket of bushes between the smaller cabin and the canoe landing. In a bed of ferns on the edge of this thicket, directly in front of the small cabin and some fifteen feet from the door, we kept a quantity of millet seed scattered about over the ground. This was visited by the Finch at frequent intervals and, no doubt, constituted his chief food supply during his stay. It may have had something to do with the *length* of his stay, also, but the weather was very cool during this period and a number of other birds stayed in the same thicket for nearly the same length of time.

The Lincoln's Finch was very shy at first and at all times exceedingly alert and suspicious but he showed a nice and, on the whole, wise discrimination in his judgment of different sights and sounds. A keen, intelligent little traveller, evidently, quite alive to the fact that dangers threatened at all times, but too cool-headed and experienced to be subject to the needless and foolish panics which seize upon many of the smaller birds. He soon learned to disregard the movements and noises which we made within the cabin, and the trains thundering by on the other side of the river did not disturb him in the least but if our door was suddenly thrown open or if a footstep was heard approaching along the river path, he at once retreated into the thickets behind the ferns, dodging from bush to bush and keeping behind anything that would serve as a screen until all was quiet again, when he would presently reappear at the edge of the covert and, after a short reconnaisance, begin feeding again.

But however busily engaged at the seed, no sight or sound escaped him. If a Chipmunk rustled the dry leaves on the neighboring hillside, he would stand erect and crane his neck, turning his head slowly from side to side to watch and listen. When a Swift, of which there were many flying about, passed close overhead with a sound of rushing wings, the Sparrow would crouch close to the ground and remain motionless for a minute or more. But when nothing occurred to excite his suspicions, he would feed busily and unconcernedly for minutes at a time. Some of the seed had sifted down among the dry leaves and for this he scratched precisely in the manner of the Fox Sparrow, making first a forward hop of about two inches and then a vigorously backward jump and kick which scattered behind him all the leaves that his feet had clutched. In this manner he would quickly clear a considerable space and then devote himself to the uncovered seeds, which he would pick up one by one and roll in his bill after the manner of most Sparrows.

He was invariably silent when at the seed bed, but within the recesses of his favorite thicket he sang freely at all hours, especially in the morning or early forenoon or when the sun had just emerged from a cloud. He never sang from the top of a bush like a Song Sparrow but usually from some perch only a yard or so above the ground in the depths of the covert and not infrequently *on the ground itself* as he rambled from place to place hopping slowly over the dry leaves.

In 1956 we arrived at Dorion before the Lincoln's sparrows had settled on their nesting territories. May 16, 17, and 18 were cool with northwest winds and showers. Lincoln's sparrows were seen on each of these cool days at Mrs. Rita Taylor's feeding station in Dorion. There they, and various other species of sparrows, had been attracted by the scattering of rolled oats on the ground. On the nesting grounds 5 miles to the north, no Lincoln's sparrows were seen or heard singing. However, on May 19 the sky cleared, the wind shifted to the south, the temperature rose, and three males were heard singing. May 20 and 21 continued warm and 9 of the 10 nesting territories under special study were occupied by singing males.

Roland C. Clement, who has observed the species in the interior of Quebec and Labrador during the breeding season writes us (in litt.):

"The birds are shy or wary, and though they sing well enough when the frequent rains and wind abate, they are difficult to see. In 1957 I heard the first song in the Knob Lake region on May 31st In 1945 I found a few birds at Indian House Lake (lat. 56° N.), where arrival was as late as June 19. This bird is much more common in that Canadian Zone pocket which is the Goose Bay region in Newfoundland Labrador. The species arrived there on May 30, 1944, and occupied alder runs or brushy brook borders near bogs."

Courtship.—At Dorion, Ontario, in 1957, we noted courtship behavior from May 28 to June 5, chiefly in mid-morning from 8:00 to 10:30 a.m. The birds were nest building.

In most cases the female appeared to take the initiative by crouching, fluttering her wings in the fashion of a baby bird begging for food, and uttering a special, excited, high-pitched, rather hoarse "dzee-dzee-dzee" note, very similar to notes song sparrows and swamp sparrows utter when inviting copulation. On June 9, 1956, a case was observed when a male appeared to take the initiative. He flew from a low stump to a small dogwood at the foot of a spruce, quivering his wings and "tit"ing excitedly. Launching forth over a bit of meadow, he planed gradually toward the ground and pounced on his mate, who rose from the grass apparently in anticipation of the pounce, just before he came to ground. In most cases the "dzzee-dzee-dzee" invitation of the female seemed sufficient to stimulate the male, but if this failed she might resort to slow, labored, fluttering flight inviting pursuit by her spouse. Pairs were seen to copulate on the ground, on brushpiles, on a picnic table, on a sign. One of our notes reads: "The mating took place about two feet off the ground along an alder branch which was in tiny leaf."

The male's behavior is very much as Margaret M. Nice (1937) describes for the song sparrow: Lincoln's sparrow males "pounce" on their mates in much the same manner, although in most cases observed, they were encouraged to do so only after special vocal and behavioral invitations by their mates. After copulating the male quite frequently sang, sometimes while on the wing immediately after flying up from the female, at other times from a nearby branch.

A typical mating was observed at Dorion on June 2, 1956. The female was perched on a brushpile, quivering her wings and uttering intense, high-pitched "dzee-dzee-dzee" notes. After about 5 minutes of this the male flew down from a nearby spruce and pounced on her from above. A short chase took them out of sight behind the brushpile where, presumably, they copulated. The male then flew back into the spruce and sang. The female mounted to the top of the brushpile calling a slow "tit-tit-tit." The male in the spruce fanned his tail as if displaying to the female, then flew off.

A pair may mate several times during the course of a morning. On May 29, 1957, a female Lincoln's sparrow busily building her nest was seen to copulate with her mate seven times between 8:00 a.m. and 10:13 a.m. Once she had her bill full of long grasses and flew directly to the nest with them after the act.

In 1956 a second courtship cycle took place between July 1 and July 7. On July 1 a female Lincoln's sparrow interrupted a heavy schedule of feeding 8-day-old young still in the nest by inviting copulation from her mate with begging flutterings. He obliged. This was probably the initial step in a second nesting that season.

Territory—Margaret M. Nice (1937) reports five stages in the establishment of territory by song sparrows. Our impressions after watching Lincoln's sparrows at Dorion for 2 months in the late spring and early summer of 1956, were that the Lincoln's sparrows did not fight among themselves for territories and that song was the only important territorial manifestation. We saw no threats of fighting between "rival" males during our many hours of observation that year.

On June 3, 1957, at least seven singing males were present on our 25-acre study area, which had no more than five in 1956. When we arrived on the territory of L3, a Lincoln's sparrow flew down toward us from a height of about 25 feet from trees to the north. Another flew in low, also from the north. Both entered a brushpile right beside our parked car and chased each other in and out of the brushpile for several minutes. From their appearance and behavior, we felt both birds were females, both birds had their crests depressed, as is usual for females, and one uttered the female characteristic "zrrr" note. Finally one then the other left the brushpile and flew to the forest edge east of us and disappeared. Our field notes read: "After waiting some time for them to come back, I went over to the place where they had disappeared to see if they could be found again. A male was singing there at the southeast edge of his territory (L3). Another male was singing about 100 feet to the southeast (L2). The two sang thus for some time, then both flew out into the open and met in mid air. They climbed vertically upward, breast to breast, fighting on the wing to a height of about twenty feet; then one turned and flew to a tall spruce with the other in hot pursuit. The chase, and presumably the fight, continued near the top of the big spruce. L3's mate called 'zrrr' from her territory, then flew to a branch of the spruce below the combatants as if to see better what was going on and cheer on her spouse. L2's mate could be heard scolding from her territory, 'tit'ing from cover."

This account shows plainly that Lincoln's sparrows are not immune from territorial fighting when competition becomes sufficiently severe. Seven pairs on 25 acres might not seem overly crowded, but one must remember that much of the area was pre-empted by other species, notably by man (this was a busy trout-rearing station) and by song sparrows that compete strongly and very successfully against the Lincoln's sparrows. Swamp sparrows were also present in the more marshy areas along the creek; whether they competed with the Lincoln's sparrows in this wetter part of the study area, we could not determine.

The nesting habitat at Dorion was the edge area between the forest and the buildings with their surrounding lawns and roads. Here were scattered bushes and small trees and a few large poplars and spruces. The area was "brushed" every few years to keep the forest from taking over the property, and the cuttings formed a layer on the ground into which at least one pair had sunk their nest. We found another nest in the grass bordering the roadside ditch. Much of the vegetation was about a foot high and included such plants as anemones, various grasses and sedges, wild roses and raspberries, small dogwood bushes and young evergreen trees, chiefly spruce and balsam fir. Some willows and alders grew along the creek. The actual species of plants are probably unimportant but their size and disposition probably are important. There should be shrub growth less than 8 feet high for concealment and from which the male can sing, openings carpeted with grasses, heaths, or annuals less than 2 feet high in which they can forage, and a substratum of brush cuttings, grass clumps, or sphagnum that the nest may be sunk into.

The actual size of the territory probably varies a good deal, as in other species. Those in the Dorion study area appeared to be about one acre in extent; some were a little larger and some a little smaller. Several of these were used for more than one year, though we did not do enough color-banding to be sure they were occupied by the same individuals.

In 1956 and 1957 Lincoln's sparrows occupied their territories in the Dorion region as soon after their arrival as the weather warmed up, as manifested by the presence of singing males. Nesting may not begin for another 10 days to 2 weeks. On cool windy days during this interval it was often difficult or impossible to find the owners of the territories, either because they temporarily abandoned territories or perhaps because they did not sing in such weather. We were not able to stay through the summer in 1956 and 1957, but in 1955 the Lincoln's sparrows were present and feeding young on the trout hatchery property until mid-September. It appears likely, therefore, that the territories are occupied until the birds migrate in autumn.

Nesting.—Lewis McI. Terrill (MS.) has found a number of nests of the Lincoln's sparrow in Quebec, most of them "in shallow depressions on sphagnum mounds concealed by *Ledum* bushes and resting on the accumulation of fallen *Ledum* leaves. The outstanding materials composing the rather frail structures were leached sedges, especially the filiform, wiry stems of such species as *Carex trisperma* and *C. leptalea,* which commonly drape the sphagnum mounds in the Lincoln's sparrow's habitat."

He writes further (MS.):

In the St. Lawrence River Valley below Quebec this sparrow becomes decidedly more common, especially in the Rivière du Loup, Matane, and Gaspé Counties. Preference is shown for the dryer, bushier portions of sphagnum bogs, particularly the older bogs suitable for the production of peat rather than the wet sphagnum of newer bogs. A typical nesting habitat is the extensive, rather dry savanne known as Caribou Plains, near Corner of the Beach, Gaspé County, where three were seen with food and about ten heard singing on July 7, 1941. Here they frequented the fringe of the bog amongst the heaths (chiefly *Ledum,* Kalmia, and *Rhodora*), with scattered shrubby conifers and a ground cover of Cloudberry (*Rubus Chamaemorus*) though somewhat farther out in the open bog than their principal nesting associates, the Yellow Palm warbler and the Yellow-throat.

At Metis, Matane County, the Lincoln's Sparrow also nests in boggy clearings where the old stumps are partly hidden in the new growth; also among low alder fringing streams. An unusual habitat was near the top of Mount Logan (Shickshock Mts.), Gaspé, where four were heard singing amongst scrubby conifers at an altitude of about 3000 feet on July 6, 1937. Several Black-poll warblers appeared to be their only companions.

In our experience, the nest of Lincoln's sparrow is very difficult to find. Although we made a special effort in the Thunder Bay District of Ontario in 1956, we failed to find a nest with eggs. By the time incubation was underway, we had settled down to watch one pair whose activities could be conveniently observed from our parked car. With black flies, "no-see-ums," and mosquitoes active and plentiful, a parked and closed car seemed the only livable observation point in the country. After several days we had the nest nearly pinpointed, but, alas, not definitely located. We determined its approximate position by making minute-by-minute notes for more than 7 hours on June 23 and June 24. On the latter day we pointed out the place where we thought the nest should be to Dr. and Mrs. A. E. Allin of Fort William. All four of us set out to comb the area on hands and knees. We flushed the bird from the indicated spot but found no nest.

After supper on June 24 Neil Atkinson came puffing into our house, having run the mile from the nest site, to announce that he had succeeded in locating the nest. Immediately we went back with him, and there the nest was, right where we had looked, but set well down into the ground under a pile of last year's brush cuttings. It looked like a little black hole.

The nest contained three young about a day old and one infertile egg. It was situated 16 feet from the access road into the trout rearing station and 8 feet from the forest edge. The main cover plants were grasses, wild rose, anemones, raspberry, cut off shrubs of dogwood, willow, alder, a little balsam, and brush one or two feet high. Brush cuttings from other years formed an interlacing mat below this new growth, which grew profusely to a height of 1 or 2 feet. The nest measured 3½ inches in outside diameter, about 2⅓ inches in inside diameter and about 1¼ inches deep outside. It was made of dried grasses. As early as June 21 we had searched for this nest but were driven back to the car by mosquitoes. The female at this time was silent while we searched but scolded us when we left off searching, so she was no help. After the young left the nest on June 2, we collected the nest and infertile egg and later presented them to the Royal Ontario Museum.

The following extracts are from the field notes of J. Murray Speirs:

On May 27, 1957, as I entered the property of the Dorion Trout Rearing Station about 8:00 a.m. E.S.T., two little sparrows flushed from the roadside just west of the Abitibi road and flew toward the alders at the forest edge north of the entrance road to the hatchery. They uttered little 'tit'ing notes characteristic of Lincoln's sparrows and one paused to eye me long enough for me to verify the identification. I thought "This must be Mr. and Mrs. A, the elusive little pair that occupied this territory in 1956 and raised a family so furtively that we saw nothing of the nesting until one day the young were seen being fed." We suspected nesting right by this same corner in 1956 and made a few searches for the nest, but found nothing.

On May 29, 1957, however, fortune smiled on us. We had finished the morning watch in the hatchery property and were about to leave when a movement caught my eye and we waited. It was a Lincoln's sparrow, sure enough, and IT HAD GRASS IN ITS BILL. So we waited.

Mrs. A, or to be more formal, L_7♀–1957, flew with her long, dried grasses trailing at each side like the tail of a comet, to the narrow vegetative border between the road and the roadside ditch. She worked along the ditch quickly toward us about eight or ten feet. She stopped briefly by a little clump of assorted bushes. This clump consisted of one sprig of alder with new green leaves about an inch across, several shoots of willow, and a small gooseberry bush, all about a foot high. After her pause here she flew off, *without* the grasses, directly away from the clump. This was at 7:40 a.m. Three more trips followed in quick succession, the last at 7:45 a.m. Each time she flew to the roadside border of the ditch and worked along the ditch, usually several feet toward the nest.

Sometimes she lit west of the nest site, sometimes east of it. When leaving she flew directly from the nest site or from a foot or so to the east of it. Just after her fourth trip, several cars carrying men to work at the hatchery passed by within inches of her nest and put a temporary stop to her nest building activities. At 7:58 a.m. and 8:02 a.m. she made two more trips with grasses to the nest-site, remaining some time after the second trip.

As she left the nest at 8:07 a.m., the male, who had been waiting in a cedar by the forest's edge, flew east about thirty feet and intercepted her as she reached the edge. He pounced on her in typical Melospizan style. There was a short skirmish, after which he mounted singing to a bough a few feet overhead while she remained on the ground, saying shurr-shurr, shurr, shurr, shurr (DHS interpretation) or ZRRRR, ZRRRR, ZRRRR, ZRRRR, ZRRRR (JMS interpretation). Both male and female of this pair have quite a pronounced centre spot. The male keeps his crest raised much of the time and has pronounced orangy-buff malar stripes. At 8:21 a.m. she made another trip to the nest with bill full of grass, stopping en route to invite copulation on a sloping alder branch about two feet off the ground. The male made three attempts to mount her and mating appeared to be successful on the second and perhaps th rd attempts. As she left the nest after delivering this load, he pounced from a vantage point about ten feet up in a spruce at the forest edge, intercepting her as she flew just above the ground before she reached the woods. More matings, with soft singing on his part and zrrring on her part followed for several minutes, until we left at 8:25 upon the approach of two school boys, Scott and Neil Atkinson. Yesterday Scott announced that he thought there must be a "ground sparrow" nest near this corner, where they wait for the school bus. He made a cursory search but stopped when other children appeared for the bus so as not to draw attention to the possibility.

We returned at 9:30 a.m. She brought nesting material at 9:48 and again at 9:59 a.m. We left at 10:40 a.m. One of the pair was seen atop a stump in the territory with two short, thick straws, very unlike the long, flexible pieces she had taken to the nest. After holding them listlessly they were dropped, one at a time. I suspect this was the male bird showing some token interest in the building. Interest in mating continued at a high pitch during this observation period: the female zrrring frequently and the male pouncing and singing quietly, chiefly following these pounces. On the 9:59 trip she flew directly to the nest, an exception to her general rule, in spite of the fact that we were parked directly across the road not more than 15 feet from the nest. The female apparently did all the nest building though the male was ever on hand.

We did not search for the nest until we were sure it would be completed. We found it with no difficulty on May 31 when it was finished but still empty. It was in a grass clump between the road and the roadside ditch, so close to the road that we could have looked right into it from our parked car had it not been concealed by the over-arching grasses. This nest was about 30 feet from the forest edge. The cover between the road and the forest was very similar to that in which the 1956 nest had been located; grasses, annuals, cut-off shrubs, and small trees. It was somewhat wetter (the ditch was usually partly full of water) and this was reflected in a greater abundance of alder. The first egg was laid on June 1 and the others on June 2, 3, and 4. Further details of this nest are given in later sections.

Eggs.—Lincoln's sparrow lays from 3 to 6 eggs with 4 or 5 comprising the usual set. They are ovate with some tendency to elongate ovate and are slightly glossy. The ground of freshly laid eggs is "pale Niagara green," but this fades upon exposure to a greenish white. The markings are of reddish browns such as "Verona brown," "cinnamon brown," "Prout's brown," or "Argus brown." These are usually heavy and may be in the form of fine speckles and spots or large clouded blotches. Often the ground is entirely obscured and appears to be a light brown. Some eggs may have undermarkings of "pale neutral gray." They are practically indistinguishable from those of the song sparrow, but in a series they will average slightly smaller. The measurements of 130 of all three races average 19.4, by 14.4 millimeters; the eggs showing the four extremes measure *21.6* by 14.9, 20.0 by *16.0*, *17.2* by 13.5, and 18.0 by *13.2* millimeter. The measurements of 50 eggs of *M. l. lincolnii* average 19.7 by 14.6 millimeters; the eggs showing the four extremes measure *21.6* by 14.9, 20.0 by *16.0*, and *17.2* by *13.5* millimeters.

Incubation.—The chief purpose of our studies at Dorion during 1956 and 1957 was to obtain information on the incubation and fledging of Lincoln's sparrow, about which practically nothing had been published prior to that time.

Edward A. Preble (1908) wrote: During their trip to the Mackenzie my brother and Cary noted it at Hay River, June 29, and the following day found a nest containing five heavily incubated eggs. The male bird was shot just after being flushed from the eggs, showing that it assists in incubation."

Nice (1943) cites six instances of male song sparrows seen *visiting* the nest during the incubation period, but gives no record of actual incubation by the male. She states that "only females regularly incubate with * * * American Sparrows." In our studies at Dorion we never saw a male Lincoln's sparrow incubating.

In a nest we found on May 31, 1957, by the side of the entrance road into the Dorion Trout-Rearing Station, the first, second and third eggs were laid on June 1, 2, and 3 respectively. We marked each egg as we discovered it in the nest using a grass blade dipped in India ink. The final (fourth) egg was laid after 7:35 p.m. on June 3 and before 7:20 a.m. on June 4. An attentivity recorder in the nest indicated that the female was on the nest during the night between 8:15 p.m. on June 3 and 2:22 a.m. on June 4, and again between 4:11 a.m. and 6:02 a.m. on June 4. On June 17 at 7:05 a.m. the nest contained three young and the unhatched fourth egg. By 12:35 p.m. the fourth egg had hatched. This established the incubation period of the fourth egg as between 13 days, 1 hour, 3 minutes and 13 days, 16 hours, 20 minutes, and most probably about 13 days and 6 hours, from about 5 a.m. June 4 to about 11 a.m. June 17.

The attentivity rhythm at this nest was determined with a thermistor bridge recorder (Speirs and Andoff, 1958) which showed that on June 5 the female spent more time off than on the nest. Four attentive periods averaged 34 minutes in length (13, 45, 46, and 33 minutes) while four inattentive periods averaged 62 minutes (83, 28, 12, and 127 minutes), this in spite of the fact that it was a cool day with some light rain. This was the second day of incubation and the attentivity rhythm apparently was not yet fully established. On June 8, the fifth day of incubation, and a clear, mild day, the 10 attentive periods averaged 20.4 minutes ranging from 17 to 40 minutes, while 11 inattentive periods averaged 6.9 minutes ranging from 2 to 15 minutes; from 9:32 a.m. to 2:12 p.m. the incubating bird spent 75 percent of its time on the nest and 25 percent off. On the morning of June 11, the eighth day of incubation, attentive periods of 25, 54, and 19 minutes were broken by inattentive periods of 3 minutes and 1 minute. The increased attentivity on this day may have been influenced by the overcast weather though temperatures remained about the same, or may have been an expression of the intensification of the incubation habit. Nice (1937) found a similar shortening of the inattentive periods in the song sparrow as incubation progressed.

We have no evidence of the male Lincoln's sparrow calling its mate off the nest at intervals during incubation as M. M. Nice (1943) writes that song sparrow males do. The Lincoln's sparrow males apparently sing very little during the incubation period; in this also they differ from the song sparrow. In fact, we did not see nor hear our particular Lincoln's sparrow male after the day the fourth egg was laid until the young hatched. The male bird at our 1956 nest did some singing during the incubation period, chiefly in the very early morning.

When the female was flushed from the nest on June 7, 1957, instead of flying, she ran out along the ditch. Again on June 9 she did not flush until the last minute and then ran along the ditch "like a little mouse" for a yard or two, then flew very low, just clearing the ground cover, to the forest edge north of the nest. She did not scold or utter any sound when flushed, and she did not leave the nest until the grass over it was parted to show it to a visiting naturalist. On June 12 while changing the chart on the nest recorder the observer twice jumped the ditch within a few feet of the nest, and the bird did not leave the nest.

Young.—Notes were made on the development of the 1956 Dorion young five times during their nest life. On June 24, when, presumably, the nestlings were a day old, they had an egg tooth on the upper mandible which had disappeared by the next day. The eyes were tightly closed on June 24 and 25, mere slits on June 27, open on June 28, and wide open on June 29. On June 24 only a dark line indicated the future whereabouts of the primary flight feathers. By June 27 the longest sheaths of the primaries measured 8½ millimeters. By June 29 these had grown to 15 millimeters.

The young in our 1957 nest at Dorion hatched on June 16 and June 17. On June 18, when 1 and 2 days old, the four together weighed 14.7 grams (average 3.7 grams apiece). One was noticeably larger than the others. At this age they were naked except for dark grey, almost black down on top of the head, along the middle of the back, on the wings (no signs of quills yet) and on the thighs. They had a sharp ridge on top of the culmen but no egg tooth. When they opened their mouths they showed a reddish mouth lining and whitish gape.

On June 19, when 2 and 3 days old, the young together weighed 23.1 grams (average 5.8 grams each). In the process, one excreted a fecal sac that weighed 0.2 grams. The young were weighed late in the evening.

On June 21, when 4 and 5 days old, the four young together weighed 40.2 grams (average 10.0 grams). This was at 8:00 p.m. One young had its eyes partly open. Their pin feathers were by this time very black and conspicuous, the primary quills estimated to be about 10 millimeters long. All feather tracts now were conspicuous: primaries, secondaries, tertials, dorsal and capital tracts, ventral, crural and even little pin feathers on the "drumsticks." Their skin was a deep tan color. The young in the nest appeared very black in contrast to young song sparrows in a nearby nest that looked mottled grey. The mouth lining of the young Lincoln's was a brilliant cherry red, the edges of the mouth creamy white.

On June 22, when the nestlings were 5 and 6 days old, we weighed and color-banded the young individually at 8:00 p.m. They weighed 13.3 grams, 13.2 grams, 12.1 grams and 11.5 grams, averaging 12.5 grams. The eyes of the two larger ones were wide open, the smallest just showed a slit, while the other had its eyes partly open. Their primary shafts were estimated to be 15 mm. long. The ventral tracts showed a buffy-tan color, while the dorsal tracts were grey black.

On June 23, when 6 and 7 days old, we weighed the young again in the evening. They weighed 15.0 grams, 14.4 grams, 12.9 grams and 13.2 grams (average 13.9 grams). A male and female Kenneth C. Parkes (1954) collected June 25, 1953, near Madawaska, N.Y., weighed 16.5 and 15.1 grams, respectively. Our adult female weighed 17.3 grams when we banded her at 9:05 a.m. on June 19.

On June 23 the eyes of all were wide open. Their mouth linings were now a very bright crimson, the cutting edge of the mandibles yellowish. Pin feathers covered most of the skin and were chiefly blackish. For fear of causing the fledglings to leave prematurely, we did not handle them again. On June 25, when we looked into the nest carefully at 5:30 p.m., they stretched their necks and gaped to be fed. The gape now appeared bright yellow instead of creamy white as earlier (June 21, above).

The female did practically all of the feeding while the young were in the nest according to our 1956 and 1957 observations. We were never positive that either male actually delivered any food to the young, although both were seen with food in their bills, and the 1957 male made several false starts as though to go to the nest. Perhaps he was unnerved by our proximity, for he never quite made it while we were watching. In both cases the female flew to and from the nest with little hesitation and both broods left the nest successfully. That the males do sometimes assist in brooding young is attested by the observations of Maurice G. Street (*in* litt.) and Lawrence H. Walkinshaw (*in* litt.). We believe that the male of our 1957 pair looked after two of the young after they left the nest, and that the female looked after the other two, but their secretive habits made this too difficult to ascertain. The color-banded female was noted near the nest as were some young, while the male (as determined by his singing) spent most of his time about 100 yards west of the nest where the two color-banded young were seen in mid July.

As nothing appears to have been written about the feeding rhythm of Lincoln's sparrow, we spent a good deal of time studying it in 1956. Although we did not actually see the 1956 nest until Neil Atkinson found it on June 24, we knew its approximate position several days previously. On June 23 at 10:22 a.m. we saw the female fly from beyond the creek to a spruce just across the road from her nest. She had in her bill a tiny white moth and a half-inch green caterpillar. These she took to the nest—the first feeding that we noticed. At 11:10 she flew east from the nest into the forest edge and at 11:40 we saw her return with a green caterpillar in her bill. During a watch of 1 hour and 55 minutes in midafternoon, we saw her make three more feedings. This was an overcast day with showers in the morning and rain in the afternoon.

It was raining on the morning of June 24, but her rate of feeding had already speeded up. In the early morning we saw her make 3 feedings in an hour and 5 minutes, and 3 more in the course of 50 minutes later in the morning. By midafternoon it had cleared and turned warmer and we saw her make three more visits during a watch of 1 hour and 15 minutes.

On June 25 between 4:37 a.m. and 7:30 a.m. she made 8 visits, averaging 22 minutes between visits to the nest. She made 7 visits between 11:00 a.m. and 12:10 p.m., averaging 11 minutes between visits. The intervals between feedings became gradually shorter day by day until by July 1 we noted 23 visits between 6:48 a.m. and 9:00 a.m., at average intervals of only 6 minutes.

On July 2 between 6:40 a.m. and 8:00 a.m. we saw 11 visits at an average interval of 7 minutes. At 2:35 p.m. the nest was empty. Twice we saw the father with food on this day but we did not see him take it to the nest. No relationship was discernible between the time of day and the rate of feeding. On some days the mother made more frequent visits to the nest near midday than early in the morning, as on June 25, and on other days the reverse was true. On July 13 and again on July 14 when the young were 12 days out of the nest we saw the mother still carrying food (green larvae) to them.

One reason for the long intervals between feedings in the early nest life of the young was the necessity for the mother to spend a good deal of time brooding because of the wet, cold weather. Also the young had smaller food requirements at that time. As we could not actually see her on the nest because of the dense growth of grasses, wild flowers, and low shrubs that surrounded it, we could not make any accurate determination of the amount of time spent brooding the nestlings. It was not determined, either, how many young were fed at each visit. These aspects of the life history remain to be determined.

The 1956 mother Lincoln's had a standard routine in her feeding trips. She would leave the nest, with or without a fecal sac, and fly to a spruce at the forest edge east of the nest. If she were carrying a fecal sac, she would leave it on a horizontal branch of this spruce, fly to a dead balsam south of the nest, then across the road to a meadow near the river where she foraged. Then she would fly to a spruce where the male usually sang across the road from the nest, then to a raspberry patch between the spruce and the road, then very low across the road to the nest. On June 25 these trips averaged 15 minutes, varying from 5 to 29 minutes. She varied this routine somewhat in the later stages of nest life, foraging fairly often in the foliage of the spruces and balsams at the forest edge and sometimes on the forest floor.

The 1957 mother also had a definite route that she usually followed in her comings and goings. This route included a slanting alder limb on which she deposited the fecal sacs in a neat row.

The young Lincoln's sparrows left the 1956 nest on July 2 and the 1957 nest on June 26. While we have no definite proof that two broods are raised at Dorion, we have circumstantial evidence of it in a second courtship cycle in early July and a September record of an immature bird.

Of a nest she found containing three newly hatched young on July 5, 1946, near Sandwich Bay, Labrador, Virginia Orr (1948) writes: "The parent allowed me to approach within two feet slipping off the nest and running back into denser growth. * * * the bird never flew away directly, but ran along the partially covered tunnel for several feet before taking wing. It used the same route when bringing food to the young. * * * The fledglings left the nest in a flightless condition on the twelfth day after discovery."

In our 1956 nest, which was not found until June 24, the young left the nest on July 2 between 8:00 a.m. and 2:35 p.m. If, as we believe, the young hatched on June 23 when we first noted the female carrying food, then these young left on the ninth day after hatching. In our 1957 nest the first young hatched on June 16 between 10:00 a.m. and 4:25 p.m. the next two between 8:55 p.m. on June 16 and 7:10 a.m. on June 17, and the final young between 7:10 a.m. and 12:35 p.m. on June 17. All four were in the nest when it was checked at 5:30 p.m. on June 25; all had left when Neil Atkinson checked it at 6:00 p.m. on June 26. Thus they left the nest on the ninth or tenth day after hatching.

In 1956, we heard the first begging calls from the young on July 14, 12 days after leaving the nest and about three weeks after hatching. We color banded the young in our 1957 nest on June 23. On July 14 we saw the blue-banded youngster about 100 yards west of the nest, and on July 15, the red-banded one in about the same place. An adult Lincoln's sparrow which we took to be the male of the pair appeared still to be accompanying these two young birds, which were then 27 to 28 days old and 19 to 20 days out of the nest. Maurice G. Street of Nipawin, Saskatchewan wrote us that he found a nest of Lincoln's sparrows that contained three eggs on June 10, 1946, that both the male (regularly) and the femalè (occasionally) visited his feeding station and "both parents were noted feeding young at my station in late July." As the three eggs could scarcely have hatched any later than June 23, this would imply a period of dependence probably in excess of the 28 days that Nice (1943) gives as the "age of independence" for Emberizines.

Lawrence H. Walkinshaw gives us in a letter some interesting data on a Lincoln's sparrow's nest with two eggs, William Dyer found on June 22, 1956. The nest still contained two eggs on June 25 and had two young on June 28. The young left the nest when they were banded on July 4 when they could not have been more than nine days old. The disturbance of banding may have caused them to leave the nest prematurely. "Both adults fed the young at the nest."

Plumages.—The natal down of the newly hatched young at Dorion appeared to be very dark grey, almost black. It was about half an inch long and covered the body rather scantily on top of the head, along the middle of the back, on the wings and thighs. The general impression upon looking into a nest of newly hatched young of this species is like looking into a black hole. The down persists for some time after the juvenal plumage is acquired, particularly on the top of the head. In specimens examined at the Royal Ontario Museum, this down appeared brownish against a black background but almost black against a light background.

Richard R. Graber (1955) describes the juvenal plumage which is acquired by a complete postnatal molt as follows: "Forehead rich brown with rather fine black streaks. Median stripe buffy, laterally rich brown, streaked with blackish. Superciliary region gray, finely streaked with blackish. Nape finely mottled, shades of brown, buff, gray, and blackish. Back streaked buffy gray, light brown, and blackish. Rump slightly darker, streaking more obscure. Upper tail coverts and rectrices brownish, black along the shaft. Remiges dark gray; primaries light edged; secondaries, tertials, and coverts edged with rusty. Median and greater coverts tipped narrowly with buff. Tertials blackish with buff tips. Lores grayish. Auriculars rich rusty brown, margined with blackish; sub-auriculars buff. Chin and throat white, finely spotted and streaked with blackish. Chest, sides, and flanks buff, finely streaked with blackish. Belly and crissum whitish, unmarked. Leg feathers light brown."

A juvenal Lincoln's sparrow 12 days out of the nest on July 14, 1956, still had a stubby, partially grown tail; the breast streaks were broader and continued lower down on the breast than in the adults. The dark lines above and below the ear coverts were also broader and more distinct than in adult plumage, the lower line having a blotchy appearance. In the juvenal plumage they are very similar to song sparrows and swamp sparrows in the same plumage. (See *Field marks.*)

According to Dwight (1900) the first winter plumage is "acquired by a partial postjuvenal moult * * * which involves the body plumage and the wing coverts but not the rest of the wings nor the tail." In eastern Canada this postjuvenal molt takes place during August. The latest juvenal plumage Lincoln's sparrow in the Royal Ontario Museum collections was taken on August 9.

Dwight continues: The first nuptial plumage is "acquired by wear * * * from the first winter dress." The adult winter plumage is "acquired by a complete postnuptial moult in August." The adult nuptial plumage is "acquired by wear as in the young bird. The sexes are practically indistinguishable in all plumages, and the moults are the same in both sexes."

Although indistinguishable by plumage, the sexes may be distinguished during the breeding season by behavioral differences (see *Behavior*). The female of the 1956 pair at Dorion had a brownish central-breast spot, while the male's breast spot was black. This was undoubtedly an individual variation: some adults of both sexes have breast spots, others have none.

Food.—The most thorough account of the food of this species in the east is in Sylvester D. Judd (1901) from which we quote:

> Only 31 stomachs of this species have been examined. These were collected during the months of February, April, May, September, and October, mainly in Massachusetts and New York. The food during these months, as indicated by the stomachs, consists of animal matter, 42 percent, and of vegetable matter, 58 percent. The animal matter is made up of 2 percent spiders and millipeds and 40 percent insects. Useful insects, largely Hymenoptera, with some predacious beetles form 4 percent of the food, and injurious insects, 12 percent. Neutral insects, including beetles, ants, flies, and some bugs, amount to a fourth of the food. More ants (principally Myrmicidae) and fewer grasshoppers are destroyed than by the song sparrow. The vegetable matter is divided as follows: grain, 2 percent; seeds of ragweed and various species of *Polygonum*, 13 percent; grass seed, 27 percent, and miscellaneous seeds, principally weeds, 16 percent.

McAtee (1911) records the "Lincoln Finch" among those species that eat the clover-root curculio *Sitones*, a beetle that does "a large amount of obscure damage" to clover.

The most frequently noted food items taken to the young of our 1956 nest were green caterpillars (probably geometrid larvae), greyish larvae (possibly noctuids), small whitish moths (possibly leaf-miners), yellowish larvae (possibly beetle larvae), small green grasshoppers, and brownish larvae (possibly spruce budworm).

Lincoln's sparrows frequent feeding stations during migration and are often taken in banding traps. At Dorion at least two frequented the feeding station of Rita Taylor daily during the latter half of May but deserted it at the beginning of June. When feeding the birds scratch with both feet at once to uncover concealed food, in the manner of most small sparrows.

On June 7, 1956 we saw a Lincoln's sparrow jump from the ground under a little spruce tree, fly almost vertically upward two or three feet, snap up a flying insect and, returning to the ground with it, carry it under the spruce tree to dispose of it.

Voice.—Audubon (1834) has this to say of the song of Lincoln's sparrow: "But if the view of this favoured spot was pleasing to my eye, how much more to my ear were the sweet notes of this bird as they came thrilling on my sense, surpassing in vigour those of any American Finch with which I am acquainted, and forming a song which seemed a compound of those of the Canary and Wood-lark of Europe. The habits of this sweet songster resemble those of the Song Sparrow. Like it, mounted on the topmost twig of the tallest shrub or tree it can find, it chants for hours."

F. H. Allen heard the Lincoln's sparrow sing at West Roxbury, Mass., on May 13, 1915, and sent the following notes to Mr. Bent:

> One singing near the house this morning. Heard it first when I got out, about 6.30. It was in the Norway spruces northwest of the house and kept itself hidden for over half an hour, frequently singing, sometimes with a ventriloquial effect sounding far away. Never having heard the song before, I did not recognize it and I could not satisfy myself at first as to what bird it came from. When I first heard it I thought of the northern water-thrush, but I soon perceived that it was not that. Then I thought successively of chat, catbird, house wren, goldfinch, and white-winged crossbill. It sounded most like an abbreviated and low-pitched strain from a goldfinch, but the secretive habit of the bird seemed to prove that it could not be that. It was about as long as the indigo bunting's song, perhaps a *little* longer, but more varied and of different quality. At or near the end there was a short, sweet bubbling or rippling trill suggestive of the house wren, but high-pitched, I should say. The song had two forms, one of which, the more emphatic of the two, was given more frequently than the other. There were periods of silence, and during one of these I gave the bird up for the time and went into the house. Then it began again and I went on the upper piazza to look for it. Presently it flitted into a pear tree and sang there, and I saw it was a Lincoln's sparrow. A beautiful and interesting song.

William Brewster (1936) describes four different songs, and their variations, of one Lincoln's sparrow as follows:

> 1. A simple, level, woodeny trill usually indistinguishable from the summer song of the Juncos, but at times with a resonant, lyrical quality approaching that of the Yellow-rump's song; both forms given at short but distinct intervals.
>
> 2. The same trills with the intervals completely filled with short, soft, liquid notes, the whole forming a medley *exactly* like that uttered by the Junco in *early spring* with the Junco *tsup* or *tup* coming in frequently among the short, connecting notes. This song should perhaps be regarded as a variation of No. 1, but I did not once hear this bird change from one to the other. That both songs were literal copies of those of the Junco can admit of no doubt.
>
> 3. A rapid warble, at times flowing smoothly and evenly and in general effect exceedingly like the song of the Purple Finch; at others brighter and more glancing, the notes rolling one over another and suggesting those of the Ruby-crowned Kinglet; again, with a rich, throaty quality and in form as well as tone very closely like the song of the House Wren; still again guttural and somewhat broken or stuttering and very suggestive of the song of the Long-billed Marsh Wren. Although the first and last of these songs were very unlike, I have classified them under one head because the bird often gave them all during one singing period and, moreover, changed from one to another by insensible gradations.
>
> 4. Song in slow, measured bars or cadences, separated by brief intervals, swelling and sinking, some of the notes trilled or shaken, the whole given after the manner of the songs of the Hermit Thrush and Bachman's Finch and almost equally spiritual in quality.

Aretas A. Saunders (1935) transliterates two songs of the Lincoln's sparrow as: "*ŏŏ-ōō-ŏŏ-ōō-ŏŏ eeyayeeyayeeyayeeseseeesosee*" and "*ootle*

ootle ootle weetle weetle eeteeteetyāytōō." He illustrates these with his distinctive pictographs and continues: "The song of Lincoln's Sparrow is entirely distinctive, and not particularly like that of a Song Sparrow or other bird. It consists in part of notes sung with a true musician's trill, varying up and down a half tone in pitch, with liquid *l*-like consonants between the notes. Notes that are not of the trill type are inclined to be sibilant. The voice is sweet and clearly musical, and the song often suggests the House Wren or the Purple Finch. It is decidedly more pleasing than a House Wren's song, however."

In a personal note to Mr. Bent, Saunders adds the following more detailed analysis: "Songs consist of 13 to 16 notes each, though the character of the song is such that one cannot be too sure of separating the notes and counting them exactly. Songs vary from 2.4 to 2.8 seconds in length, and from C#''' to C'''' in pitch. The pitch interval is from 3½ to 5 tones."

Roland C. Clement wrote us of his Lincoln's sparrow observations in the Goose Bay region of Newfoundland Labrador in 1944: "On August 16 I 'squeaked up' eight birds in a tall stand of streamside alders, finding them very curious. 'The song,' I wrote in my journal, 'is soft but sweet and varied.' My own crude literal rendition of it was 'phreu-u-deer-e-e, $\overline{\text{teuu}}$ $\overline{\text{teu}}$ tree,' the two overscored notes being almost bell-like in richness of tone."

Almost all accounts of this species stress its song. This is owing no doubt to the apparent belief by Lincoln's sparrows that little birds should be heard but not seen. The Lincoln's sparrows we have observed singing have done little to bolster our faith in the advertising function of song perches. Usually the singer at Dorion, Ont., was well hidden in the cover of tall grasses or low shrubs in the marsh bordering the stream along which our observations were made. Occasionally one was found, after a considerable search, singing from a perch part way up a sheltering evergreen. When we did find one singing from an overhead wire or dead tree top or other conspicous perch, it was cause for special comment in our notes, Audubon notwithstanding. In the choice of its singing perch it resembles the swamp sparrow, but differs from its other congeneric species, the song sparrow.

We transcribed the song of a Lincoln's sparrow heard at Dorion May 15, 1955, in our field notes as "churr-churr-churr-wee-wee-wee-wah; quality like house wren or purple finch." This appears to be the most typical of northern Ontario songs, although we have heard several variations. W. W. H. Gunn was good enough to provide us with tape recordings of a variety of the songs of the Lincoln's sparrow, from which we selected the song most like this typical one. From this with the cooperation of Bruce Falls and the Royal Canadian

Air Force, we had an audiospectrograph made. This gives a visual picture of the song with time as the horizontal axis and frequency of the notes on the vertical scale.

The audiospectograph showed that there were six "churrs," seven "wees" and two final "wahs," rather than the three, three, and one we thought we heard, and also a longish "taa" note between the churrs and wees that we missed. The audiospectograph further showed that all the notes were far from simple but had introductory grace notes and various harmonics. The song was about two seconds in length, about as long as it takes to say "churr-churr-churr-taa-wee-wee-wee-wah." This transliteration gives us the best picture of what the Lincoln's sparrow says. We must remember that the reaction time of small birds is about twice as fast as ours, so it gets in two notes while we register one. On May 23, 1956, one bird sang a song which steadily rose in pitch, transliterated as "churr-churr-churr-wah-wah-wah-wee?" Another variation heard at Dorion June 12, 1956, we transliterated as "cheer-cheer-cheer-wah-wah-titi-wah-tsidlee-wah." In 1957 we added mourning warbler to the list of birds whose songs were similar to that of Lincoln's sparrow, though more in quality than in pattern in this case.

Sometimes Lincoln's sparrow sings on the wing. On May 25, 1956, at Grandview we saw one launch forth from a perch about 10 feet up a little birch and sing as it flew on fluttering wings some 12 feet above the ground, in an arc of about 50 feet. The flight song was introduced by a series of high, excited "tic" notes, and we transliterated it as "tic-tic-tic-churr-churr-churr-wee-wee-wee-wah." This bird had just returned from a chase involving a neighboring Lincoln's sparrow on the border of the adjacent territory.

Another flight song we heard at Dorion appeared to be caused by our shaking some branches of a brushpile in which we suspected the bird might have a nest. Still another flight song apparently was stimulated by courtship excitement; on June 9, 1956, after pouncing on the female and mating with her in the grass, the male flew toward us on quivering wings in slightly rising flight for about 50 feet, singing his normal song as he flew.

We made several counts of song frequency at Dorion and found three or four songs per minute usual during an active singing period, very rarely five songs per minute. Frequencies less than three per minute were usually correlated with change in singing position, which is not infrequent. Birds often sang from the ground while foraging. Song perches above the ground have been noted in low evergreens, tops of stumps, once on a branch about 20 feet up in a dead Jack pine, once on an overhead power wire (two unusually conspicuous perches), and most commonly in alders, willows, and birches from 4 to 8 feet high. As a full song lasts from two to three seconds, the birds are silent about 90 per cent of the time, even during an active singing period.

Singing shows marked seasonal and daily variations in amount. Birds are seldom heard singing during migration, and we have no record of their singing in winter. Even when they first arrive in breeding territory, they may be silent for several days if the weather stays cloudy and cold. At Dorion we noted that there was little singing on cold or rainy or windy mornings but a good deal on sunny, calm, warm mornings.

At Dorion, the birds sang at all times of day, but we never heard them after dark. J. Satterly, however, writes us in a letter: "This species begins to sing very early in the morning long before sunrise, probably as early as 2 a.m." His observations were made in Michaud Township, Cochrane District, Ont., in 1946. T. M. Shortt told us in conversation that at Fraserdale, Cochrane District, Ont., all the Lincoln's sparrows burst into song as the sky clouded over. Then as the sun came out all the singing ceased, to commence again as clouds darkened the sky. Lester L. Snyder confirmed this observation.

We found that singing practically ceased during the incubation period except for a few songs early in the morning, then increased again greatly when the young were about to leave the nest.

When singing ceased we generally found the birds by tracking down their rather faint, scolding "tit—tit—tit," notes often uttered from a low perch in spruce saplings, or in alders, or grassy undergrowth by both male and female. It somewhat resembles the chipping sparrow's scold notes but lacks the "s" sound of the chipping sparrow's "tsick."

We have mentioned in other sections the special "dzeee-dzeee" note the female utters with fluttering wings and squatting position when inviting copulation. One conversational greeting when a pair met under a small sheltering spruce we transliterated as "zu-zu-zu-zu" (u as in *tut*, not as in *toot*). This apparently was an excitement note of lesser intensity than the "zeee" note inviting mating.

Behavior.—We removed the 1957 nestlings from day to day to weigh them and make notes on their plumage development. When handled on June 18 when 1 and 2 days old they gaped as if to be fed. On June 21 at 4 and 5 days of age they uttered a complaining "zeeee" when taken from the nest. The following day they really squealed when picked up. On June 23, now 6 and 7 days old, when the mother arrived at the nest to feed them they uttered a high-pitched "zizz'zizz," and for the first time they made feeble efforts to scramble out of the dish in which we weighed them. On June 25 at 8 and 9 days they were well feathered and stretched their necks up for food when we parted the grass above the nest at 5:30 p.m. to see if they were still there. They left the nest on the following day. On June 27, when the fledglings were 10 and 11 days old and one day out of the nest, both parents were feeding them, each apparently feeding two young. We heard one of the young the father was looking after utter a high-pitched "zeeee" when fed.

Most observers who have written about Lincoln's sparrow have emphasized its shy, secretive, mousy, elusive behavior during migration and on the breeding ground. For instance, Audubon (1834) states "we found more wildness in this species than in any other inhabiting the same country " and again "It moves swiftly off when it discovers an enemy; and, if forced to take wing, flies low and rapidly to some considerable distance, jerking its tail as it proceeds, and throwing itself at the foot of the thickest bush it meets." Roberts (1932) calls it: "one of the shyest and most secretive of our Sparrows * * *. It passes by rather quickly in the spring, and, although usually common, keeps so well concealed in the thickest undergrowth and matted weeds and grass that only the keenest observers can discover it. It is at this season a silent bird and scurries away over the ground or along fallen tree-trunks with the speed and agility of a mouse, which adds to the difficulty in locating it. Taverner says, 'On migration * * * Lincoln's is one of the shyest and most elusive of birds. It skulks in the brush and has reduced concealment to a fine art' (Birds of Western Canada, 1926)."

On June 6, 1956, we were observing a pair at Dorion, in thin cover which consisted mainly of grass pastured the previous summer and just starting new growth, some low raspberry bushes just coming into leaf, and a small group of three or four spruces not over 3 feet high. We watched steadily from 6:12 a.m. to 6:37 a.m., when the male pounced on the female in the raspberry canes and returned to the spruce. We saw nothing stir from that time until we became restless at the lack of activity at 7:05 a.m. We then searched both the raspberry canes and the spruces, and could flush neither bird yet neither had been seen to leave. We had many similar demonstrations of their almost magical ability to disappear. This facility is due in part, no doubt, to their habit of "mousing off" through the grass instead of flying. Their behavior in their winter quarters, however, appears to differ from that familiar to observers in Canada and the United States. Alexander Wetmore (1944) writes:

> On their wintering grounds these sparrows seem completely at home, and here in Mexico I was able to fully appreciate the statements of E. A. Preble that this species is the song sparrow of the far north. * * * at Tres Zapotes in less than two months I actually learned more of their mannerisms than in 35 years of pre-

vious observations. Here instead of being shy skulkers that never left the dense shelter of weeds and shrubbery, their habit in migration, they came out like song sparrows to feed around the borders of the little clearing that we had made about our camp. At any time of the day if all was peaceful I had only to raise my eyes to see one or two feeding quietly on the ground, sometimes only 15 feet away. They pecked steadily at the earth, often scratching in typical finch fashion by jumping forward and then back, dragging the forward claws on the earth on the return, and then feeding again in the soil disturbed by this action. Others remained under the thin screen of leaves of the bordering shrubbery, and sometimes I found them running along on the earth in the protecting shelter of cornfields. When alarmed they retreated instantly to cover, where sometimes I heard them scolding sharply, the notes being suggestive of those of the swamp sparrow. I saw one driving petulantly at a little blue-black grassquit (*Volatinia jacarina atronitens*) that came too near. At dusk sometimes several came down from a weed grown field back of camp to roost in or near dense clumps of bushes. The daily appearance of this bird is to me one of the many pleasant memories of my work in this interesting locality.

So far as we have been able to determine, the Lincoln's sparrow hops and never, or rarely, walks. It seldom ventures far from cover, into which it retreats with amazing speed at the least sign of disturbance, crouching low and hopping so fast as to appear a mere streak of brown.

The nervous side-to-side tail-twitching so characteristic of agitated song sparrows is not customary for Lincoln's sparrows, which instead tend to crouch with neck outstretched and crest raised, muttering "tit—tit," followed by one of their celebrated exits.

The flight behavior of this species, at least near the nest, appears to be characterized by a fluttering directness rather than the bouncy flight of some fringillids. The females noted at Dorion during their foraging expeditions merely skimmed the tops of the low vegetation. Compared with the tail-pumping action of a song sparrow in flight, the Lincoln's sparrow's normal flight seems much more purposeful and direct.

On June 6, 1956, we watched a rather bedraggled, wet female perched in a little spruce energetically preening herself, concentrating on the upper breast with its characteristic buffy band. As this was a fine sunny morning with little dew, she had no doubt just come from a bath in the nearby creek edge. The male was seen preening in the same tree on the following morning, again concentrating on its upper breast as well as the base of the tail behind the wings. Our field notes for June 7, 1956, say: "Scratches behind both ears with both feet." Our notes for June 27, 1956, comment on the "very fast preening" of a parent that had just fed its young in the nest. "Not only does it use its beak in preening, but the feet come into play to scratch areas not easily reached with its bill."

The behavior of the female changes noticeably in the course of the breeding season. When flushed from a nest with eggs she usually utters no note while the observers are near the nest, but may begin to scold as they leave. When we flushed the female from the nest on June 18, 1957, when the young were just 1 and 2 days old, she ran through the grass about half way to the forest edge, fluttering part of the way as if she had a broken wing, but was too concealed by the grass to be seen well. She then flew the rest of the way to the forest edge where she emitted the first of several "tit" notes. The male answered with a quiet "tit." This was our only observation of injury feigning by Lincoln's sparrow.

This nesting female always came to the nest on foot, after mousing along the ditch, but she flew directly from the nest after feeding. She displayed great agitation when we handled the young for weighing and banding, "tit"ing loudly from the forest edge nearby.

On June 29, 1956, the mother was observed shielding the 5-day-old nestlings from the strong sun, at 12:25 p.m.

After the young had left the nest the parental solicitude continued to increase for a few days. On June 28, 1957, when the young were two days out of the nest, the mother scolded within 15 feet of the observer, and in plain sight, from a bare branch of a shrub by the roadside. The quality of the scold note had changed from the very weak "tit" heard early in the season, to the loud "tit," and after the young left the nest it approached the quality of a scolding chipmunk's "cork-pulling" note—"tot."

The behavior of the male also changes with the nesting season. He is very inconspicuous during most of the incubation period, generally singing only in the early morning and very spasmodically later in the day. He takes no part in incubation so far as we could determine. When the young hatched we not infrequently saw the male near the nest with food but in both of the 1956 and 1957 nestings, the father was very hesitant actually to go to the nest. After the young were fledged, however, the father became a good provider and appeared to play as active a part as the mother in rearing the young.

Field marks.—Peterson (1947) writes:

The Lincoln's Sparrow is a skulker, "afraid of its own shadow," and often hard to glimpse. Like Song Sparrow, with shorter tail; streakings on under parts *much finer* and often not aggregated into a central spot; best identified by broad band of *creamy buff* across breast.

Similar species.—The buffy band and fine breast-streakings distinguish it from most Sparrows except the immature Swamp and Song Sparrows. It is grayer-backed than either, with a more contrastingly striped crown A narrow *eye-ring* is also quite characteristic. The immature Swamp Sparrow in spring migration is continually misidentified as the Lincoln's Sparrow, but its breast is duller with dull blurry streaks (Lincoln's fine and sharp). In the South the juvenile Pine Woods Sparrow can easily be mistaken for Lincoln's.

Most of the salient field marks are mentioned in the above account:

The buffy breast band which also continues down the sides, the narrow and black streaking which is found not only on the breast but on the back and on top of the head, the short tail and the pronounced eye-ring which gives Lincoln's sparrow a characteristically wide-eyed astonished expression enhanced by its tendency to stare at the observer with neck stretched and crest raised, semi-crouched, as if to dash off at the slightest movement.

The really difficult plumage in which to determine this species with accuracy is the juvenal plumage, as Peterson and others have pointed out, for this plumage very closely resembles that of the juvenal song and swamp sparrows. Peterson, in the account quoted, wrongly states: "The immature Swamp Sparrow in spring migration * * *" is misidentified as Lincoln's. This should read "in autumn migration." James L. Baillie kindly checked the immature swamp sparrows in the collection of the Royal Ontario Museum and found that the latest date on which an immature swamp sparrow showed a streaked breast was September 10. After the end of September there should be little cause for confusing swamp with Lincoln's sparrows.

In late summer and early autumn, however, it is really very difficult to distinguish the juvenals in the field. Wendell Taber wrote us: I am exceedingly skeptical about sight records of Lincoln Sparrows in autumn. I remember, vividly, a sparrow I just could not identify on the shore of a pond in Ipswich many years ago. I went and got my father-in-law, Dr. C. W. Townsend, from his house 200 yards distant. HE couldn't identify the bird. I kept an eye on the bird until Dr. T. could get a gun. The bird was a Swamp Sparrow. But, even in the hand, Dr. T. couldn't identify it until he had spent a good deal of time reading."

The resemblance of juvenal song and swamp sparrows to Lincoln's is vividly illustrated in Allan Brooks' painting (Plate 72) in Forbush (1929) and his sketch of a juvenal Lincoln's sparrow on page 98 where Forbush writes: "*Young*: Often indistinguishable in the field from young Song Sparrow, unless by narrowness of dark streaks on either side of throat."

The crown pattern seems to be a good way for bird banders to distinguish the juvenals of swamp, song, and Lincoln's sparrows. The crown is mostly black, like a black cap, in swamp sparrows. It is brown with no black streaks in song sparrows. In the Lincoln's sparrow the crown is distinctly striped with about six fine black streaks on a brown background with a gray stripe in the center.

Enemies.—Predatory mammals, chiefly red squirrels, and birds, notably pigeon hawk, sparrow hawk, broad-winged hawk, gray jay, crow, and raven, were observed on or flying over the territories of our nests at Dorion, but the sparrows all survived successfully. The secretive habits of the adults and silence of the young no doubt help them avoid predation. They do not always escape, however, as Frank W. Braund and John W. Aldrich (1914) mention "young being eaten by sharp shinned hawk" from a nest in the Upper Peninsula of Michigan.

Apparently cowbird parasitism is comparatively rare. Herbert Friedmann (1963) writes:

> This sparrow has been recorded as a cowbird victim only a small number of times. S. S. Stansell, A. D. Henderson, and T. E. Randall informed me independently of parasitized nests, six in number, which they had found in Alberta. Dr. Ian McTaggert Cowan wrote me of a parasitized nest found at Elk Island Park, Alberta, the notes on which are in the files of the University of British Columbia. The late J. H. Bowles wrote me that he had in his collection a parasitized set of eggs taken at Kalevala, Manitoba, on June 6, 1920. G. Bancroft informed me of set found in Monroe County in northern New York on June 1, 1903. Street (Houston and Street, 1959, p. 195) found a nest at Nipawin, Saskatchewan, on June 3, containing only 1 egg of the sparrow; two days later it held 2 sparrow eggs and 2 cowbird eggs; and two days later, again, it held 3 cowbird eggs, no sparrow eggs, and the shell of another cowbird egg outside but near the nest. The New York Record refers to the eastern race of the Cowbird, *M.a.ater;* the others, to *M.a.artemisiae.* All refer to the typical race of the sparrow.

At Dorion the song sparrow appeared to be the Lincoln's sparrow's chief competitor. A song sparrow frequently sang from the same small spruce tree the male of our 1956 nesting pair favored as a singing perch. The Lincoln's sparrow never disputed possession of this tree but always beat a hasty and unobtrusive retreat. On various occasions song sparrows were seen chasing Lincoln's sparrows. The two species frequently had overlapping territories and, so far as could be determined, had identical territorial requirements. Possibly song sparrow competition is a factor determining the southern border of the nesting range of Lincoln's sparrow. Some territories occupied by Lincoln's early in the season were found later in undisputed possession of song sparrows. The smaller sparrows were able to remain in the same area in the face of song sparrow aggression only by dint of persistent passive resistance: they always fled and returned later by stealth. "The meek shall inherit the earth."

The Lincoln's sparrows at Dorion frequently hunted for food in the territory of the other congeneric species there, the swamp sparrow, but no conflicts were observed between the two. Chipping sparrows nested within the territory of our 1956 pair but did not conflict, as they nested at a greater height and foraged largely high up in tall spruces. White-throated sparrows were observed to chase even the song sparrows when their ranges overlapped, though the white-throats tended to confine most of their activities to more heavily forested areas.

Roy C. Anderson (1959) reports finding the air sacs of a Lincoln's sparrow infested with the nematode *Diplotriaena bargusinica.* He believes that in some cases this may be an important disease factor. L. R. Penner (1939) reports a fluke, *Tamerlania melospizae,* from the ureter of a Lincoln's sparrow found dead at Minneapolis May 1, 1938. Joseph C. Bequaert (1954) lists the species as host to louse flies (Hippoboscidae) of the following species: *Ornithomyia fringillina* and *Ornithoica vicina.* G. Robert Coatney and Evaline West (1938) write that the blood parasite *Haemoproteus* was found in a Lincoln's sparrow collected near Peru, Nebr., in 1937: "but there were too few to allow for detailed study."

Fall.—We were never able to remain at Dorion until the Lincoln's sparrows left for their autumn migration. When we departed Sept. 6, 1955, the birds were still active on their summer territories. Rita Taylor, a resident of Dorion, wrote us: "We have had Lincoln's sparrows feeding here quite often this fall, three at one time at the kitchen window. The last one was Sept. 19."

The peak of the autumn migration in the Toronto region is generally in the third week of September, when they may be found in marshy places and in weedy fields, often in company with white-throated and white-crowned sparrows. We used to flush them from the former Ashbridge's Bay marsh on the Toronto waterfront. They would keep well in cover, usually but some would yield to curiosity long enough to perch in some low bush, peek out at the observers with craned necks, raised crest, and wide-eyed wonderment, then drop down out of sight or dash away ahead to repeat the performance. The latest Toronto record is Nov. 19, 1932 (Speirs, *in* litt.).

Bird banders probably see more Lincoln's sparrows on migration than most bird watchers. Ruth Brown, of Toronto, Ont., took them on Sept. 22, 23, and 30 in 1956 at her city banding station. Two banding recoveries are of interest to fall migration. One banded at Wantagh, Long Island, N.Y. May 8, 1935, was recovered Oct. 1, 1935. in Gaspé County, Quebec. Another banded at Treesbank, Manitoba, Aug. 29, 1937, was recovered at Canarem, Iowa, Dec. 16, 1937.

Roberts (1932) has an interesting account of the fall migration through Minnesota:

> In the fall it is rather easier to find for then it is very abundant and keeps company with the other migrating Sparrows, but it is still silent and much more timid than its companions. Mr. Kendall finds it common on the Mesabi Iron Range in the fall and speaks of its quiet ways and resemblance to the Song Sparrow, especially when the spot on the breast is well marked. Dr. Hvoslef refers frequently in his notes to its abundance at Lanesboro, in the valley of the Root River, occasionally for a couple of weeks rivaling in numbers the White-throat. It is often abundant in the vicinity of the Twin Cities in late September and early October, frequenting hedgerows, weed-patches, borders of woods, tamarack

swamps, and similar dense coverts. Dr. Guilford found many at Lac qui Parle Lake, Chippewa County, early in October, feeding on the mud-flats just outside of the grass where the lake had dried; when flushed they took refuge in the grass farther back. From September 25 to October 3, 1907, the writer found it abundant at Heron Lake, Jackson County, frequenting thick, tangled weeds and grass on low places and also keeping company with Harris's Sparrows and White-throats in high brushy and weedy places and plum thickets. It was common in corn-fields and old grass-grown gardens. It was sprightly and quick in its actions, never still, twitching and jerking all the time, and timidly inquisitive. When flushed in the open it flew low in the same halting manner and with the same pumping of the tail as the Song Sparrow. When excited it erected the feathers of the crown to form a noticeable topknot. No sounds were heard from it except an occasion weak *tsup*.

William A. Squires (1952) gives the latest record for New Brunswick as a specimen in the American Museum taken on the Tobique River Sept. 28, 1894. For Maine Ralph S. Palmer (1949) writes: "As birds have been seen or collected in late August at places where they do not breed, there is some wandering or migration by then. A definite southward movement begins by the second week in September, with most birds seen from September 24 to October 13. * * * Late dates are: * * * October 17, 1918, on Monhegan (Wentworth in Jenney, 1919: 29)." Griscom and Snyder (1955) give autumn dates for Massachusetts as "September 12 (specimen)—October (November 1)." Norman A. Wood (1951) says that in Michigan: "The fall migration, for which the records are more numerous than for the spring, occurs mainly between the last of August and early October." The latest record for the Upper Peninsula is a report by Oscar M. Bryens (1939) near McMillan in Luce County, on October 17, 1937. The latest record for the Lower Peninsula appears to be one banded by E. M. Brigham, Jr. on October 17, 1938 (Walkinshaw, 1939). In central Pennsylvania Merrill Wood (1958) describes the Lincoln's sparrow as "fall transient from early-September to late-October."

Frances Westman (1960) records 7 Lincoln's sparrows among the 936 birds killed during four late September nights at the Barrie, Ontario, television tower. This indicates that Lincoln's sparrow is a night migrant.

Winter.—Griscom (1932) writes of the Lincoln's sparrow in Guatemala as "A not uncommon winter visitant, which has been taken as late as April 8. Alfred W. Anthony reports that he found it chiefly in the pine woods above 3000 feet."

Wetmore (1943) writes that Lincoln's sparrows are common winter residents in southern Veracruz, Mexico. He collected a small series in grassy clearings near the village of Tres Zapotes Mar. 8, 18, and 30 and Apr. 3 and 13, 1939, and on Jan. 23, 1940; also by the riverside at Titacotalpam on Feb. 5, 1940, and in grassy pastures on old dunes at El Conejo on Feb. 12, 1940. About the migration through Veracruz he writes: "On March 30 there was sudden increase in their number, evidence of migration from farther south, as on that morning half a dozen came skipping about on the ground in our clearing. They were passing in increased numbers through the early days in April and were still present on April 15, when I left for return home."

Dale A. Zimmerman (1957) describes his experience with Lincoln's sparrow in Tamaulipas, Mexico: "In 1955, at Pano Ayuctle, we found Lincoln Sparrows familiar door-yard birds that were easily studied at close range as they fed on the lawn and about the buildings. Two individuals that frequented a much-used path leading from the house, seldom moved more than a few feet out of the way when people walked by. They were as fearless as House Sparrows of city parks. The contrast between this behavior and that of the species during migration, and particularly on its breeding grounds, was striking."

Very rarely one of these sparrows remains north during the winter. On Jan. 3, 1960 Mrs. Else Rohner identified a Lincoln's sparrow at her feeding station near Rochester, New York. It remained into April and was seen by a number of qualified observers from the Rochester and Buffalo areas. Mrs. Rohner reported (fide Allen Kemnitzer) that the bird was fairly responsive to the placing of seed in the feeder, that it held its own with other feeding birds and that it was not overly shy. Its behavior appeared to be quite typical of a Lincoln's sparrow on its wintering grounds.

Distribution

Range.—Western Alaska, central Yukon, Mackenzie, northern Ontario, northern Quebec, central Labrador, and Newfoundland south to southern Mexico, El Salvador, the Gulf Coast, and central Florida.

Breeding range.—The eastern Lincoln's sparrow breeds from western and interior Alaska (upper Kobuk River, Iliamna Lake; Cordova Bay, intergrades with *M. l. gracilis*), central Yukon (Forty Mile), western and southern Mackenzie (Fort Good Hope, Fort Providence), northern Manitoba (Churchill), northern Ontario (Fort Severn), northern Quebec (Great Whale River, Fort Chimo), central Labrador (Hopedale), and Newfoundland (St. Anthony) south through interior British Columbia (Atlin, Chilcotin Lake) to the mountains of central and northeastern Washington (Mount Rainier, Windy Peak), northern Idaho (Potlatch River), northwestern Montana (Flathead Lake), southern and central Alberta (Waterton Lake Park, Battle River region), central Saskatchewan (Big River), southern Manitoba (Margaret), northern Minnesota (Leech Lake, Duluth), northern Wisconsin (Madeline Island, Oconto), central Michigan (Missaukee County), southern Ontario (casually to Pottageville and Wainfleet Marsh), western New York (Monroe County 15 miles northeast of Wilmurt), central and eastern Maine, and Nova Scotia (Advocate Harbour).

Winter range.—Winters from northern California (Chico, Sebastopol), southern Nevada (Searchlight), northern Arizona (Flagstaff), northern New Mexico (Shiprock), northern Oklahoma (Copan), eastern Kansas, central Missouri (Kansas City), south-central Kentucky (Bowling Green), and northern Georgia (Kirkwood; Chatham County) south to southern Baja California (Victoria Mountains), El Salvador (Los Esesmiles), Quintana Roo (Camp Mengel), southern Louisiana (Cameron), southern Mississippi (Gulfport), Alabama, and central Florida (Orlando); casually north to Washington (Foster Island), northern Illinois (Beach), southern Ontario (Kingston), Pennsylvania (Jeffersonville), and North Carolina (Raleigh), and south to Canal Zone, southern Florida (Goulds), and Bermuda.

Accidental in Greenland (Nanortalik) and Jamaica (Blue Mountains).

Migration.—The data deal with the species as a whole. Early dates of spring arrival are: Florida—Tallahassee, April 26. Alabama—Huntsville, May 2. South Carolina—Aiken County, April 24. Virginia—Lynchburg, April 4; Blacksburg, April 5. District of Columbia—April 21 (average of 10 years, May 5). Maryland—Laurel, May 3. Pennsylvania—Beaver, May 6; State College, May 7. New Jersey—Princeton, May 8. New York—New York City, April 11; Ontario County, April 28; Orient, April 29. Connecticut—East Hartford, April 24. Massachusetts—Cambridge, May 7. New Hampshire—New Hampton, May 15 (median of 5 years, May 20). Maine—Bangor and Lake Umbagog, May 15. Quebec—Montreal area, May 6. New Brunswick—Grand Manan, May 2. Nova Scotia—Antigonish, May 19. Newfoundland—Tompkins, May 19. Arkansas—Little Rock, April 10. Tennessee—Nashville, April 25; Knox County, May 12. Missouri—St. Louis, April 1 (median of 13 years, April 20). Illinois—Urbana, April 1 (median of 19 years, May 3); Chicago, April 19 (average of 16 years, April 30). Indiana—Wayne County, April 28. Ohio—Oberlin, April 14 (median of 12 years, May 9); central Ohio, April 16 (median of 40 years, May 5). Michigan—Battle Creek, April 22; Detroit area, May 4 (mean of 10 years, May 7). Ontario—Meadowvale, April 14. Iowa—Sioux City, April 12. Wisconsin—Oconto County, April 12. Minnesota—Minneapolis-St. Paul, April 19 (average of 6 years, April 26). Oklahoma—Norman, April 2. Kansas—northeastern Kansas, April 14 (median of 7 years, April 18). Nebraska—Holstein, April 18; Red Cloud, April 20 (average of 11 years, May 1). South Dakota—Sioux Falls, April 17 (average of 7 years, April 27); Mellette, April 20. North Dakota—Lower Souris Refuge, April 14; Cass County, April 27 (average, May 1). Manitoba—Treesbank, April 25 (average of 12 years, May 9). Saskatchewan—Eastend, May 1. Mackenzie—Hay River, May 12. New Mexico—Los Alamos, March 20. Colorado—Fort Lyon, April 2. Utah—Salt Lake City, March 21. Wyoming—Laramie, April 8 (average of 9 years, May 1). Idaho—Lewiston, April 1 (median of northern Idaho, April 13). Montana—Libby, April 28; Miles City, May 4. Alberta—Carvel, April 29. Nevada—Mercury, March 18. Oregon—Malheur National Wildlife Refuge, April 14. Washington—Bellingham Bay, April 23. British Columbia—Okanagan, April 18. Alaska—Nulato, May 16.

Late dates of spring departure are: Florida—Lower Keys, May 14. Alabama—Florence, May 11. Georgia—Athens, May 13. North Carolina—Morganton, May 14. Virginia—Lexington, May 18; Blacksburg, May 16. District of Columbia—May 30 (average of 10 years, May 20). Maryland—Brookeville, June 1; Prince Georges County, May 30. Pennsylvania—Crawford County, May 24. New York—New York City area, June 7. Connecticut—Hartford, May 30. Massachusetts—Belmont, May 26. New Hampshire—New Hampton, June 1; Concord, May 23. Maine—Portland, May 12. New Brunswick—Grand Manan, May 26. Louisiana—Baton Rouge, April 14. Mississippi—Deer Island, May 7. Arkansas—Little Rock, May 16. Tennessee—Nashville, May 28 (median of 13 years, May 17). Kentucky—Bardstown, May 16. Missouri—St. Louis, May 30 (median of 13 years, May 14). Illinois—Chicago, June 1 (average of 16 years, May 27); Urbana, May 28 (median of 19 years, May 15). Indiana—Wayne County, May 22. Ohio—central Ohio, May 28 (median of 40 years, May 18); Oberlin, May 23 (median of 12 years, May 14). Michigan—Detroit area, May 24 (mean of 10 years, May 22). Ontario—London, May 19. Iowa—Sioux City, May 20. Wisconsin—Sheboygan, May 29. Minnesota—Minneapolis-St. Paul, May 22 (average of 6 years, May 19). Texas—Sinton, May 16 (median of 5 years, May 4); Amarillo, May 12. Oklahoma—Norman, May 12. Kansas—northeastern Kansas, May 19 (median of 9 years, May 6). Nebraska—Holstein, May 17. South Dakota—Sioux Falls, May 23 (average of 6 years, May 20). North Dakota—Cass County, May 30 (average, May 24). New Mexico—Los Alamos, May 27. Arizona—Cibola, April 7. Utah—Uinta Basin, April 15. Idaho—Moscow, May 15 (median for northern Idaho, May 1). Montana—Libby and Columbia Falls, May 15. California—Mount Hamilton, May 3. Nevada—Esmeralda County, May 9. Oregon—Ashland, May 6. Washington—Okanogan, May 6.

Early dates of fall arrival are: Washington—Mount Adams, August 27; Everson, September 5. Oregon—Portland, September 9. Nevada—Hidden Forest, September 17. California—Berkeley, September 8. Montana—Dawson County, August 27; Libby, August 28. Idaho—Lewiston, August 29 (median for northern Idaho, September 1). Utah—Standrod, August 25. Arizona—Chiricahua Mountains, August 24. New Mexico—Los Alamos, September 2 (median of 6 years, September 11). North Dakota—Cass County, August 22 (average, August 26); Jamestown, August 25. South Dakota—Sioux Falls, August 27. Nebraska—Holstein, September 5. Kansas—northeastern Kansas, September 5 (median of 6 years, October 1). Oklahoma—Copan, September 29. Texas—Austin, September 11; Sinton, September 17 (median of 9 years, October 8). Minnesota—Minneapolis-St. Paul, August 17 (average of 5 years, September 1). Wisconsin—Waukesha County, September 3. Iowa—Sioux City, August 31. Ontario—Toronto, September 18. Michigan—Detroit area, September 7 (mean of 10 years, September 20). Ohio—Buckeye Lake, September 4 (median of 40 years for central Ohio, September 23). Indiana—Wayne County, September 18. Illinois—Chicago, September 1 (average of 16 years, September 10). Missouri—St. Louis, September 18 (median of 12 years, September 28). Kentucky—Bowling Green, September 20. Tennessee—Nashville, September 29; Knox County, October 5. Arkansas—Fayetteville, October 8; Little Rock, October 14. Mississippi—Deer Island, November 1. Louisiana—Baton Rouge, October 11. Maine—Portland, September 25. New Hampshire—New Hampton, September 2 (median of 18 years, September 19). Massachusetts—Belmont, September 9. Connecticut—Stanford, September 2; East Windsor Hill, September 9. New York—Orient, September 9; Tiana, September 11. New Jersey—Princeton, September 21. Pennsylvania—State College, September 5; Beaver, September 30. Maryland—Laurel, September 12. District of Columbia—September 30. Virginia—Blacksburg, September 18; Lexington, September 21. North Carolina—North Fork Valley, September 17. Georgia—Athens, October 6. Alabama—Dauphin Island, October 14; Livingston, October 17. Florida—Leon County, October 9; Lower Keys, October 18.

Late dates of fall departure are: Alaska—Cook Inlet, September 28. Yukon—Macmillan River, August 24. British Columbia—Chilliwack, October 21. Washington—Tacoma, November 11. Oregon—Portland, November 26. Nevada—Indian Springs, October 21. Alberta—Camrose, October 7. Montana—Libby, October 2. Idaho—Lewiston, October 16 (median for northern Idaho, October 2). Wyoming—Laramie, October 20 (average of 9 years, October 3). Utah—Deep Creek, October 5. Colorado—Colorado Springs, November 2. New Mexico—Los Alamos, October 18 (median of 5 years, October 2). Mackenzie—Fort Simpson, September 6. Saskatchewan—Eastend, September 22. Manitoba—Treesbank, October 27 (average of 11 years, October 17). North Dakota—Cass County, October 21 (average, October 5). South Dakota—Sioux Falls, October 21. Nebraska—Holstein, November 4. Kansas—northeastern Kansas, October 27. Oklahoma—Payne County, November 8. Minnesota—Minneapolis-St. Paul, October 28 (average of 6 years, October 19). Wisconsin—Milwaukee, November 6. Iowa—Sioux City, October 26. Ontario—Toronto, October 11. Michigan—Detroit area, October 27 (mean of 10 years, October 12); Battle Creek, October 17. Ohio—Buckeye Lake, November 3 (median of 40 years for central Ohio, October 23). Indiana—Wayne County, October 23 (median of 5 years, October 19). Illinois—Chicago, October 28 (average of 16 years, October 16). Missouri—St. Louis, November 10 (median of 12 years, October 28). Kentucky—Bowling Green, November 26. Tennessee—Nashville, October 29 (median of 10 years, October 11); Knox County, October 23. Arkansas—Little Rock, November 25. Newfoundland—Stephenville Crossing, September 20. New Brunswick—Tobique River, September 28. Quebec—Montreal area, October 6. Maine—Lake Umbagog, October 16. New Hampshire—New Hampton, October 17 (median of 18 years, October 17). Massachusetts—Belmont, November 1. Connecticut—East Windsor Hill, October 24. New York—Long Island, December 4. New Jersey—Princeton, October 25; Cape May, October 12. Pennsylvania—State College, October 26; Allegheny County, October 23. Maryland—Baltimore County, October 30; Laurel, October 30 (median of 4, October 12). District of Columbia—October 21 (average of 3 years, October 18). Virginia—Lexington, November 22; Blacksburg, October 26. South Carolina—Columbia, November 7.

Egg dates.—Alaska: 2 records, June 21 and June 27.

Alberta: 46 records, May 27 to June 28; 27 records, June 6 to June 14.

Mackenzie: 4 records, June 13 to June 25.

New Brunswick: 7 records, June 8 to June 15.

Ontario: 11 records, June 4 to July 11; 6 records, June 9 to June 17.

Quebec: 30 records, June 3 to June 29; 18 records, June 12 to June 21.

MELOSPIZA LINCOLNII ALTICOLA (Miller and McCabe)

Montane Lincoln's Sparrow

Contributed by Oliver L. Austin, Jr.

Habits

The 1957 A.O.U. Check-List assigns to this race the Lincoln's sparrows breeding in the mountains from Oregon and Montana southward to northern New Mexico, central Arizona, and southern California. This is essentially the distribution its describers, Miller and McCabe (1935) attribute to it. They epitomize the population as a variable "mosaic," for which they were reluctant to designate a type because "there is no such thing as a specimen typical of the race." They claim the subspecies averages slightly larger than nominate northern and eastern *lincolnii*, and "includes chiefly birds with moderately ruddy or brown backs, rarely ruddy or gray-brown backs. The greatest number are brown-backed. Varying percentages of brown backed birds are of the dull brown type with reduced light feather margins. Birds with moderately broad and narrow stripes are included, but the latter type predominates."

It must be admitted that the systematic status of *alticola* still remains open to some question, for no two recent writers who have studied the western Lincoln's sparrows agree with each other, or with the Check-List for that matter, on its characteristics and distribution. Jewett et al. (1953) assign to it the birds breeding in the mountains of Washington state, which they claim are "more grayish and slightly larger" than nominate *lincolnii*. Gabrielson and Lincoln (1959) include in it all the Lincoln's sparrows of mainland Alaska and Mackenzie, which they find "entirely lack the rich browns that characterize the eastern race." Finally Phillips et al. (1964) relegate *alticola* to the synonymy of *lincolnii* with the tart parenthetical comment: "Several earnest ornithologists have foundered on McCabe's color descriptions or have left museum work in despair."

At best the population to which the Check-List assigns this name is a poorly marked and highly variable one. Sharp geographical boundaries cannot be drawn between many of its segments, and throughout its range are many individuals that cannot be identified subspecifically with certainty on morphological grounds alone.

Its summer habitat in California Grinnell and Miller (1944) describe as "mountain meadows of boggy type, grown to fairly tall grass, *Veratrum*, and sedges, and fringed or intermixed with willow thickets. Wet ground and wet dead grass invariably are present. The ground usually is flooded shallowly by melting snow or by springs or overflow from streams at the time nest sites are chosen."

In these surroundings the species becomes somewhat less shy. W. L. Dawson (1923) notes:

> And forty years of acquaintance with the Lincoln Song Sparrow in winter and on migrations will scarcely yield one more than fleeting glimpses, baffling disappearances, or strained moments of maddening unnaturalness.
>
> Quite different is the story of the Lincoln sparrow in his summer home, an emerald meadow in the Sierras, or a lush-bound cienaga in one of the southern ranges. There he bursts upon you in a torrent of music, a flood which leaves you fairly gasping. This little, slinking, bird-afraid-of-his-shadow gets all at

once the courage of mighty convictions, when he has the mountain to back him; and though he still skulks and evades, it is henceforth rather as a modest hero shunning the plaudits of an unrestrained admiration."

Nesting.—Charles R. Keyes (1905) was one of the first to record a nest of this form. He found one in the central Sierras "with three half-fledged young * * * in a small and very wet meadow near Susie Lake, just off the Mt. Tallac trail, on July 2. It was placed in a bunch of dead grass and composed of the same material and a few hairs. Both parents approached me closely while at the nest." Wright M. Pierce (1916) writes from the San Bernardino Mountains of California, "On June 21 in a small meadow near Bluff Lake I found a nest containing five eggs of this bird, incubation just started. The nest was placed on the ground at the base of a small bunch of hellebore, and was composed mostly of grass, with a little hair and one feather for a lining."

In the mountains of southwestern Montana, Aretas A. Saunders (1910) writes in the experimental spelling of that day

* * * I flusht a Lincoln Sparrow (*Melospiza lincolni*) from its nest, situated at the base of a clump of willows and containing three eggs. At our next camp, about six miles south of Pipestone Basin, I found two more nests of this bird, one with four and one with five eggs. The nests are much like those of the Song Sparrow but a little smaller, and constructed almost entirely of grass with little or no hair in the lining. The way in which this bird flushes from her nest is very distinctive and quite unlike any other sparrow with which I am acquainted. She slips quietly from her nest and runs off thru the grass without a note or a flutter of any sort, her movements more like those of a mouse than a bird. In fact two of the three birds I flusht I supposed at first were mice, and had I not lookt at them a second time would have gone away without seeing their nests.

In his recent studies of subalpine fringillids in Colorado, Neil F. Hadley (MS.) writes:

Nineteen nests of the Lincoln's Sparrow were found. These nests were restricted to very wet, marshy areas between 9,500 and 11,000 feet. The availability of this particular habitat, plus the excellent concealment of the nest were important factors in reducing the number of nests found. The number of eggs per nest varied from 4 to 5 and averaged 4.4. The length of incubation for eggs in nests for which it was possible to follow the complete history of a brood was 12 to 13 days, with a similar amount of time spent in the nest after hatching. It was not determined whether the Lincoln's Sparrow attempted a second brood if the first was unsuccessful or if more than one brood was reared during the season.

Jewett et al. (1953) write:

Few nests have ever been found in the [Washington] state. Dawson (1908d: 483) reports a breeding colony of some 20 individuals in the swamp at Longmire Springs, Mt. Rainier. On July 1, 1908, the birds seemed to be about evenly divided between care of young out of the nest and preparations for a second nesting. Peck located a nest July 25, 1917, in a little alder bush in a swampy place along Surveyors Creek, close to Signal Peak Ranger Station. The nest was not quite 12 inches from the ground, being concealed by sedges. It was built of rather fine grasses and contained 5 eggs in an advanced stage of incubation. As the observer approached, the parent flew silently from the nest and did not reappear during the 10 minutes he spent in the neighborhood.

Eggs.—The measurements of 40 eggs average 19.1 by 14.5 millimeters; the eggs showing the four extremes measure *20.6* by 15.2, 20.1 by *15.5*, *17.8* by 13.7, and 18.0 by *13.2* millimeters.

Young.—No account of the breeding biology of this form has ever been published, but most aspects of it probably differ little if at all from those of the nominate race. A. A. Saunders (1910) continues his experiences with the species in Montana:

> Up to the time the young birds left the nest I never heard an alarm note of any sort from the Lincoln Sparrows, but after that time, which took place about June 25, one could not enter the willow thickets without being scolded from one end to the other by these birds. We had a litter of young coyotes in camp, and one Sunday they broke loose from their pen and led us quite a chase into a near-by willow swamp, before they were finally captured. As soon as they entered the swamp the Lincoln Sparrows, evidently recognizing a natural enemy, started scolding in a manner that I have seldom heard equalled in any bird. While helping to corner one of the coyotes, I notist a young Lincoln Sparrow running ahed of me thru the grass and soon captured it. In general appearance and in the manner in which it ran thru the grass this bird resembled, until actually caught, a newly hatcht game-bird rather than a young sparrow. It was unable to fly, but was very active at running and hiding in the tall grass. I took it to camp and posed it on the end of a tent peg for its picture, after which I releast it again in the swamp.

Food.—As Gabrielson and Lincoln (1959) point out, "Little is known about their food * * *. Nevertheless, it can be assumed to consist of seeds similar to those utilized by other sparrows. It probably also takes its share of such insects as are available during the summer months." The latter observation is corroborated by Grinnell (1908) who states that while camped in the San Bernardino Mountains in late June "fully a dozen adults were seen, some carrying bills full of insects and others singing a wheezy, incoherent song from the tips of dead willow stalks. They were very secretive and kept pretty much out of sight in the rank Veratrum patches and willow thickets."

Voice.—R. T. Peterson (1941) states "Song, sweet and gurgling; suggests both House Wren and Purple Finch; starts with low passages, rises abruptly, drops." Dawson (1923) gives the following more detailed account of his impressions of it in California:

> The song of the Lincoln Sparrow is of a distinctly musical order, being gushing, vivacious and wren-like in quality, rather than lisping and wooden, as are so many of our sparrow songs. Indeed, the bird shows a much stronger relationship in song to the Purple Finch than it does to its immediate congeners, the Song Sparrows. The principal strain is gurgling, rolling, and spontaneous, and the bird has ever the trick of adding two or three inconsequential notes at the end of his ditty, quite in approved Purple Finch fashion. *Linkup, tinkup perly werly willie willie weeee* (dim.) says one; *Riggle, jiggle, eet eet eer oor*, another. *Che willy*

willy willy che quill; Lee lee lee quilly willy, willy, and other such, come with full force and freshness at a hundred yards to the listeners * * *.

Jewett et al. (1953) thus describe it in Washington: "The song of the Lincoln sparrow, which may be heard in summer on favorable alpine meadows, is rendered with unique and attractive quality, and when first heard greatly piques the curiosity. On attempting to find the bird the concert stops abruptly, and the singer drops into the brush out of sight. * * * As the summer advances the song of the Lincoln loses much of its piquancy and charm, and is less often heard, A *chek* call note, with something of junco and of warbler quality about it, but different from either, is more in evidence."

Fall.—Jewett et al. (1953) continue:

The restlessness so universal with birds in the fall seems to infect the Lincoln with the rest, and migrating individuals are frequently encountered. It is less closely bound at this season by its predilections for meadow and swamp, and we have found it common in September in the flag and tule thickets of the lowlands and the mountain ash brush and dwarfed conifers close to timber line in the mountains. It is likely to be encountered, during migration, in almost any brushy or grassy situation not too far from water, although it sedulously avoids the woods. It often attaches itself to roving bands of white-crowned or golden-crowned sparrows or juncos.

Winter.—Grinnell and Miller (1944) state this race migrates to the the California lowlands in September and winters in the same type of habitat as *M. l. lincolnii,* which they characterize as: "Low-growing bushes and clumps of annuals interspersed with grass, especially on damp ground or near water. Ditch banks, brushy borders of sloughs, tangles of driftwood, and sedge clumps are typical situations. The birds adhere closely to cover and make the fullest use of its protection when alarmed, only momentarily exposing themselves in flight low over the ground between cover. In foraging they work inconspicuously and solitarily through the grass about the bases of bushes or within brush tangles."

Distribution

Range.—Oregon and Montana south to southern Mexico, Guatemala, and El Salvador.

Breeding range.—The Montane Lincoln's sparrow breeds in mountains from north-central and eastern Oregon (Breitenbush Lake, Wallowa Mountains), central Idaho (Payette Lake), southwestern and south-central Montana (18 miles northwest of Dillon, Shriver), and north-central Wyoming (Big Horn Mountains) south to California (west to the inner northern coast ranges, South Yolla Bolly Mountain; south to the San Jacinto Mountains), west-central Nevada (Galena Creek), southwestern Utah (Cedar Breaks), east-central Arizona (White Mountains), and northern New Mexico (Pecos Baldy).

Winter range.—Winters from central California (Hayward, Modesto), southern Nevada (Boulder City), southern Arizona (Phoenix, Patagonia), Chihuahua (Chihuahua), and southern Texas (Kerrville) south to southern Baja California (El Sauce), Guatemala (Finca La Primavera), and El Salvador (Los Esesmiles). In migration in western Kansas.

Egg dates.—California: 29 records, May 24 to June 30; 22 records June 13 to June 25.

Colorado: 21 records, June 12 to July 14; 11 records June 20 to June 26.

Oregon: 6 records, June 13 to June 25.

MELOSPIZA LINCOLNII GRACILIS (Kittlitz)

Northwestern (Forbush's) Lincoln's Sparrow

Contributed by Oliver L. Austin, Jr.

Habits

The Lincoln's sparrows breeding on the Pacific coast and islands from southeastern Alaska to Vancouver Island average slightly smaller in wing and tail measurements than the other two subspecies. P. A. Taverner (1926) calls *gracilis* "a faintly defined race, slightly more olivaceous on back and with the dark streaks heavier and more numerous."

J. Grinnell (1910) reports that Miss Alexander found the birds at the head of Cordova Bay "occupying the upper end of the tide flat, where they found cover in the low, stiff, willow-like brush that skirted the sloughs." In the Sitka region George Willett (1914) says: "It is apparently a fairly common summer visitant during some years, and much less plentiful during others. In the summer of 1912 I found it common in the grass around Swan Lake and in marshes at the head of Silver Bay. Young birds just out of the nest were noted in the former locality July 28. During 1913 I visited both of these localities several times but failed to find the species at all, nor did I note it anywhere else in the region."

H. S. Swarth (1922) describes *gracilis* as probably occurring throughout the upper Stikine Valley but, "judging from our experience, in small numbers and at widely scattered points." When he reached Sergief Island August 18th many birds were present, and "they greatly increased in numbers within the next few days. At the upper margin of the marshes, that section which is but rarely inundated by the tides, there is much willow brush, increasing in density and size of the trees as the salt water is left behind. The lower edge of this strip, where the willow brush was about waist high and rather scattered, and with thick grass beneath, was the preferred habitat * * * and here the birds literally swarmed. I was accustomed to think of this species as being rather solitary in its habits, but here, whether or not the birds were in constantly associated flocks, their choice of surroundings brought hundreds of them closely together." He counted 15 birds in view at one time. The species was still present in reduced numbers September 7th.

Grinnell (1909) states "On Chichagof Island it was not uncommon along the edge of the timber near the river at Hooniah, June 21 to 27, where it was breeding. Littlejohn found a nest there June 26, in the moss on the side of a fallen, half-buried log just above high-water mark. It was well concealed by overhanging vegetation. The nest was located by watching the female parent feed the five young which were thought to be about six days old. She was very shy about approaching the nest." The same author (1910) describes a nest Miss Alexander found at the head of Cordova Bay June 10 as:

well concealed in a rather straggling clump of the stiff brush characterizing the local habitat of the species. It was located at the base of a low-lying branch that almost completely covered it. The nest (no. 39) presents a firm structure, externally 67 mm. deep by 100 in width. This does not, however, probably include whatever peripheral loosely laid material there may have been. The cup-shaped cavity is 38 mm. deep by 53 wide. Externally the nest consists of layers of brown willow leaves of the previous season. Within this and making up the rim, is a basket-work of rather coarse, weathered grayish stems and blades of grass. Finally the nest-lining is of fine, round, yellowed grasses.

The measurements of 40 eggs average 19.4 by 14.2 millimeters; the eggs showing the four extremes measure *20.8* by 14.7, 19.8 by *15.5*, *17.8* by 13.7, and 18.0 by 13.2 millimeters.

Distribution

Range.—Southeastern Alaska to central California.

Breeding range.—The northwestern Lincoln's sparrow breeds in the coastal district of southeastern Alaska (Yakutat Bay, Juneau) and central British Columbia (Doch-da-on, intergrades with *M. l. lincolnii;* Queen Charlotte Islands, Porcher Island); rarely on Vancouver Island (in mountains).

Winter range.—Winters chiefly in central California (Lakeport, Colusa, Morro Bay, Walker Basin); rarely south to southern California (Tia Juana River), northern Baja California (El Valle de la Trinidad), southwestern Arizona (The Needles), central Sonora (Maicoba), and Coahuila (Sierra del Carmen).

MELOSPIZA GEORGIANA ERICRYPTA Oberholser

Northern Swamp Sparrow

PLATE 74

Contributed by DAVID KENNETH WETHERBEE

HABITS

"In this moderately well marked race," (Godfrey, 1949) "breeding adults differ from *Melospiza georgiana georgiana* in their paler upper parts, the browns of back and rump averaging grayer, the pale dorsal feather edgings whiter and apparently broader. Autumn specimens of *ericrypta* are distinguishable by their paler dorsal and rump coloration, and by the paler feather edgings of the back which provide more contrast with the black dorsal streaking than in *georgiana*, which average darker and duller above. In juvenal plumage the differences are somewhat less obvious but *ericrypta* averages paler." Wetmore (1940) finds that Oberholser's (1938) statement that the western birds are smaller is not confirmed by measurements.

DISTRIBUTION

Range.—Southern Mackenzie, northern Ontario, central Quebec, and Newfoundland south to central Mexico, the Gulf coast, and northeastern Florida.

Breeding range.—The northern swamp sparrow breeds from southwestern and central southern Mackenzie (Fort Norman, Hill Island Lake), northern Saskatchewan (Lake Athabaska), northern Manitoba (Churchill), northern Ontario (Fort Severn, Attawapiskat Post), central Quebec (Paul Bay, Mingan Island), and Newfoundland (Pistolet Bay, St. John's) south to northeastern British Columbia (Nulki Lake, Tates Creek), central Alberta (Red Deer), southern Saskatchewan (Indian Head), southern Manitoba (Margaret, Indian Bay), northeastern North Dakota (Fargo), northern Minnesota, western and central Ontario (Big Fork, Chapleau), and south-central Quebec (Lake St. John, Gaspé Peninsula).

Winter range.—Winters south to Jalisco (Ocotlán), Tamaulipas (Altamira), eastern Texas (Beaumont), southern Louisiana (Buras), southern Mississippi (Cat Island), southern Georgia (Grady County, Folkston), and northeastern Florida (Gainesville, Palatka). Northern limits in winter imperfectly known; recorded from Tennessee (Nashville), South Carolina (Anderson County), Virginia (Manassas, Alexandria, Mount Vernon), and Massachusetts (Wayland); casually to northwestern Oregon (Tillamook), California (Morro Bay; San Diego County; Riverside, Salton Sea), central Nevada (Ruby Lake), and southern Arizona (Tucson).

Erie County, N.Y., June 1928 S. A. Grimes

NEST AND EGGS OF SWAMP SPARROW

Crawford County, Pa., June 1949 H. H. Harrison

SWAMP SPARROW INCUBATING

Madison County, Ill., May 24, 1936 J. H. Gerard

NEST AND EGGS OF SONG SPARROW

Lake Summit, N.C., July 1950 D. J. Nicholson

SONG SPARROW AT NEST

Egg dates.—Ontario: 28 records, May 19 to July 25; 14 records, May 30 to June 9.

Quebec: 26 records, May 9 to June 26; 18 records, May 20 to June 2.

MELOSPIZA GEORGIANA GEORGIANA (Latham)

Southern Swamp Sparrow

Contributed by DAVID KENNETH WETHERBEE

HABITS

Because the specimen he described came from Georgia, John Latham named this species *Fringilla georgiana* in 1790. Known earlier by William Bartram as the "reed sparrow," it was first called the swamp sparrow by Alexander Wilson when he redescribed it as *Fringilla palustris* (swampy) in 1811. Recognizing its close taxonomic relationship to the song and Lincoln's sparrows, Spencer Fullerton Baird placed all three species in his new genus *Melospiza* (song finch) in 1858. Because of the similarity of their juvenal plumages, Richard Graber (pers. comm.) would unite *Melospiza* and *Passerelle*, as J. M. Linsdale (1928) and others have recommended on morphological and behavioral grounds. Graber considers *georgiana*, on the basis of plumage characteristics, to be evolutionarily the "most advanced" member of the combined genera. Though this group is famous for geographical variation in color and size, only three subspecies of the swamp sparrow are recognized by the current (1957) A.O.U. Check-List: the nominate southern race, *georgiana*, a lighter northern race, *ericrypta*, and a darker coastal race, *nigrescens*. The habits of all three are treated together here.

In comparison to its much-studied congener, the song sparrow, the swamp sparrow is rather poorly known, a simple consequence of the ankle- to waist-deep morass that is its usual habitat. As E. H. Forbush (1929) aptly expresses it:

> The Swamp Sparrow is not a public character. He will never be popular or notorious. He is too retiring to be much in the public eye, and too fond of the impassable bog and morass to have much human company; and so he comes and goes unheralded and to most people unknown. He is the dark little bird that fusses about in the mud when spring floods have overflowed the wood roads, or slips through the grasses on marsh-lined shores of slow-flowing, muddy rivers. Any watery, muddy, bushy, grassy place where rank marsh grasses, sedges and reeds grow—any such bog or slough where a man will need long rubber boots to get about—is good enough for Swamp Sparrows. In such places they build their nests. But in migration they may appear almost anywhere, though seldom distinctly seen and recognized by ordinary observers, because of their retiring habits. When they are looked for, they sneak about, mostly under cover, and hardly show themselves sufficiently for identification, but if the observer

apparently takes no interest in their whereabouts and sits quietly down, curiosity may overcome their suspicions and bring them into view.

Spring.—The "swamp song sparrows" are first heard in the breeding range in March, and they reach a numerical peak in New England in mid-May. At this time they can be found in many swamps where there will be none during the nesting season. The sparse northern wintering population is probably migratory; a bird banded at Athol, Mass. in January remained at the banding station until April when it disappeared (Bagg and Eliot, 1937). One banded at Lisle, Ill., May 1, 1931, was found dead a year and a day later in Clarion, Mich.

P. L. Hatch (1892) states, perhaps without critical evidence, that the females arrive a few days later than the males in spring.

LeRoy C. Stegeman (1955) notes that swamp sparrows are lighter in weight in the spring than they are in the fall. This condition, the reverse of that in its near relative, the song sparrow, he attributes to the fact that the swamp sparrow is more insectivorous and less granivorous than the song sparrow.

Nesting.—The swamp sparrow breeds in fresh water marshes, swamps, bogs, and wet meadows, and about the low swampy shores of lakes and streams, more rarely in coastal brackish meadows. Usually only a few pairs occupy a given locality, but occasionally it seems to nest semi-colonially where conditions are suitable. Chandler S. Robbins (1949) reports a breeding density of 21 per 100 acres (2 in 9½ acres) of "open hemlock-spruce bog" in Maryland. J. W. Aldrich (1943) determined that in northeastern Ohio it shares seasonal predominance with the redwinged blackbird and Virginia rail in the *Decodon-Typha* Associes; with the short-billed marsh wren, redwinged blackbird, and Virginia rail in the *Juncus-Scirpus* Associes; with the song sparrow, yellowthroat, and yellow warbler in the *Nemopanthus-Alnus* Associes; with the song sparrow, American goldfinch, robin, yellow warbler, yellowthroat, redwinged blackbird, kingbird, and Traill's flycatcher in the *Cephalanthus-Alnus* associes; and with the song sparrow and yellowthroat in the *Chamaedaphne-calyculata* Consocies. G. M. Allen (1925) states more simply that in most New England swamps "The Swamp Sparrows are found in the inner grassy ring; Song Sparrows and Yellowthroats in the bushy border." George M. Sutton writes me that he believes, from observations at the George Reserve in Michigan that this species requires mixed vegetation, a more complete overhead shelter than a pure stand of *Chamaedaphne* affords, and that adequate nest-sites are not provided by a pure stand of cat-tails.

Practically nothing is known of territorial behavior in this species, nor has its courtship been described. The male generally sings from a conspicuous position on an alder or willow or cat-tail, and often adopts this perch as its habitual singing place. While singing the bird spreads its tail noticeably. G. M. Sutton writes me that he once observed a male chasing a female with a dry grass-blade in her bill.

Sutton (1928) based the following generalized description on some 66 nests he found in the Pymatuning Swamp area of Pennsylvania:

> Nests were almost never placed on the ground, but were built between the cat-tail stalks, or upon the bent-down clumps of stalks and leaves, and were often completely hidden from above by the broad, dead leaf-blades. Entrances to the nests were almost always from the side, and rarely from above. The material of the lining varied but little. It was always of fine grasses, and not varied with plant-fiber, roots, or hair, as might have been expected. The material forming the foundations of the nests was often coarse and bulky, and some of the structures were huge, sprawling affairs. Nests were often built directly above the water, where the depth varied from six to twenty-four inches, and were usually built about a foot or more above the surface.

In the less alkaline swamps I have found many nests built in green sedge tussocks of *Carex*. The broad bushy flood-plain along the meandering Quabog River in central Massachusetts, where literally thousands of swamp sparrows breed, is the only place I have found them nesting consistently in bushes, and usually at heights reached only by standing in a boat.

Though the foundation is occasionally huge and sprawling, the nest proper is usually smaller than that of the song sparrow, being on the average 4.0 inches in outside diameter, with the inside cup 2.4 inches across and 1.5 inches deep. All those I have found have had the foundation and the thick outer cup built entirely of tightly woven coarse dead marsh "grasses," and the inner cup of fine round grass stems, often still showing green. Isaac E. Hess (1910) states that each of four nests he found in Illinois "had an appendage or handle constructed of grass stems protruding from one side about three inches." I also have noticed this characteristic loose tag on many nests. The entrance to the nest is characteristically from the side. The parents circled a Chardoneret banding trap I placed over a nest of fledglings in frustration for an hour until I rigged an inclined stick from a nearby perch that led them to the top entrance.

P. L. Hatch (1892) writes that the nest is "jointly built" by the pair, but this is probably an uncritical observation. Most of the evidence suggests that, as in most of the closely related sparrows, nest building in the swamp sparrow is entirely or almost entirely by the female.

Eggs.—(The data refer to the species as a whole.) The swamp sparrow lays from 3 to 6, usually 4 or 5 ovate and slightly glossy eggs. The ground color of freshly laid eggs is usually "pale Niagara green," but this pales out to a greenish-white upon exposure. They are spotted, blotched, clouded, and frequently marked with scrawls of reddish browns such as "Verona brown," "Prout's brown," "Brussels brown," or "Argus brown," with undermarkings of "pale neutral gray." They vary considerably, but are generally boldly marked, and practically indistinguishable from those of the song sparrow, except in a series it is noticeable that the blotchings and cloudings are heavier; also they are frequently marked with clouded scrawls and they average slightly smaller. The measurements of 50 eggs average 19.4 by 14.6 millimeters; the eggs showing the four extremes measure *21.8* by 5.1, 20.0 by *16.4*, *17.8* by 15.0, and 19.3 by 13.1 millimeters.

In one clutch that I incubated artificially, the eggs floated when tested 10 days before hatching. The complete clutch of four eggs weighed 8.25 grams, and the individual eggs from 1.85 to 2.15 grams. I found them more difficult to candle than the eggs of many song birds. The three young that hatched averaged 1.46 grams apiece at hatching.

Two clutches are laid each year and sometimes more, particularly when early clutches are destroyed by flooding or by predators.

Young.—Incubation is apparently by the female alone, at least I have never seen the male incubate. I have, however, often seen the male feed the slightly smaller and duller female on the nest while she brooded. Her mouth lining appeared to be the same orange color as that of her 4-day-old young.

How well the length of the incubation period has been measured is questionable. Lynds Jones (1892) gives it as 13 days, Ora W. Knight (1908) as 12 to 15 days, T. S. Roberts (1936) as 12 to 13 days. The three of a clutch of four eggs that hatched successfully in my incubator hatched over an interim period of 12 plus or minus 8 hours; the fourth egg did not hatch.

During early incubation the female slips off the nest quietly and unobtrusively while the intruder is still some distance away. Later she waits to be flushed and scolds the intruder busily and boldly. At one nest in advanced incubation that was tipped badly by the differentially growing substrate, the female returned to incubate immediately after I righted it; indeed she seemed as oblivious to my presence in my crude blind as she was to the green frog croaking beside her. Her attentive periods varied from 6 to 15 minutes, her inattentive periods from 11 to 34 minutes. On hot days she spent much of her attentive time sitting high as though to shade the eggs, although no direct sunshine reached the nest. Her departure was sometimes in response to calls of the male, and sometimes without apparent external provocation, though there was usually vocal communication between the pair whenever she left or returned. Her return to the nest was often noisy.

Nothing has been written of nest sanitation, which probably does not differ from that in the song sparrow. G. M. Sutton writes me that he found bits of shell in a nest after the young had fledged, suggesting that the shells may sometimes be crushed rather than carried away by one of the adults.

The chicks hatch with their eyes closed and are very helpless. They make no sound as they gape for food. The inside of the mouth is pink with a very pale yellowish border. The pinkish skin is so transparent the viscera and blood vessels show clearly through the abdomen wall. The tiny egg tooth is about 1 millimeter from the tip of the bill. The upper mandible is pigmented sooty gray anteriorly; the toenails are horn color. The flight feather tracts show pigmentation where the feathers will appear. As the young grow older their mouth lining becomes much brighter orange with a yellow border than in the newly-hatched fledglings.

E. H. Forbush (1929) states:

> The young ordinarily remain in the nest about 12 or 13 days, if undisturbed. Swamp Sparrows nest near water so frequently that the callow young in their first attempts at flight are likely to fall into it and struggling as they do on the surface, they sometimes fall a prey to large frogs, fish or turtles. The following from one of my note books shows how one little bird bravely struggled to safety: Concord, August 28, 1907. This morning early as I stood on the river bank, a bird flying toward me fell and struck the water about half way across the stream. Immediately it fluttered swiftly along on the calm surface of the water for about a rod, and then, apparently exhausted and unable to raise itself from the water, it lay there for a few seconds, head under and tail a little raised. I looked to see some fish seize it, but no! Suddenly by a vigorous struggle it raised its body clear of the water and fluttered almost ashore, alighting on the pickerel weed at the water's edge. A few minutes later, having regained its breath and courage, it flew up into the bushes, and I saw that it was one of a brood of young Swamp Sparrows in juvenal plumage, which were flitting along the shore.

G. M. Sutton (1935) presumes that the young leave the nest "on or about their ninth day." I have found them still in the nest on the 7th day but gone on the 11th day.

Plumages and molts.—The natal down is blackish brown. Seven specimens had neossoptiles one-half inch long with the following average distribution: coronal region 9, occipital 4, mid-dorsal 6, upper pelvic 1, lower pelvic 6, femoral 8, scapular 5, greater secondary coverts 7, ventral abdominal (these were white) 3. Sporadic pterylal loci were the posterior orbital region, the distal middle secondary coverts, and the proximal secondaries.

To speak of a postnatal molt is a misnomer, as no passerine bird actually "molts" its natal down. The loss of neossoptiles is by abrasion, a process which, although inevitable, is an accidental external phenomenon of a different order than physiological molt. Some loss of neossoptiles is postponed until the first *sensu strictro* molt, when the juvenal plumage is replaced.

Dwight (1900) describes the juvenal plumage as follows: "Above, cinnamon-brown, dull chestnut on the crown, streaked with black. No obvious median crown stripe. Superciliary line olive-gray duskily spotted. Wings and tail black, edged largely with chestnut, the wing coverts and tertiaries paler. Below, dull yellowish white washed with deep buff on sides of chin, across jugulum, on sides, flanks and crissum and narrowly streaked with black except on the chin and mid-abdomen. Bill and feet pinkish buff, the former becoming dusky, the latter sepia-brown." This plumage is similar to that of the song sparrow, but darker expecially on the crown, more washed with buff below, and more narrowly streaked with deeper black on the throat. Richard R. Graber (1955) notes that birds of this genus retain the juvenal plumage "for a rather long period by comparison with most migratory passerines."

The first winter plumage is acquired by a partial postjuvenal molt that starts the end of August and involves the body pumage and wing coverts, but not the flight feathers; G. M. Sutton (1935) says possibly the tail. Dwight (1900) describes this garb as:

"Above, similar to the previous plumage, the back and the lateral crown stripes showing more chestnut; a grayish nuchal band. Below, unlike previous plumage, grayish white, cinereous on throat obscurely streaked with a darker gray, washed on the flanks and often on the breast with olivaceous wood-brown obscurely streaked or spotted with clove-brown. Rictal and submalar streaks black bordering a grayish or yellow tinged chin. Superciliary line clear olive-gray or yellow tinged; postocular streak black; auriculars bistre."

E. G. Rowland (1928) made many observations on fall birds probably in their first but some possibly in their second winter plumage, that showed abonormal amounts of yellow coloring (xanthochromatism). He summarizes the literature on this peculiar color phase, which was first figured by Baird, Brewer and Ridgway (1874) who named it *Passerculus caboti* after the collector, Dr. Samuel Cabot, Jr. E. G. Rowland (1925) and L. B. Bishop (1889) also describe melanistic individuals, and J. H. Sage (1913) and A. T. Wayne (1922) describe partial albinos. J. Dwight (1900) continues:

"First Nuptial Plumage acquired by a partial prenuptial moult which involves chiefly the crown, chin and throat, but not the wings nor the tail. The amount of renewal varies according to individual, and may be quite extensive; a few feathers of most of the body tracts are usually renewed. Early April specimens from the south show the prenuptial moult in progress. The chestnut cap with black forhead, white chin, and clear cinereous gray of the throat, sides of head and neck are assumed, and a nearly complete renewal is indicated in some cases judging by the freshness of the feather borders." Many adults of both sexes lack the reddish brown cap in the spring and have the entire top of the head striped with black and reddish brown with a median gray stripe as in winter plumage. This may represent a first-year nuptial plumage.

The adult winter plumage according to Dwight is "acquired by a complete postnuptial moult in August and September. Practically indistinguishable in many cases from first winter, but usually with more chestnut on the crown, the superciliary line and sides of neck a clearer darker gray, the chin not yellow tinged but white and a grayer cast of plumage everywhere perceptible."

Mean body weights are given in grams as 17.61 (Wetherbee, 1934), 15.88 (Stewart, 1937), and 18.5±2.49 (Hartman, 1946). G. B. Becker and J. W. Stack (1944) give the average temperature of two birds as 110.2° F.

Food.—The swamp sparrow is the most highly insectivorous species in its genus. This is reflected in the reduced size of its skull and bill and bulk of jaw muscle in comparison to those of the seed-cracking song sparrow (Beecher, 1951). Banders note its absence from grain-baited traps during the nesting season (Commons, 1938). Martin, Zim, and Nelson (1951) show its diet to be 55 percent insects in winter, 88 percent in spring and early summer. "Beetles, ants and other *Hymentoptera*, caterpillars, grasshoppers, and crickets appeared most commonly as items in the insect part of the diet." In late summer and fall the diet becomes 84 percent to 97 percent granivorous, with seeds of sedges, smartweed, panicgrass, and vervain heading the list. Sylvester D. Judd (1901) writes: "[It] takes more seeds of polygonums than most birds, and eats largely of the seeds of the sedges and aquatic panicums that abound in its swampy habitat. The giant ragweed (*Ambrosia trifida*) is also well represented in its stomach contents."

Thomas Nuttall (1840) noted it ate "the smaller coleopterous kinds" of insects, as did I in my examination of nestling stomachs. The ready recognizableness and relative indestructibility of the chitinous remains of Carabid and Curculionid beetles perhaps biases uncritical examinations. Forbush (1929) credits this species with "control over the increase of such marsh insects as the army worm." C. C. Abbott (1895) describes the birds picking at dead drying herring, and A. H. Howell (1932) mentions their coming to bread crumbs at one of his camps in Florida.

Voice.—F. H. Forbush (1929) describes the swamp sparrows voice as: "Call note a *chink*, *chip* or *cheep*, with a metallic ring; song *weet-weet-weet-weet-weet*, etc., a little like that of Chipping Sparrow, but less dry, louder, a trifle more musical and more varied; also a limited variety of twittering notes." F. Schuyler Mathews (1904) calls the song a monotonic chip repeated in rapid succession with "a very perceptible *accelerando*." Aretas A. Saunders (1935) says "Some songs are double; that is, notes are sung on two pitches at once, the higher notes being slow and sweet in quality, and the lower notes faster and somewhat guttural. There are generally three notes of the lower part to one of the upper. The two notes are harmonious and usually about a third apart in pitch." He states further (*in* Roberts, 1936) "If one listens carefully to a number of these birds on their breeding grounds he will soon be likely to find one that sings, "tolit lit lit lit" etc., and with it a lower "tururur tururur tururur" about two or two and a half tones below the upper notes. From a distance the higher note is usually the only one audible, whereas near the bird only the low one can be heard, and at a medium distance both are heard at once." This peculiar anatomy of the swamp sparrow song lends itself to ventriloquial effects.

The male sings in spring from a few special prominent perches on its territory, with tail expanded and evidence of great effort apparent over all its body. T. S. Roberts (1936) claims: "Occasionally the Swamp Sparrow indulges in a flight song, when it rises a few feet in the air and utters a brief, ecstatic jumble of notes surprisingly unlike the usual simple, broken trill." However E. P. Bicknell (1884) classes the species among those "with which aerial song-flight appears to be only occasional or exceptional."

The song of this species is one of the first to come from the swamps on summer mornings, and it is often heard past midnight. Indeed M. G. Brooks (1930) notes that "On moonlit nights this bird sings as freely as in the daytime." G. M. Sutton writes me: "On June 24, 1946, I heard the first Swamp Sparrow song of the day (a full ringing song) at 3:40 a.m., the second at 3:45, and so many immediately thereafter that I felt sure the whole population must have been awake by 3:50, despite the darkness. While spending the night of July 9–10, 1946, awake in a blind at a Whip-poor-will nest, I heard the latest Swamp Sparrow song of the evening at 9:05 o'clock, fully five minutes later than the last song of the veery. * * * In late summer the songs were all delivered from well down in the cat-tails or shrubbery rather than from prominent song-perches."

E. P. Bicknell (1885) gives the following account of late summer and fall singing in the Riverdale, New York City area:

> The song of the Swamp Sparrow comes up from the swamps and marshes until early August, then it becomes less frequent. Usually it ceases about the middle of the month, sometimes a little before, but not unfrequently it continues later, and I have heard songs even so late as early September. About a month of silence now ensues; then the species comes again into voice. My record gives dates for the recommencement of singing from September 11 (?) and 18, to 28. The time of final cessation is carried into October—15th and 17th are latest

dates; but often the song is not heard after the first part of the month. In this supplementary season of song, singing is by no means general, and is usually confined to the early morning hours. But the birds seem more ambitious in their vocalism than earlier in the year. In the spring and summer the song is a simple monotone; in the autum this is often varied, and extended with accessory notes. A few preliminary *chips*, merging into a fine trill, introduce the run of notes which constitutes the usual song, which now terminates with a few slower, somewhat liquid tones. This seems to be the fullest attainment of the birds, and is often only partially or imperfectly rendered.

Behavior.—T. S. Roberts (1936) points out the swamp sparrow "is more secretive in its habits than the Song Sparrow and is loath to leave the concealment of its retreats. It climbs up and down the coarse stems of the reeds and bushy shoots in a nimble, mouse-like manner and, when alarmed, descends into the dense marsh grass, runs rapidly away, and disappears for good and all. It rarely flies from the nest but slips quietly off and silently creeps away, keeping well under cover." The abrasive action of the coarse marsh grasses and sedges in which it lives keep the birds' tail feathers continually worn.

It does much of its feeding by wading in shallow water like a sandpiper and picking insects and seeds from the surface. These activities are doubtless facilitated by its femur and tibiotarsus being proportionately longer than those of the song sparrow. Though E. T. Seton (1890) thought they showed great fear of getting wet, A. Allison (1904) describes them "splashing through the water like little muskrats." S. D. Judd (1901) relates that a captive bird "showed an aversion to picking up seeds from its seed cup, preferring to take them from the surface of its drinking vessel."

Except when migrating the swamp sparrow rarely flies more than a few dozen yards at a time, and rarely rises more than a few feet above the grass tops. In flight it pumps its tail rapidly up and down in a characteristic manner. Yet E. L. Poole (1938) shows that its wing-loading (ratio of wing area to body weight) of 4.30 square centimeters per gram is appreciably greater than the 3.94 square centimeters per gram in the larger congeneric song sparrow, which should make it an appreciably better flier.

Their behavior toward other species is little known. During fall migration they are often found flocking with other sparrows in dry fields. Yet on the wintering grounds in coastal Mississippi J. D. Corrington (1922) reports they "did not associate with other birds." William Brewster (1937) relates that a Lincoln's sparrow often drove swamp sparrows from a feeding plot in May.

While they do not trap as readily as some of their more granivorous relatives, swamp sparrows are not overly shy about repeating at bands ing stations. Over a 2-year period Marie A. Commons (1938) reports banding 104 individuals, 40 of which repeated a total of 162 times.

They enter traps with ground entrances more readily than those with top entrances.

Field marks.—Adult birds are readily separable from other sparrows in the field by their dark, chunky aspect, their reddish cap and wings, clear gray breast, and white throat. Other aids to identification are the hard call notes that have the quality of cut-glass percussion, and the bird's characteristic manner of pumping the tail in flight. Juvenile birds in summer are easily confused with young song sparrows and young Lincoln's sparrows, for all have similar fine breast streakings, but as R. T. Peterson (1947) points out, the juvenal swamp sparrow is "usually darker on the back and redder on the wings." In the hand the swamp sparrow's smaller and more curving bill is diagnostic, as is its smaller size and, according to Olive P. Wetherbee (pers. com.), its softer texture to the touch.

Enemies.—The main decimating factor of swamp sparrow populations on the breeding grounds are those related to changing water-levels, both natural and man-induced. While the creation of mill ponds and other bodies of water by artificial damming during the 19th century probably increased the range and density of the swamp sparrow within and beyond the glaciated areas of North America, the draining of morasses for housing developments is currently reducing its habitat markedly.

As the swamp sparrow usually nests just above the water level, a rise of only a few inches in that level can drown out every nest over wide areas. E. H. Eaton (1910) records that the birds had their nests thus flooded out in New York twice in 1906. I observed the same thing in Connecticut in 1956. Each year the birds take two or three of these 20-day gambles, that the waters will not rise until their young are fledged.

Herbert Friedmann (1963) states:

The swamp sparrow is generally an uncommon victim of the brown-headed cowbird. * * * Although the cowbird frequents marshes during migration, it tends to leave marsh nests alone. At Ithaca, New York, where both the swamp sparrow and the cowbird are common, there were no records of parasitism on the species.

* * * In Michigan, Berger (1951, p. 28) reported an unusual degree of parasitism on the swamp sparrow: he observed five nests, four of which had been victimized by the cowbird.

Although the swamp sparrow appears to be a rather uncommon victim of the brown-headed cowbird in most areas where the two exist together, it has been found to be a frequent and submissive host in southern Quebec. Here L. M. Terrill (1961, p. 10), between 1897 and 1956, found 322 nests of the swamp sparrow, of which 34, or roughly 10 percent, contained eggs of the cowbird. He wrote that the swamp sparrows in his area nested chiefly in sedgy tussocks among small willows in shallow water. Apparently this environment was more acceptable to the cowbirds than are the usual marshy areas.

The banding files show banded birds reported killed by: cats, dogs, hawks and owls, shrikes, rodents, cars, and weather conditions. Migratory calamities such as the 1906 fall storm over Lake Huron (Lincoln, 1950) that killed many swamp sparrows must take their toll fairly regularly. E. G. Rowland (1925) described two individuals that succumbed to a "pea-green diarrhoea" (botulism?).

The Communicable Disease Center at Atlanta, Georgia, reports that the swamp sparrow has been found to carry antibodies of one or more of the American arthropod-borne encephalitides. The species has been found to be host to the following ectoparasites: four species of bird louse (Mallophaga): *Degeeriella vulgate*, *Menacanthus chrysophaeum*, *Philopterus subflavescens*, and *Ricinus* sp.; three species of bird fly (Hippoboscidae): *Ornithoica confluenta*, *Ornithomyia anchineuria*, and *Ornithomyia fringillina;* and one tick, *Haemaphysalis leporis-palustris*.

Fall.—As Cruikshank (1942) notes, the swamp sparrow on migration "regularly leaves the marshlands and occurs in all types of habitat with the exception of deep woodlands." The crest of the autumn migration occurs throughout the northern states usually during the first week of October (Brewster, 1937 and Mason, 1938). The high percentage of immature birds in the population at this time attests the species' high annual reproductive capacity. From his banding studies at Belchertown, Mass., E. G. Rowland (1925, 1928) concluded that local breeding birds disperse locally before September 19th, and most depart by September 23. Autumnal migrants average about a week's stopover, as determined by repeat captures, and some individuals remained 2 weeks before moving on.

A swamp sparrow banded at Shirley, Mass., Oct. 4, 1937 was shot the following January at Plant City, Fla. One banded at Branchpost, N.Y., Oct. 7, 1926, was found dead at Renfrew, Ont., May 2, 1928. Numerous returns to the same banding stations during successive spring and fall migrations suggest the birds retrace the same migration routes each year in both directions.

Winter.—The species is a common winter resident in the Gulf States. In Georgia, T. D. Burleigh (1958) notes: "Its preference for the vicinity of open marshes and streams, however, limits its distribution, for rarely, if ever, will it be found in thickets or underbrush far from water. Cattail marshes are favored spots, and here its numbers during the winter months are limited only by the size of the area covered by the cattails. Bottomland fields overgrown with broom sedge likewise have their winter quota of Swamp Sparrows, provided a stream is close by and the ground is damp." In Florida, A. H. Howell (1932) writes: "Swamp Sparrows are by no means confined to swamps in the winter season, but are found most frequently in fields overgrown with brush and briers, and particularly in patches of broom sedge where the ground is moist. The birds are silent at this season and quite inconspicuous as they feed on the ground, threading their way through the brush like mice." In Louisiana, S. C. Arthur (1931) says "it is found not only in swamps but in old fields, overgrown with brush and briars, and particularly in wet patches of broom sedge. It leaves the salt-water tidal marshes, of course to the seaside sparrows."

The uncommon but regular occurrence of a few swamp sparrows within the northern breeding range in winter may (Abbott, 1895) or may not (Bagg and Eliot) indicate that these individuals are nonmigratory. In Cambridge, Mass., William Brewster (1906) writes:

> During the earlier years of my field experience Swamp Sparrows were not known to occur in midwinter near Cambridge, but on January 11, 1883, Mr. Charles R. Lamb met with a flock of seven birds in some dense maple woods on the western side of Pout Pond. Not long after this the cattail flags began to increase and spread in the Fresh Pond Swamps; since they became widely dispersed over the marshes lying to the north and west of the Glacialis, Swamp Sparrows have been constantly present there in winter. The birds vary considerately in numbers with different years, but one may be reasonably sure of starting at least three or four during a morning walk in December, January, or February, and under exceptionally favorable conditions as many as a dozen or fifteen may be seen.

Cruikshank (1942) says: "After the first killing frost in early November the Swamp Sparrow is purely casual in the highlands of the interior, but in the spring-fed marshes around New York City many regularly linger until Christmas, and some always remain to brave the winter."

While no correlation is apparent between the number of such overwintering birds and weather conditions, their survival probably depends largely on the comparative mildness of the season, or on their finding a suitable refuge with enough food and protection. Many individuals have repeated through the winter at banding stations on Cape Cod and Long Island. E. A. Mearns (1879) records a bird in the Hudson River Valley that remained through the severe winter of 1874–75 "* * * about a roadside drain, which, owing to a continual inflow of water, was not often frozen. The water was supplied through a small passing beneath the road, in which the bird doubtless found a desirable and effectual retreat in severe weather, as I several times started it from within the opening of this passageway, where the water was quite shallow."

Distribution

Range.—Eastern South Dakota, northern Wisconsin, northern Michigan, southern Quebec, and Nova Scotia to southern Texas, the Gulf coast, and southern Florida.

Breeding range.—The southern swamp sparrow breeds from eastern South Dakota (Yankton), central Minnesota, northern Wisconsin (Herbster, Outer Island), northern Michigan (Isle Royale), southern Ontario (Biscotasing, Eganville), southern Quebec (Kamouraska), northern New Brunswick (Miscou Island), Prince Edward Island, and Nova Scotia (Sydney) south to eastern Nebraska (Neligh), northern Missouri (St. Charles County), northern Illinois (Philo), northern Indiana (Crawfordsville, Richmond), south-central Ohio (Circleville), south-central West Virginia (Fayette and Greenbrier counties), western Maryland (Accident; Allegany County), southeastern Pennsylvania (intergrades with *M. g. nigrescens;* Delaware County), and southern New Jersey (intergrades; Salem, Cape May).

Winter range.—Winters from eastern Nebraska, central Iowa (Sioux City), southern Wisconsin (Madison), southern Michigan (Grand Haven, Ann Arbor), southern Ontario (Toronto), central New York (Rochester, Schenectady), and Massachusetts (Danvers) south to southern Texas (Del Rio), southern Louisiana (New Orleans), southern Mississippi (Gulfport), southern Alabama (Petit Bois Island, Orange Beach), and southern Florida (Aucilla River, Cape Sable); casually north to New Brunswick (Sackville).

Casual records.—Accidental in California (Niland) and Bermuda.

Migration.—(The data treat of the species as a whole.) Early dates of spring arrival are: Virginia—Blacksburg, March 21. West Virginia—Avalon, April 8. District of Columbia—March 9 (averages of 29 years, March 31). Maryland—Laurel, March 16. Pennsylvania—Meadville, March 23; State College, March 28 (average, April 15). New Jersey—Cape May, March 14. New York—Nassau County, March 23; Tompkins County, March 29. Connecticut—Portland, March 14. Rhode Island—Providence, March 10. New Hampshire—Concord, April 12; New Hampton, April 14 (median April 20). Maine—Bangor, March 20. Quebec—Montreal area, April 13 (median of 7 years, April 20). New Brunswick—St. John, April 6. Kentucky—Bowling Green, April 5. Illinois—Urbana, February 23 (median of 20 years, March 19); Chicago, February 26 (average of 16 years, March 27); Rantoul, March 5. Ohio—Buckeye Lake, March 17 (median of 40 years for central Ohio, April 1). Michigan—Battle Creek, March 23 (median of 34 years, April 6). Ontario—London, March 29. Iowa—Sioux City, April 12 (median of 38 years, May 1). Wisconsin—Madison, April 14. Minnesota—Minneapolis-St. Paul, March 12 (average of 27 years for southern Minnesota, April 6). Oklahoma—Okmulgee and Tulsa counties, March 20. Nebraska—Neligh, March 24. South Dakota—Sioux Falls, April 23. North Dakota—Cass County, April 13 (average, April 19). Manitoba—Margaret, April 9; Treesbank, April 9 (average of 11 years, May 1).

Saskatchewan—Davidson, April 23. Alberta—Glenevis, April 21. British Columbia—Tupper Creek, May 15.

Late dates of spring departure are: Florida—Tallahassee, May 15; Daytona Beach, May 9. Alabama—Florence and Birmingham, May 11. Georgia—Athens, May 20. South Carolina—Charleston, May 19 (median of 9 years, April 24). North Carolina—Asheville, May 21; Raleigh, May 19 (average of 11 years, May 11). Virginia—Richmond, May 17. District of Columbia—May 27 (average of 42 years, May 11). Maryland—Laurel, May 26 (median of 6 years, May 21). Pennsylvania—Blair County, May 20. New Jersey—Cape May, May 14. Connecticut—New Haven, May 23. Massachusetts—Martha's Vineyard, May 14 (median of 5 years, April 18). Louisiana—Baton Rouge, May 5. Mississippi—Bay St. Louis, May 4. Arkansas—Arkansas County, April 29. Tennessee—Knox County, May 7; Nashville, May 5 (median of 8 years, April 27). Kentucky—Bardstown, May 12. Missouri—St. Louis, May 15 (median of 13 years, May 6). Illinois—Chicago, May 31 (average of 16 years, May 27); Port Byron, May 24. Indiana—Wayne County, May 19 (median of 13 years, May 11). Ohio—central Ohio, May 30 (median of 40 years, May 16). Iowa—Sioux City, May 20. Wisconsin—Racine May 24. Texas—Cove, May 5; Sinton, April 28. Kansas—northeastern Kansas, May 9 (median of 21 years, April 5). South Dakota—Vermilion, May 6. North Dakota—Cass County, May 25 (average, May 22). California—Salton Sea, May 9.

Early dates of fall arrival are: British Columbia—Vanderhoof, September 2. California—Daly City, October 21. Utah—Washington, October 23. Colorado—Mosca, October 2; San Luis Valley, October 23. Arizona—Bill Williams Delta, November 28. North Dakota—Jamestown, August 18; Cass County, September 11 (average, September 15). South Dakota—Sioux Falls, September 24; Yankton, October 10. Kansas—northeastern Kansas, September 24 (median of 21 years, October 1). Texas—Cove, October 13; Sinton, October 30. Wisconsin—Meridian, September 1. Iowa—Sioux City, September 25 (median of 38 years, October 5). Ohio—central Ohio, September 1 (median of 40 years, September 20). Indiana—Wayne County, September 23 (median of 9 years, September 30). Illinois—Glen Ellyn, September 2; Chicago, September 14 (average of 16 years, September 22). Missouri—St. Louis, September 25 (median of 13 years, October 2). Kentucky—Bowling Green, October 15. Tennessee—Knox County, September 26. Arkansas—Fayetteville, October 12. Mississippi—Rosedale, October 22 (mean of 19 years, October 24). Louisiana—Baton Rouge, October 10. New Hampshire—New Hampton, October 30. Massachusetts—Martha's Vineyard, August 28 (median of 5 years, September 15). Connecticut—New

Haven, September 16. New York—Tiana Beach, October 13. New Jersey—Cape May, September 21. Pennsylvania—State College, September 19. Maryland—Anne Arundel County, August 24; Laurel, September 18 (median of 6 years, September 24). District of Columbia—August 21 (average of 20 years, October 8). Virginia—Lexington, September 23. North Carolina—Asheville, October 2; Raleigh, October 10 (average of 11 years, October 21). South Carolina—Charleston, September 28 (median of 6 years, October 17). Georgia—Athens, October 2. Alabama—Fairfield, September 29; Livingston and Mobile Bay, October 6. Florida—Tallahassee, September 18; Chipley, October 4.

Late dates of fall departure are: British Columbia—Indianpoint Lake, October 9. California—near Riverside, November 13; near Keeler, November 1. Alberta—Glenevis, September 29. Saskatchewan—Yorkton, October 3. Manitoba—Treesbank, October 20 (average of 18 years, October 4). North Dakota—Cass County, October 28 (average, October 18). South Dakota—Aberdeen, November 5. Nebraska—Ravenna, October 28. Oklahoma—Norman, November 23. Minnesota—Minneapolis-St. Paul, October 26 (average of 8 years, October 23). Wisconsin—Delavan, November 3. Iowa—Sioux City, October 26. Ontario—Toronto, October 24. Michigan—Battle Creek, November 21 (median of 31 years, October 26). Ohio—central Ohio, November 13 (median of 40 years, November 4). Illinois—Chicago, December 6 (average of 16 years, October 31). Tennessee—Pulaski, November 4; Nashville, October 17 (median of 11 years, October 5). Prince Edward Island—Murray Harbour, October 26. New Brunswick—St. John, November 7. Quebec—Montreal, October 29 (median of 7 years, October 13). Maine—Lake Umbagog, October 31. New Hampshire—Concord, November 4. Rhode Island—Westerly, November 11. Connecticut—Portland, November 28. New York—Central Park, November 23; Monroe County, November 10. New Jersey—Cape May, November 26. Pennsylvania—State College, November 28. Maryland—Laurel, November 30. District of Columbia--December 3 (average of 14 years, November 7). West Virginia—Bluefield, October 25. Virginia—Blacksburg, November 12.

Egg dates.—Illinois: 25 records, May 9 to June 29, 16 records, May 26 to June 10.

Maine: 17 records, May 21 to July 1; 10 records, June 8 to June 15.

Massachusetts: 36 records, May 9 to July 18; 18 records, May20 to June 3.

Michigan: 8 records, May 1 to June 25.

Minnesota: 11 records, May 18 to June 17.

New Brunswick: 5 records, May 27 to June 17.

Pennsylvania: 26 records, May 20 to June 20.

Wisconsin: 22 records, May 17 to June 20; 16 records, May 23 to May 20.

MELOSPIZA GEORGIANA NIGRESCENS Bond and Stewart

Coastal Plain Swamp Sparrow

Contributed by DAVID KENNETH WETHERBEE

HABITS

This subspecies is similar to the nominate race but in breeding plumage according to G. M. Bond and R. E. Stewart (1951) the black streaking of the upper parts is distinctly heavier, especially on the nape and dorsal region; feather edgings of the upper parts, much grayer, less rufescent and buffy; tail and bill average darker; flanks, noticeably less buffy. In November specimens, the brown of their upper parts is somewhat richer and darker, and the light edgings of their dorsal feathers are considerably less distinct. This race is similar also to the pale form, *M. g. ericrypta* Oberholser but in both breeding and winter plumage, feather edgings of the upper parts are considerably narrower, not so whitish. General coloration of dorsal region is even darker than when compared with *M. g. georgiana.* Measurements based on a very small sample indicate that *nigrescens* may be slightly larger than the nominate race.

This race breeds in the Nanticoke River marshes, Wicomico County, across the river from Vienna, Md., and possibly also in other brackish tidal marshes where vegetation is suitable along the east shore of Chesapeake Bay in Maryland and Delaware.

DISTRIBUTION

Range.—Southern New Jersey to eastern Maryland.

Breeding range.—The coastal plain swamp sparrow breeds in tidal marshes of the Nanticoke River in southeastern Maryland and adjacent southwestern Delaware, and also around Delaware Bay (Delaware City and Bombay Hook, Delaware; Hancocks Bridge, Port Norris, and Delmont, New Jersey).

Winter range.—Winters in the breeding range; also recorded on the Maryland coast (Ocean City), in east-central Virginia (Shirley), and once in the mountains of west-central Virginia (Lexington).

Egg dates.—Maryland: 7 records, June 5 to June 22; 5 records, June 10 to June 15.

MELOSPIZA MELODIA (Wilson)

Song Sparrow

PLATE 75

Contributed by VAL NOLAN JR.

On any list of North American birds selected for their general familiarity, the song sparrow would have few peers. Although relatively small and not very conspicuously marked, this species combines a readiness to dwell near humans and a persistent and attractive song with a breeding range extending from Mexico to the outer Aleutians and from the islands off the Atlantic coast to those off the coast of the Pacific. Further, the territories of the males are small and the suitable habitats extensive, with the result that the song sparrow is abundant in most of its range. Add to the foregoing the fact that these sparrows are readily trapped, and it is not surprising that some populations have been studied in meticulous detail.

Not only is the song sparrow one of our best-known birds; it is also our most variable, with 31 subspecies recognized as occurring within the territory covered by the A.O.U. Check-List (1957) and 3 additional subspecies in Mexico (Friedmann, et al., 1957). Robert Ridgway (1901) writes, "No other bird of the Nearctic Region has proven so sensitive to influences of physical environment," and Alden H. Miller (1956) cites the song sparrow as "one of the best examples of substantial racial diversification" among terrestrial vertebrates on this continent. Most of the subspecies occur west of the Rocky Mountains and in Alaska. Thus 9 races are found exclusively in California, to which may be added in California 8 other races that are not confined to that state. As a result of this plasticity, the song sparrow figures prominently in literature dealing with the origin of species and with ecologic gradients. The frontispiece in Joseph Grinnell and A. H. Miller's (1944) work on California birds will repay examination for its portrayal of variations in eight of the races of that state. Ira N. Gabrielson and F. C. Lincoln (1951) put the extent of the intra-specific variation in the following way: "it is probably true that if all the resident Song Sparrows between Kodiak Island and the Imperial Valley in California were suddenly destroyed, there are few observers who would believe that there was any close relationship between the large dusky Aleutian birds and the small pale form about the Salton Sea."

It will assist the reader if he is aware of the following decisions as to the manner of presenting this life history of the song sparrow:

(1) Most subspecies are treated separately in order to permit the use of the detailed information that is available for some populations

and to maintain the integrity of three contributed accounts, Margaret M. Nice's summary of her seminal study of *euphonia*, Richard F. Johnston's report of his investigation of *samuelis*, and Robert W. Dickerman's account of *fallax*.

(2) When two or more geographically proximate and ecologically similar subspecies are believed not to differ in the essentials of their life histories, they are sometimes grouped and information about them is pooled or is otherwise generalized, as indicated.

(3) When published studies have treated some aspect of the species as a whole rather than of subspecies, e.g., its food habits or its molestation by the cowbird, these results are presented under the first subspecific history, i.e., of the nominate race *M. m. melodia*, which also includes data that cannot be referred to subspecies and material that appears to be of general applicability.

Thus, the life history of *M. m. melodia* is to a degree broadly descriptive of the species. Mrs. Nice's treatment of *euphonia*, on the other hand, contains a wealth of detail about a small population of a widely distributed migratory race. Dr. Johnston's life history of *samuelis* treats in similar detail a rather specialized, sedentary race with a very limited range. For a general view of the song sparrow and its "wonderful adaptability" (Taverner, 1934), therefore, the reader might wish to consult the life histories of the races just mentioned, as well as the accounts of the races grouped as "Alaskan song sparrows" and "Pacific insular song sparrows." Finally, *M. m. rivularis* might be referred to as an example of the several subspecies inhabiting the deserts of the United States and Mexico.

MELOSPIZA MELODIA MELODIA (Wilson)

Eastern Song Sparrow

PLATE 75

Contributed by VAL NOLAN JR.

HABITS

The breeding song sparrow of eastern Canada and of the United States west to the Appalachians displays the typical preference of this species for moist ground and for a low, irregular, dense plant configuration considerably exposed to the sun. "No land bird seems more fond of water," writes E. H. Forbush (1929). Everywhere it is "primarily a bird of the lower lands * * *" (Knight, 1908), along the banks of streams, the brushy shores of ponds, and in shrubby wet meadows or cattail swamps. Even on the central Atlantic coast, where the race *atlantica* replaces the present subspecies on the beaches, *melodia* seems to be the song sparrow found back in the thickets (Stone, 1937), and Dexter (1944) has reported a nest of this race in a salt marsh on a tidal inlet at Gloucester, Mass. But these lowland situations are only a first preference, for the bird is tolerant of a wide range of conditions. It is often found in brushy fence rows and along country roads; and it sometimes breeds even in rocky wooded clearings in Maine, in small wooded openings only a few rods in diameter in New York (Eaton, 1914), and in second-growth woodland in Pennsylvania (Todd, 1940). Gardens and yards offer the song sparrow sunny, bushy, moist cover, and the bird is a common nesting species in suburbs and small towns. On Mount Mitchell, North Carolina, the highest point in the eastern half of the United States, Burleigh (1941) observed individuals of the race *euphonia* as high as 6,300 feet above sea level during the summer.

Spring.—Although a few song sparrows winter far north, most withdraw from that part of the range in Canada and northern New England. M. M. Nice (1933) has cited the evidence, from banding records, that some individuals of this subspecies are resident "in regions where most of their kind are migratory." Hervey Brackbill (1953) has found that the breeding population of Maryland contains both migratory and sedentary individuals. In the Hudson River valley and around New York City the species is a common winter resident. The arrival of migrants, and the return to their breeding territories of birds that have wintered, normally begins in the latter half of February in the southern part of the range, while the first spring arrivals appear in Maine in mid- and late March and in Canada in March and early April. In Maine migration continues into early May (Palmer, 1949).

Carl H. Helms (1959) weighed song sparrows captured in Massachusetts just before and just after a large night migration in April. Birds weighed before the flight averaged 1.41 grams heavier than those that arrived as the result of the movement. These post-flight individuals were noticeably less fat.

The song sparrow sings even on cold clear mornings of late winter, and its voice is a characteristic sound of early spring. Aretas A. Saunders (1947) reports singing in Connecticut when the temperature was −2° F.

Territory.—Territory appears to be established principally or entirely by the male. E. H. Forbush (1929) has described behavior that probably includes elements both of territorial defense and of courtship or pair formation: "There is considerable rivalry among the males, but their contests appear to be mainly competitions in song and flight. They chase the females and each other about through the air with fluttering wings, often sailing and singing. Their pursuit seems not to be in earnest, as, notwithstanding the rapid movement of their wings, their progress is slow. Now and then a bird pauses in his flight to sing, supported for an instant on his widespread pinions. Flight-songs also carry them up into the air. Occasionally a battle ensues between two rival males, and sometimes they even roll and tumble in the dust with locked bills and beating wings." In the section on courtship is a description of behavior that probably has territorial functions as well. The song sparrow's persistent songs, six to eight per minute at dawn in spring (Forbush, 1929), are, of course, associated with the maintenance of territory.

The size of the individual territory in favorable habitat is less than an acre. Robert E. Stewart and Chandler S. Robbins (1958) give an interesting series of data on the population density of breeding song sparrows in Maryland. (Population densities provide a basis for estimating only maximum territory size, for it does not follow that all the area censused actually fell within the boundaries claimed by the males.) In 19.2 acres of " 'shrubby field with stream-bordered trees' " were 21 territorial males; in 9.5 acres of " 'open hemlock-spruce bog' (brush-meadow stage * * *)" were 3 males; and in 20.5 acres of " 'moderately sprayed apple orchard with infrequently mowed ground cover * * *' " were 4.5 territorial males.

Courtship.—Witmer Stone (1937) writes as follows of his observations on Cape May: "In late March and April the air seems simply filled with Song Sparrow song and at this time we see male birds flying from bush to bush with neck stretched out, head and tail held high, and wings vibrating rapidly. This seems to be a part of the courtship display and as soon as the bird alights it bursts into song. On March 21, 1925, and April 2, 1914, I have noted this performance and the birds were evidently paired * * *." This behavior probably was associated also with territory defense. To the account from Forbush quoted in connection with territory may be added the same author's statement that song sparrows "spend much time in the pleasant pastime of courtship. The females seem to be modest and coy." The duration of the periods of pair formation and between pair formation and nesting seem not to have been recorded. A comparison of the dates given for the height of the return of spring migrants and for the beginning of general nesting in a given locality suggests that a month or more often elapses in these "prenuptial" and "preliminary" periods (Nice, 1943).

The same males and females have been found mated to each other in successive years (Hamill, 1926; Higgins, 1926).

Nesting.—Building is carried on principally by the female, but Ora W. Knight (1908) once saw a male apparently assisting his mate. He was "more inclined to shirk his share, picking up material, dropping it and picking it up again, singing meanwhile." During building, says Forbush (1929), "the male devotes himself more to song than to labor."

The duration of building is variously given, with 5 days the lowest figure and 10 days a commonly accepted maximum. Weather is known to influence the speed of building; and it may be supposed that the time-advance of the season, the number of nesting attempts already made, and the presence or absence of an earlier brood might all affect the female's building behavior. As mentioned below, females of the race *melodia* commonly raise three broods in a season and sometimes deposit the eggs for a later brood in a previously successful nest. Andrew J. Berger (1951) found five nests built in one season by the same female of the subspecies *euphonia;* not all succeeded.

The heights of nests range from ground level to at least 12 feet high. Most nests are placed on the gound, usually concealed under a tuft of grass, a bush, or a brush pile; and elevated structures are rare or absent early in the season. Eaton (1914) reports that 99 percent of the nests in New York are on the ground, but most writers use words suggesting only that something over half are located there. Elevated nests are "at a height of generally not over two or three feet" (Knight, 1908), but numerous references to somewhat higher sites can be found. Locations over water are not uncommon.

Plants in which nests are placed are grasses, sedges, cattails, a great assortment of bushes and shrubs, and, more rarely, trees of many species. Nests are occasionally built in cavities. Hollows in old apple trees are apparently the commonest such locations (Knight, 1908; Todd, 1940; Eaton, 1914); but hollow logs and rails, unoccupied buildings such as woodsheds, and even nest boxes (Palmer, 1949) have been resorted to.

The materials used for the outer, bulky part of the nest, as opposed to the lining, are most commonly leaves, strips of plant bark, and weed and grass stems. The lining is of fine grasses, rootlets, and horse or other animal hair. W. E. C. Todd (1940) states that nests "when above the ground * * * are often quite bulky." Knight reports the dimensions of one nest placed on the ground: the diameter of the cavity was 2½ inches, while the overall diameter varied between 5 and 9 inches; the cavity depth was 1½ inches, the overall depth 4½ inches.

Eggs.—The statements in this paragraph are applicable to the song sparrow without regard to race. The female lays from 3 to 6 eggs. They are slightly glossy and range from ovate to short ovate. The ground color of freshly laid eggs is "pale Niagara green" but this fades upon exposure to a greenish-white. Most eggs are very heavily speckled, spotted, or blotched with reddish browns such as "Verona brown," "russet," "cinnamon brown," or "Brussels brown." Some eggs have undermarkings of "pale neutral grey." The spottings generally are more or less evenly distributed over the entire surface, sometimes obscuring the ground color and making it appear to be a light buffy brown. They vary considerably both in shape, size, and intensity. The measurements of 400 eggs average 20.4 by 15.6 millimeters; the eggs showing the four extremes measure *25.9* by 17.8, 24.5 by *18.3*, *16.9* by 15.4, and 19.6 by *12.8* millimeters.

Turning to the race *melodia*, the measurements of 50 eggs average 19.5 by 15.1 millimeters; the eggs showing the four extremes measure *21.9* by 14.5, 20.1 by *16.8*, *17.8* by 14.2, and 18.0 by *14.0* millimeters.

Incubation.—Forbush (1929) states that incubation is "by both sexes, female chiefly" and that "some males assist the females a little * * *." However, there is no evidence that males have an incubation patch, without which they would be ill-equipped to supply heat to the eggs. Mrs. Nice (1937) found males of the race *euphonia* lack this patch, and her unequivocal statement that only the female *euphonia* incubates casts doubt on Forbush's contention. The role of the male during incubation is probably confined to the defense of territory and nest.

Incubation seems to start sometime not many hours from the laying of the last egg of the set, if this inference may be drawn from the failure of observers to report differences in development in the young of a brood. In *euphonia* Mrs. Nice observed that most often a clutch hatched over a 2-day span, indicating that incubation had begun before all eggs were laid.

The incubation period is said by Knight and Forbush to be from 10 to 14 days, but it is doubtful if accurate measurements of the period, as it is presently defined, would be less than 12 days, as in *euphonia* (Nice, 1937). W. E. Schantz (1937) watched a female *euphonia* incubate three eggs (laid July 10–12) for 24 days; the eggs failed to hatch.

Young.—Most of our knowledge of the development of the behavior of nestling song sparrows comes from Mrs. Nice's work, devoted chiefly to *euphonia*. The following paragraph is based on her report (1943). The development of the plumage is described below under the heading *Plumage*.

Newly hatched song sparrows can grasp, gape, swallow, defecate, and change location "by means of uncoordinated wrigglings." A feeding note has been heard in 2-day-old birds. The eyes begin to open at age 3 or 4 days. Incipient preening motions appear at age 5 days, as do, rarely, cowering and the ability to utter a location call. At age 7 days many motor coordinations are acquired, and henceforth the bird "is capable of leaving the nest." Among the behaviorisms of the 7-day-old are cowering, stretching of the wings, head-scratching, yawning, and climbing to the nest rim. Birds 8 and 9 days old acquire new types of wing-stretching, engage in wing-fluttering and -fanning, and body-shaking, and utter new feeding notes.

Both parents feed the nestlings, chiefly on "insects, worms, beetles, grubs, flies, caterpillars, grasshoppers, and similar insects" (Knight, 1908). The period in the nest varies, its minimal limit being given as 7 days by Forbush (1929) and its maximum as 14 days by most writers. Seven days undoubtedly does not represent a natural, undisturbed nestling period, but is probably the youngest age at which nestlings will leave the nest when disturbed. Knight says that young leave ground nests earlier than they do elevated nests, and that this early age is 10 days. At this time they are still unable to fly, and newly fledged birds remain hidden in plant cover. Mrs. Nice (1937) states that young *euphonia* "when * * * about 17 days old * * * are able to fly and come out of hiding."

Dependence on the parents continues until after the post-juvenal molt (Todd, 1940). The parental bond may be assumed to be severed at the age of about 28 to 30 days as in *euphonia* (Nice, 1937).

As in other species, juvenile song sparrows occasionally engage in some of the behavior of nest building (Hoyt, 1961).

As second and third broods are produced regularly, and fourth broods probably occasionally, as far north as Massachusetts, the matter of timing successive families is of interest. "When the young of the first brood are able to fly, the female immediately begins to deposit eggs for the second brood, often in the same nest, leaving the male to care for the first, and he attends them usually until the young of the second brood have hatched, when he leaves them to help feed and care for the younger brood" (Forbush, 1929).

Plumages.—In the following description of the plumages and molts, material involving both *melodia* and *euphonia* has been used. The sexes are identical in their molts and practically identical in their plumages. Females average a little later than males in date of molt. Minor sexual differences in plumage will be mentioned.

Natal down, described as both sepia-brown in color (Dwight, 1900) and black (Nice, 1943) is present at hatching. Mrs. Nice (1943) writes that this down "is prominent on the dorsal, femoral and occipital regions and on the coverts. For the first two days there is little change except in increased length of down."

The progress of the molt into the juvenal plumage is described in detail by G. M. Sutton (1935), who writes:

> * * * the nestling-stage of the juvenal plumage is * * * notable for its dullness, the feathers of the loral, malar, and superciliary regions being still for the

most part in their sheaths, and the tertials so short that their rich edgings are not yet apparent. The streaking of the chest is quite sharp, but on the sides it is, if anything, less marked than in later stages. Male and female birds are apparently not distinguishable at this age. The pectoral streaking is so much intensified because the feathers lie close together and are partially sheathed, that the actual width of the streaks is difficult to determine.

By the time the tail is an inch long the feathers of the face are almost altogether unsheathed, the tertials and secondaries are practically of full length, the pectoral plumage is fully fluffed out, and the bird is, therefore, much more colorful in appearance. At this stage males may, with a fair degree of certainty, be distinguished from females by the heavy streaking of the chest. Chapman * * * tells us that the "breast blotch is wanting" in this plumage. While this is no doubt to a considerable extent true, two individuals in a series of eleven specimens at hand show a definite blotch and two others exhibit a tendency toward convergence of streaks in the middle of the chest.

Sutton considers that song sparrows have a rather definite and complete juvenal plumage. "By the time the juvenal rectrices are of full length the body plumage is comparatively complete with all the feathers unsheathed and with no noticeable intrusion of pin-feathers of some subsequent plumage." He says that "specimens in juvenal feather may be taken during a long period of the summer," but is cautious about concluding how long the individual bird wears the plumage.

The foregoing is essentially an account of the molt, not the plumage, of which Dwight (1900) gives a good description. The bird "resembles *Z. albicollis*, but lacks chestnut above" and is "paler on [the] crown and less streaked below. Above, including sides of head, wood-brown or sepia broadly striped on back, narrowly on crown, nape and rump with dull black, the feathers centrally black with a narrow zone of walnut and wood-brown and grayish edgings. Indistinct median crown and superciliary stripes dull olive-gray with dusky shaft streaks. Rictal and submalar streaks black; orbital ring buff. Wings dull black with walnut edgings, the wing coverts and tertiaries buff tipped. Tail olive-brown broadly edged with walnut and indistinctly barred. Below, dull white washed with pale or yellowish buff deepest on the throat and flanks and streaked on sides of chin, throat, breast and sides with dull black. Feet and bill pinkish flesh, becoming dusky with age, the lower mandible remaining partly flesh-color." Dwight believes this plumage is worn several months; it fades considerably.

The first winter plumage is acquired, according to Dwight, "by a partial, sometimes complete, postjuvenal moult" beginning in some birds in mid-August, in others not until the last of September. These latter will still show new feather growth late in October or early in November, although "the whole period of moult does not cover much more than two months in the majority of cases." The molt "involves the body plumage and the tail and very often, part at least, of the remiges. The renewal of five or six outer primaries occurs in nearly all young birds of this species and is very likely characteristic of the first brood. * * * The secondaries are rarely found in moult, the tertiaries, alulae and wing coverts regularly so. * * * [Occasionally] the renewal of primaries, secondaries and even of rectrices, might easily be overlooked as the new feathers are nearly of the same pattern and color as the old and not in contrast * * *."

In appearance, the first winter plumage is like the previous one, "but is whiter below and richer in chestnut streakings both above and below. The lateral crown stripes are distinct with black streaks, the median and superciliary stripes distinctly olive-gray. Below, white washed with pale vinaceous cinnamon on sides of head, across jugulum and on sides, and streaked, except on chin and mid-abdomen, with clove-brown bordered with chestnut, the streaks becoming confluent at sides of chin and on mid-throat forming three nearly black spots. Old and young become absolutely indistinguishable in most cases, young birds with the wing edgings perhaps a trifle duller and with a yellowish tinge." In this plumage females are "apt to be more washed with brown or to have a yellowish cast when compared with males" in the same plumage.

The first nuptial plumage is acquired, according to Dwight, by wear, which is marked; "by the end of the breeding season the birds are in tatters. The buff is lost and the streaking below comes out in strong contrast on a white ground."

The adult winter plumage is "acquired by a complete postnuptial moult beginning usually about the middle of August and completed before the end of September. Old and young cannot be told apart with any certainty, adults however with wing edgings that may perhaps average darker and browner and the throat markings blacker."

The adult nuptial plumage is "acquired by wear as in the young birds with the same results."

The following description of the adult plumage is by Robert Ridgway (1901):

Adults, (sexes alike):—Pileum brown (mummy brown to almost burnt umber), narrowly streaked with black and divided by a narrow median stripe of gray, this also narrowly streaked with black; hindneck brownish gray, more or less streaked or washed with brown; scapulars and interscapulars black medially, producing streaks of greater or less width, these margined laterally with brown (like the color of the pileum), the edges of the rectrices, more or less broadly, brownish gray; rump olive-grayish, more or less streaked with brown (sometimes with blackish also); upper tail-coverts browner than rump and more distinctly streaked; tail brown (broccoli brown to russet brown), the middle pair of rectrices with a narrower median stripe of dusky brown, the inner webs of the other rectrices darker brown than outer webs; lesser wing-coverts brown; middle coverts brown, margined terminally with pale brownish gray, and marked with a more or less distinct median streak or spot of dusky; greater coverts brown, margined terminally with paler and marked with a broad median tear-shaped (mostly concealed) space of blackish; tertials mostly blackish, but outer webs chiefly brown, passing into a paler (sometimes pale grayish or almost grayish white) hue terminally; rest of remiges dusky, edged with paler or more grayish brown; edge of wing white; a broad superciliary stripe of olive-gray, sometimes approaching grayish white on lower portion; loral, suborbital, and auricular regions darker olive-grayish, the latter margined above and below by narrow postocular and rictal stripes of brown, these brown stripes sometimes narrowly streaked with black; a broad malar stripe of dull white or pale buffy, margined below by a conspicuous submalar stripe or triangular spot of black or mixed brown and black; under parts white, the chest marked with wedge-shaped streaks of black, more or less broadly edged with rusty brown, these streaks more or less coalesced in the lower central portion of the chest, or upper breast, forming a more or less conspicuous irregular spot; sides and flanks streaked with black and rusty brown, the ground color, especially on flanks, more or less tinged with pale olive-grayish or buffy; under tail-coverts white or pale buffy, more or less streaked with brown; maxilla dusky brown, paler on tomia; mandible horn color; iris brown; tarsi pale brown, toes darker.

Albinism occurs in song sparrows, and Root (1944) reports a banded individual that acquired a considerable degree of whiteness during a 28-day period in early autumn, presumably as the result of molt.

Food.—S. D. Judd (1901) has described the diet of song sparrows without regard to race. For the year, animal matter constitutes 34 percent of the total food, the greatest amount being taken from May to August, when insects represent about half the bird's food. Ground-, leaf-, and clickbeetles, weevils, and other beetles rank first in number; grasshoppers, locusts, larvae such as the cutworm and army-worm, ants, wasps, ichneumon flies, bugs, leaf-hoppers, larvae and imagos of horse-flies, etc., are also taken. The remaining two-thirds of the diet is composed of seeds of crabgrass and pigeon-grass, timothy, old-witch grass, barnyard grass, panic-grasses, orchard and yard grasses; knotweeds, wild sunflower, lamb's quarters, gromwell, purslane, amaranth, dandelion, chickweed, dock, ragweed, sheep-sorrel and wood-sorrel; a little grain, largely waste; and, before the seeds have ripened, wild berries and fruits such as blackberries, strawberries, blueberries, elderberries, and raspberries, wild cherries and grapes, and woodbine berries. The species is very beneficial as a destroyer of injurious insects and weed seeds. Judd says, "Only 2 per cent of the food consists of useful insects, while 18 per cent is composed of injurious insects; grain, largely waste, amounts to only 4 per cent, while the seeds of various species of weeds constitute 50 per cent."

W. L. Dawson (1923), writing of song sparrows of no specified race, says that a bird "sometimes seizes and devours small minnows."

Behavior when foraging reflects the seasonal dietary preferences already described. Eaton (1914) states that in summer song sparrows cease to feed largely on the ground and sometimes forage for insects among foliage as high as 20 and 30 feet, although usually among bushes and grass. These birds scratch the ground by kicking simultaneously with both feet. Charles H. Blake writes of watching a song sparrow catch winged termites as they emerged from their subterranean colony in early June.

Behavior.—Song sparrows are often furtive in manner, and Knight (1908) gives a good description of the behavior of alarmed birds. He states that they prefer to "work downward into the bushes with bobbing tail, hopping along from twig to twig, or skulking through the underbrush, grass and leaves. They do not fly, save from bush to bush, unless closely pursued with evident intention to flush them or do them harm." Witmer Stone (1937) speaks of "how well adapted [song sparrows] are for a terrestrial life and how rapidly they can run, mouse-like, through the grass."

Despite their sometimes secretive behavior, birds dwelling near humans often develop considerable tameness. Forbush (1929) states that they may be conditioned by feeding to come when called and tells of one song sparrow that learned to associate the sound of a bell with the fact that food was to be scattered and of another that learned to peck at a window to be fed.

The behavior of females on the nest is often cryptic, according to Knight (1908). Sometimes the bird sits until almost stepped on; at other times, when the male gives the alarm, she slips off, sneaks a few feet away, and then begins to call. Johnston (1957) in long experience with the shrub-nesting race, *samuelis*, saw only one case of rodent-like distraction display. Both adults protest intrusions into the vicinity of the nest, and Forbush (1929) describes the posture of nest defense as involving "outspread wings and depressed tails." This threat, if unsuccessful, may be replaced by attack. Birds as large as the catbird and hairy woodpecker happening to approach the nest are attacked, and Forbush mentions a successful attempt by a song sparrow to drive five house sparrows from a feeding station.

Bathing, states Forbush, occurs "during the day whenever opportunity offers" and, if there is water, "every night after sunset." Puddles, including salt water along the shore, are used; and the song sparrow is one of many species that bathe in drops of water on grass and leaves by striking the foliage with the wings and body and thus throwing water on the plumage.

Scratching of the head by song sparrows is "indirect," with the foot brought over the wing to reach the head, and Hailman (1959) has observed song sparrows and other emberizines scratching the head against perches.

Anting has often been noted in song sparrows; Whitaker (1957) has summarized the details.

"Helping," i.e., the feeding of young both of other song sparrows and of other species, has been noted several times and summarized by Brackbill (1952) and Skutch (1961). Perhaps the most surprising instance, reported by Brackbill, involved the cooperative building and joint use of a nest by a pair of cardinals and a pair of song sparrows. Both females incubated, the cardinal sometimes sitting on the sparrow. The cardinal eggs succeeded, and all four adults fed the nestlings. Forbush (1929) describes an instance in which two females laid a total of eight eggs in one nest; one of these birds had its own nest 30 feet away but did not use it. The females took turns incubating, and all eggs were said to have produced fledglings.

The flight speed of song sparrows has been measured by O. P. Pearson (1961) as 15.9 miles per hour and possibly as much as 21 miles per hour.

Manwell and Herman (1935) found that individual song sparrows displaced and released in spring as much as 1½ miles returned quickly to the point of capture; at an intermediate trapping station on the presumed line of flight none were caught.

Body temperatures of 64 individuals of the race *euphonia* averaged about 109.6° F., varying 10° F. within the sample (Becker and Stack, 1944). There is a considerable literature on song sparrow weights; Mrs. K. B. Wetherbee (1934) gives many data. Mrs. Nice (1935) lists an average weight of 21.3 grams for 267 adults. LeRoy C. Stegeman (1955) reports weight fluctuation amounts at times to 20 percent in 24 hours, with peak weights in the spring recorded in the late morning and late afternoon.

Voice.—Male song sparrows sing their variable repertoire not only during the breeding season but at other times. Songs may be heard in much of the breeding range during any month of the year (Saunders, 1947), and dawn singing on clear, cold mornings in January and February is especially noticeable. Regular singing in spring begins in Connecticut in late February or in March (Saunders, 1947) and generally closes, for a time, in the third week of August (Saunders, 1948a). There follows a revival of song, beginning in Connecticut on the average date of September 30 and continuing until November 21 (average). Aretas A. Saunders, who is responsible for these dates, writes (1948b): "This species is the most regular and dependable fall singer of all our birds."

Forbush (1929) states that the birds sing "no matter how very stormy the weather" and sometimes even "in the darkness of night."

Six to eight songs per minute is the frequency during the dawn hours of the breeding period (Forbush), with singing continuing, but less frequently, all day. Knight (1908) reports that in summer in Maine most singing occurs during the dawn and evening hours. Forbush says that occasionally molting birds sing a whisper song.

When singing, the male mounts to a position typically between 7 and 15 feet from the ground (Eaton, 1914); trees, shrubs, fences and boulders are among the song posts used. Singing has often been observed in birds on the wing, and Forbush's description, quoted under *Territory*, indicates that this form of behavior may have become an element in some displays.

Female song sparrows have been known to sing, and Mrs. K. B. Wetherbee (1935) has written of a female in Massachusetts that sang "a clear series of whistled notes" from April to mid-June.

Not only the vociferousness of the species but also the unusual variability of the repertoires of the individual males are responsible for an abundant descriptive literature. Further, the use of electronic recording and analysis of songs has thrown light on the extent to which song sparrow vocalizations are modifiable as opposed to innate. For the present account, two authorities on bird song are quoted. Aretas A. Saunders wrote Mr. Bent: "I have 885 records of the song, no two of them alike. If we count trills as single notes, the number of notes per song varies from 4 to 20, averaging about 11. The length of songs varies from 1.8 to 5.2 seconds, the average being 2.7. The pitch varies from D″ to F″″. The pitch interval varies from 1 to 7½ tones, the average about 3½ tones. Each individual song sparrow sings a number of different songs. It commonly sings the same song over a half a dozen times or so, and then takes up a different song. The number of songs per individual varies from 6 to 24, the latter being an unusual bird."

The same author writing elsewhere (1951b) goes into additional detail and reports the following: Pitch varies from 1150 to 5450 vibrations, in notes audible to man, and pitch intervals are similar to those in human music. There is little variation in intensity. "Quality is usually sweet and musical * * * . Consonant sounds are not very noticeable. * * * The song has three parts: strongly rhythmic introductory notes, a central trill, and a final series of rather irregular and indefinite notes. * * * Songs are of five types * * * [differing] primarily in the position and relative pitches of the introductory notes and the trill."

Donald J. Borror (1961), who analyzed 889 tape recording of songs from 113 different individual song sparrows of the races *melodia* and *euphonia*, writes,

The songs of this sparrow consist of a series of different phrases (mostly 1- to 4-noted), and usually a trill; many of the notes are buzzy. * * * A given bird has a vocabulary of a large number of notes and phrases, and these are variously combined to produce up to a dozen or more different song patterns; the different patterns of a given bird are often quite different. The songs of a given pattern may vary * * *.

Song Sparrow songs are of two general types, those beginning with two to four (rarely one or five) similar and equally spaced phrases, and those beginning with four to twenty similar phrases that increase in tempo * * *. Songs of the first type were much more common, making up 83.8 percent of the Ohio [*euphonia*] patterns and 86.7 per cent of the Maine [*melodia*] patterns * * *.

A Song Sparrow apparently has an inborn tendency to sing songs of two general types, but it learns its phrases by listening to other, nearby Song Sparrows. As a result, the songs of different birds in a local population contain similar notes and phrases (but usually arranged differently), while the songs of birds in separated populations contain different phrases. The farther away two populations are, the less likely they are to use similar phrases in their songs.

In a later, very detailed analysis of variation in the songs of Maine song sparrows, Borror (1965) found 544 song patterns represented in 7,212 tape-recorded songs of 120 birds.

A description of autumnal song by Forbush (1929) probably is applicable not to adults but only to birds of the year: Most of the singing [in fall] is quite different, ranging from a low connected warble to a song resembling that of the Purple Finch, and (rarely) one like that of the Vesper Sparrow. There is a particularly low, sweet melancholy warble uttered just before the bird departs for the south." Formless, continuous warbling of the kind described is commonly a stage in the ontogeny of song in passerines (Lanyon, 1960).

Call notes are described as "tchenk," "tchip," "tchunk," "chip," "tcheek," "chuck." Forbush also mentions a note "sst"; a similar note given by California races is regarded by Dawson (1923) as functioning as a flocking or recognition call.

Field Marks.—A medium-sized sparrow, the song sparrow is best recognized by the heavily streaked breast, on which the streaks are "confluent into a *large central spot*" (Peterson, 1947). In flight, which is usually for short distances between perches or into cover, the bird is distinguished by its manner of pumping its rather long, rounded tail up and down. Witmer Stone (1937) describes this flight graphically as "'brokenbacked' * * * as if the tail were hinged at the base."

Banding—The longevity record for banded song sparrows appears to be about 8 or 9 years. Mrs. Nice (infra) reports a male that was at least 7½ and possibly 9½ years old at death. A song sparrow Mrs. K. C. Harding (1943) banded April 27, 1936 at Cohasset, Mass., and recaptured there on April 5, 1943, was in at least its 8th year.

Recaptures and recoveries at points other than the original banding station have been reported with some frequency in the journal,

Bird-Banding. Some of the most interesting of these follow: The number of such "recoveries" and "foreign retraps" from a total of 3,614 song sparrows banded in Montgomery County, Pennsylvania, was 12 (Middleton, 1956); from 6,109 banded in Groton, Mass., 7 (Wharton, 1953); from over 1,200 banded on Cape Cod, Massachusetts, 1 (Broun, 1933). Some of the Pennsylvania birds were caught in Georgia, North Carolina, Maryland, and New Jersey. The Groton, Mass., birds were caught in Arkansas, South Carolina, North Carolina, Nova Scotia, and New Brunswick. The Cape Cod bird was caught in South Carolina. May Thacher Cooke (1943) reports a bird banded in Massachusetts and captured in Newfoundland. Wendell P. Smith (1942) caught a bird in Vermont in April, and it was recaptured 90 miles southward in New Hampshire in June of the same year, an interesting case of reversal in the direction of migratory movement.

Enemies.—Perhaps the most interesting and surely the most well documented hazard in the song sparrow's environment is exposure to the parasitic brown-headed cowbird and bronze cowbird. Herbert Friedmann's latest report (1963) on the cowbirds states that the song sparrow (all races) shares with the yellow warbler the claim to being the most frequently reported host of *M. ater*. Friedmann's summary of the relations between all races of the song sparrow and the brown-headed cowbird is quoted substantially in full:

> The song sparrow is one of the most frequent, if not the most frequent, victim of the brown-headed cowbird. Since the former is sympatric with the latter throughout the entire breeding range of the parasite, it is parasitized probably more often and over a greater area than any other bird. The total number of records is very great. After accumulating over 900, I stopped noting them except for records of special interest. The data came from every province of Canada and every state of the United States included in the breeding ranges of both birds. All three races of the parasite are involved, and no less than 17 races of the song sparrow: *melodia*, *atlantica*, *euphonia*, *juddi*, *montana*, *inexpectata*, *merrilli*, *fisherella*, *morphna*, *cleonensis*, *gouldii*, *samuelis*, *pusillula*, *heermanni*, *cooperi*, *fallax*, and *saltonis*. So far, none of the purely Mexican races have been reported as fosterers of the cowbird, but this fact is probably due more to a lack of human observation than to any actual immunity of the bird to cowbird parasitism.
>
> There is no need to detail actual instances for the various races of the song sparrow since such cases already have been given in my earlier summaries [Friedmann, 1929, 1934, 1938, 1943, 1949]. However, a few additional records of infrequently reported races of the host species should be mentioned * * * [viz. *cleonensis*, *fallax*, *morphna*, *saltonis*, *samuelis*, and *inexpectata*].
>
> In recent years, not only many hundreds of additional cases, but also much more quantitative data on the host-parasite relations have become available. Hicks (1934) found that 135 out of 398 nests (34 percent) of this sparrow were parasitized in Ohio. Nice (1937a***, 1937b***), also in Ohio, reported that 98 out of 223 nests (43.9 percent) contained eggs or young of the cowbird (the annual percentage varied from 24.6 to 77.7 percent). Sixty-six unparasitized nests raised an average of 3.4 song sparrows, whereas 28 successful but parasitized

broods averaged only 2.4 song sparrows, indicating that each cowbird was reared at the expense of one song sparrow. In one instance Nice *** found that a pair of song sparrows raised a young cowbird together with five of their own young. Apparently here no loss of sparrows was involved. In another paper, Nice (1936) noted that, in all the song sparrow nests which she had watched during a period of five years, adult cowbirds removed 5.7 percent of the song sparrow eggs and nestling cowbirds crushed or starved 3.5 percent of the young sparrows. The cowbird eggs did not succeed as well as those of the host; only 30.7 percent of the former, but 35.8 percent of the latter, reached the fledgling stage. In 1930–31, there was one female cowbird to about 11.5 pairs of suitable hosts, but in 1934–35 there was one to 8.6 pairs of suitable victims.

Of all song sparrow nests parasitized, Nice reported that 70 percent held a single cowbird egg each, 27 percent held 2 each, and 3 percent held 3 each. In the area of study—near Columbus, Ohio—the song sparrow was the most important host of the paeasite [sic]. Norris (1947***) noted that 11 out of 27 nests (40.7 percent) in Pennsylvania were parasitized, and Berger (1951***) recorded 37 out of 59 nests found in Michigan (62.7 percent). In the Detroit area, as reported by the Detroit Audubon Society (1956***), the average frequency of parasitism of the song sparrow was 40.1 percent of all the nests found * * *.

One is drawn toward attempting an over-all estimate of the frequency with which the song sparrow is victimized, but to do so with any feeling of accuracy is difficult because the incidence of parasitism appears to vary geographically (or, at least, the frequency with which it is reported varies). From this it follows that the over-all percentage depends on how many geographically different areal data are used in the estimation. [With one group of studies from the eastern United States] ***, we come up with a total of 323 parasitized nests out of 804 nests observed, or a little over 40 percent. On the other hand, in southern Quebec (Terrill, 1961, p. 11), out of 486 nests observed, only 62, or 12.7 percent, were parasitized. If we put all these studies together, we get a total of 382 out of 1,285 nests victimized, or 29 percent. This figure becomes yet smaller when we attempt to include data from other parts of the continent.

[One color-banded song sparrow in a single summer] *** had no fewer than five consecutive nests * * *. It would seem that, if none of these nests had been interfered with, there would not have been sufficient time for four or five in one season. * * * It appears that one of the effects of parasitism may be to increase the "nesting potential" of the host. * * *

As many as 7 cowbird eggs have been found in a single nest of this sparrow; there are numerous records of 3, 4, and 5 parasitic eggs to a nest. Occasionally, but not often, song sparrows may partly bury cowbird eggs by building a new nest lining over them—if the alien egg is laid before any eggs of the host.

Salmon (1933, p. 100) has reported seeing a song sparrow feeding three fledgling cowbirds; no young sparrows were mentioned. Lees (1939, p. 121) recorded that near Wetaskiwin, Alberta, he watched a song sparrow feeding no less than five young cowbirds. This must be a record of fledgling success for any host species.

Friedmann (1963) lists no instances of parasitization by the bronze cowbird of subspecies of the song sparrow covered by these life histories. Only the Mexican race *mexicana* has been involved.

Other enemies of the song sparrow are at least four species of hawks (Munro, 1940; Randall, 1940; Hamerstrom and Hamerstrom, 1951; Heintzelman, 1964) and at least five species of owls (Allen, 1924; Hawbecker, 1945; Johnston, 1956; Fisler, 1960; Graber,

1962). S. A. Altmann (1956) has reported mobbing of mounted specimens of both screech and great horned owls, and F. Hamerstrom (1957) witnessed mobbing of a tame red-tailed hawk. Forbush (1929) mentions nest defense against snakes and turtles; he does not indicate what turtles may be involved, but box turtles of the middle west (*Terrapene o. ornata*), at least, have been known to eat birds and their eggs (Legler, 1960).

A curious case in which a garter snake (*Thamnophis s. sirtalis*) disgorged an adult song sparrow is reported by Carpenter (1951), who suggests that the bird must have been found dead and then eaten. Mahan (1956) discovered a milk snake (*Lampropeltis triangulum*) eating song sparrow eggs in a nest 15 inches above the ground.

A number of external parasites taken from song sparrows east of the Mississippi River, most of them within the range of *melodia*, have been reported by Harold S. Peters (1936). These include the Mallophaga *Degeeriella vulgata* (Kell.), *Machaerilaemus maestum* (Kell. and Chap.), *Menacanthus incerta* (Kell.), *Philopterus subflavescens* (Geof.), *Ricinus melospizae* (McGregor); the bloodsucking hippoboscid flies *Ornithoica confluenta* Say, and *Ornithomyia anchineuria* Speiser (syn. *O. fringillina*); the mites *Analgopsis* sp., *Liponyssus sylviarum* (C. and F.), *Trombicula bisignata* Ewing, *Trombicula cavicola* Ewing; and the ticks *Haemaphysalis leporispalustris* Packard, *Ixodes brunneus* Koch, and *Ixodes* sp. Herman (1937) gives further data on the hippoboscids parasitizing song sparrows, as does Boyd (1951); the latter would apparently refer the records of *Ornithoica confluenta* to *Ornithoica vicina*, as the parasite of song sparrows.

Nestling song sparrows are among the many species victimized by the maggots of blow flies (Calliphoridae). Johnson (1932) found larval *Protocalliphora splendida* (Macq.) in a nest, and George and Mitchell (1948) report *Apaulina metallica* (Townsend) (syn. *Protocalliphora metallica*).

Blood protozoa found in song sparrows (Herman, 1944) include a number of species of the genera *Haemoproteus*, *Leucocytozoon*, *Plasmodium*, *Toxoplasma*, and *Trypanosoma*.

Cats, other predatory mammals, and man are often responsible for song sparrow deaths; and the physical environment takes its toll in starvation (Forbush, 1929) and in the flooding of ground nests.

Song sparrows are among the birds whose feet occasionally exhibit large, rough, wart-like swellings. H. and J. R. Michener (1936) have described the appearance and effect of this disease, which they also imply may affect the wings and heads of song sparrows, and which they regard as mildly contagious and epidemic. Their observations were made in California. The disease runs its course between from 1 to 5 months. Apparently it often produces no noticeable after effects, but it may cause the loss of the nails and sometimes the phalanges. These authors quote a pathologist's histological analysis of a foot of an unspecified species. The opinion was that the lesions were not true tumors but were the result of an unrecognized irritant or infection. Viruses are now known to produce comparable effects in some birds (Herman, 1955).

Fall.—In Massachusetts, a few song sparrows begin moving away from their breeding places in mid-July. The fact that nests have been found in New York as late as August 25 (Eaton, 1914) suggests that it may be the young of the year that move at so early a date. There is some conflict in the evidence as to when the fall migration is at its peak. The data of Stewart and Robbins (1958) are perhaps the most recently reported and based upon the most voluminous and varied factual data. These authors state that in Maryland and the District of Columbia the normal period of fall migration is between Sept. 20–30 and Nov. 20–30, with its peak between October 10 and 30. More northerly latitudes would, of course, be correspondingly earlier, e.g., in Maine "throughout September and most of October" (Palmer, 1949).

Winter.—Most song sparrows that pass the winter in Massachusetts (Forbush, 1929) remain near the sea, where there are usually patches of ground clear of snow. In Ontario (Snyder, 1951) and New York (Eaton, 1914) the habitat at this season is principally marshes and swamps. In Pennsylvania, Todd (1940) says brushy thickets and fields with corn shocks are frequented by song sparrows. The birds are not especially social, but they are often seen in loose flocks of mixed composition and, particularly in severe weather, may assemble in small companies with other song sparrows.

South of the breeding range, in the deep south and southeast of the United States, *melodia* is found with *euphonia*, *juddi*, and, in places, *atlantica*. Here the birds seek the same brushy, moist, riparian and marshy situations that they prefer for breeding. Sprunt and Chamberlain (1949) describe such habitat in South Carolina and say the song sparrow "often * * * is found with swamp sparrows * * *. The thoroughly characteristic song is delivered throughout the winter except in very cold weather or on freezing days." In contradiction Arthur H. Howell (1932) in his work on Florida says, "The Song Sparrow, so well known in the North by its cheery song, is practically silent during its stay in the South, except for its metallic, characteristic *tchip*." Howell adds that the birds associate "in small loose companies, but not in compact flocks." George H. Lowery, Jr., (1960) of Louisiana, emphasizes the "entirely different personality" of the song sparrow that winters in the south and describes it as a shy and, it seems, silent skulker that prefers the depths of thickets or "a rank growth of broom sedge."

Distribution

Range.—Southeastern Ontario, central Quebec and southwestern Newfoundland south to eastern Texas, the Gulf coast, and southern Florida.

Breeding range.—The eastern song sparrow breeds from southeastern Ontario (Muskoka District, intergrades with *M. m. euphonia*), central Quebec (Lake St. John, Romaine, Blanc Sablon), and southwestern Newfoundland (Parson's Pond) south through eastern New York (intergrades with *M. m. euphonia* in central section) and Pennsylvania to extreme northeastern West Virginia (Halltown) and central Virginia (Lynchburg, Petersburg).

Winter range.—Winters from southern Ontario (Barrie, Arnprior), southern Quebec (Montreal), central New Brunswick (Memramcook), Prince Edward Island (North River), and Nova Scotia (Pictou) south to eastern Texas, eastern and southern Louisiana (Kisatchie, New Orleans), southern Mississippi (Saucier), southern Alabama (Petit Bois Island), and western and southern Florida (Pensacola, Flamingo); casually north to Newfoundland (Mobile)

Casual records.—Casual in Bermuda.

Migration.—The data deal with the species as a whole. Early dates of spring arrival are: Virginia—Lynchburg, March 2. West Virginia—Wellsburg, March 21. Maryland—Laurel, February 19. New York—Monroe County, February 21; Suffolk County, February 22. Massachusetts—Martha's Vineyard, March 14; Essex County, average of 5 years, March 10. Vermont—Bennington, March 11. New Hampshire—Concord, February 22; New Hampton, March 2 (median of 21 years, March 21). Maine—Lake Umbagog, March 25. Quebec—Montreal area, March 27. New Brunswick—St. John, March 16; St. Andrews, March 17. Nova Scotia—Yarmouth, March 15. Prince Edward Island—North River, March 19. Newfoundland—Codroy River, May 2. Illinois—Chicago, March 5 (average of 16 years, March 15). Indiana—Elkhart, March 7. Ohio—Buckeye Lake, February 27. Iowa—Sioux City, March 14 (median of 38 years, March 25). Minnesota—Minneapolis-St. Paul, March 14 (average of 15 years, March 22); Lincoln County, March 14 (average of 27 years for southern Minnesota, March 22). Nebraska—Holstein, March 5; Red Cloud, March 11 (average of 21 years, April 3). South Dakota—Sioux City, March 20 (average of 7 years, March 27). North Dakota—Cass County, March 25 (average, April 2); Jamestown, March 31. Manitoba—Treesbank, April 4 (average of 25 years, April 14). Saskatchewan—Sovereign, April 5.

Arizona — Baboquivari Mountains, February 16. Utah — Kanab area, February 21. Montana—Columbia Falls, March 19. Washington—Destruction Island, March 10. British Columbia—Arrow Lake, March 7. Alaska—Kupreanof, April 18.

Late dates of spring departure are: Florida—Enterprise, April 17. Alabama—Jasper, May 10; Wheeler National Wildlife Refuge, May 4. Georgia—Savannah, May 10; Atlanta, May 9. South Carolina—Charleston, May 5 (median of 5 years, May 3). North Carolina—Raleigh, April 29 (average of 14 years, April 4). Virginia—Lawrenceville, April 12. Maryland—Laurel, April 29. Louisiana—Baton Rouge, April 8. Mississippi—Rosedale, May 26; Gulfport, April 4. Arkansas—Washington County, May 4; Arkansas County, April 28. Tennessee—Athens, April 28 (average of 6 years, April 24). Kentucky—Bowling Green, April 29. Missouri—St. Louis, April 19. Illinois—Chicago, May 19 (average of 16 years, May 6). Ohio—Buckeye Lake, median April 5. Texas—Tyler, April 28; Sinton, April 8 (median of 5 years, March 29). Oklahoma—Payne County, May 4; Cleveland County, April 24. Kansas—northeastern Kansas, May 9 (median of 18 years, April 26). Nebraska—Holstein, April 25. New Mexico—Mesilla Park, March 20. Arizona—Tucson, May 2. Utah—Washington County, May 1. California—Death Valley, April 6. Oregon—Netarts, April 14. Washington—Cathlamet, May 22.

Early dates of fall arrival are: California—Fortuna, September 19. Arizona—Tucson, September 18. Nebraska—Red Cloud, September 7. Kansas—northeastern Kansas, September 2 (median of 20 years, October 7). Oklahoma—Payne County, September 27; Cleveland County, October 13. Texas—Sinton, September 17 (median of 5 years, October 1); Midland, September 24. Iowa—Sioux City, September 4. Ohio—Buckeye Lake, median, October 1. Missouri—St. Louis, September 30. Illinois—Chicago, August 4 (average of 16 years, August 16). Kentucky—Bowling Green, October 4. Tennessee—Nashville, October 4 (median of 11 years, October 11); Athens, October 7. Arkansas—Washington County, October 14; Arkansas County, October 15. Mississippi—Rosedale, October 2 (mean of 42 years, October 6); Gulfport, October 24. Louisiana—Baton Rouge, October 23. New York—Tiana Beach, October 10. New Jersey—Island Beach, September 26. Maryland—Laurel, September 20 (median of 5 years, September 30); Ocean City, October 4. West Virginia—French Creek, October 10. Virginia—Lawrenceville, October 14. North Carolina—Raleigh, October 2 (average of 18 years, October 13). South Carolina—Charleston, September 21 (median of 7 years, October 10). Georgia—Athens, October 2; Savannah, October 12. Alabama—Birmingham, September 22;

Marion, September 29. Florida—Tallahassee, October 8; St. Marks, October 9.

Late dates of fall departure are: Alaska—Tenakee Inlet, September 29. British Columbia—Arrow Lake, November 29. Montana—Fortine, November 5. Arizona—Oak Springs, October 12. Saskatchewan—Eastend, October 22. Manitoba—Treesbank, October 28 (average of 22 years, October 15). North Dakota—Cass County, November 1 (average, October 24); Jamestown, October 23. South Dakota—Lennox, November 4; Sioux Falls, November 1 (average of 6 years, October 12). Nebraska—Holstein, November 28. Minnesota—Minneapolis, November 28 (average of 14 years for southern Minnesota, November 7). Ohio—Buckeye Lake, median, November 7. Indiana—Roanoke, November 19. Illinois—Chicago, November 17 (average of 16 years, November 3). Newfoundland—Codroy River, October 10. Prince Edward Island—North River, November 25. New Brunswick—Scotch Lake, November 4. Quebec—Montreal area, November 22. Maine—Lake Umbagog, October 27; Bangor, October 26. New Hampshire—New Hampton, median of 21 years, November 12. Vermont—Rutland, November 21. New York—Suffolk County, November 5; Ontario County, November 1. Maryland—Laurel, November 19. Florida—Leon County, November 27.

Egg dates.—The data deal with the species as a whole:

Alaska: 21 records, April 29 to July 3; 11 records, June 1 to June 26.

Alberta: 51 records, May 18 to July 28; 30 records, May 18 to June 6; 13 records, June 17 to July 26.

Arizona: 33 records, April 9 to August 22; 14 records, May 16 to May 29; 10 records, June 2 to June 29.

British Columbia: 15 records, April 7 to June 26.

California: 352 records, February 12 to July 7; 73 records, April 12 to April 30; 163 records, May 12 to May 31; 62 records, June 1 to June 20.

Illinois: 116 records, April 22 to August 7; 58 records, May 10 to May 31; 30 records, June 8 to July 18.

Maryland: 210 records, April 12 to August 21; 105 records, May 7 to June 19.

Massachusetts: 156 records, May 5 to August 17; 68 records, May 16 to May 31; 42 records, June 6 to June 20; 30 records, June 26 to July 10.

Michigan: 205 records, April 21 to August 29; 100 or more records, May 7 to June 14.

New Brunswick: 36 records, May 10 to July 16.

New York: 147 records, May 2 to August 24; 65 records, May 10 to June 21; 26 records, June 4 to June 27.

Nova Scotia: 60 records, April 20 to August 6; 30 records, May 24 to June 25.

Ontario: 140 records, April 28 to August 3; 72 records, May 21 to June 20.

Oregon: 80 records, April 7 to July 15; 36 records, May 1 to May 22; 32 records, May 25 to June 29.

Washington: 82 records, April 5 to July 14; 32 records, April 5 to April 19; 30 records, May 2 to May 29.

MELOSPIZA MELODIA ATLANTICA Todd

Atlantic Song Sparrow

PLATE 75

Contributed by VAL NOLAN JR.

HABITS

This race breeds on the ocean beaches and barrier islands of the central Atlantic states and shifts its range only a little southward in winter. Witmer Stone (1937) writes that on Cape May, N.J., the bird inhabits "possibly the inner edges of the salt marshes" as well as the coast islands, and other writers have found *atlantica* in or near salt marshes. Stone proceeds to give the following interesting ecological information about this race and *melodia:* "To illustrate how environment affects the distribution of these birds it may be mentioned that a series of breeding Song Sparrows collected in 1891 on the edge of the old Cape Island Sound and on the salt meadows that formerly existed southwest of Cape May are all typical of the Atlantic Song Sparrow * * *. Since * * * the meadows [were filled and] replaced by dry ground with thickets of bayberry, etc., the common Eastern Song Sparrows of the interior have spread out and occupied the area."

"[*M. atlantica* is] rarely, if ever, found far from salt water. It nests in myrtle thickets and in willows at the edge of the salt marsh, obtaining much of its food in the marsh itself, somewhat in the manner of the Seaside Sparrow" (Burleigh, 1958). Alexander Sprunt, Jr. wrote Mr. Bent that "the nest of *atlantica* resembles that of *melodia* in construction, being made of grasses at low elevations, but always in or near tide water. The eggs are practically indistinguishable from those of *melodia.*" The measurements of 40 eggs average 19.6 by 15.4 millimeters; the eggs showing the four extremes measure *21.6* by 15.5, 20.1 by *16.8*, and *17.8* by *14.2* millimeters.

The voice is similar to that of *melodia*, according to Sprunt, but Murray (1941) found the song distinguishable "by a buzzing quality, definitely reminiscent of the song of the Bewick's Wren."

The winter habitat is much the same as that of the summer, although Sprunt's note says that in South Carolina the bird "frequents the same habitat as *melodia*, showing a predilection, however, for salt and brackish marshes and environs."

Writers disagree as to whether *atlantica* and *melodia* are distinguishable in the field. W. E. C. Todd (1924) described the subspecies *atlantica* as "much grayer above, with the blackish streaking more distinct, and the reddish brown feather-edging reduced to a minimum. More nearly resembling *Melospiza melodia juddi*, but more grayish above * * *"

Distribution

Range.—Tidelands from Long Island, New York, to Georgia.

Breeding range.—The Atlantic song sparrow breeds in the tidelands along the Atlantic coast from Long Island, New York (Shelter Island) south to North Carolina (vicinity of Beaufort), including lower Chesapeake Bay and the lower Potomac River in Maryland (Morgantown) and Virginia.

Winter range.—Winters on breeding grounds north at least to Maryland, ranging south along Atlantic coast to South Carolina (Mount Pleasant, Yemassee) and Georgia (Savannah).

MELOSPIZA MELODIA EUPHONIA Wetmore

Mississippi Song Sparrow

Contributed by Margaret Morse Nice

Habits

From 1928 to 1936 at Columbus, Ohio, I studied a population of song sparrows on a 40 acre tract known as "Interpont." The habitat consisted of weeds, shrubs and trees; the area adjoined the Olentangy River. Over 500 adults were color-banded and 353 nestlings given aluminum bands (Nice, 1937). Later a number of nestlings were hand-raised and kept in captivity; several belonged to the eastern subspecies *melodia*, having been hatched in Massachusetts; the others were *euphonia* from southern Michigan (Nice, 1942).

Migratory status.—About half the resident males proved to be permanent residents on Interpont, and about 20 percent of the females. Six males and one female changed status during the study. Banding of two and three successive generations gave no evidence of a migratory or resident strain. The migratory impulse seemed to be latent in all the birds, cold weather in October stimulating it in the majority of the individuals, mild weather in October inhibiting it in some.

Spring.—The spring migration normally showed two main flights: an early migration of breeding males in late February or early March, and the main flight of breeding males and females, and also transients, in the middle of March. The early migration was absolutely dependent on a warm wave the last of February or the first of March, but the main migration was only relatively dependent on a rise in temperature. Severe cold waves stopped migration short. The early males migrated at markedly higher temperatures, an average of 50° F., than did the later males, which migrated at an average of 43° F. High temperatures in December, January, and early February never brought a flight, so it is clear that migration was dependent on both increasing day-length and rising temperature. Fifty-seven migration dates for 22 banded males were obtained; 5 birds came consistently early and 6 consistently late, while the others varied in different years depending both on the weather and on their ages, older birds coming earlier than younger ones.

Territory.—The holding of territory is a fundamental trait with these song sparrows, enforced by innate behavior patterns consisting of song, display and fighting. This territoriality is essential for the undistrubed carrying out of the reproductive cycle (Nice, 1939). Although highly territorial for over half the year, and inclined, if a resident, to remain on or near his territory permanently, yet in fall and winter the male becomes somewhat social, particularly in times of severe cold and snow. Occasionally females hold territory for themselves; sometimes one helps defend the male's boundaries; sometimes females ignore the boundaries established by males. Male and female song sparrows were recorded as driving from their territories their own and 21 other species, ranging in weight from 6 to 42 or even 50 grams. (The song sparrow's own weight averages 22 grams.) Yet several of these species nested among the song sparrows.

Some male song sparrows keep the same territories year after year, while others make slight changes. Females returned to their former nesting territories in 20 of 54 cases, settled next door almost as often, and in 19 instances settled at distances of from 100 to 800 yards. Twenty-two males banded in the nest took up territories from 100 yards to nearly a mile from their birth places, while 12 females banded in the nest settled from 50 yards to nearly a mile from their birthplaces. The minimum size of a territory was some 2000 square meters (½ acre), the average size in a region well filled with song sparrows about 2700 square meters (⅔ acre), and the maximum size about 6000 square meters (1½ acres). In years of low population density, territory size was somewhat larger.

Pair Formation.—In pair formation, the territorial male gives the same initial reaction to all intruders of his species, that is, he flies at them. Migrating song sparrows respond by leaving; a male in breeding condition puffs out his feathers, sings, and waves a wing, while a female seeking a mate stands her ground and gives special notes and postures. The male "pounces" upon his mate, sometimes colliding with her, sometimes only swooping over her, then flies away with a loud song; she stands still and either gives her copulation note or a threat note. Copulation, however, never occurs in connection with pouncing. The male stops singing as soon as joined by a mate.

The pair normally stays together throughout one nesting season. Yet a female may sometimes follow her young into a neighbor's territory and if he is unmated she may remain with him for the next brood. Remating of pairs a second year has been known in only 8 out of 30 possible cases, probably due to the many chances a male has of getting a mate before the return of his last year's mate. A female finding her former mate already mated to another female does not drive off the new female, as does the brown thrasher (Thomas, 1952), but joins another male. There were 4 cases of bigamy, apparently arising when an incubating female lost her mate and attached herself to a neighboring male.

Nesting.—Typically the nest is built entirely by the female. An exceptional male, while unmated, built 2 incomplete and one complete nest; later he helped his mates built 3 nests (Schantz, 1937). The nest is a rather simple affair built largely of dead grass and weeds, with a few fine roots and pieces of grape-vine bark, and lined with fine grass and occasionally horse hair. Renesting regularly occurs if a nest fails, until the nesting season is at its end. The song sparrow shows its adaptability in the nest sites chosen. The requisites are secure support and concealment. In April almost the only situations on Interpont offering these characteristics are on the ground; here under tufts of grass, weed stalks or thistles, and often in a natural depression, nine-tenths of the nests of the first attempt have been situated. One-third of the nests of the second attempt were placed above the ground, as were two-thirds of the third attempt. Few nests were built more than 3 feet above the ground. Replacement nests were built at 10 to 55 yards from the nests replaced, averaging 25 yards.

Reginald F. James wrote Mr. Bent from Willowdale, Ontario: "The Song Sparrow begins to nest around April 20th, and its first nest is usually placed on the ground. The second nest is built about 18 inches above the ground level. If and when a third nest is constructed, it may be placed as much as 3 feet above ground level, usually in a thorn bush."

One nest, however, he found 9½ feet above ground in a horizontal hole in a willow. One banded song sparrow nested for 3 years in his garden: "On May 18, 1947 it was found sitting on three lightly marked eggs in a perfect replica of an ovenbird's nest. On June 14th she was found sitting on three heavily blotched eggs and one cowbird egg, eighteen inches from the ground in a wild rose bush."

A different picture is given in a letter to Mr. Bent by D. J. Nicholson of small colonies of song sparrows observed from June 10 through August at Lake Summit, near Tuxedo, Henderson County, North Carolina, at an elevation of 2,000 feet. Nests were often placed 2 to 4 feet up in small pine saplings. Three nests were found "in very large tall pines 25 or 28 feet above the ground," and two others at 20 feet; these were built 8 to 15 feet from the trunk of the tree. Around Tuxedo many nests were found "well up in apple trees 6 to 12 feet above ground."

The nest is usually pretty well completed in two days and lined on the 3rd and perhaps the 4th. A female will engage in building for from 15 to 23 minutes, then interrupt her work for 5 to 8 minutes.

In the matter of nest building, the young female is in every way the equal of the older and experienced bird in choice of site, skill in construction, quality of the finished structure, and excellence of its concealment.

The start of egg-laying with the song sparrows on Interpont was closely correlated with the temperature in April; in one year, 1929, it was also affected by the temperature in the last third of March. In 6 years the first egg was found between April 15 and 19, but in 1929 it was found on April 10, and in 1932, April 23. The start of general laying was closely correlated with temperature. The "normal" date was April 25, but this was accelerated nearly 2 weeks in 1929 and 4 or 5 days in 1930 and 1931, but was delayed 4 or 5 days in 1933 and 1934.

In eastern North America between the latitudes of Maine and North Carolina, the races of the song sparrow normally nest through July and into August. Drought curtails nesting, however, as it did on Interpont in 1930, when adults began to molt two weeks early. George M. Sutton (1960) found the same to be true on the Edwin S. George Reserve near Ann Arbor, Mich., where nests were active in July and August of 1934, 1935, and 1940, but not in the extremely dry summers of 1936 and 1946.

Eggs.—The ground color of the eggs on Interpont ranges typically from blue through blue-green to grey-green. The spots are brown to red-brown and rarely lilac, and are arranged in an endless variety from small speckles nearly uniformly distributed over the whole egg to a few large splotches irregularly placed, usually the larger part of the pigment being around the large end, sometimes in quite a regular ring. Measurements of 503 eggs ranged from 17.5 to 22.5 mm. in length and from 14 to 17 mm. in width, the median being 19.9 x 15.5. As to weight, 44 fresh eggs varied from 1.8 to 2.85 grams, the average being 2.28, the median 2.23.

In 211 nests on Interpont sets of 5 eggs were found in 30 percent of the cases, 4 eggs in 50 percent, and 3 eggs in about 20; the average size was 4.1 eggs. In North Carolina in 175 nests D. J. Nicholson discovered only one 5-egg set; 4-egg sets were in the majority, although there were several of 2 eggs and once he collected a single well incubated egg. When a song sparrow's nest is destroyed the first egg of the next set is laid 5 days later.

The weight of a set was approximately half the weight of the bird that laid it.

Young.—Incubation, which is performed by the female alone, usually lasts slightly over 12 or 13 days but rarely has taken 14 and 15 days with unusually inattentive females. The bird stays on the eggs for 20 to 30 minutes, then leaves for 6 to 8 minutes. The total percentage of daylight hours spent on the nest averages 75 to 80. The male guards his territory, nest, and mate, and does considerable singing. He often calls her off the nest with a sudden loud song.

The young are brooded by the female for the first 5 or 6 days of nest life. The rate of feeding increases with the age of the nestlings; in 7 broods the rate for the first 5 days averaged 7.2 times an hour, for the second 5 days 17.8; the average for the whole period was 11.1 times an hour. The weight of the nestling increases more than tenfold in the first 10 days of life. Young usually stay in the nest 10 days, leaving before they can fly. They become independent of the parents at the age of 28 to 30 days.

After a nest was destroyed, the young of the replacement nest were usually fledged just 30 days later. Periods between the fledging of two broods successfully raised ranged from 30 to 41 days. *M. m. euphonia* might be called three-brooded, although Schantz (1937) reports that one pair raised four broods in one nest in one season. D. J. Nicholson writes of a similar observation near Tuxedo, N.C. in 1956, his only such record in 56 years of experience.

Plumages.—Alexander Wetmore (1936b) described *euphonia* as similar to *melodia* but distinctly darker above, being grayer, with the dark markings generally more distinct; sides of head grayer, less buffy or brown; tail averaging darker. In common with other races of the song sparrow in the east, many individuals of *euphonia* show a distinctly rufescent phase. One breeding bird collected has the brown markings (auburn in color) predominating over any other shade on the dorsal surface.

Behavior.—Female song sparrows arose about 5 minutes after civil twilight in clear weather and 7 minutes after civil twilight in cloudy weather. Males did likewise in January and early and late fall; but in early spring they arose *at* civil twilight, and later in spring and in mid-fall when in full song they rose 4 minutes before civil twilight. Roosting took place at about 10 times the light values of the rising time of the female. From December through May and again in October the last notes of the males came with surprising regularity 13–14 minutes after sunset in clear weather.

Song sparrows use several methods for defense of nest and young. They may sometimes threaten an enemy with posture and sound. They attack cowbirds that approach the nest site. Some individuals attack small snakes, while others ignore them. Typically solicitude for the nest reaches its peak when the young are ready to leave it. Warning notes from the parents at the approach of an intruder induce silence in the young. Distraction display, in which the bird runs about close to the observer with wings held stiffly erect and tail depressed, was typically shown when young of 6 or 7 days shrieked when being banded. Occasionally parents will try to lure young to safety by bringing food near, then hurrying away with it.

Experiments with enemy recognition, as well as observations in nature, led to the conclusion that owls are recognized by song sparrows largely through an inborn pattern, hawks through their rapid movements, and cats and cowbirds through conditioning. With a hand-raised bird, memory of circumstances connected with strong alarm persisted after 4 to 19 months, a response that has definite biological value (Nice and ter Pelkwyk, 1941).

Anting wás observed in 3 of the hand-raised song sparrows; both ants and sumach berries were used. Anting first appeared at the age of 36 to 37 days (Nice and ter Pelkwyk, 1940).

Although the song sparrow is only slightly gregarious, it shows the basic mechanisms for social integration (Nice, 1943.)

Voice.—Eight different kinds of vocalizations were heard from young song sparrows, 16 from adult males, and 15 from females. Songs are given at the rate of 5 to 7 a minute when the bird is singing steadily, but occasionally during encounters involving territory establishment, the rate may be 10 times a minute. Sometimes a primitive-sounding, irregular flight song is uttered. Young birds change often from one song to another; at the height of vigor there is sustained effort and one song may be sung 60 or even 70 times in succession; an old bird may change from one song to another somewhat more often. The greatest number of songs in one hour was 325, and in one day 2,305 from a bird 8 or 9 years old.

Female song sparrows occasionally sing early in the season before nesting begins; the song is given from an elevation and is short, simple, and unmusical. The most energetic singers were also zealous in chasing male neighbors.

There are 5 chief stages in the development of song in the young bird: continuous warbling, advanced warbling with some short songs, predominantly short songs, songs practically as in adult but with repertoire undetermined, songs as in adult with repertoire fixed.

This species, where each male has a quota of songs peculiar to himself, but where there are occasional duplications in a community, offers an opportunity to test the matter of inheritance or learning of song with banded birds. The possession of similar songs was no proof of close relationship between the singers, as neither brothers, fathers and sons, nor grandfathers and grandsons had similar songs, while birds known to be unrelated occasionally had similar songs. With two hand-raised brothers (*melodia*) from Massachusetts exposed only to records of songs of English birds, the form, length, and timing of their songs were typical of the species, but the quality was atypical and may have been suggested by the recorded songs. The following year, a nestling *euphonia* hatched 600 miles from the hatching site of the two brothers, heard one of them sing a small amount in the fall but heard no other singing; in December this *euphonia* burst into song with all of the 6 songs he had heard and with nothing else. It is evident that the pattern is innate, but that quality may be imitated. Particular songs may be improvised, or they may be adopted from some other song sparrow.

Enemies.—The song sparrow, like other small passerines, suffers from a multitude of adverse factors: weather; predators, native and introduced; the brood parasite, the cowbird; and man with his destruction of habitat, his inventions—windows, rat traps, automobiles, lighthouses, ceilometers at airports—shooting by his offspring in mistake for "English sparrows." The introduced predators—cat, rat, and dog—appeared to be more destructive than native predators—snakes, birds, and mammals. On Interpont about 26 percent of the song sparrow nests found were parasitized by the cowbird in 1930 and 1931, 58 percent of the early nests in 1932, 36 percent in 1933 and 69 to 78 percent during the next 3 years. From 0 to 5 song sparrows were raised in 28 nests along with 1 cowbird, from 0 to 2 song sparrows along with 2 cowbirds. Sixty-six successful nonparasitized nests raised an average of 3.4 song sparrows, while 28 successful parasitized nests raised an average of 2.4 song sparrows. So each cowbird appears to have been raised at the expense of one song sparrow.

D. J. Nicholson found no cowbird eggs or young in any nests during 9 years of observation in North Carolina. But in July, 1954, he saw a fledging cowbird being fed by a Mississippi song sparrow. "Apparently cowbirds are extremely scarce in that region of North Carolina and have just come there," he wrote.

Turning to egg and nestling losses from all causes, 44 percent of the eggs laid left the nest as fledged young during the first 2 years of the Interpont study and 29 percent during the next 4 years; 36 percent of the eggs yielded fledglings during the 6 years. The first 2 years, during which conditions for reproduction were favorable, correspond well with results of other studies on altricial young in open nests. The poor success afterwards reflected the disturbed conditions of the environment. The percentage losses suffered by eggs and nestlings of 906 eggs laid during 7 years was: flood 2.8 percent, predators 36.7 percent, cowbird 6.1 percent, sterile and addled eggs 5.6 percent, parental failure 2.4 percent, man 4 percent, parents killed 3.7 percent, young starved 3.1 percent. For all eggs laid these figures represent a death of 40.9 percent in the egg stage, and of 23.5 percent after the nestling stage was reached—64.4 percent in all.

The survival of the adult breeding males averaged over 60 percent during the first 2 years, but after that dropped to 48, 23, 30, and 20 percent. The loss of breeding males from April to June averaged 15 percent during the first 3 years, 30 percent during the next 3; the loss of breeding females averaged 30 percent and 35 percent during the same periods. The proportion of first year males in the population ranged from about 26 to 55 percent.

Out of 317 fledged nestlings 26 males and 14 females were later found as breeders. The late arrival of young females doubtless raises difficulties in the way of return to the vicinity of the birth place. The percentage of yearly return of birds, without regard to sex, ranged from 4.5 to 20, averaging 12.6; and 4.5 percent of the eggs laid produced birds that returned to breed on the area. If the population is to be maintained it is estimated that an average of 20 percent of the fledged young should survive to adulthood. It is believed that 50 to 60 percent of the young song sparrows that survived to breed returned to the place of birth to do so.

In a well-situated group of song sparrows the average life of the breeding males was 2½ to 2¾ years. Individuals have been known to have reached 7 years of age, while one male was at least 7½, and perhaps 9½ years old at his death.

Fall.—There was always singing in the fall from the males on their territories, much in mild weather, little in bleak. Usually the summer residents sang for only a few days the last of September and first of October, but some residents might sing well into November. In each of 5 years one banded male sang for periods lasting 40 to 65 days. The character of the autumn singing differed little from that of the height of the nesting season, except that there were more incomplete songs.

The fall migration of the transients in central Ohio takes place in late September and throughout October. Summer resident females left by the middle of October, males a little later. Bleak weather tended to hasten migration, mild weather to delay it or even occasionally to supress it.

Winter.—Resident song sparrows stay on or near their territories throughout the year, although they do not defend them in winter. At this season they may range over an area 6 to 10 times as large as their breeding territories. In cold spells they sometimes come more than a quarter of a mile to a feeding station. In snowy weather they assemble in loose flocks which are neither family parties nor neighborhood groups, as they are composed of both residents and winter residents. (Families break up at the end of the nesting season.) The resident males start their singing and take up territories during warm weather in late January or early February, but a return of winter brings a return to winter behavior.

I never had a recovery away from Interpont of the 870 birds banded. A song sparrow banded June 8, 1932 near Cleveland, Ohio, was taken in Janesboro, Ga., Dec. 25, 1933.

[*Note.*—Because Mrs. Nice's account of *euphonia* is essentially a summary of her banding study of an Ohio population, it is desirable to add a word about the race in other places, and especially in the Appalachian Mountains. Indeed, the old vernacular name Mississippi Song Sparrow was rejected by some (see Burleigh, 1958) as being less appropriate than "Appalachian Song Sparrow."—V.N.]

Arthur Stupka (1963) writes that this race is common in the lower altitudes of the Great Smoky Mountains National Park but breeds at any heights there. The habitat above 6,000 feet is "brushy openings in these moist highlands." In the mountains of Georgia, on the other hand, Burleigh (1958) states that the bird is fairly common in "thickets and underbrush in the valleys. It has no liking for thick woods and will never be seen on mountainsides or in wooded ravines."

Interestingly, both the foregoing authors have noted an extension of *euphonia's* range. It appears to have moved into the high altitudes in only recent years, and Stupka discusses the possibility that large-scale habitat changes attributable to lumbering and chestnut blight have thinned the forest overstory and produced the changed distribution of the bird. In Georgia, the breeding range of the species has been extended even more markedly. "Less than fifty years ago, it was not known to breed in Georgia * * * (Burleigh, 1958), but by

1945 it had penetrated southward beyond the mountain valleys to the northern edge of the Piedmont."

Milton B. Trautman (1940) has given a most comprehensive description of the habitat preferences of this race in a large and varied area around Buckeye Lake in central Ohio:

In winter the bird was abundant in brushy thickets, fallow fields of rank weed growth, weedy fields of uncut corn, brushy edges and openings of woodlands, brushy fence rows, brushy and weedy swamps, weedy edges of the canal, and cattail marshes. It was less numerous or entirely absent from the bleak snow-swept fields and pastures, from the vicinity of farmhouses containing little shrubbery, and from orchards and woodlots which had no ground cover. During spring and fall it was also noted in small numbers in more barren localities, such as pastures, meadows and last year's forage and grain fields.

In the nesting season, from late March to early August, the species was found in the greatest concentrations in lowland weedy situations. Many pairs nested on the islands and lowland shores of the lake where herbaceous plants and brush were present, about weedy and brushy borders and isolated brushy areas of cattail swamps, in weedy and brushy inland swamps, in brushy edges and openings of woodlands, along brushy fence rows, in fallow and weedy fields, and in the openings and borders of brushy thickets. A few also nested along weedy or brushy fence rows, in fields of smaller grains and forage crops, and in woodlots containing little ground cover. It was only in the barren upland fields and on the crests of wooded hills that nesting birds were absent.

Distribution

Range.—Northern Wisconsin, northeastern Michigan, southern Ontario, and western New York south to south-central Texas, the Gulf coast, and southern Georgia.

Breeding range.—The Mississippi song sparrow breeds from northern Wisconsin, northeastern Michigan (Marquette, Whitefish Point), central southern Ontario (Bruce County, Hamilton), and western New York (east to Keuka Lake) south through southeastern Minnesota and Iowa to northeastern Kansas (Bendena), southwestern Missouri (Jasper County), and northwestern and north-central Arkansas (Winslow, Newport); through western Pennsylvania, western Maryland (Accident), West Virginia (except extreme northeast), southwestern Kentucky (Paducah, Glasgow), southwestern Virginia (Pulaski, Marion), southeastern Tennessee (Chattanooga, Crab Orchard), northeastern Alabama (Valley Head), and western North Carolina to northern Georgia (Milledgeville) and northwestern South Carolina (Clemson); casual in summer in south-central Kansas (Harper) and northern Louisiana (Tallulah).

Winter range.—Winters from southern Wisconsin (Viroqua, Green Bay), southern Michigan (Alicia), southern Ontario, and western New York southwest and south through southeastern Nebraska, eastern Kansas (Douglas County), and central Oklahoma (Norman) to south-central Texas (Fort Clark, Matagorda), southern Louisiana (Main Pass), southern Mississippi (Biloxi), southern Alabama (Petit Bois Island), southern Georgia (Grady County, St. Simons Island), and South Carolina (Kershaw County, Mount Pleasant); casually in northern Michigan (McMillan) and western Kansas (Seward County).

MELOSPIZA MELODIA JUDDI Bishop

Dakota Song Sparrow

Contributed by VAL NOLAN JR.

HABITS

This breeding race of the great plains of Canada and of the northern United States withdraws from much of its range in winter and spreads southward and eastward as far as Florida. Early migrants return to Canada in mixed flocks with tree sparrows, juncos, fox sparrows, and other fringillids in March and April (Houston and Street, 1959).

Thomas S. Roberts (1936) has described the habitat in Minnesota: "Bushy meadows and the banks of lakes and streams are the chosen dwelling-places, but it is not confined to such surroundings and may be found almost anywhere about prairie groves, upland fields, clearings, and gardens, shunning only the deep shade of heavy timber." Roberts also quotes T. Martin Trippe, a pioneer Minnesota bird student, who in 1871 noted that this shy bird of the brush prairies and thickets, near water, was changing from "almost the wildness and timidity of a wild-duck" to a confiding neighbor of man.

Territory sizes under favorable conditions would probably approximate those stated above for *euphonia* and suggested for *melodia.* However, Beer et al. (1956) report that song sparrows nesting on small islands in Basswood Lake, Minn., regularly hold territories as small as 0.04 acre, which is the total area of each of two of the islands. Indeed, territories of 0.05 acre each were held by two pairs present on a single island, but one male was "definitely subordinate." Suthers (1960) measured lake-shore territories on Lake Itasca, Minn., "to retain the effects of shore line on size" while avoiding the probable effects of insularity; territory sizes varied from 0.34 to 0.68 acre, averaged 0.47 acre, and were thus intermediate between those of island and mainland territories. Comparison with work of Tompa (1962) on the race *morphna*, below, is suggested.

M. m. juddi is among the first birds to sing in spring, and descriptions of the song resemble those of the eastern races. However, Louis B. Bishop (1896), who described the race, found the song "quite different,

* * * clearer, sweeter, more powerful. * * * I could not believe [it] was a song sparrow until I had the bird in my hand."

No differences between the reproductive cycle of *juddi* and of *melodia* and *euphonia* are apparent in Roberts (1936) and other literature. Beer and his colleagues (1956) state that on the small islands in Basswood Lake, Minn., "Nesting, while normally on the ground, may take place in holes in trees or in small evergreens as much as seven feet off the ground where there are not suitable open areas."

Roberts describes an interesting instance of predation on a nest by a garter snake which suddenly appeared, and seized and made off with a newly hatched nestling "in spite of a vigorous attack by one of the parents. When pursued the snake quickly swallowed the tiny nestling." Roberts opened the snake (a gravid female) and found a second song sparrow nestling in it. As garter snakes are common in the nesting habitat of song sparrows, the episode was probably typical.

L. B. Bishop (1896) described *juddi* as being similar to the race presently known as *M. m. melodia*, "but with the ground color of the upper parts paler, especially the superciliary streak and sides of neck, and the white of the lower parts clearer; the interscapulars with the black center broader, the reddish-brown portions narrower, and the gray edgings paler; the dark markings on the breast restricted, and more sharply defined against the ground color."

Distribution

Range.—Northeastern British Columbia, southern Mackenzie, northern Manitoba, and northern Ontario south to southern Texas, the Gulf coast, and central Florida.

Breeding range.—The Dakota song sparrow breeds from northeastern British Columbia (near Peace River), central southern Mackenzie (Great Slave Lake), northern Saskatchewan (Lake Athabaska), northern Manitoba (Knee Lake; casual at Churchill), and northern Ontario (Fort Severn, Attawapiskat Post) south through the plains of Alberta (Grand Prairie, Calgary, Milk River) and eastern Montana (Miles City) to northern Nebraska (Sioux County, Dakota City), northwestern Iowa, southern Minnesota, extreme northwestern Michigan (Baraga County), and southwestern Ontario (Amyot); casual in southern Nebraska (Red Cloud).

Winter range.—Winters from southeastern Montana (Miles City), South Dakota (Yankton), and southern Minnesota (Cambridge) south and east to western and southern Texas (Fort Davis, Boquillas, Del Rio; Atascosa County; Longview), Louisiana (Lake Charles), southern Mississippi (Petit Bois Island), Georgia (Ila, Tifton), central Florida (Enterprise), and southwestern Virginia (Blacksburg); casually to Manitoba (Burnside) and southern Arizona (Tucson).

Accidental on Banks Island, Franklin District.

MELOSPIZA MELODIA MONTANA Henshaw

Mountain Song Sparrow

Contributed by VAL NOLAN JR.

HABITS

This is the breeding subspecies of most of the Rocky Mountains of the United States, from the states bordering Canada to those adjoining Mexico. Although it may nest at least as high as 9,000 feet (Betts, 1912), the song sparrow is replaced in the Canadian life zone by the congeneric Lincoln's sparrow and is ordinarily found at somewhat lower altitudes. In Yellowstone, for example, Milton Skinner (1925) found *montana* only up to 6,500 feet. At the other extreme, some individuals breed on the plains of Colorado at the eastern edge of the mountains (W. W. Cooke, 1897; Niedrach and Rockwell, 1939).

The habitat of *montana* is water-edge vegetation, whether it be in marshes around mountain lakes as at Lake Tahoe, Nev. (W. W. Price *in* Barlow, 1901), in streamside willows as in eastern Oregon (Peck, 1911), or in boggy areas of cultivated fields and meadows as in Colorado (Rockwell, 1908; Niedrach and Rockwell, 1937). Alexander Wetmore (1920) describes the habitat at Lake Burford, N. Mex., as clumps of dead tule (*Scirpus occidentalis*) fringing the lake, although occasionally birds ventured up into sagebrush to feed or nest.

In the marshes of the Grand Tetons of Wyoming, Salt (1957) studied the ecologic relations of song sparrows (believed to have been *montana*, because of the location), Lincoln's sparrows, and fox sparrows. Song sparrows occupied the dense thickets 6 to 10 feet high along open water, where they foraged "often with their feet in the water." Population density was approximately 3 individuals per 10 acres, and Salt estimated plant food comprised 60 percent of the summer diet.

Spring.—Some birds winter throughout the breeding range, while others migrate as far south as the northern states of Mexico. Reoccupation of breeding territories takes place in late March in Colorado (Cooke, 1897) and extends into early April in Montana (Saunders, 1921).

Nesting.—Nesting habits are like those of the races already discussed. Ground nests appear to be the commonest and are built in grass, alfalfa, in hollows under sage and willows, among ferns under fallen trees, and in cattails at slight elevations. Elevated nests have been found as high as 11 feet, and willows and lodgepole pines are numbered among the nest trees. The nest itself is described in the same terms as are the nests of the eastern races and apparently does not differ significantly. As an example, M. S. Ray (1910) has reported a nest in a flooded alfalfa field. It was made "of grasses and weed stems with a lining of horsehair, was placed on slightly higher ground," and well concealed, and contained an unusual clutch of 6 eggs. Nests are sometimes built over water (Rust, 1917). Jean M. Linsdale (1936), in testing the hypothesis that colors of nest linings and downy plumage of nestlings are adapted to the degree of exposure to sun, studied these points in the Toyabe Mountains of Nevada, where the breeding race of the song sparrow is *montana*. Linsdale found five nests "close to the ground" and "covered" so they were not exposed to sun. The down of the nestlings he classed as intermediate between light and dark in color, but the nest linings were dark, with the result that they would absorb warmth rather than reflect it.

Nesting continues until mid-summer, e.g., in Oregon until at least mid-July.

The male is said by Niedrach and Rockwell (1937) to help in nest building.

Eggs.—The measurements of 40 eggs average 19.9 by 14.9 millimeters; the eggs showing the four extremes measure *22.6* by 15.2, 20.8 by *15.5*, *18.3* by 14.2, and 19.3 by *13.5* millimeters.

Incubation.—Courtship feeding by the male of the female as she sits on the eggs has been attributed to this race by Niedrach and Rockwell (1937). However, because these authors give no details and because Mrs. Nice (1943) did not observe such behavior in *euphonia*, confirmation seems desirable. David Lack (1940b) in his review of courtship feeding states, "Typically [it] seems absent in * * * American sparrows, including the well-studied * * * Melospiza (Song Sparrow)."

Plumage.—Ridgway (1901) states that *montana* is similar to *melodia*, "but wing, tail and tarsi averaging decidedly longer, bill smaller and relatively more slender, and coloration grayer; young with ground color or under parts dull white or grayish white, instead of more or less buffy, that of upper parts less tawny than the young of * * * *melodia*." H. W. Henshaw (1884) states that fall specimens of *montana* are "browner" than the race *fallax* with the markings generally less distinct, i.e., more diffused. The black streaks of the back are always present. M. S. Ray (1913) found a partially albino nestling in a brood of three; "the entire underparts were pure white and iris light reddish."

Fall and winter.—Some birds are found in fall above the breeding altitude, e.g., at 10,000 feet in Park County, Colorado (Warren, 1915). Those that remain in the breeding range through the winter apparently survive by staying close to the moderating influences of water, including warm springs where these occur. Rockwell and Wetmore (1914) found this race common in the mountains along Clear Creek near Golden, Colo., on Nov. 14 "though there was six inches of snow and the bushes were veritable snow banks." Stanley G. Jewett (1912) has written of seeing several *M. m. montana* that in December frequented the warm spring flats of the Wood River in Idaho and obtained insects from the muddy ground. The birds were "often seen feeding in the shallow water, while on all sides the snow was piled four feet deep." Birds that migrate to southeastern California inhabit "thickets of arrowweed, and willows and reeds at the edges of ditches and river courses. The birds forage short distances out into grassy or weedy places and about root tangles and piles of driftwood" (Grinnell and Miller, 1944).

Distribution

Range.—Northeastern Oregon and north-central Montana to southeastern California, northern Sonora, central Chihuahua, and western Texas.

Breeding range.—The mountain song sparrow breeds from northeastern Oregon (Union and Wallowa counties), central western Idaho (New Meadows), and north-central Montana (Missoula and Teton counties, intergrades with *M. m. merrilli*) south to eastern Nevada (Toiyabe Mountains, Lehman Creek), southwestern Utah (Pine Valley Mountains, Kanab), central eastern Arizona (White Mountains), and northern New Mexico (Santa Fe, Raton).

Winter range.—Winters throughout the breeding range and south to southeastern California (Death Valley, Riverside Mountain), northern Sonora (Caborca, headwaters of Bavispe River), central Chihuahua (Chihuahua), and western Texas (Fort Davis, Ingram); east casually to western Nebraska (Crawford), western Kansas (Trego County), and western Oklahoma (Cimarron County).

MELOSPIZA MELODIA INEXPECTATA Riley

Yellowhead or Riley Song Sparrow

Contributed by Val Nolan Jr.

Habits

Although *M. m. inexpectata* occurs as a breeding bird on the coast and inner islands of the southeastern extension of Alaska, the range of this race also includes much of interior British Columbia and reaches into the mountains of Alberta. This distribution and a difference in its nesting ecology are responsible for the separation of this life history of *inexpectata* from the combined account of most other subspecies that occur in Alaska.

Both on the breeding and the winter ranges, which do not overlap, this race seems to prefer a marshy or brushy habitat like those, for example, of *melodia* or *juddi*. George Willett (1928) writes that *inexpectata* occurs in southeastern Alaska in inland locations several miles from salt water. "Nests * * * found at Ketchikan were often placed several feet up in trees." Apparently nests were built near the ocean, as well, for the same writer found a nest "inside a roll of wire netting that was lying just above the high tide line." Harry S. Swarth (1922) found this song sparrow in relatively few places in the upper Stikine River valley in British Columbia, but near one tributary creek and in the marshy meadows a mile or so back from the river it was abundant. Between July 8 and 26, 1921, Swarth considered full grown young more numerous than adults; the latter were apparently engaged in tending second broods, many probably still in the nest. The adults were very shy and stayed in the nesting areas, which were sloughs grown up with reeds and surrounded by willows. By mid-July, the presumed first-brood young were spreading farther and farther from the marshes and down the river. Another example of the dispersal of young from the breeding habitats is Swarth's collection of juveniles between July 26 and August 8 in fireweed patches near Flood Glacier where no suitable nesting areas were observed.

Swarth (1924) reported that on the Skeena River near Hazelton, British Columbia, this song sparrow found little suitable habitat and nested only in scattered pairs along small streams. Nesting seemed in progress on May 26, and a young bird was seen being fed by an adult as late as Aug. 29. Most birds had left by the third week of September. Swarth found no song sparrows nesting in the mountains.

Jewett et al. (1953) describe the winter habitat in western Washington as "alder brush and berry tangles of second-growth localities, as well as brush along roadsides and in partly cleared places."

J. H. Riley (1911) described *inexpectata* as being "similar to *Melospiza melodia rufina*, but the browns of the upper parts lacking the reddish tinge, thus giving to the back a gray cast; below not so heavily streaked; averaging smaller."

Distribution

Range.—Southeastern Alaska and southern Yukon south to northern Oregon.

Breeding range.—The yellowhead song sparrow breeds from the coast and inner islands of southeastern Alaska (Glacier Bay, Admiralty Island, Revillagigedo Island), southern Yukon (Squanga Lake), and northwestern British Columbia (Atlin, rarely) southeast through interior British Columbia to lat. 51° N. (Horse Lake, Yellowhead Pass) and the mountains of southwestern Alberta (Henry House, Banff).

Winter range.—Winters from southern British Columbia (Comox, Alta Lake, Okanagan Landing) south through Washington to northern Oregon (Portland, Prineville); casually north to Caribou district, British Columbia (Indianpoint Lake).

MELOSPIZA MELODIA MERRILLI Brewster

Merrill's Song Sparrow

Contributed by Val Nolan Jr.

Habits

This migratory race breeds in the interior of the three northwestern states adjoining Canada and of the two southwestern provinces of the latter country. As is true of so many other subspecies of *Melospiza melodia*, individuals can be found in winter in locations virtually throughout the breeding range, while others migrate, in the case of this race, to the southwestern United States. Descriptions of the habitat would be generally applicable to those of most of the other inland subspecies: tangles of willows, cottonwood, and alder; open, sedge-grown, brushy meadows; hawthorn brush bordering clearings; and lakeside marshy associations. H. J. Rust (1919) tells of seeing these birds hopping from pad to pad of water lilies and wading into shallow water "reminding one of the Water Ouzel except in color." At the opposite extreme, they occur in Washington, possibly as breeders, in brush succeeding deforestation at altitudes of 4,000 feet (Jewett et al., 1953). James C. Merrill (1898), for whom the bird is named, states, "There is nothing in their general habits to distinguish them from the Song Sparrows in other parts of the country," but he notes their very marked preference for the immediate vicinity of water in the type locality, Fort Sherman, Idaho.

Spring.—Rust (1919) believed birds that wintered near Fernan Lake, Idaho, to be principally old males, and these started to sing on sunny February days. Females began to join males in mid-March, and the earliest nest was found on Apr. 12, 1918, a year with an unusually warm spring. A like date is given for Washington by W. L. Dawson and J. H. Bowles (1909). At these dates few other species are nesting in the song sparrow's habitat.

Nesting.—Dawson and Bowles (1909) describe a pattern of nest placement that prevails for many other races: First nests are usually built on the ground under cover of vegetation, and elevated nests (up to 20 feet high) become commoner as the season advances. Occasional ground nests may be found at any date, e.g., on Aug. 3, in Washington. On the other hand, Rust (1919) gives an interesting portrayal of a different kind of seasonal change in nest location, with heights tending to move downward from elevated positions to the ground. At Fernan Lake, Idaho, the onset of breeding coincided with high water levels, and early nests invariably were in spirea shrubs and willows whose bases were partly submerged. Receding water in mid-May exposed clumps of sedge, which were then used for some nest sites, although shrubs and willows also continued to be selected throughout the season. J. C. Merrill (1898) never found a nest on the ground, and most were in bushes growing in water. Dawson and Bowles and also Merrill describe clumps of debris stranded in willows by flood water as common nest sites.

J. C. Merrill (1898) writes that nests near Ft. Sherman, Idaho, were "unusually large for a song sparrow" and were built largely of dead leaves and strips of cottonwood bark, deeply cupped and with finer materials for the linings. Rust found sedge the most used plant material and reported that nests built later in the season were more compact and less precariously wedged in forks and supports; horsehair was a common lining.

Eggs.—The measurements of 40 eggs average 20.1 by 15.0 millimeters; the eggs showing the four extremes measure *22.4* by 15.5, 20.8 by *16.3*, *18.3* by 15.2, and 19.3 by *13.7* millimeters.

Rust (1919) found 4-egg clutches more numerous than 5-egg clutches at Fernan Lake, Idaho. Near Ft. Sherman, Idaho, Merrill (1898) reports 5 as the common size of the first clutch, 3 or 4 as the usual later sizes.

Incubation, young.—The incubation period is set by Dawson and Bowles (1909) and by Rust (1919) at 12 days, but Rust's nestling period, 14 to 16 days, seems remarkably long in view of the periods known for *euphonia*, 10 days, and *melodia*, 10 to 14 days. Dawson and Bowles' statement that young can "fly" when 12 days old should be compared with Mrs. Nice's finding that 17 days is the age at which young of *euphonia* commonly begin to fly. Fledglings remain in dense underbrush and sedge until fairly strong on the wing.

Plumage.—Ridgway (1901) states that *merrilli* is "very similar to * * * *montana* but slightly darker and more uniform above, with the grayish edgings to the interscapulars and scapulars less strongly contrasted with the darker mesial streaks, the latter usually with more brown than black."

Food.—Jewett et al., (1953) tell of the methodical dismemberment, limb by limb, of a moth by a *merrilli* song sparrow.

Enemies.—Both Merrill (1898) and Rust (1919) regard nest losses to flooding as very numerous. As enemies Dawson and Bowles (1909) list the usual nest predators of small passerines, i.e., mammals, snakes, and corvids.

Fall and winter.—Individuals wintering in the breeding range resort to tule beds, thickets, brush piles, and the vicinity of outbuildings. Outside the breeding range in California, Grinnell and Miller (1944) report the habitat as "weed thickets, old rice fields, tule beds and willow tangles. In general favors riparian growth and damp places."

Distribution

Range.—Southern interior British Columbia and southwestern Alberta south to southern California, southern Utah, and northern New Mexico.

Breeding range.—The Merrill's song sparrow breeds from southern interior British Columbia (south of lat. 51° N.; Alta Lake, Shuswap Falls) and southwestern Alberta (Waterton Lakes Park) south to eastern Washington, east of the Cascade Range (Yakima, Wallula; intergrades with *M. m. fisherella*), northern Idaho (South Fork Clearwater River), and northwestern Montana (Flathead Lake).

Winter range.—Winters from southern interior British Columbia (Okanagan Landing) and northwestern Montana (Fortine) west to western Washington (Destruction and Orcas islands) and south to southern California (Altadena, Victorville), southern Nevada (Charleston Mountains), southern Utah (Santa Clara), and northern New Mexico (Las Vegas, Hot Springs); casually to southern Arizona (Quitobaquito) and northern Sonora (Upper Bavispe River).

MELOSPIZA MELODIA FISHERELLA Oberholser

Modoc Song Sparrow

Contributed by Val Nolan Jr.

Habits

A song sparrow of the interior of the northwestern United States (as far south as Nevada), *M. m. fisherella* appears in its life history to resemble closely *merrilli*, one of the races with which it intergrades. Many individuals winter throughout the breeding range, but others migrate, occasionally as far as northern Sonora.

Breeding altitudes in California range between 300 and 8,000 feet above sea level. But everywhere "riparian vegetation, marshes, and lake borders" are sought out, for "the combination of dense low cover and surface water with wet ground is essential for this race" (Grinnell and Miller, 1944). Philip C. Dumas (1950) has documented the foregoing statement about the habitat in a series of detailed density indices for this and other birds in the various environments of southeastern Washington.

Moisture-loving plants such as willows and cattails are the most usual nest sites, which in California "commonly are above ground in the branch-work of bushes" (Grinnell and Miller, 1944). Near Pullman, Wash. (Jewett et al., 1953), nests are often placed between 8 and 12 inches high in willows. Plants of dry associations, e.g., small conifers and shrubs, are also sometimes used for nests, which have been found as high as at least 7 feet (Mailliard, 1919b). Ground nests are also found. Nests are described as loosely woven of weeds and grasses. L. R. Dice (1918) once found a structure in which some of the material had been picked green. W. L. Dawson (1923) reports a most unusual nest in Modoc County, California; it had been built into the side of a large paper wasp nest hanging 5 feet up in a willow, and scraps of newspaper were among the materials used in the construction of the outer surface. In Washington full sets of fresh eggs have been found as early as March 30, and L. R. Dice (1918) found well feathered young in a late nest on July 13.

Feeding "occurs on the moist ground or at the water's edge, or on plants over the water or floating in it," state Grinnell and Miller (1944); and Jewett et al. (1953) describe some birds as "almost semiaquatic" in their foraging on the floating green leaves of water plants. H. C. Bryant (1911) found only insects in one stomach he examined.

Grinnell and Miller state: "In winter, restriction to riparian growth is less rigid, but seldom are the birds found far from moist situations and the associated plant species."

H. C. Oberholser (1911) described *fisherella* as being similar to *heermanni*, "but larger; upper surface paler, less rufescent; streaks on lower parts less blackish (more brownish)." *M.m. fisherella* differs from *montana* "in its darker upper parts, more blackish brown streaks of under surface, heavier bill, and shorter wing."

Distribution

Range.—Northeastern Oregon and southwestern Idaho south to southern California.

Breeding range.—The Modoc song sparrow breeds from northeastern Oregon, east of the Cascade Range and west of the Blue Mountains (The Dalles, Pendleton; intergrades with *M. m. merrilli* in southern interior Washington, and with *M. m. montana* in central Baker County, Oregon), and extreme southwestern Idaho (Weiser, Jordan Creek) south to south-central Oregon (Medford), north-central and central eastern California (Hayfork, Red Bluff, Mohawk, Olancha), and western Nevada (Santa Rosa Mountains, Fish Lake Valley).

Winter range.—Winters throughout the breeding range and south to western and southern California (Laytonville, Hayward, El Monte, Calipatria); rarely to northern Sonora (Caborca) and southern Arizona (Tucson).

MELOSPIZA MELODIA (Wilson)

Song Sparrow: Alaskan Subspecies*

Contributed by Val Nolan Jr.

Habits

The six races grouped for the purposes of this life history have in common the facts that they breed only in Alaska and that they are largely birds of the ocean beaches. Two of the races, *kenaiensis* and *caurina*, are migratory to some extent and breed, in part, on the mainland, whereas the other four races are almost exclusively island inhabitants and are resident. Otherwise the life histories of these six subspecies are probably much alike. Information referable to a particular race is so indicated.

Two additional races that breed both in Alaska and in British Columbia, *inexpectata* and *rufina*, are treated separately, because of the differences in their habitats, which are sometimes "inland localities several miles from salt water * * *," according to George Willett (1928). The same experienced observer states that the other Alaskan races (recognized at the date he wrote) "appear to be strictly beach birds, nesting and feeding within a few yards of the beach."

Gabrielson and Lincoln in their work (1959) on Alaskan birds write:

---

* The following subspecies are discussed in this section: *Melospiza melodia maxima* Gabrielson and Lincoln, *M. m. sanaka* McGregor, *M. m. amaka* Gabrielson and Lincoln, *M. m. insignis* Baird, *M. m. kenaiensis* Ridgway, and *M. m. caurina* Ridgway.

The Alaskan Song Sparrows have become rather specialized birds, adhering very closely to the sea beaches throughout most of their range, and only in the southeastern district from Yakutat Bay south do they show any resemblance to the habits so familiar to bird students elsewhere. * * * The species has one of the most curious ranges of any in Alaska. It is found along a narrow coastal strip from Dixon Entrance [at the boundary of Alaska and British Columbia] to Attu [the outermost Aleutian] * * * and only as straggling individuals in the Bristol Bay area, on the Pribilofs, or on the north side of the Alaska Peninsula.

It is also one of the most variable of Alaskan birds. The races of southeastern Alaska are dark and relatively small * * *. Northward and westward from Yakutat, however, the birds become larger and paler, reaching the grayest race in the Alaska Peninsula and in the easternmost of the Aleutian Islands [*sanaka*], and then becoming browner but not much darker in the western Aleutians [*maxima*].

Ridgway's measurements of the length, although taken from dried skins, give some indication of the variation in the size of these birds as one passes to the west. Males of the southeastern race (*rufina*) average 159 mm. in length while those of the Aleutian Islands (*maxima*) average 187 mm. * * * These big birds * * * with the normal markings greatly obscured and softened look entirely unlike their more sharply marked relatives to the east; and yet, they sing about the same song. It is an unusual experience for an ornithologist to watch one of these comparatively gigantic Song Sparrows behave exactly as do their small counterparts far to the south.

Spring.—Those individuals of the two migrant races that have wintered in southeast Alaska, British Columbia, and the Pacific states of the United States probably return to the breeding range in March and April. Thus *caurina* is found in California until March, and Swarth (1911) took specimens of that race in the Alexander Archipelago just south of the breeding range in middle and late April. Gabrielson and Lincoln (1951) mention a specimen of *kenaiensis* collected in southeastern Alaska outside the breeding range on Feb. 6.

The spring behavior of the resident races may perhaps be typified by that of *maxima* on Attu, as described by Sutton and Wilson (1946) for the period Feb. 20 to March 18. "As a rule we saw the birds in twos, and we believe that most of these were actually mated pairs. They were not in breeding condition, however (the gonads of specimens examined being unenlarged), and we saw little in the way of courtship, few pursuit flights of any sort, and no copulation. Singing we heard now and then on windy days, but it was especially noticeable in calm, sunny weather."

Nesting.—Richard F. Johnston (1954), from a study principally of egg collections, fixes the duration of nesting in the Alaskan Peninsula and the Aleutians (presumably, *sanaka* and *maxima*, and possibly *kenaiensis*, *insignis*, and *amaka*) at about 7 weeks and indicates that breeding in Alaska begins on about May 15, reaches a peak on about June 10, and ends about July 5.

Gabrielson and Lincoln (1959) say,

Nests are almost invariably placed either on the ground or very close to it in a clump of grass. Those in the Aleutians and along the south side of the Alaska Peninsula are usually built in the beach grass just above the high tide line or in the same grass in the little bays and stream bottoms which it occasionally follows for a short distance into the interior. In southeastern Alaska, it builds in similar situations, although sometimes the nests are woven around the taller grass stems, and elevated a few inches above the ground. The nests are rather bulky and rough on the outside, and are usually built of coarse grass stems not too well put together. They are usually lined with finer dried grasses that are more carefully woven into the interlining.

Joseph Grinnell (1910b) describes two nests of *M. m. kenaiensis*. Both were placed in beach grass growing on sand spits and both were alike in structure, composed principally of coarse, dry, mildewed grass stalks, arranged concentrically but not intertwined, "so that if roughly handled the nest would readily fall to pieces. The inner lining is thin and of fine, round, yellow grass stems, the majority approaching a position parallel to the rim of the nest. Although many stems are also incorporated cross-wise, the interweaving is not a conspicuous feature. The inner wall of the nest has a slippery feeling because of the smoothness of the grass-stems and the ease with which they slide, one over another; and it is extremely porous. Yet there is a moderate firmness about the whole structure." The dimensions of one nest were taken after shipment and may have been inaccurate; the diameter externally was 142 millimeters and internally 70 millimeters, while the depths were 67 and 32 millimeters externally and internally.

Two ground nests of *sanaka* that Swarth (1934) examined were made of grass, one built in a hollow, fairly well concealed by overhanging ferns and salmon berry on a steep mossy bank, the other on a hillside 30 feet above the water. One of these had an external diameter of about 150 millimeters and an internal diameter of 80 millimeters. R. C. McGregor (1960) describes a nest of *sanaka* in similar terms; it was in the face of a low cliff and had external and internal diameters of 140 and 160 millimeters and depths of 100 and 60 millimeters, respectively.

J. C. Howell (1948) found eight nests of *insignis* on the ground on Kodiak Island.

Eggs.—The measurements of 20 eggs of *M.m. sanaka* average 24.1 by 17.4 millimeters; the eggs showing the four extremes measure *25.9* by 17.8, 24.5 by *18.3*, and *21.8* by *16.3* millimeters.

The measurements of 20 eggs of *M.m. insignis* average 22.5 by 16.7 millimeters; the eggs showing the four extremes measure *23.9* by 16.3, 23.4 by *17.3*. *21.3* by 16.8, and 21.8 by *15.8* millimeters.

Johnston (1954), from 17 records of clutch size of unspecified Alaskan races, found an average first clutch of 4.00 eggs and an average second clutch of 4.33 eggs, with the mean clutch size of the sample being 4.17 eggs. The nest of *sanaka* McGregor found, described above, had three eggs, and those found by Howell contained from three to five eggs.

Young.—Swarth (1934) tells of finding families of young *sanaka* hopping about the face of a cliff and among boulders on the shore of Unalaska on June 15.

Plumage.—This summary of descriptions of the races under consideration is taken from the paper by Gabrielson and Lincoln (1951), which described *maxima* and *amaka* and reviewed the Alaskan song sparrows, and from Ridgway (1901).

M. m. maxima: "Separable from *sanaka,* to which it is most nearly related, by the following characters: bill slightly heavier and averaging somewhat longer, especially in the males; in breeding plumage back and head distinctly brownish in tone rather than grayish. This is due to the wider and heavier brown stripes in the center of the feathers of the back and to a darker brown color of the head. In specimens of *sanaka* in comparable plumage, the brown feather markings are narrower and more obscured, so that the general effect is an over-all grayish tone of the head and back.

"The brownish appearance also is conspicuous in the fall, * * * [and] a comparable difference is noticeable in the juvenal plumage" (Gabrielson and Lincoln, 1951).

M. m. sanaka: Ridgway's (1901) description of *sanaka* (at that date *cinerea*) is that the "general color above [is] olive-gray (almost ash-gray in summer), the back broadly streaked with brown (usually inclosing narrow blackish shaft-streaks), the pileum usually with two broad lateral stripes of light vandyke or mummy brown (these often obsolete in worn summer plumage); streaks on chest, etc., varying from light grayish brown to rusty brown. Young similar to the young of * * * *insignis,* but paler above and streaks of under parts grayish brown instead of sooty brown." The bird is similar to, but larger and grayer than, *M.m. insignis.*

M. m. amaka: "Resembles *maxima* from the western Aleutians in color and extensive brown markings, but somewhat more heavily marked with brown than that race both on back and breast * * *. Closer in color to *maxima* than to the geographically closer race *sanaka.* Bill short and stubby as in *sanaka*" (Gabrielson and Lincoln, 1951).

M. m. insignis: "This race is somewhat smaller than *sanaka* and is darker, with a sooty wash that noticeably obscures the markings and tends to make the color more uniform. It is, however, paler and grayer than [*kenaiensis*] * * *" (Gabrielson and Lincoln, 1951).

M. m. kenaiensis: Ridgway (1901) states that this race is smaller and browner than *insignis* with the streaks on the chest and elsewhere darker. It is intermediate between *kenaiensis* and *caurina,* being larger with the upper parts more uniform in color and less streaked than *caurina.* "Young, much resembling * * * *insignis* but more heavily streaked below; much paler and browner above than young of * * * *caurina,* with streaks on back much narrower, those on chest, etc., much browner."

M. m. caurina: This subspecies is intermediate between *kenaiensis* and *rufina,* which is a sooty brown form of the outer islands of Alaska and British Columbia. *Caurina* "is smaller and darker, with the streaks more distinct on the back [than *kenaiensis*], whereas it has a longer bill and grayer coloration than *rufina*" (Gabrielson and Lincoln, 1951).

Food.—Although the song sparrows of Alaska eat seeds when they are available, Gabrielson and Lincoln (1959) note that they take a considerable amount of small marine life, particularly in western Alaska. "Gabrielson has seen them picking up small mollusks or crustaceans as well as such seeds and berries as may be found close to the water line." Reported food items are beach fleas, crowberries, seeds of wild rye grass, and "many of the smaller alpine and tundra plants that grow close to the water's edge." The birds also undoubtedly eat insects. G. M. Sutton and R. S. Wilson (1946) state that *maxima* on Attu in February and March feeds on tidal flats side by side with rock sandpipers. A specimen examined smelled like the sandpipers and had eaten tiny snails. Swarth (1912) quotes Allen Hasselborg as saying that winter song sparrows around Juneau were very fat and had masses of unrecognized slimy matter in their stomachs, food that had been gathered on the beaches.

Behavior.—Ornithologists familiar with song sparrows in other environments will find the beachcombing habit of the Alaskan races of special interest. Thus Gabrielson and Lincoln (1959) state that "the Song Sparrows most frequently seen at Seward * * * are those that live along the beach and under the main dock of that town. On the west side of the Kenai Peninsula, [they] * * * are usually seen only around the wharves and waterfronts of * * * towns * * *. From Kodiak west through the Aleutians and the other islands * * * it is most frequently seen as a beach bird which, when disturbed, flies up into the rocks or disappears into the openings of a talus slope." The same authors state that the birds of southeastern Alaska, presumably *inexpectata, rufina,* and perhaps *caurina,* are sometimes found in the same bushy habitats, including ornamental shrubs around buildings, frequented by more southern races. The behavior of such birds is correspondingly like that of the southern forms.

Sutton and Wilson (1946) give a notably interesting and detailed report of the behavior of *maxima* on Attu in February and March, when

> The only vegetation is coarse grass, most of which has been blown flat and buried under the snow, and the bare stalks of high weeds which offer little shelter. * * * Its manner is not quite orthodox [for a song sparrow]. It seems to move too slowly and it keeps under rocks too much of the time. * * *
>
> Most of them lived along the shore, spending virtually all their time between the water's edge and the snow—a coastal strip varying in width from a few feet at high tide to a hundred yards or so at low tide. * * *
>
> Certain pairs lived about scrap heaps of metal, piles of gasoline drums, and so forth, as Song Sparrows might be expected to live about brush piles. * * * The usual roosting place was a niche or crevice on the face of a big rock, or under a tussock on a turfy headland. * * * Between 5 o'clock in the afternoon and dark, * * * we frequently saw the sparrows going to roost or flushed them from their roosting places. One which we saw asleep was fluffed up, with the bill stuck between the back and scapular plumage, chest against the bare rock, and tail out, down and slightly spread. Others, which flew out as we climbed about the rocks in the twilight must have been sleeping under the rocks or on the bare ground.

Voice.—Gabrielson and Lincoln (1959) state that the song is "rather persistent" during the breeding season, but not heard at other times. On the other hand, Sutton and Wilson (1946) heard it in February from males of *maxima* whose gonads were not in breeding condition. The song is variable and to Gabrielson and Lincoln "enough like that of the same species on the Atlantic coast * * * to be easily recognized * * *." (These authors make this statement only about birds of the western Aleutians [*maxima*] but presumably select this most remote race in order to make the general point.) Sutton and Wilson speak of a slight initial unfamiliarity in the song of *maxima* but seem to attribute this to the unfamiliar environment and conclude that the vocalization is "fairly average after all * * *." They also state that an ornithologist from the eastern United States will instantly recognize the Aleutian song sparrow's husky, alto "chirp of alarm." "He will recognize also a higher pitched *chip*, which indicates greater excitement, and certain beady cries which accompany pursuit flights."

Fall.—A specimen of *sanaka* collected July 28 had a very short, new tail, and a male and female of that race collected Aug. 3 had half-grown tails, new feathers of primaries 3 through 7, and were undergoing body molt (McGregor, 1906).

The resident races of the western islands leave the immediate vicinity of the shore after the young have been raised and wander some distance up the side of the mountains until snows force a return to the beaches (Gabrielson and Lincoln, 1959; R. D. Taber, 1946, referring to *maxima*).

Winter.—The behavior of *maxima,* as Sutton and Wilson (1946) describe it, may be inferred to be typical of that race during the winter and not likely to differ much from that of any of the other sedentary Alaskan races. Wilson, in another paper (1948) states that on Attu song sparrows usually stayed in pairs the year round and that he noted them only "occasionally singly, never in a flock."

Those birds of *caurina* (and apparently *kenaiensis*) that migrate remain essentially shore dwellers on the winter range. Thus Alfred Shelton (1915) reports collecting two specimens of *caurina* in Oregon after he saw one fly up to elude a breaker and then light again at the surf's edge. A similar observation made by C. I. Clay is reported by Grinnell (1910a), who also indicates that the bird was adhering closely to a winter foraging range 200 yards long on a strip of shore in California. The bird was seen repeatedly feeding among driftwood, and it could never be driven beyond the bounds of its range. Its flights were short and apparently undertaken reluctantly, and it preferred to skulk on foot. Interestingly, song sparrows were said by Allen Hasselborg, quoted by Swarth (1912), to have been distributed singly along 200-yard stretches of stony beach at Juneau, Alaska, in winter.

Distribution

Giant Song Sparrow (*m. m. maxima*)

Range.—The giant song sparrow is resident in the Aleutian Islands, Alaska, from Attu Island to Atka Island.

Aleutian Song Sparrow (*M. m. sanaka*)

Range.—The Aleutian song sparrow is resident in the eastern Aleutian Islands, Alaska (Seguam Island to Unimak Island), the Alaska Peninsula east to Stepovak Bay, and the islands south of the Alaska Peninsula from Sanak Island to the Semidi Islands.

Casual records.—Casual in fall and winter on the Pribilof Islands (St. George) and the coast of western Alaska (Nushagak).

Amak Song Sparrow (*M. m. amaka*)

Range.—The Amak song sparrow is resident on Amak Island, north of the western end of the Alaska Peninsula.

Bischoff's Song Sparrow (*M. m. insignis*)

Range.—The Bischoff's song sparrow is resident in the Kodiak Island group (Barren Islands to Sitkalidak Island) and the adjacent Alaska Peninsula (Kukak, Katmai).

Kenai Song Sparrow (*M. m. kenaiensis*)

Range.—Cook Inlet to southeastern Alaska.

Breeding range.—The Kenai song sparrow breeds on the coast of southern Alaska from Cook Inlet (Seldovia, Hope) to the mouth of the Copper River.

Winter Range.—Winters in the breeding range and southward in southeastern Alaska (Sitka); rarely to the coast of western Washington (Marysville).

Yakutat Song Sparrow (*M. m. caurina*)

Range.—Coast from Yakutat Bay in southeastern Alaska to northern California.

Breeding range.—The Yakutat song sparrow breeds on the coast of southeastern Alaska from Yakutat Bay to Cross Sound.

Winter Range.—Winters from southeastern Alaska (Chichagof Island, Juneau, Wrangell, Howkan) south along the marine shore lines of British Columbia, Washington, and Oregon to northern California (Fortuna); rarely to central California (Bay Farm Island).

MELOSPIZA MELODIA RUFINA (Bonaparte)

Sooty Song Sparrow

Contributed by Val Nolan Jr.

Habits

This race, although it breeds on the outer islands of southeastern Alaska and British Columbia, is not confined to the beaches. George Willett (1928) states that *rufina* occurs "in inland locations several miles from salt water * * *." Near Sitka, the same observer (1914) found the bird common in summer "in brush and grass lands on islands and along the shore." Individual birds occur in winter in the breeding range, but some migrate as far south as western Washington. George Willett (1921) reports that *rufina* and *caurina* both remained at Craig, Alaska, through the winter of 1919, but that in 1920 at Wrangell, *rufina* had departed by early November. "This latter place, though only about a hundred miles distant from Craig is, by virtue of its proximity to the mainland, considerably colder."

Willett (1928) says all nests of *rufina* are "either flush with the ground or in short grass a few inches up." Gabrielson and Lincoln (1959) quote the same observer as having found nests with eggs or young from June 2 to July 22.

The post-breeding and winter habitats of *rufina* are substantially unlike those of the six races reported immediately preceding. Of birds found in September on Mt. Rainier, Washington, Jewett et al. (1953) write: "It seemed to prefer the alder and huckleberry brush of moist, spongy meadows, as well as willows about lake margins." They add: "Coastal records of the sooty song sparrow are notably scarce, though it appears to be of general occurrence in winter on the islands of Puget Sound and at certain lowland localities in western Washington away from the coast." Specimens have been collected in Washington between Sept. 3 and Feb. 20.

Ridgway (1901) describes *rufina* as being "Similar to *M. c. morphna* but decidely larger (except bill), with coloration darker (sooty rather than rusty), and more uniform above; general color of upper parts deep sooty brown or bister, brightening into rusty brown or chestnut on outer webs of greater wing-coverts and tertials, the back obsoletely streaked with darker, and the median crown-stripe indistinct or obsolete; streaks on chest, etc., deep prouts brown."

Distribution

Range.—Outer islands of southeastern Alaska and of central British Columbia south to western Washington.

Breeding range.—The sooty song sparrow breeds on the outer islands of southeastern Alaska (Chichagof to Forrester and Duke islands) and of central British Columbia (Queen Charlotte Islands, Porcher Island, Spider Island).

Winter range.—Winters in breeding range (north to Sitka), ranging south to western Washington (Whidbey Island, Toledo).

MELOSPIZA MELODIA MORPHNA Oberholser

Rusty Song Sparrow

Contributed by VAL NOLAN JR.

Habits

Another race from the Pacific Northwest, *M. m. morphna* breeds in southwest British Columbia and western Washington and Oregon. Bird banders have found many wholly sedentary individuals, but there is also a migratory element. The winter range reaches to California and, rarely, Nevada.

The habitat is well described by Jewett et al. (1953): "Distinctly a ground bird, it prefers to hide in the brush along the bank of some trickling creek, though it is often observed in dry brushy localities at some distance from water, and has been noted in such diverse places as weedy lots and about dooryards in towns, on the tide flats, among the logs and brush of a windfall, in a log jam on a river, among stranded dry logs on the sea beach, along roadsides and in partly cleared places, in tule swamps, about beaver ponds, and even in the dense Douglas fir forest. Everywhere it keeps fairly close to the ground, and in general it remains in wet or marshy places." Frank S. Tompa (1962), in an important study of the population on Mandarte Island, B. C., found that the birds defended territory in shrubby growth, included grassland within their home ranges, and foraged in the tidal zone as a common feeding ground.

Territory.—Tompa's work on the sedentary population of Mandarte Island provides the following data: Territorialism revived in late January, when singing and chasing began in males. At this time adults with previous breeding experience were occupying their territories and home ranges of the year before, substantially without change in the former boundaries. Land left vacant by mortality was occupied by birds hatched the preceding year, and a surplus of such young birds was distributed in loose groups of five to ten individuals. With the revival of territorial behavior, most young birds that were still unsettled on a site emigrated; one was found 1,300 meters from its hatching site and another 6 kilometers. Pair formation occurred in February and March.

Territory size of mated males averaged 288 square meters for 47 cases, and home range averaged 473 square meters. This average territory area is one-tenth the minimum size Nice reported for territories of *euphonia* in Ohio. Unmated males on Mandarte Island had territories averaging only 82 square meters. Tompa suggests that the amount of shrubbery defended determined whether a male could attract a female.

Territorial behavior gradually declined during the breeding season until it reached its minimum in late July and August when molt began in adults. Song was very rare by late June and early July, except in unmated males. Aggressive behavior revived in October. Some young of the year became territorial in late summer, and from late August until October there was an emigration of certain of these birds, apparently as a result of mutual aggressiveness and the shortage of vacant habitat on which to settle. Aggressiveness declined again after October and reached the minimum in November and December.

Tompa's investigation establishes that the upper limit of territory size in this local population is fixed primarily by territorial behavior.

Details of early spring behavior of birds at Vancouver, B.C., are reported by William M. Hughes (1951). Males sing on bright winter mornings, and other signs of territoriality appear early in the season. Hughes remarked aggressiveness in birds in January and color-banded three, which he sexed as males. He found that these marked birds fed amicably with other song sparrows (he caught all three again on Feb. 8, together in the trap) but that each then returned to a particular area in which it attacked and pursued others of the species. This territorial behavior persisted even in a late-February and early-March period of cold and snow, during the sunny intervals. Song first became frequent on March 13, courtship of females was first noted on March 17, and by March 27 the three banded males all had mates that were carrying nest material.

Song posts of males are 10 to 15 feet high (Jewett et al., 1953).

Nesting.—On Mandarte Island, B.C., Tompa found that the breeding season "normally extends from the second half of March to late July." As many as three broods are raised by some pairs.

In Washington, eggs have been found as early as April 2, and a fresh set of four eggs has been recorded on July 16. Gabrielson and Jewett (1940) set extreme dates of fresh eggs as April 15 and July 10 in Oregon. G. W. Gullion (1951) states that breeding dates of song sparrows in the southern Willamette valley, Oregon, range from Feb. 28 to Aug. 13; the subspecies is not identified but is inferred from the locality to have been *morphna*.

Nests are said to be very well concealed, and are located both on the ground in grass or tules or by a log, in shrubs such as blackberries, in trees such as spruces, and in brush piles. The seasonal pattern of nest location already described for *melodia* and many other races, in which the elevated nests are to be expected later in the season, prevails in *morphna*. Heights are rarely greater than 5 feet, more commonly 1 or 2 feet (Jewett, 1916; Gabrielson and Jewett, 1940). William H. Kobbe (1900) measured an elevated nest made of grasses and found its external diameter was 5 inches, its internal diameter 3 inches, its external depth 3½ inches, and internal depth 2 inches. The same author, as well as Alexander Wetmore (quoted in Jewett et al., 1953), described nest construction in terms closely resembling descriptions of nests of *melodia*. Hughes (1951) found a most unusual nest on April 16; it was the previous year's nest of a Swainson's thrush, 6½ feet high in a yew.

Eggs.—The measurements of 40 eggs average 20.2 by 15.1 millimeters; the eggs showing the four extremes measure *21.8* by 15.2, 20.3 by *16.0*, *18.0* by 14.2, and 18.8 by *13.8* millimeters.

Young.—Song has been noted in young of the year as early as July 9, in a bird that could not have been more than 2 months old. William E. Sherwood (1929) felt that the first songs he heard were subdued in volume, but within a few minutes the songs had become indistinguishable from those of an adult. This early beginning of song correlates well with Tompa's observation of the onset of territorial behavior after the post-juvenal molt.

Outside the breeding range, in California, *morphna* "Has been noted specifically in weedy thickets, along grassy ditch banks, in old cornfields, and in wooded or brush-bordered gardens. This race is not noticeably restricted to the vicinity of water in the winter season in California" (Grinnell and Miller, 1944).

Mortality.—Tompa found that 29 of 55 birds (53 percent) banded as adults survived from one summer until the beginning of the following breeding season. During the next approximately 10 months, from the onset of breeding until the end of January, adult mortality was only 22 percent. Emigration of the young apparently prevented accurate determination of first-year mortality. One year Tompa recaptured 21 of 113 young that he had banded the preceding season, 19 on Mandarte, 2 on adjacent islands. Egg and nestling losses on Mandarte Island, where nest predators and parasites were virtually lacking, were less than 40 percent.

Plumage.—Ridgway (1901) describes *morphna* as being similar in color to the race *cleonensis*, "but much larger and colors more uniform above, the rusty brown or chestnut streaks on back, etc., less strongly contrasted with the rusty olive ground color and the black mesial streaks less distinct (often obsolete); under parts with the chestnut streaks on chest, etc., usually without blackish shaft-streaks, and the flanks olivaceous rather than tawny. Young, slightly rufescent bister brown above, the back streaked with blackish; beneath dull whitish or very pale buffy grayish, the chest, sides, and flanks more or less tinged with buffy or pale fulvous and streaked with sooty brownish."

Food.—L. M. Huey (1954) collected a female of this subspecies near San Diego, Calif., on Oct. 13, and states that "the entire digestive tract was found to be thoroughly stained red from a diet of the ripe [*Opuntia*] cactus fruit." Tompa mentions caterpillars and lacewings as food items.

Fall.—Mainland birds show a tendency to wander in the fall, as indicated by records from altitudes of 4,000 feet in the Cascade Mountains of Washington and from heights in the Olympics, as well as from records east of the Cascades. Most of these wanderers are thought to be young birds (Jewett et al., 1953), as Tompa's work suggests.

Winter.—Winter habitats are varied and include most of the places itemized by Jewett et al. (1953), as quoted in the second paragraph of this life history. Gabrielson and Jewett (1940) regard *morphna* as a conspicuous member of the mixed winter flocks of sparrows in Oregon. Songs are heard there on bright winter mornings. In another paper, Jewett (1916) says that birds of this race "are very plentiful on the ocean beach, feeding amongst the driftwood."

Distribution

Range.—Southwestern British Columbia to northern California.

Breeding range.—The rusty song sparrow breeds from southwestern British Columbia (Alert Bay, Chilliwack) south through western Washington (Tatoosh Island, Longmire) to southwestern Oregon (North Santiam River at 3,400 feet, Grants Pass, Wedderburn).

Winter range.—Winters chiefly in the breeding range, extending south to northern California (Paicines, Snelling), rarely to southern California (Riverside, Yaqui Wells) and western Nevada (Fallon).

MELOSPIZA MELODIA CLEONENSIS McGregor

Mendocino Song Sparrow

Contributed by Val Nolan Jr.

Habits

This permanent resident of the coastal districts of the extreme southwest corner of Oregon and of three counties of northern California inhabits a variety of low dense cover, listed by Grinnell and Miller (1944) as "blackberry patches, ceanothus clumps, bracken, weeds and brush-piles in logged or burned-over land, pasture fence-row tangles, baccharis brush, willow thickets, and fresh- and salt-water marshes. Within the narrow coastal range of this race prevailing fogs and rain supply amply the moisture requirements of Song Sparrows even in cover some distance from streams or marshes. Undergrowth in forests is generally not occupied, the birds apparently seeking brush in openings and at forest edges." Walter K. Fisher (1902), commenting on the abundance of the bird, writes that it "fairly swarms in some places, and is the commonest bird in deforested areas."

Ridgway (1901) describes *cleonensis* as being "similar in size and proportions to *M. m. samuelis*, but averaging slightly smaller with larger legs and feet, and coloration very different, being much more rufescent; general color of upper parts deep rusty olive, conspicuously and broadly streaked on back, etc., with dark rusty brown, or chestnut, and black; streaks on chest, etc., dark rusty brown or chestnut (black medially), and sides, flanks, and under tail-coverts strongly fulvous."

Distribution

Range.—The Mendocino song sparrow is resident in the coastal district of extreme southwestern Oregon (mouth of Pistol River) and northwestern California (Del Norte, Humboldt, and western Mendocino counties, south to Gualala).

Casual record.—Casual in Marin County, California (Olema).

MELOSPIZA MELODIA GOULDII Baird

Marin Song Sparrow

Contributed by Val Nolan Jr.

Habits

Except in the marshes around San Francisco Bay, the song sparrow of the long coastal district of central California is this resident race. Here it inhabits fresh water marshes, fog-drenched brush on westward-facing slopes down to the shore or to the edges of salt marshes, streamside growth such as willow clumps and shrubby weedy tangles, and garden shrubbery. As Grinnell and Miller (1944) observe, "An essential combination of dense, tangled vegetation, and moist ground or surface water is provided by each of these types of habitat." Toward the interior the birds are limited to streamsides and freshwater marshes, but near the coast the fogs, seepage, and damp ground provide enough moisture to free them of such restrictions.

Nests are built "on the ground or in bushes a few feet up" (Ray, 1908). Richard F. Johnston, in his study of the breeding seasons and clutch sizes of western song sparrows (1954), indicates that the season extends from about February 25 to about June 25 in south central California and from about March 25 to about July 5 in the northern part of the range; the peaks of breeding are in mid-April in both sections with a second, greater, peak in the first half of May in the north. Mean clutch sizes in the sets Johnston examined were 3.71 and 3.53 in the south and the north, respectively; first clutches were somewhat smaller and second clutches larger than the means.

Grinnell and Miller (1944) say that cover "is often hunted through in almost wren-like fashion; crevices, holes and branch tangles are entered and inspected for insect food." H. C. Bryant (1921) stated at Berkeley, "The worst egg eater yet discovered in my aviary is a Santa Cruz Song Sparrow [now *M. m. gouldii*]."

"In fall and winter some scattering to drier situations is noted, especially to thickets of dead grass and annuals in fairly open fields" (Grinnell and Miller, 1944).

Grinnell (1909) describes *gouldii* as: "Similar to *M. m. cleonensis*, but less rufescent, the black element much stronger on feathers of back, scapulars, and exposed quills, that of pileum taking form of streaks alternating with browns; the streaking of underparts also more decidedly black, often scarcely rufescent on edges." The race is depicted by Dawson (1923).

Distribution

Range.—The Marin song sparrow is resident in the coastal district of central California (exclusive of tidal and brackish marshes of San Francisco Bay area), from interior Mendocino County (6 miles southwest of Laytonville), northern Sonoma County (Cazadero), and Lake County (Blue Lakes) south through San Mateo and Santa Clara counties to northern San Benito County (Paicines); east to the edge of Sacramento Valley (Stonyford, Vacaville).

MELOSPIZA MELODIA (Wilson)

Song Sparrow: San Francisco Bay Marsh Subspecies*

Contributed by Richard Fourness Johnston

[Nowhere have song sparrows become adapted more interestingly to a specialized environment than they have in the salt and brackish marshes ringing San Francisco Bay. Here, as Joe T. Marshall, Jr. (1948) has written, "the spatial isolation of different habitats, particularly bay salt-marsh from upland fresh-water growth is correlated with a marked differentiation of very local races." Marshall's paper analyzes the differences in the ecologies of these sedentary marsh song sparrows, but their essential similarities have led to their being grouped for present purposes. The race *samuelis* is selected to represent the group because of Dr. Johnston's knowledge of it. A few details regarding other races are inserted into the Johnston account; these are set apart in brackets.—V.N.]

Habits

Melospiza melodia samuelis is one of the many distinctive morphological segregates of this widespread species found in the central Californian region. One of the smaller, darker subspecies (Marshall, 1948), it is closely restricted to a peculiar habitat-type found only on the salt marshes fringing the northern reaches of San Francisco Bay. As these marshes are inhabited by no other subspecies, any song sparrow seen there is almost certain to be *M. m. samuelis.*

The salt marshes of the north part of the bay are flat expanses of alluvial soil seldom more than 7 feet in elevation above mean sea level. They are exposed to a varying amount of wetting each day

* The following subspecies are discussed in this section: *Melospiza melodia maxillaris* Grinnell, *M. m. samuelis* (Baird), and *M. m. pusillula* Ridgway.

by tidal flux of the brackish bay waters. The marsh vegetation in response to these conditions is arranged in three zones, corresponding roughly to the amount of daily submergence each zone experiences. Fringing the lower edge of the marsh adjacent to the bay is a broad expanse of cordgrass (*Spartina foliosa*), and on the higher reaches of marsh grows pickleweed (*Salicornia ambigua*). Lastly, along the raised banks of tidal sloughs, which carry water into and out of the marsh, grows a gumplant (*Grindelia cuneifolia*). This gumplant, which reaches the size of a small bush, affords a great deal of cover when mixed with the pickleweed; here the marsh song sparrows find conditions most suitable for their existence.

The tides thus set the pattern assumed by the dominant plants on the marsh, and in so doing strongly influence the areas in which the song sparrow lives. High tides also have other effects on the birds. High spring tides, which can flood nests of song sparrows, occur in late April, May, and June in nocturnal hours; high winter tides, which may influence the amount and direction of movements of song sparrows, occur mainly in December during daylight hours.

Nesting, territory, eggs.—In lowland California song sparrows tend to begin breeding activities fairly early in the year, ordinarily in late March, but the song sparrows that breed earliest are those living on salt marshes (Johnston, 1954). The first date for a completed clutch of *M. m. samuelis* is February 28, and the modal date for population-wide completion of clutches is March 28; corresponding dates for song sparrows living in the hills around the San Francisco Bay area are March 25 and April 15, respectively. The marked earliness of breeding in the salt marsh birds probably is an adaptation to tidal conditions, for if these song sparrows bred at the same time that the upland birds do, spring flood tides would destroy many eggs and young (Johnston, 1956a). Birds hereditarily endowed for earliness of breeding thus leave more offspring than those breeding late. [*M. m. pusillula* also breeds early.—V.N.]

Salt marsh song sparrows are double-brooded; almost all pairs nest twice in a season. If replacement nests are considered, each pair will nest on the average 2.5 to (rarely) 3 times each season.

The song sparrows place their nests in clumps of pickleweed, among stalks of cordgrass, or in crotches of gumplant. All nests are low to the ground, as the average height of marsh vegetation is less than 2 feet. Nests in fact average only 9½ inches above the ground; they are higher on the lower marsh, averaging there about 12 inches high. Nests are not used more than once, and the two or more nests of any one season are built at different sites within a territory.

On one occasion (out of about 130 possible occasions) a song sparrow gave a "rodent run" distraction display as it left the nest when the observer visited it.

[The measurements of 40 eggs of *samuelis* average 21.5 by 15.9 millimeters; the eggs showing the four extremes measure *24.4* by 16.3, 22.9 by *17.3*, *19.1* by 15.8 and 20.1 by *15.0* millimeters.—W.G.F.H.]

Mean clutch-size for salt marsh song sparrows is 3.20 ± 0.05 eggs, on the basis of 157 records collected between 1950 and 1955 (Johnston, 1956a). The range in mean clutch-size is from 2.91 to 3.42 eggs. In any one season the earliest clutches are relatively small (to 2.83 eggs), clutches completed in mid-season are relatively high (to 3.66 eggs), and those of the late season low (to 2.60 eggs). Pairs of *samuelis* averaged from 7.5 eggs to 9.1 eggs per season from 1950 to 1955. Owing to unpredictable mortality to eggs and young, these figures are not a reliable guide to productivity, which is best defined as the number of fledglings per pair of adults per season. On the salt marsh this productivity is from three to five fledglings per pair per year.

[*M. m. pusillula* also has a low mean clutch size, 3.3 eggs.—V.N.]

Territorial relationships of salt marsh song sparrows are similar to those of the species in general. In late winter and spring, male singing and chasing increase. By late February and March most males have established themselves on territories; pair-formation ordinarily has already taken place, but those birds not yet mated now form pairs. Singing decreases in late March and April, but territorial strife continues sporadically throughout the remainder of the breeding season. Territorial activity ceases in July, but becomes evident again in late August and September. Although in many instances true territories are not staked out the quarters most birds, adults and juveniles alike, occupy in September are identical with those of the following breeding season.

The territories of salt marsh song sparrows are small, and the borders of some sloughs may support as many as 8 to 10 pairs of birds per acre; most territories are thus about 30 feet wide by 150 feet long, a little over 0.1 acre. Territories are larger where vegetation is sparser at the heads and mouths of the sloughs than along the middle reaches.

Adults show a strong tendency to remain permanently in the territories they take up their first autumn. Very few birds move more than 10 meters from this first autumn territory, no matter how long they live. The longest movement recorded on banded birds (Johnston, 1956a) is 35 meters.

The incubation period is about 12 (12 to 14) days. Young remain in the nest 9 to 12 days, but will leave prematurely at 8 days if disturbed. Fledglings remain under parental care for 5 to 8 more days; this gives a total parental period of attention per brood of about 30 days. The adults start second broods in short order, and the first young then gradually move out into other parts of the marsh.

Dispersal by the young occurs from time of fledging until autumn, when the adults again begin to show territoriality. The median distance of dispersal in these young is 185 meters. The longest distance on record is 960 meters (Johnston, 1956a).

Enemies.—Adults are preyed upon by marsh hawks, short-eared owls, and probably Norway rats. Much predation must occur for which there is little record, for although adult mortality is about 42 percent per year (Johnston, 1956) very few birds are known to have died through a specific agency. Only four skulls of song sparrows appeared in 491 pellets of short-eared owls collected in a 4-year period (Johnston, 1956b).

Eggs and nestlings are subject to higher mortality than full-grown birds, and for these the mortality factors are easier to determine. In a sample of 504 eggs and young, about 20 percent of eggs and young were killed by some predatory agent (probably Norway rats), 11 percent by flood tides, 5 percent by desertion of adults, 5 percent by rainstorms, and about 4 percent by accidental loss of eggs from the nest and parasitism by cowbirds (*Molothrus ater*). Total mortality was 50 percent of all eggs laid.

Plumages.—The sequence of plumages in salt marsh song sparrows has not been studied, but probably is the same as for other subspecies of the species. The annual molt begins in early July, almost immediately following cessation of breeding, at which time adults are in extremely poor feather owing to heavy abrasion on rough marsh plants. The annual molt is completed in late August or early September, and at this time most juveniles have completed the post-juvenal molt.

[Grinnell (1909) described *maxillaris* as resembling the race "*gouldii* closely in coloration and *M.m. heermanni* in general size; differs from *M.m. samuelis* * * * in having the browns more extended and of a deeper tone (bay rather than hazel) and in much greater size and, especially, bulkier bill; differs from *M.m. gouldii* * * * in much greater size throughout; and from *M.m. heermanni* * * * in that the base of the maxilla is more swollen, the black streakings everywhere broader, and the general tone of coloration darker." Ridgway (1901) states that *samuelis* is "exactly like" the race *heermanni* in coloration, but is "much smaller, with the bill more slender." He describes *pusillula* as being "Most like *samuelis* but still smaller, the wings and tail decidedly so; coloration much less rusty, the general color of upper parts olive-grayish, the black dorsal streaks not distinctly, if at all, margined with rusty brown, the lateral crown-stripes and wings less distinctly rufescent, under parts more heavily streaked (streaks usually wholly black) and flanks paler fulvous; under parts usually more or less tinged with yellowish. Young much paler and grayer than that of *N. c. samuelis*, with the broad black streaks on back and scapulars much more strongly contrasted with the ground color; ground color of under parts dull yellowish white or pale yellowish buff, without brownish tinge on breast or sides."—V.N.]

Behavior: foraging.—Salt marsh song sparrows forage on the marshes in the same fashion as do song sparrows in upland situations. Upland races frequently scratch vigorously with their strong feet at the ground surface to expose invertebrate and plant foods within and under the surface litter. Salt marsh song sparrows perpetuate this foraging mannerism; these birds scratch, typically with both feet in unison, on the soft slough mud, and peck frequently at the disturbed surface. One bird, for a period of 40 seconds, alternately scratched 3 to 6 seconds and pecked 1 to 5 times between each scratching period. The bird was hunting small snails, and it furrowed and turned over the top $\frac{1}{32}$ inch of mud covering about 8 square inches. Foraging on harder mud comprising the true marsh surface most closely resembles the scratching performed by song sparrows in upland habitats. The birds also forage in "typical" fashion, i.e., slowly progressing by short hops accompanied by wing flicks and tail flicks and punctuated by frequent pecks at possible food items.

Another type of foraging on soft mud could be called "terrestrial flycatching." In midsummer on salt marshes large numbers of various Diptera occur. Some of these frequent exposed mud at low tide, flying just above the mud or resting on it. Song sparrows catch these flies, by making short, jerky hops or runs with tail elevated and sometimes with wings half outstretched, but without leaving the ground. Aerial flycatching is also a small part of foraging behavior in these birds, but the half-outstretched wings are probably used to maintain balance rather than to remain ready to resume flight.

Salt marsh song sparrows feed at dried heads of the gumplant (a composite) and eat the peeled seeds, perching on the edges of the larger heads or on nearby stalks or heads. They look much like siskins or goldfinches when foraging in this fashion.

In autumn these song sparrows eat fleshy fruits and seeds of pickleweed or salicornia. The birds perch quietly in a patch of salicornia and slowly and methodically chisel the fruits out of the succulent, cylindrical spikes with their bills. They seem to prefer plants within 6 feet of the tidal sloughs, and they consume most of the available fruits along the sloughs in 2 or 3 weeks, ordinarily at the end of November. This feeding is possibly of some importance as a source of free water; it comes at a time when insect foods with their free water are at an ebb.

The birds also eat the almost unbelievably enormous numbers of seeds of salicornia released when the spikes wither in winter. The birds probably take these seeds whenever they find them, but their consumption is especially noticeable after the high winter tides when the loose seeds have gathered in great, floating windrows up to a foot thick and form a concentrated food source. Song sparrows spend almost all the morning hours foraging, mostly on the masses of salicornia seeds; they also eat invertebrate animals they find within the seed masses.

Reactions to high tides.—It is possible to mention only the diurnal behavior evident during the daytime high tides in December; presumably equally important behavior patterns occur when breeding adults and young contend with the night high tides in spring, but they have not been witnessed. It is known that nestling song sparrows about 8 days old escape flooding by climbing up into vegetation above their nests.

The tallest salt marsh vegetation is leafless in December. When tide water rises within a foot to a few inches from the tops of these plants, little cover remains for song sparrows. When no potential avian predators are in evidence, the sparrows usually maintain an active, vigorous foraging pattern. Occasional birds splash in the water in typical bathing routines, and others loaf. A few birds apparently wander beyond their autumnal territories, and occasional examples of territorial strife are evident. Such occurrences end in a chase, and the intruder moves back to his presumed point of origin. One banded bird was seen under such circumstances to have moved about 150 yards, and thus made a round trip of 300 yards.

I reviewed the influence of winter high tides on two distinct populations of salt marsh song sparrows before completing my observations on the behavior of *M. m. samuelis.* In a marsh where extensive, man-made levees existed, the song sparrows accumulated on them, but on a marsh where only emergent vegetation and floating timbers were available, no such concentrations were seen. Later observations on this marsh from a 6- by 30-foot raft floating at high tide showed that the song sparrows there did indeed congregate; at one time immediately after a marsh hawk passed, 17 song sparrows were perched on the raft. The birds apparently felt exposed in the thin emergent vegetation, and those from as far as 60 yards away streaked toward the raft in full, powered flight. After the hawk passed the birds gradually left the raft, but each time a hawk approached they returned to it. At the same time, the foraging or loafing song sparrows practically ignored short-eared owls; this difference in reaction to the raptors lends support to the idea that short-eared owls are unimportant predators on song sparrows.

The sparrows reacted to marsh hawks just as strongly during normal tides. They always detected an oncoming hawk well before the human observer did and, giving thin, *chip* alarm notes, moved down to soil level, quite out of sight and reach of any hawk.

Distribution

Suisun Song Sparrow (*M. m. maxillaris*)

Range.—The Suisun song sparrow is resident in brackish marshes surrounding Suisun Bay in central California (Southampton Bay, Grizzly Island, Port Costa, Pittsburg).

Casual record.—Casual in Santa Clara County, California (Palo Alto).

Samuel's Song Sparrow (*M. m. samuelis*)

Range.—The Samuel's song sparrow is resident in central California in salt marshes on the northern side of San Francisco and San Pablo bays (Richardson Bay to Vallejo) and on the south side of San Pablo Bay (southwest to San Pablo Point).

Egg dates.—San Pablo Salt Marsh, Contra Costa County, California: 157 records, February 28 to June 18; 78 records, March 20 to April 10.

Alameda Song Sparrow (*M. m. pusillula*)

Range.—The Alameda song sparrow is resident in salt marshes surrounding the south arm of San Francisco Bay, California (San Francisco, Alviso, Stege).

MELOSPIZA MELODIA MAILLIARDI Grinnell

Modesto Song Sparrow

Contributed by Val Nolan Jr.

Habits

This non-migratory race is confined to the central lower basin of the Great Valley of California, the lowland between the Coast Range and the Sierra Nevada Mountains. Grinnell and Miller (1944) state that it breeds "chiefly, perhaps entirely, below 200 feet elevation" but may occur rarely at greater altitudes along streams of the Sierran foothills. The same authors state that the habitat is "Fresh-water marshes and riparian thickets. Predominant plant cover consists of willow and nettle thickets and growths of tules and cattails." No other material on the life history has been found.

J. Grinnell (1911b) described the race *mailliardi*, giving as diagnostic characters the generally large size, large bill, and broad and dark markings; "resembles *Melospiza melodia maxillaris* closely in these respects, but shape of the bill different, more nearly like that in *M. m. heermanni.*" He considered the bill the distinctive feature of *mailliardi*. Although the bills of *mailliardi* and *maxillaris* appear practically identical when viewed from the side, "when viewed dorsally the bill of *mailliardi* presents a very much narrower outline, there being scarcely any indication of the lateral swellings of the maxilla characterizing the bill of *maxillaris* * * *. In coloration *mailliardi* is very much darker than *heermanni*, having the streaking everywhere broad and black, with edgings of deep bay, the latter color showing dorsally to the almost entire exclusion of ashy marginings, there being mere traces of the latter. In coloration, *mailliardi* differs from *maxillaris* only in being a trifle less heavily marked on an average * * *."

Distribution

Range.—The Modesto song sparrow is resident in the Central Valley of California, from Glenn and Butte counties (Glenn, Biggs) south to Stanislaus County (Modesto, Lagrange); west to the deltas of the Sacramento and San Joaquin rivers.

Casual record.—Casual in western Nevada (Fallon).

MELOSPIZA MELODIA HEERMANNI Baird

Heermann's Song Sparrow

Contributed by Val Nolan Jr.

Habits

Still another non-migratory song sparrow from California, this race lives between the north-south mountain ranges in the San Joaquin valley. In this arid region the bird adheres closely to stream-, lake-, and marsh-side vegetation at altitudes of from 100 feet to 5,000 feet. In 1944 Grinnell and Miller reported that "numbers have greatly increased in the last thirty-five years owing to development of irrigation systems in previously unoccupied parts of its general range." In an earlier paper (1911) Grinnell had noted the absence of song sparrows in great stretches of dry prairies in the San Joaquin valley and predicted range extensions along canals.

The breeding habits of *heermanni* appear to fit the generalized pattern for riparian song sparrows. Grinnell (1911a) describes two nests, at 2½ and 4 feet, built in low vegetation in which drift trash had lodged. He also reports finding two females with nests, but only one male, at a reservoir 3 miles distant from any other song sparrow habitat. Among other possibilities was that of polygyny attributable to the surplus of females.

The measurements of 20 eggs average 20.4 by 15.4 millimeters; the eggs showing the 4 extremes measure *23.1* by *17.2* and *19.6* by *12.8* millimeters.

The food habits of *heermanni* are among those Beal (1910) investigated and reported in the life history of *M. m. samuelis* and the other salt marsh song sparrows.

Ridgway (1901) describes *heermanni* as being similar to *melodia* "but smaller and coloration much darker and browner, the black streaks on back, etc., averaging broader, and streaks on chest, etc., darker (black or brownish black in summer); young similar to that of * * * *melodia* but deeper tawny brown above with black streaks on back broader, the under parts more or less tinged with brownish buff, especially on chest, where the dusky streaks are broader." Grinnell (1911a) states that *heermanni* has a "much paler 'ground color' * * *, narrower black-streaking both above and below and * * * slightly smaller bill" than *mailliardi*.

Distribution

Range.—Heermann's song sparrow is resident in the southern San Joaquin Valley of California, from Merced and Mariposa counties (Los Baños, Yosemite Valley) south to Kern County (Fort Tejon, Walker Basin); east to Kings Canyon (Zumwalt Meadow).

MELOSPIZA MELODIA COOPERI Ridgway

San Diego Song Sparrow

Contributed by Val Nolan Jr.

Habits

Melospiza melodia cooperi is a resident race in southern California and northern Baja California in the valleys of the coast ranges and on the Pacific slopes; it extends eastward to streams penetrating the Mojave and Colorado deserts. Its habitat is river bottom vegetation, fresh water marshes, "at least margins of salt marshes" (Grinnell and Miller, 1944), and garden shrubbery. Settlement of the coastal plain, with a consequent development of water systems, has contributed to an increase in numbers in relatively recent times. Breeding occurs from sea level to altitudes of 5,000 feet, and vagrants have been collected in late summer at 7,500 feet. Nests found in pampas grass (Myers, 1910) and 10 inches high in a dock plant (Chambers, 1917) have been described.

R. F. Johnston (1954) has reported that the breeding season begins about Feb. 5 and lasts until about July 5, with the great majority of nesting records falling between late March and early June, the peak about May 1. First clutches averaged 3.74 eggs, second clutches 3.58; the seasonal mean was 3.69 eggs. The interval between completion of the first nest and the laying of the first egg has been reported for one nest as about 5 days (Lamb, 1922). W. C. Hanna (1924) weighed 48 eggs; the extremes were 2.87 and 2.05 grams, the average 2.41 grams.

A number of diverse but interesting points have been recorded about *cooperi*. Josephine R. Michener (1926) describes her efforts to raise a young bird unable to fly. Among details of its behavior is the fact that its response to the first standing water it saw was to hop into the dish and bathe, at an age inferred to be about 20 days. E. L. Sumner, Jr. and J. L. Cobb (1928) in the fall and winter of 1927 displaced 25 banded birds about 4 miles and recaptured 3 at the original trapping stations within a few days; 8 birds were released 34 miles west of the point of capture, to which none was known to have returned. More interestingly, 2 were still present at the point of release 7 days later.

J. Mailliard (1919a) observed that a bird that habitually flew against a window pane on cool mornings was in fact gathering sluggish house flies apparently attracted by the warmth of the glass on the preceding evenings. R. S. Woods (1932) saw song sparrows of this race drinking sugar solution put out for hummingbirds. W. L. Dawson (1923) picked three ticks from the head of a *cooperi* song sparrow in April 1917, but gives no further details.

Ridgway (1901) describes *cooperi* as being similar to *heermanni* "but slightly smaller and coloration much lighter and grayer; prevailing color of the back, etc., grayish olive, the back broadly streaked with black, the black streaks with little, if any, rusty external suffusion; young similar to that of *M. m. montana*."

Distribution

Range.—The San Diego song sparrow is resident in the coastal districts of southern California from Santa Cruz County (Santa Cruz) southward to northern Baja California, as far as lat. 30° N. (San Fernando); east to streams penetrating Mohave and Colorado deserts (Manix, Palm Canyon, Vallecitos, east base of Sierra San Pedro Mártir).

MELOSPIZA MELODIA (Wilson)

Song Sparrow: Pacific Insular Subspecies*

Contributed by VAL NOLAN JR.

HABITS

On each of the San Miguel, San Clemente, Santa Barbara and Coronados Island groups off the California and Baja California coasts lives a sedentary subspecies of the song sparrow. These four races, about whose life histories not a great deal is known, are treated together here.

Although the habitats these islands afford are not uniform, in general the birds dwell in a sparsely vegetated environment characterized by its aridity. Cover is afforded by herbs and coarse grasses, cacti, and, particularly on San Clemente Island, brush and shrubs. On Los Coronados Islands no fresh water is to be found (Grinnell and Daggett, 1903), and fresh moisture must come only from the condensation of fog. Indeed fog seems to supply most of the moisture needs for all these races (Grinnell and Miller, 1944).

C. B. Linton (1908) writes that *M. m. clementae* was abundant on San Clemente. He continues: "Common in the yards at Howland's, nesting in the scrub cacti and vines within a few yards of the hacienda. March 31, three nests were found in the corral near the stables; one contained four young one week old, the others having incomplete sets. These nests were built a few inches from the ground in the center of the cacti beds, which, being covered with a thick growth of vines, completely hid the nests."

Wright and Snyder (1913) report *M. m. graminea* occurs on Santa Barbara wherever bushes provide cover, and Grinnell and Miller (1944) add that "Bushes are used for nesting."

Grinnell and Daggett (1903) visited Los Coronados Islands on Aug. 6 and 7, 1902, and collected the type specimen of *coronatorum*. The following quotations are from their account of their field work:

> Juvenals were seen along the path * * *. An old and weather-beaten nest was found under a bush. * * * As we landed, an individual was fearlessly hopping close at hand among the boulders almost at the edge of the surf. Most of the Song Sparrows, however, were seen higher up toward the crest of the island, where they were haunting the sparse growth of shrubs on the shaded northeast slope. We saw no trace of fresh water anywhere, and the scanty vegetation presented anything but an inviting appearance. Yet here we heard the familiar notes and full song of these birds which on the mainland keep so close to verdant water courses and damp lowlands. The Rock Wren, always a bird

---

*The following subspecies are discussed in this section: *Melospiza melodia micronyx* Grinnell, *M. m. clementae* Townsend, *M. m. graminea* Townsend, and *M. m. coronatorum* Grinnell and Daggett.

of the dryest localities, did not seem out of place, but the Song Sparrow seemed altogether foreign to such surroundings.

Nelson K. Carpenter (1918) described and photographed two nests of *coronatorum*, one of grasses placed 3 feet up in a bush, the second on the ground and "constructed entirely of feathers and the skin of a lizard * * *. This nest was found in the midst of the large colony of California Brown Pelicans and Western Gulls." Pingree I. Osburn (1909) found three young just able to fly on April 8.

Joseph Grinnell (1928) describes *micronyx* as the race with grayest coloration among song sparrows in general: "brown or brownish tones almost wanting; dark markings black and sharply contrasted against gray of dorsal surface or white of lower surface; bill, feet and especially claws weak; wing showing extreme of bluntness (longest primary not much longer than outermost)." *M. m. micronyx* is most nearly like *graminea* of Santa Barbara Island, "but differs from it in broader and blacker dark streaking everywhere, in grayer ground-color dorsally, especially on the pileum, in paler flanks, in decidedly smaller claws, in blunter wing, and in slightly greater size." From *clementae* the race *micronyx* differs as it does from *graminea*, "only for the most part (save as to general size) in greater degree. Especially on the top of the head is the greater amount of grayness apparent; the broad brown capital side-stripes in *clementae* are in *micronyx* reduced to very narrow ones, which play out altogether on the nape instead of extending back to blend (in *clementae*) with the brownish tone of the dorsum. The broad gray occipital area is in *micronyx* lined sharply with black shaft streaks which are thus thrown into conspicuous contrast."

Ridgway (1901) describes *clementae* as being similar to *cooperi* "but slightly larger and coloration still grayer, the back light olive-grayish, with black streaks narrower, the black streaks of chest, etc., also narrower; young similar to that of *cooperi* but paler above."

Ridgway (1901) describes *graminea* as being similar in coloration to *clementae*, but much smaller.

J. Grinnell and F. S. Daggett (1903) describe *coronatorum* as "most nearly resembling in coloration *melospiza clementae*, and general size about the same, but tarsus decidely shorter and bill smaller; differs from * * * *cooperi* of the adjacent mainland in much paler ground color, narrower streaking and smaller bill."

Distribution

San Miguel Song Sparrow (*M. m. micronyx*)

Range.—The San Miguel song sparrow is resident on San Miguel Island, Santa Barbara County, California.

San Clemente Song Sparrow (*M. m. clementae*)

Range.—The San Clemente song sparrow is resident on Santa Rosa, Santa Cruz, Anacapa, and San Clemente islands off the coast of southern California.

Casual record.—Casual on the California mainland (Santa Barbara).

Santa Barbara Song Sparrow (*M. m. graminea*)

Range.—The Santa Barbara song sparrow is resident on Santa Barbara Island, Los Angeles County, California.

Coronados Song Sparrow (*M. m. coronatorum*)

Range.—The Coronados song sparrow is resident on the four islands of Los Coronados group off northern Baja California.

MELOSPIZA MELODIA FALLAX (Baird)

Tucson Song Sparrow

Contributed by Robert William Dickerman

Habits

The pale reddish desert song sparrow race, *fallax*, is a resident of riparian and marsh associations at low to moderate elevations from extreme southeastern Nevada and extreme southwestern Utah southwards to central Sonora. In the period before the introduction of cattle, the rivers of central Arizona had lush bottomlands that supported beaver marshes and their attendant wildlife. Trapping by man, overgrazing by cattle, and, most recently, the demand for irrigation water have reduced the major portions of these rivers to dry eroded beds. As a result, some populations of *fallax* are extinct (those of the Santa Cruz River and of sections of the San Pedro and Salt Rivers) and others much reduced. The largest populations are now found along the Salt River above Tempe at Coon Bluff and in marshes along the Gila River near Palo Verde, both locations in Maricopa County.

Allan R. Phillips (1943) described a subspecies *bendirei* from the Salt River at Tempe Butte, Maricopa County, Ariz., as a population intermediate between *fallax* and *saltonis*. Later, when it was realized that *saltonis* migrates regularly to southeastern Arizona, the type of *bendirei* was reexamined and proved to be a fresh-plumaged migrant of *saltonis*. Examination of a large series of fresh-plumaged birds from Arizona and Sonora has revealed no positive geographic variation within the population here considered *fallax*.

J. T. Marshall, Jr., and W. H. Behle (1942) describe the habitat of song sparrows in the Virgin River valley as "the vicinity of cattail swamps with standing water and with brushy thickets such as mesquite or rose in the immediate dry-land surroundings. Both the thickets and the cattails are frequented by the Song Sparrows, the latter being resorted to especially for greater protection * * *. Bird associates are Marsh Wrens, Yellow-throats, Yellow Warblers, and Red-winged Blackbirds * * *. The swamps where these birds do occur are few in number and widely scattered. If the swamps are of any extent at all, Song Sparrows are numerous in them, but the total * * * population cannot be great. This spotty distribution of suitable swampy habitat * * * makes for discontinuous distribution of the colonies within the general range of the race."

Nesting.—The nesting habits of *fallax* are similar to those of other populations in more temperate areas. The nest is always built close to open water. Francis C. Willard (1912) found a nest in a low bush. The same author (1923) writes "The Song Sparrow sometimes deserts the ground and low bushes in favor of a tree, and the desert subspecies (*Melospiza melodia fallax*) also has this trait. One nest was built fifteen feet up in a large willow tree, on a horizontal branch. The bird was on the nest when I found it and remained until I was nearly up to it. * * * There were four of the song sparrow's eggs and four of the Long-tailed Chat * * *."

Herbert Brandt (1951) describes the site of a nest he found on the Slaughter (San Bernadino) Ranch 20 miles east of Douglas, Cochise County, Ariz., in an "irrigation project near cattail pond in grassy meadow; surrounding flora, small mesquites, sacaton and other grasses, beyond which are rows of black willow and cottonwood, and in near-by pond, cattails and other water plants; date, May 23, 1948. Nest situated 18 inches up in a low dense mesquite brush, 25 feet from artesian pond rim; nest placed in a four-pronged fork of dead wood; made in a crude, bulky manner of coarse plant stems and leaves; rim substantial but ragged and irregular, shaped to fit the supports; lining of brown rootlets and white cow-tail hair arranged circularly; interior well cupped. Apparently the only pair present in the area. Contents, 3 eggs, unevenly incubated 6 to 8 days." A female taken March 26 near La Casita (27 miles south of Nogales, Sonora) contained ova measuring 7 and 4 millimeters. Full grown young have been collected by May 30 (Feldman, San Pedro River).

Eggs.—There are 15 sets of eggs of *fallax* in the United States National Museum and one set in the University of Arizona collection. These sets contain 2, 3, and 4 eggs, with 3 being the most frequent number and the average. These eggs measure in millimeters 14.1 to 15.7 by 17.4 to 21.7. The average of the 48 eggs is 15.00 by 19.03.

Plumages.—The molts and plumages of the desert populations are similar to those of the species elsewhere, save for the light coloration of the plumage. Adults are in heavy molt in September, and first molt may continue until December, but the time of instigation of these molts is not known. Young in juvenal plumages are to be found in September and possibly later. Wear and fading are extreme in the desert subspecies. This is probably due to coarse vegetation, sun, and possibly higher alkaline content of the soils. Adults taken after March are virtually worthless for taxonomic purposes.

Ridgway (1901) describes *fallax* as being similar to *montana* in the slender bill, "but wing and tail averaging decidedly shorter and coloration conspicuously paler and more rusty, the rusty streaks, both above and below, without blackish shaft-streaks, or else with these merely indicated on the interscapular region; young dull brownish buffy or pale wood brown above, the back streaked with rusty brown or dark brown; beneath buffy white, the chest streaked with rather light brown."

Winter.—The Tucson song sparrow winters throughout much of its breeding range, but some movement does occur, especially from the northern part of the breeding range. The breeding population at Tucson has been extinct for more than 5 decades, but an occasional winter specimen is taken there, and a winter specimen of *fallax* has been taken at Bard, Calif.

Distribution

Range.—Southeastern Nevada and southwestern Utah south to Arizona and northeastern Sonora.

Breeding range.—The Tucson song sparrow breeds from southeastern Nevada (Pahranagat Valley) and southwestern Utah (St. George) south in the Virgin River Valley and the Colorado River Canyon of Nevada and north-central Arizona, and locally through the lowlands of central and southeastern Arizona to northeastern Sonora. It intergrades with *saltonis* along the Colorado River from southern Nevada to Topock, Arizona, along the Big Sandy River, and a little south of Arlington along the Gila River. In central Arizona it nests below the Mogollon Plateau (Indian Gardens, Oak Creek Canyon, and possibly formerly Walnut Creek north of Prescott), along the Verde and Salt Rivers, the Gila River (Geronimo, San Carlos, Safford, Phoenix, Palo Verde), the San Pedro River (near Feldman, formerly south to Fairbank), along the Sante Cruz River (formerly at Tucson), and at Picacho Reservoir. In extreme southern Arizona it has nested at Patagonia and San Bernardino. In Sonora it breeds along the Rio Magdalena (Caborca) and along its tributaries (Rancho la Arizona, Saric, Magdalene, La Casite, and Agua Caliente), along the Rio Sonora (Hermpsillo, Ures, Arizpe), the Rio Moctezum

(Oposura, Cumpes), and the Rio Bevispe (Husebes, Grenados, and Pilares).

Winter range.—Winters apparently over most of the breed range, but in reduced numbers northward.

MELOSPIZA MELODIA SALTONIS Grinnell

Desert Song Sparrow

Contributed by Val Nolan Jr.

Habits

Melospiza melodia saltonis is a resident of the lower Colorado River valley. The summary of its habitat in California by Grinnell and Miller (1944) gives an idea of its life: "Riparian plant associations, most notably those dominated by arrow-weed (*Pluchea*), guatemote (*Baccharis*) and young willows, and tule beds and cattails in marshes, overflow sumps and along irrigation systems. Nests are placed in the vegetation above the mud which marks flood level. Development of irrigation has undoubtedly increased the total population of this race in the last 30 years. Although usually sharply limited to water-seeking plants, and most abundant in cover growing over or at the edge of water, this Song Sparrow has occasionally been noted in mesquite thickets at some distance from water."

The measurements of 40 eggs average 18.9 by 14.9 millimeters; the eggs showing the four extremes measure *20.8* by 15.2, 18.5 by *15.5*, *17.8* by 15.0, and 18.0 by *14.0* millimeters. Robert W. Dickerman reports three sets of eggs of this race from Yuma, Ariz., in the collection of the University of Arizona, two of which contain eggs of the brown-headed cowbird.

J. Grinnell (1909) described *saltonis* as resembling *fallax*, "but very much paler throughout, the 'ground-color' being white ventrally and ashy dorsally, with streakings of pale hazel; supercilliary stripe wholly white; general size much less than in either *M. m. fallax* or *M. m. montana*."

Distribution

Range.—The desert song sparrow is resident in the lower Colorado Valley in extreme southern Nevada (east of Searchlight), southeastern California, western Arizona (east to Big Sandy River at 2,000 feet; Alamo), northwestern Baja California (Mexicali, mouth of Hardy River), and northwestern Sonora (Colorado River delta), extending northwest through the Imperial Valley of California (Mecca, Calexico).

Casual records.—Casual in the desert area of southeastern California (Death Valley, Oro Grande), south-central Arizona (Tucson), and northwestern Sonora (Sonoyta River, Caborca).

MELOSPIZA MELODIA RIVULARIS Bryant

Brown's Song Sparrow

Contributed by VAL NOLAN JR.

HABITS

This race inhabits "west-flowing stream courses" (Grinnell, 1928) in a very limited region of central Baja California. Here, as Griffing Bancroft (1930) writes, "there are several systems of dry river beds which have an important influence on the biology of this region. Even though the country be arid beyond anything known in the United States there is still enough rainfall to provide some moisture. This water, as well as a part of that from the cloud-bursts that come once in a decade, finds its way to the sea by means of a subterranean flow. * * * Occasionally the subterranean flow encounters bed rock formations which force the water to the surface."

G. Bancroft (1930) gives the following description of the breeding biology of *rivularis* in this restricted range:

> This light-breasted type of *Melospiza* occurs wherever there are pools of water with tule or willow. * * * It is by no means as abundant * * * as is, for instance, *M. m. cooperi* in the willow bottoms of southern California. Still it can hardly be regarded as rare.
>
> The birds begin to lay the latter part of April and continue for at least six weeks. Most of the nests are bulky affairs of tule, usually lined with palm fibre or cow hair. They are normally placed in tule about four feet above the water. * * * [Some were] surrounded by loose and fairly long dead tule leaves. These more than equaled the bulk of the nest * * * . Some of the nests found were in willow trees and one was in a thick weed clinging to a rock and overhanging a pool. In general, excepting the unusual size of their nests, the habits of the Brown Song Sparrow were much like those of the San Diegan form [*cooperi*]. They lay either two or three eggs, with four the record.
>
> The eggs themselves are unlike those of any other Song Sparrow I have examined. They are more brilliant than those of the northern birds, a brighter blue, and altogether lacking in the common tan type, in which the spots are so close together as to give the appearance of a reddish egg.

G. Bancroft's measurements of 35 eggs from San Ignacio yielded an average size of 21.2 x 15.9 mm., and of 250 eggs from El Rosario an average size of 20.1 x 15.2 mm.

Ridgway (1901) describes *rivularis* as being similar to *fallax* "but larger, with longer, more slender, and more compressed bill, still less strongly contrasted markings, and duller, less rufescent colors."

DISTRIBUTION

Range.—The Brown's song sparrow is resident in south-central Baja California (Santa Agueda Canyon and San Ignacio south to Comondú).

Casual record.—Casual in the Cape District of Baja California (Todos Santos).

RHYNCHOPHANES McCOWNII (Lawrence)

McCown's Longspur

PLATE 76

Contributed by HERBERT KRAUSE

HABITS

Whether on its winter range or summer breeding ground, McCown's longspur is a bird of the plains, of the "big sky" country where the land flattens to the blue haze of mesa or plateau; where distance is the hawk's flight from a line of craggy "breaks" to the horizon. Amid the features of such a vast landscape it was first collected about 1851. It happened apparently as much by accident as by design. "I fired at a flock of Shore Larks," writes Capt. John P. McCown, U.S.A. (1851), "and found this bird among the killed." For this, in the first published description of the bird, George N. Lawrence (1851) announced, "It gives me pleasure to bestow upon this species the name of my friend, Capt. J. P. McCown, U.S.A." He adds, "Two specimens were obtained * * * on the high prairies of Western Texas. When killed, they were feeding in company with Shore Larks. Although procured late in the spring, they still appear to be in their winter dress."

Very likely this is the bird that the fatigued Captain Meriwether Lewis saw on the Marias River (near Loma, Choteau County, Mont.). Had he been more explicit in his description he might have added McCown's longspur to the magpie and the prairie dog on the list of species new to science the Lewis and Clark Expedition was to bring out of the vast northwestern wilderness. As it happened, the company was footsore and weary, slightly rebellious, and nearly at the rope's end of its resources when on June 2, 1805, with its usual unpredictableness, the Missouri River divided in front of the explorers. One branch bore down on them from the right or north, the other seemed to come from the south or left, each flow about equally wicked in its rolling turbidity. Which was the Missouri and which its affluent? An incorrect decision meant days of toil and pain spent for nothing, incalculable delay, the threat of spending winter in the mountains. On June 4, 1805, Lewis and six men, taking the right-hand fork, the Marias River, explored upstream. A day's march brought him to extensive "plains" where prickly pear tore his feet through his "Mockersons," where rain soaked, and a windstorm chilled

A. D. Du Bois

McCown's Longspur Incubating

Johnson River, Alaska, June 8, 1946 L. H. Walkinshaw

Nest and Eggs of Alaska Longspur

the party. What with haste, the fear of Indian attack, the distraction of bear, deer, elk, and "barking squireels" continually under their gunsights, it is perhaps hardly surprising that when he encountered a new bird in the short grass, Lewis did not collect it and later was less precise in his report than was his custom. He listed (Thwaites, Lewis and Clark Journals, II: 119–120) several sparrows and

Also a small bird which in action resembles the lark, it is about the size of a large sparrow of a dark brown colour with some white feathers in the tail; this bird or that which I take to be the male rises into the air about 60 feet and supporting itself in the air with a brisk motion of the wings sings very sweetly, has several shrill soft notes reather of the plaintive order which it frequently repeats and varies, after remaining stationary about a minute in his aireal station he descends obliquely occasionally pausing and accomnyng his descension with a note something like *twit twit twit;* on the ground he is silent. Thirty or forty of these birds will be stationed in the air at a time in view. These larks as I shall call them add much to the gayety and cheerfullness of the scene. All those birds are not seting and laying their eggs in the plains; their little nests are to be seen in great abundance as we pass. there are meriads of small grasshoppers in these plains which no doubt furnish the principal aliment of this numerous progeny of the feathered creation.

While Lewis' notation describes McCown's generally (though it lacks the precise detail necessary for positive identification), Elliott Coues in his annotation of the Biddle edition of the Lewis and Clark "JOURNALS" in 1893 unhesitatingly identified the bird: "This is the black-breasted lark-bunting or longspur, *Centrophanes* (*Rhynchopanes*) *maccowni,* which abounds in Montana in the breeding seasons." Reuben G. Thwaites, the editor of the "ORIGINAL JOURNALS OF LEWIS AND CLARK (1904–05)," accepts his conclusion. Between 1806, when Thomas Jefferson announced the news of the progress of the Expedition in a message to the Congress, and 1851, when George N. Lawrence published the discovery of the longspur, only the Biddle version of the "JOURNALS" (published in 1814) appeared in print. The Biddle edition, however, is a paraphrase, a popular account of the most important events of the expedition. It omits the scientific data, including the zoological material, among which is the account of McCown's longspur. While the avian specimens collected on the Expedition were becoming well known, the scientific data remained in darkest obscurity.

For almost a hundred years Lewis' description of "a small bird" with a treasury of other ornithological information lay hidden in the unpublished portions of the "JOURNALS" in the library vaults of the American Philosophical Society in Philadelphia. In 1892 Elliott Coues, his new Biddle edition largely completed, learned of the original papers, secured them, and from their largely untapped resources enriched his volume with pages of annotations. One of the notes pertains to the identification of Lewis' "small bird." But the actual text of Lewis' account of the discovery was not published until Thwaites brought out the original Lewis and Clark "JOURNALS," uncut and intact, in 1904–05. By that time Captain McCown's discovery of the longspur was firmly established in the literature. With no specimen of McCown's from the expedition at hand, ornithologists since then seem indisposed to reopen the question whether the "small bird" Lewis saw on its breeding grounds really was, as Coues stoutly maintained, *Centrophanes* (*Rhynchophanes*) *maccowni*.

If his identification of the species lacks detail, Lewis' description of its habitat is certainly that of McCown's longspur. For McCown's is a bird of the land where mirages on miles of sage and salt flats deceive the eye with the illusion of gleaming tree-bordered lakes; where, as Lewis observed, "the whole country appears to be one continued plain to the foot of the mountains or as far as the eye can reach; the soil appears dark rich and fertile yet the grass * * * is short just sufficient to conceal the ground. Great abundance of prickly pears which are extremely troublesome; as the thorns very readily pierce the foot through the Mockerson; they are so numerous that it requires one half of the traveler's attention to avoid them;" a land where the temperature, as unpredictable as a cowboy's flapjacks, rises breathlessly high in summer and drops to icy lows in winter. In Custer County, Montana, in the late 1880s, Ewen S. Cameron (1907) watched McCown's longspurs in the heat waves of a temperature standing at 114 degrees. In July 1911 near Choteau, Teton County, in the same state, Aretas A. Saunders (1912), caught in one of those thunderstorms which suddenly and commonly lash the plains, fled to cover under a sheep herder's shed to escape the rain which quickly changed to hail. Soon "a small flock" of McCown's longspurs joined him, "feeding on the ground under the shed as though they were out in the open in the best of weather."

I remember the flock of McCown's I saw in 1958 in a late April squall. According to my field notes:

Mr. and Mrs. Herman Chapman, Dr. N. R. Whitney, Jr., and I drove near Casper, Wyoming. With the unexpectedness characteristic of prairie weather, a spring storm hurled wind and snow upon us; the road ahead vanished. We no more than crawled along a road where side-banks, car high, were topped with sage.

Suddenly we saw birds struggling into view over and into the road. Some came down no more than a car's length away. Chapman stopped altogether. We saw they were McCown's Longspurs, the black caps and dark smudgy crescents on the breast marking the gray fronts of the males. Farther away were others, their bodies so light in color that frequently they were invisible, lost in the folds of snow. Several dozen swooped out of a gust. Through snow on the windshield and snow driven in windy sheets we watched. Perhaps as many as two hundred birds drifted into the road and up the side of the opposite bank.

The wind ripped at the sage above them, but here in the lee of the bank, in a sort of microclimate less severe than the white fury above, they fed, apparently on seeds; walked rather than hopped about, now in, now out of view in the white spirals the wind flung down the roadway. Now and again two males squared off in what seemed to be threat postures, head down, beaks open, wings laid back and fluttering slightly. There was some chasing presumably of McCown's females by males. A male pursued a female across the road and back again; then both flew down the road; the white area in the tail and the black terminal band were sharply revealed in flight; both vanished in the obscurity of snowdust. A female faced an approaching male; male promptly veered aside, lifting his wings slightly but enough to show the white linings momentarily.

About five minutes passed. When the squall abated, the birds moved in short flights above the road and along the bank; appeared restless. As the road ahead cleared, the birds arose above the sage and met the hard push of the wind. For a moment they hung there, swinging sidewise, dark shapes moving at a cord's-end, without advancing. Then in a slacking wind or in an extra spurt of driving power, they swept low over the sage and vanished. By the time we drove beyond the cutbank, though the storm had lifted somewhat, the birds had become indistinguishable from the driven gusts.

It is a bird of a landscape dominated by rolling prairies where sage and buffalo grass are the characteristic floristic types, and chestnut-collared longspurs, horned larks and sage grouse are the characteristic birds. Saunders (1912), riding on horseback across the divide between the drainages of the Dearborn and Sun Rivers, gives an excellent account of the approach to prairie habitat for which McCown's seems to have a preference: "The rolling, round-topped hills changed to fantastically shaped, flat-topped, prairie buttes, the tall grass and blue lupine changed to short buffalo-grass and prickly pear, and the bird voices changed from Vesper Sparrows and Meadowlarks, to Horned Larks and McCown Longspurs."

Called McCown's bunting, rufous-winged lark bunting, black-breasted longspur, black-throated bunting, and "ground larks" (Raine, 1892) by "the natives" at Rush Lake in Saskatchewan, in southern Alberta it is often "one of the few common, widespread birds of the open country" (Rand, 1948); sometimes "on flattopped prairie benches, this is the only bird found" in Teton and Northern Lewis and Clark counties (Saunders, 1914).

The monotypic status of *Rhyncophanes mccownii* has been questioned several times. In his general discussion of the genus *Plectrophanes*, S. F. Baird (1858) suggested in 1858 a new genus, *Rhyncophanes*. In his description of the species, Baird says: "The *Plectrophanes Maccownii* is quite different from the other species of the genus in the enormously large bill and much shorter hind claw, so much so, in fact, that Bonaparte places it in an entirely different family. As, however, many of the characteristics are those of *Plectrophanes*, and the general coloration especially so, I see no objection to keeping it in this genus for the present."

Coues (1880) writes: "As Baird exhibited in 1858, there is a good deal of difference among the birds usually grouped with *Plectrophanes* *nivalis*, enough to separate them generically in the prevailing fashion. * * * Maccown's Bunting has precisely the habits of *C. ornatus*, with which it is associated during the breeding season in Dakota and Montana."

When in 1946 Olin S. Pettingill, Jr., collected in Saskatchewan what proved to be a hybrid between the chestnut-collared and McCown's longspurs, the problem was discussed again. Enumerating similarities and differences, Sibley and Pettingill (1955) argue that, despite the difference in the size of the bill, the point of distinction between the two longspurs, "It is demonstrable that it merely represents the extreme development in a graded series." The authors conclude that "it seems doubtfully valid to separate the members of the genus *Calcarius*, including the Chestnut-collared, Lapland (*C. lapponicus*) and Smith's (*C. pictus*) longspurs from the monotypic genus *Rhyncophanes*." They recommend a return to the genus *Calcarius*.

Once the species ranged in the breeding season over the wide prairie interiors of the western United States and the southern expanses of the Canadian prairie provinces: Oklahoma (Nice, 1931), Colorado (Bergtold, 1928; Bailey and Niedrach, 1938), Wyoming (McCready, 1939; Mickey, 1943), Nebraska (Carriker, 1902), South Dakota (Visher, 1913, 1914), Minnesota (Brown, 1891; Currie, 1890), North Dakota (Allen, in Coues, 1874; Coues, 1878), Manitoba (Taverner, 1927), Saskatchewan (Raine, 1892; Macoun, 1909) and Alberta (Macoun, 1909).

If the foregoing is an indication of its former nesting grounds, then the breeding range of McCown's has been drastically reduced. It is no longer included among the breeding birds of Kansas (Johnston, 1964), if indeed it ever nested there, nor of Nebraska, where it is now designated a migrant and a winter resident (Rapp, Rapp, Baumgarten, and Moser, 1958).

In South Dakota it was last recorded by Visher (1914) in 1914; since 1949, no authenticated nesting has been reported (Krause, 1954; Holden and Hall, 1959). It vanished from the Minnesota scene after 1900 (Roberts, 1932) except for a single observation of two fall stragglers in October 1936 near Hassem (Peterson and Peterson, 1936). The first authentic specimen for Manitoba was not collected until May 1925 according to P. A. Taverner (1927); its status as a breeding bird in the province is at the moment unclear.

In North Dakota it has been reported from the southwest (Allen, in Coues, 1874), northeast (Peabody, in Roberts, 1932, at Pembina), and northwest (Coues, 1878). But Robert E. Stewart, wildlife research biologist of the Northern Prairie Wildlife Research Center at Jamestown, writes me (1964): "During the first quarter of this century, the species gradually disappeared over the greater portion of its former range, leaving only a small remnant population of scattered pairs in the extreme western part of the State near the Montana line."

It is sobering to reflect on his next statement: "At the present time, there is some doubt as to whether McCown's Longspurs breed anywhere in North Dakota, although spring and fall migrations are of regular occurrence in the western areas. If breeding populations are present they must be either very rare and local or irregular in occurrence. While searching for them during the past two summers, I have combed the native prairies in the northwest quarter of the State, but without success."

At this writing, Montana seems to be the last stronghold of McCown's longspur in the United States. Stewart (letter, 1964) says that it is "common and widespread over most of the short grass prairies" there; "in the northeast portion, considerable numbers may be found within 50 miles of the North Dakota boundary. On July 3, 1953, I made a detailed list count of breeding birds occurring in approximately 200 acres of lightly grazed short-grass prairie, located in Roosevelt County, about 18 miles northeast of Wolf Point."

How numerous McCown's was in the study area as compared with other emberizine forms can be seen in Stewart's list of relative abundance:

Savannah Sparrow	7
Clay-colored Sparrow	1
Chestnut-collared Longspur	44
McCown's Longspur	20

Is it significant that this area of comparative abundance is contiguous to the area in the Canadian Provinces where McCown's longspur still maintains itself with something of its former vigor? The center of population seems to be northeastern Montana westward, the adjacent regions in Saskatchewan from Willow Bunch northwest to Gull Lake and Golden Prairie, and the southeastern portion of southern Alberta. Whether the density of population is contiguous or broken into widely distributed breeding colonies seems not to be known. C. Stuart Houston writes me (letter, 1964) that in Saskatchewan there appears to be additionally a wide area of lesser density which apparently runs from Estevan northward to Fort Qu'Appelle, northwest to Outlook and Rosetown, and westward to the Alberta border. This would include the "elbow" region of the South Saskatchewan River.

In this "fringe" area the bird seems to show considerable fluctuation in numbers and in appearances in a given locality. M. Ross Lein (letter, 1964) says that in the Estevan region during the period 1958–

1962, "I never saw a McCown's Longspur," although he believes the bird may be resident but very much restricted. Writing about the South Saskatchewan River sector, Frank Roy (1958) comes to the conclusion that "longspurs, once the most common bird in the Coteau, are now a rare and local species." However, in a letter (1964) he adds, "I now believe that the fluctuations in numbers in the area north of the South Saskatchewan River are attributable to the birds being near the edge of their normal range."

Apparently McCown's is a bird that responds to not easily discernible environmental changes. Perhaps this is involved in the unpredictableness of its appearances at certain times and in certain places. Although not enough data seem to be at hand to draw conclusions, it appears to arrive in numbers more often in dry years than in wet. Roberts (1932) says that it visited western Minnesota "only in dry seasons—when very dry it was most abundant, and in wet seasons it was entirely absent."

In North Dakota Dr. and Mrs. Robert Gammell (letter, 1964), bird banders at Kenmare, are of the opinion that they secure McCown's "mostly during the dry years * * *. During the dry year of 1961 we caught 6 in July." This is contrasted with years of average or above average moisture when one bird was banded in June in 1959 and none in the years 1960, 1962, 1963, and 1964 until August; after the breeding season, that is, and at the beginning of the flocking and migration period. Frank Roy (1964) states that its abundance in the "Elbow" region of Saskatchewan apparently depends on the year—an inference, I take it, to a wet or a dry year.

Another factor seems to complicate the problem. Writes Stewart (letter, 1964): "Certainly there seems to be ample habitat left, since large tracts of native prairie are still present in many areas, including the high, drier types that were preferred. * * * The reason for the gradual disappearance of this species in North Dakota is not apparent to me." He adds: "Possibly, some subtle climatic change may be involved."

Willard Rosine (MS) suggests that certain of the emberizine forms, such as lark bunting and grasshopper sparrow, may detect minute and subtle changes in the complex of soil and vegetation as well of climate—changes too minute to be easily recognized—to which they respond. It may be that McCown's longspur is a member of this group.

I have been thinking about the effects of fire in the regeneration of the prairie environment and whether this may be one of the "changes" involved here. Early travelers on the plains have left many and vivid depictions of "oceans of flame" rolling over the prairie swales, from Kansas (Sage, 1846) to the Canadian Provinces where Henry W.

Hind (1860) describes one such holocaust which "extended for one thousand miles in length and several hundreds in breadth."

In the last 40 years at least, agricultural methods have largely prevented uncontrolled prairie fires or have contained them to the smallest area possible. One wonders if fire and its effect on the grasslands' environment, however minute and subtle, may be involved in the changing boundaries of the breeding range of McCown's longspur; whether fire is implicated in the environmental requirements of this species as there is the possibility that it may be in the requirements of Kirtland's warbler in Michigan (Van Tyne, 1953), although these have not yet been determined.

Nor can one ignore such factors as Frank Roy (1958) underscores in his query concerning the Coteau region of Saskatchewan: "Has cultivation brought about this rather sudden decline in the longspur population? Do newer methods of cultivation, and more frequent tilling to eradicate weeds, make it impossible for longspurs to rear their young in regions where they were abundant as recently as fifteen years ago?" Also the possible effects of aerial spraying, pesticides, herbicides, and fertilizers upon the vast and still somewhat mysterious complex of soil composition and vegetational relationships have still to be assessed.

Once McCown's longspur apparently ranged a country where fences were farther apart than rivers or the far plateaus; today it nests where barbed and woven wire proclaim the domesticity of plowed acres. Once it bred on the plains where its associates included the antelope and the buffalo; today it is neighbor to the Hereford and the baby Angus.

Spring.—Even while the blusters of spring are still raging on its summer range, McCown's longspur leaves its wintering grounds. In Texas watchers report that it usually leaves the San Antonio region late in March or early in April (Dresser, 1865; N. C. Brown, 1882, 1884) and the western areas, such as Tom Green and Concho counties, in March (Lloyd, 1887). An occasional straggler might be encountered as late as May (Cruickshank, 1950). In Arizona it apparently departs the southeast region late in February (Monson, 1942) and the central east in March (Swinburne, 1888). In New Mexico H. K. Coale (1894) collected a pair in March 1892 near Fort Union in the northwestern part of the state while A. W. Anthony (1892) writes that he saw them only until February in the southwestern region.

Apparently McCown's responds early to subtle environmental and physiological stimuli toward migration, for it arrives in numbers on "the Laramie Plains during the first week in April" (Mickey, 1943), in east and north central Montana from mid-April to the third week in the month (DuBois, 1937a; Saunders, 1921), in southwestern North Dakota at Dickinson between April 9 and May 3 (9 years, Sorenson, letter, 1964), and in the Regina, Saskatchewan, environs during the last two weeks of the month (Belcher, 1961). The earliest data for spring arrivals in southern Alberta seem to be that of the Macouns (1909) who saw two individuals at Medicine Hat Apr. 21, 1894. That same year Spreadborough (Rand, 1948) collected this species at the same place on April 26. These dates correspond pretty well with Margaret Belcher's (1961) observations in the Regina, Saskatchewan, region where she cites Ledingham's April 15 as an early date (letter, 1964).

In Saskatchewan dates recorded by Belcher (1961)—the last two weeks of April—presumably hold comparatively true for that part of the province west and south of Regina. W. Earl Godfrey (1950) lists two adult male specimens in the National Museum of Canada taken at Crane Lake near the Alberta border Apr. 25, 1894.

In its usual penetration northward in spring McCown's apparently stays well south of Saskatoon (Bremner, letter, 1965). Houston and Street (1959) have no records for the Saskatchewan River between Carlton and Cumberland. In the grasslands east and west of the "elbow" region of the South Saskatchewan River it still finds suitable habitat for breeding purposes, although Roy (1964) finds that it ranges "from rare to fairly common depending on the area and the year." I am greatly indebted to C. Stuart Houston of Saskatoon and his indefatigable researches which include data on nearly all of my Saskatchewan references. On a vegetation distribution map C. S. Houston laid out the range of McCown's longspur in terms of greater and lesser densities of population. In a note (1965) he reminds me: "Notice how well range corresponds to yellow prairie area of enclosed map."

Cameron (1907) regards McCown's as "seemingly a most punctual migrant." Writing about its spring appearance in Dawson and Custer Counties, Montana, he adds, "My notes give April 26, 27, and 29, for 1897, '98 and '99 as dates of first appearance." Davis (letter, 1964) collected a specimen near Judith Gap on April 26.

In Montana McCown's is frequently in the vanguard of spring, arriving during the last harsh vestiges of winter. Perley M. Silloway (1902) in Fergus County remembers that:

> It was on April 24, 1889, on a cloudy, raw afternoon, when I had gone out upon the neighboring bench to look for evidence of belated spring. In the bed of a miniature coulee that crossed my path was a bank of snow, sullenly giving way before the weak assaults of the advancing vernal season. Crouching under the lee of a small stone, and hugging the edge of the snow-bank, a new bird caught my eye. The stranger was apparently as interested in the featherless biped as I was in him, for he allowed me to approach until I could observe every detail

of his handsome breeding plumage, so that there was no call for me to deprive him of the life he was supporting with so much hardihood along the line of melting snow. I can yet remember how the great tears crossed down my cheeks as I faced the raw south wind in my efforts to watch every movement of the longspur and to take in every detail of his dress. Presently I observed a second McCown's longspur lurking near the first, the advance guards of the troops that were soon to throng the prairies to rear their broods.

The following Sunday afternoon * * * while walking over the bench I suddenly found myself in the midst of a flock of McCown's Longspurs. They were crouching silently in the hollows of the road and in depressions of the ground, and I was not aware of their presence until I startled several near me. When flushed at my approach, after sitting undisturbed until I was only five or six feet away from them, six or eight of them would flitter farther away, uttering a sharp chipping note as they flittered to stations beyond me.

When I discovered myself among them, by looking carefully around me I could see them crouched upon the ground on all sides of me, their gray attire assimilating them as closely with the background that only by their black crescentric breast markings could I detect them. Frequently, however, some of them would emit their chipping call in a gentle tone, and thus I could note their positions. In several instances there were fifty of the flock crouched around me, their black breasts showing as black spots on the dreary gray herbage and prairie soil.

E. S. Cameron (1907) who witnessed their arrival in Custer and Dawson counties in Montana says that "the birds scatter over the ground as they alight, hide in the horse and cattle prints, or other holes, and allow themselves to be almost trodden upon before rising."

Frances W. Mickey (1943), whose work on the breeding habits of McCown's is the most complete study to date, describes the arrival near Laramie, Wyo. "By the third week in April large flocks of male longspurs were common. These flocks spent most of their time feeding. However, those among them who were selecting territories sang a great deal, not only in characteristic flight song, but also from perches on the tops of rocks or shrubs within their chosen areas."

Mickey observes that at about the time flight song is initiated and territorial selection begins, "scattered groups of females made their appearance. By the last of April the females became numerous. Later than this, females were seldom seen in groups, for the transients had moved on, and the resident females had separated and spread out over the areas being defending by singing males."

Extremes for southern Wyoming are March 12 and April 24 (Mickey, 1943; McCreary, 1939). In Montana both sexes are common by the first week in May, with early arrivals berween April 13 and 18 in Teton county (DuBois, 1937), on April 22 at Terry, and April 28 at Big Sandy in the north central part of the state (Saunders, 1921).

In Alberta John Macoun (1909) found them "in thousands at Medicine Hat and numbers of males were in full song" on May 2, 1894. In Saskatchewan C. G. Harrold (1933) found them "fairly common from May 20 to 26 in the Lake Johnston area south of Moose Jaw." Macoun (1909) reports them as "common at Crane Lake in June", presumably the first part of June. Crane Lake lies in the southwestern part of the Province north of Highway No. 1 at the village of Piapot. Early dates are Apr. 7, 1947 and Apr. 16, 1948 at Bladworth, some 50 miles southeast of Saskatoon; however, P. L. Beckie (1958), an observer there, writes, "Although I often see the McCown's in migration * * * I have no records of resident birds for this area."

In these northern latitudes there are intriguing records of McCown's wandering rather widely from its wonted purlieus. Macoun (1909) reports that "one was seen on the shore of an island in Lesser Slave Lake" and Salt and Wilk (1958) call attention to the fact that "wanderers have been taken * * * on an island in Lesser Slave Lake." This is nearly 500 miles from what seems to be its area of greatest density in southeastern Alberta. Other points where McCown's has been collected in the province are Beaverhill Lake and Sandy Creek near Athabasca, the first east and the second about 100 miles north of Edmonton. In British Columbia Major Allan Brooks (1900) took a male and two females "on the lower Fraser River Valley at Chilliwack", the male on June 2, 1887, and the females on the same day, 1889. William Brewster (1893) acknowledged this unusual record in the AUK, adding Brooks' postscript to the observation: "I passed this place every day but saw no others, either there or elsewhere in British Columbia." Robert R. Taylor points out in a letter (1964) that during the summer of 1964 members of a party from the Saskatchewan Museum of Natural History at Regina "collected a McCown's longspur on the Hanson Lake Road, in northern Saskatchewan."

In Alberta Salt and Wilk (1958) extend the range of McCown's as far north as "Youngstown on the east" and "Calgary on the West." The inclusion of Calgary brings up the matter of McCown's somewhat erratic appearances and disappearance. In 1897 Macoun (1909) "Observed a number at Calgary, Alta., on June 19"; and Salt and Wilk (1958) report "Eggs * * * (Calgary, May 28)". Whether these records are sporadic appearances, a trait that seems characteristic of this species, is intriguing in the light of an observation by Timothy Myres of the University of Alberta at Calgary. Dr. Myres writes in a letter (1965) that "there is nothing known on McCown's Longspur by local naturalists."

Territory.—As F. W. Mickey (1943) observed on the Plains of Laramie, during the third week in April with large flocks of males already present, the beginning of territorial selection soon became evident. Alert to their behavior on first arriving in Fergus County, Mont., Silloway (1903) writes:

This longspur appears in this locality late in April. At first the birds keep in flocks, sitting on the ground so closely that an observer can get among them without detecting their presence until he startles one or more almost under his feet. On such occasions the startled birds will fly a few feet, while the remainder of the flock will continue to crouch upon the ground. As the days pass, the males utter a low, trilling song, not greatly different from that of the horned larks. Soon the longspurs scatter over the prairie and the peculiar flight-songs of the males begin. Rising with twittering hurried chant after an ascent of a few yards, they will drop downward with out-spread, unmoving wings, uttering their gush of song, thus descending parachute-like to earth.

From shrubs, rocks and piles of stone as well as from the air, those males early inclined toward the selection of territory fling their chiming notes across the benches, proclaiming their chosen plots of prairie habitat. Mickey (1943) describes the activity—I am indebted to her "Breeding Habits of McCown's Longspur," a paper meaty with information about this subject:

The male proclaimed his right to a territory chiefly by a characteristic flight-song. In the early spring he was a persistent and exuberant singer. He mounted into the air, spread his wings and floated downward, repeating over and over the phrases of his song, *see, see, see me, see me, hear me, hear me, see.* Sometimes the bird did not alight after one descent, but rose immediately for another song.

* * *

The first males to settle in a region claimed territories that were larger than necessary. As more and more resident males arrived, they tried to establish themselves on ground already claimed by others.

The result was increased tension among the males and a subsequent "squeezing" of available space into smaller and smaller units to accommodate the most recent arrivals. "The newcomers that I observed," Mickey continues, "succeeded in holding the territories that they appropriated. As their territories decreased in size the birds increased the vigor of their defense, in order to keep an area of sufficient size around the nest from which the adults could secure the large quantities of food needed by the young nestlings and still be able to brood them for long periods." Adjusted territories, in Mickey's judgment, were seldom less than 250 feet in diameter. But such close proximity, wing by beak, as it were, was enough to increase the possibility of tension and the necessity for defensive behavior.

"For the male longspurs, who held small territories in areas where more birds congregated, the conspicuous flight-song and occasional chasing of an intruder were not sufficient to hold their territories; they often had to fight neighboring males. The bird defending a territory challenged the trespasser by flying at him, singing and rapidly fluttering his wings. If the intruding bird was easily intimidated, he was chased off the territory; if not, the two males rose in the air fighting." Thus high above the grass and the blue lupine, where earlier the birds had performed in graceful solo, but now in fierce combativeness, "bill to bill, singing and fluttering their wings," they disputed the patch of prairie habitat which for each, holding dominantly a mate and a nest, was "his."

Mickey describes the progress of one of these conflicts:

> An interesting situation arose early in June, 1938, when a new bird, M10, attempted to encroach upon the territory of an established bird, M2, at the same time and close to the same place that a nest was being constructed by M2's mate. M10 was an aggressive bird and finally succeeded in establishing himself in a small area * * *. When he secured a mate, it so happened that she chose a site for her nest close to the disputed boundary. On July 7, I watched these two pairs of birds for an hour or more. M10 was engaged in flight-song within his own territory when I arrived. After each descent, he hovered over the nest site, and then flew directly over into M2's territory, uttering a sharp *tweet-twur* on the way. M2 immediately flew toward M10, singing. They met head on and rose high in the air; then, bill to bill, singing lustily and with wings beating vigorously, they dropped to the ground, and each retired to his own territory. This performance was repeated eight times within twenty minutes.

Once boundaries were firmly laid out and apparently recognized by the adjoining claimants, an alert kind of truce apparently prevailed, broken only now and again by aerial encounters. Not that this put a stop to the singing. On the contrary. Writes Mickey, "after longspurs settled on their territories, they sang from or over these areas at intervals throughout the day and well into the evening." Thereafter apparently less and less energy was directed toward the maintenance of defensive attitudes and more and more toward the center of interest in the territory, the mate, and later the nest.

Courtship.—In its own way, the courtship display of McCown's longspur, while it does not have the drama of the parachute descent, is in the terrestial world of buffalo stems, blue lupine and sage, a spectacle in minature. In early June A. D. DuBois (1937b) came upon a "very pretty demonstration" of this amatory manuevering: "On the ground * * * a male McCown longspur pranced around his mate in a circle about one foot radius, holding the nearer wing stretched vertically upward to its utmost, like the sail of a sloop, showing her its pure white lining, while he poured forth an ecstatic song."

It is the unexpectedness of the behavior that intrigues the beholder. The quick upraising of the dark wing and the sudden revelation of the white lining, shining silver in contrast to the darker body, is a rather astonishing performance, made all the more fanciful by the comparative diminutiveness of the actors. It reminds me of the courtship ballet of the buff-breasted sandpiper I saw in South Dakota where the male, with both wings elevated almost like an upland plover just alighting on the ground and the body held almost perpendicular, moved in a half-circle about the female, the white wing-linings satin shiny beside the buff of the body.

On another occasion DuBois (1937b) "saw a male standing at rest on a rock, holding one wing aloft and singing softly. Presumably his mate was in the grass nearby. * * * The same day I saw a female raise both wings and hold them quivering; and immediately her mate ran past her, singing, and hoisting his white sail toward her."

F. W. Mickey (1943) tells about a male that "was frequently seen singing softly from the top of a small rabbitbrush, meanwhile making little bows to the female in the grass below. Occasionally, he would hold up one wing while he sang. At another time, while on the ground, he raised the wing nearest the female and held its silver lining before her. Then he ran over to the female; they both flew up and settled in the grass some ten feet away."

Sometimes what DuBois (1923) calls "a popular movie situation" develops where a second male intrudes upon the domesticity of a mated pair. One such incident occurred while nest building was still going forward; another took place so late in the season that the mated pair were brooding young.

Mickey relates how on May 20 she encountered a pair of McCown's, apparently a mated pair. They were:

feeding side by side at the edge of the field. The female flushed and was followed by the male; as they settled in the grass, another male alighted beside them. Both males rose fighting; finally one was driven off. The victorious male returned to the female, which had remained on the ground, and started bowing to her. The other male returned; again they fought and chased each other about until the female flew a short distance into the field. One male followed and dropped close beside her; the other perched on the nearby fence. On May 24, the nest in this territory was practically finished, but the two males were still fighting each other.

In this instance the affair ended somewhat inconclusively. Mickey says that "two weeks later, this nest was destroyed and one of the males disappeared."

DuBois (1923) has an account of a Don Juan among the McCown's which apparently was undismayed by an advanced season or a female attentive upon a nest of young. DuBois writes:

This morning, while she stood in the garden with a grasshopper in her bill, an audacious stranger ran past her, making his bow with the wing nearer her. He quickly made another advance with the evident intention of bowing to her again, but she ran at him and drove him away. Her mate was on the nest, panting and sweltering in the hot sun while bravely shading the young. He seemed in a position to observe this attempted flirtation with his spouse, but he paid no attention to it. I afterward saw the stranger again. * * * This time [he] came marching into view ostensibly oblivious of the presence of the female which stood upon the rock at the edge of the garden. He made no advances toward her * * *. But she flew at him this time also, and he went away.

Nesting.—The nest J. A. Allen (Coues, 1874) discovered in North Dakota, July 7, 1873, probably the first McCown's longspur nest to be described, "was built on the ground and is constructed of decomposing woody fibre and grasses, with a lining of finer grasses." Grinnell (1875), who encountered the species southwest of Fort Lincoln in North Dakota in 1874, found that the nest "resembles, both in position and construction" that of the Chestnut-collared longspur. In Minnesota Rolla P. Currie (1890) found two nests: "Composed of fine round grasses and fine dried weed stems, lined with very fine grasses a few horse-hairs. One nest was on the ground in a clump of grass and the other in a small bush." Currie's observation is interesting; no where else have I found reference to McCown's building a nest above the ground.

In Nebraska M. A. Carriker (1902) located a nest in the dry hills of the northwest corner of the state near the Wyoming line. The nest was "sunken flush with the surface of the ground and made of dried prairie grass blades and rootlets." There was "no attempt whatever at concealment or protection by weed or tuft of grass." DuBois (1935) and Mickey (1943) also remark on nests where concealment was at a minimum. DuBois writes that one such nest was placed "in a grazed pasture" with "no standing grass about it—just three or four scant shoots. At another the growing tufts nearby had been cropped off by stock."

Of a nest in Fergus County, Montana, Silloway (1903) writes, "The site was a depression among grass-blades, open above. The nest was made of dried grass felted at the bottom with a few downy pistils, the style of architecture being very similar to that followed by the horned lark. The cavity was two and one-half inches in diameter and two inches in depth". In Saskatchewan the Mocouns (1909) came upon a nest that was "a rather deep hole in the prairie, lined with a little dried grass." And Barnes, quoted by Ferry (1910), took a nest on June 4 near Regina. "It was located in a depression near the road on the open prairie where there was practically no grass. It had been run over by a wagon, crushing the nest out of shape. The bird, however, was on the nest and the eggs were uninjured."

DuBois (1935) speaks of the oddity of nests "placed near old dried heaps of horse droppings; one was a foot away, one was quite close, one was at the edge of such a point of vantage, while another was in the midst of a scattered pile which had become very dry and weathered."

In Wyoming Mickey (1943) found that of a group of 40 nests, "nineteen were beside grass clumps, fifteen beside rabbitbrush, five beside horsebrush and one between rabbitbrush and horsebrush." In Montana Silloway (1902, 1903) found nests in shallow depressions at the base of small Coronilla bushes. "A very common site," he adds, "and one most generally selected by this longspur." In Colorado Bailey and Niedrach (1938) found them frequently "beautifully placed near prairie asters, phlox, or flowering cactus."

Where the advance of the plow has turned the short buffalo grass and blue-joint and sage into wheat and legumes, McCown's longspur clings somewhat precariously to the transitional areas or edges. DuBois (1935) found a nest "in a narrow strip of sod between two wheat fields, at the extreme edge of the grass, against the bare dirt turned over by the plow; another was found in a strip between a wheat field and new breaking, while another, though in the prairie grass, was near the edge of the wheat field. Even more notable was a nest on a narrow dead furrow of prairie sod, missed by the breaking plows, in the middle of a field of winter wheat." On the basis of such observations in Montana DuBois (1935) concludes, "no nests were found on cultivated ground." However, C. G. Harrold (1933), reporting his experiences in the Lake Johnston region south of Moose Jaw, Saskatchewan, during April and May, 1922, writes that the bird is "found chiefly in stubble fields on high ridges."

Roberts (1932) says that in the last reports of the species in western Minnesota McCown's nested "only in the high parts of wheat fields." He quotes a letter from A. D. Brown who writes that after 1899 "only a few were seen, even when quite numerous, as it hid most of the time in the growing grain." Margaret Belcher (1961), reviewing the opinions held by a number of writers that McCown's prefers "the drier and more sparse prairie vegetation," notes, "It is interesting that McCown's longspurs in the Regina area nest regularly in the cultivated fields." And in a letter (1964) she calls my attention to the report of George Fairfield on the breeding bird census conducted "in a 28-acre field of uncultivated prairie grassland at Moose Jaw." G. Fairfield (1963), in commenting on "the McCown's preferred nesting habitat," says that no horned larks "or McCown's were seen on the census plot, but a few of both species had territories on the plowed (summer-fallow) fields close by."

Mickey (1943) found that "The majority of the nests were constructed entirely of grasses, the body consisting of coarse stems and blades, and the inner lining of finer grasses." As exceptions, however, occasional nests contained bits of lichen, "shredded bark of horsebrush and rabbitbrush", down feathers and tag-ends of wool, with one nest "lined entirely with wool." Comments Mickey: "Very likely the nests constructed entirely of grass represented the primitive type of material used for nests before sheep, horses, and cattle were introduced into this region. However, when such materials as wool and hair became available, the birds made use of them." She notes too that the birds collected "bits of wool which clung to the barbed-wire fence bordering the territories in which these nests were located."

Not only does the female gather the nesting material within the territory but occasionally she helps to scrape out a shallow depression for the nest when such excavation seems necessary (Mickey, 1943; Silloway, 1902). "A new nest was constructed for each brood," writes Mickey, "usually at some distance from the old one, either within the previous boundaries of the territory or close enough to it so that, in uncrowded portions of the field, adjustments in the boundaries could easily be made."

Bailey and Niedrach (1938) found that "It is an easy matter to locate nests * * * after the song perches have been discovered, for the females are almost sure to be tucked away in the near vicinity, and it is only a matter of walking about until they flush from under foot." But, as they found, this is the beginning, not the end of the problem. Nests are hard to locate, they learned. "Even when in the open, cut by only a few blades of wiry grass, they are difficult to see." To which Mr. Bent (1908) and DuBois (1937b) agree. In DuBois' opinion, "Typical nests are not effectively hidden by grasses; but * * * a nest may be effectively camouflaged by scant grass-clusters slanting over the top of it, or by dry blades of grass hanging loosely over it. It is surprising how few such blades are necessary to make an effective camouflage."

Parasitism of the nests by cowbirds does occur although apparently only a few instances have been recorded. Currie (1890) in Minnesota found a cowbird's egg in a nest from which he had removed four McCown's eggs the previous day. And John Macoun (1909) in Saskatchewan, in April 1894, discovered a cowbird egg in a nest of four longspur eggs.

Eggs.—The usual number of eggs per clutch is three or four, occasionally five, though Sclater (1912) mentions six. Walter Raine (1892) says that in the nests he discovered at Rush Lake, southwest Saskatchewan, "the number of eggs to a clutch is usually five, sometimes only four. In my collection I have seven clutches of five eggs, and four clutches of four." Farther west at Crane Lake Macoun (1904) found two nests with four eggs each. Brown (Roberts, 1932) reported 11 sets gathered in Minnesota between 1891 and 1899, of which 6 sets numbered three eggs each and 5 held four eggs each. Of 52 nests DuBois (1935) studied in Montana between 1915 and 1918, 24 had sets of three eggs, 26 had sets of four eggs and 2 contained sets of five eggs. In Oklahoma M. M. Nice (1931) found one nest with five eggs and one with six eggs.

Average size of eggs seems to vary from .80 by .65 inch, as reported by G. B. Grinnell (1875) from North Dakota, to .81 by .57

inch as measured by Brown (Roberts, 1932) of 11 sets in Minnesota. The 72 eggs Mickey (1943) recorded in Wyoming averaged .8089 by .6086 inch. Harris gives the average measurements of 100 eggs as 20.4 by 15.0 millimeters, with eggs showing the four extremes measuring *22.9* by *15.9*, *18.8* by 14.6 and 19.8 by *13.7* millimeters.

Egg size and weight within a clutch may vary somewhat, according to Mickey (1943). At one nest she found that "one large egg was deposited the first day, followed on the second and third days by lighter, smaller eggs." Concerning the egg weight Mickey (1943) writes: "Fresh eggs varied in weight from 2.3 to 2.5 grams; the average of six was 2.4. Eggs weighed the day before hatching varied from 1.7 to 2.15 grams; the average of seven was 1.914 grams. * * * The average total weight of a three-egg set was 7.21 grams as compared to 9.5 for a four-egg set and to 11.4 for the one five-egg set weighed."

There seems to be some geographical variation in the ground color of the eggs. Raine (1892) found that in the eggs near Rush Lake in Sasketchewan "the ground colour varies from white to greyish white, pinky white, clay and greyish olive, usually boldly spotted with umber and blackish brown; many of the eggs are clouded over with dark purple grey which almost conceals the ground colour, and many of the eggs have scratches and hair-like streaks of brown." The ground color of the eggs in the Brown (Roberts, 1932) collection from Minnesota is a "pale greenish-white of varying intensity, more or less obscured in three of the eleven sets by a buffy tinge." In Wyoming Mickey (1943) discovered that "The ground color * * * varied from white to pale olive. The markings consisted of various combinations of lines, scrawls, spots, and speckles of lilac, rusty-brown, mahogany, and in one case black." In general, Harris writes that "the ground may be grayish white or a very pale green such as 'tea green.' There is considerable variation in coloring and pattern." Raine (1892) found one set near Rush Lake in Saskatchewan which "is remarkable in having all the markings at the larger end of the egg where they form a zone."

The earliest date for full clutches of eggs is May 9 in a listing by DuBois (1935) for Montana, the latest being July 28. In the same state near Lewistown, Silloway (1903) reports a nest of three fresh eggs on May 29. In Wyoming, McCreary (1937) quotes Neilson as finding "full sets of 4 eggs near Wheatland by May 20." Near Laramie, Mickey (1943) came upon a nest with one egg on May 20 and a full complement of four on May 25. She reports the latest date for a full clutch as August 6. In Saskatchewan, Raine (1892) "flushed a McCown's longspur from its nest and five eggs" on June 10, 1891. Brown (Roberts, 1932) collected "five sets of eggs, all nearly fresh" in early June 1891 in Minnesota.

Apparently eggs are laid early in the morning. In a nest DuBois (1937a) visited "both morning and evening, they were laid before 6:00 or 7:00 a.m." Mickey (1943) writes:

> On July 8, 1939, at 7 a.m. I observed F18 flying about in small circles just above the top of the grass in the vicinity of her nest. When I came into the territory, she flew away. Then her mate flew around me as if he were trying to drive me off; so I walked a short distance away and sat down. About five minutes later the pair returned to the nest site; the female dropped into the grass, the male perched on top of a nearby rabbitbrush. After a while he dropped down and fed. I walked over and flushed the female from her nest, which contained one warm egg.

Incubation.—DuBois (1937a) states that "the eggs are deposited at the rate of one each day" and "incubation begins when the last egg is laid." There seems to be room for latitude here, for Mickey (1943) sees it differently. "It seemed to me that the birds were somewhat erratic in this respect; for I found that the eggs of a complement were not always deposited on successive days, nor did the female always wait for the completion of the clutch before starting to incubate."

Incubation seems to be the duty of the female. DuBois (1937a) writes, "I have never seen a male on the nest before hatching time," and Mickey (1943) concurs: "I did not at any time flush a male from a nest containing eggs."

Information on the length of the incubation period is confined to the detailed observations of Mickey (1943) who states, "I have data on two pairs that were successful in hatching more than one brood. Nests 3 and 23 were thought to be those of the same pair * * *. The length of the incubation period was twelve days. This was calculated from the laying of the last egg until the time of its hatching, from June 22 to July 4, at nest 3." While the female incubates, "she turns around very often in the nest, and sometimes erects the feathers of her crown," writes DuBois (1923). He adds, "the female sometimes sings at her nest when the male is approaching."

During this period, writes Mickey,

> the male longspur spent a great deal of time (a) guarding the nest from some nearby rock or shrub, (b) engaging in flight-song, or (c) defending his territory, particulary if nests were close together.
>
> Sometimes the male was seen guarding the nest during the female's absence; at other times neither bird was near the nest. M4 was never in the vicinity of of the nest when the female was absent. M6 was usually on guard from a pile of stones close to the nest, not only while the female was off the nest, but also while she incubated. He often sang from this stone pile. Whenever I came near the nest * * * he either flew about over the nest or circled about in the grass nearby, making some pretense of collecting food.
>
> * * *
>
> Male longspurs sang during the incubation period, but with less intensity than prior to mating.

On one occasion DuBois (1923) watched while "a male came to the nest and presumably fed the female, for she was on the nest."

On the hatching of the eggs Mickey (1943) writes:

> On July 5, 1938, at 6:30 a.m., after flushing the female from nest 9, I found that her eggs were in the process of hatching. One young bird had already emerged from the shell; its down was still wet and clinging to the body. There was a large hole in the side of a second egg, through which could be seen the bill and part of the head of its occupant. A small, circular, cracked area, not yet broken through, was observed in the side of a third egg. Sounds and faint tappings could be detected coming from the fourth egg. When I visited the nest the following morning, all four had successfully hatched.

DuBois (1923) observes that during the early stages of the second nesting young birds are sometimes seen near the nest. On June 28 he discovered "a young bird, fully grown and 'on the wing'" on the ground near an incubating female, "presumably her offspring, from an earlier nest, although no more definite evidence could be secured to prove this assumption." On June 29 at a second nest from which the female had been flushed, "Two birds, able to fly, were in the grass near her; the nest contains four eggs which are apparently incubated." These eggs hatched on July 5.

In her studies on the Laramie Plains, Mickey (1943) found that climatic conditions might effect hatching success to a considerable degree, as might an increase in the number of predators in the area. During a three-year period, 11 of 45 nests were completely successful, 16 were partially successful, and 18 were failures. "A total of 153 eggs were deposited in 45 nests, averaging 3.4 eggs per nest. Of these 92, or 60 percent of the total number laid, were hatched; 71 birds, representing 46.4 per cent of the eggs laid, were fledged, giving an average of 1.58 birds per total nest, or 3.5 birds per successful nest."

Young.—Details concerning the young have been chronicled discerningly by DuBois (1937a) and Mickey (1943), especially by the latter who writes:

> The young were hatched blind but not entirely naked, for the dorsal feather tracts were covered with long, buffy down. The skin appeared dark where it was stretched over the body, yellowish where it lay in loose folds. The light, tan-colored egg-tooth was very prominent on the grayish bill. The egg-tooth was shed the fifth day. * * *
>
> The nestlings were blind for two days. Occasionally on the third day they momentarily opened their tiny, slit-like eyes. By the fourth day they could keep their eyes open for several minutes, although, if undisturbed, they rested quietly in the bottom of the nest with eyes closed. On the fifth day they appeared much more alert for even though they sat quietly in the nest, they peered over the rim with bright, beady eyes.
>
> When eight days old, the nestlings were no longer content to sit quietly in the nest, but moved about considerably, preening, stretching their necks,

raising themselves up and fluttering their wings. By the ninth day, fear instinct was evident. Before this they had not been much disturbed at the weighing process but now they either crouched on the scale with neck drawn down between the scapulars, or fluttered about trying to escape, cheeping constantly. At this the adults became quite alarmed and circled low over the box containing the scales, uttering sharp alarm notes.

Regarding the progressive increase in the growth of feathers, DuBois (1937b) has this to say:

> The newly hatched young, as soon as dry, are protected above by fluffy natal down, about one-fourth inch long, of a whitish buff or pale dead—grass color similar to that of young Desert Horned Larks. The invisibility afforded by this covering is truly marvelous. The skin is light-colored but reddish. The tongue and inside of the mouth are of a strong pink color, without spots or marks of any kind. This distinguishes them from young of Desert Horned Larks.
>
> When the nestlings are four days old, the feathers of their underparts become well sprouted, forming a longitudinal band along each side. When six days old, the natal down of the upper parts has been pushed out on the feather tips so that the covering is a combination of down and feathers. The young are well feathered at the age of eight or nine days.

Mickey adds:

> By the sixth day, the feather tips had broken from all sheaths except those on the capital tract. Another day was needed for the head feathers to emerge, otherwise, on the seventh day the bird appeared well feathered. Down still clung to the head and occasionally to some of the back feathers on the eighth day. * * *
>
> The wing feathers developed at a slightly different rate from those on the body proper. The developing flight feathers, enclosed in their sheaths, appeared on the wings on the second day. These sheaths grew from one-sixteenth of an inch on the third day to one-fourth of an inch by the fifth day. On the sixth day, feather tips had broken from the sheaths of the primary coverts and on the inner margins of the secondaries. * * * By the time the bird was ready to leave the nest, the feathers of the secondaries protruded one-half an inch beyond the end of the sheaths and those of the primaries one-fourth of an inch. The primary feathers of a bird captured when eighteen days old measured two inches in length.
>
> The caudal feathers were the slowest of all to grow. The nestlings were six days old before the tail feathers could be measured. * * * The tail of an eighteen-day-old bird measured one inch in length. At this time the characteristic color pattern of the tail was clearly indicated.

Early dates for the discovery of young in the nest appear in a tabulation by DuBois (1935) for Teton County, Montana. May 22 appears to be the earliest, other dates being May 26, 27, and 31. In the same state for Chouteau County, A. A. Saunders (1921) has May 23 as the first day on which young were found, but, he adds, "the young were already half grown," which suggests a hatching date as early as May 18 or 19.

Care of the young is assumed by both male and female, especially during the nestling period. "The female brooded most of the first two days after the young hatched," observes Mickey (1943), "but she was relieved at intervals by the male. From the third day on, more and more time was spent by both adults gathering food for the young and less time brooding them. During showers the female brooded the nestlings even after they were well feathered. At nest 22, where the female had either deserted or been killed while away from the nest, the male fed the young, but apparently failed to brood them during a downpour, for the young were found wet and dead after the rain."

The young were shielded not only against the rain but against the heat of the July prairies also. DuBois (1923) has several notations regarding this behavior.

July 8. * * * The mother bird stood in the nest sheltering the young from the sun, but she left every few minutes to go for food for them * * *.

As the parent stands on the nest in the hot sun, she usually keeps her mouth open, panting. Her breathing is rapid, and when there is no wind her puffing is audible * * *.

The male, as well as the female, goes on the nest after feeding and stands with his wings partly spread, if the sun is hot, until his mate comes with more food to relieve him. She then takes his place and remains until he returns * * *.

July 12. This evening after supper I watched for awhile from the tent-blind. Both parents were feeding hastily and in rapid succession. A thunder shower was brewing, night was coming on, and drops of rain, striking the nestlings made them stretch up their heads and open their mouths when both parents were away. The female sat on the nest a few minutes between meals, and the thunder did not seem to startle or disturb her * * *.

The position of the male while brooding is to stand astride the nest with a foot on each side, at the rim, the young filling the cavity between. Once, while the female was brooding, the male came with food which he fed to the young at her side. At another time under similar circumstances he gave the food to his mate and she fed it to the young under her breast, the food being nearly always grasshoppers. On one occasion, after feeding, the female stood at the edge of the nest facing the young, and, stooping over them, sang a little warble close to their heads while the male was approaching with another ration. She was obviously tired and sleepy, as she frequently yawned and dozed while brooding in the short intervals between feedings.

At another nest on July 8, DuBois (1923) found "at noon the male standing in the nest with his feathers all 'fluffed up', shading the young from the hot, penetrating rays of the noonday sun." Mickey (1943) observed a similar position in the female which straddled "the nest while brooding. She placed one foot on either side of the rim of the nest."

For about half of their nestling life the young are brooded at night also, as Mickey learned:

On the night of July 10, 1938, my husband and I visited the field at ten o'clock. We had previously marked the nests so that they could be found easily in the dark. When a nest was located, a flashlight was turned on it. The young birds in nest 9, which were five days old, were being brooded. The adult bird left the nest, but the young birds did not open their eyes. The seven-day-old nestlings in nest 3 were not being brooded. The adults were on the ground in the immediate vicinity. The male, evidently disturbed, sang a short snatch of song. From this night visit it seems that the young birds are brooded at night until they are well feathered, or until about six or seven days old.

Both DuBois (1923) and Mickey (1943) agree that the young are fed insects from the very start and that the food is not regurgitated. Both parents feed the young. "Moths and grasshoppers furnished the bulk of the food," says Mickey. In addition to this menu DuBois includes larval worms. On one occasion, he adds, "I thought I recognized a spider as it went into one of the throats." He declares the female gives as a food call "a brief twitter. The young, which must be less than twenty-four hours old, have a note which can be easily heard from the tent: it is a clear 'peep.' They frequently give utterance to it while their mother is standing in the nest shading them." As they grew, "the food call of the young longspurs," Mickey notes, "changed from the continuous chippering of the nestling to the shriller intermittent call of the fledgling."

Mickey (1943) weighed and tabulated the young from 13 nests. The minimum weight of nestling at hatching was 1.6 grams, the maximum was 2.9 grams, while the average was 2.03 grams. Sometimes a nestling had to cope with the drawback of hatching out a day later than its nest mates. "A nestling never overcame such a handicap," states Mickey; "in fact, it often did not make normal daily gains in either weight or length. * * * The chances of the survival of these underlings were closely associated with the amount of food that they received. In cases where the adults did not respond readily to their weaker food calls, they died either before leaving the nest (as in the nests 24 and 28), or shortly afterward (as the one from nest 3, which was found dead six inches from the nest)."

Sanitation of nests is maintained by both parents. "The nests are kept quite clean until the last two days of nest life," reports Mickey. "By this time the young so filled the nest cavity that an occasional excrement sac was often overlooked. * * * Ants were omnipresent. From the observation blind at nest 13, the female was seen picking them from the young and out of the nest." DuBois (1923) has these additional notes on sanitation: "The excrement is sometimes swallowed and sometimes carried away, the two methods in about equal proportions. * * * At this state of the development of the young (age six days) the parents begin carrying the excrement away from the nest, after one feeding the male being observed to fly away with it, but at the next trip he swallowed it as formerly. * * * The practice of swallowing excrement has been entirely discontinued.

It is being carried away and is usually dropped while the bird is on the wing."

The solicitude of the male and the female for the young increases as the nestlings become more and more feathered. DuBois (1937a) writes:

When I caught a fledgling near nest 59, on the day it left, * * * its father flew at my head, excitedly singing the trio of notes that is so characteristic. One day I managed to catch a youngster that was an excellent runner. Upon turning it loose I gave forth the most distressing squeaks of which I was capable. Quickly five adults appeared upon the scene and tried to lead me away. They alighted approximately in a row, well deployed, as though for battle; and when I followed, they all ran through the grass ahead of me, in company front, in a manner that was very amusing.

Mickey (1943) found that

an incubating female would normally leave the nest and settle in the grass some distance from her nest during my visit to it. The brooding female would leave the nest if disturbed, but fed close by. By the time the nestlings were nine days old, both adults kept close to the nest during my visit, alternately feeding nearby and circling low over the nest, uttering sharp calls. On the day the young left the nest, both adults continually flew about me calling, *chip-pur-r-r-r chip-pur-r.* They were just as excited at my intrusion on the following day, although later than this I did not notice any anxiety on the part of the adults, unless I accidentally flushed a young bird.

In their Montana and Wyoming observations, DuBois (1935) and Mickey determined that, with some exceptions, the normal period of nestling life was 10 days. At that time the nestlings "can run at a lively rate, fluttering their wings if pursued," says DuBois. "Two days later (age 12 days), as observed at nest 59, they are able to fly for short distances." One bird in Mickey's study area, an 11-day-old fledgling, had a very weak flight but "in another day it could fly thirty feet or more." A fledgling DuBois (1923) caught 6 feet from the nest on the 10th day, when released scrambled "over the ground at a lively rate, fluttering its wings as it runs, although it is not very large." Two days later he concluded his notations with: "The young longspurs are now able to fly for short distances."

Plumages.—The following descriptions appear in Ridgway (1901):

Tail (except middle pair of rectrices) white, broadly tipped with dusky.

Adult male in summer.—Forehead and anterior portion of crown, more or less distinct rictal streak, and crescentic patch across chest, black; posterior portion of pileum and hindneck pale brownish gray, streaked with dusty, especially the former; back and scapulars, pale wood brown, or pale buffy brown, broadly streaked with dusky; rump and upper tail-coverts grayer (especially the latter), less distinctly streaked; more anterior lesser wing-coverts ash gray with dusky (mostly concealed) centers; posterior lesser coverts and middle coverts chestnut; rest of wing grayish dusky with pale brownish gray edgings, the primaries narrowly edged with white (outer web of first primary almost entirely white), the greater coverts and secondaries rather broadly (but no distinctly) tipped with white;

middle pair of rectrices dusky grayish brown margined with paler; rest of tail white, broadly tipped with dull black, except outermost rectrices, where the blackish, if present, is very much reduced in extent; under parts (except chest) white, tinged with pale gray laterally, the plumage deep gray beneath the surface; bill brownish, dusky at tip; iris brown; tarsi brown; toes dusky.

Adult male in winter.—Black areas concealed by broad tips to feathers, brown on pileum, buffy on chest; otherwise not essentially different from summer plumage.

Adult female in summer.—Above, light buffy brown (pale wood brown or isabella color), streaked with blackish, the streaks broadest on back and scapulars; wings dusky, with light buffy brown edgings (broadest on greater coverts and tertials, narrower, paler and grayer on primaries, and primary coverts), the middle coverts broadly tipped with buffy, the lesser coverts pale brownish gray; tail as in adult male; sides of head (including broad superciliary stripe) light dull buffy, relieved by a rather broad postocular streak of brownish; under parts pale buffy, passing into white on abdomen and under tail-coverts; a brown or dusky streak (submalar) along each side of throat.

Adult female in winter.—Similar to summer plumage, but dusky streaks on back, etc., narrower and less distinct, and under parts rather more strongly tinged with buffy.

Young.—Back, scapulars, and rump dusky, with distinct pale buffy margins to the feather; pileum and hindneck streaked with dusky and pale buffy; middle wing-coverts broadly margined, and greater coverts broadly tipped with pale buffy or buffy whitish; chest rather broadly streaked with dusky; otherwise much like adult female.

Food.—The principal items in the diet of McCown's longspur, according to Roberts (1932), consists of weed seed: pigweed, ragweed, bindweed, goosefoot, wild sunflower, sedges, foxtail, and other grass seeds; grain; grasshoppers, beetles, and other insects. On their wintering grounds in New Mexico A. L. Heermann (1859) says that the birds include berries in their diet. Richard H. Pough (1946) states that "Grasshoppers are generally their staple summer food, seeds of grasses and weeds at other seasons." DuBois (1937a) considers the food of the young to be principally grasshoppers "with now and then a moth or a caterpillar." Mickey (1943) lists the grasshoppers which seemed to predominate in the bulk of the food: *Arphia pseudonietanus*, *Gamnula pellucida*, *Melanoplus femur-rubrum*, and *Trimerotropis* sp.

From such data one can only conclude that economically McCown's longspur is to be counted among the beneficial species of birds, despite the comment of Arthur L. Goodrich, Jr. (1946) on wintering birds in Kansas: "It is reported that this race and other longspurs may be responsible for the destruction of large quantities of winter wheat in some areas of the west." Perhaps the subject has not yet been sufficiently investigated.

Behavior.—The following account by Grinnell (Ludlow, 1875) suggests the kind of mate attachment in McCown's attributed to the mated Canada goose and the bald eagle pair. He writes:

The male and female manifest an unusual degree of attachment for one another. While watching them feeding in the early morning, for they were very unsuspicious and would allow me to approach within a few yards of them, I noticed that they kept close to one another, generally *walking* side by side. If one ran a few steps from the other to secure an insect or a seed, it returned to the side of its mate almost immediately.

On one occasion, a pair were startled from the ground while thus occupied, and I shot the female. As she fell, the male which was a few feet in advance, turned about, and flew to the spot where she lay, and, alighting, called to her in emphatic tones, evidently urging her to follow him. He remained by her side until I shot him.

Nest tenacity, developed to a high degree in the female of this species, is described by Raine (Macoun, 1908), DuBois (1937a) and Mickey (1943). "The female is a close sitter, not leaving the nest until the intruder has stepped close up to it," declares Raine.

Mickey (1943) remarks on the bird's awareness of the human gaze. "I was standing less than a foot from the incubating bird when I saw her. Not until I looked directly at her did she fly."

DuBois (1937b) describes a female apparently employing pretended food hunting as a distraction display. "After I had flushed her from the eggs, and had been seated for some time at the nest, she approached and deported herself very much as do the larks, running in the grass and pretending to hunt food, while she watched me."

Both male and female sometimes display remarkable intrepidity. DuBois (1923), taking pictures and having his camera set up near the nest, was surprised at the male's lack of concern. "He now permits me to sit at the camera, which is only three or four feet from him, as he stands or sits on his brood."

At a pond in north central Montana in 1911 Saunders (1912) found horned larks and McCown's longspurs feeding about the edge, "the longspurs walking daintily over the green scum at the edge and eating the small insects that swarmed there. Several young longspurs, barely able to fly, were here with their parents, and one such had evidently come to grief in its efforts to imitate its parents' example, and was drowned in the midst of the scum."

In eastern Alberta, A. L. Rand (1948) saw McCown's longspurs fly in "commonly to drink at the irrigation reservoirs, along with horned larks and the chestnut-collared longspurs."

G. B. Grinnell (Ludlow, 1875) asserted that he "did not see these birds hop at all. Their mode of progression was a walk rather hurried, and not nearly so dignified as that of the cow-bunting [brown-headed cowbird]."

Where Grinnell in 1874 found this species "unsuspicious" and fairly easy to approach on the prairies of southwestern North Dakota, Bailey and Niedrach (1938) in 1936 and 1937 found them "extremely wild" in northeastern Colorado.

Voice.—To the dweller on the north central great plains, few experiences after a long hard winter equal the pleasure and the promise of the song bursts of certain early spring birds. Chaucer had his "smale foule" which "maken melodie" but the prairie-dweller has his horned larks and Sprague's pipits with their spectacular singing flights high aloft, seemingly cloud-high, and their dizzy plummeting to earth. He has his lark buntings and chestnut-collared longspurs with their less spectacular but more graceful and butterfly-like descent to earth, bubbling with sound. With them McCown's forms a trio in the grace and musical quality of the aerial performances.

Writes P. M. Silloway (1902) of Montana:

In a wagon trip across many miles of prairie in the last week of May 1899 I was regaled by the well-known flight-songs of the males of this species. Numbers of them were frequently seen in the air at one time, some of them mounting upward in irregular, undulating, star-like lines of movement, pouring forth their hurried bursts of song; others could be seen floating downward with out-spread, elevated wings, uttering their ecstatic measures as they slowly floated to earth without moving a feather.

E. S. Cameron (1907) recalls that near Terry, Montana, "On June 22, 1894, I had ample opportunity for observing this species, as, my horse having run away, I was compelled to walk home, ten miles across the prairie. My way was enlivened by the handsome males, which hung above me, before sinking into the grass with a burst of song."

One of the earliest to describe the song of McCown's longspur was George Bird Grinnell (Ludlow, 1875). Traveling as zoologist with the Custer Expedition into the Black Hills in 1874, on observing the bird near Fort Lincoln (present day Bismarck) in North Dakota, he calls it "by far the most melodious songster" on "the high dry plains. It rises briskly from the ground, after the manner of *C. bicolor* until it attains a height of 20 or 30 feet, and then, with outstretched wings and expanded tail, glides slowly to earth, all the time singing with the utmost vigor."

In July of 1911, Aretas A. Saunders (1912) took a horseback ride "nearly across the State of Montana"—one of those adventures which the more sedentary only dream about. In the flat open prairie of Broadwater County where the "principal vegetation was buffalo-grass and prickly pear," he found McCown's longspur

in full song, a charmingly sweet song, that tinkled across the prairie continually and from all sides. The song has been compared to that of the Horned Lark, but to my mind it is much better. The quality is sweeter and richer; the notes are louder and clearer, and above all, the manner in which it is rendered is so different from that of the lark or of any other bird, that the lark passes into insignificance in comparison. The song is nearly always rendered when in flight. The bird leaves the ground and flies upward on a long slant till fifteen or twenty feet high, then spreads both wings outward and upward, lifts and spreads its white tail feathers, erects the upper tail coverts and feathers of the lower back, and bursting into song, floats downward into the grass like an animated parachute, singing all the way.

In Teton County, Montana, DuBois (1937b) also noted the parachute-like descent as well as "the usual song," which he says,

is a variety of warbles, clear and sweet. It is a joyous song. In the height of the nesting season it ripples through the air from many directions. It is usually delivered in course of a special flight.

The song-flight is a charming feat of grace. The male bird flies from the ground, in gradual ascent, to a height of perhaps six or eight yards, then spreads his white-lined wings, stretching them outward and upward, and floats slowly down to earth like a fairy parachute made bouyant with music. He continues to pour forth his song all the way down into the grass, and seems to swell with the rapture of his performance. Sometimes the descent is perfectly vertical. The song is delivered both while fluttering the wings and while making the parachute descent. The birds let their legs hang down beneath them while in flight. The floating descent was unique in my experience with birds, for though the Chestnut-collared Longspur also has a songflight, it lacks the parachute descent.

In two records DuBois (1923, 1937a) describes a characteristic feature of the song: "Occasionally, while the bird is in the air, he utters a trio of staccato notes, each of decidedly different pitch, and separated by equal time intervals. The three notes are louder than the usual song; they are so short and clear, and have so pronounced a pause between them that the effect is very striking."

In the Prairie Provinces of Canada Raine (1892) seems to be the first to mention the song of this longspur. In June of 1891 near a slough north of Moose Jaw, he found the song "very cheering * * * the male always sings as he descends to the ground with outstretched, motionless wings." Mr. Bent (1908), investigating the prairies in the vicinity of Maple Creek in southwestern Saskatchewan in 1905–06, considered McCown's song similar to the chestnut-collared longspur's "but somewhat louder and richer". The male "rises slowly and silently to a height of 10 or 15 feet and then floats downward, on outstretched wings and widespread tail, pouring out a most delightful, rich, warbling, bubbling song." But Harrold (1933), while mentioning the "remarkable butterfly-like flight", says that the song "consists of only a few notes one of them having a peculiar squeaky sound quite unlike that of any other bird in tune."

Olin S. Pettingill, Jr., (Sibley and Pettingill, 1955) describes the mechanics of the flight, comparing it with the chestnut-collared longspur's:

The flight songs of typical McCown's and Chestnut-collared longspurs differ in movements and in song pattern. Both species fly gradually upward, their wings beating rapidly. From the peak of the ascent McCown's proceeds to sail downward abruptly with wings held stiffly outstretched and raised high above the back. The Chestnut-collared, after reaching the peak of the ascent, prolongs the flight by circling and undulating, finally descending with the wings beating

as rapidly as before. Both species sing after the ascent, but the song of the McCown's is louder with the notes uttered more slowly.

During the peak of breeding intensity, as calculated by Mr. Bent (1908), "the male makes about three song flights per minute, of about 8 or 10 seconds duration, feeding quietly on the ground during the intervals of 10 or 12 seconds."

A. A. Saunders, remembering his days in Montana, writes in a note that the general quality of the song is "sweet and musical, and is a broken warble, that is a group of several rapid, connected notes, then a short pause and another group, and so on to the end of the song. In this the song differs from the Chestnut-collared Longspur, whose song is continuous, without a break. It also differs in that the general pitch is maintained at about the same level throughout the song, where that of the Chestnut-collared grades downward in pitch."

DuBois (1923) seems to be the only observer to record singing in the female. In Teton County, Montana, from a tent which served as a blind, he kept a series of nests under surveillance. On July 2, 1917, watching a female incubating, he notes, "I was surprised to hear her begin to sing. She sang a very pleasing little song." On July 5 when the male approached, "she again sang a little twittering, musical song." DuBois takes into consideration that at each of these occurrences the male was near. In the first instance, at the close of the song he saw the male drop suddenly into view; "he walked up to her and gave her a large insect, apparently a grasshopper with amputated legs." In his detailed study of 61 nests over three seasons (1915, 1916, 1917) Dubois mentions the female singing only in this one instance.

Though Saunders' (1922) observation lead him to believe that this species "sings from a perch only rarely" and that "the Chestnut-collared Longspur * * * sings from a perch more frequently than McCown's, but still rarely," he writes in a later note that occasionally McCown's will sing from "a wire fence or a stone." Salt and Wilk (1958) note in Alberta, that in its choice of song sites McCown's is similar to the chestnut-collared longspur's. "Both prefer low perches either on the ground or on a fence but not on bushes." The last part of the observation is interesting in its difference from the experience of Mickey (1943) who found in her Wyoming study that perches included shrubs as well as rocks and in one instance the top of a stone pile. She mentions the rabbitbrush (*Chrysothamnus* sp.?) specifically.

In Montana, DuBois (1923) discovered that a favorite singing spot was often a rock. Apparently some individuals are more concerned about its actual location than in the kind of perch they choose. Thus DuBois noted that the male of one nest under observation "has an habitual perch on an old kettle which has lodged at the edge of the garden some twenty feet from the nest. The kettle and Longspur combination, although perhaps picturesque, struck me as rather incongruous and I replaced the kettle by a rock which pleased me better and seemed to suit the Longspur just as well. He came repeatedly to perch there after descending from his song flight or returning from an absence * * *."

In May 1899 in Montana, Silloway (1902) found the longspurs singing from the ground. A concentration remained hidden by the blending of their coloration with the background of bare gray ground and last year's dead vegetation:

> When * * * about sixty yards to one side of their position, I was attracted by a series of strange songs, uttered with unusual force. Walking in the direction of the unfamiliar music, I found that the Longspurs were the authors, and for many minutes I watched different songsters twittering their pretty little songs. The performance was a continuous chatter, having some resemblance to portions of Meadowlark music. It was quiet similar to the continuous, hurried measures of the Horned Larks, though louder and clearer. In some instances the performer uttered the act of singing while pecking for seeds among the dead herbage, thus showing a further resemblance in habit to the Horned Larks. A noticeable feature of the performance was the movements of the white throats as the spirited measures bubbled forth.

Field Marks.—Silloway (1903) describes the male as: "Upper parts chiefly grayish brown, streaked with darker; top of head, and large crescent on breast, black; wing coverts reddish-brown; lower parts grayish white." DuBois (1937b) has this description of the female:

> The upper surface of the head is uniformly covered with faint, fine, wavy streaks * * *. The face has a buffy appearance, with a line over the eye that is more whitish. * * * The throat is white. There is just a faint suggestion of darker gray on the breast where the black patch adorns the male. The wrist of her wing shows a little of the reddish brown "shoulder" patch worn by her mate. * * * When the bird takes flight, she shows, conspicuously, an almost black T-shaped design at the end of the white spread tail. The sexes are alike in this tail pattern, which constitutes the best field mark.

Enemies.—Various plundering marauders play havoc with the nests and eggs of McCown's longspurs. DuBois (1937a) relates that in Montana "carcasses of [Longspur] fledglings were seen at a Short-eared Owl's nest, and at a nest of Swainson Hawks" but concludes that raptores were in general "almost neglible factors in the lives of the longspurs at this place." Among the mammals considered predatory, DuBois points his finger at the weasel and the skunk. He adds, "Punctured eggs or broken shells showing tooth marks, noted in several instances, were thought to be the work of the common ground squirrels [the thirteen-lined (*Citellus tridecemlineatus*) and Richardson's (*C. richardsonii*)], though I have never caught one of these rodents in the act of plundering a nest. Whenever a ground squirrel approached a nest, the longspurs drove him away by swooping at him repeatedly, sometimes actually striking his back." Adds Mickey (1943), "On several occasions the birds were seen hovering over a ground squirrel, chirping and darting at it in an effort to drive it away from the nest site," suggesting that the birds recognize these animals as predators.

While the elements and the animal predators undoubtedly take a yearly toll of McCown's longspurs, the species has been subject to their onslaughts for millenia with little evidence of any serious reduction of the population. The real threat, whether recognized, minimized, or ignored, as DuBois (1936), states, is man—"man whose poisoned baits set out for ground squirrels apparently kills more birds than spermophiles." Man with his plow and his agricultural achievements: "Many nests were of course plowed under by the breaking plows of pioneer farmers," DuBois remembers. "I have seen one or two go over with the turning sod, when it was too late to prevent it."

To DuBois' list of enemies Mickey (1943) adds the cat, the badger (*Taxidea taxus*), and among birds the prairie falcon and western crow. "A pair of Swainson's Hawks, *Buteo swainsoni*, and a pair of Marsh Hawks, *Circus hudsonius*, were frequent visitors to this field. They swooped over the field in search of rodents, quite indifferent to the smaller birds. A Prairie Falcon, *Falco mexicanus*, occasionally visited the field, but did not seem to bother the longspurs. Sometimes the longspurs ignored the hawks, but oftener a group of birds would rise and twitter noisily as they flew around the hawk. * * * Although I did not actually witness any depredations by the crows, it is my belief that they were responsible for the disappearance of some of the eggs and young of the smaller birds."

Frequently the forces of nature itself are antagonistic. Unseasonably cold rainstorms and late spring snows often bring disaster to the young of McCown's longspur. DuBois (1937a) describes a Montana storm that brought a deep fall of snow on May 25 and continued into the 26th.

I had previously marked a nest in which the bird was known to have begun incubating her four eggs on the morning of the 19th. The snow covered everything so completely that I could not find my marker; but in the afternoon of the 26th the marker-rock showed through the melting snow, and I uncovered the nest. The eggs had been in cold storage all of one day and part of another; but an hour or two after the nest was uncovered the female was sitting on the eggs. She continued to incubate until the 8th of June. That day she was absent morning and evening, though in the nest at noon. Before my return early the next morning the eggs and nest had been mysteriosly destroyed. The bird had continued incubation about nine days beyond the normal period. Perhaps it was her first experience with eggs under snow.

Fall.—No sooner are the fledglings on the wing, fortified against the ardors of the migration journey, then they begin the annual flocking. In the Canadian Provinces the gathering begins by the first of August; by the early part of the month, writes Mr. Bent (1908), in southwestern Saskatchewan "almost all of the Longspurs of both species, had disappeared from the plains."

As they continue their southerly movement, their ever-increasing numbers growing larger and larger, they string out over the prairies like tiny black pepper kernels flung across the sky, rising up high and thickening darkly into compact groups, masses twisting and turning, then slanting down, lightening as they thin out, sometimes so near the ground that an obstruction like a fence sends them bending upward to flow serpentlike over the obstacle; at other times they sweep tree-high from one seed-rich area to another. At last the groups swell into the hundreds, so that by the time they leave southern Montana in September they are seen in immense congregations like that which P. M. Thorne (1895) reports on the Little Missouri in 1889.

After August 10, Visher (1912) considered them numerous on the plains of south central South Dakota in the years from 1901 to 1911. In Montana, Saunders (1921) has a September 27 date for the north central portion. By September the birds have reached Oklahoma (Sutton, 1934) although W. W. Cooke (1914) during 1883–84 dates the arrival there as January 19. By October 16 they have arrived in Arizona and by November 5 (Lloyd, 1887) in the western part of Texas. Here as well as in New Mexico and northern Old Mexico they await the stimulus that will send them north again.

Winter.—A. L. Heermann (1859) who was with the topographical surveyors along the 32nd parallel of north latitude during the season of 1873–74 declares: "I found this species congregated in large flocks * * * engaged in gleaning the seeds from the scanty grass on the vast arid plains of New Mexico. Insects and berries form also part of their food, in search of which they show great activity, running about with ease and celerity. From Dr. Henry, U.S.A., I learned that in spring large flocks are seen at Fort Thorne, having migrated hither from the north the fall previous."

George B. Sennett (1878), who was on the lower Rio Grande during the season of 1877, writes of McCown's longspur:

I found these only about Galveston. They were in large flocks, and associated with them were *Eremophila chrysoloema,* Southwestern Skylark, and *Neocorys spraguii,* Missouri Skylark. They frequented the sandy ridges adjoining the salt-marshes. In habits they reminded me of *P. lapponicus,* Lapland Longspur, as I saw them in Minnesota last year. When flushed, they dart from side to side, taking a swift, irregular course, never very high, and suddenly drop down among the grass-tussocks, with their heads towards you. They are so quiet and so much the color of their surroundings that they are seen with difficulty. They fly in such scattered flocks that a single discharge of the gun can seldom bring down more than one or two. That they extend farther south than the vicinity of Galveston I very much doubt, for we would, in all probability, have noticed them if they had been farther down the coast.

In winter its peregrinations must occasionally have been extensive, for Coale (1877) has a note about its appearance at Champaign and Chicago, Illinois, which suggests a field of study as yet largely untouched:

While looking over a box of Snow-buntings and Shore Larks in the market, January 15, 1877, I found a specimen of *Plectrophanes maccowni*, shot at Champaign, Illinois. January 17, another box containing Lapland Longspurs was sent from the same place, and among them was a second specimen of *P. maccowni*, which is now in the collection of C. N. Holden, Jr., Chicago. January 19 I obtained a third specimen from the same source, which has been sent to Mr. E. W. Nelson, of this city. They were all males, showing plainly the chestnut coloring on the bend of the wing and the peculiar white markings of the tail. This is, I think, the first record of the occurrance of this bird in Illinois, if not east of Kansas.

That some birds may overwinter within the breeding range or near its borders is indicated by the Christmas Bird Counts listing 200 birds from Huron, S. Dak., in 1953 and 15 from Billings, Mont., in 1956.

Distribution

Range.—Southern portions of Prairie Provinces south to northeastern Sonora, northern Durango, and southern Texas.

Breeding range.—McCown's longspur breeds from southern Alberta (Calgary, Medicine Hat), southern Saskatchewan (Davidson), southwestern Manitoba (Whitewater Lake), and central northern North Dakota (Cando) south to southeastern Wyoming (Laramie), northeastern Colorado (Pawnee Buttes), northwestern Nebraska (Sioux County), and central North Dakota (Fort Lincoln); formerly east to southwestern Minnesota (Pipestone County).

Winter range.—Winters from central Arizona (Camp Verde), southwestern, central, and northeastern Colorado (Durango, Fort Morgan), west-central Kansas (Hays), and central Oklahoma (Cleveland County) south to northeastern Sonora (Pozo de Luis), Chihuahua, northern Durango (Villa Ocampo), and southern Texas (Rio Grande City, Corpus Christi, Galveston).

Casual records.—Casual in southern British Columbia (Chilliwack), Oregon (Malheur National Wildlife Refuge), Idaho (Birch Creek), northern Alberta (20 miles south of Athabaska Landing), and Illinois (Champaign).

Migration.—Early dates of spring arrival are: Wyoming—Cheyenne, March 12 (average of 9 years, April 14); Laramie, April 6.

Late dates of spring departure are: Minnesota—Lac Qui Parle County, May 8. Texas—Amarillo, April 4; Austin, March 27. Oklahoma—Camp Supply, March 8. Kansas—northeastern Kansas, April 3 (median of 5 years, February 17). New Mexico—Fort Union, March 22. Arizona—Bowie, March 7.

Early dates of fall arrival are: New Mexico—Mescalero Indian Agency, September 12. Kansas—northeastern Kansas, October 29 (median of 4 years, November 7). Oklahoma—Comanche County, November 21. Texas—Amarillo, October 18; Austin, November 15.

Late dates of fall departure are: Wyoming—Laramie, October 27 (average of 6 years, October 12).

Egg dates.—Montana: 10 records, May 9 to July 28; 5 records, May 9 to May 26.

North Dakota: 17 records, May 17 to July 22; 9 records, May 27 to June 10.

Saskatchewan: 7 records, May 28 to June 14.

Wyoming: 5 records, May 17 to June 29.

CALCARIUS LAPPONICUS LAPPONICUS (Linnaeus)

Common Lapland Longspur

Contributed by FRANCIS S. L. WILLIAMSON

HABITS

In North America the range of the Lapland longspur extends from northwestern Mackenzie over the vast expanses of tundra of the arctic and subarctic regions northward to Ellesmere Island and eastward to the Atlantic Ocean in Labrador. The following remarks show the habitat this species prefers remains essentially the same over this enormous region. T. H. Manning, O. Hohn, and A. H. Macpherson (1956) found longspurs most numerous on Banks Island in "marshes and better vegetated country." It occurs throughout Prince of Wales Island except on the barren disintegrated limestone uplands (Manning and Macpherson, 1961). J. Dewey Soper (1946) remarks that the species is scarce in the mountainous eastern half of Baffin Island and reaches the height of its abundance on the great tundras of the west where "it inhabits localized flats of a swampy nature, but its favorite breeding grounds are wide, moist tundras interspersed with ponds and streams and studded with grassy tussocks."

V. C. Wynne-Edwards (1952) states that the most suitable habitats at Clyde Inlet on Baffin Island are wet tussocky meadows, and in the southern part of that island Sutton and Parmelee (1955) found the longspur inhabiting all wet grasslands of the vicinity. They remark:

> Precisely why wet grasslands are so all-important to the longspur may be difficult to say. Availability of insect food for the nestlings, of dead grass for building material, of nest sites not readily accessible to certain predators: these probably have a part in determining the matter. To be attractive the terrain must be more than low and flat; if too well drained, too gravelly, too bare, it will not do. Dry, firm, thinly grassed areas just north of the Base were inhabited by Horned Larks and Semipalmated Plovers, but the longspurs lived elsewhere—a stone's throw away, in the wet grassy places.

W. H. Drury (1961) describes the preferred and somewhat different habitat on Bylot Island as follows: "Longspurs occupied the thick, moss-floored vegetation of dry places in the uplands, primarily on the east- and south-facing slopes, not the bogs. Their distribution was similar to that of the Bell Heather [*Cassiope tetragona*], but Bell Heather grew over large areas where we found no longspurs."

On Southampton Island, Sutton (1932) found that nesting-sites were restricted to the grassy margins of streams, or to hummocks of grass in the little marshes.

I would add to these generally consistent remarks only my belief that many references to "grasses" actually refer to the numerous sedges (*Carex*) of the arctic, and that the species generally nests in those moist areas that are not excessively wet. The situation on Bylot Island Drury describes seems exceptional and somewhat at variance with the notes of others. However, Adam Watson (1957) states that longspurs attained peak densities on the Cumberland Peninsula of Baffin Island wherever the ground became slighly drier and more heathy with a good growth of willows (*Salix*) and became uncommon on drier ground where the heath was closed. Drury (1961) suggests that the breeding sites on Bylot Island were selected "because the wet meadow sites were snow-covered too late in the species' breeding cycle and because the species, displaced from ideal nest sites, selected a form resembling the overhang of a tussock."

In the extreme northern part of the range on Ellesmere Island, habitat apparently suitable for longspurs is unoccupied. David F. Parmelee observed about 20 pairs breeding on the Fosheim Peninsula (80° N.), but recorded none in roughly 400 square miles of seemingly suitable tundra between Slidre and Greely Fiords. J. S. Tener (1961) recorded an extreme northern nesting on Ellesmere Island when he saw a female feeding a flightless young a few miles north of Hazen Lake at approximately 85° N.

Spring.—A sampling of the scattered records of spring arrival show a synchrony consistent with that observed in the ensuing nesting activities. At Bathurst Inlet, Mackenzie District, E. H. McEwen (1957) observed the first longspur to arrive, a female, on May 21, and

10 days later saw four males feeding in a sedge-covered flat. T. H. Manning et al. (1956) were present on Banks Island (De Salis Bay) in 1952 when the first longspurs arrived on May 29, when three were seen. The next day they counted 115 in 7½ hours, mostly in flocks of 25. Males outnumbered females on that date and on May 31, but on June 1 the sexes were about equally represented. In 1953 the first longspur (a male) was seen at Sachs Harbor on May 19, and one was heard at Cape Kellett on May 21. Their numbers increased thereafter, and most of the birds seen up until May 26 were males. The migration was essentially over by June 3, at which time the birds were seen in pairs. Manning and Macpherson (1961) first observed longspurs on Prince of Wales Island on June 14, and remarked that the late date of arrival was likely due to the late thaw on the northern part of the mainland barrens. The males outnumbered the females by 4 to 1 for 3 or 4 days.

The severe climatic conditions arriving longspurs frequently meet throughout their range is well-described by Sutton (1932) from observations on Southampton Island:

On May 20, 1930, during a snow-storm, which eventually developed into one of the worst blizzards I ever experienced, I saw and collected a male Lapland Longspur at Itiujuak. The bird was associating with a large flock of Snow Buntings, practically all of which were males. It was fat. The gonads were much enlarged. The stomach and crop held particles of vegetable food and some bits of quartz crystal, but food had evidently been difficult to find. I noted the brightness of the yellow bill, the base and culmen of which had a slight greenish cast. I looked carefully for other longspurs in this flock of buntings, but saw none.

On May 27 an adult male was seen perched on the very edge of the ice, perhaps six miles from land, at the floe west of Native Point. We heard one (perhaps the same individual) from our tent on May 28. On the following day a male was seen at the Post, feeding with the Snow Buntings during a wind-storm. This bird was very weak, probably from starvation, and I nearly caught it in my hands. During the midst of the storm it flew upward, was caught in a blast of wind, was hurled southward, and did not return.

On May 30 I collected a specimen from a flock composed of five longspurs and a few Snow Buntings. *All* these birds were males. On May 31 a male longspur was seen at the Roman Catholic Mission and another at the Factor's dwelling.

On June 1 large, loose flocks, entirely composed of males, assembled on the bare ground about three miles north of the Post. There must have been two hundred birds in all. I collected seven. The gonads of all were considerably enlarged; and all were fat, but their gizzards were not full of food. The birds worked their way through the short grass diligently, walking for a time, then stopping to look round, only to continue their search. When they came to the edge of a bare patch, they usually flew over the snow to the next bit of open ground. In some places the tundra had many snowless patches, and here with almost mathematical precision each such patch of open ground harbored its single longspur, which searched carefully over all its chosen space, not neglecting the shadowy spots at the edge of the snow.

The retention of substantial deposits of subcutaneous fat by arriving migrants has been remarked upon by other writers dealing with arctic passerine birds, and this phenomenon can readily be seen to have considerable importance to the welfare of the birds settling upon a wintry landscape.

In southern Baffin Island Soper (1928) observed the first longspurs at Cape Dorset on June 3, and saw them sparingly the following few days. Soper (1946) states that they arrived at nearby Bowman Bay on June 4, and in three days both sexes were common. By June 10 they swarmed in thousands over the restricted strips of snow-free tundra. The numbers increased "up to the middle of the month, when the majority moved on to more northern resorts. Large numbers remained to breed, however, and by a wide margin were the most abundant summer residents of the tundra. On June 11, the males were first heard singing half-spirited snatches of song, but the first mad outbursts of their full and brilliant repertoire was not general until June 20." In central Baffin Island, Wynne-Edwards (1952) observed the first longspur, a male, on May 29; three days later most of the males had arrived and females were seen.

D. B. O. Savile (1951) states that two males and a female appeared at Chesterfield Inlet, Keewatin on May 19, 1950; on May 21 there were eight males and two females, and thereafter numbers increased; males were still somewhat predominant on June 7. The early arrivals frequented mainly the wind-swept beach ridges where there was little snow and seeds of the sea-beach sandwort, *Arenaria peploides*, provided abundant food.

Courtship and nesting.—The courtship and nesting habits do not appear to differ from those described for the Alaskan race of this species. The same general and striking synchrony of activities in any single locality is apparent over the entire range of the species. Dates of the onset of courtship and nestbuilding may vary between years at the same or nearby localities, apparently because of weather, and consistent variation between populations may be due to latitude (indirectly to weather), or perhaps to local habits.

Sutton's (1932) comments on the breeding schedule on Southampton Island are pertinent for the species as a whole: "On June 8 I collected another female and observed the first flight-songs. In the North Country, the program of the individual is virtually that of the species. When one male bird begins to sing, they all begin to sing; by the time one pair mates, all the pairs are mating; when the first egg is laid by one female, all the females of that species are laying the first egg, and so on throughout the length and breadth of the tundra." This is certainly the first impression an observer of this species gets, and it can be carried further to include the molt of young and adults. Although the onset of particular activities among individual birds in the same population usually varies somewhat more than Sutton describes, his remarks point out fairly enough what is to me the most striking single adaptation birds have made to life at high latitudes—the general synchrony of events on the nesting ground and the compression of the time intervals between them.

On Banks Island, Manning et al. (1956) found pairs occupying nesting territories as early as June 1, although prior to June 2 the largest ovum found in a female was 1.5 millimeters. On June 5 a female was taken with a complete egg in the oviduct and three or four others had fully developed eggs in the next few days. Manning and Macpherson (1961) in their study of late-arriving longspurs on Prince of Wales Island (discussed previously) state that: "On June 26 a male was seen copulating with NMC 43094, a female with no empty follicles and rather small ova. When she was shot he turned his attention to NMC 43095, which had six empty follicles. The first nest was found on June 28. It contained six eggs. Another with six eggs was seen on June 30. Males continued to perform their nuptial flights regularly until the end of June, and some were singing until about July 10."

Drury (1961) arrived at Bylot Island while the longspurs were still in flocks and their numbers were still increasing daily. Males took up territories between 15 and 25 June, copulation was observed on June 21, and eggs were laid as early as June 17 with clutches completed 22 June to 4 July. Wynne-Edwards (1952) found egg-laying starting as early as June 6 on Baffin Island.

More extensive variation in nest-lining materials than that noted for the Alaskan subspecies is interesting to note. Field notes of J. R. Cruttenden mention the use of caribou hair in a nest at Churchill, Manitoba. Wynne-Edwards (1952) noted ptarmigan and longspur feathers, plant down from willows, and hair from the arctic hare. Sutton and Parmelee (1955) observed linings of raven feathers and dog hair, while Watson (1957) found ptarmigan feathers, hare wool, lemming hair, and plant down from willows in nests on Baffin Island.

Eggs.—Clutch size of the Lapland longspur remains generally consistent over the entire range. Drury (1961) observed an average clutch size of 4.6 (15 nests) on Bylot Island and found that the removal of eggs during and after laying had no effect on the number laid. Sutton and Parmelee (1955) found the average to be 4.4 in 22 nests on Baffin Island; all of these figures agree closely with the 4.7 average observed in northern Alaska. Wynne-Edwards (1952) based his larger figure of 5.4 on Baffin Island on only ten nests, Sutton (1932) obtained bonafide evidence of a larger average clutch size in an eastern population on Southampton Island, where 78 nests held an average of 5.8 eggs and 71 of these clutches, found between June 21 and July 21, contained six eggs. It is of interest that while no seven-egg clutches were observed in Alaska, Watson (1957) and Wynne-Edwards (1952) observed one and two of this size, respectively.

Wynne-Edwards (1952) presents evidence of a decline in clutch size as the season progresses: "five clutches begun between June 6 and 15 numbered 5, 6, 6, 7, 7, and five begun between June 19 and July 2 numbered 4, 4, 5, 5, 5. (The probability is about 30 to 1 against the apparent difference being due merely to chance.)" Drury (1961) states: "Early nests (hatching 3-9 July) contained consistently larger clutches (6, 6, 6, 6, 5, 4) than later nests hatching 10–15 July (5, 5, 4, 4, 4, 4, 4, 3, 3)." Sutton and Parmelee's (1955) data show 11 clutches hatching before July 3 averaged 4.7 eggs and ones hatching later averaged 4.3 eggs.

Egg color and pattern seems to be so generally variable over the range of the species as to merit no special discussion for this race. The measurements of 50 eggs average 20.9 by 15.3 millimeters; the eggs showing the four extremes measure *23.9* by *16.8*, *18.8* by 15.8, and 19.4 by *14.2* millimeters.

Incubation.—Considerable variation exists in the onset of incubation with respect to number of eggs laid, which may be a matter of adjustment by individual females to local climatic conditions. If so, it could be construed as an interesting adaptation to arctic conditions. Wynne-Edwards (1952) states that "Incubation begins with the first egg" because, as he elaborated in his discussion of the redpoll, "the temperature in June is below freezing for much of the 24 hours." He found, however, that the actual hatching period in six cases ranged between 2 and 4 days. Watson (1957) found that the females at two nests definitely started to incubate from the laying of the first egg, and early incubation was suspected in most other nests, although in a few it definitely did not occur. At one nest the eggs were cold on many visits during the first two days of laying, but warm after the third day. At another nest the female did not sit for at least all of the two afternoons of the days she laid the first two eggs; here three young hatched the same day followed by the fourth early the next day. A much greater spread in hatching resulted from the early incubation at most nests. At the nest where all 5 eggs hatched, the hatching occupied at least 3 full days, and about 3 days at another nest where 5 eggs out of 7 hatched.

Drury (1961) notes similar variation in the onset of incubation and he discusses it for other populations throughout the range of the species.

The length of the incubation period appears to be generally the same throughout the range, 10 to 13 days (Drury, 1961), 12 days (Wynne-Edwards, 1952), 12 days (Sutton and Parmelee, 1955), 13 to 14 days (Sutton, 1932).

Young.—Nearly every author has commented on the early departure of the longspur young from the nest: 9 days (Drury, 1961), 9 to 10 days (Wynne-Edwards, 1952), and 9 to 10 days (Sutton and Parmelee, 1955). Watson's (1957) observations on Baffin Island are generally appropriate for the species. He states that nestlings showed a marked gradation in size, at some nests so great as to suggest periods of hatching in excess of 2 days. This gradation was evident in 8- to 10-day-old broods at the time of leaving the nest. In at least four nests the smallest individual was left behind in the nest and was apparently deserted and no longer fed for up to a day after the others had gone. Two such young died, one in the nest and one outside. Another that fluttered from the nest after most of a day alone was not more than 7 days old and had all retrices and primaries ensheathed. Most of the young left when 8 or 9 days of age, when the retrices and primaries were just beginning to appear. About the third week of July most of the young being fed by the adults were unable to flutter more than a few yards and their tails scarcely showed. Many seemed to have been deserted and dead young were often found.

Wynne-Edwards (1952) suggests that the habit of leaving the nest early may in part be directly correlated with increasing the clutch size without increasing the size of the nest.

> Certainly towards the end the impression was given, both by the redpolls and the longspurs, that the nest was ready to burst and I was prepared at once to assume that dead chicks found in redpolls' nests had been suffocated. There is moreover the growing danger of attracting the arctic weasel as the young become daily noisier and as the odor of feces mounts. (The latter probably also attracts the blowflies, whose larvae were found in all the examined nests of longspurs, snow buntings, redpolls, and wheatears.) It is not difficult therefore to see advantages in scattering the brood as early as possible, since it reduces the danger both from predators and from overcrowding in the nest. But the parents are probably presented with a more difficult task in providing enough food for each of the young after they are scattered, and the young are also deprived of the protection from cold and wet, and in general the uniform environment which they have previously enjoyed in the nest. It may be presumed that the advantages outweigh the dangers, and that once the young have acquired sufficient control of body-temperature their chances of survival are increased by dispersal.

Two additional important points must not be overlooked: that the frequent marked disparity in size of the nestlings can result in one or more remaining in the nest only to be abandoned as Watson noted, and that the chief predators of fledged longspurs are avian ones, mainly jaegers, to which dispersed young are certainly more vulnerable than those in nests.

Density.—A number of authors have remarked on the generally high density of this species throughout the tundra regions. Manning et al. (1956) believed it to be by far the commonest and most generally distributed bird on Banks Island, and estimated the total adult summer population at 700,000. Likewise, Manning and Macpherson (1961) believed that the Lapland longspur was the commonest summer resident on Prince of Wales Island and from density figures of up to 56.8 birds per square mile estimated 250,000 present when nesting began. Sutton (1932) states that it was the most abundant bird on Southampton Island and comments on its general distribution. Drury (1961) refers to the longspur as the most numerous nesting species near his camp on Bylot Island (60 pairs in 7 square miles), and Wynne-Edwards (1952) states that at the head of Clyde Inlet on Baffin Island longspurs were the commonest birds, and in the most suitable habitats reached a density of one pair in 5 to 15 acres.

Much greater densities were recorded in Alaska, though this may have been due to the careful and intensive census methods used. The total population figures of young and adults can be exceedingly great in late summer, as mentioned in the account of the Alaskan subspecies.

Plumages.—As mentioned in the account of the Alaska longspur, the two races are only doubtfully distinguishable. The eastern race is somewhat darker and, according to Manning et al. (1956) the eastern *lapponicus* have wider and more deeply black centers in the dorsal feathers, and narrower more tawny and less buckthorn brown, but not markedly darker margins. The sequence of molts and plumages is the same in both races.

Winter.—In Minnesota, T. S. Roberts (1932) writes:

> During October and November immense flocks are passing southward across the state to winter in the southern Mississippi Valley beyond the winter range of the Snow Bunting. A very considerable number, however, remain in the southern half of Minnesota where they pass the winter months in the prairie and semi-prairie regions, generally in great flocks, often mingling with the Snowflakes or feeding about the corn-and-weed-fields with the hardy Horned Larks. * * * The northward movement begins in Minnesota in late February and early March, and during the latter month and April countless myriads of these birds are traversing the state toward their Arctic homes, going in great, endless flocks, generally by night but often by day as well, passing steadily onward, sometimes high in the air, sometimes low over the earth, an incessant, twittering, hurrying stream of birds.

On February 25, 1878, Roberts "Found a flock in an old corn-field where, rising from the ground, they circled around and around for some time, occasionally crossing and recrossing the circle, parting above and around me and streaming by within a few feet. At length, they settled on a near-by fence and showed very little fear at my presence." Again, he says on March 16, 1880:

When disturbed they would fly up two or three at a time and perch in the bushes, where, if not further molested, they would make an attempt at singing. On being startled into the air the whole flock circled about for a time, now and then leaving as if for good and as often returning to alight on the ground, or, in two or three instances, in the tops of a neighboring grove of small oaks. No sooner were they fairly settled in the trees than all burst out singing, and, although thus early in the season the individual effort was neither full nor continuous, the general chorus was quite loud and pleasing and kept up without breaks. The effect was very much like that produced by a flock of Blackbirds. These birds were not in very full plumage.

By April 23 the birds "were then in nearly full spring plumage and uttering an agreeable musical song." E. T. Seton (1891) describes generally similar behavior of spring migrants in Manitoba.

In Maine, R. S. Palmer (1949) quotes A. H. Norton's notes to the effect that: "the small flocks at Scarborough are found in sheltered places about the edges of grassy areas and out on the sand where vegetation is sparse. Here their food is mainly the seeds on the long spikes of marram grass (*Ammophila* sp.) and the seeds of orache (*Atriplex* sp.). Inland, they have been seen in fields where ragweed (*Ambrosia* sp.) and other weed stalks protrude above the snow. Associates, in decreasing order of frequency noted, are Horned Larks, Pipits, and Snow Buntings."

C. W. Townsend (1905) says that in Massachusetts "Lapland Longspurs, although occasionally found by themselves, are more apt to be associated with Horned Larks and Snow Buntings. Flying and feeding with these birds, they generally keep together, however, in one part of the flock, although a few scattered birds are not uncommon. They frequent the dunes at Ipswich and the neighboring hills by the sea * * *."

In a letter to Mr. Bent, Wendell Taber wrote: "On February 3, 1935, following a long spell of below-zero weather, I saw five of these birds on Ipswich beach in Massachusetts, accompanied by one snow bunting. My wife and I walked right up to the birds. A number of times I was within 4 to 6 feet of a bird. Ultimately I laid down and stretched out on my stomach near a bird. The bird kept right on feeding within a few feet of me, and came within 18 inches of my elbow. I watched it take a mouthful of snow and, seemingly, 'chew' it up and swallow it."

Geoffrey Carleton writes in a letter from New York:

On March 28,1965 Mr. John L. Bull, Eugene Eisenmann and I were on a remote part of the Kennedy International Airport. It was a sunny afternoon with a sharp, cold sea breeze. About 25 Lapland longspurs showed a preference for the tops of rocks piled along the shore as a breakwater, many of them evidently quarried for the purpose and 3 or 4 feet thick. Some of the longspurs were singing, particularly those most advanced into breeding plumage. Some were crouched so as to be more sheltered from the wind, and I believed they were taking advantage of the warmth of the rocks in the sun. After short flights or periods of feeding on a nearby grassy bank, the birds returned to the rocks and resumed singing.

Distribution

Range.—Central Franklin, Greenland, northern Russia, and northern Siberia south to northeastern Texas, southern Louisiana, northwestern Mississippi, southwestern Ohio, eastern West Virginia, and Virginia.

Breeding range.—The common Lapland longspur breeds from central Franklin (Banks, Prince Patrick, Melville, and Devon islands), Greenland (north to Thule and Scoresby Sound), Norway (lat. 71° N.), northern Russia (Arkhangelsk Government), Franz Josef Land, Novaya Zemlya, and the tundra of northern Siberia, including the New Siberian Islands and Wrangel Island, south to central western Keewatin (between Casba and Baker Lake: Hanbury River), northeastern Manitoba (Churchill), northern Ontario (Little Cape, Cape Henrietta Maria), northern Quebec (Cape Jones, Fort Chimo), northern Labrador (Okak), southern Greenland (Cape Farewell), southern Norway (Dovre), and central Sweden (lat. 63° N.); in eastern Siberia around the Gulf of Anadyr; recorded in summer north to Ellesmere Island (Slidre Fiord, Lake Hazen), and in Greenland to Germania Land.

Winter range.—Winters from central northern Colorado (Barr), central northern Nebraska (Wood Lake), central Minnesota (Otter Tail County), central Wisconsin (Oconto County), central Michigan (Newaygo and Tuscola counties), southern Ontario (Kitchener), southern Quebec (Aylmer), Vermont (St. Johnsbury), Maine (Lubec), New Brunswick (St. John), and central Nova Scotia (Grand Pré) south to Oklahoma, northeastern Texas (Dallas), southern Louisiana (Jennings, New Orleans), northwestern Mississippi (Rosedale), Alabama (south to Marion and Montgomery), western Tennessee (Memphis), southwestern Ohio (Hamilton County), eastern West Virginia (Moorefield), and Virginia (Blacksburg, Shenandoah National Park, Falls Church, Back Bay); casually to Utah (Tooele County), Georgia (Augusta), Florida (Wilson), and Bermuda; and from England, northern Europe, and central eastern Siberia to France, northern Italy, Rumania, southern Russia, and Altai, casually to Iceland.

Casual records.—Accidental in Baja California (Isla Cerralvo).

Migration.—The data deal with the species as a whole. Early dates of spring arrival are: Pennsylvania—State College, March 22. New York—Nassau County, February 7. Massachusetts—Martha's Vineyard, February 27. New Hampshire—New Hampton, March 15. Quebec—Seven Islands, May 25. Illinois—Urbana, February 12; Chicago, March 20 (average of 6 years, April 19). Michigan—Battle Creek, March 27. North Dakota—Red River Valley, February 19. British Columbia—Okanagan Landing, March 9; Mackenzie Delta,

May 16. Yukon—Sheldon Lake, April 29; Old Crow, May 4. Alaska—Yakutat, April 6; Unimak, April 16; Homer, April 19; Dyca, April 21; Amchitka Id., April 25; Adak, April 25; Cape Thompson May 2; Attu, May 2; Cold Bay, May 5; Fort Yukon, May 4; St. Michael, May 1; Pt. Barrow May 20.

Late dates of spring departure are: Alabama—Courtland, March 27. Georgia—Oysterbed Island, March 24. South Carolina—Long Island Fill, April 20. North Carolina—Raleigh, February 20. Virginia—Blacksburg, May 1. Maryland—Baltimore County, February 10. Pennsylvania—State College, April 4; Erie, March 25. New Jersey—Cape May, March 24. New York—Long Island, May 9. New Brunswick—Grand Manan, March 28. Louisiana—Baton Rouge, February 4. Missouri—St. Louis, April 15 (median of 8 years, March 2). Illinois—Chicago, May 13 (average of 6 years, May 7); Urbana, April 21. Ohio—central Ohio, April 12 (median of 40 years, March 25). Michigan—Detroit, April 24 (mean of 10 years, April 19). Iowa—Sioux City, April 4. Minnesota—Lac Qui Parle County, May 30 (average of 16 years for southern Minnesota, April 8). Oklahoma—Payne County, March 31. Kansas—northeastern Kansas, April 12 (median of 10 years, March 12). Nebraska—Red Cloud, April 18. North Dakota—Cass County, May 21 (average, May 18); Jamestown, April 25. Manitoba—Treesbank, February 20. Wyoming—Laramie, April 3 (average of 5 years, March 17). Montana—Gallatin County, April 17. Washington—Destruction Island, April 28. British Columbia—Atlin, May 15.

Early dates of fall arrival are: British Columbia—Kispiox Valley, September 1. Washington—Westport, September 5. Oregon—Siltcoos Lake, October 15. Nevada—Mercury, October 10. California—San Diego County, October 2. Montana—Deer Lodge County, October 30. Idaho—Fort Sherman, November 13. Wyoming—Laramie, October 7 (average of 8 years, November 2). Arizona—Coconino County, November 15. Manitoba—Treesbank, August 24 (average of 22 years, September 6). North Dakota—Cass County, September 10 (average, September 18); Jamestown, September 18. Nebraska—Red Cloud, November 28. Kansas—northeastern Kansas, November 1. Texas—Austin, November 27. Minnesota—Kittson County, September 8 (average of 5 years for northern Minnesota, October 21). Iowa—Sioux City, October 26. Michigan—Detroit area, September 25 (mean of 10 years, October 20). Ohio—central Ohio, November 1 (median of 40 years, November 15). Illinois—Chicago, September 17 (average of 11 years, October 4). Missouri—St. Louis, October 28 (median of 10 years, November 10). Tennessee—Nashville, December 31. Arkansas—Arkansas County, November 16. New Brunswick—Memramcook, October 1. New

Hampshire—Pittsburg, September 30; New Hampton, October 22. Massachusetts—Martha's Vineyard, October 18 (median of 5 years, November 1). New York—Long Island, October 3. New Jersey—Cape May, November 14. Pennsylvania—Erie, October 3; State College, October 26. Maryland—Laurel, December 3. Virginia—Shenandoah National Park, October 22. North Carolina—Swannanoa, November 14. South Carolina—Chester, January 1. Georgia—Augusta, January 1. Alabama—Gadsden, November 14; Marion, December 1. Florida—northwestern Florida, October 25.

Late dates of fall departure are: Alaska—Demarcation Point, September 2; Point Barrow, September 4; Nome, September 10; Attu, August 30; Glacier Bay, October 11; Kodiak, October 23; Cold Bay, October 25. Yukon—Macmillan Pass, September 4. British Columbia—Atlin, November 1. Manitoba—Treesbank, December 31 (average of 21 years, November 16). Kansas—northeastern Kansas, November 26. Illinois—Chicago, December 14 (average of 11 years, November 21). New York—Nassau County, November 26.

Egg dates.—Baffin Island: 52 records, June 12 to July 9; 25 records, June 22 to July 2.

Victoria Island: 61 records, June 11 to July 21; 31 records, June 15 to June 24.

Banks Island: 3 records, June 18 to July 10.

Bylot Island: 15 records, June 22 to July 4.

Manitoba: 15 records, June 12 to June 29.

Prince of Wales Island: 3 records, June 28 to July 1.

Southampton Island: 78 records, June 21 to July 17.

CALCARIUS LAPPONICUS ALASCENSIS Ridgway

Alaska Longspur

PLATES 76 AND 77

Contributed by FRANCIS S. L. WILLIAMSON

HABITS

It is frequently said that every biologist should, at least once during his life, visit the tropics, particularly an equatorial rain forest with its amazing wealth of plant and animal species and its concomitant ecological complexity. More than elsewhere on earth the tropical environment affords unequalled opportunity to gain appreciation for evolutionary diversification. I think, however, it must also be said that every naturalist should at some time visit the arctic tundra, a relatively bleak and windswept environment characterized by a striking diminution of species of plants and animals and a concomitant ecological simplicity. These are factors which tend to make studies of adaptation and of ecological relations especially rewarding.

For the vertebrate ecologist or zoologist there is no more suitable subject for studies of such relations than the Lapland longspur, in all likelihood the most characteristic species of vertebrate animal to be found throughout the arctic. The extensive circumpolar breeding range of this species is equaled by few other birds, and the generally consistent high density of individuals over such a vast area is likely not equaled at all. The Lapland longspur is found on the tundra of Kamchatka west through Siberia to Scandinavia, Franz Joseph Land, Greenland, northern Canada, and Alaska. In winter it can be found occupying large areas of southern Europe, Russia and China as well as most of the United States.

The great bulk of this imposing range is occupied by one subspecies, *lapponicus*, while two others, *coloratus* (Commander Islands, Kamchatka), and *alascensis* (Alaska, N. Yukon, N. W. Mackenzie) occupy more restricted areas. In Alaska, principal breeding area for the race *alascensis*, the distribution conforms essentially to the treeless coastal regions and islands. These include a relatively broad belt of tundra extending from the Arctic coast south and west along the Chukchi and Bering Sea to the base of the Alaska Peninsula. Westward in the Aleutian Islands the range extends to Attu (Murie, 1959). More peripheral range includes a small nesting group on Middleton Island in the Gulf of Alaska (Rausch, 1958), St. Lawrence Island (Fay and Cade, 1959), and the Pribilof Islands (Preble and McAtee, 1923). In the interior of Alaska longspurs occupy areas above timber in scattered localities including the Talkeetna Mountains (Schaller, MS) and the central Alaska Range (Dixon, 1938).

The habitat these small birds occupy within this geographic range includes nearly all that of open character. Generally excluded are the extremely wet marshlands and meadows except as these contain more elevated areas such as hummocks or ridges where nests can be placed. The very xeric communities such as the *Dryas* and lichen-clad rocky fellfields of the hills and mountains are also avoided. Otherwise, in such widespread arctic and sub-arctic vegetation as sedge tussocks (*Eriophorum*), the meadow-like tundra of *Carex*, low, ankle-high areas of willow (*Salix*), and in expanses of low dwarf-birch (*Betula*) intermixed with various heaths, the Lapland longspur is the most numerous bird of the north.

The subspecies of Lapland longspurs are differentiated primarily on the basis of color. For the most part the differences are slight, as pointed out by the following brief review. F. G. Salomonsen (1950) believes the longspurs of Greenland, on the basis of a larger bill and paler color, are separable from those of Scandinavia and for these he utilizes the name *C. l. subcalcaratus* (Brehm). He includes all the birds of Canada and Alaska within this subspecies and states: "The N. American population comes nearest to *C. l. subcalcaratus* and is best referred to that form; *C. l. alascensis* Ridgway is hardly worth recognition." H. Johansen (1958) adopts this system and states "Three population groups can be separated: *lapponicus* in Eurasia, *subcalcaratus* in North-America and Greenland, and *colaratus* on the Commander Islands and Kamchatka." Portenko (1960) believes that the birds from Kamchatka are subspecifically distinct and has given them the name *kamtschaticus*. Manning et al. (1956) indicate that the birds of Baffin Island are even paler, and thus further removed from the nominate race than those of Greenland, although they prefer to leave the nomenclature unchanged pending a direct comparison of good series of specimens. They suggest that the failure of Salomonsen to recognize *alascensis* might be due to his lack of specimens in fresh autumn plumage for the comparison that demonstrates their distinctness.

In general, a weak cline of increasing paleness extends from Greenland to the Aleutian Islands. Over this vast area, there is no convenient or realistic point at which to make a subspecific distinction and, indeed, allocation to subspecies of specimens from Banks Island (Manning et al. 1956) is difficult under the present system. It seems reasonable that Salomonsen and Johansen have made the best interpretation of the situation.

With respect to differences in habits or behavior it is apparent that these vary little or none at all among the different races. Familiarity with the extensive literature dealing with this species combine with my own field experience over a period of 9 years, including 3 years when I conducted an intensive study of populational phenomena at Cape Thompson, Alaska, confirm this belief. The bulk of the account which follows derives from my own study at the latter locality.

Spring.—The wintering ground of the Alaska longspur includes the southern part of British Columbia and the bulk of the western United States south to New Mexico and Texas. Migration from this area in spring must begin in March and early April as longspurs appear as early as April 6 in southeastern Alaska (Grinnell, 1910). I have observed migrants at Anchorage, Alaska, as early as April 24, and at Homer, Alaska, on April 19.

The general course of travel appears to be northwestward through British Columbia and Yukon Territory and northward through the western Mackenzie Valley (Irving, 1961). There is also a coastal movement of birds whose arrival times are somewhat different from

Johnson River, Alaska, June 15, 1946

L. H. Walkinshaw

ALASKA LONGSPUR FEEDING YOUNG

those of longspurs moving through the interior. Irving has taken latitude 50° N. and longitude 134° W. as representing the northwestern sector of the wintering area and points out that from that locality migration extends 20° north and 14° west to the eastern border of the breeding range in Mackenzie, while to the west in the Aleutian Islands, migration extends 67°, but represents only a 4° northward advance. The average arrival time for four years at Atlin, British Columbia was April 22 (Swarth, 1936). This station is located in the path of large migratory flights moving westward to Alaska and from whence the general sequence of northward movement may be traced (Irving, 1961).

Arrival in western and northern Alaska varies from the last of April until mid-May with an average arrival date of about May 10. The consistent arrival in April in southeastern and south-central Alaska and the Aleutian Islands indicates a coastal migration independent of the major movements of birds through the interior.

The first flocks are entirely or preponderantly comprised of males, and these are followed in a few days by flocks that are preponderantly females. Arrival of the longspurs coincides with the rapidly retreating snow cover and the increasing availability of nesting habitat. Late snowfall, especially in the arctic, is not uncommon and the weather is characteristically unsettled when the birds appear.

Courtship.—Courtship and pair formation take place after the birds have arrived on the nesting ground. Scattered males take up residency on the tundra and show signs of increasing territoriality. At this time, usually mid-May, small groups of males continue to remain together quietly feeding, and intermittent stormy weather may cause others to leave the newly established or forming territories and regroup temporarily in sheltered areas such as willow-clad stream bottoms. Singing on the wing, or less commonly from more elevated parts of the territory such as sedge tussocks, commences rather abruptly after the males arrive. Territorial disputes, including spirited chasing of neighboring males at the borders of the territories, and alternate singing with adjacent males are commonplace. Some of the chases are long-lived with the pursuing male seemingly within inches of the fleeing adversary, and maneuvering adroitly to remain there as they are lost from view.

Actual contact between rival males is not uncommon and one intruder was seen to land on the back of a silently feeding male, thus initiating a prolonged and erratic chase during which he was routed. On another occasion two males approached to within a foot of one another on the ground; both crouched down in a threat posture for a moment, whereupon the intruder flew off a short distance and the remaining bird resumed his feeding between the tussocks. The intruder returned promptly and struck the feeding bird. This initiated new threat posturing with the birds crouching low and spreading their wings slightly.

As the females continue to arrive in increasing numbers and disperse over the tundra, the attention of the males is attracted more and more toward them. Courtship flights are common, and two or three males are frequently involved in chases of an individual female. The male pursues the female in frequently lengthy and circuitous flights and finally lands a few feet from her. Common behavior during these pauses is for the male to peck at the ground and move closer to the female until she flies up to the top of a tussock thus initiating a new flight. His actions seem to indicate that he is physiologically predisposed to copulation and is so motivated by the female's presence. When her response is not one soliciting copulation, his actions may be carried over into the displacement activity of pecking. Later, as the female becomes motivated toward breeding, probably largely due to the persistence of the chasing male, she may react by reciprocal chasing.

Drury (1961) states that:

> Pursuit flights were obviously mutual affairs and, I believe, closely associated with pair formation. They were longer, slower, and with less zigzagging than territorial skirmishes. If the male caught up, there was a burst of rapid zigzagging but if he fell far behind, the female slowed down until he overtook her. We saw these flights before any displays on the ground, and throughout the period of ground displaying. Male No. 6, displaying to his female, ran across in front of her or up to her side, standing at about a 60° angle to the horizontal, with his breast feathers fluffed out, head held high and bill pointed slightly up, wings about half spread, drooped and quivering. While he ran in this way he was singing his regular flight song. The female ran slowly ahead of him, crouched in a horizontal position with her head partly lowered, wings partly spread, tail cocked just above horizontal, calling *zeep, zeep.* * * * She and the male often pecked stiffly at the ground. * * * The chestnut nape emphasized the stiff bow by the male. The female ran around and ahead of him; then flew; if he did not follow, she came back and repeated her actions until he did chase. During the chases she landed several times, ran along the ground, then flew again, fast and darting, or slowly and on quivering wings. During the period of pursuits, because their attention was on the females, males sang less often and chiefly on the ground.

In the presence of a female the advertising and/or territorial song flight was seen to be modified into a courtship display. The male performed this flight in the usual manner, with the tail spread and wings near the horizontal in a gliding path. The entire flight is only a few feet in length; it is performed only a short distance above the ground a few feet from the female, and the male often carries nest material, apparently sedge or grass, in his bill. The chases, both aerial and on the ground, together with the modified display flights wherein the male may carry nesting material, ultimately result in the female becoming receptive to copulation.

Drury (1961) describes similar behavior as precopulatory:

> Above nest No. 3 * * * I saw the male rise with fluttering flight straight up into the air, flying with difficulty because of a wad of dark material in his bill * * * . Before flying, he stood vertically, bill horizontal or pointed up, wings drooped at his sides, and tail spread and lowered. He sang with this material in his bill and succeeded in getting about 20 feet off the ground, then sang as he fluttered down again. He picked up even more material, and hopped onto a stone. He had so much in his bill now that he could not get off the ground, but he could sing. He stood a few moments and readjusted the material in his bill, put it down and picked it up again; then he pointed his bill up and fluttered his wings without getting off the ground. * * *
>
> When approaching the female the male held his head high, neck extending and bill horizontal, with all the accumulation of dark material in his bill. He dropped the load and pointed his bill straight up, showing his black throat, while he dragged his wings as he walked up to her. Then he lowered his head, ruffled his scapular, back and rump feathers, and widely spread his tail * * * . She crouched with head low, tail cocked up, wings quivering and partly spread. He fluttered over and, without hovering, mounted on her back in the same position he had assumed in front of her, and copulated. After copulation he hopped off and walked in front of her in the same crouched position, while she stood up, raised her bill straight up and cocked her tail as high as possible, chattering.

Belligerence of a male toward a female was witnessed on one occasion when pairs from adjoining territories came into contact. The male of one of these pairs assumed a crouching threat posture with wings slightly spread before the female of the other pair. No other aggressive action was taken.

On another occasion the quiet side-by-side foraging of a male and female was interrupted by a violent struggle between them. They chattered loudly and actually seized one another with their bills. The male routed the female and came away with a bill full of feathers. Whether or not these birds constituted a pair was not determined, but in any event the hostile, defensive motivation of the male was apparently released by the female's proximity.

Toward the end of May, as early as the 26th, the intensity of song and other territorial behavior of the mated males begins to subside. This becomes marked by the end of May, and as early as June 3 mated males were seen to tolerate the presence of other males singing around and over their territories. By June 12 song and territoriality virtually cease. In late May and early June it is commonplace to see two, three, or less frequently four males following a single female as she forages about the territory. The resident male often tries to drive off these intruders, but apparently a diminished agressiveness in the face of unfavorable odds nullifies his efforts. One explanation for the presence of these seemingly surplus males is that they are unmated, but this implies an unusually disproportionate sex ratio not at all consonant with what is known of passerine birds generally, and when all longspur nests on a given area are censused, the number of males in the area, whether counted in small groups or singly, generally agrees with the nest count.

Coincident with incubation and the general subsidence of territorial behavior, the males are attracted to any female who happens to be away from a nest. Undoubtedly a few males and females are unmated, and these together with birds that have lost nests, may commence flocking by mid-June. Males collected from obvious small flocks in generally uninhabited areas had testes smaller than those of the breeding component of the population.

Nesting.—A striking feature of arctic bird life generally is the sudden onset of nesting after the arrival of the migratory birds. The Lapland longspur is an example of a species that has compressed this interval to a minimum. With the arrival of the females, which may be as much as two weeks after that of the males, the nesting cycle is set rapidly in motion. The females start nest-building as promptly as four days later, and many records show nest-building spans just three days.

Edward W. Nelson's (1887) comments on general nest structure indicate that considerable size variation is commonplace:

> The walls are thick and strong, composed of an abundance of material, or they may be a mere cup-shaped shell, barely sufficient to hold the eggs. The majority of nests are composed of rather coarse grass, sometimes with moss interwoven, forming a thick layer, which was frequently as thoroughly water-soaked as a wet sponge when the nest was collected. The amount of material used depends greatly upon the locality; in damp places a much greater amount is made use of, while in dry places the nests are much lighter. Though the outer part of the nest was frequently formed of old and often grimy or partly decayed vegetable matter, the interior was invariably composed of fine, soft, dry, yellow blades of last year's grasses. These in many instances are unmixed with other material, and in others are combined with feathers of the Ptarmigan or other wild fowl. In a few cases the lining of the nest is a warm cup of feathers resting upon fine grass, and one has a thick lining of feathers and dogs' hair. Some nests are so small that they may be inclosed in the hand, while others can scarcely be inclosed by both, and the smallest nest collected may be inserted entire into the cavity of the largest one.

I feel that much of this size variation can be attributed to the use of a nest from a previous year. Nest depressions, and undoubtedly the old material they contain, are used repeatedly. This material may be carried to a new site and made into a more compact nest, or it may be simply left in place, slightly modified, and then lined with fresh grass. Such a nest would be considerably larger both in bulk and size of the opening than a new one. The virtual impossibility of finding old, unoccupied nests suggests that the premium placed on particular nest locations is great and their reuse routine. Nevertheless, my examination of many nests failed to reveal variation in size of the magnitude Nelson indicates.

Further variation in lining, apparently depending on availability of materials, is indicated by the remarks of J. W. Bee (1958) who found nests lined with snowy owl feathers and caribou hair, and A. M. Bailey (1943) who also found a nest lined with caribou hair. The slightly more than 100 nests I have found were all lined with nothing but willow or rock ptarmigan feathers.

Herbert Brandt (1943) gives the measurements in inches for 21 nests as follows: height 3 to 7, outside diameter 4 to 6.5, inside diameter 3 to 3.5, and depth of cup 2.5 to 3.5.

The nests are nearly always placed in depressions in the sides of small hummocks of moss or sedge (*Carex*) or in the sides of tussocks of grass (*Calamagrostis*) or sedge (*Eriophorum*). Invariably some vegetation hangs over the nest, usually grass or sedge, or it may be hidden by the leafy twigs of willow (*Salix*) or various ericaceous plants. Nests are also placed in more level terrain such as *Carex* meadows or alluvial flats grown to low willows, usually in the drier parts, and well hidden beneath the vegetation.

The nest nearly always has one conspicuous entrance, which compass readings showed to be generally on the south side. The prevailing wind in the study area was from the north, but longspurs at other locations tended to orient the nest opening similarly, probably to take advantage of the greater insolation from that direction. A. V. Mikheev (1939), working in Russia, observed that the bowls of the nests were inclined to the east, south, or southeast, a phenomenon he attributed to the rarity of southeast winds during the nesting season. At Cape Thompson south winds are also uncommon, but nonetheless they are the ones associated with summer storms and precipitation.

The general habitat utilized for nesting has been described earlier in this paper. In summary, it can be said that longspurs are adaptable in their choice of nesting locations, requiring primarily only open terrain with concealing vegetation, either hillside or flatland, and there preferring the more xeric sites with microrelief such as tussocks, hummocks, and low ridges. The use of the term xeric here is decidedly relative. Truly xeric areas such as rocky hillsides are assiduously avoided, and the remainder of the northern landscape, all mesic by general terminology, is inhabited. Here, however, a distinction must be made between areas with actual standing water and those only moist underfoot. The latter are most densely occupied, and the preference for elevated sites is conspicuous. Thus the comment by many authors that the Lapland longspur requires and selects moist areas for nesting is misleading.

Eggs.—The Lapland longspur usually lays five eggs although in my experience the mean number is somewhat less. In 44 nests I studied at Cape Thompson in 1960 the average clutch size was 4.7. Although slightly more than 50 percent were 5-egg clutches the number of eggs laid ranged from 1 to 6. The clutch of one egg, and another of only two, were dutifully incubated and apparently were not the result of eggs having been lost. In 1961 the average clutch size was 4.9 eggs in 64 nests, and the range was from 2 to 6; slightly more than 60 percent were 5-egg clutches. Herbert Brandt (1943) studied 28 nests at Hooper Bay and found an average clutch size of 5.5 with 16 nests containing 6 eggs and 12 containing 5 eggs.

It seems likely that had Brandt observed a larger number of nests this mean number would not have been so much higher (nearly one egg) than the average per clutch at Cape Thompson. Clutches of three or fewer eggs generally represent renesting attempts and perhaps should not be included in these computations. They do not necessarily represent late nestings, and no evidence was obtained to indicate that clutch size declined as the season advanced. True second nestings are apparently nonexistent, renesting is uncommon, and such variation as exists in number of eggs relates only to the single clutch laid by each female at very nearly the same time during the nesting period.

The shape, color, and size of the eggs are extremely variable as the following descriptions will indicate. The shape is ovate tending to elongate, to ovate and the surface is slightly glossy. The ground color is pale greenish-white, but on most eggs it appears to be "buffy brown" owing to the confluence of spots, blotches, and cloudings of "Hay's brown," "Saccardo's umber," "bister," or "mummy brown." This is not to imply a blotchy appearance, as generally the background color tends toward uniformity. Most eggs have scattered spots or scrawls of black. Undermarkings when visible are "light mouse gray," and occasionally this is the predominant color of the egg, with only a few spots or scrawls of dark brown or black. The markings are fairly evenly distributed over the entire surface.

Gabrielson and Lincoln (1959) describe the eggs as "light greenish-gray, heavily marked with shades of brown."

Joseph Grinnell (1900) describes a clutch of eggs as nearly oblong-ovate in shape with a ground color, disclosed only at the ends of the eggs, as very pale blue. He states further that "Otherwise the eggs are so completely covered with pigment as to be almost uniform isabella-color. Overlying this are scattered scrawls and dots of bistre."

Nelson (1887) described the ground color of the eggs as light clay with a pale greenish tinge. He found eggs covered with a coarse blotching of reddish brown, principally at the large end, some with a fine reddish brown specking, and others with varying types and intensities of marking including spots, spots and blotches, and irregular zigzag markings of dark umber brown. The markings become heavier and darker colored (chocolate brown) until the ground color may be entirely concealed, or revealed as only a faint mottling of olive-brownish.

The measurements of 40 eggs average 21.1 by 15.1 millimeters; the eggs showing the four extremes measure *22.9* by 15.3, 22.8 by *16.3*, 20.8 by *13.7*, and *19.3* by 14.2 millimeters.

Incubation.—A few records indicate a one-day pause between the completion of the nest and the laying of the first egg, but usually the first egg is laid the day the nest is finished, and one is then laid each successive day until the clutch is complete. Effective incubation apparently begins with the 3rd or 4th egg in the usual 5-egg clutch. In some cases it may start with the second egg, but apparently almost never with the laying of the first egg. The variation in the time of onset of incubation is evidenced by the commonly observed spread of hatching over a 1- to 3-day period. Incubation is by the female alone and is of 12 or 13 days duration, measured between the laying and hatching of the last egg in the clutch. Data from 14 complete nest-histories showed eight 12-day incubation periods and six of 13 days.

As both Nelson (1887) and Brandt (1943) point out, the male stays nearby during incubation and utters alarm notes when danger threatens. Early during the incubation period the female's usual reaction is to leave the nest when an intruder is still some distance away, fly 10 to 20 or more yards, alight often near the male, and begin foraging. Both birds may utter alarm calls, and the female may fly from tussock to tussock or other vantage points while watching the intruder. Usually within 5 or 10 minutes after the intruder retires, she returns to the nest in a series of short flights interspersed with brief periods of foraging and watching. The last abrupt flight takes her directly to the nest; only once have I seen a female walk to the nest.

As the time of hatching approaches the attentiveness of the incubating female increases noticeably. She shows a marked reluctance to leave the nest and frequently remains on it until approached very closely. Then she flies only a few feet, often chattering loudly and plaintively. Alighting with wings slightly spread and drooped and tail fanned against the ground, she runs fluttering in this position away from the nest. The responses of individual females when forced from the nest vary considerably. Some may omit either the alarm notes or the distraction display, or both.

Clutches of four or more eggs take between 24 and 48 hours to hatch, and may take as long as 72 hours. While I have no definite evidence of longer hatching periods, a few of the nest histories from Cape Thompson suggest that it could have run to a maximum of 96 hours. Only one nest with 4 eggs was observed to hatch completely in 24 hours.

Young.—The most striking single feature in the development of young longspurs is their early departure from the nest, well before the plumage develops enough to permit flight.

My records from Cape Thompson show that most young leave the next after 8 to 10 days, with an average nest life of 9 days. A few histories show departure as early as the 7th day and as late as the 11th. The young left two nests in 6 days, probably because the nests were disturbed. W. J. Maher (1964) reported the nestling period at Barrow, Alaska, averaged 7.4 days with a range of 6 to 8 days. This relatively brief time was undoubtedly influenced somewhat by nest disturbance. Maher reported that the average weight of longspurs at hatching is 2.3 gm. and increases to 18.8 gm. 7 days later. When the longspur is able to fly on about the 12th day it averages about 21.9 gm. or 80.5 per cent of its adult weight. Maher noted that the gaping response is weak on the day of hatching and grasping with the feet appears on the 2nd day. The fear response of huddling down in the nest appeared on the 5th day and escape was attempted by the 7th day.

My records show that the young usually leave the nest over a two-day period, although in some instances all young left the nest within 24 hours. In one case the departure of six young apparently spanned 3 to 4 days. It is not uncommon for one young bird to remain in the nest a day or two longer than his nestmates, especially in the larger broods. This might be due to later hatching and/or to difficulty in getting a proportionate share of the food, for disparity in nestling size is commonplace.

The sexes share equally in the feeding of the young birds. After leaving the nest the brood is often split and each adult cares for a portion of the young. Maher (1964) inclosed nests with a fence and observed that the young begin to fly on the 12th day. At Cape Thompson fledging success was 1.68 young per pair of adults in 38 nests in 1960 and 1.9 in 53 nests in 1961.

Density.—The following figures may bear out the belief expressed earlier that the Lapland longspur is very likely the most numerous bird in the north. At Cape Thompson the density per 100 acres was 14 pairs in low riparian willows, and up to 59 and 65 pairs in the widespread plant formations of *Eriophorum* tussocks and *Carex* meadow. Extrapolating these figures for larger areas of generally uniform habitat, such as *Eriophorum* tussock tundra, yields such total population figures as 11,800 breeding birds in 10,000 acres. With 1.9 young reared per pair, the total number of fledglings and adults present on this expanse in mid to late summer is about 22,200. *Eriophorum* tundra is the dominant plant communtiy not only of the Cape Thompson area, but of the entire foothill region of the arctic slope of Alaska (Spetzman, 1959). The lowland areas that are largely covered with *Carex* meadows may support even greater population densities.

Plumages.—The natal down is basally light tan in color, shading to yellow and gray for the distal third (Maher, 1964). Dwight (1900) states that the juvenal plumage is acquired by a complete post-natal molt. Maher shows that the nestlings appear feathered by the 7th day and can fly by the 12th day, although the primaries are still growing. The juvenal plumage is described by Gabrielson and Lincoln (1959) and by Dwight (1900) generally as follows: upper parts and sides of head rich buff, tawny buff, or clay-colored, streaked heavily with black; wings and tail deep clove brown; tertiaries and greater coverts edged with "Mars brown" and white-tipped; lesser coverts edged with white, primaries and tail with pale cinnamon; outer rectrices terminally buffy white; below dull white, washed with buff across the throat; the chin, throat, chest, and sides streaked with black.

The postjuvenal molt begins about 3 weeks after fledging and involves mainly the body plumage and part of the wing coverts. It coincides generally with the timing of the complete molt of the adults. At its end the adults and immatures become, for all practical purposes, indistinguishable.

Dwight (1900) describes the first winter plumage of the male as follows:

> Above, wood-brown and cinnamon streaked with clove-brown, the nape and sides of neck chestnut concealed by wood-brown edgings; lesser coverts edged with wood-brown. Median crown stripe, superciliary line, and anterior auriculars buff, posterior auriculars black. Below, white, the feathers everywhere dusky basally, the sides of chin and a crescentic area on the throat jet black veiled almost completely by long white edgings; the sides and flanks streaked with black.

Dwight further states that the first nuptial plumage is

> acquired by a partial prenuptial moult beginning in March in the United States which involves the anterior parts of the head, chin and throat. The black feathers of these areas and the creamy white ones of the sides of the head are acquired by moult contrasting with the chestnut collar which is assumed by loss of feather edgings. This moult does not usually extend to the posterior portion of the black throat patch where old black feathers with partly worn-off edgings are regularly found. Wear produces a distinctly black and white streaked appearance above with the collar clear chestnut as if unveiled.

The adult winter plumage is acquired by a complete post nuptial molt in July and August. Dwight notes it as "practically indistinguishable in many cases from the first winter plumage, but the black on the chin and throat is more extensive, and the colors richer and deeper, especially the wing edgings." At Cape Thompson the complete molt begins during the last part of June and is essentially complete in all members of the population by the end of August. Timing of molt is similar for both sexes and takes about 50 days to complete. The earliest dates for inception of the annual molt of males and females were June 25 and July 2, respectively, while molt started as late as July 5 in males and July 11 in females. Postjuvenal molt was observed to begin as early as July 10. The striking degree of synchrony manifest in the timing of molt accords with the brevity of the arctic summer and the short time available for this activity.

The adult nuptial plumage of the male is acquired by a partial prenuptial molt as in the young birds. Gabrielson and Lincoln (1959) describe this plumage as follows:

Head and chest deep black, relieved by a broad white or buffy stripe behind eye, continued downward (vertically) behind ear coverts and then backward along sides of chest; ground color of upperparts light grayish brown, with little if any rusty tinge, even on wings; sides narrowly streaked or striped with black; rest of underparts white; hindneck deep chestnut rufous; lesser wing coverts grayish, feathers black in center. Outer tail feathers white, dusky along midrib and on inner web toward base; the tail feathers narrowly edged with grayish white; lining of wing and axillaries grayish white. Bill dark, lighter at base; legs and feet black; iris brown.

The plumages and molts of the female according to Dwight (1900)

correspond to those of the male, but the black throat patch is never so extensive and usually merely outlined with dull black streaks. The juvenal plumage is indistinguishable from that of the male. The first winter plumage is much veiled and streaked above with clove and cinnamon brown, the nape vinaceous; below it is white obscurely black on the sides of the chin and with a small throat patch, the sides and flanks black streaked. The first nuptial plumage is chiefly the result of wear, a few white feathers being acquired by moult on the chin.

Gabrielson and Lincoln (1959) describe the plumage of the adult breeding female as follows: "A dull-colored bird, striped above with dull black, rufous, and grayish white; an indistinct median light line on crown; collar on hindneck pale rufous, finely streaked with dusky; feathers of throat and breast black, concealed in part by grayish white and pale buffy margins of feathers, producing a mottled or streaked appearance; sides and flanks striped with dull black and pale rufous; rest of underparts white; tail and wings as in male." The adult winter plumage of the female is like that of the first winter with perhaps more black on the throat.

H. S. Swarth (1934) records colors of the soft parts quite accurately, noting that in the young male the upper mandible is yellowish brown with pale yellow edges, the lower mandible a grayish flesh color, and the tarsus and toes brownish flesh color. The adults in summer have a lemon-yellow bill with a black tip, the iris is brown, and the tarsus and toes are dark brown.

Food.—Gabrielson (1924) made an exhaustive examination of 656 stomachs, including 113 previously reported on by S. D. Judd, taken from birds collected in Alaska, five provinces in Canada, and 15 states of the United States, during every month of the year. He classifies 56 stomachs from Alaska and northern Canada, June to September inclusive, as representing "summer," with the remainder being "winter." Beetles, mostly chrysomelids and weevils, constituted 11.91 percent of the summer food. Fly remains, almost entirely the eggs and adults of crane-flies (Tipulidae) constituted 17.77 percent. Caterpillars, spiders, bugs, and fragments of other insects accounted for 17.75 percent. Total animal food was thus 47.43 percent of all food. Grass seeds formed 12.02 percent, seeds of sedges 4.16 percent, seeds of a variety of other plants 27.86 percent. Bits of grass and unidentified vegetable debris formed the remaining 8.53 percent.

These foods differ little from those observed through study of the contents of 90 stomachs taken at Cape Thompson during the summer of 1960. Animal and plant food were taken in approximately equal amounts with only a slight preference shown for the former. Important animal groups selected in order of occurrence in the stomachs were beetles (Coleoptera), flies (Diptera), wasps (Hymenoptera), bugs (Homoptera), and spiders (Araneae).

Gabrielson points out that over half of the 600 "winter" stomachs were taken in Kansas under very similar conditions. They contained largely millet and crabgrass seeds; animal food comprised only 3.97 percent, and four birds that had fed almost exclusively on carabid beetles of the genera *Platynus* and *Amara* accounted for half this total. Other animal food was chrysomelids, weevils, fly larvae, caterpillars, and spiders taken in varying quantities in every month except February. Goose-grass (*Eleusine*) was an important item, as were also sedge seeds. Seeds of purslane (*Portulaca*) were common but, owing to small size, made up only 0.82 percent of the bulk. Seeds of pigweed (*Amaranthus*) comprised 6.03 percent. Goose-foot (*Chenopodium*) and ragweed (*Ambrosia*) seeds were favored. Wheat formed 8.33 percent of the food and was eaten in every one of the eight months except October.

At Cape Thompson the young appeared to be fed animal food exclusively. This was also the observation of Rowell (1956) who noted that young longspurs were fed mainly adult Diptera, particularly culicids and chironomids, and were also given some beetles and caterpillars.

During 1960 the adults showed no clear pattern of food preference with the changing season. For approximately two weeks during late May and early June animal foods were taken to the near exclusion of plant foods, while prior to and following that period nearly equal amounts of both were eaten. The important point is that this arctic species is markedly adaptable in its diet and, depending on the day to day availability of certain items, readily switches to the most easily acquired foods.

G. W. Rawson (1954) comments on feeding behavior of this species in the Brooks Range of northern Alaska as follows:

> Mosquitoes collected in large numbers on the outside of a white canvas tent two of us were using as living quarters. Several small flocks of immature Alaska Longspurs soon "caught on" to the fact that the tent acted as an ideal trap or concentration camp for mosquitoes and diligently fed on them both day and night. At first (before knowing what was causing the disturbance) the longspurs were quite perturbing because one or more would lose their footing and slide down the inclined roof of the tent causing a ripping sound suggestive of someone or something trying to rip open the canvas.

More commonly observed feeding behavior consists of constant walking about quietly concealed in such vegetation as sedge tussocks, often seemingly quite oblivious to the observer. Extremely strong winds seem to have no effect on the birds' ability to find insects, and the young are fed just as constantly during gales that make flight difficult much above the ground.

Behavior.—The general pattern of breeding behavior as detailed in the preceding sections, together with other facets of the annual cycle of the Lapland longspur, can be briefly reviewed as follows:

After a winter spent in flocks on the open country of the western and mid-western United States the birds begin the spring migration north to the breeding grounds of Alaska, Yukon Territory, and the Northwest Territories in March and April.

At Cape Thompson, in northwestern Alaska, the males arrived as early as May 5th, an event marked by the abrupt onset of song and display. Territorial disputes become commonplace, and defensive behavior involves chases, sometimes with actual physical contact, and threat posturing. Singing on the wing or from elevated points in the area seems virtually incessant. In less suitable habitat a male may defend an area roughly seven acres in size, while in favorable vegetation the territory is reduced to approximately two acres.

The females arrive as early as May 18. The attention of the males is turned toward them, courtship flights begin, and copulation may be observed as early as May 21. The end of May sees a marked subsidence of territorial behavior. Nest-building begins as early as May 23 and takes three days; only the female performs this task. The eggs are laid on successive days immediately following the completion of the nest. The average clutch consists of 4.7 to 4.9 eggs and these are incubated for 12 days. The young birds remain in the nest for an average of 9 days and begin flying at the age of 12 days. Molt is initiated promptly in late June and early July, and the birds gather in small flocks by mid-July.

The longspur flocks feed quietly on the ground and may go unnoticed until approached closely. Gabrielson and Lincoln (1959) describe this flocking behavior very well:

> After the breeding season, they gather in small groups, which gradually unite into flocks that sometimes consist of thousands of individuals by the time they reach their wintering grounds in the northern States. These flocks have the characteristic habit of taking flight when alarmed, flying in great sweeping circles, and then returning to alight on the same spot or very close to it. At other times, however, they may take off and go straight away, completely out of sight, before alighting again.

As the birds move morthward in spring the behavior differs somewhat as the compact flocks pause only to feed for a short time before moving on.

These aggregations take flight readily and seem unusually wary when contrasted with the tameness of the individuals scattered on their nesting territories. Their behavior is frequently like that Grinnell (1900) observed at Kotzebue Sound: "I would frequently meet with a male longspur standing motionless on some conspicuous hummock. If I approached too close he would attempt to get out of my way by stealthily running to one side, but if pressed he would take flight and mount upwards, circling high overhead and uttering his pleasing song." I also have noted that territorial males pressed into flight often respond by initiating the flight song.

Voice.—The varied vocalizations of this species include the conspicuous song of the breeding male, call notes, the alarm notes of both sexes, the alarm notes of the female when frightened from the nest, and flocking notes used during the non-breeding season.

Nelson (1887) writes vividly of the song of the male:

> The males, as if conscious of their handsome plumage, choose the tops of the only breaks in the monotonous level, which are small rounded knolls and tussocks. The male utters its song as it flies upward from one ofthese knolls and when it reaches the height of 10 or 15 yards it extends the points of its wings upwards, forming a large V-shaped figure, and floats gently to the ground, uttering, as it slowly sinks, its liquid tones, which fall in tinkling succession upon the ear, and are perhaps the sweetest notes that one hears during the entire spring-time in these regions. It is an exquisite jingling melody, having much less power than that of the Bobolink, but with the same general character, and, though shorter, it has even more melody that the song of that well-known bird.

This quotation is slightly misleading in that the bird seldom begins the song during the preliminary, upward flight.

The behavior of singing birds I witnessed at Cape Thompson did not differ from that Drury recorded (1961) on Bylot Island, which is briefly as follows: males occasionally sing from conspicuous perches on the ground, but the usual song is given in a flight during which the male rises to a height of 20 to 40 feet and then settles slowly to the ground singing several songs in rapid succession. During windy periods the birds often sing several songs while hovering overhead. Drury notes that "Songs started with a ringing and metallic *zing*, followed by a rolling and rapidly descending *zizeleeaw*; then a rolling, sustained *zizelee-ee* (ending with the highest note of the song *ee*), and closed with another rapid rolling and descending *zizeleeaw*." Drury also uses the syllables *see*, *serilee-aw*, *serilee-ee*, *serileeaw* to describe the rapidly descending flight song, and these seem to me excellent word representations of the sounds. He also reports a "whisper" song containing the same elements as the full song, but usually shorter, and given only by the male when in close company with the female before the start of nest-building. This I never heard at Cape Thompson where, over a two-year span, full song began as early as May 5 and continued as late as June 28.

The peak of song seems to occur during the period of greatest territorial activity, prior to the laying of eggs. Singing diminishes conspicuously after the female begins incubating. The last songs of the season, heard on July 21 and again on August 12, were weak and abbreviated.

The alarm note sounds to me like a plaintive *peer* and is given near the nest or elsewhere on the territory when the birds are disturbed. The same call is given by members of a flock when they are pressed into flight. Salomonsen's (1950) descriptions of these and other notes for the birds on Greenland are applicable as well to the Alaskan members of the species and are generally more accurate representations than other published versions. He states:

> The common call-note, used at the breeding-place, is a soft melodious *ee-yü* or only *yü* or *chüp*, uttered by both sexes on the ground and during flight, but more slurred and not so frequently by the female. Another note is a bunting-like *dír-rit*, uttered also on ground and in flight, used as a contact-note, during flight often as a lengthened, chirping *dirrirrirrirrit*. A short and more harsh *pirrh* uttered by the male on the wing is sometimes heard, as well as an exited sparrow-like note during pursuing-flight. The call-note and the contact-note are often combined during flight, alternating like *dit-ü-dit-ü*. Birds moving about in flocks in the autumn use *chüp* when alighting, when foraging and at rest, *dír-rit* when rising and in flight.

Almost as memorable as the full song of the male are the alarm notes sometimes given by the female when she is startled from the nest late in incubation. These and the associated display are described by Nelson (1887): "In one instance a parent was driven from her eggs just as they were about to hatch, and she ran along the ground for a few yards, uttering a plaintive note, like *chēē chēē chēē*, in a fine, vibrating, metallic tone, at the same time dragging her outspread wings and tail upon the ground, and fluttering as though in mortal agony."

Field marks.—P. A. Taverner (1934) writes:

The adult male has the throat black like the face, instead of white as in McCown's, or buffy as in Smith's and the Chestnut-collared Longspurs. Harris's Sparrow has a similar black face and bib, but is otherwise an entirely different-appearing bird, with light grey ear-coverts, and no chestnut collar. Females and juveniles with the distinct or semi-obscured chestnut collar are easily separated from McCown's and Smith's, but may be very similar to the Chestnut-collared. They are distinctly larger birds, however, wing 3.50 and over instead of 3.25 or under, and the collar is well developed instead of vaguely defined or absent. The whole bird is more sharply streaked. The black suffuses around ear-coverts and across the lower neck, and the underparts are solid white. Female and juvenile Chestnut-collared Longspurs may have a veiled black spot below a light throat, but the abdomen is a dusty buffy and usually shows more or less irregular intrusion of black. Autumn juveniles are still more confusing. They have a general appearance of a streaked buffy bird, with white, rarely cream, abdomen, with but traces of veiled black down sides of throat from corners of bill, and across upper breast. The tips of the ear-coverts are bordered by a conspicuous brown or black patch that is absent in the Chestnut-collared and McCown's Longspurs and much smaller or absent in Smith's. The best test for the species, in this plumage, is the white or faintly cream abdomen. * * * In addition to details previously mentioned, other plumages are more streaky than other longspurs, and never as evenly buffy as Smith's. * * * The subspecific distinction is slight.

R. T. Peterson (1941) notes that the spread tail is predominently black with white edges, whereas the amount of white in the tail of McCown's and the chestnut-collared longspurs exceeds the amount of black. The flight is undulating.

T. S. Roberts (1932) points out that female or autumn birds can be confused with vesper sparrows, but the longspurs have different tail patterns, customarily occur in flocks, and have different call notes. He also says they "resemble the House Sparrow more closely than anything else, but habits and notes are very different." Further, the "bird hops or runs instead of walks."

Additional features brought out by H. F. Witherby et al. (1938) are the absence of white in the wing, the comparatively thick upper mandible, and the long, lark-like, hind claw.

Enemies.—Observations at Cape Thompson indicated that the greatest losses of nests were caused by predation, which accounted for approximately 77 percent of the losses over a 2-year period. Arctic foxes (*Alopex lagopus*), ground squirrels (*Citellus undulatus*), and weasels (*Mustela erminea, Mustela rixosa*) were the predators believed mainly responsible, although the activities of the ground squirrels were restricted entirely to the gravel-covered stream bottoms where longspurs were relatively scarce.

After the young leave the nest they are particularly vulnerable to avian predation, and at Cape Thompson two species of jaegers, the parasitic and the long-tailed, feed on them regularly. James W. Bee (1958) reported that he observed short-eared owls and pigeon hawks preying regularly on longspurs in the vicinity of Point Barrow, Alaska. I watched a northern shrike capture and kill a young longspur in Mt. McKinley National Park.

Heavy precipitation at the time of hatching caused many nest losses at Cape Thompson. In 1961 rain associated with wind and low temperatures fell June 14 to June 21 following the peak of hatching on June 13. In the 66 nests under observation, 10 nest losses resulted from this storm, while only one before and one after that period were attributed to weather. Considering the relatively small number of nests I was able to observe, the loss must have been very great on a regional basis. At such times the females brood the young effectively for a while, but nevertheless must leave to feed, and frequently the resulting exposure is sufficient on a cumulative basis to cause losses of young. By contrast, in 1960 with 46 nests being watched, only one nest loss was attributed to the heavy rain that fell June 19 to 27, apparently because the young birds were by then sufficiently well feathered to endure the sporadic absence of the female.

Stormy weather is a well-known peril for migrating passerine birds, and the Lapland longspur is no exception. T. S. Roberts (1932) describes a spectacular mass kill in Minnesota during a March snowstorm in 1904:

> On two small lakes, with an aggregate area of about two square miles, the ice was still intact and nearly bare from the melting snow. This exposed surface was thickly and evenly strewn with dead longspurs. By measuring a number of squares, counting the birds in each, and averaging these counts, it was possible to make a fair estimate of the number of bodies on the whole area. A conservative calculation showed that there were at least 750,000 dead longspurs lying on these two lakes alone! The adjoining uplands, the streets of the town, and the roofs of the buildings were strewn with bodies in equal numbers. And this was only one locality in the extensive area throughout which the birds were killed.

Roberts adds that the total area involved was found to be approximately 1,500 square miles. This mass mortality had no noticeable effect on the numbers of migrating longspurs in succeeding years. With respect to such winter kills Lincoln (1939) writes "Almost every winter brings reports of storm destruction of thousands somewhere in the Middle West until it seems amazing that the species is able to survive * * * catastrophes have been reported from eastern Colorado, Nebraska, and North Dakota."

Winter.—While much of the available literature on wintering Lapland longspurs cannot be referred to a specific subspecies, it is well known that eastern and western forms overlap broadly in the mid-western prairies where they occur in great numbers. Nearly every author mentions the great abundance of these birds in winter. A. L. Goodrich, Jr. (1945) remarks that in Kansas "They frequent the wind-swept plains and prairies, occurring in large flocks. Skimming or running over the ground, they range widely in search of seeds and berries of available grasses, weeds and low plants." W. W. Cooke (1897) states that in Colorado "When it first arrives it passes up into the lower mountain parks, but in severe weather it is confined to the plains extending to southern Colorado." The species apparently moves rather extensively in winter, opportunistically seeking localities where the food supply can sustain the very large numbers present. This seems especially true in the northern perimeter of the winter range (latitude 50° N.) where they may occur in abundance in some years and only uncommonly in others.

Distribution

Range.—Alaska, northern Yukon, and northwestern Mackenzie south to Oregon, Nevada, Utah, Arizona, New Mexico, and northern Texas.

Breeding range.—The Alaska lapland longspur breeds from southwestern, western, and northern Alaska (Aleutian, Shumagin, Pribilof, Nunivak, and St. Lawrence islands; St. Michael, Cape Lisburne, Barrow) to northern Yukon (Herschel Island) and northwestern Mackenzie (Mackenzie Delta, Rendezvous Lake); recorded in summer farther south in Alaska (Semidi Islands, Fort Kenai) and in Mackenzie (Fort Franklin).

Winter range.—Winters from southern British Columbia (Lulu Island, Okanagan Landing), northwestern and central Montana (Fortine; Custer County), southwestern South Dakota (Rapid City), central northern Nebraska (Wood Lake), and northeastern Kansas (Hamilton and Douglas counties) south to California (rarely, Litchfield, Death Valley), central Utah (Tooele; Duchesne County), Arizona (rarely, Imperial Dam, Meteor Crater), east-central New Mexico (Picacho), and northern Texas (Canyon); casually west to western California (Eureka, False Bay) and east to Tennessee (Memphis) and Ohio (Columbus).

Egg dates.—Alaska: 159 records, May 23 to August 1; 90 records. June 5 to June 22; 112 records May 25 to July 7.

Mackenzie: 12 records, June 14 to July 1.

CALCARIUS PICTUS (Swainson)

Smith's Longspur

FRONTISPIECE

Contributed by EMERSON KEMSIES

HABITS

This obscure species well deserves Ira N. Gabrielson and Frederick C. Lincoln's (1959) characterization of it as "one of the least known of North American birds." In many ways a bird of mystery, it is nowhere plentiful, and its elusiveness makes it hard to find in the field, even where it is known to be present. Hence the dearth of information in the literature about its habits is not surprising. This account combines the available material on all three subspecies, whose respective ranges are detailed in the distribution section.

William Swainson described the species in 1831 as *Emberiza picta*, meaning "painted buntling," from a specimen Sir John Richardson's exploring party collected in Saskatchewan. Some 13 years later J. J. Audubon gave it its common name in honor of his friend Gideon B. Smith of Baltimore, when he described as new, specimens he obtained in southwestern Illinois.

South of their northern breeding grounds, Smith's longspurs are encountered only in open, grassy fields and pastures. Of recent years airports have offered them suitable wintering habitat where they are frequently reported. Nowhere, however, are they easy to observe. W. Rowan of Edmonton, Alberta, commented on their evasiveness thusly in a letter to Mr. Bent: "Like the Lapland longspur the flock indulged in elaborate aerial evolutions, though not nearly so spectacular, which they continued over their favorite field for a great while until they either settled down or disappeared altogether. They always settled with great abruptness and without any warning that we could note. Once in the stubble, although it happened to be very thin after last year's drought, they were impossible to see, even when right amongst them."

Spring.—P. A. Taverner (1926) calls the species

"Only a migrant in cultivated Canada, passing th[r]ough quickly in spring * * * Not nearly so common nor so generally distributed as the Lapland Longspur, but appearing in flocks of considerable size when it does occur." Edward A. Preble (1908) describes their migrating past Fort Simpson, Mackenzie, in May. "When disturbed, the birds flew in a loose flock, not nearly so fast as the Lapland longspurs, and usually only a short distance. When feeding they were very difficult to detect. Their characteristic note was heard only a few times."

According to Laurence Irving (1960) they reach their breeding grounds in northern Alaska two to three weeks later than the Lapland longspurs. He estimated them to be "* * * about a twentieth as numerous as Alaskan [Lapland] longspurs which would rank them as about the second species in abundance over the open wet grassy part of the tundra at the level of the floor of Anaktuvuk Valley.

"They did not frequent the dry places, but were often seen in wet grassy places." He also notes that the testes of the males "showed all to be at breeding size at the time of arrival. In this they were unlike the Alaska longspurs which had been reported two weeks before the time all males were at breeding size."

Nesting.—Irving (1960) continues:

In four females examined between May 27 and June 1, eggs were recorded at 2 mm. in length (that is, to have undergone a little growth), but on June 5, a bird contained a fully formed egg.

The nests collected * * * in 1949 were located on hummocks in the grassy tundra, slightly raised above the wet or damp surroundings and not concealed. They were rather bulky and were constructed of grass lined with fine round grass, some caribou hair, and a few ptarmigan feathers. The sets of eggs were observed for two or three days before being taken and were complete in number by about June 15. This places the nesting date about 10 days later than that of Alaskan longspurs.

S. F. Baird, Brewer, and Ridgway (1874) write of what were probably the first nests of this species discovered:

These birds were observed in large numbers at Fort Anderson, and on the Lower Anderson River, by Mr. MacFarlane, and a large number of their nests obtained. These were all on the ground, and usually in open spaces, but also in the vicinity of trees. The usual number of eggs found in a nest appears to have been four. The nests, for the most part, were constructed of fine dry grasses, carefully arranged, and lined with down, feathers, or finer materials similar to those of the outer portions. In a few there were no feathers; in others, feathers in different proportions; and in a few the down and feathers composed the chief portion of the nest, with only a few leaves as a base to the nest. They were sometimes sunk in excavations made by the birds, or placed in a tussock of grass, and, in one instance, placed in the midst of a bed of Labrador tea.

* * * * * * *

When their nests are approached, the female quietly slips off, while the male bird may be seen hopping or flying from tree to tree in the neighborhood of the nest, and will at times do all he can to induce intruders to withdraw from the neighborhood.

On his experiences with the nominate race in the Hudson Bay region in 1931, Olin S. Pettingill, Jr., has sent me the following notes from his field journal:

June 29. I accidently flushed a female from her nest this afternoon at Mosquito Point. She flushed almost at my feet and alighted 5 feet away. I recognized her woodeny rattle at once. The nest contained four eggs.

July 1. I found a nest with three eggs. Discovered it by watching the female only a few minutes. She returned to it by flying first to a tree for a brief stay, then to the ground.

July 4. I found a nest with four eggs near the Gravel Pit.

July 9. Today I photographed the Gravel Pit nest and female. The nest contained three young with one egg lying alongside. The nest was placed in the open with a clump of grass at the north side. It was constructed of grasses, lined with five white Willow Ptarmigan feathers, and sunk in dry moss not two feet from the edge of a small pond. When I first approached the nest I was greeted with a sudden rush and flight from beneath my feet. Alighting just four feet away, the female spread her tail downward so that it touched the ground, dropped her wings slightly and lowered her head as well. She then crept about slowly, her rump feathers lifted slightly, and uttered her rattling cries.

For the first hour the female did not come to the nest, but having gained courage, she returned repeatedly. She always approached on foot, stopping at intervals. Once she remained "glued" near the nest for about four minutes, making no motion except flickering her eyelids. The male came near the nest with food in his beak, but after eyeing the blind a short while, swallowed the food and departed. The female fed the young at least five times during my two hours in the blind. She found the food always in the near vicinity of the nest, and was seldom out of my view.

Eggs.—Most subsequent descriptions of the eggs of this species seem to have been copied from Baird, Brewer, and Ridgway (1874), who state they "have a light clay-colored ground, are marked with obscure blotches of lavender and darker lines, dots, and blotches of dark purplish-brown." Coues (1903) considers them "less heavily colored than those of *lapponicus* usually are, and thus closely resembling those of *ornatus*." The usual clutch size is four or five, and rarely six eggs. W. G. F. Harris reports by letter: "The measurements of 50 eggs average 21.0 by 15.0 mm.; the eggs showing the four extremes measure *23.9* by 15.5, 22.4 by *16.3*, *18.8* by 14.7, and 20.9 by *13.7* mm."

Young.—J. R. Jehl, Jr., and D. J. T. Russell (1966) say of the incubation period: "Previously unknown, the periods at three nests were 11½, 11½, and 12 days." Irving (1960) notes that young birds in Alaska "had reached adult weight on July 27."

In August, 1958, I had the opportunity to visit Churchill, Manitoba, where Mrs. H. L. Smith kindly showed me the areas Smith's longspur inhabits. At one place a male flew up from the ground, steadily giving the alarm rattle. A few moments later two nearly full-grown young and a female flew up from the ground near the base of a spruce. The male meanwhile perched near the top of a black spruce 8 feet high, which surprised me considerably, for I had seen the species previously only on the ground or flying overhead.

Food.—Martin, Zim, and Nelson (1951) report that 21 stomachs collected in Illinois in winter contained mainly seeds of dropseedgrass (*Sporobolus*), bristlegrass (*Silaria*) and panicgrass (*Panicum*), with lesser amounts of wheat, timothy, clover, crabgrass, common ragweed, bulrush, millet, and sedge. Of animal food they say "Beetles (particularly ground beetles), caterpillars, and spiders are prominent among the invertebrates eaten by this species."

Two birds Ben Coffey collected, one in Tennessee, the other in Mississippi, had eaten mainly seeds of three-awn grass (*Aristida*). Horace H. Jeeter found the birds inhabiting patches of this same grass on a Shreveport, La., airport. W. D. Klimstra of Southern Illinois University reports on the stomachs of two November birds Jay Sheppard collected in Ohio: "We have examined the crops of the two Smith's Longspurs. In the case of both there were two species of plants represented: *Sporobolus vaginiflora* and *Digitaria isclaemum*. In both cases *Sporobolus* represents over 99 per cent of the seeds." It is of interest to note that although *Aristada* was growing in the field where these birds were collected, no seeds of it were found in them.

Voice.—Most observers encountering this species note as does Preble (1908) in Athabasca: "My attention was first attracted to them by their characteristic notes, several sharp 'chirps' uttered in quick succession."

R. T. Peterson (1960) says of its voice: "Rattling or clicking notes in flight (suggests winding of cheap watch). Song, sweet and warbler-like; ends like a Chestnut-sided Warbler's (*we' chew*).

The rattling notes characteristically given as the birds take wing are also heard on the ground. These notes are similar to those of the Lapland longspur, but some observers believe they can detect a difference in quality between the two. To me the notes of Smith's seem more staccato, louder, and more intense than those of the Lapland, though the differences may not be apparent on first meeting with the birds. A flock of birds calling overhead may induce others on the ground to join them in flight, or vice-versa.

Behavior.—Alexander Wetmore wrote me in a letter:

In late February and early March, 1905, I found between 20 and 30 Smith's longspurs scattered through large pastures near Independence in southeastern Kansas. They ranged in wet ground, in slight depressions, and around small ponds where grassy vegetation had been grazed closely by cattle. In this rather open cover the longspurs remained so concealed that I came upon the first ones seen by chance, so that it is possible that they had been present there throughout the winter. I located them first by their low calls, sufficiently different from those of the Lapland longspur, present in numbers, to attract attention. Often they allowed approach, without moving, to within a dozen steps; occasionally I found that one had remained hidden while I passed within a dozen feet.

They flushed suddenly, with low calls that were repeated at times by hidden birds which remained in the grass, and flew with a swift, erratic flight that for a few yards reminded me of the zigzag course of a common snipe as it flushed. Often the longspurs dropped immediately to the ground. If they remained in the air, the flight became undulating and they circled for several minutes. Usually then calls from companions hidden in the cover brought them again to the ground. They were especially averse to taking flight if the wind was high. They seemed to remain apart from the Savannah and LeConte sparrows, other longspurs, and horned larks that were also present in small numbers in these fields.

In a letter to Mr. Bent, W. Rowan remarks that "they have a peculiar habit of running suddenly for a short distance before again becoming immobile. The run is always accompanied by a musical little twitter, a useful prelude that helped us materially to pick out the bird the moment it moved. The birds always scattered widely on settling. We collected specimens entirely at random, picking off the birds as they revealed themselves, so that theoretically we should have had equal numbers of both sexes, yet we got about three males to one female. This seems to indicate that males are in excess. The same thing applies to both flocks noted."

At the Oxford, Ohio, airport we have found the birds often quite unwary, and have approached them to within 15 or 20 feet. When first flushed they usually fly close to the ground for a distance of only 5 or 10 yards before settling again, but after repeated flushing they generally spiral high into the air, sometimes almost out of sight, and may remain aloft for several minutes. In Ohio and in northwestern Indiana fields, Smith's longspurs seldom associate with the Lapland longspurs, unless they are forced into close proximity by such circumstances as a general disturbance of a migratory concentration, or by crowding during the peak of the Lapland's massive migration.

Field marks.—Smith's longspur has the white outer tail feathers of the other longspurs, but in all plumages is generally a much buffier bird, with a slightly slenderer, more pointed bill, and yellowish legs. The male in spring is unmistakable with his striking triangular black and white head marking; adult males often retain their distinctive white-tipped black lesser wing coverts in winter. Females and immatures closely resemble their Lapland counterparts, but may be distinguished by their greater buffiness, and particularly by their buffy abdomens, which are concolor with the breast, and not almost white as in the Lapland.

Fall and winter.—As Worth Randle and I have pointed out (Kemsies and Randle, 1964), regrettably little is known of the migratory movements and winter distribution of Smith's longspur. The recent efforts of Coffey (1954), Jeeter (1953), Imhof (1962), and Sheppard (1959) have added greatly to our knowledge of seasonal movements and shown the wintering grounds to be considerably more extensive than was previously thought (see distribution section). But whether individual birds follow the same migratory paths in spring and fall, or whether they return to the same wintering grounds in subsequent years is unknown. So far the species has proved even more difficult to band than it generally is to observe, and too few have been banded to contribute materially to our information.

Previous to 1958 the only Smith's longspurs ever banded were five nestlings at Churchill, Manitoba, three in 1933 and two in 1941. In April 1958, Ronald Austing and Edward Johnstone tried to catch some with mist nets at the Oxford, Ohio, airport. They were plagued by the constant strong seasonal winds, but finally, on the 14th, they managed to herd the birds and suddenly flush three of them into the nets, two males and a female. The following year they put out cracked corn as bait, which the birds were quick to find and come to. Between March 28 and April 23 they banded 39 birds and took 5 repeats of individuals from 6 to 19 days after banding.

They tried again in the spring of 1960, but the birds showed no interest in the cracked corn put out, nor in other baits offered them—seeds of clover, orchard grass, and lespedeza. Again unfavorable winds interfered with their efforts, but finally they managed to net six new birds at a nearby puddle where 70 to 80 birds came regularly to drink at noon. Thus over a 3-year period only 48 individuals were banded which to date have produced no returns or recoveries.

Distribution

Range.—Northern Alaska, northern Yukon, northwestern Mackenzie, and southeastern Keewatin, southeastward to central Texas, northwestern Louisiana and Mississippi, and southwestern Tennessee.

Breeding range.—The Smith's longspur breeds from northeast-central Alaska (nests recorded from Anaktuvuk Pass), northern Yukon (Herschel Island), northwestern and central northern Mackenzie (Caribou Hills west of Mackenzie Delta, mouth of Kogaryuak River on Coronation Gulf), and southeastern Keewatin, southeast to south-central Mackenzie, northeastern Manitoba (Churchill), and the Hudson Bay coast of northern Ontario (Fort Severn, Cape Henrietta Maria, and Little Cape).

Winter range.—Winters from Kansas, central Iowa (Linn and Poweshiek counties), and Illinois, south to central Texas (Giddings), northwestern Louisiana (Shreveport), central Arkansas (Lonoke), northwestern Mississippi (Walls), and southwestern Tennessee (Memphis).

Casual records.—Casual west to central and southeastern British Columbia (Kispiox Valley, Boundary Pass), north to central northern Alaska (Umiat on the Colville River), east to southern Ontario (Elmvale) and South Carolina (Chester), and south to central Alabama (Birmingham, Montgomery) and northeastern New Mexico (Clayton).

Migration.—Early dates of spring arrival are: Illinois—Urbana, March 29; Chicago, March 30. Indiana—Jasper County, April 24. Ohio—Oxford, March 19 (median arrival for central Ohio, April 1). Wisconsin—Sauk Prairie, April 27. Minnesota—Jackson County, April 18. North Dakota—Cass County, April 28. Manitoba—Treesbank, April 30 (average of 5 years, May 6); Whitewater Lake, May 4; Churchill, May 6. Saskatchewan—Indian Head, May 14. Mackenzie—Hay River, Great Slave Lake, May 12. Alberta—Beaverhill Lake, May 15. British Columbia—Tupper Creek, May 27. Alaska—Tolugak Lake, May 27.

Late dates of spring departure are: Arkansas—Fayetteville, February 28. Illinois—Chicago, May 15; Urbana, May 12. Ohio—central Ohio, median, May 1. Minnesota—Marshall County, May 6. Oklahoma—Cleveland County, April 1. North Dakota—Red River Valley, May 12. Arizona—White Mountains, April 24.

Early dates of fall arrival are: Alberta—Beaverhill Lake, August 28. Manitoba—Oak Lake, September 15. Saskatchewan—Lake Athabaska, August 17; Indian Head, September 11. North Dakota—Red River Valley, October 5. Oklahoma—Tulsa, December 1. Texas—Gainesville, November 19; Tyler, December 6. Minnesota—Kittson County, September 15. Alabama—Birmingham, December 5.

Late dates of fall departure are: British Columbia—Kispiox Valley, August 25. North Dakota—Cass County, October 18. Minnesota—Kittson County, October 13. Ohio—Oxford, November 27.

Egg dates.—Mackenzie: 28 records, June 9 to July 2; 18 records, June 20 to June 26.

Manitoba: 5 records, June 2 to July 3.

Regarding the Frontispiece

The A.O.U. Check-List Committee has not as yet assessed the validity of the three races of Smith's longspur pictured in the frontispiece to this volume. Just before going to press we received a copy of a manuscript by Joseph R. Jehl, Jr., entitled "Geographic and Seasonal Variation in Smith's Longspur," which he has submitted for publication in the Transactions of the San Diego Society of Natural History. Jehl's study presents strong evidence that no geographical variation exists in this species. The color differences on which Kemsies' (1961) proposed races are based are apparently the result of seasonal feather wear and fading of the breeding plumage. The brightly colored birds that Kemsies named *"roweorum"* are in relatively fresh, unworn breeding plumage and were collected in May and early

June. The birds with the palest underparts and darkest backs (*C. p. "mersi"*) are in worn faded plumage and were collected in July and early August just before the postnuptial molt. The describer was apparently misled by inadequate material and biased sampling.—O.L.A., Jr.

CALCARIUS ORNATUS (Townsend)

Chestnut-collared Longspur

PLATE 78

Contributed by George M. Fairfield

Habits

When he investigated the birds of the Saskatchewan prairies in 1905, Mr. Bent (1908) wrote of the chestnut-collared longspur: "This and the following species [McCown's longspur] were a constant source of enjoyment and interest; we never ceased to admire their beautiful plumage and their delightful little flight songs, during our long drives across the grassy plains."

Indeed, the male chestnut-collar, with his black underparts, white winglinings and tail, and rich chestnut nape, adds a pleasant note of contrast to the rather monotonous aspect of the northern prairies. Where the grass is sparse and preferably less than 8 inches high, we see dotted here and there across the plain the black breasts of birds perched on low weeds guarding their territories. As we approach they take off and circle around with undulating flight, giving their short lively song and their high clear alarm call.

When the northern prairies became the great wheat-producing region of the continent, the amount of grassland available for the chestnut-collar was reduced proportionately. The McCown's longspur and the horned lark, adapted to sparser, more open ground than the chestnut-collar, were able to continue nesting in the summer-fallow ploughed fields. The chestnut-collar, needing elevated song perches and a little cover for its nest, found the plowed lands too open. As the fields of growing wheat were too dense and confining for such an open-country bird, all that remained for its use were uncultivated pastures and wastelands. In heavily settled regions today the only suitable habitat for the chestnut-collar is on the outskirts of towns and cities where golf courses, airports, and idle lands provide the needed degree of cover.

T. S. Roberts (1932) thus describes the effect on the chestnut-collar of the agricultural altering of the virgin prairie in Minnesota: "Formerly an abundant summer resident throughout the prairie region of

Minnesota * * *. It has entirely disappeared in recent years from this range, except for a few small isolated colonies on the first sand ridge along the Red River Valley in western Pennington and eastern Polk counties * * * and in central Norman County."

Frank Roy (1958) of Saskatoon, Saskatchewan, reports: "The Chestnut-collared longspur was an abundant bird in the Lucky Lake-Birsay region from the year 1937 to 1944. As many as 15 pairs used to nest in a fifty-acre pasture on our farm. By 1945, not more than seven or eight pairs nested in the same area. In 1946 five pairs remained. In 1947 not a single bird nested in the pasture (which, by the way, has been reduced to 20 acres in extent). Since that date, the Chestnut-collared Longspur has become progressively more scarce, even in the extensive tracts of pasture west and south of Lucky Lake and Beechy."

Nonetheless, large areas of suitable grassland still exist on the northern prairies, and where conditions are favorable the breeding population of chestnut-collars can be quite heavy. Elmer T. Fox (in Belcher, 1961) found 11 nests on about 20 acres of pasture near Regina, and we found 19 territories (16 nests located) on 50 acres of waste land at Moose Jaw, Saskatchewan. As several of the early writers mention it as "abundant locally," perhaps the species has always tended to nest in loose "colonies" in concentrated groups of territories. E. T. Seton (1886) notes that in Manitoba it was "Local in distribution, many pairs sometimes affecting a limited area of dry prairie, while again for miles no more of the species are to be seen."

Much of the following information has been extracted from an unfinished study of the chestnut-collar in Saskatchewan. D. J. T. Russell cooperated with me on the breeding biology work, and several other friends have given help and advice.

Spring.—Very little information is available on the northward migration of the chestnut-collared longspur. Comparatively few of the species have been banded (1,067 to 1962, with only 3 returns to the place of banding and no recoveries reported). The summer and winter ranges meet in northeastern Colorado and Nebraska, and much of their migration seems to consist merely of a northward drifting, in company with the flocks of other longspurs and of horned larks, from their winter home on the deserts and plateaus of northern Mexico and the plains of the southwestern United States to the northern prairies.

Several writers have noted their habit of stopping for several days at favorable feeding and watering places. W. H. Osgood (1903) says of their migration through Cochise County, Arizona: "In February and March the chestnut-collared longspur was exceedingly abundant. They were seen flying over at all times and at nightfall clouds of them

Woodrow, Saskatchewan, June 1947 H. O. Todd, Jr.

NEST AND EGGS OF CHESTNUT-COLLARED LONGSPUR

Lake Bowdoin National Wildlife Refuge, Malta, Mont. A. D. Cruickshank

MALE CHESTNUT-COLLARED LONGSPUR AT NEST

would sweep over the house and on down to the grass at the edge of the alkali lake, whence they straggled out at daybreak."

The birds pass northward through western Texas and Oklahoma, New Mexico, and eastern Arizona, across Colorado and Kansas, and arrive on their breeding grounds about the second week of April. R. D. Harris (1944) describes their arrival at Winnipeg, Manitoba: "On the first day of migration, no more than a single individual was usually noted, but afterward 10 or 12 were counted in a day. They arrived principally during the forenoon, either singly or in groups of two or three."

Territory.—We found that the chestnut-collared longspur usually defends a nesting territory of between 1 and 2 acres of prairie, though two of our pairs occupied territories of almost 10 acres of rather unsatisfactory habitat at the margin of the nesting area. As with other territorial species, the more the pairs are crowded together and the smaller the individual territories, the more defensive behavior is to be seen.

An important aspect of territorial defense consists of advertising by singing from conspicuous perches. Rival males spent many hours singing at each other from weed clumps, small shrubs, boulders, fences, or farm refuse. Our wire nest markers were favored perches, and one longspur even sang from the top of the car when it was parked near the nest. The birds rarely sang from the transmission line that crossed our study area; possibly its 20-foot poles were too high to suit their purposes. The birds stand out so strikingly against the pale prairie grass when singing that I believe the black breast is almost as important as the song in advertising territorial occupancy.

L. J. Moriarty writes in a letter of his observations of the species in eastern South Dakota:

> The birds nearly always nest on the higher areas in our rolling short-grass lands. Seldom do I find them in hay land as they prefer open places with poor soils and short-spaced vegetation. Each male appears to have what I call his "singing rock" upon which he sits, flies up from to sing or to defend his territory and returns to constantly. These rocks are usually the largest ones in each pair's territory, and are soon marked by a ring of droppings around the highest peak. Occasionally when no rock is available, a weed or a post will be substituted. The nest is usually within 25 feet of the singing rock. Each pair's territory appears to be about 100 yards across. Of the many nests I have found, none have been closer together than 100 yards.

In Saskatchewan we observed chases of two types. The commoner occurs when a neighboring bird flies over an occupied territory. The male, and sometimes the female as well, take wing and follow him at a distance of a few feet. The chase usually continues over at least one more territory, from which another male will rise to join the chase. It is common to see three to five longspurs circling round and round after one another in undulating flight high above the fields, then dropping back to their own territories.

Occasionally a much more violent chase takes place, apparently when a male bird discovers a trespasser on the ground within his territory. He flies at the offending bird and chases it in a fast, erratic course low over the ground until he has driven it well away from his boundaries.

Fights occur frequently along territorial boundaries. Two males, each probably on his own territory, may be foraging only a few feet apart. Suddenly one of them, possibly considering the other to be trespassing, runs at him with lowered head. Facing each other, the two join battle with fluttering wings. They may rise together to a height of 4 to 15 feet before dropping separately to the ground, either to go their own ways or to start the fracas again. I have never seen a bird hurt in these exchanges.

We experimented with setting up a mounted male chestnut-collar about 50 feet from an active nest. The male first threatened the dummy. Facing it with his head held high, he pointed his bill up at a 45-degree angle and raised his breast to show as much of the black as possible. He then dived repeatedly at the interloper, delivering blows to the head and back. Such continued chastisement would be unlikely under natural conditions where the intruder would retreat or fight back.

Courtship.—Courtship in the chestnut-collared longspur seems largely a matter of staying close together. Up to the time incubation starts, when the male isn't singing we can usually find the pair foraging together quietly in the more open parts of their territory. We saw a number of sexual chases, in which the male chased the female low over the prairie in fast, erratic flight, apparently trying to force her down. After a minute or so the male was seen to fly back to the foraging area, the female following along behind. As Tinbergen (1939) found with snow buntings, these chases probably result from the male's unsuccessful attempt to copulate when the female is not in the right state of physiological receptiveness. The only display we saw a male make under natural conditions was to lift the tail high over the back momentarily on two occasions.

That a much more intense display is possible was shown by a male's reaction to a mounted female placed near the nest. Approaching the dummy female in a zigzag course, he erected his chestnut collar, stretched his head high, and looked down at her over his lowered bill from directly in front. He then fluttered to her back and attempted to copulate. Dismounting, he ran away from her holding his body level with the ground, wings and wide-fanned tail almost dragging. He then circled back and tried once more to copulate, dismounted, and circled to the front. There he assumed an exaggerated "female precopulatory posture," in which he raised his closed tail as high as possible until his chest almost touched the ground, bent his head back on his shoulders with bill pointing straight up, and the wings projecting back and down. In this remarkable posture he rocked slowly from side to side several times. He then pecked at the dummy's head, rump, and cloacal area as if in annoyance, and repeated the display. Possibly this behavior is elicited only when resistance is met, for I saw one pair copulate a dozen times without performing any such preliminary display.

In the matings I witnessed the female took the initiative. Typically she flies over and lands beside the singing male, lifts her tail straight up and tilts her head backward with bill pointing up and wings held low and quivering. The male mounts for a few seconds, dismounts, and stands beside her with his chestnut collar erect and bulging out from the rest of his plumage. The female holds the copulatory position for two or three seconds after the male dismounts, then assuming normal posture, fluffs out her feathers momentarily and assumes normal posture again. I once saw a female hold a piece of grass in her bill during coition.

The female's reaction to a mounted female placed near her nest was to attack it fiercely, pecking at the head and throat. This suggests that the female drives off rival or trespassing females. I have found no reports of polygamy in the literature, nor did we find any indication of it in the field.

Nesting.—The chestnut-collared longspur nests typically in uncultivated grasslands. At Winnipeg, Manitoba, R. D. Harris (1944) describes its favored habitat as consisting of "* * * prairie, its flatness relieved by occasional low ridges and shallow sloughs. The dominant vegetation was composed of grasses of the following species: *Panicum virgatum*, *Poa arida*, *Agrostis hyemalis*, and *Agropyron tenerum*. Wolfberry (*Symphoricarpos occidentalis*) in straggling patches, prairie sage (*Artemisia gnaphalodes*), goldenrod (*Solidago canadensis* and *S. hispida*), and gum-weed (*Grindelia squarrosa*) were also present."

In Montana, A. Dawes DuBois (1935) writes: "The Chestnut-collared Longspurs prefer to nest in the low and slightly moist situations where the thicker and taller grasses afford adequate concealment. If the meadow is wet or flooded the nests are placed on higher ground but are often near the moist margins. * * * twelve nests out of eighteen were in low places. However, one nest was high and dry on a knoll of the rolling prairie, one was on sloping land near a coulee, one in a fence border of native sod between wheat fields, and one was in a patch of grass on a dead-furrow left by the breaking plows, in the midst of a field of winter wheat which was almost knee high at the time the nest was found."

At Regina, Saskatchewan, Margaret Belcher (1961) found the birds preferred sparse to heavy grassland: "* * * I noted with interest that the longspurs were more numerous in a 160-acre pasture that had been over-grazed than in an adjacent 320-acre pasture with a good stand of grass. Fox had a similar impression when checking a small pasture near Regina View School, southeast of the city, for Chestnut-collared Longspurs' nests. In 1960 when there were no cattle in the pasture and the grass was long, no nests were found when the area was checked with a rope; in 1961 when the pasture was patchy from grazing, it was noted that the longspurs had chosen the bare patches for their nests."

We found a few nests at Moose Jaw, Saskatchewan, in very sparse pasture with little cover for the nests. Though one nest was in quite thick grass over a foot high, the preferred habitat seemed to be ungrazed fields of medium thickness up to eight inches tall which offered good concealment and yet allowed the birds easy walking. The nests were built on level or gently sloping prairie, and not in the low areas that would flood in heavy rains. The steeper slopes were not suitable for the cup-shaped hollows they dig for their nests.

The nest is built by the female alone. Three different females we watched gathered the material a short distance from the nest site, mostly within 100 feet, and usually walked with it to the nest. DuBois (1935) describes the nest-building process as follows:

On the afternoon of May 22 I discovered a nicely rounded hollow in the ground, amidst the grass. There was no loose dirt near it. When I returned the next morning the nest proper had been started at the rim. There were only two weed stems at the bottom of the hole. Two and a half days later, at 9:30 a.m., the entire excavation has been lined with dead grass blades and stems, but the material was as yet rather loose in the bottom, while the rim was apparently finished. The grass material of the rim had been interwoven with the basal stems of the standing grass which grew around the nest. It seems especially noteworthy that the weaving of the rim was the first work done upon the nest structure. By 8 a.m. on May 27 (about four days after construction had started) the nest was apparently finished, with some white hairs added to the lining. The first egg was probably laid early the next day, as there were two eggs on the evening of the 29th, three on the morning of the 30th, and four on the morning of the 31st.

* * *

The body of all nests examined was composed entirely of dried grasses. These grass materials consist of both blades and stems, varying in different nests as to age and texture. One nest was made of old, soft, and shredded grasses; others had very old grass around the rim but fresher grasses in the bottom. Old, weathered grass in the rim is clearly an aid to concealment.

* * *

The materials used for linings include grasses, rootlets and hair, in various combinations and proportions. * * * The rim of the nest is usually flush with the surface of the ground.

The main building material for the nests seems always to be dried grasses, with animal hair or feathers added to the lining when they are available. Of 33 nests I examined only 3 contained material other than grass—one had seven gray partridge feathers in the lining and the other two each contained one small passerine feather. All these nests were circular in shape except one that was slightly oblong. Seven nest excavations I measured varied from 75 to 100 millimeters (average 88) in diameter, and from 43 to 55 millimeters (average 51) in depth. Nine nests I measured varied from 45 to 70 millimeters (average 60) in inside diameter, and from 38 to 45 millimeters (average 43) in depth of cup.

The nest is usually well concealed under a clump or tuft of grass. Even when placed in an open spot the nests blend so well with the pale prairie earth they are very hard to see, and the general sameness of the surroundings makes them even more difficult to find. L. J. Moriarty writes (*in* litt.):

> A good way of locating the nest, if you don't find it when the female flushes—and she usually walks away from it before flying—is to sit quietly not too far away and watch with binoculars her return. She will not fly directly to the nest, but will alight some distance from it and walk around apparently unconcerned, nonchalantly picking up food. As soon as she is convinced that no danger threatens, she will go to the nest and disappear into it to resume incubating. The nest is usually placed in a tuft of longer grass beside a stone of perhaps baseball size. I believe such sites are selected partly for the shade offered by the grass or rock during the noonday heat, and also because cattle will not step or lie down on stones of this size.

The female sometimes builds the nest close enough to the boundary of the territory to involve the male in a continual battle with his neighbor. In one such case the two nests were only 130 feet apart.

Eggs.—The chestnut-collared longspur lays from three to five and sometimes six ovate eggs that may show considerable variability even within a single clutch. The ground is creamy white, spotted, blotched, clouded, and with small scrawls of dark purplish-browns such as "dusky drab," "bone brown," or "olive brown" and black. The undermarkings are often very prominent blotches of "pale neutral gray," or "deep purplish gray." Some eggs have the entire surface clouded with gray undermarkings and with only scattered spots of the purplish-browns and black; others will show considerable ground with the markings concentrated toward the large end where they often form a loose wreath. The measurements of 90 eggs average 18.7 by 14.2 mm; the eggs showing the four extremes measure *20.8* by 14.7, 18.3 by *15.9*, and *16.2* by *12.7* mm.

Incubation.—The eggs are laid early in the morning, one each day on successive days until the clutch is complete. At Moose Jaw,

Saskatchewan, the laying time, as nearly as we could determine, was between 6:00 a.m. and 7:30 a.m., central standard time.

Incubation generally does not start until the clutch is completed, and is entirely by the female alone. Some confusion has resulted apparently from the occurrence of male plumage characteristics in an occasional female.

The male spends his time during the incubation period in foraging, singing, defending the territory against encroachment by neighboring pairs, and chasing off small mammals and birds that approach the nest. One male approached the incubating female with a mouthful of insects, but was deterred by the close proximity of the blind. This behavior was not seen again during many hours of watching and may have been anomalous, perhaps anticipatory of later nestling feeding.

As Harris (1944) notes, the male

> * * * selects one or two definite stations near the nest. He watches attentively for his mate, and when she flies to or away from the nest, he follows and alights beside her. Now and then throughout the day he launches himself into the air, rises to a height of 10 to 50 feet, spreads wings stiffly, and, floating slowly to earth, delivers his short, clear melody. At the approach of a human intruder, the male retires to his favorite perch, from which he marks the intruder's progress. With uneasiness growing stronger, he takes wing and flies back and forth over his territory, giving utterance to a warning *wheer* note and sometimes a song. Some males have a habit on these occasions of reaching the highest point of their flight directly over the nest.

As incubation progresses the female sits very closely and leaves the nest only when almost trodden upon. Sometimes she flutters away in a distraction display with half-spread wings as though crippled. She leaves the nest of her own accord, however, every half hour or so and joins the male feeding, or she may fly to a nearby pond for a drink. If the female has not returned after a few minutes, the male appears agitated and flies to the nest, or he chases the female until she returns.

DuBois (1935) found the incubation period at one nest to be 12½ days. Harris (1944) reports the period "from the laying of the last egg to the hatching of the last" to be 10 days at three nests. Our observations at one nest support DuBois's 12½-day period—the last two marked eggs in a four-egg clutch were 12 days 13 hours, and 11 days 13 hours old the evening before they hatched. This is confirmed also by Moriarty's (1965) timing of a marked clutch: "(2:30 p.m.). Egg No. 1 was hatched, 14 days plus 6 hours after laying. This was 11 days and 6 hours after I was sure incubation started. Eggs No. 2 and No. 3 were pipped at this time and hatched, young still moist at 5:30 p.m. By this time No. 4 was pipped, to hatch and dry by 7 p.m. It took about 1 to 1½ hours to complete hatching after the egg was pipped."

The young may hatch over a period of a day or two. As Harris (1944) describes the process:

"In one observed case, hatching of one egg required over half a day, but in the majority of cases it seemed to take a shorter time. An irregular series of perforations is made by the young bird around the circumference of the shell about mid-way down the main axis. When the cut is completed, and the young bird has finally extricated itself, the two halves of the shell are carried away by the parent; pieces of shell have been found as far as a hundred feet away from the nest."

Young.—Both parents feed the young and tend to nest sanitation. The fecal sacs may be either eaten or carried away and dropped at a distance. For the first few days the female broods the young up to 50 percent of the daylight hours, and the male makes most of the trips with food. Daytime brooding, which is exclusively by the female, ends about the fifth day, except during cold and rainy periods and thereafter the female makes more trips with food than the male. At one nest the young were fed 7.2 times per hour (5-hour watch) when 3 days old, and 16 times per hour (9-hour watch) when 9 days old. Watches at two nests of 8- or 9-day-old young on June 13 and June 23 showed the daily feeding period to last 17 hours.

The parents feed the young whatever insect food is available. Harris (1944) found his birds feeding their young almost exclusively on grasshoppers, but this was at a time when they were very abundant. At our study area the most common food seemed to be small green caterpillars and small brown segmented worms. The parents subdued these by biting them and beating them on the ground before giving them to the nestlings.

The following account of development is based on daily observations at four nests of individually color-marked young:

First day: The newly hatched young are very weak. They have just strength enough to gape for food as they lie in the nest. They appear well covered with down on the head and back after the down dries. They weigh about 1.6 grams at hatching, and gain 0.6 to 0.7 grams the first day. (Moriarty, (1944) reports four young weighed a total of 5.48 grams, or 1.37 grams each at hatching.)

Second day: The young are much stronger and gape for food at any noise made near the nest. They now weigh between 2.0 and 2.5 grams and will gain about 1.4 grams during the day.

Third day: The young are growing rapidly and the down is now about half an inch long. They will gain about 1.8 grams daily from the 3rd through the 8th day.

Fourth day: The eyes of the more developed young are open a slit. The feather sheaths are beginning to protrude from the skin. The nestlings begin to call with a soft "peeping."

Fifth day: The eyes are about half open, but the nestlings still gape at sound rather than sight. Daytime brooding has almost stopped. Barring strong territorial competition with neighboring males, the male will stop singing about this time.

Sixth day: The eyes are now open and the nestlings will gape at the wave of a hand. The body feathers are beginning to break from their sheaths, but there are bare areas between the feather tracts.

Seventh day: The young gape at any movement near the nest. The feathers of the back and side are out and the primary sheaths are 10 to 15 millimeters long. The nestlings call when the parents bring food.

Eighth day: The young now crouch in the nest when disturbed, and can scramble away if placed on the ground outside the nest. The head feathers are out and the primaries beginning to protrude from their sheaths. There are still tufts of down above the eyes and a few bits elsewhere on the body.

Ninth day: The young are very active, moving around in the nest and preening. They are noisy when the parents bring food. They weight about 14.0 grams, and daily weight gain reduces to about 0.7 grams.

Tenth day. This is the day the young are most likely to leave the nest. R. D. Harris (1944) found the young left in 9, 10, or 11 days. L. J. Moriarty (1965) reports them remaining through the 14th day, when they each weighed 12.21 grams. The young we observed weighed from 15.3 to 16.1 when ready to leave the nest.

The above account refers to normally developing young. Frequently, however, one nestling is smaller than the rest (possibly the last to hatch), and less successful than his siblings in competing for food. He either dies shortly after hatching, or may fall further and further behind to die later in the nestling period. A. D. DuBois (1937) writes:

"On July 19 I witnessed the removal of the dead fledgling from nest no. 14. It was a surprising feat of strength, for the fledgling was very heavy, being eight or nine days old. Upon rapidly fluttering wings the parent rose with his burden straight upward from the nest; then it flew horizontally, and, while flying low, dropped the carcass at a spot about fifty feet away."

I saw a similar occurrence at Moose Jaw, when a female weighing about 20 grams carried a dead 14-gram nestling for about five feet before dropping it. Another dead young she dragged away from the nest.

Harris (1944) describes a nest-leaving he witnessed thusly:

The movement, perhaps stimulated by my activity around the nest, began without warning. The birds suddenly became very restless, kicking violently, and soon were panting hard for breath. After a few minutes they stopped simultaneously, and were quiet for about ten minutes. Again they began, and this time one bird, curiously enough the smallest of them all, pushed itself over the rim and crawled and hopped away from the nest in a wildly erratic course, finally coming to rest beside me two feet from the nest. Meanwhile, another bird, which had projected itself over the opposite side of the nest, turned back, and, shoving itself across the backs of its fellows in the nest, went toward the first one. The birds began to utter the *chi-eep* note and were answered by their parents, which were flying about overhead. After a general period of rest, a third one managed to scramble out, and the second one, in amazingly strong hops, followed an aimless course around the nest.

Of the post-nestling period he writes:

On the day of nest leaving, the bird is quite incapable of flight, and, except for occasional attempts at hopping, it remains crouched in the grass, receiving food from its parents. It grows, however, with extraordinary rapidity. After another day it is able to fly, when alarmed, for 100 feet or more. The flight is direct and labored. After alighting, the bird crouches upon the ground—I did not determine the age at which it is able to stand upright and walk.

Fourteen days after hatching (four days after leaving the nest), the young bird begins to use the *til-lip* call note characteristic of the species. Its flight has now become undulating.

On the fifteenth day the bird is still being fed regularly by the male parent and occasionally by the female. If another nest is to be started, the female stops caring for the young at a time varying from two to seven days after they have left the nest; thenceforth they are in the sole care of the male.

By the twenty-fourth day, the bird appears to be fully grown. It may still be attended by the male parent, but it has sometimes to assume a begging posture, with wings outspread and fluttering, before the parent will give it food.

It begins to wander at large on about the twenty sixth day. If the parents are finished nesting, young and old go off together, but otherwise the young bird joins roving bands of juveniles.

The first clutches are usually laid about the middle of May. DuBois's (1935) earliest clutch in Montana was May 6th. In Saskatchewan we found two clutches apparently completed about May 11th. New nests are started until well into July, which allows ample time for a second brood, or for several relayings after unsuccessful nesting attempts. Whether more than two broods are ever raised in a season is not known. Harris (1944) watched two pairs complete at least two nesting in a season. He notes "a second nest built by one pair was placed 40 feet away from the first nest; another pair built their second nest 100 feet from the first." Two second nests we found were 50 and 100 feet respectively from each pair's first nest.

Plumages.—Harris (1944) says newly-hatched young

are covered with buffy gray down about one-fourth-inch long. On the capital tract two rows of down, beginning at the loral region, run posteriorly to the occipital region, where they join a transversely placed tuft. An isolated tuft stands above each eyelid. A wide patch occurs in the spinal region, narrowing as it enters the pelvic region. Down is abundant in the humeral tract. In the alar tract, it is distributed in two rows on the dorsal surface. A prominent patch is found in each femoral tract, and scattered tufts can be detected in the crural tract. Mandibles are flesh color, darkening at the tip. Tarsi, toes, and claws are pale flesh color.

L. J. Moriarty (1965) adds that the mouth lining is "yellowish-orange."

T. S. Roberts (1932) describes the juvenal plumage as:

"Feathers of upper parts dusky centrally, edged with buffy and grayish-white producing a scaled rather than striped appearance; throat, abdomen, and under tail-coverts plain white; pale buff on breast, more or less thickly streaked and spotted with dusky-black; wings, including greater coverts, buffy-gray, the latter tipped with pale buff; middle and lesser coverts dark, tipped and edged with buffy-white, producing two rather indistinct buffy wing-bars; tail as in adult."

He notes that in the first fall and winter plumage of the male: "The black of crown and underparts and the chestnut collar are largely acquired at the postjuvenal molt but are almost entirely obscured by buffy-white edgings of feathers. * * * The *first nuptial plumage* is assumed before spring by the wearing off of the light feather-edgings and a partial molt on head and breast. The adult male, after the postnuptial molt, is similar, but the concealed black is more extensive, and the middle and lesser wing-coverts are purer black and white."

He describes the male in breeding plumage as:

Top of head, a broad line back of eye, a spot below ear-coverts, and underparts from chin to belly black; a small spot on occiput, a broad line over eye, lores, and a collar across throat white; chin pale buff (the white collar separating the buff from the black of lower throat); a collar across hindneck deep clear chestnut; back striped with dull black and gray, indistinctly so on rump and upper tail-coverts; wings, including greater coverts, brownish-gray; middle and lesser coverts black, tipped with white, broadly on the lesser forming a white patch; tertiaries brown, tipped and edged with light; the closed tail appears dark above, white below; spread it is largely white except middle pairs of feathers; the two outer pairs of feathers are almost wholly white, the others white at base with terminal oblique dark areas, decreasing in extent outward, thus not producing the terminal barred appearance seen in McCown's longspur. The wing-lining, a patch on either side of the breast, belly, and under tail-coverts white. The black of the abdomen is sometimes streaked with chestnut. Bill dusky above, light on cutting-edges and at base below; legs and feet dusky-flesh color; iris brown.

The female he describes as:

"A dull-colored bird, smaller than the male, striped throughout above with dull black, pale rufous, and grayish; a slightly paler collar across hindneck; below dull buff, lighter on chin and upper throat; faintly streaked on sides and across breast with fine dark lines. Some females are mottled with concealed black on breast and upper abdomen, and obscurely streaked on sides. Wings and tail as in male, except two very faint wing bars. Bill, legs, and feet dusky-flesh color, lighter than in male."

We found great variation in the breeding plumages of both male and female birds in Saskatchewan, so much so that we could recognize many individual birds. Some males had white areas of various sizes and shapes in the otherwise black underparts, and their throats varied from white to buffy yellow. Many females showed vestiges of such male plumage characteristics as black breast markings or dull chestnut collars, but we saw none that reached the extremes reported by DuBois in Montana and R. D. Harris in Montana. As Harris (1944) tells it:

> Occasionally a male is encountered in summer with areas of chestnut on the black underparts. Another anomaly is the occurrence of females in male plumage. DuBois (1935: 69, and 1937: 107) observed at least three female of this type, one "with all the male markings"; the others in an intermediate plumage, with the black underparts, but lacking the chestnut collar. A female with this intermediate type of plumage was collected on June 14, 1933, by T. M. and A. H. Shortt on my study area (it was carefully sexed). * * * The whole plumage was like that of a male, except that all the browns were paler.

C. G. Sibley and O. S. Pettingill, Jr. describe a hybrid between the chestnut-collared and McCown's longspur they collected in an area where the two species are sympatric near Regina, Saskatchewan. The specimen was a male and showed intermediate characteristics between the two species in each area where they normally differ. The bird acted like a McCown's, but had a flight song like that of the chestnut-collared.

Food.—Very little has been published on the food of the chestnut-collar. F. M. Bailey (1928) describes it as "Largely weed seeds and insects, including crickets and grasshoppers, leaf beetles and weevils." Roberts (1932) lists: "Seeds of grasses and other prairie plants; goosefoot, pigweed, witchgrass and grains; grasshoppers, crickets, beetles, bugs, caterpillars, wireworms, ants, etc."

Martin, Zim, and Nelson (1951) give the analysis of 43 stomachs from various times of year as showing the diet 100 percent plant food in winter, and 72 percent animal food in summer. The animal food consists of "many beetles, grasshoppers, and spiders, as well as numerous other kinds of invertebrates." Leading the plant foods are dropseedgrass, wheat, sunflower, and needlegrass, with lesser amounts of panicgrass, three-awn, pigweed, bristlegrass, and grama-grass, goosefoot, and sedge.

Voice.—Sibley and Pettingill (1955) give the following comparison of the flight songs of the chestnut-collared and McCown's longspurs: "The flight songs of typical McCown's and Chestnut-collared longspurs differ in movements and in song pattern. Both species fly gradually upward, their wings beating rapidly. From the peak of the ascent McCown's proceeds to sail downward abruptly with wings held stiffly outstretched and raised high above the back. The Chestnut-collared, after reaching the peak of the ascent, prolongs the flight by circling and undulating, finally descending with the wings beating as rapidly as before. Both species sing after the ascent, but the song of the McCown's is louder with the notes uttered more slowly."

The chestnut-collar does not use the flight song as often as the McCown's does, nor does his performance appear as formal. The McCown usually nests on flat, open places such as very sparse prairie or plowed, summerfallow fields where it must make frequent, short song flights to advertise its presence. The chestnut-collared's habitat is usually well supplied with song perches from which the singing male is easily seen.

D. J. Borror (1961) found the pitch range in the chestnut-collared's song to vary between 2,300 and 6,500 cycles per second. He gives the following comprehensive description of the song:

> The song is loud, rather musical, somewhat similar in quality to the song of the western meadowlark, and is generally 2 to 2.5 secs in length. It consists of 5 to 10 (usually 7 or 8) phrases uttered 3 to 4 per sec; the phrases may contain from one to several notes. The 3 or 4 introductory phrases contain clear notes, and are of decreasing pitch; the final phrases are usually buzzy. The first phrase or two of the song are usually quite weak. The phrases are not repeated in a given song, but some phrases contain repetitive elements. The songs of a given bird are essentially alike, differing only in the character of the final weak phrases; the songs of different birds usually contain slightly different phrases.

I was pleased to see that Borror disagrees with the earlier published accounts that seem to follow Coues' (1903) description of the song as "weak and twittering." From the inside of a blind, the song of a bird singing on the roof can be deafening! I could distinguish no difference between the songs given in flight and those while perched.

The male chestnut-collared spends a great deal of his time singing. Throughout the nesting season song continues from one hour before sunrise until shortly after sunset with little regard to the weather. The only significant break occurs when the nestlings get so large that most of his time and energy is taken up with providing food for them. At one nest, however, the male was still singing 54 times per hour when the young died eight days after hatching.

Harris (1944) gives the following accurate account of other notes: "The common call note is a *til-lup* or *til-lip* (the accent on the first syllable), sometimes lengthened to *til-lil-lip*. It is a general flocking and flight note, and in the breeding season it seems to express anxiety. The usual alarm note is a whistled *wheer*, used mostly by the male. A *tzip* and a rattling *tri-ri-rip* indicate extreme alarm and perhaps anger. On coming to the nest with food, the female sometimes utters a soft *lu*, and the young then stretch open their mouths. Low, conversational notes are exchanged between the parents at the nest." To which it should be added that birds also utter continuous *buzz-buzz-buzz* notes during sexual and territorial chases.

Behavior.—The different roles the male and female chestnut-collared longspurs play on the nesting grounds result in wide differences in their behavior. The male is well suited to his role of guarding the territory against encroachment by rival males. He makes himself conspicuous as possible by his flight songs and by perching above the level of the grass. The female is quiet and tame. She rarely perches above the ground level and she seldom flies.

The female is so protectively colored and so agile afoot that she does not have to be very timid. As she walks through the grass near the nest she can be extremely hard to follow. As you approach she will usually walk quietly away from you, occasionally flying 10 or 15 feet to avoid being stepped on if you get too close. Her close sitting during incubation and brooding also has survival value in foiling potential predators. In one extreme case a female allowed me to photograph her from a distance of 18 inches, and then catch her by hand on the nest for weighing and color marking.

The only time the female makes herself conspicuous is when trying to attract your attention away from the nest. I have five records of distraction displays by females in my notes, each when the young were hatching. In each case the bird fluttered two or three feet into the air in a series of six-foot jumps with head held low and tail flicked wide to show all its white. John Horton of Moose Jaw told me of a male doing a "broken-wing act" and trying to lead him away from a nest containing young about a week old.

Although the chestnut-collared lives peacefully with the other grassland birds and animals, it tries to drive away any that approach its nest too closely. Our study area supported a heavy population of Richardson's ground squirrels, and whenever one came near a nest, one of the pair, usually the male, immediately attacked it. Fluttering and chattering over the "gopher's" head, the bird drops down to peck its head and back. Sometimes the gopher rears up at the bird, and I saw one actually jump into the air at the attacker. Or there may be a pause while bird and squirrel stand facing each other a few feet apart. Eventually the longspur gets the animal running away from the nest, and keeps chivvying it from above its back until it is a safe 80 or 100 feet away from the nest. I saw one bird pause after attacking a ground squirrel flick his bill several times as though to clear it of hair.

I have seen the longspurs similarly attack gray partridges, meadowlarks, cowbirds, and Savannah sparrows. On the other hand I have seen chestnut-collareds being chased by meadowlarks and Baird's sparrows whose nests they probably approached too closely.

Though a resident of the dry prairies, the chestnut-collar is strongly attracted to water and will visit regularly any that happens to be nearby to drink and bathe. I kept watch at a pool left by recent rains on our study area when the females were incubating their first clutches. Birds visited the pool periodically from a few minutes after sunrise until just before sunset, and their appearances seemed fairly evenly distributed. In 5½ hours of watching I never saw two male or two female longspurs at the pool at the same time. One female bathed and preened herself twice over while the male watched impatiently. After five minutes he finally crowded up to her and chased her back toward the nest, as if urging her to return to the eggs.

Field marks.—The male in spring with his chestnut collar, black underparts, and white tail can be mistaken for no other species. In other plumages the birds are rather nondescript, and can best be told from the vesper sparrows, pipits, and other longspurs that frequent open ground by the tail pattern. The spread tail is mostly white, with a small dark triangle in the center with its base at the end of the tail.

Enemies.—By reducing the amount of grassland habitat, man and his agricultural practices are undoubtedly the chestnut-collar's worst enemy. Yet the birds must suffer heavily from the depredations of badgers, skunks, weasels, and snakes, as do all ground-nesting birds. Though as related, the birds will not tolerate Richardson's ground squirrels near their nest, I have no real proof of any predation by these animals. Such nest-robbing birds as crows and magpies must also take their toll. One morning a crow crouched in the grass with just his head showing about 150 feet from a nest with four eggs. The parents investigated him, and then went about their affairs apparently unconcernedly. The crow watched quietly for almost an hour, and then flew off without discovering the nest. Of the 31 nests we had under observation for more than one day, eggs or young disappeared from 11.

Young birds found dead in the nest are usually covered with ants. Though this is no proof that they caused the deaths, the female may often be seen cleaning ants out of the nest and picking them off the nestlings.

Hawks, owls, and shrikes also take a few birds without doubt, though the only record in the literature is M. F. Gilman's (1910) report of a Cooper's hawk preying on a flock in Arizona.

Cases of cowbird parasitism are rare. None of the 36 chestnut-collared nests we found in Saskatchewan was parasitized, though three of the four lark-bunting nests we found in the same area contained cowbird eggs. None of the 38 nest-record cards in the Regina Museum of Natural History mentions cowbird eggs. Of the 23 nests Harris (1944) studied in Manitoba, only one was parasitized. Herbert Friedmann (1963) concludes "This longspur is probably a not uncommon local victim of the northwestern race of the brown-headed cowbird. The paucity of records seems to be due to a scarcity of observers in the breeding range of the host. * * * North Dakota is the only area where this longspur has been observed repeatedly as a cowbird victim."

Fall.—Harris (1944) gives the following fine description of the start of autumn migration in Manitoba:

> The birds collected into flocks before turning southward. Young birds were the first to gather, frequenting the outskirts of the nesting areas. With the termination of nesting about the middle of August, adults joined the flocks of juveniles. The species then entirely abandoned the grassy breeding grounds, and was found in adjacent ditches, dried-up sloughs, and similar low-lying, rough ground (though rarely stubble or plowed land). This rather remarkable change of habitat may be due to the availability of the autumn crop of weed seeds, combined with the reduced number of grasshoppers, which constitute the bulk of the species' food in summer; but the cause may lie deeper than that, and involve the psychological and physiological changes bound up with migration. Young and old together spent the last half of August in the new habitat, in loose, restless flocks numbering up to 30 or more individuals. During September, southward migration began, and the latest date on which I noted the species at Winnipeg was September 28.

The birds wander southward in large flocks to their winter range, pausing at good feeding and watering point en route. Some remain on the southern plains of the United States, the rest continue on to northern Mexico.

Distribution

Range.—Southern portions of Prairie Provinces south to northern Sonora, central Chihuahua, southern Texas, and northern Louisiana.

Breeding range.—The chestnut-collared longspur breeds from southern Alberta (Lundbreck, Beaverhill Lake), southern Saskatchewan (Conquest, Quill Lakes), and southern Manitoba (Brandon, Winnipeg) southeast to northeastern Colorado (Weld County), central northern Nebraska (Holt County), and southwestern Minnesota (Jackson County), formerly to western Kansas (Ellis County).

Winter range.—Winters from northern Arizona (San Francisco Mountain, Springerville), central New Mexico (San Mateo Mountains), northeastern Colorado (Fort Collins), and central Kansas (Larned, Manhattan) south to northern Sonora (Pozo de Luis; San Pedro River at boundary), central Chihuahua (Chihuahua), southern Texas (Rio Grande City, Brownsville), and northern Louisiana (Gilliam); occasionally south to Puebla and Veracruz (Orizaba).

Casual records.—Casual west to California (Point Reyes; Darwin) and central British Columbia (Kispiox Valley), north to northern Alberta (Fort McMurray), east to the Atlantic coast in Nova Scotia (Cape Sable), New Brunswick (Nantucket Island near Grand Manan), Maine (Scarborough), Massachusetts (Magnolia), New York (four Long Island localities), and Maryland (Ocean City), and south to northern Florida (Tallahassee).

Migration.—Early dates of spring arrival are: New York—Orient, April 21. Minnesota—Jackson County, April 12 (average of 5 years for southern Minnesota, April 30). North Dakota—Jamestown, March 26. Manitoba—Treesbank, March 24 (average of 23 years, April 11). Saskatchewan—Indian Head, March 30. Wyoming—Laramie, March 16. Montana—Big Sandy, April 21; Terry, April 26.

Late dates of spring departure are: Texas—Austin, April 26. New Mexico—Gage, April 17. Arizona—Huachuca Mountains, May 3.

Early dates of fall arrival are: California—Inyo County, September 28. Arizona—San Francisco Mountain, September 18; Mount Graham, September 24. New Mexico—Willis, September 12. Oklahoma—Copan, November 11. Texas—Austin, November 12. Maine—Scarborough, August 13. Massachusetts—Magnolia, July 28. New York—Miller Place, September 14. Maryland—Ocean City, August 20.

Late dates of fall departure are: Montana—Miles City, September 27; Terry, September 23. Manitoba—Treesbank, October 12 (average of 24 years, October 3). North Dakota—Jamestown, October 7. Minnesota—Lac qui Parle County, October 12.

Egg dates.—Alberta: 6 records, May 27 to June 11.

Minnesota: 23 records, May 19 to June 16.

Montana: 36 records, May 6 to July 19; 19 records, June 6 to July 7.

North Dakota: 27 records, May 23 to June 30; 19 records, May 26 to June 10.

Saskatchewan: 55 records, May 10 to July 9; 36 records, May 20 to June 10.

South Dakota: 19 records, May 20 to June 17; 13 records, May 22 to June 5.

PLECTROPHENAX NIVALIS NIVALIS (Linnaeus)

Snow Bunting

Contributed by DAVID FREELAND PARMELEE

HABITS

To those who dwell in the North Temperate Zone, the snow bunting is the very epitome of an arctic bird, a true creature of the snows for which it is so aptly named. It usually appears only in the dead of winter, often on the heels of a storm that has blanketed the countryside with white. Though certainly capable of flying southward to warmer climes, it remains with the cold and snow, and seldom strays below the northern two tiers of the United States, content to glean its hardy livelihood from the few seed-spikes of grasses and weeds the carpet of winter leaves exposed. And as soon as the warming spring sun begins to melt the wandering drifts, the vagrant flocks disappear as suddenly as they came, on route back to their northern home.

But to those who know it on its northern breeding grounds, the snow bunting is the harbinger of warmer times to come. As George M. Sutton (1932) wrote after spending the long winter on Southampton Island: "Only the North Countryman knows how welcome is the cheerful greeting of the little *Amauligak* when it returns in the Spring. The whole world may be white, the sky overcast, and the wind boisterous or cruel; but when the *Amauligak* comes, winter is near its end. All of us, even the fatalistic, phlegmatic Eskimos, found ourselves listening every morning in February for the familiar note of this bird. But *Amauligak's* vital problems are not easily solved, when he returns too early; so he waits until he is sure the drifts are soon to melt. And it often seems that he is a long time in coming."

Much of the following account of this species is based on my own experiences shared with G. M. Sutton (Sutton and Parmelee, 1954) on Baffin Island and with S. D. MacDonald (Parmelee and MacDonald, 1960) on Ellesmere Island. Other detailed sources referred to repeatedly by author only in the following pages are those by Niko Tinbergen (1939), H. F. Witherby et al. (1941), Finn Salomonsen (1950–1951), and Alfred Watson (1957).

Spring.—T. S. Roberts (1932) thus describes the species' departure from its wintering grounds in Minnesota: "Migrating by day as well as by night, the Snow Bunting may be seen on days in March and early April passing in a continuous stream at no great height above the earth. It is not in flock formation but scattered, the birds calling to one another as they move steadily onward in undulating, erratic flight, a few dropping out now and then to alight and feed."

The arrival date of snow buntings on the breeding grounds may vary considerably from year to year in a given locality. Salomonsen notes "When the spring is especially inclement the Snow-Bunting can be delayed almost a month." Tinbergen cites the careful records kept by Johan Petersen, first governor of Angmagssalik in southern Greenland, which showed first arrivals as early as February 10th and as late as April 8th, with an average arrival date for 17 years of March 21st. While Pleske (1928) attributes such variation to climatic conditions in the breeding area, Tinbergen thinks it "may be due to a considerable extent to weather conditions at the last stage of the migration route." The birds often arrived in southern Greenland following stormy weather from the east. He adds: "The arrival of new birds always occurred during the early morning, up to about 6 or 7 A.M.; during the first three hours after midnight, flocks were often observed that did not alight but passed on."

MacDonald and I observed very much the same arrival pattern in Ellesmere Island, and also noted some diurnal migration in mid-afternoon. In Greenland according to Salomonsen: "The migration covers more than one month and usually continues over the greater part of May * * *. The first birds to arrive are always males, as normal in many passeres. However, the sexual difference in migration is more pronounced in the Snow-Bunting than in any other bird. The females do not arrive until 3–4 weeks after the males." At 80°N. in Ellesmere we found the arrival period covered a span of at least 46 days. We first noted a male on April 16, a female on May 21.

Plumage characteristics show the first males to arrive are mostly those more than one year old. Few in numbers at first, they flock near the coast while their numbers gradually increase; some then disperse to higher country inland. When the first females arrive some weeks later, they are often accompanied by newly arriving males, many returning for the first time. We found mixed flocks common in Ellesmere at the end of the migration period in late May. The birds in these mixed flocks did not appear to be mated on arrival.

Arrival dates in the Canadian Archipelago correspond roughly to those recorded for Greenland and other parts of the species' circumpolar range, being generally later at higher latitudes. A few birds occasionally reach low-arctic localities in February, but the first usually appear in March. The snow buntings seldom reach the high arctic before April, Greely's (1886) report of one in Hall Land beyond 81° N. on March 14th being a notable exception. MacDonald (1953) recorded the species on the north coast of Ellesmere Island beyond 83° N. on April 27, and there are earlier April records for more southern parts of Ellesmere and for high-arctic Greenland. Most birds probably reach the northernmost breeding grounds in mid- to late May.

Territory.—The nesting habitat of the snow bunting is confined at low latitudes to bare, stony mountain-tops, rarely below 3,500 feet in Scotland according to Witherby et al. (1941). In its arctic home, however, the species nests from sea level along the coasts to considerable elevations inland. Salomonsen notes they are found higher in the Greenland mountains than any other bird, having been observed at 1,027 meters. On Baffin Island Watson recorded females at 1,050 meters, males at 1,800–2,000 meters. On Bylot Island Van Tyne and

Drury (1959) recorded birds above 900 meters, and at Ellesmere MacDonald and I frequently saw pairs at 600–700 meters elevation. Its preferred habitat is rough, rocky country with interrupted vegetation, as near stony beaches or in sea cliffs in coastal areas, or in rocky outcrops at higher levels. Some of the lowest breeding densities occur in grassy tundra with little broken or rocky ground.

The size of the individual bunting territory may be surprisingly large, commonly as much as 300 to 400 meters in diameter. In optimum habitat where the population pressure is great, Tinbergen records territory diameters "diminished to about 50 to 100 m. in most of the observed cases." Nevertheless Van Tyne and Drury's (1959) report of two occupied nests "within five yards of each other in the stone wall of one Eskimo house" on Bylot Island must be regarded as exceptional.

The early arriving males wander about the breeding grounds in flock for several weeks before showing signs of territorial behavior. Tinbergen notes that as the season progresses, certain individuals in the flock become noisier, begin to sing softly, grow more excitable, and quarrel occasionally with their companions, threatening them with head lowered between the shoulders, bill pointed toward the enemy, and occasional fluttering of wings. Such birds leave the flock in a day or two and isolate themselves on territory of their choosing.

Each male proclaims his occupancy by perching on favored conspicuous lookout perches within the territory, singing, and driving off trespassing males. Newly established territories may not be occupied continuously. Tinbergen observed defending males that fed on their territories in the morning and often left by midday to forage elsewhere, but returned later in the day, also that "The males slept within their territories, using the same hole for several nights successively, but now and then moving to a new site." Roosting males that MacDonald and I flushed at this stage on Ellesmere Island often flew off and alighted beside the roosting defender of another territory. Surprisingly no fighting ensued, and both birds simply turned their heads back and went to sleep again. But when the two were flushed together, they made a show of animosity, chasing each other and even singing until both settled down again, sometimes side by side. This behavior pattern was not seen after the females arrived.

As the season advances the males remain and feed within their territories for longer periods and become increasingly jealous of their boundaries. Song increases in intensity, and the defenders savagely attack other males that approach. The defender often flies toward its adversary from afar, singing and posturing during flight, a phenomenon Tinbergen calls "song-flight," in which the defender "rose steeply with frequent wing-strokes, then stopped wing-action, sailed in the direction of the stranger, body curved upward, loudly singing, and keeping its slightly trembling wings in an approximately horizontal position." The intruding bird usually flees, and the incident is over. But the fighting that may follow such an attack, especially between males of adjacent territories, may be fierce and prolonged. The birds may rise into the air on fluttering wings, clinging to each other with bills and feet, or tumble together across rocks and snow. Feathers fly, but serious injury probably seldom results.

While sight of an intruder is usually enough to provoke attack, Niko Tinbergen (1939) points out the great importance of sound. A calling or especially a singing trespasser is certain to evoke attack, but "Sometimes a male, though foraging on an occupied territory, remained unnoticed by the owner for some time. This was especially the case when several birds intruded on one territory at the same time. We observed in such cases that an intruder, although he was not attacked himself, crouched every time the owner of the territory performed a ceremonial flight, keeping quite flat and motionless, only moving his head slightly to follow the singing bird with the eyes. This was the first proof we got of the warning function of the display of a bird holding a territory."

According to E. M. Nicholson (1930) male buntings on territory are indifferent to other nonpredatory species, and Tinbergen adds "Lapland Longspurs, Greenland Wheatears and Redpolls often lived in Snow Bunting territories but I never noticed any hostilities." We observed no such interspecific tolerance in either Baffin Island or Ellesmere Island. In both regions the male buntings chased other small passerines from the territory. They were particularly adamant in driving off any wheatears (*Oenanthe oenanthe*) which, as Salomonsen points out, occupy a type of habitat similar to that the bunting prefers.

It is difficult to interpret Watson's observations on Cape Searle Island, near Baffin Island, after a heavy influx of migrants in late May. He states "The males occupied territories and paired with the females though they were clearly migrants; nearly all had gone by May 25th." Our observations in Ellesmere indicated that the newly arrived mixed flocks contained only unpaired birds, but some buntings certainly pair before arriving at the breeding ground. These probably include those pairs that roam in the breeding areas before settling on territories.

Courtship.—Some male buntings may continue to sing ardently for several weeks before the females arrive. When the females first appear, the males threaten them as they would trespassers. But the females remain close by instead of fleeing, though they may move from one territory to another until paired. The males then exhibit a new type of behavior, which Tinbergen describes as follows: "He assumed an erect, strangely stretched attitude, spreading his tail widely and spreading the conspicuously colored wings backward and downward. In this attitude he directed the piebald surface of back and tail toward the female and then ran quickly away from her. Having run for some meters, he abruptly turned, came back without any display, and then repeated the performance. This specialized display apparently served to demonstrate the conspicuous color patterns of the plumage."

Sutton and Parmelee describe similar behavior on Baffin Island: "Males who were with females sometimes lifted their wings high above their backs, or scuttled rapidly through the snow, with head lowered, as if showing off. 'Scuttling' males sometimes ran swiftly in one direction, stopped, turned at a right angle, and scuttled off again." Witherby et al. express it as: "Courting male also observed 'dancing' down a scree, raising wings."

Another display of the male before the female closely resembles the territorial song-flight already described. He ascends 15 to 30 feet or so into the air and, with wings set high or horizontally, flutters to the ground singing mostly during the descent and often after landing. Or he may sing while fluttering down from a precipitous ledge. As Gabrielson and Lincoln (1959) describe it: "the males start courtship performance, usually rising from a perch somewhere on the ground to a point high in the air and then singing at frequent intervals their rather simple but musical song as they descend, ending it as they reach the ground. The song is given on the upward flight as well as on the descent."

Immediately following pairing, the male buntings temporarily but dramatically stop singing and remain quiet, except when their mates leave the territory. This led Tinbergen to conclude that the primary function of the song on territory is to attract a mate, to which its warning function is of secondary importance, and he therefore calls it "advertising song."

After pairing the birds move about and forage together on the territory. The females leave the territory from time to time, but the males seldom do. Mated males seldom court other females, but exceptions are known. The males continue their strong defense of the territory against other males, and the mated females against other females. As Tinbergen writes:

> Mated females do not tolerate other females in their neighborhood. Fights between two females were of common occurrence. When two pairs met on their common boundary, a fight often resulted, and these fights of pair against pair really consisted of two fights: one of male against male, the other of female against female. Although we witnessed hundreds of fights of male Snow Buntings *inter se* and females *inter se*, we only once saw a female attacking a male, and this attack consisted of a short pursuit of a retreating male after a prolonged fight between two pairs. We never saw a male attacking a female.

The females at this stage are not yet sexually receptive, and rebuff the males' frequent attempts to copulate. This results in the conspicuous sexual flights, in which the males chase their mates swiftly both close to and high above the ground in a most dazzling manner. These flights according to Tinbergen invariably follow unaccomplished coition. They may continue for several weeks, but they decline rapidly when the female becomes oestrously receptive.

During this period paired birds, often one following the other, explore the various niches and fissures on the territory, presumably searching for nest sites. Even unpaired males on territory show interest in holes by entering them. Tinbergen describes the nest stage thus:

> The beginning of this new period was marked by a change in the behavior of the female. She had until now shown interest in holes, but never had picked up nesting materials. On a certain day, the female suddenly took some moss in her bill, carried it for a few seconds or even less, and then dropped it again. On this same day she did not flee when the male, as on previous days, approached her, but adopted an attitude which was never seen before: she kept her back quite flat and horizontal, pointed her bill upward and lifted the tail. The male mounted and coition was accomplished.
>
> The carrying of nesting material therefore indicated, in all instances studied, the beginning of the female's oestrous period.
>
> * * *
>
> After this first day the birds regularly performed coition, most frequently during the early morning, between about 2 and 6 A.M., and not more than 2 to 5 times a day.
>
> Shortly after the first copulations the female started building, that is, she not only collected pieces of moss, but she really carried mouthfuls of it to a hole. What she did with it when she entered the hole, we were unable to see. Nesting activities were most persistent immediately after coition.

Nesting.—The female snow bunting builds the nest alone, though the male often accompanies her to and from the nest site and occasionally even picks up nesting material and offers it to her. She may gather nesting material from afar, in which case the male does not follow her much beyond territorial limits. Also she may start several nests and abandon them before choosing the one she finishes.

The species utilizes a variety of sites, but almost always hides the nest in some hole or cranny, though sometimes only under moss. The nest is often a foot or more back in a narrow rock fissure where it is inaccessible. Frequently it is built under loose rocks on the ground or in scree, and not infrequently in stone foundations or buildings. Nests have been reported in skulls and in such artificial sites as wooden boxes, metal containers, wire coils, construction rubble, and other debris. Where rock or artificial sites are lacking, the buntings will use cracks or holes in soft ground, especially where the earth is frost-heaved into piles of mud. Nests in soft ground rest in depressions that presumably the buntings themselves scratch out.

Exposed nests are exceptional. Watson noted one "open to the sky" in a hollow between a shrub and a boulder on Baffin Island. Of three that MacDonald and I found on Ellesmere, one was between two hummocks on the tundra far from rocks or mud mounds, and two were on narrow rock ledges. The tops of all three were completely open and exposed. We found several others in shallow sandstone niches that were partially exposed, but not from above.

The rather large, loosely constructed, thick-walled nest is composed chiefly of dry grasses, sometimes partially or mainly of mosses, lichens, roots, or leaves. A considerable amount of grass often projects from its sides, adding to its bulky appearance. In some localities it is characteristically sandy, in others it may contain bits of mud. The deep nest cup is variously lined, thickly or thinly, with finer dry grasses, rootlets, occasionally downy willow seeds, and invariably with one or more kinds of feathers or fur. White ptarmigan feathers are commonly used, also feathers of jaegers, gulls, and snowy owls. The fur of dogs, arctic foxes, lemmings, and hares, and the coarse guard hairs and soft wool of the musk ox have all been reported. No doubt the birds find suitable the feathers and fur of any other species at hand.

The buntings sometimes re-use their old nests, though this phenomenon has not been widely reported. Watson found a nest on Baffin Island with two linings, the older one from the previous year. Two active nests MacDonald and I found on Ellesmere Island were old ones lined afresh, with the bases of the old structures still frozen to the ground when found. This re-use of old nests is probably not related so much to the shortness of the breeding season as to the lack of good, perhaps preferred nest sites in certain situations. The common occurrence of several old unoccupied nests in some nesting areas, however, attests the frequent abundance of nest sites.

A nest Sutton and I found on Baffin Island, started on June 15, was ready for lining June 19; by June 20 much hair had been added, by June 22 feathers had also been added and the first egg laid. Watson reports another Baffin Island nest built and lined in 4 days and the first egg laid on the 5th day. The brief time of 14 hours with the first egg laid the 2nd day Joseph S. Dixon (1943) reports for nest building at an Alaskan site must be exceptional. G. T. Kay (1944) reports captive birds taking up to 6 days. Tinbergen notes that females may continue to add lining to the nest for 2 or 3 days after laying the first egg. In extreme cases, according to Watson, the first egg may be laid on dry sand before nest building even starts, and the nest built around it while the clutch is completed.

Tinbergen found that in two cases the interval between the first observed copulation and the laying of the first egg was 13 days in one, 8 days in the other. He also states that females do not allow the males to copulate after they lay the first egg. Observers agree that eggs are laid during the early morning, as early as 3:00 a.m., and that generally one is laid each day until the clutch is complete. Watson reported 2 days between laying of two eggs at one nest.

The spread of egg laying at any one locality, even at high latitudes, may be considerable, in some cases more than a month. Tinbergen quotes Manniche's finding eggs at Danmarks Havn, Greenland, from June 6 to July 18. Though eggs may be laid earlier at low latitudes—mid-May in Iceland and late May in Scotland—egg laying is not necessarily late at high latitudes. MacDonald and I believe egg laying started at 80° N. in Ellesmere in early June, certainly no later than June 10, which is earlier than many reports for lower latitudes.

The peak of egg laying appears to be mid-June in west-central Ellesmere and in southern Baffin Island at the opposite end of the Canadian Arctic Archipelago, but Watson found it to be late June in eastern Baffin Island. Of interest also is Salomonsen's observation that egg laying in Greenland averages at least a week earlier in the sunny interior than on the colder outer coast.

Data on clutch size from various parts of the species' range, summarized by Tinbergen and by Watson, indicate that, as Lack (1947) pointed out for this and other species, the average size of the clutch increases with latitude. Our observations from Ellesmere substantiate this. Eight clutches we found at 80° N. varied from 6 to 8 eggs and averaged 6.8—a significantly high sample.

Eggs.—The snow bunting usually lays 4 to 7 eggs, but sometimes only 3 or as many as 9. The ground color is greenish, pale bluish, grayish, or creamy white with spots, blotches, and occasional small scrawls of greenish and purplish browns such as "dusky drab," "Natal brown," "olive brown," "Rood's brown," "Clove brown," and black. The undermarkings of "purplish gray" or "pale Quaker drab" are frequently very prominent. There is much variation; some eggs will be heavily marked with scrawls, others only with spots. The markings generally are scattered over the entire surface, although they frequently tend to concentrate at the large end where they may form a loose wreath, or make a solid cap over the top of the egg. Some types are very pale and marked only with light browns such as "wood brown" or "fawn color" and without undermarkings. The measurements of 50 eggs average 22.9 by 16.5 mm; the eggs showing the four extremes measure *26.4* x 17.3, 23.4 x *18.3*, *20.3* x 15.8, and 21.3 by *15.2* millimeters.

Young.—Though one or two observers have reported seeing males on the nest, most are agreed that incubation is entirely by the female. The males feed their mates frequently during egg laying and incubation, and are conspicuous in carrying food. On and off the nest the females will beg for food by calling and fluttering their wings just as the young do later. The females also feed themselves; Watson noted one that left the nest regularly to feed for an hour in mid-afternoon.

Opinions differ as to when incubation starts. Tinbergen states that in southeast Greenland it "begins from one to three days after completion of the clutch." Watson reports that in eastern Baffin Island: "At nearly every closely watched nest the female began to sit from the time the first egg was laid. The sole exception was at one sheltered nest where incubation did not start till the third egg was laid, though the nights were cold and frosty and light snowfalls frequent." Our experiences in both Baffin and Ellesmere islands showed incubation usually started with the laying of the third or fourth egg.

The incubation period, that is the interval between the laying and the hatching of the last egg, varies from 10 to 15.5 days, apparently dependent on the attentiveness and effectiveness of the female in her duties. Witherby et al. note it recorded as 10 to 12 days by Ekblaw, 12 to 13 days by Thompson, and 14 to 15 days by Sutton. One we timed at Baffin and one at Ellesmere each fell somewhere between 12 and 13 days. All these variations are close to or within the range Watson gives as 10.25–10.5 to 14.5–15.5 days. The 21-to-22-day incubation period Gabrielson and Lincoln (1959) report for Alaska is confusing, and probably measured from the laying of the first to hatching of the last egg.

Regarding hatching, Watson comments: "At most nests the habit of incubating the eggs during the laying period resulted in a marked spread in hatching. For example, a clutch of four produced three young in over 4 and probably 5 days; other periods, for clutches of 5 and 7 eggs from which 5 and 6 hatched, were 3–4 days and at least 4½ days." The greatest spread undoubtedly results when incubation of a large clutch starts with the first egg and all the eggs hatch.

Newly hatched bunting are thinly covered with down and quite helpless. When touched they open their mouths wide but produce no audible sound. When 2 days old they make faint food cries which gradually become louder as the birds develop. Tinbergen writes: "While the young were being fed, they uttered a long, high note, which became louder as they grew older, and which called attention to the nests from a great distance." Nicholson (1930) says "The loud metallic chittering of nestlings carried quite 150 yards."

The many young calling conjointly produce the great noisiness so characteristic of a heavily populated breeding ground.

Both parents feed the nestlings, the female being at first the more active and persistent. The food consists of various insects and arachnids gathered both on and off territory. The males at this time are somewhat less adamant in defense of their nesting territories, and may forage together amicably in favored nearby areas—a sort of no man's land among territories. Females still beg food, sometimes successfully from males other than their mates, and then give it to the young. Food begging at this time apparently has little or no sexual function.

The females frequently brood after feeding and during cold periods. At one Baffin Island nest Watson writes: "The female was often seen sitting on the young during the coldest few hours of the night till a time when in one nest the oldest young was 12 days old, and the youngest 8 days old and only three days from finally leaving this nest."

Both parents tend to nest sanitation by carrying fecal sacs from the nest. Shortly before the young leave the nest, their feces lose the mucous sac and resemble adult feces. At this time the young also develop a new and distinctive food cry which enables the parents to find them more readily after they start to disperse.

The brood may leave the nest en masse, but more often only part of it leaves, followed by the rest considerably later. Some young may leave the nest and even the nest crevice, and then return to it later. This complex dispersal pattern makes it difficult to determine the duration of the fledging period. Watson found that the interval from hatching until the individual left the nest for the last time varied from 10 to 17 days. Generally young buntings leave the nest proper before they can fly well, though they may remain in the nest crevice for another day or so. Some young fly strongly when 13–14 days old.

Once outside the nest crevice the brood soon scatters, even beyond the male's territorial boundaries. Those advanced young that disperse early are largely or entirely cared for by the male parent, who readily locates them through the food call. The remaining siblings are probably tended by the female until parent-offspring relations dissolve, for Tinbergen found fledglings fed by the same parent each time. The young still flutter their wings and call noisily when begging food.

Territorial defense by the males now declines rapidly, singing becomes lax, and some males may start their prenuptial molt while still feeding young. The fact that territorial defense declines at fledging, a most critical time in the breeding cycle, has led some investigators to question the food function of the territory, though its sexual function is widely held.

A first sign of coming fledgling independence is when the young buntings start to show interest in insects, which they do well before their remiges are full grown. Tinbergen noted that one young that left the nest on June 28, tried to catch a mosquito July 2, though its male parent fed it until July 10. On July 9 this chick uttered its first "trembling note" similar to that of adults living in flocks, and the parent-offspring relationship dissolved by July 11. There can be no doubt that this new "contact-note" functions to bring the young together in the loose flocks they now form.

The swarming of young buntings in large flocks at this time has been widely reported. MacDonald and I found them particularly conspicuous in the Slidre Fiord area of Ellesmere Island in early August. The fiord shores had comparatively few buntings during the nesting period, for most of them bred in the rocky interior. When the species started returning to the fiord shores on August 5, most of the birds were full-tailed, unattended juveniles, presumably of early broods. They came by the hundreds, appearing near the beaches in the early morning and fanning out in small groups over the low country during the day, and their numbers increased daily. Here they remained until they completed their postjuvenal molt in early September.

Not all young buntings flock as described above. Some remain with the adults, when the latter retire to secluded places to complete the postnuptial molt. Whether these represent family groups or simply mixed flocks is not certain. By this time, although an occasional fragment of song may still be heard, the sexual bonds between pairs have been broken.

Both Witherby et al. and Salomonsen cite evidence that the snow bunting is occasionally double brooded, that is the female may proceed with a second nesting after successfully fledging its first brood. Tinbergen noticed one case of double-broodedness, which was not clearly defined; the female abandoned her first brood, which perished, and proceeded with another nesting with a second mate. Apparently bigamy may occur in either sex when one of the pair remains sexually potent longer than usual. But as Tinbergen points out, the rigid division of labor between the two sexes in caring for the young does not permit effective double-broodedness. Despite the shortness of the summer season, early nesting snow buntings, even at 80° N., might have time for a second brood, but apparently they rarely do. The sudden decline of sexual flights and song as nesting progresses and the failure of either to recur more than spasmodically is also good evidence that single broods each summer are the rule in the true Arctic.

Plumages and molts.—The natal down is variously described as grayish or brownish. Witherby et al. describe the nestling as "Down, dark grey, fairly long; distribution, inner supra-orbital, occipital, humeral, spinal, ulnar, femoral, and crural. Mouth, externally gape yellow; beak (pale) yellow." Van Tyne and Drury (1959) describe an 8-day-old nestling as "bill, Cadmium Yellow to Cartridge Buff (at rictus); mouth lining, near Deep Corinthian Red; legs and feet, near Ecru Drab. The head, back, and lesser wing coverts of this bird were covered (along the usual tracts) with long natal down, Hair Brown in color. Not the slightest trace of down remained on an eleven-day female in the same nest (nor on an older fledgling collected nearby two days later). The eleven-day nestling weighed 32.3 grams and was extremely fat (2.3 grams of free fat were removed from the underparts). The fledgling was also very fat."

Juveniles differ from first-year birds chiefly in body plumage. Their upper parts, according to Witherby et al., are dusky or buffish-gray streaked with black, the mantle being most buffy and heavily streaked; the underparts are buffy with dusky markings on upper breast and flanks, whitish-buff in the center of breast and belly, dusky gray on chin and center of throat. The median wing coverts are grayish-black tipped with white, not white as in first winter birds; the lesser coverts differ in being grayish-black fringed with grayish-white, rather than black with buffish-white tips or white flecks. The sexes are similar, but the females have more black on the secondaries and outer rectrices. In comparing five juveniles from Frobisher Bay, Baffin Island, with three from Wainwright, Alaska, Richard Graber (MS. 55) found the Alaskan specimens tended to be "buffier" throughout, the buffiness being especially noticeable on the auriculars.

The first winter plumage is acquired by an incomplete postjuvenal molt in which the juvenal wings (except the median and lesser coverts) and tail are retained. The resulting plumage strongly resembles that of adults, but in young males the flight feathers are darker than those of adults, and the brown of the upper parts may be darker. First-year females have darker secondaries than older females.

The juveniles molt while flocking, often near the coast, though some may complete it inland. At high latitudes in Canada and Greenland the juveniles molt very rapidly, and acquire their new plumage by late August or early September. One young bird we collected at 80° N. in Ellesmere Island had nearly completed its postjuvenal molt by August 17.

The adults acquire their fall plumage by a postnuptial molt that is complete or nearly so. The males start molting about fledging time, as early as mid-July in parts of the Canadian Arctic Archipelago and Greenland, the females slightly later. By late July and early August both sexes are molting heavily, and they seek secluded places where they are met singly or in small groups that may include both sexes and young birds. The adults often molt so many flight feathers within a short interval that they become temporarily almost flightless, and escape their enemies only by scurrying swiftly over the rocks.

Salomonsen notes that though the molt may not be completed by early October at lower latitudes and in Iceland, it is particularly rapid at high latitudes in Greenland where migration starts in early September. This is also true in Ellesmere Island, where we found adults in fresh new plumage by late August.

The fresh adult fall plumage is essentially the breeding dress heavily overlaid with brown above and, to a lesser degree, below (pectoral band more or less prominent). The plumage is immediately sensitive to abrasion, which produces a great variation of plumages both individually and seasonally. As abrasion continues, certain colored areas become whiter and the wing pattern more pronounced. The bill, which is black during the breeding season, becomes yellowish, often with a dusky tip.

According to Witherby et al., an incomplete molt affecting the throat and facial region takes place in March, the new feathers being pure white except the ear coverts, which are buffy in males, tawny in females. Continued abrasion in spring produces the boldly black and white breeding plumage of the male. The female becomes a less striking gray and white, characteristically speckled and streaked with brownish to grayish-black above and white below.

The spring molt, according to Salomonsen, is aided to some extent by the bunting's habit of feeding on hard snow, which wears down the facial feathers. Newly arriving males reach the breeding ground in spring, still veiled with brown, some heavily, and a few individuals may retain traces of the veiling well into the nesting season. Others are in breeding dress complete with black bills as early as April 26, possibly earlier. Changes in plumage and appearance can be sudden. One Ellesmere Island male had considerable brown about the head and neck when we banded it April 29th; only a trace of the brown remained when we recaptured it two days later on May 1st.

Male buntings are dimorphic in that their primary coverts grade from pure white through black-tipped and largely dark, to almost or completely dark (Manning et al., 1956). Salomonsen considers the pure white and black-tipped to be the normal adult condition, and the uniform black-brown coverts a "retarded" condition frequently, though not invariably, found in first-year birds. Most early arrivals on the breeding grounds have white or lightly black-tipped coverts, indicating that the old birds commonly are the first to migrate north.

Food.—The deep snows of the low arctic are a great obstacle to the buntings moving northward in spring, and many observers have noted the difficulties the birds encounter in their search for food. In coastal

Alaska for instance, A. M. Bailey (1948) notes of their arrival in early April: "winter seems to have a firm grip upon the barren land at this time, with frozen ground offering little in the way of food, but the flocks of birds scatter throughout the native villages, securing a precarious living where the winds have blown the snow clear." They fare no better in Greenland, where Salomonsen notes the early arrivals depend extensively on Eskimo villages and wind-blown snow fields.

Though the layman might assume conditions to be even more severe at higher latitudes, the opposite is true. Lack of precipitation makes the high arctic a desert with very little snow and the land is a refuge for birds arriving in the early spring. The buntings move among the grass tops exposed by the thin snow, gleaning an easy food supply. On the coastal slopes of Ellesmere Island, MacDonald and I noted thousands of bunting tracks leading from one grass tuft to another. The newly arrived birds were obviously hungry, and those near our camp fed ravenously at the banding traps for several days before joining the flocks of those already fattened.

Food in the early spring consists primarily of various seeds, especially of the grass *Poa* in the far north. In summer and fall the birds eat a mixed diet of insects (mainly Coleoptera, Lepidoptera, Hemiptera, and Diptera), spiders, and seeds and buds. They feed their nestlings and young fledglings animal food exclusively, so far as known. Gabrielson (1924) found the summer food of a few buntings collected near Hudson Bay and the Pribilof Islands to be one-third animal (beetles, crane flies, spiders) and two-thirds vegetable (seeds of grasses, sedges, smartweed). Martin, Zim, and Nelson (1951) list bristlegrass, ragweed, pigweed, sandgrass, goosefoot, and oats as the leading plant species in the diet, and "Fly larvae and pupae, particularly of the cranefly, caterpillars, beetles, and true bugs constitute the major portion of the animal diet. Crustaceans are also consumed, particularly sand fleas." Nichols (in Pearson et al., 1936) reports that they eat "locust" eggs in Nebraska. The winter food is primarily grass and weed seeds, but Forbush (1929) notes that "along the coast [it] takes tiny crustaceans and other small forms of marine life, sometimes following the retreating waves or gleaning in pools like sandpipers."

Voice.—Witherby et al. characterize the male snow bunting's song as: "short, but musical, bold and loud for size and with fair variety of phrasing. Typical version might be rendered 'tūr*ee*-tūr*ee*-tūr*ee*-tūri*wee*.' From rock or other low perch and on wing." Salomonsen describes it as a "short rippling warble of distinct structure, but rather varying, consisting of 9–14 syllables, repeated sometimes with intervals of 5–10 seconds or delivered 3–4 times without pauses as a long continuous song." He writes several versions: "*ditrée-ditréedipi-tree-ditrée-ditrée*" and "*déeiti-dée-ditréeditréeditrée.*"

To Sutton and myself on Baffin Island "Songs seemed invariably to include a repetition of certain polysyllabic phrases. Ordinary songs (*i.e.*, songs not given in flight) sounded like (1) *sir plee si-chee whee-cher; sir plee si-chi whee-cher* and (2) *chor-i-bee-chee, chor-i-bee-chee, chip-i-deer.* Flight songs were more complex." Tinbergen speaks of locally restricted song "dialects" among the Greenland buntings which, he points out, the young males must either inherit or learn in the nest.

The species' call notes have been variously written as *chee, tee, djjj,* a loud, high-pitched *tweet,* a rather rippling twitter tĭrrĭrrĭr*ripp,* and a rippling yet rather hard *stĭrrrp,* among others. According to Tinbergen they are of two main types, a long monosyllabic *peee,* and a trembling note that Salomonsen transcribes as *pirrr* or *pirrr-rit.* Given on the ground or in flight, these function as communication signals between individuals or contact notes between members of the flock.

Males on territory have a threatening note Tinbergen writes *pEEE,* which they direct at trespassers of both sexes, but whether the males discriminate between sexes in such cases is uncertain. Tinbergen also notes that the actual attack on one male by another is often preceded by a special shrill, trembling *cherr.*

Most peculiar from singing males newly on territory is a long, high note that Tinbergen says "resembled more or less the screaming of a Swift, though it was much softer, and which I therefore will call the 'Swift' call. It was often performed two or three times in rapid succession and was often accompanied by trembling of the wings and panting. Both Swift call and wing trembling sometimes occurred separately. * * * this behavior must be considered as an outlet for unsatisfied sexual impulse."

On Baffin Island when a male brought food to an incubating female on the nest, as he disappeared into the nest crevice Sutton and I "heard odd, rather angry-sounding cries of *churr, churr.*" We described the food cry of young buntings after leaving the nest crevice as "*zhip* or *zhi-dip.*" Salomonsen thinks the fledgling's food call sounds like *pitt-pitt.*

Witherby et al. add: "Anxiety-note a musical, plaintive, piping 'tüü.' " Nichols (in Pearson et al., 1936) says the buntings call *beez-beez* when disturbed. Gabrielson and Lincoln (1959) state: "The alarm note is a hard, rattling *chir-r-r.*" Tinbergen observed that whenever a predator appeared the birds "uttered a special call, a monosyllabic, soft *weee,*" which he heard elicited by the appearance of a peregrine falcon, a merlin, roaming Eskimo dogs, and occasionally by his own approach to a nest or fledged young.

Behavior.—Of its behavior in Minnesota, T. S. Roberts (1932) writes:

"The Snowflake is a ground-loving bird, seldom alighting in trees, and roosting at night on the earth or snow beneath the shelter of some weed or tuft of grass. It is gregarious in the highest degree, and the vast flocks that formerly assembled in springtime almost obscured the skies as they towered above the weed fields from which they had arisen, whirling and circling in perfect unison, now up, now down, making with their thousands of wings a noise like the rushing of the wind."

Despite their marked gregariousness when away from the breeding grounds, the snow buntings do not associate much with other species. When they do, it is most often with the Lapland longspur. Wendell Taber wrote me that he usually looked for one to a half dozen longspurs in a New England flock of buntings. Ralph Palmer (1949) writes that in Maine: "Most common associates seen in flocks of this species are Horned Larks and Lapland Longspurs. On March 23, 1929, at Brunswick, I saw a single Snow Bunting with a flock of Bronzed Grackles."

The compact migrating and wintering flocks wheel and circle in characteristic fashion over the upland fields and sea beaches, descending abruptly and skimming low over the ground before settling. The flight of the individual bird is somewhat undulating, but hardly swift. B. Nelson (1944) timed one at 20 mph, another at 26 mph. On the ground the birds may scatter widely while feeding. Their normal gait is a walk or a quick run, and they occasionally hop or jump over the snow surface.

While they spend most of their time on the ground, in the south the buntings sometimes perch in trees or on the roofs of buildings, and may even line up on an electric wire like so many swallows. Forbush (1929) states: "I have seen an apple tree almost covered by a great flock of these birds, and they may be seen now and then on fences or stone walls, but I have never seen a Snow Bunting in the woods."

In a letter to Mr. Bent from Colebrook, New Hampshire, Hildegarde C. Allen describes their snow-bathing: "Whenever the mercury drops and the wind blows snow, in they come with their sweet calling in the wind, space themselves neatly on the ridgepole, and are with us on feeders, porch, and lawn till the next real thaw. They so love to swim in the light snow, particularly if it is both snowing and blowing and about zero. They seem almost like chickens dusting."

According to Scholander et al. (1950a, 1950b) snow buntings under cold stress can tolerate −40° F, but at −58° F their body temperatures drop seriously within an hour. Thus at very low temperatures the birds must depend on behavioral thermoregulation to some extent, and particularly to avoid windchill which must often be a hazard to them. A. M. Bagg (1943) reports their burrowing into snowdrifts during −35° F weather in Massachusetts and remaining huddled in their individual holes throughout the day, emerging "only occasionally to feed on a nearby chaff pile." Salomonsen states: "The birds in a flock have often a common roosting-place in which they spend the night, as a rule in cavities or crevices in rocks, in which they crouch close together in order to take shelter against the cold of the night."

Witherby et al. state "Roosts, sometimes singly, but often in parties, in shelter of stones, clods, grass-tussocks, etc., on ground; also recorded in quarry." Forbush (1929) writes: "When the snow is soft, these birds are said to dive into it (as they do sometimes when pursued by hawks), and there pass the night. When the snow is frozen hard, the flocks sleep in the open, protected from the north wind only by some slight rise in the ground, by sand dunes, or by a stone wall. * * * Snow Buntings are necessarily very light sleepers; when caged, they are said to be always awake and moving, when approached in the night. The wild birds leave their resting place at the first hint of light in the east, and begin feeding while it is still quite dark. They have never been known to roost in trees at night."

Roosting during the winter and at low latitudes probably coincides with and is governed by the hours of darkness. Conceivably in the continuous daylight that shines on much of their northern breeding grounds the birds might stay awake and active indefinitely, but they usually go to roost and sleep part of each day, usually when the sun is lowest. Tinbergen found that in southeastern Greenland the buntings "awoke earlier from day to day during April, until at the beginning of May their activities started at about 1 A.M. Although the nights grew lighter until the end of June, the birds did not rise any earlier from about the middle of May onward; a certain amount of sleep, about 2 to 3 hours, apparently is necessary."

Roosting behavior on the high northern breeding grounds has not been widely reported. The following paragraphs are adapted largely from the account MacDonald and I prepared of our observations near Slidre Fiord in west-central Ellesmere Island between April 16 and September 27, 1955.

When the first male buntings returned to Slidre Fiord, apparently the same day we arrived there, the sun was continuously above the horizon. When it was low these early arrivals roosted at Eureka Weather Station in a lumber pile, as many as 28 of them at once.

Away from the station they roosted out of the wind in shallow niches in sandstone outcrops. A single gully often had several such roosts. During the early spring the number of buntings at a given roost fluctuated considerably; anywhere from 1 to 24 birds might be found roosting together, and even the most favored sites were unoccupied at times. The birds slept squatted down with their heads turned back and their bills tucked under their scapulars. Most slept in shadowy niches, but some in direct sunlight. Even at −25° F we never saw them huddled together for warmth as Salomonsen reports.

After territories were established in the gullies near the coast, only a few buntings roosted there, but these continued to occupy the same roosts. New flocks were arriving daily, and more buntings than ever inhabited the coastal slopes during late May. Although daily maximum air temperatures did not reach thawing until May 28, evaporation and heat absorption from imbedded grains of wind-blown sand produced deep pits along the fronts of snowbanks that made excellent shelters where the newcomers of both sexes roosted together. The largest number of buntings seen in one of these snow roosts was 14. While these banks were accessible to predators, mammals could not climb them without noisily shattering the ice crystals that formed during the cool hours.

During May the buntings roosted principally between 9 p.m. and 2 a.m. A few birds, especially the hungry new arrivals, moved about at all hours. Most birds seemed to feed heavily between 6 and 8 p.m., just before going to roost. With the influx of new males and females and the start of courtship, roosting became less regular. By early June it was decidedly irregular, but even then most buntings roosted when the sun was lowest. Once courtship was over, roosting became regular again. No communal roosting was observed during the nesting period. The males usually roosted on a rock or bank within their territories while the females incubated or brooded on the nests.

In August the mixed flocks of adults and young fanned out to roost among the rocks on steep banks. As these flocks gradually became larger, some birds roosted on rocky slopes, others among boulders in the nearly dry stream beds. On August 21st we flushed 30 or more buntings roosting under a huge snowbank undercut by running water; the number of droppings showed this roost had been used for some time.

During August and September a few birds continued to roost singly or in small groups in the sandstone outcrops, rock piles, and mud cracks, and the gully roosts near the coast again became popular. But the large flocks, some containing a hundred or more birds by September, commonly roosted on the open tundra where the ground was eroded and hummocky. Occasionally Lapland longspurs roosted with the buntings. As in spring, the birds fed heavily from 6 to 8 p.m. before retiring. By September they started going to roost somewhat earlier, usually between 8 and 9 p.m., and the coming of night made them roost even earlier. By late September they were roosting by 7:30 p.m.

Enemies.—Probably the snow buntings' greatest foe in spring is the elements. Sutton (1932) describes dramatically how hundreds of buntings succumbed from starvation or exposure on Southampton Island during stormy weather in late May and early June. Weak from lack of food and dazed by the wind, they were easily caught by hand, and many were destroyed near the settlement by Eskimo children and dogs. Under normal spring conditions when the birds are healthy and the weather clement, predators probably catch few buntings. MacDonald and I watched dogs and arctic foxes stalking buntings unsuccessfully on Ellesmere Island, though one fox track led to a bunting kill.

Arctic foxes are doubtless one of the principal destroyers of bunting nests and of young buntings. When a fox appears on the nesting grounds, the old birds flock together in common defense. We watched some 20 fluttering over and behind one hunting fox, but how successful their distraction displays are is speculative. Where weasels are plentiful they also take their toll of young birds. Unpretentious despoilers of bunting and other small passerine ground nests are the brown and collared lemmings. These small rodents may only partially destroy a clutch of eggs, but this causes the parents to desert the nest. They may destroy all or part of a brood of small young.

Among potential avian predators on the breeding grounds are snowy owls, the several arctic falcons, and the jaegers that quarter the tundra so fast and low. On Ellesmere Island, Tener (*in* Godfrey, 1953) found the remains of an adult snow bunting in an adult long-tailed jaeger, and a long-tailed jaeger chick regurgitated a bunting fledgling while MacDonald and I were handling it. Bunting remains are often numerous at gyrfalcon and peregrine falcon aeries. The gyrfalcons commonly follow the bunting hordes along the coasts in the fall; one that MacDonald and I shot had just eaten four buntings.

Though buntings are still used for food occasionally in parts of Europe and Asia, happily they are no longer hunted for market in North America. William Dutcher's (1903) report of 80,000 buntings for the gourmet trade "found by a State game warden in a cold storage warehouse in one of the larger eastern cities" staggers the imagination.

Fall and winter.—On Southampton Island Sutton (1932) comments: "The prompt fall departure of the passerine birds surprised me. I had expected to find Snow Buntings, Lapland Longspurs, and horned larks all through the fall, and perhaps irregularly throughout the winter. But with the coming of the snows these hardy species disappear just as definitely as do the familiar birds of the Eastern United States, when September frosts begin to be sharp * * *."

At the high latitude of Ellesmere Island, most buntings leave for the south by the middle of September. Prior to migration, mixed flocks of buntings of both sexes and all ages may gradually combine to form the enormous numbers sometimes seen along the coasts in fall. A single flock seldom numbers more than a hundred birds, usually much less, but occasionally upward of a thousand or more buntings will form a more or less loose flock. These great hordes may linger for some days, the flocks constantly breaking up into smaller ones and then regrouping.

On the other hand, Sutton (1932) notes that at Southampton Island "Premigratory flocks are not usually formed until the very eve of departure for the south. Family-flocks are to be seen during most of the fall. Buntings linger throughout October, and even until November, though most of them depart by the last of September." Salomonsen reports that the majority migrate from Greenland from late September to mid-October.

A few buntings may remain at or near the breeding areas after the main body has left. Late departure dates even at high latitudes may extend well into October or later. Personnel at the Alert Weather Station at 83° N. on the north coast of Ellesmere Island told me of seeing two buntings there November 27, feeding on spilled oats. The birds flew off into total darkness beyond the station lights and were not seen again. C. G. and E. G. Bird (1941) report from MacKenzie Bay in northeast Greenland "still a few around the station on 10 December." Salomonsen notes that "The greater part of the Snow-Buntings leave Greenland in the autumn, but a small minority stay in winter in the southern parts of the country. Wintering specimens have been recorded in all parts of the low-arctic region."

On the more southerly wintering grounds the flocks may vary from a few to hundreds, sometimes thousands of individuals. Alexander DuBois wrote Taber in a letter of a flock of 400 near Ithaca, N.Y. Gabrielson and Lincoln (1959), T. S. Roberts (1932) and others have commented on species' varying in abundance from year to year; regions where they winter commonly one year may find them scarce or wholly absent the next.

Though there is no territorial fighting in winter, aggressive individuals in the flocks often fight in much the same manner, usually over food. These fights are motivated by the establishment of peck-order and apparently have no sexual connotation.

DISTRIBUTION

Range.—Arctic islands of North America, southern Greenland, Jan Mayen, Spitsbergen, and Franz Josef Land, south to Oregon, Utah, New Mexico, Kansas, Indiana, Ohio, Tennessee, Virginia, the British Isles, France, Italy, Yugoslavia, Rumania and the Caucasus.

Breeding range.—The common snow bunting breeds from Prince Patrick Island, Ellef Ringnes Island, northern Ellesmere Island and northern Greenland (to Peary Land) south to southwestern Alaska (Cold Bay, Kodiak Island), central Mackenzie (Mackenzie Mountains, Lake Campbell), central Keewatin (Baker Lake, Southampton Island, Coats Island), northern Quebec (Cox Island, Fort Chimo), north-central Labrador (Bowdoin Harbour, Okak); and southern Greenland (Ivigtut); and in the higher mountains of northern Scotland, Faeroes, Jan Mayen, Norway (south to lat. 60° N.), northern Sweden, Finland, Spitsbergen, Franz Josef Land, and northwestern Russia (Arkhangelsk Government). Occurs in small numbers in summer on coasts of southern Hudson and James bays.

Winter range.—Winters from central western and southern Alaska (Nulato, Nushagak, Sitka), northwestern British Columbia (Atlin), central Saskatchewan (Dorintosh, Emma Lake), southern Manitoba (Lake St. Martin), western and southern Ontario (Port Arthur, Lake Nipissing), southern Quebec (Montreal, Gaspé), southern Labrador (Battle Harbour), and Newfoundland south to northwestern California (casually, Humboldt Bay), eastern Oregon (Camp Harney), northern Utah (Bear River Refuge, Provo), north-central New Mexico (Las Vegas), central Kansas (Hays), southern Indiana (Bloomington), Ohio, Tennessee, North Carolina (Big Bald and Round Bald mountains), Virginia, and casually to Alabama (Birmingham), Georgia (Columbia, Richmond, Liberty, and Chatham counties), and coastal South Carolina (Charleston County), and from southern Scandinavia and central Russia to Ireland, Wales, England, France, northern Italy, Yugoslavia, Rumania, and the Caucasus.

Casual Records.—Casual in Bermuda, the Azores, Canary Islands, Morocco, and Malta.

Migration.—Early dates of spring arrival are: Pennsylvania—State College, March 19. Greenland—Angmagssalik, March 11. Illinois—Chicago, March 4. Iowa—Grinnell, April 25. British Columbia—Cranbrook, February 18. Alaska—Mt. McKinley, April 8.

Late dates of spring departure are: Alabama—Birmingham, January 24. Georgia—Grovetown, January 28. South Carolina—Charleston, February 12. North Carolina—Clarkton, February 4. Virginia—Back Bay and Rockingham County, February 9. Maryland—Ocean City, April 1. Pennsylvania—Crawford County, April 9; State College, March 24. New Jersey—Cape May, February 22.

New York—Idlewild, April 14; Lewis County, March 30. Connecticut—New Britain, April 21; South Glastonbury, April 13. Massachusetts—Plum Island, May 3. New Hampshire—New Hampton, April 5 median, March 8. Maine—Piscataquis County, April 29. New Brunswick—Newcastle, May 28; Tabusintac, May 16. Illinois—Urbana, April 9; Chicago, March 19. Ohio—central Ohio, March 19 (median, February 14). Michigan—Detroit area, March 30. Minnesota—Wadena, May 21 (average of 7 years for northern Minnesota, April 9). North Dakota—Cass County, April 3 (average, March 18). Manitoba—Treesbank, May 23 (average of 19 years, April 30). Wyoming—Cheyenne, March 19. Montana—northern Montana, May 2 (average of 6 years, March 17). Oregon—Wallowa, March 10. Washington—Chelan, March 17. British Columbia—Cranbrook, March 29.

Early dates of fall arrival are: British Columbia—Arrow Lake, October 22. Washington—Skagit County, October 19. Oregon—Malheur County, November 17. Montana—northern Montana, October 26 (average of 6 years, October 30). Manitoba—Treesbank, September 24 (average of 21 years, October 11). North Dakota—Red River Valley, October 9; Cass County, October 16 (average, October 20). Minnesota—Hibbing, September 3; Lake County, September 18 (average for 15 years for northern Minnesota, October 24). Ohio—central Ohio, October 13 (median, November 20). Illinois—Chicago, October 14 (average of 14 years, October 28). Tennessee—Nashville, November 19. New Brunswick—Revous River, October 13; St. John County, October 15. Maine—Brunswick, September 24. New Hampshire—New Hampton, October 12 (median of 16 years, October 28). Massachusetts—Sharon, September 15. Connecticut—South Windsor, October 20; New Haven, October 22. New York—Cayuga County, September 28; Idlewild, October 3. New Jersey—Cape May, November 7. Pennsylvania—Erie, October 17; State College, October 20. Maryland—Anne Arundel County, October 31; Ocean City, November 2. Virginia—Shenandoah National Park, October 31; Cobb Island, November 4; Alexandria, November 6. North Carolina—Marshallberg, November 23. South Carolina—Charleston, November 12. Georgia—Blythe, November 10.

Late dates of fall departure are: Alaska—Wainwright, October 5. British Columbia—Okanagan Landing, November 2. Illinois—Chicago, December 28 (average of 14 years, November 25).

Egg Dates.—Alaska: 77 records, May 20 to July 14; 39 records, June 14 to June 28.

Franklin: 9 records, June 10 to July 24.

Greenland: 12 records, May 25 to July 24; 6 records, June 15 to June 25.

Hudson Bay: 9 records, June 22 to July 6.

Keewatin: 8 records, June 18 to July 4.

Mackenzie: 4 records, June 18 to July 22.

Quebec: 6 records, June 20 to July 3.

PLECTROPHENAX NIVALIS TOWNSENDI Ridgway

Pribilof Snow Bunting

Contributed by DAVID FREELAND PARMELEE

HABITS

This subspecies is identical in color to the nominate race and differs only in size, being larger bodied and notably larger billed. It is believed to be resident over much of its range, which consists of a rather limited land area scattered over a vast body of water, the Bering Sea. As its numbers may fluctuate considerably from time to time at any one place and the birds gather in flocks in winter, some limited migratory movement apparently takes place within the breeding area. When flocks of the nominate race and of McKay's buntings migrate to or through its range in winter, it is possible to find all three buntings in proximity.

Ira N. Gabrielson and Frederick C. Lincoln (1959) present the following summary of the available information on its movements and life cycle:

It is a permanent resident of the Pribilofs where between June 4 and 24, many nests and eggs have been taken from the elevated parts of the islands. Dall (Dall and Bannister 1869) was the first American to list it from the Pribilofs, but it is quite certain that Russian observers had reported it long before that time.

Harrold found it common on Nunivak with young ready to leave the nest by July 1 (Swarth 1934), and Gabrielson found it common on the same island on July 10 and 11, 1940, and on July 14, 1946, collecting specimens on both visits.

It is also a common resident throughout the Aleutians where it has been noted by all observers since Dall (1874) reported a nest on June 20, 1873 at Attu. Murie and his parties found nests on Kiska on June 4 and on Agattu on June 12 and 14, while Wetmore found them obviously nesting on Unalaska and at Morzhovoi Bay in 1911. Krog (1953) found them nesting in considerable numbers on Amchitka. Beals has found them regularly throughout the seasons on Unimak and Sanak Islands and around Cold Bay, and he states that they were common on the Shumagins in May 1944. There are specimens in the National Museum from Dolgoi Island taken by Murie on May 24, 1937, one from Nagai in the Shumagins taken by Townsend on June 24, 1893, and the first one from Little Koniuji, taken by T. H. Bean on July 16, 1880. Gabrielson saw three birds and collected an adult on Chowiet Island in the Semidis on June 18, 1940; and secured specimens at Frosty Peak on June 21, 1940, and at King Cove on June 13, 1946.

He has seen them on numerous islands in the Aleutians, including a nesting pair on Ogliuga Island on June 27, 1940, and also on the Pribilofs.

Turner (1885) considered it a common resident of the Near Islands, but Sutton and Wilson (1946) called it infrequent on Attu between February 20 and March 18, 1945. Taber (1946) published January records for Adak; and Cahn (1947) considered it a regular but not abundant winter resident at Dutch Harbor.

Beals' notes contain many winter records of this race. In 1941 he saw them at King Cove on January 10; small flocks on Unimak on January 11 and 12; a number of flocks—including one of more than one hundred birds—on Unalaska between January 15 and 27; one on Akutan at one thousand feet elevation on January 17; four near Atka Village on January 31; a flock of twenty-five at Nikolski Village on Umnak on February 16; twenty birds in two flocks on Unalaska on February 18; and he found it common on Unimak when he returned to False Pass on March 1. In 1942, he found them in flocks on Unalaska from January 20 to April 20.

The Pribilof snow bunting's breeding habitat is treeless tundra superficially resembling that of the nominate race. Notable differences, however, are the higher summer temperatures and greater precipitation on the Bering Sea islands. The vegetative cover differs from arctic tundra not only in its plant components, but also in its more copious and luxuriant growth. The cold surrounding waters and strong winds prevent any forest growth, but the dwarfed woody plants, mainly willows and birches, form dense mats in places.

From what little is known of its habits and behavior, these apparently differ little if any from those of the nominate race. Olaus J. Murie (1959) gives the following details of its nesting:

> The nest of the snow bunting may be placed among lava rocks, in crevices or cliffs, or under a ledge of a rock on fairly level terrain. On June 4, 1937, Douglas Gray found a nest with three eggs under an overhanging rock on Kiska Island.
>
> On June 12, 1937, on Agattu Island, I found two nests. One was in the form of a deep grassy cup, with a few feathers worked in, placed under a ledge of a flat rock on fairly level ground. It contained four eggs.
>
> The other nest was located under an overhanging boulder, and it had feathers of a forked-tailed petrel woven into the structure. This nest also contained four eggs.
>
> On June 14, also on Agattu Island, a similar nest made of grass was found in a hollow under a flat rock. There were four eggs.

Harry S. Swarth (1934) adds the following on Harrold's experiences on Nunivak: "Young in juvenal plumage were taken up to August 7. The annual molt of the adult is represented by specimens taken during the first half of August, but it must have lasted until about the end of the month. The flight feathers seem to be lost almost all at once and Harrold's comments upon this condition read as follows: "The adults are now (August 10) in full molt and individuals seem hardly capable of flight. While in this condition they skulk in the rock piles and are very inconspicuous."

Distribution

Range.—The Pribilof snow bunting is resident in southwestern Alaska from the Pribilof and the western Aleutian Islands (west to Attu) east to the tip of the Alaska Peninsula at Morzhovoi Bay, the Shumagin Islands, and Nunivak Island; also on the Komandorskie Islands and in parts of Siberia adjoining the Bering Sea.

PLECTROPHENAX HYPERBOREUS (Ridgway)

McKay's Bunting

Contributed by Ira Noel Gabrielson

Habits

The McKay's bunting, whitest of all North American passerine birds, lives in such remote country that relatively few ornithologists ever have a chance to see it. This is especially true of its summer home on the relatively inaccessible Hall and St. Matthew Islands in the Bering Sea. When the opportunity came to visit these islands in 1940, I looked forward to the trip with uncommon interest. No bird known or recorded from these islands was anticipated with more interest than the McKay's bunting. Previous visitors had found it to be fairly common, but birds are subject to such great annual numerical variation in the arctic that they might well be present only in small numbers. As our time was limited, there was considerable speculation as to whether it would be found at all, and if so, in what numbers.

Our first landing was on a little beach on St. Matthew Island near Cape Upright on July 8. As the small boat touched shore and the party stepped out beneath the overhang of an old snowbank, the first bird to greet us was a McKay's bunting perched on the drift and scolding at this invasion of his territory. Needless to say, we were delighted to meet this relatively rare bird so promptly. In the two days that we tramped the island, we were seldom out of sight of one or more of these little finches, either flitting over the grass and tundra vegetation ahead of us or feeding along the slopes of the ridges. One day we climbed Cape Upright and found them scattered sparingly even over the barren rocky, scree-like surface of the summit, but they were more plentiful on the flatter lands along the shore and in the low intervals between the more rugged parts of the island.

The adult males in their pure white plumage, decorated with the black primaries, black in the tail, and jet black bill, were a striking contrast to all other birds, and the most exciting one of all on the visit to St. Matthew. They made one think of giant white butterflies as they flitted about over the landscape going about their various businesses, feeding themselves or their young, or singing at least a part of their song. Young of all sizes, from bobtailed ones that were still uncertain of the distance or direction of their flight to those that could fly as well as their parents, were scattered over the islands. On both my 1940 and 1946 visits the gray youngsters were much more abundant than the whiter adults; the fuzzy grayness of their plumage and the indistinct breast streaks easily distinguished them from their parents.

The first known specimens of McKay's bunting were taken at Nulato and St. Michael in April 1879 by E. W. Nelson (1887). His notes recorded at the time that they were odd birds, but although he commented on their differences from the more common *P. nivalis*, he did not suspect that they represented a new species. These specimens, and others that Charles L. McKay took at Nushagak Nov. 16 and Dec. 10, 1882, were the basis for Ridgway's (1885) description of the species. Its breeding ground was discovered by Charles H. Townsend (1887), the first ornithologist to visit Hall Island, when he collected adults and juveniles there Sept. 8, 1885.

John Burroughs et al. (1901) wrote of his visit to Hall Island with the Harriman Alaska Expedition in 1899:

> After we had taken our fill of gazing upon the murres came the ramble away from the cliffs in the long twilight through that mossy and flowery solitude. Such patterns and suggestions for rugs and carpets as we walked over for hours; such a blending of grays, drabs, browns, greens, and all delicate neutral tints, all dashed with masses of many-colored flowers, it had never before been my fortune to witness, much less to walk upon. Drifting over this marvelous carpet or dropping down upon it from the air above was the hyperborean snowbird, white as a snowflake and with a song of great sweetness and power. With lifted wings, the bird would drop through the air to the earth pouring out its joyous ecstatic strain.

Charles Keeler (1901), another member of the expedition who wrote a running account of the birds seen, described the visit to Hall Island as follows:

> Upon climbing up the slopes from the shore, we found ourselves upon an Arctic tundra—a great rolling plateau of bog, with pools of water in every hollow, and flowers growing in bewildering profusion. A bed of moss spread across the island from cliff to cliff carpeting everything with its soft tones of gray, brown, purple, and green—parts of it like velvet, soft and yielding to the tread, and other parts spongy and soggy. The masses of flowers wove richly flowing patterns into the carpet, in purple, blue, yellow, and white—the purple primrose and pedicularis the blue polemonium, the yellow poppy, a fine golden cowslip, and the white cupped dryas.
>
> It was fitting that this fairy garden in the midst of a stormy sea should be inhabited by one of the most chastely adorned of birds, the hyperborean snowflake. Verily a snowflake this exquisite creature is, as it whirls through the mystic glow of night among the wastes of flowers. Its plumage is as candid as a freshly opened lily. The spotless white shows more perfectly by contrast with

the jetty bill and the blackness of the wing tips. At the edge of its snowy tail are two other black dots. It is a sparrow transformed into a wraith of snow. It is adorned with the ermine of kings, and a king it seems amid the realm of flowers. Its little mate has the back streaked with black and more of the same on her wings and tail, but otherwise her plumage is white like that of her lord and master.

Courtship.—Nothing has been written on the courtship of this species, and my two visits to its breeding grounds in July and August were both too late in the season to observe courting behavior. In my July visit a male, or occasionally two males, pursued a female briefly, probably a part of the courtship pattern. Likewise the males occasionally sang a bit on the wing, although I did not witness any elaborate, song flight. Burrough's description and Brandt's account (see *Voice*) of the song flight are the only specific information available on this point. Quite probably the courtship behavior is similar to that of the nearly related snow bunting.

Nesting.—Few nests of this island-nesting species have been discovered. Keeler (1901) reported one nest found by the Harriman Expedition was "* * * placed far back in a crevice in the rocks upon the cliff wall. The nest was made of grasses and contained five rather light greenish eggs dotted with pale brown. Later in the evening another nest was found containing young birds which came to the edge of the hole to be fed. The abundance of the Arctic fox upon the island no doubt explains the unusual places in which the snowflakes tuck away their homes." G. Dallas Hanna (1917), one of the few other persons who have visited the nesting grounds of this bird, reported it that it was most common along the shingle beaches where it nested in old hollow drift logs. He remarked: "One nest was found in an old hollow spruce which had been excavated by some woodpecker on the mainland when the tree was standing. A few birds were found to the tops of the highest mountains. Flying young and fresh eggs were found, indicating that two broods are reared."

Eggs.—Keeler's (1901) description of "light greenish eggs dotted with pale brown" is the only one ever published. W. G. F. Harris writes in a letter: "The measurements of 7 eggs average 23.2 by 17.3 millimeters. The eggs showing the four extremes measure *24.0* by *18.2* and *22.2* by *16.5* millimeters."

Plumages.—In breeding dress the adult male is almost entirely white except for the black bill, black outer part of the primaries, and occasionally some black on the back and scapulars. The breeding female is much like the summer female *P. nivalis*, except that the black or dusky areas on the back and scapulars are more restricted and mingled with more white.

Juvenile birds are much like the young of the eastern snow bunting. Their general pattern is somewhat like that of the adults, with the pure whites replaced by grays, obscure dusky streaks on the breast, and the primaries dusky rather than black.

In winter the adult male has more or less of a brownish or rusty wash on the head and back, but otherwise is much like the summer bird. The adult female has more black or dusky streaks and patches on the back and scapulars and a brownish wash over most of the back.

Food.—Nothing definite is known about its food preferences, though it obviously feeds on grass, sedge, and weed seeds as do other arctic fringillids, and probably eats a goodly proportion of insects in summer.

Voice.—Keeler (1901) writes: "Nor did the song of this snowflake prove disappointing. It was a loud, sweet, flutelike warble, frequently uttered on the wing, and much resembles the notes of the western meadowlark, although rather higher, shriller, and shorter."

I am not sure that I ever heard the full song, as both my visits to the nesting ground occurred after the young were well fledged. The adults had a sharp, metallic, sparrow-like note, and one occasion gave a partial song, to me much like the song of the snow bunting.

Herbert Brandt (1943) says:

> Suddenly a beautiful white bird, evidently a male, began to sing vigorously its Eastern Goldfinch-like song, and leaping into the air, bounded directly away, causing me to wonder where in that vast sea of snow it could possibly be going? A few minutes later I heard a distant song approaching, and soon a fine white bird settled into the flock, preened itself, and began to search for food.
>
> Almost at once another individual left, and this time I followed the bird with my glasses until lost to view, noting that it flew toward our headquarters. Finally I saw it returning from a direction nearly opposite that in which it had departed. Recalling the birds that had bounded past the schoolhouse without pausing, led me to discover that the McKay Snow Bunting has a wide, circular, nuptial flight-song which, on this occasion, covered a diameter of considerably more than a mile.

In another passage Brandt refers to the species "uttering a wild sweet warble" while on the wing.

Fall and winter.—In winter McKay's bunting reaches to the shores of Bristol Bay and travels through the Yukon-Kuskokwim Delta in migration. It probably winters in this area also. Away from the breeding grounds it has been taken at St. Michael, Hooper Bay, Bethel, and on Bristol Bay either in winter or on migration. Brandt (1943) found it present in numbers at Hooper Bay from April 30 to May 20. Outside of this, the species has been found only on the Pribilofs and Nunivak Island.

Distribution

Range.—Hall and St. Matthew islands to the mainland of western Alaska.

Breeding range.—The McKay's bunting breeds on Hall and St. Matthew islands, Alaska.

Winter Range.—Hall, St. Matthew, and Nunivak islands and western coastal Alaska (St. Michael, Kuskokwim River, and Nushagak).

Casual record.—Casual in the Pribilof Islands (St. Paul Island).
Egg dates.—St. Matthews Island: record, June 10.

EMBERIZA RUSTICA LATIFASCIA Portenko

Eastern Rustic Bunting

Contributed by MATTI HELMINEN

HABITS

The rustic bunting is widely distributed across northern Eurasia from central Fenno-Scandia in the west eastward to the shores of the Pacific. Though some students (Dementiev et al., 1954) consider it a monotypic species, its division by Portenko (1930) into an eastern and a western subspecies seems generally accepted and is recognized by the most recent (1957) A.O.U. Check-List. The form that has occurred within the Check-List limits in the Aleutian Islands is apparently the eastern race, about which regrettably little seems to have been written. Thus it has been necessary to prepare this report largely on observations made of the western form. The Russian handbooks, however, (Dementiev et al., 1954, and Portenko, 1960) mention no essential differences in habits or ecology between the two populations.

The admission of the species to the American list was based originally on three specimens collected on Kiska Island in the western Aleutians in 1911. Of these Mr. Bent (1912a) writes: "Two specimens of this bird, at that time unknown to us, were picked up dead and partially dried on Kiska Island. On June 19, at the same place, Alexander Wetmore saw and collected a living specimen. I saw two or three birds on Adak Island, which I thought were this species, but they were exceedingly shy and I did not collect any." Olaus J. Murie (1959) quotes the following version of the same incident from Alexander Wetmore's field notes:

> On June 19, while making the rounds of my traps, I flushed a small bird that flew up with a faint *tsip*, and dove immediately into the grass along a creek. The flight was quick and with an up-and-down motion, and the bird showed two white outer tail feathers. I flushed it again after some tramping, and shot it on the wing, and found it a fine specimen of the bird found on the seventeenth. A hundred yards farther I flushed another on a grassy slope, and missed it the first time. When it got up again I shot it, but the wind carried it so that I was not able to find it, though I searched carefully. No others could be found. The one taken was a female, in fine plumage, but exceedingly fat.

More recently Walter M. Weber (1956) saw a flock of five on Adak Island Oct. 22, 1951, and Gabrielson and Lincoln (1959) report that Karl W. Kenyon collected two specimens on Amchitka Island Oct. 20 and 27, 1957. As these few widely scattered records are the only ones reported from the Aleutians, which have been visited and studied by a number of alert and competent naturalists, they must be regarded merely as stragglers that wandered or perhaps were blown east of their normal route during migration.

Spring.—The rustic buntings evidently begin to leave their wintering grounds in March. They usually travel in small flocks, and the males are sometimes heard singing during migration. They generally reach their northern nesting grounds between late April and late May. The first migrants often appear in Finland while the ground is still snow covered, and are ready to start nesting immediately after the spring thaw.

Their preferred breeding habitat is marshy, ragged, mixed forest with plenty of beard lichen (*Usnea*) and undergrowth. Often they inhabit the fringes of muskeg-type bogs and the thickets bordering streams. Trees characteristic of their habitat in Finland include spruce, birch, alder, and willows. In the Okhostk area according to Portenko et al. (1954) they also nest in stands of fir, and may be found in the mountains up to 1,800 feet.

Nesting.—Soon after their arrival the males settle down, select their territories, and begin to sing actively. The nest is built on or near the ground, sometimes in the thick moss carpet or in a grass tussock usually hidden under a small shrub, sometimes slightly above it in a bush or stump. Of 26 nests found by Lars von Haartman (MS.), 20 were on the ground, 5 were from one to three feet above it, and 1 was in a stump almost six feet from the ground.

The nest is made largely of grasses or sedges with bits of moss added occasionally. It may be lined with finer dry grasses, and in Finland often with animal hair of reindeer, moose, or snowshoe hare. Eight nests that E. S. Nyholm (*in* litt.) measured varied from 10 to 12 cm. in outside diameter, from 6.5 to 8.5 cm. in outside depth, from 5 to 6 cm. in inside diameter, and from 4.5 to 5.5 cm. in inside depth.

Eggs.— The clutch usually contains four or five, less often six eggs. Of 40 clutches Haartman (MS.) reports, there were 10 with four eggs, 22 with five, and 8 with six. Witherby et al. (1938) describe the eggs as "ground-colour greenish-grey to bluish-green, spotted and blotched thickly with greyish-olive and violet shell-marks, but no streaks. Average of 64 eggs * * * 20.16×15.1. Max.: 21.8×15.2 and 20.7×15.7. Min.: 18×14.5 and 17.6×14 mm." Most striking is the rustic bunting's eggs' lack of the wreath of hair lines that is so characteristic of the eggs of most other *Emberiza* species.

Haartman's (MS.) data show nests with eggs found in Finland from May 11 to July 10, with the main laying period the last week of May and the first week of June. Few data are available for the far east populations. According to the Russian handbooks, breeding usually takes place from late May to early July, but fledglings have been seen as late as August.

Incubation and young.—According to Witherby et al. (1938) incubation is chiefly by the female. Bertil Haglund (1935) reports the length of the incubation period as 12 to 13 days, and that the young remain in the nest another 14 days. The species usually has only one brood each summer, but a few pairs may occasionally rear second broods.

Plumages.—The natal down has not been described. The juvenile birds acquire their first winter plumage by molting their body feathers and wing-coverts in August, but not the primary coverts, remiges, or rectrices. A partial molt in April (sometimes March) and May is confined to the head and throat. The adults undergo a complete postnuptial molt in August. (Niethammer, 1937; Witherby et al., 1938).

Food.—The food habits of the rustic bunting are inadequately known. H. F. Witherby et al. (1938) say only "Seeds, including rice; young said to eat oats and other grain." Dementiev et al. (1954) quote Novikov's findings to the effect that in summer the species feeds mainly on animal matter, chiefly curculionid beetles, lepidopteran larvae, and spiders, with lesser amounts of aphids, flies, and gnats, and in September shifts to a vegetative diet of plant buds and seeds of grasses and other herbs. The observations of E. N. Teplova (1957) are essentially the same.

Voice.—The song of the rustic bunting is more varied and melodious than those typical of most emberizines, and bears some resemblance to the songs of the European robin (*Erithacus rubecula*), European redstart (*Phoenicurus phoenicurus*), and even of the blackcap (*Sylvia atricapilla*). As the male delivers it from his singing perch, which is often within the canopy, it is not very loud, and may easily be overlooked when heard. K. E. Kivirikko (1947) describes it as roughly "dilludiludilutytyty", delivered with an accelerating tempo. This short song is repeated at frequent intervals at the height of the singing season. The alarm note is a sharp, high-pitched, easily recognized "tic-tic-tic" or "dic-dic-dic."

Behavior.—The rustic bunting is not easily observed during the breeding season, for it is shy and retiring and usually remains under cover in the thickets it inhabits. The male remains near the nest, sometimes singing, but nervously uttering warning notes at the approach of an intruder. The female incubates closely, and stays on the nest until approached within a very short distance. She will then run along the ground and through the lower branches giving the usual distraction display with the typical "broken wing." Both birds move restlessly close to the ground through the underbrush and rarely come into the open.

Field marks.—The rustic bunting has the white outer tail-feathers characteristic of all members of its genus. It may be distinguished from other buntings by the large bright rusty spots that form a well-marked breast-band and contrast on the flanks with the white underparts. The male in summer is readily identified by the broad white eye-stripe in the otherwise dark head, white throat, and chestnut upper parts streaked with black. The female and the male in winter have a similar color pattern but are much duller.

Fall and winter.—The rustic buntings start to leave Finland in late August and, as Olavi Hilden (1960) shows, most are gone by early October. Dementiev et al. (1954) state that the peak of the autumn flight in central Siberia and from the Kamchatka and Okhotsk areas is usually in late September and early October. Late migrants have been reported in the Kurile Islands November 5, in Sakhalin November 10, and in the Primorsk area November 24.

In southern Korea, Austin (1948) "found it by far the commonest of the wintering small birds * * *. When you encountered Fringillids at all, you found Rustic Buntings. From December through March flocks numbering upward of 500 birds lived among the weeds in the mulberry fields, and smaller bunches could be found wherever there was cover at almost any time. They began to depart in mid-March, and by early April had all disappeared except for the usual few stragglers."

Austin and Kuroda (1953) write: "The Rustic Bunting is a common winter visitor in Japan, arriving in late October or early November and moving northward again in late March, a few remaining until early May. It is encountered most often feeding on the ground in open cultivated fields and dormant paddies along the edges of woodlands, in flocks of 20 to 30 or fewer birds. As winter wanes and the spring movement begins, the flocks join together until they contain several hundred or more birds. Its call note is a high, sweet, somewhat plaintive *tweet*, and just before it leaves in the early spring snatches of its melodious little song can be heard."

Distribution

Range.—Eastern Siberia to northern China and Japan.

Breeding range.—The eastern rustic bunting breeds in eastern Siberia from west-central Yakutsk (Verkhoyansk; east through Verkhne Kolymsk) to northern Khabarovsk, and Kamchatka.

Winter range.—Winters to northwestern Irkutsk (Taishet), southern Yakutsk (Olekminsk), Ussuriland, northern China (casually south to Fukien), and southern Japan.

Casual records.—Casual in the Komandorskie Islands, and in the Aleutian Islands (Kiska, Amchitka).

Literature Cited

Abbott, Charles Conrad

1895. The birds about us.

Abbott, Charles H.

1959. The 1958 migration of the painted lady butterfly, *Vanessa cardui* (Linnaeus), in California. Pan-Pacific Ent., vol. 35, pp. 83–94.

Abbott, Clinton Gilbert

1902. [Note] Abstr. Proc. Linn. Soc. New York, 1900–1902, Nos. 13–14, p. 17.

1931. Birds caught in spiders' webs. Condor, vol. 33, p. 169.

Abbott, Jackson Miles

1958. Hybrid white-crowned white-throated sparrow. Atlantic Nat., vol. 13, pp. 258–259.

Adams, Andrew Leith

1873. Field and forest rambles, with notes and observations on the natural history of eastern Canada.

Adams, Ernest

1899. House finches again. Bull. Cooper Ornith. Club, vol. 1, p. 24.

Adams, Lowell

1947. Food habits of three common Oregon birds in relation to reforestation. Journ. Wildlife Management, vol. 11, pp. 281–282.

Adney, Edwin Tappan

1886. Naturalization of the European goldfinch in New York City and vicinity. Auk, vol. 3, pp. 409–410.

Agersborg, G. S.

1885. The birds of southeastern Dakota. Auk, vol. 2, pp. 276–289.

Aiken, Charles Edward Howard

1937. Birds of the southwest. Colorado College Publ., No. 212.

Aiken, Charles Edward Howard, and Warren, Edward Royal

1914. The birds of El Paso County, Colorado. II. Colorado College Publ., Nos. 75 and 76, pp. 497–603.

Alcorn, Joseph R.

1940. New and noteworthy records of birds for the state of Nevada. Condor, vol. 42, pp. 169–170.

1946. The birds of Lahontan Valley, Nevada. Condor, vol. 48, pp. 129–138.

Aldrich, John Warren

1943. Biological survey of the bogs and swamps of northeastern Ohio. Amer. Midland Nat., vol. 30, pp. 346–402.

1948. Distribution of North American birds. The breeding distribution of the dickcissel. Audubon Field Notes, vol. 2, pp. 12–13.

Aldrich, John Warren, and Nutt, David C.

1939. Birds of eastern Newfoundland. Cleveland Mus. Nat. Hist., Sci. Publ., vol. 4, pp. 13–42.

Alexander, Gordon

1935. An influx of Dickcissels into central Colorado. Condor, vol. 37, p. 38.

Allard, H. A.

1928. Unusual singing of the eastern chewink. Condor, vol. 30, pp. 247–249.

Allen, Amelia Sanborn

1915. Birds of a Berkeley hillside. Condor, vol. 17, pp. 78–85.

1920a. The rusty song sparrow in Berkeley, and the return of winter birds. Condor, vol. 22, pp. 16–18.

1920b. Red crossbills at Berkeley, California. Condor, vol. 22, p. 73.

1933. Arrival and departure of avian visitants in the San Francisco Bay region. Condor, vol. 35, pp. 225–227.

1943. Additional notes on the birds of a Berkeley hillside. Condor, vol. 45, pp. 149–157.

Allen, Arthur Augustus

1924. A contribution to the life history and economic status of the screech owl (*Otus asio*). Auk, vol. 41, pp. 1–16.

1928. Mother goldfinch tells her story. Bird-Lore, vol. 30, pp. 287–293.

1930. The book of bird life.

1932. Random notes on tanagers and finches. *In* Grosvenor and Wetmore (eds.), The book of birds, vol. 2, p. 257.

1933. The indigo bunting. Bird-Lore, vol. 35, pp. 227–235.

1934. American bird biographies.

1939. The golden plover and other birds.

1951. Stalking birds with color camera.

Allen, Francis Henry

1888. Tameness of the pine siskin. Auk, vol. 5, p. 426.

1916. A nesting of the rose-breasted grosbeak. Auk, vol. 33, pp. 53–56.

Allen, Glover M.

1892. Fringillidae in Newton, Middlesex County, Mass. Oologist, vol. 9, pp. 244–246.

1909. Fauna of New England, No. 11. List of the *Aves*. Occas. Pap. Boston Soc. Nat. Hist., vol. 7.

1919. Boston region. *In* The season. Bird-Lore, vol. 21, pp. 50–51.

1925. Birds and their attributes.

Allen, Joel Asaph

1869. Notes on some of the rarer birds of Massachusetts. Amer. Nat., vol. 3, pp. 505–519, 568–585, 631–648.

1872. Geographical variation in North American birds. Proc. Boston Soc. Nat. Hist., vol. 15, pp. 212–219.

1874. Notes on the natural history of portions of Dakota and Montana Territories. Proc. Boston Soc. Nat. Hist., vol. 17.

1875. [Note.] Proc. Boston Soc. Nat. Hist., vol. 17, pp. 292, 293.

Allen, Joel Asaph, and Brewster, William

1883. Lists of birds observed in the vicinity of Colorado Springs, Colorado, during March, April, and May, 1882. Bull. Nuttall Ornith. Club, vol. 8, pp. 151–161, 189–198.

Allen, W. T.

1881. Bird notes from Virginia. Ornith. and Ool., vol. 6, No. 3, p. 22.

Allison, Andrew

1904. The birds of west Baton Rouge Parish, Louisiana. Auk, vol. 21, pp. 472–484.

Altmann, Stuart A.

1956. Avian mobbing behavior and predator recognition. Condor, vol. 58, pp. 241–253.

Amadon, Dean

1943. Bird weights and egg weights. Auk, vol. 60, pp. 221–234.

AMADON, DEAN, and ECKELBERRY, DON R.
1955. Observations on Mexican birds. Condor, vol. 57, pp. 65–80.
AMADON, DEAN, and PHILLIPS, ALLAN ROBERTS
1947. Notes on Mexican birds. Auk, vol. 64, pp. 576–581.
AMERICAN ORNITHOLOGISTS' UNION
1910. Check-List of North American birds, ed. 3.
1931. Check-List of North American birds, ed. 4.
1944. Nineteenth supplement to the A.O.U. Check-List of North American birds. Auk, vol. 61, pp. 441–464.
1949. Twenty-fourth supplement to the A.O.U. Check-List of North American birds. Auk, vol. 66, pp. 281–285.
1957. Check-List of North American birds, ed. 5.
AMSTUTZ, AGNES
1957. A clay-colored sparrow summers in the Adirondacks. Kingbird, vol. 6, p. 117.
ANDERSON, ANDERS HAROLD, and ANDERSON, ANNE
1944. "Courtship feeding" by the house finch. Auk, vol. 61, pp. 477–478.
1946. Late nesting of the Pyrrhuloxia at Tucson, Arizona. Condor, vol. 48, p. 246.
1957. Life history of the cactus wren: Pt. I. Winter and pre-nesting behavior. Condor, vol. 59, 274–296.
ANDERSON, ROY C.
1957. Taxonomic studies on the genera *Aproctella* Cram, 1931 and *Carinema* Pereira and Vaz, 1933 with a proposal for a new genus *Pseudaproctella* n. gen. Canadian Journ. Zool., vol. 35, pp. 25–33.
1959. Preliminary revision of the genus *Diplotriaena* Henry and Ozoux, 1909 (Diplotriaenidae: Diplotriaeninae). Parassitologia, vol. 1, pp. 195–307.
ANDERSON, RUDOLPH MARTIN
1907. Birds of Iowa. Proc. Davenport Acad. Sci., vol. 11, p. 330.
ANDERSON, W.
1942. Rediscovery of the Cape Sable seaside sparrow in Collier County. Florida Nat., vol. 16, p. 12.
ANONYMOUS
1957. Point Pelee banding station—spring—1956. Ontario Bird-Banders' Assoc. Banding Newsletter No. 4, pp. 3–10 (mimeo).
ANTHONY, ALFRED WEBSTER
1886. Field notes on the birds of Washington County, Oregon. Auk, vol. 3, pp. 161–172.
1887. Winter plumage of *Leucosticte australis*. Auk, vol. 4, pp. 257–258.
1889. New birds from Lower California, Mexico. Proc. California Acad. Sci., vol. 2, pp. 73–82.
1890. The nests and eggs of Townsend's junco (*Junco townsendi*) and San Pedro partridge (*Oreortyx pictus confinis*). Zoe, vol. 1, pp. 5–6.
1892. Birds of southwestern New Mexico. Auk, vol. 9, pp. 357–369.
1893. Birds of San Pedro Martir, Lower California. Zoe, vol. 4, pp. 228–247.
1895. Birds of San Fernando, Lower California. Auk, vol. 12, pp. 134–143.
1897. New birds from the islands and peninsula of Lower California. Auk, vol. 14, pp. 164–168.
1906a. Where does the large-billed sparrow spend the winter? Auk, vol. 23, pp. 149–152.
1906b. Stray notes from Alaska. Auk, vol. 23, pp. 179–184.

ANTHONY, ALFRED WEBSTER—Continued
1923. Ants destructive to bird life. Condor, vol. 25, p. 132.
1925. Expedition to Guadalupe Island, Mexico, in 1922. Proc. California Acad. Sci., vol. 14, No. 13, pp. 277–300.

APOLLONIO, SPENCER
1958. Notes from the North Polar region. Auk, vol. 75, p. 468.

APPLETON, J. S.
1911. Brewer sparrow breeding in Simi valley. Condor, vol. 13, p. 76.

ARLTON, ALEXANDER V.
1949. Songs and other sounds of birds.

ARNOLD, JOHN R.
1937. Birds of the Coalinga area, Fresno County, California. Condor, vol. 39, pp. 31–35.

ARTHUR, STANLEY CLISBY
1931. The birds of Louisiana. Louisiana Dep. Conservation, Bull. 20.

ARVEY, DALE
1938. Color changes in a captive Cassin purple finch. Condor, vol. 40, p. 263.
1947. A check-list of the birds of Idaho. Univ. Kansas Publs., Mus. Nat. Hist., vol. 1, no. 10, pp. 193–216

ATKINSON, GEORGE E.
1894. The fox sparrow in Toronto. Biol. Rev. Ontario, vol. 1, pp. 57–63.

ATKINSON, WILLIAM LEROY
1901. Nesting habits of the California shrike (*Lanius ludovicianus*). Condor, vol. 3, p. 9.

ATTWATER, HARRY P.
1887. Nesting habits of Texas birds. Ornith. and Ool., vol. 12, pp. 103–105, 123–125.
1892. List of birds observed in the vicinity of San Antonio, Bexar County, Texas. Auk, vol. 9, pp. 229-238, 337–345.

AUDUBON FIELD NOTES
1956. Middle Atlantic coast region (Bird-Banding Notes), vol. 10, pp. 240–242.

AUDUBON, JOHN J.
1829. Birds of America.
1831. Ornithological Biography.
1832. Birds of America, vol. 1.
1833. The birds of America, vol. 2.
1834. Macgillivray's finch. Ornithological Biography, vol. 2, pp. 285–286.
1839. Ornithological biography, vol. 5.
1841. The birds of American, vol. 3.
1843. Birds of America, vol. 6.
1844. The birds of America, vol. 7.

AUDUBON, MARIA A.
1897. Audubon and his journals, vol. 2, pp. 116–117.

AUGHEY, SAMUEL
1878. Notes on the nature of the food of the birds of Nebraska. Rep. U.S. Ent. Comm. (1877), pp. 13–62.

AUSTIN, OLIVER LUTHER, JR.
1931. Clay-colored sparrow on Cape Cod. Auk, vol. 48, pp. 126–127.
1932a. The birds of Newfoundland Labrador. Mem. Nuttall Ornith. Club, No. 7, pp. 189–190.

1932b. Tree sparrow movements on Cape Cod. Bird-Banding, vol. 3, pp. 81–85.

1947. Mist netting for birds in Japan. GHQ (Nat. Res. Sec.) Report No. 88.

1948. The birds of Korea. Bull. Mus. Comp. Zool., vol. 101.

1961. On the American status of *Tiaris canora* and *Carduelis carduelis.* Auk, vol. 80, pp. 73–74.

Austin, Oliver L., Jr., and Kuroda, N.

1953. The birds of Japan, their status and distribution. Bull. Mus. Comp. Zool., vol. 109, pp. 277–637.

Averill, Charles K.

1933. Geographical distribution in relation to number of eggs. Condor, vol. 35, pp. 93–97.

Axelrod, Daniel I.

1939. A Miocene flora from the western border of the Mohave Desert. Carnegie Inst. Washington, vol. 516.

Baepler, Donald H.

1962. The avifauna of the Soloma region in Huehuetenango, Guatemala. Condor, vol. 64, pp. 140–153.

Baerg, W. J.

1930. Bird migration records in northwest Arkansas. Wilson Bull., vol. 42, pp. 45–50.

1931. Birds of Arkansas. Agric. Exper. Sta., Univ. Arkansas Bull. 258.

Bagg, Aaron Clark, and Eliot, Samuel Atkins, Jr.

1933. Notes from the Connecticut Valley in Massachusetts. Auk, vol. 50, p. 455.

1937. Birds of the Connecticut Valley in Massachusetts.

Bagg, Aaron Moore

1943. Snow buntings burrowing into snow drifts. Auk, vol. 60, p. 445.

1955. Airborne from Gulf to Gulf. Bull. Massachusetts Audubon Soc., vol. 29, pp. 106–110, 159–168.

1958. The changing seasons: A summary of the spring migration. Audubon Field Notes, vol. 12, pp. 320–333.

Bagg, Egbert, Jr.

1878. Lincoln's finch (*Melospiza lincolni*) breeding in Hamilton County, N.Y. Bull. Nuttall Ornith. Club, vol. 3, pp. 197–198.

1881. *Melospiza lincolni* breeding in New York again. Bull. Nuttall Ornith. Club, vol. 6, p. 246.

Bailey, Alfred M.

1925. A report on the birds of northwestern Alaska and regions adjacent to Bering Strait, pt. 1. Condor, vol. 27, pp. 20–32.

1926. A report on the birds of northwestern Alaska and regions adjacent to Bering Strait, pt. 10. Condor, vol. 28, pp. 165–170.

1927. Notes on the birds of southeastern Alaska. Auk, vol. 44, pp. 351–367.

1928. Early nesting of the redpoll in Alaska. Condor, vol. 30, p. 320.

1943. The birds of Cape Prince of Wales, Alaska. Proc. Colorado Mus. Nat. Hist., vol. 18.

1948. Birds of Arctic Alaska. Colorado Mus. Nat. Hist., pop. ser., No. 8.

Bailey, Alfred Marshall, Baily, A. Lang, and Neidrach, Robert J.

1953. The red crossbills of Colorado. Denver Mus. Pict., No. 9.

Bailey, Alfred Marshall, and Neidrach, Robert J.
1936. Community nesting of western robins and house finches. Condor, vol. 38, p. 214.
1938. The chestnut-collared longspur in Colorado. Wilson Bull., vol. 50, p. 243–246.

Bailey, Alfred Marshall, and Wright, Earl G.
1931. Birds of southern Louisiana. Wilson Bull., vol. 43, pp. 190–219.

Bailey, Florence Merriam
1902. Handbook of birds of the western United States.
1904. Additional notes on the birds of the upper Pecos. Auk, vol. 21, pp. 349–363.
1906. Nesting sites of the desert sparrow. Condor, vol. 8, pp. 111–112.
1910. The yellow pines of Mesa del Agua de la Yegua. Condor, vol. 12, pp. 181–184.
1916. Meeting spring half way. Condor, vol. 18, pp. 151–155.
1918. Birds. General information regarding Glacier National Park, pp. 52–64.
1923. Birds recorded from the Santa Rita Mountains in southern Arizona. Pacific Coast Avifauna, No. 15, pp. 1–60.
1928. Birds of New Mexico.
1939. Among the birds in the Grand Canyon country.

Bailey, Harold Harris
1913. The birds of Virginia, p. 245.
1921. Congratulations, Brother Bailey. Oologist, vol. 38, p. 129.
1925. The birds of Florida.

Bailey, Robert E.
1952. The incubation patch of passerine birds. Condor, vol. 54, pp. 121–136.

Baillie, James Little, Jr.
1940. The summer distribution of the eastern evening grosbeak. Canadian Field-Nat., vol. 54, p. 24.

Baillie, James Little, Jr., and Harrington, Paul
1937. The distribution of breeding birds in Ontario. Trans. Royal Canadian Inst., No. 46, vol. 21, pp. 199–283.

Baily, A. Lang
1954. Indigo bunting nesting in Colorado. Auk, vol. 71, p. 330.

Baird, James, and Nisbet, Ian C. T.
1960. Northward fall migration on the Atlantic Coast and its relation to offshore drift. Auk, vol. 77, pp. 119–149.

Baird, Spencer Fullerton
1852. *In* Stansbury, Exploration and survey of the Valley of the Great Salt Lake of Utah . . . , Appendix C, Birds, pp. 314–335.
1859. Notes on a collection of birds made by Mr. John Xantus, at Cape St. Lucas, Lower California, and now in the museum of the Smithsonian Institution. Proc. Acad. Nat. Sci. Philadelphia, vol. 11, pp. 299–306.
1869. On additions to the bird fauna of North America, made by the scientific corps of the Russo-American telegraph expedition. Trans. Chicago Acad. Sci., vol. 1, p. 316.

Baird, Spencer Fullerton, Brewer, Thomas Mayo, and Ridgway, Robert
1874. A history of North American birds: Land birds, vols. 1 and 2.

BAIRD, SPENCER FULLERTON, CASSIN, JOHN, and LAWRENCE, GEORGE NEWBOLD
1858. Birds. *In* Reports of explorations and surveys . . . for a railroad from the Mississippi River to the Pacific Ocean, vol. 9, pp. 515–516.
1860. The birds of North America.

BAKER, BERNARD W., and WALKINSHAW, L. H.
1946. Bird notes from Fawcett, Alberta. Canadian Field-Nat., vol. 60, pp. 5–10.

BALDWIN, SAMUEL PRENTISS, and KENDEIGH, SAMUEL CHARLES
1938. Variations in the weight of birds. Auk, vol. 55, pp. 416–467.

BALDWIN, P. H., and REED, E. B.
1955. A chronology of nesting for the hoary redpoll (*Acanthis hornemanni*) at Umiat, Alaska, in 1953. Journ. Colorado-Wyoming Acad. Sci., vol. 4, No. 6, pp. 62–63.

BALL, STANLEY C.
1943. Further bird notes from Gaspé, Quebec. Canadian Field-Nat., vol. 57, pp. 1–4.

BANCROFT, GRIFFING
1922. Some winter birds of the Colorado Delta. Condor, vol. 24, p. 98.
1927. Breeding birds of Scammons Lagoon, Lower California. Condor, vol. 29, pp. 29–57.
1930. The breeding birds of central Lower California. Condor, vol. 32, pp. 20–49.

BANGS, OUTRAM
1903. The Louisiana cardinal. Proc. New England Zool. Club, vol. 4, pp. 5–7.

BANKS, RICHARD C.
1959. Development of nestling white-crowned sparrows in central coastal California. Condor, vol. 61, pp. 96–109.
1960. Notes on birds from Hart's Pass, Washington. Condor, vol. 62, pp. 70–71.
1963a. New Birds from Cerralvo Island, Baja California, Mexico. Occas. Pap. California Acad. Sci., No. 37.
1963b. Birds of Cerralvo Island, Baja California. Condor, vol. 65, pp. 300–312.
1963c. Birds of the Belvedere Expedition to the Gulf of California. Trans. San Diego Soc. Nat. Hist., vol. 13, pp. 49–60.
1964a. Birds and mammals of the voyage of the "Gringa." Trans. San Diego Soc. Nat. Hist., vol. 13, pp. 177–184.
1964b. Geographic variation in the white-crowned sparrow, *Zonotrichia leucophrys*. Univ. California Publ. Zool., vol. 70, pp. 1–123.

BARBOUR, THOMAS
1923. The birds of Cuba. Mem. Nuttall Ornith. Club, No. 6.
1943. Cuban Ornithology. Mem. Nuttall Ornith. Club, No. 9.
1945. A naturalist in Cuba.

BARGER, N. R.
1941. April field notes. Passenger Pigeon, vol. 3, p. 45; May field notes, ibid., p. 60; Quest of the worm-eating warbler in Wisconsin, ibid., p. 75.

BARLOW, CHESTER
1900. Some additions to Van Denburgh's list of the land birds of Santa Clara County, California. Condor, vol. 2, pp. 131–133.
1901. A list of the land birds of the Placerville-Lake Tahoe state road. Condor, vol. 3, pp. 150–184.

BARLOW, CHESTER—Continued

1902. Some observations of the rufous-crowned sparrow. Condor, vol. 4, pp. 107–111.

BARLOW, JON C.

1960. Courtship feeding in the lark sparrow. Bull. Kansas Ornith. Soc., vol. 11, p. 2.

BARROWS, WALTER BRADFORD

1912. Michigan bird life. Spec. Bull. Dept. Zool. and Physiol. Michigan Agric. College.

BARTHOLOMEW, GEORGE A., JR., and CADE, TOM JOE

1956. Water consumption of house finches. Condor, vol. 58, pp. 406–412.

BASSETT, FRANK N.

1920. Variations in the song of the golden-crowned sparrow. Condor, vol. 22, pp. 136–137.

1923. Pine siskins as "foliage-feeders." Condor, vol. 25, pp. 137–138.

BATCHELDER, CHARLES F.

1885. Winter notes from New Mexico. Auk, vol. 2, pp. 121–128, 233–239.

BATES, JOHN MALLORY.

1901. Additional observations on the birds of northwestern Nebraska. Proc. Nebraska Ornith. Union, vol. 2, pp. 73–75.

BATTS, HENRY LEWIS, JR.

1948. Some observations on the nesting activities of the eastern goldfinch. Jack-Pine Warbler, vol. 26, pp. 51–58.

1953. Siskin and goldfinch feeding at sapsucker tree. Wilson Bull., vol. 65, p. 198.

1955. A simple study in winter bird ecology. Jack-Pine Warbler, vol. 33, pp. 115–126.

1958. The distribution and population of nesting birds on a farm in southern Michigan. Jack-Pine Warbler, vol. 36, No. 3, pp. 131–149.

BAUMGARTNER, A. MARGUERITE

1937a. Enemies and survival ratio of the tree sparrow. Bird-Banding, vol. 8, pp. 45–52.

1937b. Nesting habits of the tree sparrow at Churchill, Manitoba. Bird-Banding, vol. 8, pp. 99–108.

1937c. Food and feeding habits of the tree sparrow. Wilson Bull., vol. 49, pp. 65–80.

1938a. A study of development of young tree sparrows at Churchill, Manitoba. Bird-Banding, vol. 9, pp. 69–79.

1938b. Experiments in feather marking eastern tree sparrows for territory studies. Bird-Banding, vol. 9, pp. 124–135.

1938c. Seasonal variations in the tree sparrow. Auk, vol. 55, pp. 603–613.

1939. Distribution of the American tree sparrow. Wilson Bull., vol. 51, pp. 137–149.

1942. Sex ratio in Oklahoma tree sparrows. Bird-Banding, vol. 13, pp. 181–182.

1952. A five-year study of winter Harris sparrows (MS).

BAUMGARTNER, FREDERICK M.

1934. Bird mortality on the highways. Auk, vol. 51, pp. 537–538.

BAUMGARTNER, FREDERICK M. and A. MARGUERITE

1950. Lark bunting in central Oklahoma in Winter. Wilson Bull., vol. 62, p. 36.

BEAL, F. E. L., MCATEE, WALDO LEE, and KALMBACH, EDWIN RICHARD

1916. Common birds of southeastern United States in relation to agriculture. U.S. Dep. Agric. Farmers' Bull. 755, p. 16.

BEAL, FOSTER ELLENBOROUGH LASCELLES

1897. Some common birds in their relation to agriculture. U.S. Dep. Agric. Farmers' Bull. 54.

1907. Birds of California in relation to the fruit industry, pt. 1. U.S. Dep. Agric. Biol. Surv., Bull. 30, pp. 13–17.

1910. Birds of California in relation to the fruit industry, pt. 2. U.S. Dep. Agric. Biol. Surv., Bull. 34, pp. 1–96.

BEALS, MARIE V.

1939. Ten years of banding at Birdwood. Bird-Banding, vol. 10, pp. 13–14.

BEAN, T. H.

1882. Notes on birds collected during the summer of 1880, in Alaska and Siberia. Proc. U.S. Nat. Mus., vol. 5, pp. 144–173.

BECK, ROLLO H.

1896. Western evening grosbeak *Coccothraustes vespertinus montanus*. Nidologist, vol. 4, pp. 3–4.

BECKER, GEORGE B., and STACK, JOSEPH W.

1944. Weights and temperatures of some Michigan birds. Bird-Banding, vol. 15, pp. 45–68.

BECKIE, P. L.

1958. Observations of Longspurs at Bladworth. Blue Jay, vol. 16, pp. 55–56.

BECKMAN, C. W.

1885. Notes on some of the birds of Pueblo, Colorado. Auk, vol. 2, pp. 139–114.

BEE, J. W.

1958. Birds found on the Arctic slope of northern Alaska. Univ. Kansas Publ., vol. 10, No. 5.

BEE, R. G., and HUTCHINGS, J.

1942. Breeding records of Utah birds. Great Basin Nat., vol. 3, pp. 61–85.

BEEBE, C. WILLIAM

1906. The bird, its form and function.

1907. Geographical variation in birds, effects of humidity. Zoologica, vol. 1, pp. 20–21.

BEECHER, WILLIAM J.

1942. Nesting birds and the vegetation substrate. Chicago Ornith. Soc.

1951. Adaptations for food-getting in the American blackbirds. Auk, vol. 68, pp. 411–440.

1955. Late-Pleistocene isolation of salt-marsh sparrows. Ecology, vol. 36, pp. 23–28.

BEER, JAMES ROBERT, FRENZEL, LOUIS D., and HANSEN, NORMAN

1956. Minimum space requirements of some nesting passerine birds. Wilson Bull., vol. 68, pp. 200–209.

BEHLE, W. H., BUSHMAN, J. B., and GREENHALGH, C. M.

1958. Birds of the Kanab area and adjacent high plateaus of southern Utah. Univ. Utah Biol. Ser., vol. 11, No. 7.

BEHLE, WILLIAM HARROUN

1940. Extension of the range of the black-chinned sparrow into Utah. Condor, vol. 42, p. 224.

1943. Birds of Pine Valley Mountain region, southwestern Utah. Bull. Univ. Utah, vol. 34.

1944. Check-list of the birds of Utah. Condor, vol. 46, pp. 67–87.

1958. The birds of the Raft River Mountains, northwestern Utah. Univ Utah Biol. Ser., vol. 11, No. 6.

BEHLE, WILLIAM HARROUN, and SELANDER, ROBERT KEITH

1952. New and additional records of Utah birds. Wilson Bull., vol. 64, pp. 26–32.

BEHREND, FRED W.

1946. Wintering of the evening grosbeak in northeast Tennessee. Migrant, vol. 17, pp. 1–4.

BEIDLEMAN, RICHARD GOOCH

1957. Winter bird-population study: Isolated ponderosa pine woodland. Audubon Field Notes, vol. 11, pp. 305–306.

1960. Open ponderosa pine forest. Audubon Field Notes, vol. 14, pp. 494–495.

BELCHER, MARGARET

1961. Birds of Regina. Saskatchewan Nat. Hist. Soc., Spec. Publ. No. 3.

BELDING, L.

1884. Second catalogue of a collection of birds made near the southern extremity of Lower California. Proc. U.S. Nat. Mus., vol. 6, pp. 344–352.

1890. Land birds of the Pacific district. California Acad. Sci., Occas. Pap., pt. 2.

1900. A part of my experience in collecting. Condor, vol. 2, pp. 1–5.

1901. Chipmunks. Condor, vol. 3, p. 3.

BELL, JOHN

1852. On the *Pipilo Oregonus* as distinguished from the *Pipilo Arcticus* of Swainson. Ann. Lyc. Nat. Hist. New York, vol. 5, pp. 6–8.

BENCKESER, HAROLD R.

1955. Keith County notes. Nebraska Bird Rev., vol. 23, p. 22.

1957. Keith County notes. Nebraska Bird Rev., vol. 25, pp. 24–25.

BENDIRE, CHARLES EMIL

1882. The rufous-winged sparrow. Ornith. and Ool., vol. 7, pp. 121–122.

1888. Notes on the nests and eggs of *Peucaea aestivalis bachmani* Aud., Bachman's sparrow. Auk, vol. 5, pp. 351–356.

1889. Notes on the general habits, nests and eggs of the genus *Passerella*. Auk, vol. 6, pp. 107–116.

1890. Notes on *Pipilo fuscus mesoleucus* and *Pipilo aberti*, their habits, nests, and eggs. Auk, vol. 7, pp. 22–29.

1895. Life histories of North American birds. U.S. Nat. Mus. Spec. Bull. 3.

BENNETT, FRANK MARION

1909. A tragedy of migration. Bird-Lore, vol. 11, pp. 110–113.

BENNETT, G. F.

1957. Studies of the genus *Protocalliphora* (Diptera: Calliophoridae). PhD thesis, Univ. of Toronto.

1961. On the specificity and transmission of some avian trypanosomes. Canadian Journ. Zool., vol. 39, pp. 17–33.

BENNETT, G. F., and FALLIS, A. M.

1960. Blood parasites of birds in Algonquin Park, Canada, and a discussion of their transmission. Canadian Journ. Zool., vol. 38, pp. 261–273.

BENT, ARTHUR CLEVELAND

1907–08. Summer birds of southwestern Saskatchewan. Auk, vol. 24, pp. 407–430; vol. 25, pp. 25–35.

1912a. Notes on birds observed during a brief visit to the Aleutian Islands and Bering Sea in 1911. Smithsonian Misc. Coll., vol. 56, No. 32.

1912b. A new subspecies of crossbill from Newfoundland. Smithsonian Misc. Coll., vol. 60, No. 15, p. 1.

1938. Life histories of North American birds of prey: Orders Falconiformes and Strigiformes, pt. 2. U.S. Nat. Mus. Bull. 170.
1942. Life histories of North American flycatchers, larks, swallows, and their allies: Order Passeriformes. U.S. Nat. Mus. Bull. 179.
1943. My Aleutian holiday: A summer in forbidding seas. Bird-Life, vol. 39, pp. 193–209.
1958. Life histories of North American blackbirds, orioles, tanagers, and allies. U.S. Nat. Mus. Bull. 211.

Bequaert, Joseph C.
1954. The Hippoboscidae or louse-flies (Diptera) of mammals and birds. Pt. II. Taxonomy, evolution and revision of American genera and species Ent. Americana, vol. 24, pp. 1–232.

Berger, Andrew J.
1951a. The cowbird and certain host species in Michigan. Wilson Bull., vol. 63, pp. 26–34.
1951b. Ten consecutive nests of a song sparrow. Wilson Bull., vol. 63, pp. 186–188.
1953. Three cases of twin embryos in passerine birds. Condor, vol. 55, pp. 157–158.

Bergman, Sten
1935. Zur Kenntnis nordostasiatischer Vögel.

Bergtold, William Henry
1913. A study of the house finch. Auk, vol. 30, pp. 40–73.
1916. Cassin's sparrow in Colorado. Auk, vol. 33, p. 435.
1917a. The birds of Denver. Wilson Bull., vol. 29, pp. 113–129.
1917b. A study of the incubation periods of birds.
1926. Avian gonads and migration. Condor, vol. 28, pp. 114–120.
1927. A house finch infected by fly larvae. Auk, vol. 44, pp. 106–107.
1928. A guide to Colorado birds.
1929. Egg weights from egg measurements. Auk, vol. 46, pp. 466–473.

Bernhoft-Osa, A.
1956. Om en syngende hun av konglebit, *Pinicola enucleator*. (Notes on a singing female pine-grosbeak.) Vår Fågelvårld, vol. 15, pp. 245–247.

Bernier, J. E.
1909. Report on the Dominion Government Expedition to Arctic Islands and the Hudson Strait on board the C.G.S. "Arctic."

Betts, Norman de Witt.
1912. Notes from Boulder County, Colorado. Auk, vol. 29, pp. 399–400.

Bicknell, Eugene P.
1880. Remarks on the nidification of *Loxia curvirostra americana*, with a description of its nest and eggs. Bull. Nuttall Ornith. Club, vol. 5, pp. 7–11.
1884. A study of the singing of our birds. Auk, vol. 1, pp. 328–329.
1885. A study of the singing of our birds. Auk, vol. 2, 144–154.

Bigelow, Henry Bryant
1902. Birds of the northeastern coast of Labrador. Auk, vol. 19, pp. 24–31.

Bird, C. G., and Bird, E. G.
1941. The birds of north-east Greenland. Ibis, ser. 14, vol. 5, pp. 118–161.

Birtwell, Francis J.
1901. Nesting habits of the evening grosbeak (*Coccothraustes vespertinus*). Auk, vol. 58, pp. 388–391.

Bishop, Louis B.

1889. Notes on the birds of the Magdalen Islands. Auk, vol. 6, pp. 144–150.

1896. Descriptions of a new horned lark and a new song sparrow, with remarks on Sennett's nighthawk. Auk, vol. 13, pp. 129–135.

1900. Birds of the Yukon region, with notes on other species. North American Fauna, Bull. U.S. Dept. Agric. Biol., No. 19, pp. 47–100.

1901. A new sharp-tailed finch from North Carolina. Auk, vol. 18, pp. 269–270.

1905. Notes on a small collection of California birds with description of an apparently unrecognized race of Hutton's vireo. Condor, vol. 7, pp. 141–143.

1915. Description of a new race of Savannah sparrow and suggestions on some California birds. Condor, vol. 17, pp. 185–189.

Blackwelder, Eliot

1916. Late nesting of the Montana junco. Auk, vol. 33, p. 77.

1919. Notes on the summer birds of the upper Yukon region, Alaska. Auk, vol. 36, pp. 57–64.

Blain, Alexander W.

1948. On the accidental death of wild birds. Jack-Pine Warbler, vol. 26, pp. 58–60.

Blair, H. M. S.

1936. On the birds of east Finmark. Ibis, ser. 13, vol. 6, pp. 280–308, 429–459, 651–674.

Blake Charles Henry

1955. Notes on the eastern purple finch. Bird-Banding, vol. 26, pp. 89–116.

Blanchard, Barbara D.

1936. Continuity of behavior in the Nuttall white-crowned sparrow. Condor, vol. 38, pp. 145–150.

1941. The white-crowned sparrows (*Zonotrichia leucophrys*) of the Pacific seaboard: environment and annual cycle. Univ. California Publ. Zool., vol. 46, pp. 1–177.

Blanchard, Barbara D., and Erickson, Mary M.

1949. The cycle in the Gambel sparrow. Univ. California Publ. Zool., vol. 47, pp. 255–318.

Bleitz, Donald L.

1958a. Indigo bunting breeding in Los Angeles County, California. Condor, vol. 60, p. 408.

1958b. Treatment of foot pox at a feeding and trapping station. Auk, vol. 75, pp. 474–475.

Blincoe, Benedict Joseph

1921. Two Bachman's sparrow's nests near Bardstown, Kentucky. Wilson Bull., vol. 33, pp. 100–101.

1925. Birds of Bardstown, Nelson County, Kentucky. Auk, vol. 42, pp. 404–420.

Bohlman, Herman Theodore

1903. Nest habits of the Shufeldt junco. Condor, vol. 5, pp. 94–95.

Bolander, Louis

1906. The Nuttall sparrow around San Francisco. Condor, vol. 8, pp. 73–74.

Bole, B. P., Jr.

1941–42. Nesting habitat of slate-colored junco (*Junco hyemalis hyemalis*) on Little Mountain. Bird Calendar of the Cleveland Bird Club 38th year, No. 1, p. 9.

BONAPARTE, CHARLES LUCIAN

1828. American ornithology, or the natural history of the birds inhabiting the United States, not given by Wilson, vol. 2, p. 75.

1837. Notices and descriptions of new or interesting birds from Mexico and South America. Proc. Zool. Soc. London, vol. 5, p. 111.

1838. A geographical and comparative list of the birds of Europe and North America, p. 33.

1850. Conspectus generum avium, vol. 1, p. 500.

BOND, FRANK

1885. Birds. *In* Report of the governor of Wyoming to the Secretary of the Interior (Annual report of Secretary of Interior. 1885, vol. 2), pp. 1138–1140.

BOND, GORMAN M., and STEWART, ROBERT EARL

1951. A new swamp sparrow from the Maryland coastal plain. Wilson Bull., vol. 63, pp. 38–40.

BOND, JAMES

1937. Lincoln's sparrow nesting in Maine. Auk, vol. 54, pp. 102–103.

1938. Nesting of the white-winged crossbill. Canadian Field-Nat., vol. 52, pp. 3–5.

1949. Summer residents of Mt. Desert. Maine Audubon Soc. Bull., vol. 5, p. 7.

1961. Birds of the West Indies.

BOND, RICHARD M.

1939. Observations on raptorial birds in the lava beds—Tule Lake region of northern California. Condor, vol. 41, pp. 54–61.

1940. Food habits of horned owls in the Pahranagat Valley, Nevada. Condor, vol. 42, pp. 164–165.

1947. Food items from red-tailed hawk and marsh hawk nests. Condor, vol. 49, p. 84.

BOND, RICHARD R.

1957. Ecological distribution of breeding birds in the upland forest of southern Wisconsin. Ecol. Monogr., vol. 27, pp. 351–384.

BONHOTE, J. LEWIS

1903. On a collection of birds from the northern islands of the Bahama group. Ibis, ser. 8, vol. 3, pp. 273–315.

BORELL, A. E.

1936. A modern La Brea tar pit. Auk, vol. 53, pp. 298–300.

BORROR, DONALD J.

1959. Songs of the chipping sparrow. Ohio Journ. Sci., vol. 59, pp. 347–356.

1961a. Intraspecific variation in passerine bird songs. Wilson Bull., vol. 73, pp. 57–78.

1961b. Songs of finches (Fringillidae) of eastern North America. Ohio Journ. Sci., vol. 61, pp. 161–174.

1965. Song variation in Maine song sparrows. Wilson Bull., vol. 77, pp. 5–37.

BORROR, DONALD J., and GUNN, WILLIAM W. H.

1965. Variation in white-throated sparrow songs. Auk, vol. 82, pp. 26–47.

BORROR, DONALD J., and REESE, CARL R.

1954. Analytical studies of Henslow's sparrow songs. Wilson Bull., vol. 66, pp. 243–252.

BOUTEILLER, JAMES

1905. Bird migration, 1904. Observations made on Sable Island, Nova Scotia. Ottawa Nat., vol. 19, p. 119.

BOUTEILLER, JAMES—Continued

1906. Bird migration, 1905. Observations made on Sable Island, Nova Scotia. Ottawa Nat., vol. 20, pp. 127–129.

1909. In Macoun, Catalogue of Canadian birds.

BOWDISH, B. S.

1906. Bird tragedies. Bird-Lore, vol. 8, p. 208.

BOWLES, CHARLES WILSON

1903. Notes on pine siskins. Condor, vol. 5, p. 15.

BOWLES, JOHN H.

1901. Bird notes from Tacoma gulches. Condor, vol. 3, pp. 1–3.

1911. Notes extending the range of certain birds on the Pacific slope. Auk, vol. 28, pp. 169–178.

1920. The eastern Savannah sparrow and the Aleutian Savannah sparrow at Tacoma, Washington. Condor, vol. 22, pp. 108–109.

1921. Breeding dates for Washington birds. Murrelet, vol. 2, pp. 8–12.

1924. Tacoma notes on the spring of 1924. Murrelet, vol. 5, No. 2, pp. 7–8.

BOWNAN, CHARLES WILSON

1904. Nelson's sharp-tailed sparrow in North Dakota. Auk, vol. 21, pp. 385–386.

BOYD, ELIZABETH M.

1951. The external parasites of birds: a review. Wilson Bull., vol. 63, pp. 363–369.

BRACKBILL, HERVEY GROFF

1942. Goldfinch and field sparrow rifle small galls. Auk, vol. 59, pp. 445–446.

1944. The cardinal's period of dependency. Wilson Bull., vol. 56, pp. 173–174.

1947. Evening grosbeaks and purple finches at Baltimore. Auk, vol. 64, pp. 321–322.

1952. A joint nesting of cardinals and song sparrows. Auk, vol. 69, pp. 302–307.

1953. Migratory status of breeding song sparrows at Baltimore, Maryland. Bird-Banding, vol. 24, p. 68.

1954. On white-throated sparrow plumages. Bird-Banding, vol. 25, pp. 148–149.

BRADBURY, WILLIAM CHASE

1922. Field notes of W. C. Bradbury, 1914 to 1922. (Typewritten, Denver Mus. Nat. Hist., Denver, Colorado.)

BRADLEY, HAZEL L.

1940. A few observations on the nesting of the eastern chipping sparrow. Jack-Pine Warbler, vol. 18, pp. 35–46.

1948. A life history study of the indigo bunting. Jack-Pine Warbler, vol. 26, pp. 103–113.

BRAND, ALBERT RICH

1936. More songs of wild birds.

1938. Vibration frequencies of passerine bird song. Auk, vol. 55, pp. 263–268.

BRANDT, HERBERT

1940. Texas bird adventures in the Chisos Mountains and on the northern plains.

1943. Alaska bird trails.

1951. Arizona and its bird life.

Braund, Frank W., and McCullagh, E. Perry
1940. The birds of Anticosti Island, Quebec. Wilson Bull., vol. 52, pp. 96–123.

Braund, Frank William, and Aldrich, John Warren
1941. Notes on the breeding birds of the upper peninsula of Michigan. Oologist, vol. 58, pp. 86–93, 98–105.

Breckenridge, W. J., and Kilgore, W.
1929. Nelson's sparrow nesting in Minnesota. Auk, vol. 46, p. 548.

Breckenridge, Walter John
1930a. Breeding of Nelson's sparrow (*Ammospiza nelsoni*) with special reference to Minnesota. Occas. Pap. Univ. Minnesota Mus. Nat. Hist., No. 3, pp. 29–38.
1930b. A hybrid *Passerina* (*Passerina cyanea* × *Passerina amoena*). Occas. Pap. Univ. Minnesota Mus. Nat. Hist., No. 3, pp. 39–40.
1935. An ecological study of some Minnesota marsh hawks. Condor, vol. 37, pp. 268–276.
1955. Birds of the lower Back River, Northwest Territories, Canada. Canadian Field-Nat., vol. 69, pp. 1–9.

Breiding, George H.
1946. Moonseed fruits as bird food. Auk, vol. 63, p. 589.

Breninger, George F.
1901. A list of birds observed on the Pima Indian Reservation, Arizona. Condor, vol. 3, p. 44.
1904. San Clemente Island and its birds. Auk, vol. 21, pp. 218–223.

Brewer, T. M.
1878. Notes on *Junco caniceps* and the closely allied forms. Bull. Nuttall Ornith. Club, vol. 3, pp. 72–75.

Brewster, William
1877a. Northern range of the sharp-tailed finch. Bull. Nuttall Ornith. Club, vol. 2, p. 28.
1877b. Two undescribed nests of California birds. Bull. Nuttall Ornith. Club, vol. 2, pp. 37–38.
1877c. Northern range of the sharp-tailed finch (*Ammodromus caudacutus*). Bull. Nuttall Ornith. Club, vol. 2, p. 28.
1879. Notes on the habits and distribution of the rufous-crowned sparrow. (*Peucaea ruficeps*). Bull. Nuttall Ornith. Club, vol. 4, pp. 47–48.
1881. On the relationship of *Helminthophaga leucobronchialis*, Brewster, and *Helminthophaga lawrencei*, Herrick; with some conjectures respecting certain other North American birds. Bull. Nuttall Ornith. Club, vol. 6, pp. 218–225.
1882a. On a collection of birds lately made by Mr. F. Stephens in Arizona. Bull. Nuttall Ornith. Club, vol. 7, pp. 193–212.
1882b. Impressions of some southern birds. Bull. Nuttall Ornith. Club, vol. 7, p. 100.
1883. Notes on the birds observed during a summer cruise in the Gulf of St. Lawrence. Proc. Boston Soc., vol. 22, pp. 364–368.
1886. An ornithological reconnaissance in western North Carolina. Auk., vol. 3, pp. 94–112.
1890. The Acadian sharp-tailed sparrow and Scott's seaside sparrow on the coast of South Carolina. Auk., vol. 7, p. 212.
1893. On the occurrence of certain birds in British Columbia. Auk, vol. 10, pp. 236–237.

BREWSTER, WILLIAM—Continued

1895. A remarkable flight of pine grosbeaks (*Pinicola enucleator*). Auk, vol. 12, pp. 245–255.

1902. Birds of the Cape region of Lower California. Bull. Mus. Comp. Zool., vol. 41, No. 1, pp. 1–242.

1906. The birds of the Cambridge region of Massachusetts. Mem. Nuttall Ornith. Club., No. 4.

1918. Nesting of the red crossbill (*Loxia curvirostra minor*) in Essex County, Massachusetts. Auk, vol. 35, p. 225.

1936. October Farm. From the Concord journals and diaries of William Brewster.

1937a. The birds of the Lake Umbagog region of Maine, pt. 3. Bull. Mus. Comp. Zool., vol. 66, pp. 403–521.

1937b. October Farm.

1937c. Concord River.

1938. The birds of the Lake Umbagog region of Maine, compiled from the diaries and journals of William Brewster by Ludlow Griscom. Bull. Mus. Comp. Zool., vol. 66, pt. 4, pp. 525–620.

BRIDGEWATER, DONALD D.

1962. Master's thesis, Oklahoma State University, Stillwater, Okla.

BRIMLEY, CLEMENT SAMUEL

1890. Nesting of the blue grosbeak in 1888 and 1889 at Raleigh, N.C. Ornith. and Ool., vol. 15, p. 22.

BROCKMAN, CHRISTIAN FRANK

1941. Interesting records from high elevations on Mount Rainier, Washington. Auk, vol. 58, p. 270.

BRODKORB, PIERCE

1948. Some birds from the lowlands of central Veracruz, Mexico. Quart. Journ. Florida Acad. Sci., vol. 10, pp. 31–38.

BROOKS, ALLAN

1900. Notes on some birds of British Columbia. Auk, vol. 17, pp. 104–107.

1914. A sadly neglected matter. Condor, vol. 16, pp. 115–117.

1917. Birds of the Chilliwack District, B.C. Auk, vol. 34, pp. 28–50.

1922. Notes on the American pine grosbeaks with the description of a new subspecies. Condor, vol. 24, pp. 86–88.

1923a. Notes on the birds of Porcher Island, B.C. Auk, vol. 40, pp. 217–224.

1923b. Some recent record sfor British Columbia. Auk, vol. 40, pp. 700–701.

1933. Some notes on the birds of Brownsville, Texas. Auk, vol. 50, pp. 59–63.

1939. Juvenal plumage of the evening grosbeak. Auk, vol. 56, pp. 191–192.

BROOKS, ALLAN, and SWARTH, HARRY S.

1925. A distributional list of the birds of British Columbia. Pacific Coast Avifauna, No. 17.

BROOKS, EARLE AMOS

1920. White-winged crossbill (*Loxia leucoptera*) in West Virginia. Auk, vol. 37, p. 457.

1936. Observations on some Newfoundland birds. Auk, vol. 53, pp. 342–345.

BROOKS, MAURICE GRAHAM

1930. Notes on the birds of Cranberry Glades, Pocahontas County, West Virginia. Wilson Bull., vol. 42, pp. 245–252.

1938. Bachman's sparrow in the north-central portion of its range. Wilson Bull., vol. 50, pp. 86–109.

1943. The carpels of red spruce blossoms as food for birds. Wilson Bull., vol. 55, pp. 245–246.

1944. A check-list of West Virginia birds. Agric. Exper. Sta., College of Agric., Forestry, and Home Economics, West Virginia Univ., Bull. 316.

1952a. Winter season: Appalachian region. Audubon Field Notes, vol. 6, pp. 194–196.

1952b. The Allegheny Mountains as a barrier to bird movement. Auk, vol. 69, pp. 192–198.

1956. Winter foods of evening and pine grosbeaks in West Virginia. Wilson Bull., vol. 68, pp. 249–250.

BROUN, MAURICE

1933. Some interesting recoveries. Bird-Banding, vol. 4, pp. 157–158.

BROWN, A. D.

1891. The first record of McCown's longspur breeding in Minnesota. Ornith. and Ool., vol. 16, p. 142.

BROWN, HERBERT

1903. Arizona bird notes. Auk, vol. 20, pp. 43–50.

BROWN, HUBERT H.

1891–92. *In* Report of the occurrence of the evening grosbeak . . . in Ontario. Trans. Canadian Inst., vol. 3, p. 113.

BROWN, NATHAN CLIFFORD

1879. A list of birds observed at Coosada, Central Alabama. Bull. Nuttall Ornith. Club, vol. 4, pp. 7–13.

1882. A reconnaissance in southwestern Texas. Bull. Nuttall Ornith. Club, vol. 7, pp. 33–42.

1884. A second season in Texas. Auk, vol. 1, pp. 120–124.

BROWN, RICHARD McP.

1960. Black-throated sparrows in south-central Oregon. Condor, vol. 62, pp. 220–221.

BROWN, V. H.

1945. Aircraft collision with a goldfinch. Auk. vol. 62, pp. 140–141.

BROWN, WILLIAM J.

1911. Some Newfoundland bird notes—May, June, July, 1911. Ottawa Nat., vol. 25, pp. 89–94.

1912. Additional notes on the birds of Newfoundland. Ottawa Nat., vol. 26, pp. 93–98.

BROWN, WOODWARD HART

1954. Aerial feeding by white-crowned sparrows. Wilson Bull., vol. 66, p. 143.

BRUCE, MARY EMILY

1898. A month with the goldfinches. Auk, vol. 15, pp. 239–243.

BRUCE, WALTER

1923. Bird-life in the Sans Poil Valley, Washington. Bird-Lore, vol. 25, pp. 390–391.

BRYANT, HAROLD C.

1911. The relation of birds to an insect outbreak in northern California during the spring and summer of 1911. Condor, vol. 13, pp. 195–208.

1916. Habits and food of the roadrunner in California. Univ. California Publ. Zool., vol. 17, pp. 21–55.

1921. California woodpecker steals eggs of wood pewee. Condor, vol. 23.

BRYANT, HAROLD—Continued
1943. Birds eat snow. Condor, vol. 45, p. 77.
1952. Additions to the Check-list of Birds of Grand Canyon National Park, Arizona. Condor, vol. 54, p. 320.

BRYANT, OWEN
1904. Dates of nesting of Bermuda birds. Auk, vol. 21, p. 391.

BRYANT, WALTER E.
1887. Additions to the ornithology of Guadalupe Island. California Acad. Sci., vol. 2, Bull. 6, pp. 294–295.
1889. A catalogue of the birds of Lower California, Mexico. Proc. California Acad. Sci., vol. 2, pp. 237–320.

BRYENS, OSCAR MCKINLEY
1939. Some notes on the migration of the family "Fringillidae" at McMillan, Luce County, Michigan. Jack-Pine Warbler, vol. 17, pp. 102–106.

BUCKLEY, P. A.
1959. Recent specimens from southern New York and New Jersey affecting A.O.U. Check-list status. Auk, vol. 76, pp. 517–520.

BULL, JOHN L.
1963. Black-throated sparrows in the eastern United States. Auk, vol. 80, pp. 379–380.

BULLIS, HARVEY R., JR.
1954. Trans-Gulf migration, spring 1952. Auk, vol. 71, pp. 298–305.

BURDICK, AUSTIN W.
1944. Birds of the northern Cascade Mountains of Washington. Condor, vol. 46, pp. 238–242.

BURGESS, THORNTON W.
1947. [Note] *In* Evening Grosbeaks. Maine Audubon Soc. Bull., vol. 3, p. 12.

BURLEIGH, T. D., and LOWERY, G. H.
1939. Description of two new birds from western Texas. Occas. Pap. Mus. Zool. Louisiana State Univ., No. 6, pp. 67–68.
1940. Birds of the Guadalupe Mountain region of western Texas. Occas. Pap. Mus. Zool. Louisiana State Univ., No. 8, pp. 85–151.
1942. Notes on the birds of southeastern Coahuila. Occas. Pap. Mus. Zool. Louisiana State Univ., No. 12, pp. 185–212.

BURLEIGH, THOMAS DEARBORN
1921. Breeding birds of Warland, Lincoln Co., Montana. Auk, vol. 38, pp. 552–565.
1923a. Notes on the bird life of Allegheny County, Pennsylvania. Wilson Bull., vol. 35, pp. 79–99.
1923b. Notes on the breeding birds of Clark's Fort, Bonner County, Idaho. Auk, vol. 40, pp. 653–665.
1924. Migration notes from State College, Center County, Pennsylvania. Wilson Bull., vol. 36, pp. 68–77.
1925. Notes on the breeding habits of some Georgia birds. Auk, vol. 42, pp. 396–401.
1927a. Three interesting breeding records for 1925 from the Piedmont Region of northeastern Georgia. Wilson Bull., vol. 39 pp. 15–19.
1927b. Further notes on the breeding birds of northeastern Georgia. Auk, vol. 44, pp. 229–234.
1929. Notes on the bird life of northwestern Washington. Auk, vol. 46, pp. 502–519.
1930. Notes on the bird life of northwestern Washington. Auk, vol. 47, pp. 48–63.

1939. Notes on a recent trip to southern Florida. Florida Nat., vol. 12, pp. 95–96.
1941. Bird life on Mt. Mitchell. Auk, vol. 58, pp. 334–345.
1942. January 1940 in southern Mississippi. Auk, vol. 59, pp. 119–121.
1944. The bird life of the gulf coast region of Mississippi. Occas. Pap. Mus. Zool. Louisiana State Univ., No. 20, pp. 324–490.
1958. Georgia birds.

Burleigh, Thomas Dearborn, and Peters, Harold Seymour
1948. Geographic variation in Newfoundland birds. Proc. Biol. Soc. Washington, vol. 61, pp. 111–126.

Burns, Franklin Lorenzo
1895. Notes from southern New Jersey. Auk, vol. 12, p. 189.
1915. Comparative periods of deposition and incubation of some North American birds. Wilson Bull., vol. 27, pp. 275–286.
1921. Comparative periods of nestling life of some North American Nidicolae. Wilson Bull., vol. 33, pp. 4–15, 90–99, 177–182.

Burns, Robert D.
1958. Michigan cooperative cardinal study feeding station observations. Jack-Pine Warbler, vol. 36, pp. 79–81.

Burroughs, John
1886. Signs and seasons.
1901. *In* Harriman Alaska series: Narrative, glaciers, natives, vol. 1.
1904. Signs and seasons.

Burtch, Verdi
1897. Acadian sparrow in Yates County, N.Y. Auk, vol. 14, p. 93.

Bush, Clarence H.
1921. Goldfinches nest in thistles. Bird-Lore, vol. 23, p. 247.

Butler, Amos William
1888. On a new subspecies of *Ammodramus sandwichensis* from Mexico. Auk, vol. 5, pp. 264–266.
1892. Some notes concerning the evening grosbeak. Auk, vol. 9, pp. 238–247.
1898. The birds of Indiana. *In* Indiana Dep. Geol. and Nat. Res., 22d. Ann. Rep. (for 1897), pp. 515–1187.

Byrd, Elon E., and Denton, F. Fred
1950. The helminth parasites of birds. I. A review of the trematode genus *Tanaisia skrjabin*, 1924. Amer. Midland Nat., vol. 43, pp. 32–57.

Cade, Thomas Joseph
1952. Notes on the birds of Sledge Island, Bering Sea, Alaska. Condor, vol. 54, pp. 51–54.
1953a. Sub-nival feeding of the redpoll in interior Alaska: a possible adaptation to the northern winter. Condor, vol. 55, pp. 43–44.
1953b. Behavior of a young gyrfalcon. Wilson Bull., vol. 65, pp. 26–31.

Cahn, Alvin R.
1915. The status of the Harris's sparrow in Wisconsin and neighboring states. Wisconsin Nat. Hist. Soc. Bull., vol. 13, No. 2, pp. 102–108.
1947. Notes on the birds of the Dutch Harbor area of the Aleutian Islands. Condor, vol. 49, pp. 78–82.

Cameron, Ewen Somerled
1907. The birds of Custer and Dawson counties, Montana. Auk, vol. 24, pp. 241–270, 389–406.
1908. The birds of Custer and Dawson counties, Montana. Auk, vol. 25, pp. 39–56.

CAMERON, EWEN SOMERLED—Continued

1913. Notes on Swainson's hawk (*Buteo swainsoni*) in Montana. Auk, vol. 30, pp. 381–394.

CAMPBELL, LOUIS WALTER

1937. Shufeldt's junco near Toledo, Ohio. Auk, vol. 54, p. 399.

1939. Nelson's sparrow in Monroe County, Michigan. Wilson Bull., vol. 51, p. 186.

1940. Birds of Lucas County (Ohio). Bull. Toledo Zool. Soc., vol. 1, No. 1.

CAMRAS, SIDNEY

1940. A new Savannah sparrow from Mexico. Field Mus. Nat. Hist. Zool. Surv., vol. 24, No. 15, p. 159.

CARDIFF, EUGENE A.

1956. Additional records for the Imperial Valley and Salton Sea area of California. Condor, vol. 58, pp. 447-448.

CARDIFF, EUGENE E., and CARDIFF, BRUCE E.

1950. Late nesting record for the Abert towhee. Condor, vol. 52, p. 135.

CARPENTER, CHARLES C.

1951. Young goldfinches eaten by garter snake. Wilson Bull., vol. 63, pp. 117-118.

CARPENTER. NELSON K.

1907a. Concerning a few abnormally marked eggs. Condor, vol. 9, pp. 198-199.

1907b. The rufous-crowned sparrow in San Diego County, California. Condor, vol. 9, pp. 158-159.

1918. An odd nest of the song sparrow of Los Coronados Islands. Condor, vol. 20, p. 124.

CARRIGER, HENRY WARD, and PEMBERTON, JOHN ROY

1907. Nesting of the pine siskin in California. Condor, vol. 9, pp. 18-19.

CARRIKER, MELBOURNE ARMSTRONG, JR.

1902. Notes on the nesting of some Sioux County birds. Proc. Nebraska Ornith. Union, vol. 3, pp. 75–89.

1910. An annotated list of the birds of Costa Rica, including Cocos Island. Ann. Carnegie Mus., vol. 6, pp. 314–915.

CARTER, FRANCES

1937. Bird life at Twentynine Palms. Condor, vol. 39, pp. 210–219.

CARTWRIGHT, BERTRAM WILLIAM, SHORTT, TERENCE MICHAEL, and HARRIS, ROBERT D.

1937. Baird's sparrow. Trans. Roy. Canadian Inst., vol. 21, pp. 153-197.

CARY, MERRITT

1901. Birds of the Black Hills. Auk, vol. 18, pp. 231-238.

1902. Some general remarks upon the distribution of life in northwest Nebraska. Proc. Nebraska Ornith. Union, vol. 3, pp. 63–75.

1911. A biological survey of Colorado. North American Fauna, No. 33.

1917. Life zone investigations in Wyoming. North American Fauna, No. 42.

CASSEL, JOSEPH FRANK

1952. Breeding bird populations at various altitudes in north central Colorado. Ph. D. thesis, Univ. Colorado, Boulder Colo.

CASSIN, JOHN

1852. Descriptions of new species of birds, specimens of which are in the collection of the Academy of Natural Sciences of Philadelphia. Proc. Acad. Nat. Sci., Philadelphia, vol. 6, pp. 184–188.

1856. Illustrations of the birds of California, Texas, Oregon, British and Russian America.

Castenholz, Richard William

1954. Observations of sea birds off the southeastern Florida coast. Wilson Bull., vol. 66, pp. 140–141.

Castle, Gordon Benjamin

1937. The Rocky Mountain pigmy owl in Montana. Condor, vol. 39, p. 132.

Catesby, Mark

1731. The natural history of Carolina, Florida and the Bahama Islands. vol. 1, p. 34.

Chadbourne, Arthur P.

1886. On a new race of the field sparrow from Texas. Auk, vol. 3, pp. 248–249.

Chamberlain, B. R.

1946. Mecklenburg County, N.C.: summer 1946. Chat, vol. 11, p. 19.

1952. Evening grosbeaks in the Carolinas. Chat, vol. 16, pp. 30–32.

1957. Winter season: Southern Atlantic coast region. Audubon Field Notes, vol. 11, pp. 254–257.

Chamberlain, E. B., and Chamberlain, B.R.

1948. Nesting season: Carolina region. Audubon Field Notes, vol. 2, pp. 201–203.

Chamberlain, M.

1883. New Brunswick Notes. Bull. Nuttall Ornith. Club, vol. 8, pp. 6–11.

1891. A popular handbook of the ornithology of the United States and Canada. Based on Nuttall's Manual. The land birds, vol. 1, p. 298.

Chamberlin, W. J.

1916. A golden-crowned sparrow lost on Mount Shasta. Condor, vol. 18, p. 30.

Chambers, Willie Lee

1915. History of a nest of the green-backed goldfinch (*Astragalinus psaltria hesperophilus.*) Condor, vol. 17, p. 166.

1917. Early nesting of the San Diego song sparrow. Condor, vol. 19, p. 102.

Chapman, Floyd B.

1948. Eastern goldfinch feeding on June berry. Auk, vol. 65, pp. 446–447.

Chapman, Frank Michler

1891. On the birds observed near Corpus Christi, Texas, during parts of March and April, 1891. Bull. Amer. Mus. Nat. Hist., vol. 3, pp. 315–328.

1895. Handbook of birds of eastern North America.

1896. Notes on birds observed in Yucatan. Bull. Amer. Mus. Nat. Hist., vol. 8, pp. 271–290.

1897. Preliminary descriptions of new birds from Mexico and Arizona. Auk, vol. 14, pp. 310–311.

1910. Notes on the plumage of North American sparrows. Bird-Lore, vol. 12, pp. 16–18.

1911. Notes on the plumage of North American sparrows. Bird-Lore, vol. 13, pp. 89, 147–148, 202.

1912. Handbook of birds of eastern North America, rev. ed.

Chapman, Frank Michler—Continued

1914. Notes on the plumage of North American sparrows. Bird-Lore, vol. 16, pp. 268–269, 352.

1932. Handbook of birds of eastern North America, 2d rev. ed.

Childs, Henry Everett, Jr.

1948. Songs of the brown towhee evoked by nest robbing by scrub jays. Condor, vol. 50, p. 273.

Christy, Bayard H.

1930. The evening grosbeak nesting in northern Michigan. Wilson Bull., vol. 42, pp. 217–218.

1942. The cardinal: the bird itself. Cardinal, vol. 5, p. 185.

Churchill, George

1891. European goldfinch (*Carduelis carduelis*) breeding in Worcester County, Mass. Auk, vol. 8, p. 314.

Clabaugh, Ernest Dwight

1930a. Methods of trapping birds. Condor, vol. 32, pp. 53–57.

1930b. Minutes of the Cooper Ornith. Club. Condor, vol. 32, p. 75.

1933. Food of the pigmy owl and goshawk. Condor, vol. 35, p. 80.

Clark, Harold Willard

1930. Olives as food for robins and other birds. Condor, vol. 32, p. 163.

1932. Breeding range of the Yolla Bolly fox sparrow. Condor, vol. 34, pp. 113–117.

1935. Fire and bird populations. Condor, vol. 37, p. 16.

Clarke, C. H. D.

1946. Some records of blood parasites from Ontario birds. Canadian Field-Nat., vol. 60, pp. 34, 34a.

Clay, Marcia B.

1930. Evening grosbeak at North Bristol, Ohio. Bird-Lore, vol. 32, pp. 273–274.

Cleveland, Lilian

1903. Nesting of the indigo bunting. Bird-Lore, vol. 5, pp. 87–88.

Coale, Henry K.

1877. MacCown's longspur in Illinois. Bull. Nuttall Ornith. Club, vol. 2, p. 52.

1887. Description of a new subspecies of junco from New Mexico. Auk, vol. 4, pp. 330–331.

1894. Ornithological notes on a flying trip through Kansas, New Mexico, Arizona, and Texas. Auk, vol. 11, pp. 215–222.

Coatney, G. Robert, and West, Evaline

1938. Some blood parasites from Nebraska birds—II. Amer. Midland Nat., vol. 19, pp. 601–612.

Cockrum, E. Lendell

1952. A check-list and bibliography of hybrid birds in North America north of Mexico. Wilson Bull., vol. 64, p. 149.

Coffey, Ben B., Jr.

1954. Smith's longspur in the mid-south. Migrant, vol, 25, pp. 46–48.

1960. Late North American spring migrants in Mexico. Auk, vol. 77, pp. 288–297.

Cogswell. Howard L.

1946. Foothill chaparral. Audubon Mag., sect. 2, p, 146.

1947. Foothill chaparral. Audubon Field Notes, vol. 1, pp. 201–202.

1948. Foothill chaparral. Audubon Field Notes, vol. 2, p. 226.

1962. Territory size in three species of chaparral birds in relation to vegetation density and structure. Ph.D. thesis, Univ. of California, Berkeley.

COHEN, D. A.

1899a. Nesting and other habits of the Oregon towhee. Condor, vol. 1, pp. 61–63.

1899b. A northern record for the black-chinned sparrow *(Spizella atrigularis)*. Bull. Cooper Ornith. Club, vol. 1, pp. 107–108.

COMBY, JULIUS HUGH

1944. Sleeping habits of the green-backed goldfinch. Condor, vol. 46, p. 299.

COMMONS, MARIE ANDREWS

1938. The log of Tanager Hill.

COOK, HAROLD J.

1947. Notes on the effect of the snow storm of late May on birds in northwestern Nebraska. Nebraska Bird Rev., vol. 15, pp. 23–24.

COOK, MRS. HORACE P.

1934. A close up of the cardinal. Wilson Bull., vol. 46, pp. 260–261.

COOKE, C. WYTHE

1939. Scenery of Florida. Florida State Geol. Bull. 17.

COOKE, MAY THACHER

1937a. Some longevity records of wild birds. Bird-Banding, vol. 8, pp. 52–65.

1937b. Some returns of banded birds. Bird-Banding, vol. 8, pp. 144–155.

1938. Some interesting recoveries of banded birds. Bird-Banding, vol. 9, pp. 184–190.

1942. Returns from banded birds: some longevity records of wild birds. Bird-Banding, vol. 13, pp. 176–181.

1943. Returns from banded birds: some miscellaneous recoveries of interest. Bird-Banding, vol. 14, pp. 67–74.

1950. Returns from banded birds. Bird-Banding, vol. 21, pp. 11–17.

COOKE, WELLS WOODBRIDGE

1884. Migration in the Mississippi Valley. Ornith. and Ool., vol. 9, pp. 117–118.

1885. Mississippi Valley migration. Ornith. and Ool., vol. 10, p. 161.

1888. Report on bird migration in the Mississippi Valley in the years 1884 and 1885. U.S. Dep. Agric., Div. Eco. Ornith. Bull., No. 2, p. 220.

1897. The birds of Colorado. State Agric. College Bull. No. 37, Tech. Ser. No. 2.

1900. The birds of Colorado. A second appendix to Bull. 37. Colorado Exper. Sta. Bull., No. 56, pp. 179–239.

1909a. Some new birds for Colorado. Auk, vol. 26, p. 314.

1909b. The birds of Colorado—third supplement. Auk, vol. 26, pp. 400–422.

1910. The migration of North American sparrows. Bird-Lore, vol. 12, pp. 111–112.

1911. The migration of North American sparrows. Bird-Lore, vol. 13, pp. 198–201.

1913. The migration of North American sparrows. Bird-Lore, vol. 15, p. 301.

1914a. The migration of North American sparrows. Bird-Lore, vol. 16, pp. 21–22, 351.

1914b. Some winter birds of Oklahoma. Auk, vol. 31, pp. 473–493.

1928. Localities visited by observers, and State records. *In* Bailey, Birds of New Mexico.

Cooley, R. A., and Kohls, Glen M.
1945. The genus *Ixodes* in North America. U.S. Nat. Inst. Health Bull. No. 184.

Cooper, J. G.
1870. Ornithology of California (S. F. Baird, ed.), vol. 1, Land birds.
1887. Additions to the birds of Ventura County, California. Auk, vol. 4, pp. 85–94.

Cooper, William
1825. Description of a new species of grosbeak inhabiting the northwestern territory of the United States. Ann. Lyc. Nat. Hist., New York, vol. 1, pp. 219–222.
1878. Notes on the breeding habits of *Carpodacus purpureus* var. *californicus*, with a description of its nest and eggs. Bull. Nuttall Ornith. Club, vol. 3, pp. 8–10.

Copeland, Eleanor
1936. An unusual cardinal home. Nature Mag., vol. 27, p. 83.

Corrington, Julian Dana
1922. The winter birds of the Biloxi, Mississippi, region. Auk, vol. 39, pp. 530–556.

Cortopassi, Angelo J., and Mewaldt, L. Richard
1965. The circumannual distribution of white-crowned sparrows. Bird-Banding, vol. 36, No. 3, pp. 141–169.

Cory, Charles Barney
1909. The birds of Illinois and Wisconsin. Field Mus. Publ. Zool., ser. 9.

Cottam, C., Williams, C. S., and Sooter, C. A.
1942. Flight and running speeds of birds. Wilson Bull., vol. 54, pp. 121–132.

Cottam, Clarence
1953. Night migration of eastern chipping sparrows. Bird-Banding, vol. 4, pp. 54–55.

Cottam, Clarence, and Knappen, Phoebe
1939. Food of some uncommon North American birds. Auk, vol. 56, pp. 138–169.

Cottrille, Betty Darling
1958. Some additional bird observations in the northern peninsula of Michigan. Jack-Pine Warbler, vol. 36, No. 3, pp. 150–153.

Coues, Elliott
1866a. From Arizona to the Pacific. Ibis, new ser., vol. 2, pp. 259–275.
1866b. List of the birds of Fort Whipple, Arizona: with which are incorporated all other species ascertained to inhabit the territory; with brief critical and field notes, descriptions of new species, etc. Proc. Acad. Nat. Sci. Philadelphia, No. 1, pp. 39–100.
1873a. Check-list of North American birds.
1873b. Some United States birds, new to science, and other things ornithological. Amer. Nat., vol. 7, pp. 321–331.
1874. Birds of the Northwest. U.S. Geol. Surv. Terr., Misc. Publ. No. 3.
1878. Field notes on birds observed in Dakota and Montana along the forty-ninth parallel during the seasons of 1873 and 1874. U.S. Geol. Geogr. Surv. Terr. Bull., vol. 4, pp. 545–661.
1879a. History of the evening grosbeak. Bull. Nuttall Ornith. Club, vol. 4, pp. 65–75.
1879b. Southward range of Centrophanes lapponica. Bull. Nuttall Ornith. Club, vol. 4, p. 238.

1880. Notes and queries concerning the nomenclature of North American birds. Bull. Nuttall Ornith. Club, vol. 5, p. 96.

1903. Key to North American birds, ed. 5, vols. 1 and 2.

COWAN, IAN MCTAGGART

1937. The house finch at Victoria, British Columbia. Condor, vol. 39, p. 225.

1939. The vertebrate fauna of the Peace River district of British Columbia. Occas. Pap. British Columbia Prov. Mus., vol. 1, pp. 11–66.

1940. Winter occurrence of summer birds on Vancouver Island, British Columbia. Condor, vol. 42, pp. 213–214.

1946. Notes on the distribution of *Spizella breweri taverneri*. Condor, vol. 48, pp. 93–94.

COX, DANIEL G.

1891–92. *In* Report of the occurrence of the evening grosbeak . . . in Ontario. Trans. Canadian Inst., vol. 3, p. 120.

CRAWFORD, FRANKLIN G.

1950. Longevity record of Gambel white-crowned sparrow. Condor, vol. 52, p. 272.

CRIDDLE, NORMAN

1921. Birds that are little known in Manitoba. Canadian Field-Nat., vol. 35, pp. 133–135.

1922. A calendar of bird migration. Auk, vol. 39, pp. 41–49.

CROOKS, MALCOLM P.

1948. Life history of the field sparrow, *Spizella pusilla pusilla* (Wilson). Master's thesis, Iowa State College, Cedar Falls, Iowa.

CROOKS, MALCOLM P., and HENDRICKSON, GEORGE O.

1953. Field sparrow life history in central Iowa. Iowa Bird Life, vol. 23, pp. 10–13.

CRUICKSHANK, ALLAN DUDLEY

1942. Birds around New York City.

1950. Records from Brewster County, Texas. Wilson Bull., vol. 62, pp. 217–219.

CULBERTSON, ALEXANDER EDWARD

1946. Lawrence goldfinches feed on jumping galls. Condor, vol. 48, p. 40.

CURRIE, ROLLA P.

1890. Notes from northern Minnesota. Oologist, vol. 7, p. 206.

DAGGETT, F. S.

1902. Winter observations on the Colorado Desert. Condor, vol. 4, pp. 37–39.

1914. Beautiful bunting in California. Condor, vol. 16, p. 260.

DALE, E. M. S.

1924. Notes on crossbills. Canadian Field-Nat., vol. 38, pp. 119–120.

1932. Some 1930 Notes from London, Ontario. Canadian Field-Nat., vol. 46, pp. 106–108.

DALES, MARIE, and BENNETT, WALTER WALDO

1929. Nesting of the pine siskin in Iowa with remarks on regurgitative feeding. Wilson Bull., vol. 41 (N. S. vol. 36), pp. 74–77.

DALGETY, C. T.

1936. Notes on birds observed in Greenland and Baffin Land, June–September 1934. Ibis, ser. 13, vol. 6, pp. 580–591.

DALL, WILLIAM HEALEY, and BANNISTER, HENRY MARTYN

1869. List of the birds of Alaska, with biographical notes, p. 281.

DALL, WILLIAM HEALEY, and BANNISTER, HENRY MARTYN—Continued

1873. Notes on the avi-fauna of the Aleutian Islands, from Unalaska, eastward. Proc. California Acad. Sci., pp. 3, 270–281.

DAMBACH, CHARLES A., and GOOD, E. E.

1940. The effect of certain land use practices on populations of breeding birds in southwestern Ohio. Journ. Wildlife Management, vol. 4, pp. 63–76.

DANFORTH, CHARLES G.

1938. Some feeding habits of the red-breasted sapsucker. Condor, vol. 40, pp. 219–224.

DANFORTH, STUART T.

1936. Los pajaros de Puerto Rico.

DAUBENMIRE, REXFORD F.

1942. An ecological study of the vegetation of southeastern Washington and adjacent Idaho. Ecol. Monogr., vol. 12, pp. 53–79.

DAVIE, OLIVER

1885. An egg check list of North American birds.

1886. Egg check list and key to the nests and eggs of North American birds, 2nd ed.

1889. Nests and eggs of North American birds, 3rd ed.

1898. Nests and eggs of North American birds, 5th ed.

DAVIS, CLIFFORD V.

1953. Evening Grosbeak nesting in Montana. Wilson Bull., vol. 65, p. 42.

DAVIS, EDWIN RUSSELL

1926. Friendly siskins. Bird-Lore, vol. 28, pp. 381–388.

DAVIS, JOHN

1951. Distribution and variation of the brown towhees. Univ. California Publ. Zool., vol. 52, p. 120.

1957. Comparative foraging behavior of the spotted and brown towhees. Auk, vol. 74, pp. 129–166.

1958. Singing behavior and the gonad cycle of the rufous-sided towhee. Condor, vol. 60, pp. 308–336.

1959. The Sierra Madrean element of the avifauna of the Cape District, Baja, California. Condor, vol. 61, pp. 75–84.

DAVIS, JOHN H., JR.

1943. The natural features of southern Florida. Florida State Geol. Bull. 25.

DAVIS, JOHN M.

1922. Nesting of the California evening grosbeak. Condor, vol. 24, pp. 136–137.

DAVIS, L. IRBY

1939. Rio Grande Delta region. The season. Bird-Lore, vol. 41, p. 10–11.

1952. Winter bird census at Xilitla, San Luis Potosi, Mexico. Condor, vol. 54, pp. 345–355.

DAVIS, L. IRBY, and GILL, C. T.

1948. Coastal prairie. Audubon Field Notes, vol. 2, pp. 242–243.

DAVIS, WILLIAM B.

1933. The span of the nesting season of birds in Butte County, California, in relation to their food. Condor, vol. 35, pp. 151–154.

1935. An analysis of the bird population in the vicinity of Rupert, Idaho. Condor, vol. 37, pp. 233–238.

1945. Notes on Veracruzan birds. Auk, vol. 62, pp. 272–286.

DAWSON, WILLIAM LEON

1903. The birds of Ohio, vol. 1, pp. 102–104.

1908. New and unpublished records from Washington. Auk, vol. 25, pp. 482–485.

1923. The birds of California. vol. 1.

DAWSON, WILLIAM LEON, and BOWLES, J. H.

1909. The birds of Washington, 2 vols.

DAWSON, WILLIAM R., and EVANS, FRANCIS C.

1957. Relation of growth and development to temperature regulation in nestling field and chipping sparrows. Physiol. Zool., vol. 30, pp. 315–327.

DAWSON, WILLIAM RYAN

1948. Records of fringillids from the Pleistocene of Rancho La Brea. Condor, vol. 50, pp. 57–63.

1954. Temperature regulation and water requirements of the brown and Abert towhees, *Pipilo fuscus* and *Pipilo aberti*. Univ. California Publ. Zool., vol. 59, pp. 81–124.

DEADERICK, WILLIAM H.

1938. A preliminary list of the birds of Hot Springs National Park and vicinity (Arkansas). Wilson Bull., vol. 50, pp. 257–273.

DEAN, R. H.

1923. Pine siskin in Alabama in the winter of 1922–23. Bird-Lore, vol. 25, pp. 394–395.

DEARBORN, NED

1907. Catalogue of a collection of birds from Guatemala. Field Mus. Nat. Hist. Publ. 125, ornith. ser., vol. 1, p. 118.

DEARING, H., and DEARING, M.

1946. Indigo buntings breeding in Arizona. Condor, vol. 48, pp. 139–140.

DEGROOT, DUDLEY SARGENT

1934. Field observations from Echo Lake, California. Condor, vol. 36, pp. 6–9.

1935. Nesting of the Pacific evening grosbeak in the vicinity of Echo Lake, Eldorado County, California. Condor, vol. 37, pp. 40–42.

DEIGNAN, H. G.

1961. Type specimens of birds in the United States National Museum. U.S. Nat. Mus. Bull. 221.

DE LAUBENFELS, M. W.

1924. Summer birds of Brownsville, Texas. Wilson Bull., vol. 36, pp. 161–175.

DEMENTIEV, G. P., GLADKOV, N. A. ET AL.

1954. Ptichy Sovietskovo Sojuza (Birds of the Soviet Union). Vol. 5, Moscow.

DE MILLE, JOHN BLAKENEY

1926. Birds of Gaspé County, Quebec. Auk, vol. 43, pp. 508–527.

DENTON, J. FRED, and BYRD, ELON E.

1951. The helminth parasites of birds, III: Dicrocoeliid trematodes from North American birds. Proc. U.S. Nat. Mus., vol. 101, pp. 157–202.

DE SCHAUENSEE, R. MEYER

1964. The birds of Colombia, and adjacent areas of South and Central America.

DETROIT AUDUBON SOCIETY

1956. Bird survey of the Detroit region 1954.

Devitt, Otto Edmond
1935. Dickcissel influx in Essex and Kent counties. Canadian Field-Nat., vol. 49, p. 76.
1944a. An Ontario nest of the evening grosbeak. Canadian Field-Nat., vol. 58, pp. 190–191.
1944b. The birds of Simcoe County, Ontario. Trans. Roy. Canadian Inst., vol. 25, p. 94.

Devlin, Joseph M.
1954. Effects of weather on nocturnal migration as seen from one observation point at Philadelphia. Wilson Bull., vol. 66, pp. 93–101.

DeWolfe, Barbara B., and DeWolfe, Robert H.
1962. Mountain white-crowned sparrows in California. Condor, vol. 64, pp. 378–389.

Dexter, Ralph Warren
1944. Nesting of a song sparrow on a salt marsh. Auk, vol. 61, p. 646.

Dice, Lee Raymond
1918a. The birds of Walla Walla and Columbia counties, southeastern Washington. Auk, vol. 35, pp. 40–51, 148–161.
1918b. Notes on the nesting of the redpoll. Condor, vol. 20, pp. 129–131.
1920. Notes on some birds of interior Alaska. Condor, vol. 22, pp. 176–185.
1921. A bird census at Prescott, Walla Walla County, Washington. Condor, vol. 23, pp. 87–90.

Dickerman, Robert William
1961. Hybrids among the fringillid genera *Junco-Zonotrichia* and *Melospiza*. Auk, vol. 78, pp. 627–632.
1962. Identification of the juvenal plumage of the sharp-tailed sparrow (*Ammospiza caudacuta nelsoni*). Bird-Banding, vol. 33, pp. 202–204.

Dickey, Donald Ryder
1916. The shadow-boxing of Pipilo. Condor, vol. 18, pp. 93–99.
1922. Second occurrence of the Yakutat song sparrow in California. Condor, vol. 24, p. 65.

Dickey, Donald Ryder, and van Rossem, Adriaan Joseph
1923. Additional notes from the coastal islands of southern California. Condor, vol. 25, pp. 126–129.
1938. The birds of El Salvador. Field Mus. Nat. Hist., zool. ser., vol. 23.

Dickinson, Joshua C., Jr.
1952. Geographic variation in the red-eyed towhee of the eastern United States. Bull. Mus. Comp. Zool., vol. 107, pp. 273–352.

Dietrich, Albert L.
1938. Observations of birds seen in south Florida. Florida Nat., vol. 11, p. 101.

Dilger, William C.
1957. The social and hostile behavior of captive redpolls. (Unpub. MS. read at A.O.U. meeting, 1957.)

Dille, Frederick Monroe
1900. Nesting of the pine siskin at Denver, Colorado. Condor, vol. 2, p. 73.
1904. Eggs of the flammulated screech owl and western evening grosbeak taken in Estes Park, Colorado. Condor, vol. 6, p. 50.
1935. Arizona fields are virgin for bird banders. Wilson Bull., vol. 47, pp. 286–293.

DINGLE, EDWARD VON SIEBOLD

1930. Clay-colored sparrow (*Spizella pallida*) in South Carolina. Auk, vol. 47, p. 257.

DIXON, EDWIN

1930. Cat bird robs chipping sparrow. Oologist, vol. 47, p. 126.

DIXON, JAMES BENJAMIN

1934. Records of the nesting of certain birds in Eastern California. Condor, vol. 36, pp. 35–36.

1936. Nesting of the Sierra Nevada rosy finch. Condor, vol. 38, pp. 3–8.

DIXON, JAMES BENJAMIN, and DIXON, RALPH E.

1938. Nesting of the western goshawk in California. Condor, vol. 40, pp. 3–11.

DIXON, JOSEPH

1916. Mexican ground dove, western grasshopper sparrow, and California cuckoo at Escondido, San Diego County, California. Condor, vol. 18, pp. 83–84.

1924. Early nesting of the junco on the Berkeley campus. Condor, vol. 26, p. 197.

1931. Nevada Savannah sparrow breeds in Yellowstone. Condor, vol. 33, p. 38.

DIXON, JOSEPH S.

1938. Birds and mammals of Mount McKinley National Park, Alaska. Fauna of National Parks and Monuments. Fauna ser. No. 3.

1943a. Birds observed between Point Barrow and Herschel Island on the Arctic coast of Alaska. Condor, vol. 45, pp. 49–57.

1943b. Birds of the Kings Canyon National Park area of California. Condor, vol. 45, pp. 205–219.

DIXON, KEITH LEE

1959. Ecological and distributional relations of desert scrub birds of western Texas. Condor, vol. 61, pp. 397–409.

DOOLITTLE, E. A.

1920. Early date of dickcissel. Wilson Bull., vol. 32.

DOUTHITT, BESSIE PRICE

1919. Migration records for Kansas birds. Wilson Bull., vol. 31, pp. 6–20.

DOWNS, ELIZABETH HOLT

1958. Evening grosbeaks at South Londonderry, Vermont: 1956. Bird-Banding, vol. 29, pp. 27–31.

DRESSER, H. E.

1865. Notes on the birds of southern Texas. Ibis, N.S., vol. 1, pp. 312–330, 466–495.

DRESSER, HENRY EELES

1905. Eggs of the birds of Europs, including all the species inhabiting the western palaearctic area, vol. 1.

1910. Eggs of the birds of Europe, including all the species inhabiting the western palaearctic area, vol. 2, p. 106.

DREW, FRANK M.

1881. Field notes on the birds of San Juan County, Colorado. Bull. Nuttall Ornith. Club, vol. 6, pp. 85–91.

1885. On the vertical range of birds in Colorado. Auk, vol. 2, pp. 11–18.

DRUM, MARGARET

1939. Territorial studies on the eastern goldfinch. Wilson Bull., vol. 51, pp. 69–77.

DRURY, WILLIAM H., JR.

1961. Studies of the breeding biology of horned lark, water pipit, Lapland longspur, and snow bunting on Bylot Island, Northwest Territories, Canada. Bird-Banding, vol. 32, pp. 1–46.

DU BOIS, ALEXANDER DAWES

1923. Two nest studies of McCown's longspur. Bird-Lore, vol. 25, pp. 95–105.

1935. Nests of horned larks and longspurs on a Montana prairie. Condor, vol. 37, pp. 56–72.

1936. Habits and nest life of the desert horned lark. Condor, vol. 38, pp. 49–57.

1937a. Notes on coloration and habits of the chestnut-collared longspur. Condor, vol. 39, pp. 104–107.

1937b. The McCown longspurs of a Montana prairie. Condor, vol. 39, pp. 233–238.

DU BOIS, H. M.

1959. Black-throated sparrows in northwestern Oregon. Condor, vol. 61, p. 435.

DUFFEY, ERIC, and CREASEY, N.

1950. The "rodent-run" distraction-behaviour of certain waders. Ibis, vol. 92, pp. 27–33.

DUMAS, PHILIP

1950. Habitat distribution of breeding birds in southeastern Washington. Condor, vol. 52, pp. 232–237.

DUMONT, PHILIP A.

1934a. A revised list of the birds of Iowa. Univ. Iowa Studies Nat. Hist., vol. 15, No. 5, p. 139.

1934b. Migrant Nelson's sparrows in central Iowa. Wilson Bull., vol. 46, p. 62.

DUTCHER, WILLIAM

1884. Bird notes from Long Island, N.Y. Auk, vol. 1, pp. 174–179.

1886. Bird notes from Long Island, N.Y. Auk, vol. 3, pp. 432–444.

1903. Report of the A.O.U. Committee on the protection of North American birds. Auk, vol. 20, pp. 101–159.

DUVALL, ALLEN JOSEPH

1942. Records from Lower California, Arizona, Idaho, and Alberta. Auk, vol. 59, pp. 317–318.

1943. Breeding Savannah sparrows of the southwestern United States. Condor, vol. 45, pp. 237–238.

1945. Random distributional records. Auk, vol. 62, pp. 626–629.

DWIGHT, JONATHAN, JR.

1887. A new race of the sharp-tailed sparrow (*Ammodramus caudacutus*). Auk, vol. 4, pp. 232–239.

1895. The Ipswich sparrow: *Ammodramus princeps* (Maynard) and its summer home. Mem. Nuttall Ornith. Club No. 2, pp. 1–56.

1896. The sharp-tailed sparrow (*Ammodramus caudacutus*) and its geographical races. Auk, vol. 13, pp. 271–278.

1900. The sequence of plumages and moults of the passerine birds of New York. Ann. New York Acad. Sci., vol 13, No. 1, pp. 73–360.

1918. The geographic distribution of color and of other variable characters in the genus *Junco:* a new aspect of specific and subspecific values. Bull. Amer. Mus. Nat. Hist., vol. 38, pp. 269–309.

DWIGHT, JONATHAN, and GRISCOM, LUDLOW

1927. A revision of the geographical races of the blue grosbeak (*Guiraca caerulea*). Amer. Mus. Nov., No. 257.

DYER, ERNEST I.

1931. Concern exhibited by wild birds in the troubles of others. Condor, vol. 33, pp. 215–216.

EASTERLA, DAVID A.

1962a. Foods of Le Conte's sparrow. Auk, vol. 79, pp. 272–273.

1962b. Grasshopper sparrow wintering in central Missouri. Wilson Bull., vol. 74, p. 288.

EATON, ELON HOWARD.

1910. Birds of New York. Univ. New York State Educ. Dept. Mus., Mem. 12, pt. 2.

1914. Birds of New York. New York State Mus., Mem. 12, pt. 2.

EATON, STEPHEN W.

1965. Juncos of the high plateaus. Kingbird, vol. 15, pp. 141–146.

EDGE, CHESTER W.

1931. Western mockingbird, Oregon vesper sparrow, and Merrill song sparrow in Sonoma County, California. Condor, vol. 33, p. 75.

EDITING COMMITTEE

1891–92. Report of the occurrence of the evening grosbeak (*Coccothraustes vespertina*) in Ontario during the winter of 1889–1890. Trans. Canadian Inst., vol. 3, pt. 1, pp. 111–124.

EDWARDS, ERNEST P., and LEA, ROBERT B.

1955. Birds of the Monserrate area, Chiapas, Mexico. Condor, vol. 57, pp. 31–54.

EDWARDS, G.

1760. Gleanings of natural history, vol. 2, pp. 109–220.

EDWARDS, HOWARD ARDEN

1919. Losses suffered by breeding birds in southern California. Condor, vol. 21, pp. 65–68.

EDWARDS, MYRTLE SASSMAN

1925. Trapping notes from Altadena, California. Condor, vol. 27, p. 78.

EGAN, THOMAS J.

1889a. Nesting of the white-winged crossbill. Ornith. and Ool., vol. 14, p. 57.

1889b. Nesting of the American crossbill. Ornith. and Ool., vol. 14, p. 89.

EIFRIG, CHARLES WILLIAM GUSTAVE

1910. Stomach contents of some Canadian birds. Ottawa Nat., vol. 24, pp. 18–20.

1911. The birds of Ottawa. Ottawa Nat., vol. 24, pp. 198–206.

1929. Texan bird habitats. Auk, vol. 46, pp. 70–78.

ELIOT, SAMUEL ATKINS, JR.

1933. European goldfinch in western Massachusetts. Auk, vol. 50, p. 366.

1948. Green-tailed towhee at Northampton, Massachusetts. Auk, vol. 65, pp. 301–302.

ELIOT, WILLARD AYRES

1923. Birds of the Pacific coast.

ELLIOTT, JOHN JACKSON

1955. The Ipswich sparrow on the northeastern seaboard, pt. 1. Kingbird, vol. 4, pp. 91–96.

1956a. British goldfinch on Long Island. Long Island Nat., No. 5, pp. 3–13.

Elliott, John Jackson—Continued

1956b. The Ipswich sparrow on the northeastern seaboard, pt. 2. Kingbird, vol. 6, pp. 3–10.

Ellison, Lincoln

1934. Notes on food habits of juncos. Condor, vol. 36, pp. 176–177.

Embody, G. C.

1908. The accidental occurrence of the green-tailed towhee (*Oreospiza chlorura*) in Virginia. Auk, vol. 25, p. 224.

Emerson, W. Otto

1905. A bird's roost. Condor, vol. 7, p. 113.

Emlen, John Thompson, Jr.

1943. Sex ratios in wintering Gambel white-crowned sparrows. Condor, vol. 45, p. 196.

Epling, Carl, and Lewis, Harlan

1942. The centers of distribution of the chaparral and coastal sage associations. Amer. Midland Nat., vol. 27(2), pp. 445–462.

Errington, Paul L.

1932. Food habits of southern Wisconsin raptors, pt. I. Owls. Condor, vol. 34, pp. 176–186.

Esterly, C. O.

1920. A plague of rufous-crowned sparrows. Condor, vol. 22, p. 154.

Evans, F. C., and Emlen, J. T., Jr.

1947. Ecological notes on the prey selected by a barn owl. Condor, vol. 49, No. 1, pp. 3–9.

Evenden, Fred G., Jr.

1957. Observations on nesting behavior of the house finch. Condor, vol. 59, pp. 112–117.

Evermann, Barton Warren

1913. Eighteen species of birds new to the Pribilof Islands, including four new to North America. Auk, vol. 30, pp. 15–18.

Ewan, Joseph

1928. Trailside notes from the southern California mountains. Oologist, vol. 45, pp. 152–153.

1936. Summer notes from Plumas County, California. Condor, vol. 38, pp. 82–85.

Ewing, H. E.

1929. Birds as hosts for the common chigger. Amer. Nat., vol. 63, pp. 94–96.

Eyster, Marshall Blackwell

1954. Quantitative measurement of the influence of photoperiod, temperature, and season on the activity of captive songbirds. Ecol. Monogr., vol. 24.

Fairfield, George

1963. Twenty-seventh breeding bird census: Urban cemetery. Audubon Field Notes, vol. 17, p. 512.

Falls, J. Bruce

1963. Properties of bird song eliciting responses from territorial males. Proc. XIII Internat. Ornith. Congr., vol. 1, pp. 259–271.

Fargo, William Gilbert

1934. Walter John Hoxie. Wilson Bull., vol. 46, pp. 169–196.

Farley, Frank LaGrange

1921. A pine siskin invasion. Canadian Field-Nat., vol. 35, p. 141.

1930. Unusual migration of redpolls. Canadian Field-Nat., vol. 44, p. 23.

1932. Birds of the Battle River region of central Alberta.

FARNER, DONALD S., and BUSS, IRVEN O.
1957. Summer records of the golden-crowned sparrow in Okanogan County, Washington. Condor, vol. 59, p. 141.

FARNER, DONALD SANKEY
1952. Birds of Crater Lake National Park, p. 142.
1958. Breeding population of *Zonotrichia leucophrys gambelii* in the northern Cascade Mountains of Washington. Condor, vol. 60, p. 196.

FAY, FRANCIS H., and CADE, TOM J.
1959. An ecological analysis of the avifauna of St. Lawrence Island, Alaska. Univ. California Publ. Zool., vol. 63, pp. 73–150.

FAY, SAMUEL PRESCOTT
1911. Massachusetts notes. Auk, vol. 28, pp. 120–122.

FERRY, JOHN FARWELL
1907. Ornithological conditions in northeastern Illinois, with notes on some winter birds. Auk, vol. 24, pp. 121–129.
1908. Notes from the diary of a naturalist in northern California. Condor, vol. 10, pp. 30–44.
1910. Birds observed in Saskatchewan during the summer of 1909. Auk, vol. 27, pp. 185–204.

FINLEY, WILLIAM L.
1906. The golden eagle. Condor, vol. 8, pp. 5–11.
1909. Some bird accidents. Condor, vol. 11, pp. 181–184.

FIRTH, THOMAS
1936. Unpublished memorandum dated June 15, 1936, from North Bay, Ontario. On file in Ontario Fish. Res. Library, Toronto.

FISCHER, RICHARD B., and GILL, GEOFFREY
1946. A cooperative study of the white-throated sparrow. Auk, vol. 63 pp. 402–418.

FISHER, ALBERT KENRICK
1893. Report on the ornithology of the Death Valley Expedition of 1891, comprising notes on the birds observed in southern California, southern Nevada, and parts of Arizona and Utah. North American Fauna, No. 7, pp. 7–158.
1902. The redwood belt of northwestern California. Condor, vol. 4, pp. 111–114, 131–135.
1903. The editor's book shelf. Condor, vol. 5, pp. 159–161.

FISLER, GEORGE F.
1960. Changes in food habits of short-eared owls feeding in a salt marsh. Condor, vol. 62, pp. 486–487.

FITCH, HENRY S., GLADING, BEN, and HOUSE, VERL
1946. Observations on Cooper hawk nesting and predation. California Fish and Game, vol. 32, pp. 144–154.

FITCH, HENRY S., SWENSON, FREEMAN, and TILLOTSON, DANIEL F.
1946. Behavior and food habits of the red-tailed hawk. Condor, vol. 48, pp. 205–237.

FITCH, HENRY SHELDON
1947. Predation by owls in the Sierran foothills of California. Condor, vol. 49, pp. 137–151.
1948a. Ecology of the California ground squirrel on grazing lands. Amer. Midland Nat., vol. 39, pp. 513–596.
1948b. A study of coyote relationships on cattle range. Journ. Wildlife Management, vol. 12, pp. 73–78.

FITCH, HENRY SHELDON—Continued

1949. Study of snake populations in central California. Amer. Midland Nat., vol. 41, pp. 513–579.

1958. Home ranges, territories, and seasonal movements of vertebrates of the Natural History Reservation. Univ. Kansas Publ., Mus. Nat. Hist., vol. 11, pp. 63–326.

FITZPATRICK, F. L.

1930. Recent bird records from northeastern Colorado and their significance in connection with geographical distribution. Wilson Bull., vol. 42, p. 128.

FLEISHER, EDWARD

1926. Dickcissel at sea. Auk, vol. 43, p. 101.

FLEMING, JAMES HENRY

1903. Breeding of the evening grosbeak in captivity. Auk, vol. 20, pp. 213–215.

1907. Birds of Toronto, Ontario.

F. O. H.

1884. Jottings from Michigan. Oologist, vol. 1, p. 148.

FORBES, STEPHEN A.

1882. The regulative action of birds upon insect oscillations. Illinois State Lab. Nat. Hist., Bull. No. 6.

1907. An ornithological cross-section of Illinois in autumn. Illinois State Lab. Nat. Hist., Bull. No. 7, pp. 305–335.

1908. The mid-summer bird life of Illinois: a statistical study. Amer. Nat., vol. 42, pp. 505–519.

FORBES, STEPHEN A., and GROSS, ALFRED O.

1921. The orchard birds of an Illinois summer. Illinois Nat. Hist. Surv. Bull., vol. 14, pp. 1–8.

FORBUSH, EDWARD HOWE

1907. Useful birds and their protection.

1913. Useful birds and their protection, 4th ed.

1929. Birds of Massachusetts and other New England States, pt. 3.

FORBUSH, EDWARD HOWE, and MAY, JOHN BICHARD

1939. Natural history of the birds of eastern and central North America.

FORD, EDWARD RUSSELL

1936. The golden-crowned sparrow in Illinois. Auk, vol. 53, p. 223.

FOX, GLEN ALLEN

1961. A contribution to the life history of the clay-colored sparrow. Auk, vol. 78, pp. 220–224.

FRENCH, NORMAN R.

1954. Notes on breeding activities and on gular sacs in the pine grosbeak. Condor, vol. 56, pp. 83–85.

1955. Foraging behavior and predation by Clark nutcracker. Condor, vol. 57, pp. 61–62.

FRIEDMANN, HERBERT

1925. Notes on the birds observed in the lower Rio Grande Valley of Texas during May, 1924. Auk, vol. 42, pp. 537–554.

1929. The cowbirds. A study in the biology of social parasitism.

1931. Additions to the list of birds known to be parasitized by the cowbirds. Auk, vol. 48, pp. 52–65.

1934. Further additions to the list of birds victimized by the cowbird. Wilson Bull., vol. 46, pp. 25–36, 104–114.

1937. Further additions to the known avifauna of St. Lawrence Island, Alaska. Condor, vol. 39, p. 91.

1938. Additional hosts of the parasitic cowbirds. Auk, vol. 55, pp. 41–50.

1943. Further additions to the list of birds known to be parasitized by the cowbirds. Auk, vol. 60, pp. 350–356.

1949. Additional data on victims of parasitic cowbirds. Auk, vol. 66, pp. 154–163.

1963. Host relations of the parasitic cowbirds. U.S. Nat. Mus. Bull. 233.

FRIEDMANN, HERBERT, GRISCOM, LUDLOW, and MOORE, ROBERT T.

1957. Distributional check-list of the birds of Mexico, pt. 2. Pacific Coast Avifauna, No. 33.

FRITH, H. J.

1957. Breeding and movements of wild ducks in inland New South Wales. C.S.I.R.O. Wildlife Research, vol. 2, pp. 19–31.

FROST, HERBERT H.

1947. A seasonal study of the food of some birds of the Wasatch chaparral. Unpublished master's thesis, Brigham Young Univ., Provo, Utah.

FULLER, ARTHUR B., and BOLE, B. P., JR.

1930. Observations on some Wyoming birds. Sci. Publ. Cleveland Mus. Nat. Hist., vol. 1., pp. 37–80.

GABRIELSON, IRA NOEL

1915. Field observations on the rose-breasted grosbeak. Wilson Bull., vol. 27, pp. 357–368.

1924a. "Lapland Longspur." U.S. Dep. Agric. Bull. 1249, pp. 22–25.

1924b. Food habits of some winter bird visitants. U.S. Dep. Agric. Bull. 1249.

1926. Notes on certain birds nesting on wild cherry. Murrelet, vol. 7, No. 3, p. 63.

1944. Some Alaskan notes. Auk, vol. 61, pp. 270–287.

1949. Bird notes from Nevada. Condor, vol. 51, pp. 179–187.

1952. Notes on the birds of the north shore of the Gulf of St. Lawrence. Canadian Field-Nat., vol. 66, pp. 44–59.

GABRIELSON, IRA NOEL, and JEWETT, STANLEY G.

1940. Birds of Oregon.

GABRIELSON, IRA NOEL, and LINCOLN, FREDERICK CHARLES

1951. The races of song sparrows in Alaska. Condor, vol. 53, pp. 250–255.

1959. The birds of Alaska.

GALE, DENIS

1887. Notebook (unpublished). At Denver Mus. Nat. Hist.

GANDER, FRANK FOREST

1929a. The Cassin purple finch in San Diego. Condor, vol. 31, p. 131.

1929b. Notes on the food and feeding habits of certain birds. Condor, vol. 31, pp. 250–251.

1930. Notes on winter bird roosts. Condor, vol. 32, p. 64.

GANIER, ALBERT F.

1916. November bird-life at Reelfoot Lake, Tenn. Wilson Bull., vol. 28, pp. 25–30.

1921. Nesting of Bachman's sparrow. Wilson Bull., vol. 33, pp. 3–4.

1937. Further notes on a very old cardinal. Wilson Bull., vol. 49, pp. 15–16.

GANIER, ALBERT F., and BUCHANAN, FOREST W.

1953. Nesting of the white-throated sparrow in West Virginia. Wilson Bull., vol. 65, pp. 277–279.

GÄTKE, HEINRICH

1895. Heligoland as an ornithological observatory.

GAYLORD, HORACE A.
1897. Remarkable confidence of the Guadalupe junco. Osprey, vol. 1, p. 98.
GEORGE, JOHN LOTHAR
1952. The birds on a southern Michigan farm. Ph.D. thesis, Univ. of Michigan, Ann Arbor.
GEORGE, JOHN LOTHAR, and MITCHELL, ROBERT T.
1948. Notes of two species of Calliphoridae (Diptera) parasitizing nestling birds. Auk, vol. 65, pp. 549–552.
GERBRACHT, J. H.
1944. The lark bunting. Inland Bird Banding News, vol. 16, No. 6, pp. 39–40.
GIER, HERSCHEL THOMAS
1949. Lark sparrow nesting in southeastern Ohio. Auk, vol. 66, pp. 209–210.
GILLIARD, E. THOMAS
1959. Notes on some birds of northern Venezuela. Amer. Mus. Nov., No. 1927.
GILMAN, M. FRENCH
1902. The crissal thrasher in California. Condor, vol. 4, pp. 15–16.
1903. Nesting of the Abert towhee. Condor, vol. 5, pp. 12–13.
1907. Some birds of southwest Colorado. Condor, vol. 9, pp. 152–158.
1910. Notes from Sacaton, Arizona. Condor, vol. 12, pp. 45–46.
1915. A forty acre bird census at Sacaton, Arizona. Condor, vol. 17, pp. 86–90.
1935. Notes on birds in Death Valley. Condor, vol. 37, pp. 238–242.
1937. Death Valley bird notes for 1936. Condor, vol. 39, pp. 90–91.
GLEGG, WILLIAM E.
1943. Unusual site and date of goldfinch's nest. British Birds, vol. 37, p. 38
GODFREY, W. EARL
1949a. Birds of Lake Mistassini and Lake Albanel, Quebec. Nat. Mus. Canada Bull. 114, Biol. Ser. No. 38, pp. 1–43.
1949b. Distribution of the races of the swamp sparrow. Auk, vol. 66, pp. 35–38.
1950. Birds of the Cyprus Hills and Flotten Lake regions, Saskatchewan. Nat. Mus. Canada Bull. 120, pp. 1–96.
1953a. Notes on Ellesmere Island birds. Canadian Field-Nat., vol. 67, pp. 89–93.
1953b. Notes on birds of the area of intergradation between eastern prairie and forest in Canada. Canada Dep. Res. and Devel., Bull. 128.
1954a. Birds of Prince Edward Island. Nat. Mus. Canada Bull. 132, pp. 155–213.
1954b. The dickcissel on the Atlantic Coast of Canada. Auk, vol. 71, pp. 317–318.
GODFREY, W. EARL, and WILK, A. L.
1948. Birds of the Lake St. John region, Quebec. Nat. Mus. Canada Bull. 110, Biol. Ser. No. 36.
GOLSAN, LEWIS S., and HOLT, ERNEST G.
1914. Birds of Autauga and Montgomery counties, Alabama. Auk, vol. 31, pp. 212–235.
GOOD, H. G., and ADKINS, T. R.
1927. Notes on the wintering habits of the white-throated sparrow (*Zonotrichia albicollis*). Wilson Bull., vol. 39, pp. 75–78.

GOODRICH, ARTHUR L., JR.
1945. Birds in Kansas. Rep. Kansas State Board Agric., vol. 44, No. 267.
1946. Birds in Kansas. Kansas State Board Agric., vol. 64.

GOSS, NATHANIEL S.
1881. Bell's finch (*Poospiza belli nevadensis*) in New Mexico. Bull. Nuttall Ornith. Club, vol. 6, pp. 116–117.
1891. History of the birds of Kansas.

GOSSE, PHILIP HENRY
1847. The birds of Jamaica, p. 254.

GOULD, PATRICK J.
1961. Territorial relationships between cardinals and pyrrhuloxias. Condor, vol. 63, pp. 246–256.

GOVAN, ADA CLAPHAM
1940. Wings at my window, p. 165
1942. Longevity records of finches banded at Lexington, Mass. Bird-Banding, vol. 13, pp. 183–184.
1954. "Anting"—outside and inside the windowpane. Nat. Mag., vol. 47, pp. 41–43.

GRABER, JEAN W.
1953. Cassin's sparrow in Cleveland County, Oklahoma. Wilson Bull., vol. 65, p. 208.

GRABER, RICHARD, and GRABER, JEAN
1951. Notes on the birds of southwestern Kansas. Trans. Kansas Acad. Sci., vol. 54, No. 2, pp. 145–162.
1954. Baird's Sparrow in Oklahoma. Wilson Bull., vol. 66, p. 58.

GRABER, RICHARD REX
1953. Sharp-tailed sparrow in Oklahoma. Wilson Bull., vol. 65, p. 209.
1955. Taxonomic and adaptive features of the juvenal plumage in North American sparrows. Ph.D. thesis, Univ. of Oklahoma, Norman.
1962. Food and oxygen consumption in three species of owls (Strigidae). Condor, vol. 64, pp. 473–487.

GRAHAM, R.
1916. Nesting dates of Texas birds. Oologist, vol. 33, pp. 81–82.
1915. Two accidental finds of Cassin's sparrows. Oologist, vol. 32, pp. 191–192.

GRATER, RUSSELL KAY
1937. Check-list of birds of Grand Canyon National Park. Nat. Hist. Bull., No. 8.

GRAY, HANNAH R.
1948. Banding data from Wilton, North Dakota. Bird-Banding, vol. 19, pp. 159–162.

GRAY, JOHN ALBERT, JR.
1945. Land birds at sea. Condor, vol. 47, pp. 215–216.

GREELY, ADOLPHUS W.
1886. Three years of Arctic service: An account of the Lady Franklin Bay expedition of 1881–84 and the attainment of the farthest north, 2 vols.

GREEN, HORACE O.
1935. Nests of the eastern sharp-tailed sparrow. Oologist, vol. 52, pp. 98–101.

GREENE, EARLE ROSENBURG
1946. Birds of the lower Florida Keys. Quart. Journ. Florida Acad. Sci., vol. 8, No. 3.

Greene, E. R., Griffin, W. W., Odum, E. P., Stoddard, H. L., and Tomkin, I. R.
1945. Birds of Georgia. Occas. Pap., Georgia Ornith. Soc., No. 2.
Greenhalgh, Clifton M.
1948. Second record of the golden-crowned sparrow in Utah. Condor, vol. 50, p. 46.
Greulach, Victor A.
1934. Notes on the nesting of the slate-colored junco. Auk, vol. 51, pp. 389–390.
Grey, John Hugh, Jr.
1948. Sharp-tailed sparrow at Cape Henry, Virginia. Auk, vol. 65, pp. 312–313.
Griffee, W. E.
1944. Unusual nesting site for Shufeldt junco. Murrelet, vol. 25, p. 12.
1947. A high junco nest. Murrelet, vol. 28.
Griffee, W. E., and Rapraeger, E. F.
1937. Nesting dates for birds breeding in the vicinity of Portland, Oregon. Murrelet, vol. 18, pp. 14–18.
Grimes, Samuel Andrew
1931. 1930 nesting notes from the Jacksonville region—II. Florida Nat., vol. 4, pp. 77–87.
1936. "Injury feigning" by birds. Auk, vol. 53, pp. 478–480.
Grinnell, Joseph
1897a. Description of a new towhee from California. Auk, vol. 14, pp. 294–296.
1897b. New race of *Spinus tristis* from the Pacific coast. Auk, vol. 14, pp. 397–399.
1897c. Report on the birds recorded during a visit to the islands of Santa Barbara, San Nicolas and San Clemente, in the spring of 1897. Pasadena Acad. Sci., Publ. No. 1.
1898a. Land birds observed in mid-winter on Santa Catalina Island, California. Auk, vol. 15, pp. 233–236.
1898b. Rank of the sage sparrow. Auk, vol. 15, pp. 58–59.
1898c. Summer birds of Sitka, Alaska. Auk, vol. 15, pp. 122–131.
1900a. Birds of the Kotzebue Sound region. Pacific Coast Avifauna, No. 1.
1900b. New races of birds from the Pacific coast. Condor, vol. 2, pp. 127–128.
1904. Midwinter birds at Palm Springs, California. Condor, vol. 6, pp. 40–45.
1905a. Where does the large-billed sparrow spend the summer? Auk, vol. 22, pp. 16–21.
1905b. The California sage sparrow. Condor, vol. 7, pp. 18–19.
1905c. Summer birds of Mount Pinos, California. Auk, vol. 22, pp. 378–391.
1905d. Rufous-crowned sparrow near Stanford University. Condor, vol. 7, p. 53.
1908. The biota of the San Bernardino Mountains. Univ. California Publ. Zool., vol. 5.
1909a. The birds, *In* Birds and mammals of the 1907 Alexander expedition to southeastern Alaska. Univ. California Publ. Zool., vol. 5, pp. 171–264.
1909b. Three new song sparrows from California. Univ. California Publ. Zool., vol. 5, pp. 265–269.
1910a. The Savannah sparrow of the Great Basin. Univ. California Publ. Zool., vol. 5, pp. 311–316.

1910b. Birds of the 1908 Alexander Alaska expedition. Univ. California Publ. Zool., vol. 5, pp. 361–428.

1910c. Miscellaneous records from Alaska. Condor, vol. 12, pp. 41–43.

1910d. An additional song sparrow for California. Condor, vol. 12, pp. 174–175.

1911a. The linnet of the Hawaiian Islands. Univ. California Publ. Zool., vol. 7, pp. 179–195.

1911b. The Modesto song sparrow. Univ. California Publ. Zool., vol. 7, pp. 197–199.

1911c. Description of a new spotted towhee from the Great Basin. Univ. California Publ. Zool., vol. 7, pp. 309–311.

1911d. A new blue grosbeak from California. Proc. Biol. Soc. Washington, vol. 24, p. 163.

1911e. Field notes from the San Joaquin Valley. Condor, vol. 13, pp. 109–111.

1912. An afternoon's field notes. Condor, vol. 14, pp. 104–107.

1913. *Leucosticte tephrocotis dawsoni*—a new race of rosy finch from the Sierra Nevada. Condor, vol. 15, pp. 76–79.

1914a. A second list of the birds of the Berkeley campus. Condor, vol. 16, pp. 28–40.

1914b. An account of the mammals and birds of the lower Colorado Valley with especial reference to the distributional problems presented. Univ. California Publ. Zool., vol. 12, pp. 51–294.

1914c. Review: The birds of El Paso County, Colorado, by Charles E. H. Aiken and Edward R. Warren. Condor, vol. 16, pp. 264–265.

1915. A distributional list of the birds of California. Pacific Coast Avifauna, No. 11, pp. 1–217.

1917. The subspecies of *Hesperiphona vespertina*. Condor, vol. 19, pp. 17–22.

1918. Extension of known distribution in some northern California birds. Condor, vol. 20, p. 190.

1923a. Notes on some birds observed in the vicinity of Colusa, California. Condor, vol. 25, pp. 172–176.

1923b. Observations upon the bird life of Death Valley. Proc. California Acad. Sci., No. 5, pp. 43–109.

1926. A new race of rufous-crowned sparrow, from north-central Lower California. Auk, vol. 43, pp. 244–245.

1927. Six new subspecies of birds from Lower California. Auk, vol. 44, pp. 67–72.

1928a. Notes on the systematics of west American birds. I. Condor, vol. 30, pp. 121–124.

1928b. A distributional summation of the ornithology of Lower California Univ. California Publ. Zool., vol. 32.

1928c. The song sparrow of San Miguel Island, California. Proc. Biol. Soc. Washington, vol. 41, pp. 37–38.

1939a. Proposed shifts of names in *Passerculus*—a protest. Condor, vol. 41, pp. 112–119.

1939b. Notes and news. Condor, vol. 41, pp. 128–129.

GRINNELL, JOSEPH, and DAGGETT, FRANK SLATER.

1903. An ornithological visit to Los Coronados Islands, Lower California. Auk, vol. 20, pp. 27–37.

GRINNELL, JOSEPH, DIXON, JOSEPH, and LINSDALE, JEAN MYRON

1930. Vertebrate natural history of a section of northern California through the Lassen Peak region. Univ. California Publ. Zool., vol. 35, pp. 1–594.

GRINNELL, JOSEPH, and LINSDALE, JEAN MYRON

1936. Vertebrate animals of Point Lobos Reserve, 1934–35. Carnegie Inst. Washington Publ. No 481.

GRINNELL, JOSEPH, and MILLER, ALDEN HOLMES

1944. The distribution of the birds of California. Pacific Coast Avifauna, No. 27.

GRINNELL, JOSEPH, and STORER, TRACY IRWIN

1924. Animal life in the Yosemite. Contr. Mus. Vert. Zool. Univ. California.

GRINNELL, JOSEPH, and SWARTH, HARRY SCHELWALDT

1913. An account of the birds and mammals of the San Jacinto area of southern California. Univ. California Publ. Zool., vol. 10, pp. 197–406.

1926a. An additional subspecies of spotted towhee from Lower California. Condor, vol. 28, pp. 130–133.

1926b. Geographic variation in *Spizella atrogularis*. Auk, vol. 43, pp. 475–478.

GRINNELL, JOSEPH, and WYTHE, MARGARET W.

1927. Directory to the bird-life of the San Francisco Bay region. Pacifi Coast Avifauna, No. 18.

GRINNELL, LAWRENCE IRVING

1943. Nesting habits of the common redpoll. Wilson Bull., vol. 55, pp. 155–163.

1944. Notes on breeding Lapland longspurs at Churchill, Manitoba. Auk, vol. 61, pp. 554–560.

1947. A study of the common redpoll, *Acanthis flammea flammea* (L.), in comparison with other North American species of the genus *Acanthis*. Ph.D. thesis, Cornell Univ., Ithaca, N.Y.

GRISCOM, LUDLOW

1920. Notes on the winter birds of San Antonio, Texas. Auk, vol. 37, pp. 49–55.

1923. Birds of the New York City region. Amer. Mus. Nat. Hist. Handb. Ser. No. 9.

1926. Notes on the summer birds of the west coast of Newfoundland. Ibis, ser. 12, vol. 2, pp. 656–684.

1928a. New birds from Mexico and Panama. Amer. Mus. Nov., No. 293.

1928b. *Spizella taverneri* on migration in Montana. Auk, vol. 45, pp. 509–510.

1932. The distribution of bird-life in Guatemala. Bull. Amer. Mus. Nat. Hist., vol. 64, p. 365.

1934. The pine grosbeaks of eastern North America. Proc. New England Zool. Club, vol. 14, pp. 5–12.

1937. A monographic study of the red crossbill. Proc. Boston Soc. Nat. Hist., vol. 41, No. 5, pp. 77–210.

1938. The birds of the Lake Umbagog region of Maine. Bull. Mus. Comp. Zool., vol. 66, pt. 4, pp. 537–538.

1944. A second revision of the seaside sparrows. Occas. Pap. Mus. Zool., Louisiana State Univ., No. 19, pp. 313–328.

1948. Notes on Texas seaside sparrows. Wilson Bull., vol. 60, pp. 103–108.

1949. The birds of Concord.

GRISCOM, LUDLOW, and CROSBY, MAUNSELL S.
1926. Birds of the Brownsville region, southern Texas. Auk, vol. 43, pp. 18–36.

GRISCOM, LUDLOW, and EMERSON, GUY
1959. Birds of Martha's Vineyard, with an annotated checklist.

GRISCOM, LUDLOW, and FOLGER, EDITH V.
1948. The birds of Nantucket.

GRISCOM, LUDLOW, and NICHOLS, JOHN TREADWELL
1920. A revision of the seaside sparrows. Abst. Proc. Linn. Soc. New York, No. 32, pp. 18–30.

GRISCOM, LUDLOW, and SNYDER, DOROTHY E.
1955. The birds of Massachusetts, an annotated and revised checklist.

GROSKIN, HORACE
1938. Eastern purple finches as bud-eaters. Bird-Banding, vol. 9, p. 199.
1950. Banding 4,469 purple finches at Ardmore, Pa. Bird-Banding, vol. 21, pp. 93–99.

GROSS, ALFRED OTTO
1921. The dickcissel (*Spiza americana*) of the Illinois prairies. Auk, vol. 38, pp. 26, 163–184.
1937. Birds of the Bowdoin-Macmillan Arctic expedition, 1934. Auk, vol. 54, pp. 12–42.
1938. Nesting of the goldfinch. Bird-Lore, vol. 40, pp. 253–257.
1947. Late nesting of the indigo bunting at Brunswick, Maine. Maine Audubon Soc. Bull., vol. 3, pp. 44–45.

GROSVENOR, GILBERT, and WETMORE, ALEXANDER
1937. The book of birds, 2 vols.

GROTE, VON HERMANN
1943. Ueber das leben der spornammer (*Calcarius lapponicus*) in der tundra. Beiträge zur Fortpflanzungsbiologie der Vögel, vol. 19, pp 98–104.

GULLION, GORDON W., PULICH, WARREN M., and EVENDEN, FRED G.
1959. Notes on the occurrence of birds in southern Nevada. Condor, vol. 61, pp. 278–297.

GULLION, GORDON WRIGHT
1951. Birds of the southern Willamette Valley, Oregon. Condor, vol. 53, pp. 129–149.
1957. Miscellaneous bird records from northeastern Nevada. Condor, vol. 59, pp. 70–71.

GUNDLACH, JUAN
1893. Ornitología Cubana (in Spanish).

HAGEN, YNGVAR
1952. Rovfuglene og Viltpleien.

HAGERUP, ANDREAS THOMSEN
1891. The birds of Greenland.

HAGLUND, BERTIL
1935. Några bidrag till videsparvens biologi (*Emberiza rustica*). Fauna och Flora, vol. 30, pp. 134–138.

HAILMAN, JACK P.
1958. Behavior notes on the Ipswich sparrow. Bird-Banding, vol. 29, pp. 241–244.
1959. A third head-scratching method of emberizine sparrows. Condor, vol. 61, pp. 435–437.

HAILMAN, JACK P.—Continued

1960. Anting of a captive slate-colored junco. Wilson Bull., vol. 72, pp. 398–399.

HALLER, KARL WILLIAM

1949. Nelson's sharp-tailed sparrow in West Virginia. Auk, vol. 66, p. 369.

HAMERSTROM, FRANCES

1957. The influence of a hawk's appetite on mobbing. Condor, vol. 59, pp. 192–194.

HAMERSTROM, FREDERICK NATHAN, JR., and HAMERSTROM, FRANCES

1951. Food of young raptors on the Edwin S. George Reserve. Wilson Bull., vol. 63, pp. 16–25.

HAMERTON, A. E.

1937. Report on the deaths occurring in the society's gardens during the year 1936. Proc. Zool. Soc. London, vol. 107, ser. B, pp. 443–474.

1939. Review of mortality rates and report on the deaths occurring in the society's gardens during the year 1938. Proc. Zool. Soc. London, vol. 109, ser. B, pp. 281–327.

HAMILL, MRS. L. C.

1926. Notes on the mating of song sparrows and their range-limits during the nesting-period. Bull. Northeastern Bird-Banding Assn., vol. 2, pp. 7–10.

HAMILTON, WILLIAM JOHN, JR.

1933. The importance of stoneflies in the winter food of certain passerine birds. Auk, vol. 50, p. 373–374.

1940. Winter roosting habits of slate-colored juncos. Auk, vol. 57.

HANFORD, FORREST S.

1913. Sierra storms and birds. Condor, vol. 15, pp. 137–138.

HANN, HARRY WILBUR

1937. Life history of the oven-bird in southern Michigan. Wilson Bull., vol. 49, pp. 145–237.

1953. The biology of birds.

HANNA, G. DALLAS

1917. The summer birds of the St. Matthew Island bird reservation. Auk, vol. 34, pp. 403–410.

1920. Additions to the avifauna of the Pribilof Islands, Alaska, including four species new to North America. Auk, vol. 37, pp. 248–254.

1922. The Aleutian rosy finch. Condor, vol. 24, pp. 88–91.

HANNA, WILSON CREAL

1918. First occurrence of the dwarf cowbird in the San Bernardino Valley, California. Condor, vol. 20, pp. 211–212.

1924a. Some weights of eggs. Condor, vol. 26, pp. 36–37.

1924b. Weights of about three thousand eggs. Condor, vol. 26, pp. 146–153.

1933. House finch parasitized by dwarf cowbird and black phoebe nests occupied by house finch. Condor, vol. 35, p. 205.

HANTZSCH, BERNHARD

1929. Contribution to the knowledge of the avifauna of north-eastern Labrador. Canadian Field-Nat., vol. 43, pp. 52–59.

HARDING, KATHARINE C.

1943. An eight year old song sparrow. Bird-Banding, vol. 14, p. 77.

HARDY, GEORGE A.

1947. Bird notes from Saanich, southern Vancouver Island, B.C. Murrelet, vol. 28, pp. 37–38.

HARDY, ROSS

1947. Utah's Book Cliffs and bird migration. Auk, vol. 64, pp. 284–287.

1949. Ground dove and black-chinned sparrow in southern Nevada. Condor, vol. 51, pp. 272–273.

HARE, F. KENNETH

1959. A photo-reconnaissance survey of Labrador-Ungava. Geogr. Mem. 6, Dep. Mines and Tech. Surv., Ottawa.

HARGRAVE, LYNDON L.

1932. Notes on 15 species of birds from the San Francisco Mt. region, Arizona. Condor, vol. 34, pp. 217–220.

1936. Three broods of red-backed juncos in one season. Condor, vol. 38, pp. 57–59.

1939. Winter bird notes from Roosevelt Lake, Arizona. Condor, vol. 41, pp. 121–123.

HARKINS, CHARLES E.

1937. Harris's sparrow in its winter range. Wilson Bull., vol. 49, pp. 286–292.

HARLOW, RICHARD CRESSON

1918. Notes on the breeding birds of Pennsylvania and New Jersey. Auk, vol. 35, pp. 136–147.

1951. Tribal nesting of the pine siskin in Pennsylvania. Cassinia, No. 38, p. 9.

HARPER, FRANCIS

1930. A historical sketch of Botteri's sparrow. Auk, vol. 47, pp. 177–185.

1953. Birds of Nueltin Lake expedition Keewatin, 1947, 92–93. Amer. Midland Nat., vol. 49, pp. 1–116.

1958. Birds of the Ungava Peninsula. Univ. Kansas Misc. Publ. No. 17.

HARRIS, HARRY

1919. Historical notes on Harris's sparrow. Auk, vol. 36, pp. 180–190.

HARRIS, R. D.

1944. The chestnut-collared longspur in Manitoba. Wilson Bull., vol. 56, pp. 105–115.

HARRISON, HAL. H.

1948. American birds in color: Land birds.

HARROLD, C. G.

1933. Notes on the birds found at Lake Johnston and Last Mountain Lake, Saskatchewan, during April and May, 1922. Wilson Bull., vol. 45, pp. 16–26.

1934. *In* Swarth, Birds of Nunivak Island, Alaska. Pacific Coast Avifauna, No. 22, pp. 1–64.

HARTERT, ERNST

1910. Die Vögel der paläarktischen Fauna. Band 1, Heft 2.

HARTMAN, FRANK ALEXANDER

1946. Adrenal and thyroid weights in birds. Auk, vol. 63, pp. 42–64.

1955. Heart weight in birds. Condor, vol. 57, pp. 221–238.

HARTSHORNE, CHARLES

1956. The monotony-threshold in singing birds. Auk, vol. 73, pp. 176–192.

HARVEY, GERTRUDE FAY

1903. The diary of a cardinal's nest. Auk, vol. 20, pp. 54–57.

HASBROUCK, E. M.

1889. Summer birds of Eastland County, Texas. Auk, vol. 6, pp. 236–241.

HATCH, PHILO L.

1892. Notes on the birds of Minnesota, with specific characters.

HAUSMAN, LEON AUGUSTUS

1946. Field book of eastern birds.

Haviland, M. D.
1916. Notes on the Lapland bunting on the Yenesei River. British Birds, vol. 9, pp. 230–238.

Hawbecker, Albert C.
1945. Food habits of the barn owl. Condor, vol. 47, pp. 161–166.

Hawksley, Oscar, and McCormack, Alvah P.
1951. Doubly-occupied nests of the eastern cardinal, *Richmondena cardinalis*. Auk, vol. 68, pp. 515–516.

Hayward, C. Lynn
1935. A study of the winter bird life in Bear Lake and Utah Lake valleys. Wilson Bull., vol. 47, pp. 278–284.
1945. Biotic communities of the southern Wasatch and Uinta mountains, Utah. Great Basin Nat., vol. 6, p. 75.

Hayward, W. J., and Stephens, Thomas Calderwood
1914. The pine siskin breeding in Iowa. Wilson Bull., vol. 26, pp. 140–146.

Headstrom, Birger Richard
1951. Birds' nests of the west.

Heath, Harold
1915. Birds observed on Forrester Island, Alaska, during the summer of 1913. Condor, vol. 17, pp. 20–41.

Heaton, Harry L.
1928. The rufous-crowned sparrow. Oologist, vol. 45, p. 53.

Hebard, Frederick V., and Gardner, Alfred W.
1954. Mountain-top visits by birds at Aspen, Colorado, in winter and early spring. Condor, vol. 56, pp. 53–54.

Heerman, A. L.
1859. Report upon birds collected on the survey. Rep. Expl. Surv. Pacific Railroad, vol. 10, pt. 4, pp. 29–80.

Heintzelman, Donald S.
1964. Spring and summer sparrow hawk food habits. Wilson Bull., vol. 76, pp. 323–330.

Helme, Arthur Hudson
1883. Red crossbills. Ornith. and Ool., vol. 8, pp. 68–69.

Helms, Carl H.
1959. Song and tree sparrow weight and fat before and after a night of migration. Wilson Bull., vol. 71, pp. 244–253.

Helms, Carl W., and Drury, William H., Jr.
1960. Winter and migratory weight and fat field studies on some North American buntings. Bird-Banding, vol. 31, pp. 1–40.

Hendee, Russell W.
1929. Notes on birds observed in Moffat County, Colorado. Condor, vol. 31, pp. 24–32.

Henderson, J.
1906. With the birds in northeastern Colorado. Wilson Bull., vol. 18, pp. 105–110.
1912. Review of W. L. Sclater's A history of the birds of Colorado. Auk, vol. 29, pp. 277–278.
N.D. Notebooks, typewritten. Univ. Colorado Library, Boulder, Colo.

Hennessey, Frank
1909. *In* Bernier's Report on the Dominion Government expedition to the Arctic Islands and the Hudson strait on board the C.G.S. "Arctic" 1906–1907.

HENRY, THOMAS CHARLTON

1858. Descriptions of new birds from Fort Thorn, New Mexico. Proc. Acad. Nat. Sci. Philadelphia, vol. 7, pp. 117–118.

HENSHAW, HENRY WETHERBEE

1875. Report upon the ornithological collections made in portions of Nevada, Utah, California, Colorado, New Mexico, and Arizona, during the years 1871, 1872, 1873, and 1874. *In* Ann. Rep. Geogr. Geol. Expl. Surv. West 100th Mer., vol. 5, Zool., pp. 133–507.

1877. Report on the ornithology of portions of Nevada and California. Ann. Rep. Geogr. Geol. Expl. Surv. West 100th Mer. by George M. Wheeler, pp. 1303–1322.

1884. Description of a new song sparrow from the southern border of the United States. Auk, vol. 1, pp. 223–224.

1886. List of birds observed in summer and fall on the upper Pecos River, New Mexico. Auk, vol. 3, p. 75.

1894. An ingenious pair of house finches (*Carpodacus frontalis*). Auk, vol. 11, pp. 255–256.

HERING, LOUISE

1948. Nesting birds of the Black Forest, Colorado. Condor, vol. 50, pp. 49–63.

1954. Eighteenth breeding-bird census: 19. Lower foothills, ponderosa pine forest. Audubon Field Notes, vol. 8, pp. 372–373.

1956. Twentieth breeding-bird census: Lower foothills, ponderosa pine forest. Audubon Field Notes, vol. 10, p. 423.

1958. Twenty-second breeding-bird census: Open ponderosa pine forest. Audubon Field Notes, vol. 12, p. 448.

1961. Twenty-fifth breeding-bird census: Lower foothills, ponderosa pine forest. Audubon Field Notes, vol. 15, pp. 509–510.

1962. Twenty-sixth breeding-bird census: Lower foothills, ponderosa pine forest. Audubon Field Notes, vol. 16, pp. 523–524.

1963. Twenty-seventh breeding-bird census: Lower foothills, ponderosa pine forest. Audubon Field Notes, vol. 17, p. 499.

HERMAN, CARLTON M.

1937. Notes on hippoboscid flies. Bird-Banding, vol. 8, pp. 161–166.

1938. Occurrence of larval and nymphal stages of the rabbit tick, *Haemaphysalis leporis-palustris*, on wild birds from Cape Cod. Bird Banding, vol. 9, pp. 219–220.

1944. Blood protozoa of North American birds. Bird-Banding, vol. 15, pp. 89–112.

1955. Diseases of birds. *In* Wolfson, Recent studies in avian biology, pp. 450–467.

HERMAN, CARLTON M., JANKIEWICZ, HARRY A., and SAARNI, ROY W.

1942. Coccidiosis in California quail. Condor, vol. 44, pp. 168–171.

HERSEY, LUMAN JOEL, and ROCKWELL, ROBERT B.

1907. A new breeding bird for Colorado: the Cassin sparrow (*Peucaea cassini*) nesting near Denver. Condor, vol. 9, pp. 191–194.

HESS, ISAAC ELNORE

1910. One hundred breeding birds of an Illinois ten-mile radius. Auk, vol. 27, pp. 19–32.

HEYDWEILLER, A. MARGUERITE

1935. A comparison of winter and summer territories and seasonal variations of the tree sparrow (*Spizella a. arborea*). Bird-Banding, vol. 6, pp. 1–11.

HEYDWEILLER, A. MARGUERITE
1936. Sex, age, and individual variation of winter tree sparrows. Bird-Banding, vol. 7, pp. 61–68.

HICKEY, JOSEPH J.
1961. Some effects of insecticides on terrestrial birdlife in the Middle West. Wilson Bull., vol. 73, pp. 398–424.

HICKS, LAWRENCE EMERSON
1934a. The hoary redpoll in Ohio. Auk, vol. 51, pp. 244–245.
1934b. A summary of cowbird host species in Ohio. Auk, vol. 51, pp. 385–386.

HIGGINS, A. W.
1926. Nesting records of song sparrows 25935 and 39235. Northeastern Bird-Banding Assoc. Bull., vol. 2, p. 39.

HILDEBRAND, HENRY
1950. Notes on the birds of the Ungava Bay district. Canadian Field-Nat., vol. 64, pp. 55–67.

HILDÉN, OLAVI
1960. Retkeilijän lintuopas.

HILL, HAROLD M., and WIGGINS, IRA L.
1948. Ornithological notes from Lower California. Condor, vol. 50, pp. 155–161.

HILL, JAMES HAYNES
1902. The white-winged crossbill in captivity. Auk, vol. 19, pp. 13–15.

HILL, NORMAN P.
1965. The birds of Cape Cod, Massachusetts.

HIND, HENRY YOULE
1860. Narrative of the Canadian Red River exploring expedition of 1857, 2 vols.

HINDE, H. P.
1954. The vertical distribution of salt marsh phanerogams in relation to tide level. Ecol. Monogr., vol. 24, pp. 209–225.

HINES, JOHN Q.
1963. Birds of the Noatak River, Alaska. Condor, vol. 65, pp. 410–425.

HODGES, JAMES
1946. Cowbird eggs in rose-breasted grosbeak's nest. Auk, vol. 63, p. 590.
1950. Unusual accidents of birds. Auk, vol. 67, pp. 249–250.

HOFFMANN, RALPH
1904. A guide to the birds of New England and eastern New York. (New ed., 1923, under slightly different title.)
1927. Birds of the Pacific States.

HOLDEN, NELDA, and HALL, WILLIS
1959. An index to South Dakota bird notes, vols. 6–10.

HOLLAND, HAROLD MAY
1923. Black phoebes and house finches in joint use of a nest. Condor, vol. 25, pp. 131–132.
1930. Cardinals nesting in a sparrow trap. Bird-Lore, vol. 32, p. 424.
1934. Cardinals again nest in a sparrow trap. Bird-Lore, vol. 36, p. 305.

HOLLISTER, N.
1908. Birds of the region about Needles, California. Auk, vol. 25, pp. 455–462.

HOLSTEIN, OTTO
1902. Birds destroyed by pools of petroleum along railroads. Condor, vol. 4, p. 46.

HOLT, E. G., and SUTTON, G. M.
1926. Notes on birds observed in southern Florida. Ann. Carnegie Mus., vol. 16, pp. 409–439.
HOLT, ERNEST G.
1918. Birds and mulberries. Auk, vol. 35, pp. 359–360.
1932. A junco junket. Auk, vol. 49, pp. 99–100.
HOPE, CLIFFORD E.
1947. Nesting of the evening grosbeak in Algonquin Park, Ontario, 1946. Auk, vol. 64, pp. 463–464.
HOPKINS, A. D.
1938. Bioclimatics: a science of life and climate relations. U.S. Dep. Agric. Misc. Publ. 280.
HORSEY, RICHARD EDGAR
1926a. Tree sparrow migration: a comparison. Bull. Northeastern Bird-Banding Assoc., vol. 2, pp. 44–48.
1926b. Bird banding stations at Rochester, N.Y. Bull. Northeastern Bird-Banding Assoc., vol. 2, pp. 55–56.
HOSTETTER, D. RALPH
1961. Life history of the Carolina junco, *Junco hyemalis carolinensis* Brewster. Raven, vol. 32, pp. 97–170.
HOUSTON, C. STUART
1949. The birds of the Yorkton District, Saskatchewan. Canadian Field-Nat., vol. 63, p. 238.
HOUSTON, C. STUART, and STREET, MAURICE.
1959. The birds of the Saskatchewan River. Spec. Publ. No. 2, Saskatchewan Nat. Hist. Soc.
HOUSTON, STUART
1953. Co-operative spring migration study—1953. Blue Jay, vol. 11, pp. 14–15.
1954. Co-operative bird migration study—1954. Blue Jay, vol. 12, pp. 26–27.
1955. Spring migration 1955—co-operative study. Blue Jay, vol. 13, pp. 34–35.
1956. Co-operative spring migration study—1956. Blue Jay, vol. 14, p. 83.
HOWARD, H. ELIOT
1920. Territory in bird life.
HOWARD, HILDEGARDE, and MILLER, ALDEN H.
1933. Bird remains from cave deposits in New Mexico. Condor, vol. 35, pp. 15–18.
HOWE, REGINALD HEBER, and ALLEN, GLOVER MORRILL
1901. The birds of Massachusetts.
HOWELL, ALFRED B., and VAN ROSSEM, A.
1911. Further notes from Santa Cruz Island. Condor, vol. 13, pp. 208–210.
HOWELL, ALFRED BRAZIER
1911. Some birds of the San Quentin Bay region, Baja, [sic] California. Condor, vol. 13, pp. 151–153.
1914. Destruction of birds by fumigation. Condor, vol. 16, p. 54.
1916. Some results of a winter's observations in Arizona. Condor, vol. 18, pp. 209–214.
1917. Birds of the islands off the coast of southern California. Pacific Coast Avifauna, No. 12.
1923. The influences of the southwestern deserts upon the avifauna of California. Auk, vol. 40, pp. 584–592.

Howell, Arthur Holmes
1909. Notes on the summer birds of northern Georgia. Auk, vol. 26, pp. 129–137.
1919. Description of a new seaside sparrow from Florida. Auk, vol. 36, pp. 86–87.
1924. Birds of Alabama.
1928. Birds of Alabama, ed. 2.
1932. Florida bird life.

Howell, Joseph C.
1937. Early nesting of the Cape Sable seaside sparrow. Auk, vol. 54, p. 102.
1948. Observations on certain birds of the region of Kodiak, Alaska. Auk, vol. 65, pp. 352–358.

Howell, Joseph C., Laskey, Amelia R., and Tanner, James T.
1954. Bird mortality at airport ceilometers. Wilson Bull., vol. 66, pp. 207–215.

Howell, Thomas Raymond, and Cade, T. J.
1954. The birds of Guadalupe Island in 1953. Condor, vol. 56, pp. 283–294.

Hoyt, J. Southgate Y.
1948. Observations on nesting associates. Auk, vol. 65, pp. 188–196.

Hoyt, Sally F.
1961. Nest-building movements performed by juvenal song sparrow. Wilson Bull., vol. 73, pp. 386–387.

Hudson, George Elford, and Yocom, Charles Frederick
1954. A distributional history of the birds of southeastern Washington. Res. Studies, State College of Washington, vol. 22.

Huey, Laurence M.
1915. Random notes from San Diego. Condor, vol. 17, pp. 59–60.
1925. An observation on the pre-nuptial feeding habit of the California linnet. Condor, vol. 27, pp. 178–179.
1926a. Bats eaten by the short-eared owl. Auk, vol. 43, pp. 96–97.
1926b. Two species new to the avifauna of California. Condor, vol. 28, p. 44.
1926c. Notes from northwestern Lower California, with the description of an apparently new race of the screech owl. Auk, vol. 43, pp. 347–362.
1927a. Birds recorded in spring at San Felipe, northeastern Lower California, Mexico, with description of a new woodpecker from that locality. Trans. San Diego Soc. Nat. Hist., vol. 5, pp. 13–40.
1927b. The bird life of San Ignacio and pond lagoons on the western coast of Lower California. Condor, vol. 29, pp. 239–243.
1928. Some bird records from northern Lower California. Condor, vol. 30, pp. 158–159.
1930a. Comment on the marsh sparrows of southern and Lower California. Trans. San Diego Soc. Nat. Hist., vol. 6, pp. 203–206.
1930b. A new race of Bell sparrow from Lower California, Mexico. Trans. San Diego Soc. Nat. Hist., vol. 6, pp. 229–230.
1931a. Two new birds and other records for Lower California, Mexico. Condor, vol. 33, pp. 127–128.
1931b. Notes on two birds from San Diego County, California. Auk, vol. 48, pp. 620–621.
1935. February bird life of Punta Penascosa, Sonora, Mexico. Auk, vol. 52, pp. 249–256.

1936a. Notes on the summer and fall birds of the White Mountains, Arizona. Wilson Bull., vol. 48, pp. 129–130.

1936b. Notes from Maricopa County, Arizona. Condor, vol. 38, p. 172.

1938. Three noteworthy stragglers in northern Alaska. Auk, vol. 55, pp. 555–556.

1940. A new cardinal from central Lower California, Mexico. Trans. San Diego Soc. Nat. Hist., vol. 9, pp. 215–218.

1941. Notes from northern Lower California. Auk, vol. 58, p. 270.

1942. A vertebrate faunal survey of the Organ Pipe Cactus National Monument, Arizona. Trans. San Diego Soc. Nat. Hist., vol. 9, pp. 353–376.

1954. Notes from southern California and Baja California, Mexico. Condor, vol. 56, pp. 51–52.

HUGHES, WILLIAM M.

1951. Some observations on the rusty song sparrow, *Melospiza melodia morphna* Oberholser. Canadian Field-Nat., vol. 65, p. 186.

HUMPHREY, PHILIP S., and PARKES, KENNETH C.

1959. An approach to the study of molts and plumages. Auk, vol. 76, pp. 1–31.

1963. Comments on the study of plumage succession. Auk, vol. 80, pp. 496–503.

HUNN, JOHN TOWNSEND SHARPLESS

1906. Notes on birds of Silver City, New Mexico. Auk, vol. 23, pp. 418–425.

HUNT, CHRESWELL J.

1904. Goldfinch and tree sparrow—difference in feeding. Bird-Lore, vol. 6, p. 133.

HUNT, RICHARD

1920. Nuptial flight of the Anna hummingbird. Condor, vol. 22, pp. 109–110.

1921. Nesting pine grosbeaks in Plumas County, California. Condor, vol. 23, pp. 187–190.

1922. Evidence of musical "taste" in the brown towhee. Condor, vol. 24, pp. 193–230.

HUNTER, W. D., and PIERCE, W. D.

1912. Report on Mexican cotton-boll weevil. Senate Documents, No. 305. 62nd Congr., 2nd sess., p. 188.

HUSSONG, CLARA

1946. The clay-colored sparrow. Passenger Pigeon, vol. 8, pp. 3–7.

HYDE, A. SIDNEY

1939. The life history of Henslow's sparrow, *Passerherbulus henslowii* (Audubon). Univ. Michigan Mus. Zool., Misc. Publ. No. 41.

1953. Unusual records from western Colorado. Condor, vol. 55, p. 216.

ILNICKY, NICHOLAS J.

1963. Some interesting notes on birds of the upper peninsula of Michigan. Jack-Pine Warbler, vol. 41, No. 2, pp. 62–63.

IMHOF, THOMAS A.

1962. Alabama birds.

INGERSOLL, A. M.

1913. Great destruction of birds' eggs and nestlings in the Sierra Nevada. Condor, vol. 15, pp. 81–86.

Ingles, Lloyd G.
1937. Desert and Lincoln sparrows near Chico, California. Condor, vol. 39, pp. 86–87.

Irving, Laurence
1960. Birds of Anaktuvuk Pass, Kobuk, and Old Crow. U.S. Nat. Mus. Bull. 217.
1961. The migration of Lapland longspurs to Alaska. Auk, vol. 78, pp. 327–342.

Ivor, Hance Roy
1941. Observations on anting by birds. Auk, vol. 58, pp. 415–416.
1943. Further studies of anting by birds. Auk, vol. 60, pp. 51–55.
1944. Bird study and semi-captive birds: The rose-breasted grosbeak. Wilson Bull., vol. 56, pp. 91–104.

Jaeger, Edmund C.
1947. Use of the creosote bush by birds of the southern Californian deserts. Condor, vol. 49, pp. 126–127.

Jahn, Hermann
1942. Zur Oekologie und Biologie der Vögel Japans. Journ. für Ornith., vol. 90, p. 84.

Jameson, Everett Williams, Jr.
1942. Turkey bluejoint in the diet of Indigo buntings. Wilson Bull., vol. 54, p. 256.

Jardine, William
1832. The illustrative notes and life of Wilson. *In* Wilson and Bonaparte, American ornithology, 3 vols.

Jeffries, J. Amory
1883. Notes on an hermaphrodite bird. Bull. Nuttall Ornith. Club, vol. 8, pp. 17–21.

Jeffries, William Amory
1879. The Ipswich sparrow (*Passerculus princeps*, Maynard). Bull. Nuttall Ornith. Club, vol. 4, pp. 103–106.
1889. Birds observed at Santa Barbara, California. Auk, vol. 6, pp. 220–223.

Jehl, J. R., Jr., and Russell, D. J. T.
1966. Incubation periods of some subarctic birds. Canadian Field-Nat., vol. 80, pp. 179-180.

Jenkins, Hubert Oliver
1906. A list of birds collected between Monterey and San Simeon in the Coast Range of California. Condor, vol. 8, pp. 122–130.

Jenks, Randolph
1934. Unusual nesting records from northern Arizona. Condor, vol. 36, pp. 172–176.
1936. Two new records for Arizona. Condor, vol. 38, p. 38.

Jensen, Jens Knudson
1923. Notes on the nesting birds of northern Santa Fe County, New Mexico. Auk, vol. 40, pp. 452–469.
1924. The great grosbeak year. Auk, vol. 41, pp. 569–572.
1930. Third nesting record of the Rocky Mountain evening grosbeak in New Mexico. Auk, vol. 47, pp. 568–570.

Jeter, Horace H.
1953. Smith's longspur: an addition to the Louisiana list. Wilson Bull., vol. 65, p. 212.

JEWETT, STANLEY G., and GABRIELSON, IRA NOEL
1929. Birds of the Portland area, Oregon. Pacific Coast Avifauna, No. 19.

JEWETT, STANLEY G., TAYLOR, WALTER P., SHAW, WILLIAM T., and ALDRICH, JOHN W.
1953. Birds of Washington State.

JEWETT, STANLEY GORDON
1912. Some birds of the Sawtooth Mountains, Idaho. Condor, vol. 14, pp. 191–194.
1916. Notes on some land birds of Tillamook County, Oregon. Condor, vol. 18, pp. 74–80.
1928. Bird notes from Oregon. Condor, vol. 30, pp. 356–358.
1939. Additional notes on the black pigeon hawk. Condor, vol. 41, pp. 84–85.
1942. Bird notes from southeastern Alaska. Murrelet, vol. 23, pp. 66–75.

JOHANSSEN, H.
1958. Revision und Entstehung der arktischen Vogelfauna. I–II. Acta Arctica København, No. 9.

JOHNSON, CHARLES W.
1932. Notes on Protocalliphora during the summer of 1931. Bird-Banding, vol. 3, pp. 26–29.

JOHNSON, DAVID H., BRYANT, MONROE D., and MILLER, ALDEN HOLMES
1948. Vertebrate animals of the Providence Mountains area of California. Univ. California Publ. Zool., vol. 48, pp. 221–375.

JOHNSON, JOHN CHRISTOPHER, JR.
1956. Breeding of Cassin's sparrow in central Oklahoma. Wilson Bull., vol. 68, pp. 75–76.

JOHNSON, NED KEITH
1949. Loggerhead shrike steals shot sparrow. Condor, vol. 51, p. 233.

JOHNSON, ROSWELL H.
1906. The birds of Cheney, Washington. Condor, vol. 8, pp. 25–28.

JOHNSTON, DAVID W.
1949. Populations and distribution of summer birds of Latah County, Idaho. Condor, vol. 51, pp. 140–149.
1955. Mass bird mortality in Georgia, October, 1954. Oriole, vol. 20, No. 2, pp. 17–26.
1956. A preliminary study of subspecies of Savannah sparrows at the Savannah River plant, South Carolina. Auk, vol. 73, pp. 454–456.
1962. Lipid deposition and gonadal recrudescence in response to photoperiodic manipulations in the slate-colored junco. Auk, vol. 79, pp. 387–398.

JOHNSTON, DAVID W., and HAINES, T. P.
1957. Analysis of mass bird mortality in October, 1954. Auk, vol. 74, pp. 447–458.

JOHNSTON, DAVID W., and ODUM, EUGENE P.
1956. Breeding bird populations in relation to plant succession on the Piedmont of Georgia. Ecology, vol. 37, pp. 50–62.

JOHNSTON, RICHARD FOURNESS
1954. Variation in breeding season and clutch size in song sparrows of the Pacific coast. Condor, vol. 56, pp. 268–273.
1955. Influence of winter high tides on two populations of salt marsh song sparrows. Condor, vol. 57, pp. 308–309.

JOHNSTON, RICHARD FOURNESS—Continued
1956a. Population structure in salt marsh song sparrows: Part I. Environment and annual cycle; part II. Density, age, structure, and maintenance. Condor, vol. 58, pp. 24–44, 254–272.
1956b. Predation by short-eared owls on a salicornia salt marsh. Wilson Bull., vol. 68, pp. 91–102.
1957. Selection and emberizine distraction display. Condor, vol. 59, p. 266.
1960. Behavioral and ecologic notes on the brown-headed cowbird. Condor, vol. 62, pp. 137–138.
1964. The breeding birds of Kansas. Univ. Kansas Publ., Mus. Nat. Hist., vol. 12, No. 14, pp. 575–655.

JOHNSTON, VERNA RUTH
1941. Report on field projects at University of Colorado Science Lodge. (Typewritten, Univ. Colo., Boulder, Colo.)
1943. An ecological study of nesting birds in the vicinity of Boulder, Colorado. Condor, vol. 45, pp. 61–68.
1944. Observations on the courtship of four woodland birds. Auk, vol. 61, pp. 478–480.
1947. Breeding birds of the forest edge in Illinois. Condor, vol. 49, pp. 45–53.

JOHNSTONE, WALTER B.
1949. An annotated list of the birds of the East Kootenay, British Columbia. Occas. Pap. British Columbia Provin. Mus., No. 7, p. 78.

JONES, C. M.
1881. Henslow's sparrow nesting in northern Conn. Ornith. and Ool., vol. 6, pp. 17–18.

JONES, FRED MINSON
1940. Notes from southwest Virginia. Oölogist, vol. 57, pp. 88–93.

JONES, LYNDS
1892. Report of the president for the work of 1891, on the Fringillidae. Wilson Quart., vol. 4, pp. 67–84.
1895. Bird migration at Grinnell, Iowa. Auk, vol. 12, pp. 231–237.
1910. The birds of Cedar Point and vicinity. Wilson Bull., vol. 22, p. 100.
1913. Some records of the feeding of nestlings. Wilson Bull., vol. 25, pp. 67–71.

JOUY, PIERRE LOUIS
1881. Description of the nest and eggs of *Coturniculus henslowi* obtained near Falls Church, Va. Bull. Nuttall Ornith. Club, vol. 6, pp. 57–58.

JUDD, SYLVESTER DWIGHT
1898. Birds as weed destroyers. U.S. Dep. Agric. Yearbook, pp. 221–232.
1900. The food of nestling birds. U.S. Dep. Agric. Yearbook, pp. 411–436.
1901. The relation of sparrows to agriculture. U.S. Dep. Agric. Biol. Surv. Bull., No. 15, p. 98.

JUDD, W. W.
1951. White-throated sparrows at Goose Bay Labrador. Canadian Field-Nat., vol. 65, p. 80.

JUNG, CLARENCE S.
1930. Notes on birds of the delta region of the Peace and Athabasca rivers. Auk, vol. 47, pp. 533–541.
1936. European goldfinch (*Carduelis carduelis*) in Wisconsin. Auk, vol. 53, pp. 340–341.

Kaeding, Henry Barroilhet
1899. The genus *Junco* in California. Bull. Cooper Ornith. Club, vol. 1, pp. 79–81.
1905. Birds from the west coast of Lower California and adjacent islands. Condor, vol. 7, pp. 105–111, 134–138.

Kalmbach, E. R.
1914. Birds in relation to the alfalfa weevil. U.S. Dep. of Agric. Bull. 107.

Kay, G. T.
1944. Notes on the nesting of snow buntings in captivity. Avicult. Mag., vol. 9, pp. 106–107.

Keast, Allen
1960. Bird adaptations to aridity on the Australian Continent. Proc. XII Internat. Ornith. Congr., vol. 1, pp. 373–375.

Keeler, Charles
1902. Harriman Alaska Expedition. Harriman Alaska series, vol. 2, pp. 205–234.

Keeler, Charles Augustus
1890a. Song birds about San Francisco Bay. Zoe, vol. 1, p. 118.
1890b. Observations on the life history of the house finch (*Carpodacus mexicanus frontalis*). Zoe, vol. 1, pp. 172–176.
1899. Bird notes afield, p. 176.

Keller, Clyde L.
1891. Nesting of *Spinus pinus* in the North-west. Oologist, vol. 8, p. 31.

Kellogg, Peter Paul, and Allen, Arthur A.
1959. A field guide to bird songs of eastern and central America (two 33⅓ rpm recordings).

Kemsies, Emerson
1948. Northern pine siskin in Hamilton County, Ohio. Auk, vol. 65, p. 146.
1961. Subspeciation in the Smith's longspur, *Calcarius pictus*. Canadian Field-Nat., vol. 75, pp. 143–149.

Kemsies, Emerson, and Austing, G. Ronald
1950. Smith's longspur in Ohio. Wilson Bull., vol. 62, p. 37.

Kemsies, Emerson, and Randle, Worth
1964. A distributional summary and some behavioral notes for Smith's longspur, *Calcarius pictus*. Canadian Field-Nat., vol. 78, pp. 28–31.

Kenagy, Fayre
1914. A change in fauna. Condor, vol. 16, pp. 120–123.

Kendeigh, S. Charles
1941. Birds of a prairie community. Condor, vol. 43, pp. 165–174.
1947. Bird population studies in the coniferous forest biome during a spruce budworm outbreak. Canadian Biol. Bull., No. 1, pp. 75–77.

Kennedy, Clarence Hamilton
1914. The effects of irrigation on bird life in the Yakima Valley, Washington. Condor, vol. 16, pp. 250–255.

Kennerly, C. B. R.
1859. Report on birds collected on the route. Pacific Railroad Reports, vol. 10, pt. 6, No. 3, pp. 19–35.

Kenyon, Karl W.
1947. Notes on the occurrence of birds in Lower California. Condor, vol. 49, pp. 210–211.

Kessel, Brina, Cade, Tom J., and Schaller, George B.
1953. A study of the birds of the Colville River. Final report to Contract Nonr–768(00), U.S. Navy, Office of Naval Research.

Keyes, Charles R.
1888. Occurrence of *Coccothraustes vespertina* in Iowa. Auk, vol. 5, pp. 114–115.
1905b. Some bird notes from the central Sierras. Condor, vol. 7, pp. 13–17.

Keyser, Leander S.
1902. Birds of the Rockies.

Kimball, Henry Hungerford
1921. Notes from southern Arizona. Condor, vol. 23, pp. 57–58.

King, Franklin Hiram
1883. Economic relations of Wisconsin birds. *In* Geology of Wisconsin. Survey of 1873–79, vol. 1, pt. 2, ch. 11, pp. 441–610.

King, James R.
1954. Victims of the brown-headed cowbird in Whitman County, Washington. Condor, vol. 56, pp. 150–154.

King, Virgil D.
1940. A breeding bird census. Kentucky Warbler, vol. 16, p. 11.

Kinsey, Eric Campbell
1934. Notes on the sociology of the long-tailed yellow-breasted chat. Condor, vol. 36, pp. 235–237.

Kirk, George Leavitt
1917. Nelson's sparrow in Vermont. Auk, vol. 34, p. 341.

Kirn, Albert J.
1915. Notes. Oologist, vol. 32, p. 72.

Kivirikko, K. E.
1947. Suomen linnut, vol. 1.

Kiyosu, Yukiyasu
1943. On the birds as food resources (in Japanese). Inst. Nat. Res. Misc Rep., No. 4.

Klugh, A. Brooker
1926. Notes on the white-winged crossbill. Canadian Field-Nat., vol. 40, p. 19.

Knappen, Phoebe Malura
1934. Insects in the winter food of tree sparrows. Auk, vol. 51, pp. 93–94.

Knight, Ora Willis
1908. The birds of Maine.

Knight, Wilbur C.
1902. The birds of Wyoming. Univ. Wyoming Exp. Sta. Bull. 55, p. 174.

Knowles, E. H. M.
1938. Polygamy in the western lark sparrow. Auk, vol. 55, pp. 675–676.

Knowlton, George F.
1937a. Utah birds in the control of certain insect pests. Proc. Utah Acad. Sci., vol. 14, pp. 159–166.
1937b. Biological control of the beet leafhopper in Utah. Proc. Utah Acad. Sci., vol. 14, pp. 111–139.
1947. Food of the lark bunting in central Utah. Auk, vol. 64, p. 627.
1950. Insect food of the Nevada Savannah sparrow. Auk, vol. 67, p. 106.

Knowlton, George F., and Harnston, F. C.
1943. Grasshoppers and crickets eaten by Utah birds. Auk, vol. 60, pp. 589–591.

Knowlton, George F., and Nye, W. P.
1948. Insect food of the vesper sparrow. Journ. Econ. Ent., vol. 41, p. 821.

KOBAYASHI, KEISUKE
1937. Nests and eggs found around Shimo-yubetsu, Hokkaido, pt. 1 (in Japanese). Yacho, vol. 4, pp. 23–33.
KOBAYASHI, KEISUKE, and ISHIZAWA, TAKEO
1932–1940. The eggs of Japanese birds (in Japanese).
KOBBE, WILLIAM H.
1900. Birds of Cape Disappointment, Washington. Auk, vol. 17, pp. 349–358.
KOHLER, LOUIS S.
1913. Preliminary list of the birds of northern Passaic County, New Jersey. Wilson Bull., vol. 25, pp. 71–85.
1922. The birds of Greenwood Lake and vicinity (New Jersey and New York). Wilson Bull., vol. 34, pp. 148–164.
KOPMAN, HENRY H.
1907. Aspects of bird distribution in Louisiana and Mississippi. Auk, vol. 24, pp. 169–181.
1915. List of the birds of Louisiana: Pt. 6. Auk, vol. 32, pp. 15–29.
KRAUSE, HERBERT
1954. An index to South Dakota bird notes, vols. 1–5.
KRAUSE, HERBERT, and FROILAND, SVEN G.
1956. Distribution of the cardinal in South Dakota. Wilson Bull., vol. 68, pp. 111–117.
KROG, JOHN
1953. Notes on the birds of Amchitka Island, Alaska. Condor, vol. 55, pp. 299–304.
KUMLIEN, L., and HOLLISTER, N.
1951. Birds of Wisconsin, with revisions by A. W. Schorger.
KUMLIEN, LUDWIG
1879. Contributions to the natural history of Arctic America, made in connection with the Howgate polar expedition, 1877–78. U.S. Nat. Mus. Bull. 15, pp. 74–75.
KUNTZ, PAUL
1939. Migration and keeping of evening grosbeaks. Avicult. Mag., vol. 4, No. 7 (fifth ser.), pp. 225–228.
LA BRIE, W.
1931. Notes on the Acadian sharp-tailed sparrow at Kamouraska, Quebec. Canadian Field-Nat., vol. 45, p. 40.
LACEY, HOWARD
1911. The birds of Kerrville, Texas, and vicinity. Auk, vol. 28, pp. 200–219.
LACK, DAVID
1940a. Pair-formation in birds. Condor, vol. 42, pp. 269–286.
1940b. Courtship feeding in birds. Auk, vol. 57, pp. 169–178.
1943. The life of the robin.
1947–48. The significance of clutch-size. Ibis, vol. 89, pp. 302–352; vol. 90, pp. 25–45.
1954. The natural regulation of animal numbers.
LAFAVE, LYNN DALE
1960. The clay-colored sparrow, a new bird for the State of Washington. Murrelet, vol. 41, p. 30.
LAING, HAMILTON M.
1942. Birds of the coast of central British Columbia. Condor, vol. 44, pp. 175–181.

LAMB, CHESTER
1912. Birds of a Mohave Desert oasis. Condor, vol. 14, pp. 32–40.
1922. Summer record of blue-winged teal in California, and notes on other birds. Condor, vol. 24, pp. 28–29.
1927a. The birds of Natividad Island, Lower California. Condor, vol. 29, pp. 67–70.
1927b. Notes on some birds of the southern extremity of Lower California. Condor, vol. 29, pp. 155–157.
1929. Land birds of a Pacific coast sea voyage. Condor, vol. 31, pp. 36–37.

LAMM, DONALD W.
1956. Mourning dove and dickcissel on the Atlantic Ocean. Auk, vol. 73, p. 290.

LAND, HUGH C.
1962. A collection of birds from the arid interior of eastern Guatemala. Auk, vol. 79, pp. 1–11.
1963. A collection of birds from the Caribbean lowlands of Guatemala. Condor, vol. 65, pp. 49–65.

LANE, H. WALLACE
1931. Varied bunting in New Mexico. Auk, vol. 48, p. 275.

LANGDON, ROY M.
1933. The lark bunting. Bird-Lore, vol. 35, pp. 139–142.

LANGILLE, J. HIBBERT
1884. Our birds in their haunts.

LANYON, WESLEY E.
1960. The ontogeny of vocalizations in birds. *In* Lanyon and Tavolga, Animal Sounds and Communication, pp. 321-347.

LA RIVERS, IRA
1941. The Mormon cricket as food for birds. Condor, vol. 43, pp. 65–69.

LARSON, ADRIAN
1925. The birds of Sioux Falls, South Dakota, and vicinity. Wilson Bull., vol. 37, pp. 18–38.

LASKEY, AMELIA R.
1934. Eastern field sparrow migration in Tennessee. Bird-Banding, vol. 5, pp. 172–175.
1944. A study of the cardinal in Tennessee. Wilson Bull., vol. 56, pp. 27–44.
1957. Television tower casualties. Migrant, vol. 28, pp. 54–56.
1960. Bird migration casualties and weather conditions: autumns 1958–1959–1960. Migrant, vol. 31, pp. 61–65.

LASKEY, F. C.
1934. Tree sparrows again recorded at Nashville. Migrant, vol. 5, p. 12.

LATHAM, JOHN
1790. Index ornithologicus, 2 vols.

LAW, J. EUGENE
1924. Thurber juncos banded in the San Bernardino Mountains. Condor, vol. 26, pp. 232–234.
1926. Green-tailed towhee qualifies in intelligence test. Condor, vol. 28, pp. 133–134.
1929a. A query about the nest habit of the pine siskin. Wilson Bull., vol. 41, p. 192.
1929b. The spring molt in *Zonotrichia.* Condor, vol. 31, pp. 208–212.

LAWHEAD, PAUL J.
1949. Thirteenth breeding-bird census: Ponderosa pine, brush and grassland. Audubon Field Notes, vol. 3, pp. 270–271.

LAWRENCE, GEORGE N.
1851. Descriptions of new species of birds, of the genera *Toxostoma* Wagler, *Tyrannula* Swainson, and *Plectrophanes* Meyer. Ann. Lyc. Nat. Hist. New York, vol. 5, No. 4, pp. 121–123.
1874. The birds of western and northwestern Mexico. Mem. Boston Soc. Nat. Hist., vol. 2, pp. 276–277.
1889. A new name for the species of *Sporophila* from Texas, generally known as *S. morelleti.* Auk, vol. 6, pp. 53–54.

LAWRENCE, LOUISE DE KIRILINE
1949. The red crossbill at Pimisi Bay, Ontario. Canadian Field-Nat., vol. 63, pp. 147–160.
1956. An interesting displacement movement in a slate-colored junco. Auk, vol. 73, p. 267.

LEA, ROBERT BASHFORD, and EDWARDS, ERNEST PRESTON
1950. Notes on birds of Lake Patzcuaro region, Michocan, Mexico. Condor, vol. 52, pp. 260–271.

LEE, MELICENT HUMASON
1920. Notes on a few birds of the Grand Canyon, Arizona. Condor, vol. 22, pp. 171–172.

LEES, W. A. D.
1939. Song sparrow feeds five cowbirds. Canadian Field-Nat., vol. 53, p. 121.

LEFFINGWELL, DANA J., and LEFFINGWELL, ANNE MACLAY
1931. Winter habits of the Hepburn rosy finch at Clarkston, Washington. Condor, vol. 33, pp. 140–147.

LEGLER, J. M.
1960. Natural history of the ornate box turtle, *Terrapene ornata ornata* Agassiz. Univ. Kansas Mus. Nat. Hist. Publ., vol. 11, pp. 527–669.

LEOPOLD, ALDO, and EYNON, ALFRED E.
1961. Avian daybreak and evening song in relation to time and light intensity. Condor, vol. 63, pp. 269–293.

LEWIS, HARRISON F.
1920. Notes on the Acadian sharp-tailed sparrow (*Passerherbulus nelsoni subvirgatus*). Auk, vol. 37, pp. 587–589.
1924. List of birds recorded from the island of Anticosta, Quebec. Canadian Field-Nat., vol. 38, p. 127.
1939. Notes on September birds along Ontario's sea-coast. Canadian Field-Nat., vol. 53, pp. 50–53.

LEWIS, HUBERT
1943. Nesting of the thistle bird. Flicker, vol. 15, pp. 36–37.

LIGON, J. STOKLEY
1923. Nesting of the evening grosbeak in northern Michigan. Auk, vol. 40, pp. 314–316.

LIGON, JAMES STOKELY.
1961. New Mexico birds and where to find them.

LINCOLN, FREDERICK CHARLES
1916. Discovery of the nest and eggs of *Leucosticte australis.* Auk, vol. 33, pp. 41–42.
1917. Some notes on the birds of Rock Canyon, Arizona. Wilson Bull., vol. 29, pp. 65–73.

LINCOLN, FREDERICK CHARLES—Continued

1920a. Birds of Clear Creek district, Colorado. Auk, vol. 37, pp. 60–77.

1920b. Unpublished field notes, Denver Mus. Nat. Hist., Denver, Colo.

1925. Notes on the bird life of North Dakota with particular reference to the summer waterfowl. Auk, vol. 42, pp. 50–64.

1927. Returns from banded birds 1923 to 1926. U.S. Dep. Agric. Tech. Bull. No. 32.

1939. The migration of American birds.

1950. Migration of birds. Fish Wildlife Service, Circ. 16. U.S. Dep. Interior.

LINSDALE, JEAN, and HALL, E. RAYMOND

1927. Notes on the birds of Douglas County, Kansas. Wilson Bull., vol. 39, pp. 91–105.

LINSDALE, JEAN M.

1928a. Variations in the fox sparrow (*Passerella iliaca*) with reference to natural history and osteology. Univ. California Publ. Zool., vol. 30, pp. 251–392.

1928b. The species and subspecies of the fringillid genus *Passerella* Swainson. Condor, vol. 30, pp. 349–351.

1929. Roadways as they affect bird life. Condor, vol. 31, pp. 143–145.

1931. Facts concerning the use of thallium in California to poison rodents—its destructiveness to game birds, song birds, and other valuable wildlife. Condor, vol. 33, pp. 92–106.

1936a. The birds of Nevada. Pacific Coast Avifauna No. 23.

1936b. Coloration of downy young birds and of nest linings. Condor, vol. 38, pp. 111–117.

1938. Environmental responses of vertebrates in the Great Basin. Amer. Midland Nat., vol. 19, pp. 1–206.

1949. Survival in birds banded at the Hastings Reservation. Condor, vol. 51, pp. 88–96.

1950. Observations on the Lawrence goldfinch. Condor, vol. 52, pp. 255–259.

1951. A list of the birds of Nevada. Condor, vol. 53, 228–249.

1957. Goldfinches on the Hastings Natural History Reservation. Amer. Midland Nat., vol. 57, pp. 1–119.

LINSDALE, JEAN MYRON, and LINSDALE, MARY ANN R.

1956. Birds banded on the Hastings Reservation, November 1937–April 1955. News from the Bird-Banders, vol. 31, pp. 5–6.

LINTON, CLARENCE BROCKMAN

1908a. Notes from San Clemente Island. Condor, vol. 10, pp. 82–86.

1908b. Notes from Santa Cruz Island. Condor, vol. 10, pp. 124–129.

1908c. *Pipilo clementae* excluded from Santa Cruz Island avifauna. Condor, vol. 10, p. 208.

LLOYD, HOYES

1944. The Birds of Ottawa, 1944. Canadian Field-Nat., vol. 58, p. 172.

LLOYD, WILLIAM

1887. Birds of Tom Green and Concho counties, Texas. Auk, vol. 4, pp. 289–299.

LOETSCHER, FREDERICK W., JR.

1955. North American migrants in the state of Veracruz, Mexico: A summary. Auk, vol. 72, pp. 14–54.

LOGAN, STANLEY

1951. Cardinal, *Richmondena cardinalis*, assists in feeding of robins. Auk, vol. 68, pp. 516–517.

Long, W. S.
1936. Golden-crowned sparrow in Zion National Park. Condor, vol. 38, pp. 89–90.
Longstreet, Robert James
1928. Migration flight of goldfinches, kingbirds and nighthawks. Auk, vol. 45, pp. 229–230.
Loomis, Evarts G.
1945. Notes on birds of northern Newfoundland and Labrador. Auk, vol. 62, pp. 234–241.
Loomis, Leverett Mills
1885. Supplementary notes on the ornithology of Chester County, South Carolina. Auk, vol. 2, pp. 188–193.
1892. Further review of avian fauna of Chester Co., South Carolina. Auk, vol. 9, pp. 28–39.
1893. Description of a new junco from California. Auk, vol. 10, pp. 47–48.
1894. Point Pinos junco (*Junco hyemalis pinosus*). Auk, vol. 11, pp. 265–266.
Lovell, Harvey B.
1948. The removal of bands by cardinals. Bird-Banding, vol. 19, pp. 71–72.
Lowery, George H., Jr.
1945. Trans-Gulf spring migration of birds and the coastal hiatus. Wilson Bull., vol. 57, pp. 92–118.
1946. Evidence of trans-Gulf migration. Auk, vol. 63, pp. 175–211.
1947. Additions to the lists of the birds of Louisiana. Univ. of Kansas Mus. Nat. Hist. Publ., vol. 1, No. 9, pp. 179–192.
1955. Louisiana birds.
1960. Louisiana birds, 2nd ed.
Lowther, J. K.
1961. Polymorphism in the white-throated sparrow, *Zonotrichia albicollis* (Gmelin). Canadian Journ. Zool., vol. 39, pp. 281–292.
1962. Colour and behavioural polymorphism in the white-throated sparrow, *Zonotrichia albicollis* (Gmelin). Ph.D. thesis, Univ. of Toronto.
Lucas, Frederic Augustus
1891. Some bird skeletons from Guadalupe Island. Auk, vol. 8, pp. 218–222.
Ludlow, William
1875. Report of a reconnaissance of the Black Hills of Dakota, made in the summer of 1874. Ornith. Tracts, No. 52, pp. 85–102.
MacDonald, S. D.
1953. Report on biological investigations at Alert, N.W.T. Nat. Mus. Canada Bull., vol. 128, pp. 241–256.
1954. Report on biological investigations at Mould Bay, Prince Patrick Island, N.W.T., in 1952. Nat. Mus. Canada Bull., vol. 132, pp. 214–238.
MacFarlane, Roderick Ross
1891. Notes on and list of birds and eggs collected in Arctic America, 1861–1866. Proc. U.S. Nat. Mus., vol. 14, p. 440.
1908. *In* Mair and MacFarlane, Through the Mackenzie Basin, p. 398.
MacKay, George H.
1929. A spider (*Argiope aurantia*) and a bird (*Astragalinus tristis tristis*). Auk, vol. 46, pp. 123–124.

MACOUN, JOHN
1900–1904. Catalogue of Canadian birds.
MACOUN, JOHN, and MACOUN, JAMES M.
1909. Catalogue of Canadian birds, ed. 2.
MACOUN, W. T.
1899. Ornithological notes. Ottawa Nat., vol. 13, pp. 195–196.
MAGEE, MICHAEL JARDEN
1924. Notes on the purple finch (*Carpodacus purpureus purpureus*). Auk, vol. 41, pp. 606–610.
1926a. An exoneration of the purple finch. Wilson Bull., vol. 38, pp. 167–168.
1926b. Notes on the evening grosbeak. Wilson Bull., vol. 38, pp. 170–172.
1927. Bull. N.E. Bird-Banding Assoc., p. 101.
1928a. Spring molt of the evening grosbeak. Bull. N.E. Bird-Banding Assoc., vol. 4, pp. 149–152.
1928b. Evening grosbeak recoveries. Bull. N.E. Bird-Banding Assoc., vol. 4, pp. 56–59.
1930. More notes on the spring moult of the evening grosbeak. Bird-Banding, vol. 1, pp. 43–45.
1932. Some banding results after eleven years of banding at Sault Ste. Marie, Michigan, 1921–1931. Bird-Banding, vol. 3, pp. 111–113.
1939. Notes on the sex ratio and the age of the eastern evening grosbeak. Bird-Banding, vol. 10, p. 161.
MAHAN, HAROLD D.
1956. Nocturnal predation on song sparrow eggs by milksnake. Wilson Bull., vol. 68, p. 245.
MAHER, W. J.
1959. Habitat distribution of birds breeding along the upper Kaolak River, Northern Alaska. Condor, vol. 61, pp. 351–368.
1964. Growth rate and development of endothermy in the snow bunting (*Plectrophenax nivalis*) and Lapland longspur (*Calcarius lapponicus*) at Barrow, Alaska. Ecology, vol. 45, pp. 520–528.
MAILLARD, JOHN W.
1921. Notes on the nesting of the Yosemite fox sparrow, calliope hummingbird and western wood pewee at Lake Tahoe, California. Condor, vol. 23, pp. 73–77.
MAILLIARD, JOSEPH
1899. Spring notes on the birds of Santa Cruz Island, Cal., April, 1898. Condor, vol. 1, pp. 41–45.
1900. Land birds of Marin County, Cal. Condor, vol. 2, pp. 62–68.
1912. Notes from the San Joaquin Valley. Condor, vol. 14, p. 74.
1919a. Notes from the Feather River country and Sierra Valley, California. Condor, vol. 21, pp. 74–77.
1919b. Fly-catching birds. Condor, vol. 21, p. 212.
1921. Extension of breeding range of marsh sparrow and Monterey hermit thrush. Condor, vol. 23, pp. 164–165.
1922. Further record of Savannah sparrow in California. Condor, vol. 24, pp. 95–96.
1923. Expedition of the California Academy of Sciences to the Gulf of California in 1921. The birds. Proc. California Acad. Sci., ser. 4, vol. 12, pp. 443–456.
1926a. A first experience in bird banding. Condor, vol. 28, pp. 70–73.
1926b. A California pygmy owl bathes. Condor, vol. 28, p. 171.

1927. Banding of Gambel sparrows in fall of 1926. Condor, vol. 29, pp. 98–100.

1929a. Reaction toward capture among certain sparrows. Condor, vol. 31, pp. 239–241.

1929b. Golden-crowned sparrow without the gold. Condor, vol. 31, pp. 37–38.

1932. Observations on the head markings of the golden-crowned sparrow. Condor, vol. 34, pp. 66–70.

1936. Poor selection of building sites. Condor, vol. 38, p. 249.

MAILLIARD, JOSEPH, and GRINNELL, JOSEPH

1905. Midwinter birds on the Mojave Desert. Condor, vol. 7, pp. 71–77, 101–102.

MAIN, JOHN SMITH

1937. Lapland longspurs in Wisconsin in summer. Auk, vol. 54, p. 546.

MALCOMSON, RICHARD O.

1960. Mallophaga from birds of North America. Wilson Bull., vol. 72, pp. 182–197.

MANNING, T. H., HÖHN, E. O., and MACPHERSON, A. H.

1956. The birds of Banks Island. Nat. Mus. Canada Bull., vol. 143.

MANNING, THOMAS HENRY

1948. Notes on the country, birds and mammals west of Hudson Bay between Reindeer and Baker lakes. Canadian Field-Nat., vol. 62, pp. 1–28.

1949. A summer on Hudson Bay with an appendix on the birds of northwestern Ungava.

1952. Birds of the west James Bay and southern Hudson Bay coasts. Nat. Mus. Canada Bull., vol. 125.

MANNING, THOMAS HENRY, and MACPHERSON, ANDREW HALL

1952. Birds of the east James Bay coast between Long Point and Cape Jones. Canadian Field-Nat., vol. 66.

1961. A biological investigation of Prince of Wales Island, N.W.T. Trans. Royal Canadian Inst., vol. 33, pp. 116–239.

MANVILLE, RICHARD HYDE

1941. Crossbills breeding in northern Michigan. Wilson Bull., vol. 53, pp. 240–241.

MANWELL, R. D., and HERMAN, C. M.

1935. Notes on eastern song sparrow repeats. Bird-Banding, vol. 6, pp. 133–134.

MARBLE, RICHARD M.

1926. Nesting of evening grosbeak at Woodstock, Vermont. Auk, vol. 43, p. 549.

MARIE-VICTORIN, FRÉRE

1935. Flore Laurentienne, p. 522.

MARKLE, JESS M.

1946. A nesting site of the lark sparrow. Condor, vol. 48, pp. 245–246.

MARLER, PETER, and ISAAC, DONALD

1960. Physical analysis of a simple bird song as exemplified by the chipping sparrow. Condor, vol. 62, pp. 124–135.

MARLER, PETER, KREITH, MARCIA, and TAMURA, MIWAKO

1962. Song development in hand-raised Oregon juncos. Auk, vol. 79, pp. 12–30.

MARSH, CHARLES H.

1885. Notes from Silver City, N.M. Ornith. and Ool., vol. 10, pp. 163–165.

MARSH, ERNEST G., JR., and STEVENSON, JAMES OSBORNE

1938. Bird records from northern Coahuila. Auk, vol. 55, pp. 286–287.

MARSHALL, A. J.

1951. The refractory period of testis rhythm in birds and its possible bearing on breeding and migration. Wilson Bull., vol. 63, pp. 238–261.

1952. The interstitial cycle in relation to autumn and winter sexual behaviour in birds. Proc. Zool. Soc. London, vol. 121, pp. 727–740.

MARSHALL, JOE T., JR.

1942. Food and habitat of the spotted owl. Condor, vol. 44, pp. 66–67.

1948. Ecologic races of song sparrows in the San Francisco Bay region, pt. I. Habitat and abundance. Condor, vol. 50, pp. 193–215, 233–256.

1956. Summer birds of the Rincon Mountains, Saguaro National Monument, Arizona. Condor, vol. 58, pp. 81–97.

1957. Birds of pine-oak woodland in southern Arizona and adjacent Mexico. Pacific Coast Avifauna, No. 32.

1960. Interrelations of Abert and brown towhees. Condor, vol. 62, pp. 49–64.

1964. Voice in communication and relationships among brown towhees. Condor, vol. 66, pp. 345–356.

MARSHALL, JOE T., JR., and BEHLE, WILLIAM HARROUN

1942. The song sparrows of the Virgin River Valley, Utah. Condor, vol. 44, pp. 122–124.

MARSHALL, WILLIAM H., and LEATHAM, LYNDON J.

1942. Birds of the Great Salt Lake Islands. Auk, vol. 59, pp. 35–46.

MARTIN, ALEXANDER C., ZIM, HERBERT S., and NELSON, ARNOLD L.

1951. American wildlife and plants.

MARTIN, E. W.

1939. Notes from the Palo Alto sports club. Condor, vol. 41, pp. 124–125.

MARTIN, N. D.

1960. An analysis of bird populations in relation to forest succession in Algonquin Provincial Park, Ontario. Ecology, vol. 41, pp. 126–140.

MARTIN, PAUL S., ROBINS, C. RICHARD, and HEED, WILLIAM B.

1954. Birds and biogeography of the Sierra de Tamaulipas, an isolated pine-oak habitat. Wilson Bull., vol. 66, pp. 38–57.

MASON, EDWIN A.

1938a. A loggerhead shrike captures a field sparrow while in mid air. Bird-Banding, vol. 9, p. 103.

1938b. Migrating swamp sparrows at Groton, Massachusetts. Bird-Banding, vol. 9, pp. 157–158.

MATHEWS, F. SCHUYLER

1904. Field book of wild birds and their music.

MAYNARD, C. J.

1874. The birds of Florida, pt. 3, p. 88.

1875. A naturalist's trip to Florida. Rod and Gun, vol. 6, pp. 342–343, 358.

1881. The birds of eastern North America.

1882. Ornithological notes from the Magdalen Islands. Quart. Journ. Boston Zool. Soc., No. 1, pp. 52–53.

1890. Eggs of North American birds.

1896. Handbook of sparrows and finches, etc., of New England, p. 71.

MAYR, ERNST

1933. Birds collected during the Whitney South Sea Expedition. XXVII. Notes on the variation of immature and adult plumages in birds and a physiological explanation of abnormal plumages. Amer. Mus. Nov., No. 666, pp. 1–10.

1946. History of the North American bird fauna. Wilson Bull., vol. 58, pp. 1–41.

MCATEE, WALDO LEE

1908. Food habits of the grosbeaks. U.S. Dep. Agric., Biol. Surv., Bull. No. 32.

1911. Economic ornithology in recent entomological publications (rev.). Auk, vol. 28, pp. 138–142.

1913. Economic ornithology in recent entomological publications. Auk, vol. 30, pp. 128–132.

1926. The relation of birds to woodlots in New York State. Roosevelt Wild Life Bull., vol. 4.

1957. The folk-names of Canadian birds. Nat. Mus. Canada Bull., No. 149.

MCCABE, THOMAS TONKIN

1943. An aspect of collectors' technique. Auk, vol. 60, pp. 550–558.

MCCABE, THOMAS TONKIN, and MCCABE, ELINOR BOLLES

1927. Analysis of sexes in a junco migration. Condor, vol. 29, pp. 272–273.

1928a. The plumage of the pine siskin. Condor, vol. 30, pp. 221–227.

1928b. Song sparrows endure a severe winter. Condor, vol. 30, p. 358.

1929. Economic status of the pine siskin. Condor, vol. 31, pp. 126–127.

1933. Notes on the anatomy and breeding habits of crossbills. Condor, vol. 35, pp. 136–147.

MCCLURE, H. ELLIOTT

1962. Ten years and 10,000 birds. Bird-Banding, vol. 33, pp 1–21, 69–84.

MCCOWN, JOHN P.

1851. *In* Lawrance's descriptions of new species of birds. Ann. Lyc. Nat. Hist. New York, vol. 5, pp. 121–124.

MCCREARY, OTTO

1939. Wyoming bird life, rev. ed., p. 97.

MCCREARY, OTTO C., and MICKEY, ARTHUR B.

1935. Bird migration records from southeastern Wyoming. Wilson Bull., vol. 47, pp. 129–156.

MCCRIMMON, A. R.

1926. Dickcissel in western Colorado. Auk, vol. 43, p. 550.

MCEWEN, EOIN H.

1957. Birds observed at Bathurst Inlet, Northwest Territories. Canadian Field-Nat., vol. 71, pp. 109–115.

MCGREGOR, RICHARD C.

1898a. Young plumages of Mexican birds. Auk, vol. 15, pp. 264–265.

1898b. Description of a new *Ammodramus* from Lower California. Auk, vol. 15, pp. 265–267.

1900a. Description of a new *Pipilo*. Condor, vol. 2, p. 43.

1900b. A list of unrecorded albinos. Condor, vol. 2, pp. 86–88.

1901a. A list of the land birds of Santa Cruz County, California. Pacific Coast Avifauna, No. 2.

1901b. New Alaskan birds. Condor, vol. 3, p. 8.

1903. The number of feathers in a bird skin. Condor, vol. 5, p. 17.

McGregor, Richard C.—Continued
1906. Birds observed in the Krenitzin Islands, Alaska. Condor, vol. 8. pp. 114–122.
McHugh, Thomas C.
1948. A nesting census from the subalpine belt of Colorado. Condor, vol. 50, pp. 227–228.
McIlhenny, E. A.
1942. Results of 1940 bird banding at Avery Island, Louisiana, with special account of a new banding method. Bird-Banding, vol. 13, pp. 19–28.
McIlroy, Mrs. Malcolm
1961. Possible hybridization between a clay colored sparrow and a chipping sparrow at Ithaca. Kingbird, vol. 11, pp. 7–10.
McKee, Edwin D.
1934. Pinyon nuts as bird feed. Grand Canyon Nature Notes, vol. 9, pp. 272–273.
McLaughlin, Vincent P., Jr.
1948. Birds in an Army camp. Auk, vol. 65, pp. 180–188.
McMannama, Zella
1948. Notes on evening grosbeaks. Murrelet, vol. 29, p. 27.
McMinn, H. E.
1939. An illustrated manual of California shrubs.
Meade, Gordon Montgomery
1942. Calcium chloride—a death lure for crossbills. Auk, vol. 59, p. 439.
Meadows, Donald Charles
1930. Bird notes from Santa Catalina Island. Condor, vol. 32, pp. 211–212.
Meanley, Brooke
1959. Notes on Bachman's sparrow in central Louisiana. Auk, vol. 76, pp. 232–234.
Meanley, Brooke, and Neff, Johnson A.
1953. Bird notes from the Grand Prairie of Arkansas. Wilson Bull., vol. 65, pp. 200–201.
Mearns, Edgar A.
1879. Notes on some of the less hardy winter residents in the Hudson River Valley. Bull. Nuttall Ornith. Club, vol. 4, pp. 33–37.
1880. A list of the birds of the Hudson Highlands, with annotations. Bull. Essex Inst., vol. 11, pp. 200–201.
1890a. Descriptions of a new species and three new subspecies of birds from Arizona. Auk. vol. 7, pp. 243–251.
1890b. Observations on the avifauna of portions of Arizona. Auk, vol. 7, pp. 251–264.
1898. Descriptions of two new birds from the Santa Barbara Islands, southern California. Auk, vol. 15, pp. 258–264.
1902. Descriptions of three new birds from the southern United States. Proc. U.S. Nat. Mus., vol. 24, pp. 915–926.
1903. Feathers beside the Styx. Condor, vol. 5, pp. 36–38.
Mecking, Ludwig
1925. Die Polarander; *In* Nordenskjöld, The geography of the Polar Regions. Amer. Geographical Soc., Spec. Publ. No. 8, pp. 326–338.
Mengel, Robert M.
1951. A flight-song of Bachman's sparrow. Wilson Bull., vol. 63, pp. 208–209.

MERREM, BLASIUS
1786. Avium Rar. icines et descript, vol. 2, p. 37. (Latin ed. of Beytrage zur besondern Geschichte der Vögel.)

MERRIAM, CLINTON HART
1877. A review of the birds of Connecticut with remarks on their habits. Trans. Connecticut Acad., vol. 4, pp. 1–150.
1878. Breeding of the pine linnet in northern New York. Forest and Stream, vol. 10, p. 463.
1885. Bird Migration at the Straits of Mackinac. Auk, vol. 2, pp. 64–65.
1890. Annotated list of birds of the San Francisco Mountain plateau and the desert of the Little Colorado River, Arizona. U.S. Dep. Agric., North Amer. Fauna, No. 3, part 4, p. 97.

MERRILL, JAMES CUSHING
1879. Notes on the ornithology of southern Texas, being a list of birds observed in the vicinity of Fort Brown, Texas, from February, 1876, to June, 1878. Proc. U.S. Nat. Mus., vol. 1, pp. 118–173.
1880. Notes on the winter plumage of *Leucosticte tephrocotis*, Sw., and *L. tephrocotis* var. *littoralis*, Bd. Bull. Nuttall Ornith. Club, vol. 5, pp. 75–77.
1881. Oölogical notes from Montana. Bull. Nuttall Ornith. Club, vol. 6, pp. 203–207.
1888. Notes on the birds of Fort Klamath, Oregon. Auk, vol. 5, p. 359.
1898. Notes on the birds of Fort Sherman, Idaho. Auk, vol. 15, pp. 14–22.

MEWALDT, LEONARD RICHARD
1950. Bird records from western Montana. Condor, vol. 52, pp. 238–239.
1960. Recoveries and longevity. News from the Bird-Banders, vol. 35, p. 27.
1962. Displacement of white-crowned sparrows. Western Bird Bander, vol. 37, pp. 4–6.
1963a. California "crowned" sparrows return from Louisiana. Western Bird Bander, vol. 38, pp. 1–4.
1963b. Effects of bird removal on a winter population of sparrows. Bird-Banding, vol. 35, pp. 184–195.

MEWALDT, LEONARD RICHARD, and FARNER, DONALD SANKEY
1957. Translocated golden-crowned sparrows return to winter range. Condor, vol. 59, pp. 268–269.

MICHAEL, CHARLES W.
1925. Additional information concerning the birds of Yosemite Valley. Condor, vol. 27, pp. 109–113.
1927. Pigmy owl: the little demon. Condor, vol. 29, pp. 161–162.

MICHAEL, ENID
1926. Color camouflage in birds. Yosemite Nat. Notes, vol. 5, p. 3.
1928. The cherry hedge and feeding birds. Yosemite Nat. Notes, vol. 7, pp. 105–106.

MICHENER, HAROLD
1925a. Polygamy practiced by the house finch. Condor, vol. 27, p. 116.
1925b. Banding purple finches in Pasadena. Condor, vol. 27, pp. 217–223.

MICHENER, HAROLD, and MICHENER, JOSEPHINE R.
1931. Variation in color of male house finches. Condor, vol. 33, pp. 12–19.
1932. Colors induced in male house finches by repeated feather renewals. Condor, vol. 34, pp. 253–256.
1936. Abnormalities in birds. Condor, vol. 38, pp. 102–109.

MICHENER, HAROLD, and MICHENER, JOSEPHINE R.—Continued
1943. The spring molt of the Gambel sparrow. Condor, vol. 45, pp. 113–116.
MICHENER, JOSEPHINE R.
1926. Our baby song sparrow. Condor, vol. 28, pp. 65–67.
MICKEY, FRANCES WELTON
1943. Breeding habits of McCown's longspur. Auk, vol. 60, pp. 181–209.
MIDDLETON, MRS. ARCHIE
1899. Notes on the nesting of the blue grosbeak. The Nebraska Bird Rev., vol. 15, pp. 8–10.
MIDDLETON, RAYMOND J.
1956. Song sparrows at Norristown. Bird-Banding, vol. 27, pp. 73–76.
MIEROW, DOROTHY
1946. A distributional study of the pine siskin. Ann. Carnegie Mus., vol. 30, pp. 249–261.
MIKHEEV, A. V.
1939. Contributions to the biology of the Lapland longspur (*Calcarius lapponicus* L.). (In Russian) Publ. Acad. Sci. U.S.S.R., Zool. Journ. Moscow, vol. 18, No. 5, pp. 924–938.
MILLER, ALDEN HOLMES
1929. A new race of black-chinned sparrow from the San Francisco Bay district. Condor, vol. 31, pp. 205–207.
1932. The summer distributiou of certain birds in central and northern Arizona. Condor, vol. 34, pp. 96–99.
1934. Field experiences with mountain-dwelling birds of southern Utah. Wilson Bull., vol. 46, pp. 156–168.
1935. Some breeding birds of the Pine Forest Mountains, Nevada. Auk, vol. 52, pp. 467–468.
1936. The identification of juncos banded in the Rocky Mountain States. Bird-Lore, vol. 38, pp. 429–433.
1938. Hybridization of juncos in captivity. Condor, vol. 40, pp. 92–93.
1939a. The breeding leucostictes of the Wallowa Mountains, Oregon. Condor, vol. 41, pp. 34–35.
1939b. Foraging dexterity of a lazuli bunting. Condor, vol. 41, pp. 255–256.
1939c. Status of the breeding Lincoln's sparrows of Oregon. Auk, vol. 56, pp. 342–343.
1940a. The pine grosbeak of the Cascade Mountains, Washington. Auk, vol. 57, pp. 420–421.
1940b. A hybrid between *Zonotrichia coronata* and *Zonotrichia leucophrys*. Condor, vol. 42, pp. 45–48.
1941a. The buccal food-carrying pouches of the rosy finch. Condor, vol. 43, pp. 72–73.
1941b. Speciation in the avian genus *Junco*. Univ. California Publ. Zool., vol. 44, pp. 173–434.
1941c. Rufous-crowned sparrow of southeastern New Mexico. Auk, vol. 58, p. 102.
1942. Shower bathing of a spotted towhee. Condor, vol. 44, p. 232.
1945. Further records of birds from central California. Condor, vol. 47, pp. 217–218.
1946. Vertebrate inhabitants of the piñon association in the Death Valley region. Ecology, vol. 27, pp. 54–60.
1948. White-winged junco parasitized by cowbird. Condor, vol. 50, p. 92.
1949. Some concepts of hybridization and intergradation in wild populations of birds. Auk, vol. 66, pp. 338–342.

1951a. The "rodent-run" of the green-tailed towhee. Ibis, vol. 93, pp. 307–308.

1951b. A comparison of the avifaunas of Santa Cruz and Santa Rosa Islands, California. Condor, vol. 53, pp. 117–123.

1951c. An analysis of the distribution of the birds of California. Univ. California Publ. Zool., vol. 50, pp. 531–644.

1955a. The avifauna of the Sierra del Carmen of Coahuila, Mexico. Condor, vol. 57, pp. 154–178.

1955b. The breeding range of the black rosy finch. Condor, vol. 57, pp. 306–307.

1956. Ecologic factors that accelerate formation of races and species of terrestrial vertebrates. Evolution, vol. 10, pp. 262–277.

1960. Adaptation of breeding schedule to latitude. Proc. XII Internat. Ornith. Congr., vol. 2, pp. 513–522.

MILLER, ALDEN HOLMES, DAVIS, JOHN, and JOHNSON, NED K.

1963. Notes and news. Condor, vol. 65, p. 448.

MILLER, ALDEN HOLMES, FRIEDMANN, HERBERT, GRISCOM, LUDLOW, and MOORE, ROBERT T.

1957. Distributional check-list of the birds of Mexico, part. 2. Pacific Coast Avifauna, No. 33.

MILLER, ALDEN HOLMES, and MCCABE, THOMAS TONKIN

1935. Racial differentiation in *Passerella* (*Melospiza*) *lincolnii*. Condor, vol. 37, pp. 144–160.

MILLER, ALDEN HOLMES, and STEBBINS, R. C.

1964. The lives of desert animals in Joshua Tree National Monument.

MILLER, FREDERIC W.

1925. The nest and eggs of the black rosy finch. Condor, vol. 27, pp. 3–7.

MILLER, G. S., JR.

1888. Description of an apparently new *Poocaetes* from Oregon. Auk, vol. 5, pp. 404–405.

MILLER, JOHN M.

1903. Late nesting of Arkansas goldfinch. Condor, vol. 5, p. 19.

MILLER, LOYE HOLMES

1904. The birds of the John Day region, Oregon. Condor, vol. 6, pp. 100–106.

1920. Unusual conditions for southern California. Condor, vol. 22, p. 78.

1921. The biography of Nip and Tuck. Condor, vol. 23, pp. 41–47.

1952. Auditory recognition of predators. Condor, vol. 54, pp. 89–92.

MILLER, OLIVE THORNE

1904. With the birds in Maine.

MILLER, RICHARD F.

1911. Unusual nesting of the chipping sparrow. Oologist, vol. 28, pp. 87–88.

1923. Unusual nesting site of the chipping sparrow. Oologist, vol. 40, p. 152.

1933. The breeding birds of Philadelphia, Pa. Oologist, vol. 50, pp. 86–95.

MILLER, W. DE W.

1904. Breeding of the dickcissel in New Jersey. Auk, vol. 21, p. 487.

MILLS, DORIS HUESTIS

1937. European goldfinch at Hanover, New Hampshire. Auk, vol. 54, pp. 544–545.

MINOT, HENRY DAVIS

1880. Notes on Colorado birds. Bull Nuttall Ornith. Club. vol. 5, pp. 223–232.

MITCHELL, H. HEDLEY

1924. Birds of Saskatchewan. Canadian Field-Nat., vol. 38, pp. 101-118.

MITCHELL, MARGARET H.

1946. Dickcissel at Streetsville, Peel County, Ontario. Canadian Field-Nat., vol. 60, p. 136.

MITCHELL, WALTON I.

1898. The summer birds of San Miguel County, Mexico. Auk, vol. 15, pp. 306-311.

MONSON, GALE, and PHILLIPS, ALLAN R.

1941. Bird records from southern and western Arizona. Condor, vol. 43, pp. 108-112.

MONSON, GALE W.

1934. The birds of Berlin and Harwood Townships, Cass County, North Dakota. Wilson Bull., vol. 46, pp. 37-58.

1936. Bird notes from the Papago Indian Reservation, southern Arizona. Condor, vol. 38, pp. 175-176.

1942. Notes on some birds of southeastern Arizona. Condor, vol. 44, pp. 222-225.

1947. Botteri's sparrow in Arizona. Auk, vol. 64, pp. 139-140.

1951. [Note on Lawrence goldfinch.] Audubon Field Notes, vol. 5, pp. 34, 222.

1952a. [Note on Lawrence goldfinch.] Audubon Field Notes, vol. 6, p. 33.

1952b. [Note on evening grosbeak.] Audubon Field Notes, vol. 6, p. 210.

1954. [Note on Lawrence goldfinch.] Audubon Field Notes, vol. 8, pp. 35, 264.

1960. [Regional report from the] Southeast region. Audubon Field Notes, vol. 14, pp. 329-332.

MONTAGNA, WILLIAM

1940a. European goldfinch in New York. Auk, vol. 57, pp. 575-576.

1940b. The Acadian sharp-tailed sparrows of Popham Beach, Maine. Wilson Bull., vol. 52, pp. 191-197.

1942a. The sharp-tailed sparrows of the Atlantic Coast. Wilson Bull., vol. 54, pp. 107-120.

1942b. Additional notes on Atlantic Coast sharp-tailed sparrows. Wilson Bull., vol. 54, p. 256.

MONTGOMERY, THOMAS HARRISON, JR.

1905. Summer resident birds of Brewster County, Texas. Auk, vol. 22, pp. 12-15.

MONTGOMERY, VESTER

1953. The Leconte sparrow in New Mexico. Condor, vol. 55, p. 277.

MOODY, CHARLES STUART

1910. The nesting of Hepburn's rosy finch. Bird-Lore, vol. 12, pp. 108-110.

MOORE, ROBERT THOMAS

1912. The least sandpiper during the nesting season in the Magdalen Islands. Auk, vol. 29, pp. 210-223.

1913. The fox sparrow as a songster. Auk, vol. 30, pp. 177-187.

1939. A review of the house finches of the subgenus *Burrica*. Condor, vol. 41, pp. 177-205.

1946. The rufous-winged sparrow, its legends and taxonomic status. Condor, vol. 48, pp. 117-123.

MOORE, WILLIAM H.

1902. The winter Fringillidae of New Brunswick. Auk, vol. 19, pp. 199-202.

MORGAN, ALLEN, and EMERY, RUTH PRICE
1956. Winter season: Northeastern maritime region. Audobon Field Notes, vol. 10, pp. 234–236.

MORIARTY, L. J.
1965. A study of the breeding biology of the chestnut-collared longspur (*Calcarius ornatus*) in northeastern South Dakota. South Dakota Bird Notes, vol. 17, pp. 76–79.

MORRELL, CLARENCE HENRY
1899. Some winter birds of Nova Scotia. Auk, vol. 16, pp. 250–253.

MORRIS, GEORGE SPENCER
1895. Notes and extracts from a letter of Edward Harris. Auk, vol. 12, pp. 225–231.

MORRIS, R. O.
1909. *Ammodramus nelsoni subvirgatus*. Auk, vol. 26, p. 84.

MORRISON, CHARLES F.
1888. A list of some birds of La Plata County, Colorado, with annotations. Ornith. and Ool., vol. 13, p. 73.
1889. A list of the birds of Colorado. Ornith. and Ool., vol. 14, p. 149.

MORSE, ALBERT P.
1920. At a food-shelf. Bull. Essex County Ornith. Club, vol. 2, pp. 12–14.

MORSE, MINOT C., JR.
1959. Clay-colored sparrow banded in Maine. Maine Field Nat., vol. 15, p. 99.

MOUSLEY, HENRY
1916. Five years personal notes and observations on the birds of Hatley, Stanstead County, Quebec—1911–1915. Auk, vol. 33, pp. 168–186.
1930a. The home life of the American goldfinch. Canadian Field-Nat., vol. 44, p. 177.
1930b. A further study of the home life of the American goldfinch. Canadian Field-Nat., vol. 44, p. 206.

MUMFORD, RUSSELL E.
1953. Unusual nest of the red-eyed towhee. Indiana Audubon Quart., vol. 31, pp. 15–16.

MUNRO, JAMES ALEXANDER
1919. Notes on the breeding habits of the red crossbill in the Okanagan Valley, British Columbia. Condor, vol. 21, pp. 57–60.
1927. Observations on the double-crested cormorant (*Phalacrocorax avritus*) on Lake Manitoba. Canadian Field-Nat., vol., 41, pp. 102–108.
1929a. Glimpses of little-known western lakes and their bird life. Canadian Field-Nat., vol. 43, pp. 204–205.
1929b. Notes on the food habits of certain raptores in British Columbia and Alberta. Condor, vol. 31, pp. 112–116.
1930. Miscellaneous notes on some British Columbia birds. Condor, vol. 32, pp. 65–68.
1935. Bird life at Horse Lake, British Columbia. Condor, vol. 37, pp. 185–193.
1940. Food of the sharp-shinned hawk. Condor, vol. 42, pp. 168–169.
1950. The birds and mammals of the Creston region, British Columbia. Occas. Pap. British Columbia Prov. Mus., No. 8.

MUNRO, JONATHAN ALEXANDER, and COWAN, IAN MCTAGGART
1947. A review of the bird fauna of British Columbia. British Columbia Provin. Mus., Dept. Educ., Spec. Publ. No. 2.

646–737—68—pt. 3——33

Murdock, James, and Cogswell, Howard L.

1942. Foothill chaparral (breeding bird census in). Audubon Mag., sect. 2, p. 21.

Murie, Olaus J.

1944. Two new subspecies of birds from Alaska. Condor, vol. 46, pp. 121–123.

1959. Fauna of the Aleutian Islands and Alaska Peninsula. North Amer. Fauna, No. 61.

Murphey, Eugene Edmund

1937. Observations on the bird life of the middle Savannah Valley, 1890–1937. Contr. Charleston Mus., No. 9.

Murphy, Robert Cushman

1945. Middle 19th-century introduction of British birds to Long Island, N.Y. Auk, vol. 62, p. 306.

Murray, James Joseph

1941. Notes from Princess Anne County, Virginia. Auk, vol. 58, pp. 108–109.

Musselman, Thomas E.

1923. Bird-banding at Thomasville, Ga., 1923. Auk, vol. 40, p. 448.

Myers, Harriet Williams

1909. Nesting habits of the rufous-crowned sparrow. Condor, vol. 11, pp. 131–134.

1910. Notes on regurgitation. Condor, vol. 12, pp. 165–167.

1922. Western birds.

Nakamura, Yukio

1941. Food habits of wild birds (in Japanese). Yacho, vol. 8, pp. 205–210.

Nash, C. W.

1891–92. *In* Report of the occurrence of the evening grosbeak . . . in Ontario. Trans. Canadian Inst., vol. 3, p. 118.

Nauman, E. D.

1929. Birds and snakes. Bird-Lore, vol. 31, pp. 330–331.

Nehrling Henry

1896. Our native birds of song and beauty, vol. 2.

Neilson, James A.

1925. Bird notes from Wheatland, Wyoming. Condor, vol. 27, pp. 72–73.

Nelson, Bernard A.

1944. Flight speed of snow bunting. Flicker, vol. 16, p. 37.

Nelson, Edward William

1875. Notes on birds observed in portions of Utah, Nevada, and California. Proc. Boston Soc. Nat. Hist., vol. 17, pp. 338–365.

1876. Birds of north-eastern Illinois. Bull. Essex Inst., vol. 8, pp. 90–155.

1881. Door-yard birds of the far-north. Bull. Nuttall Ornith. Club, vol. 6, pp. 1–6.

1887. Report upon natural history collections made in Alaska between the years 1877 and 1881. U.S. Sig. Serv. Arctic Ser. No. 3, pt. 1, Birds of Alaska.

1922. Lower California and its natural resources. Mem. Nat. Acad. Sci., vol. 16, No. 1

Nelson, Thomas H., Clarke, W. Eagle, and Boyes, F.

1907. The birds of Yorkshire, 2 vols.

Nero, Robert W.

1956. Golden-crowned sparrow found in Saskatchewan. Blue Jay, vol. 14, pp. 79–80.

1963. Birds of the Lake Athabasca region, Saskatchewan. Saskatchewan Nat. Hist. Soc., Spec. Publ. No. 5.

NEWMAN, ROBERT JAMES
1957. [Regional report from the] Central southern region. Audubon Field Notes, vol. 11, pp. 409–413.

NEWTON, ALFRED
1864. Ootheca Wolleyana: an illustrated catalogue of the collection of bird's eggs, vol. 1.
1893–96. A dictionary of birds.
1907. Ootheca Wolleyana: an illustrated catalogue of the collection of bird's eggs, vol. 2.

NIBE, TOKUTARO
1918. Bird damage to farm crops in snow fields in Akita Prefecture (in Japanese). Tori, vol. 7, pp. 126–127.

NICE, MARGRET M.
1929a. The Harris sparrow in central Oklahoma. Condor, vol. 31, pp. 57–61.
1929b. Vocal performances of the rock sparrow in Oklahoma. Condor, vol. 31, pp. 248–249.
1931. The birds of Oklahoma, rev. ed. Publ. Univ. Oklahoma, Biol. Surv., vol. 3, No. 1.
1933. Migratory behavior in song sparrows. Condor, vol. 35, pp. 219–224.
1936. The cowbird as a subject of study (abstract of paper read). Wilson Bull., vol. 48, p. 60.
1937a. Curious ways of the cowbird. Bird-Lore, vol. 39, pp. 196–201.
1937b. Studies in the life history of the song sparrow. 1. A population study of the song sparrow. Trans. Linn. Soc. New York, vol. 4.
1939a. Territorial song and non-territorial behavior of goldfinches in Ohio. Wilson Bull., vol. 51, p. 123.
1939b. The watcher at the nest.
1943. Studies in the life history of the song sparrow. 2. The behavior of the song sparrow and other passerines. Trans. Linn. Soc. New York, vol. 6.
1945. How many times does a song sparrow sing one song. Auk, vol. 62, p. 302.
1946. Weights of resident and winter visitant song sparrows in central Ohio. Condor, vol. 48, pp. 41–42.
1948. Song sparrows at Wintergreen Lake. Jack-Pine Warbler, vol. 26, pp. 143–151.

NICE, MARGARET MORSE, and NICE, LEONARD BLAINE
1922. Some new birds for Oklahoma. Condor, vol. 24, p. 181.
1924. The birds of Oklahoma. Univ. Oklahoma Bull., new ser., No. 20.

NICE, MARGARET MORSE, and PELKWYK, JOOST TER
1940. "Anting" by the song sparrow. Auk, vol. 57, pp. 520–522.
1941. Enemy recognition by the song sparrow. Auk, vol. 58, pp. 195–214.

NICHOLS, CHARLES KETCHAM
1948. Montana junco in New York. Auk, vol. 65, pp. 138–139.
1956. Winter season: Hudson-St. Lawrence region. Audubon Field Notes, vol. 10, pp. 236–240.

NICHOLS, JOHN TREADWELL
1925. The season: New York region. Bird-Lore, vol. 27, pp. 111–113.
1936. European goldfinch near New York City, 1915-1935. Auk, vol. 53, pp. 429–431.
1954. On white-throated sparrow plumages. Bird-Banding, vol. 25, p. 60.

NICHOLS, JOHN TREADWELL—Continued
1957. A medium-dull white-throated sparrow in its seventh winter. Bird-Banding, vol. 28, p. 160.
NICHOLS, L. NELSON
1936. *In* Pearson, T. Gilbert, Birds of America, pt. 2.
NICHOLSON, DONALD J.
1928. Nesting habits of the seaside sparrows in Florida. Wilson Bull., vol. 40, pp. 225–237.
1938. An historical trip to Cape Sable. Florida Nat., vol. 11, pp. 41–44.
1946. Smyrna seaside sparrow. Florida Nat., vol. 19, pp. 39–42.
1950. Disappearance of Smyrna seaside sparrow from its former haunts. Florida Nat., vol. 23, p. 104.
NICHOLSON, E. M.
1930. Field-notes on Greenland birds, pt. 2. Ibis, ser. 12, vol. 6, pp. 395–428.
NICHOLSON, WRAY H.
1936. Notes on the habits of the Florida grasshopper sparrow. Auk, vol. 53, pp. 318–319.
NICKELL, WALTER PRINE
1951. Studies of habitats, territory and nests of the eastern goldfinch. Auk, vol. 68, pp. 447–470.
NIEDRACH, ROBERT JAMES, and ROCKWELL, ROBERT BLANCHARD
1939. The birds of Denver and mountain parks. Colorado Mus. Pop. Ser. No. 5.
NIETHAMMER, GÜNTHER
1937. Handbuch der deutschen Vogelkunde, vol. 1, Passeres.
NIGHSWONGER, PAUL
1959. Eleven years of banding. Scissortail, vol. 9, p. 43.
NOLAN, VAL, JR.
1958. Singing by female indigo bunting and rufous-sided towhee. Wilson Bull., vol. 70, pp. 287–288.
1961. A method of netting birds at open nests in trees. Auk, vol. 78, pp. 643–645.
NORRIS, J. PARKER
1887. Discovery of the eggs of the evening grosbeak. Ornith. and Ool., vol. 12, p. 144.
NORRIS, ROBERT A.
1951. Distribution and populations of summer birds in southwestern Georgia. Occas. Publ. Georgia Ornith. Soc. No. 2.
1953. Chipping sparrows at Tifton: a note on weights and foot-pox in early spring. Oriole, vol. 18, p. 46.
1954. New information on the white-crowned sparrow in southern Georgia. Oriole, vol. 19, pp. 25–31.
1960. Density, racial composition, sociality and selective predation in nonbreeding populations of Savannah sparrows. Bird-Banding, vol. 31, No. 4, pp. 173–216.
1963. Birds of the AEC Savannah River plant area. Charleston Museum.
NORRIS, ROBERT A., and HIGHT, GORDON L., JR.
1957. Subspecific variation in winter populations of Savannah sparrows: A study in field taxonomy. Condor, vol. 59, pp. 40–52.
NORRIS, RUSSELL T.
1947. The cowbirds of Preston Frith. Wilson Bull., vol. 59, pp. 83–103.

NORTON, ARTHUR H.
1897. The sharp-tailed sparrows of Maine. Proc. Portland Soc. Nat. Hist., vol. 11, pp. 97–104.

NORTON, ARTHUR HERBERT
1904. Notes on the finches found in Maine. Journ. Maine Ornith. Soc., vol. 6, No. 1, pp. 3–5.
1918. The evening grosbeak (*Hesperiphona vespertina*) in Maine, with remarks on its distribution. Auk, vol. 35, pp. 170–181.
1927. Nesting of the Acadian sharp-tailed sparrow (*Passerherbulus nelsoni subvirgatus*) in Maine. Auk, vol. 44, pp. 568–570.

NOWELL, J. ROWLAND
1899. Song season of the Cardinal (*Cardinalis cardinalis*). Auk, vol. 16, p. 278.

NUTTALL, THOMAS
1832. A manual of the ornithology of the United States and of Canada. The land birds.
1840. A manual of the ornithology of the United States and of Canada.
1903. A manual of the ornithology of the United States and Canada.

OAKESON, BARBARA BLANCHARD
1954. The Gambel's sparrow at Mountain Village, Alaska. Auk, vol. 71, pp. 351–365.

OBERHOLSER, HARRY CHURCH
1903. The North American forms of *Astragalinus psaltria* (Say). Proc. Biol. Soc. Washington, vol. 16, pp. 113–116.
1911. Description of a new *Melospiza* from California. Proc. Biol. Soc. Washington, vol. 24, pp. 251–252.
1919a. Description of an interesting new junco from Lower California. Condor, vol. 21, pp. 119–120.
1919b. Description of a new subspecies of *Pipilo fuscus*. Condor, vol. 21, pp. 210–211.
1919c. A revision of the subspecies of *Passerculus rostratus* (Cassin). Ohio Journ. Sci., vol. 19, pp. 344–354.
1927. Our friend the cardinal. Cardinal, vol. 2.
1931a. *Ammospiza caudacuta diversa* (Bishop) a valid race. Auk, vol. 48, pp. 610–611.
1931b. The Atlantic coast races of *Thryospiza maritima* (Wilson). Proc. Biol. Soc. Washington, vol. 44, pp. 123–128.
1937. Descriptions of two new passerine birds from the western United States. Proc. Biol. Soc. Washington, vol. 50, pp. 117–119.
1938. The bird life of Louisiana. Dep. Conserv., Bull. 28.
1942. Description of a new Arizona race of the grasshopper sparrow. Proc. Biol. Soc. Washington, vol. 55, pp. 15–16.
1946. Three new North American birds. Journ. Washington Acad. Sci., vol. 36, pp. 388–389.

ODUM, E. P.
1950. Bird populations of the Highlands (North Carolina) Plateau in relation to plant succession and avian invasion. Ecology, vol. 31, pp. 587–605.
1958. The fat deposition picture in the white-throated sparrow in comparison with that in long-range migrants. Bird-Banding, vol. 29, pp. 105–108.
1960. Lipid deposition in nocturnal migrant birds. Proc. XII, Internat. Ornith. Congr., pp. 563–576.

ODUM, E. P., CONNELL, C. E., and STODDARD, H. L.
1961. Flight energy and estimated flight ranges of some migratory birds. Auk, vol. 78, pp. 515–527.
ODUM, EUGENE P., and HIGHT, GORDON L.
1957. The use of mist nets in population studies of winter fringillids on the AEC Savannah River area. Bird-Banding, vol. 28, pp. 203–213.
OLSEN, O. WILFORD
1939. *Dispharynx pipilonis,* a new spiruroid nematode from the red-eyed towhee. Amer. Midland Nat., vol. 21, pp. 472–475.
OLSEN, RICHARD E.
1935. Records of rare Michigan birds, 1934. Auk, vol. 52, pp. 100–101.
ORNITHOLOGICAL SOCIETY OF JAPAN
1942. A hand-list of the Japanese birds, 3d rev. ed.
1958. A hand-list of the Japanese birds, 4th and rev. ed.
ORR, VIRGINIA
1948. Notes on birds of Sandwich Bay and vicinity, Newfoundland Labrador. Auk, vol. 65, pp. 220–225.
ORTEGA, JAMES LEROY
1945. Lawrence goldfinch eating egg of mourning dove. Condor, vol. 47, p. 41.
OSBURN, PINGREE I.
1909. Notes on the birds of Los Coronados Islands, Lower California. Condor, vol. 11, pp. 134–138.
OSGOOD, WILFRED HUDSON
1903. A list of birds observed in Cochise County, Arizona. Condor, vol. 5, pp. 128–151.
OVER, WILLIAM HENRY, and CLEMENT, G. M.
1930. Nesting of the white-winged junco in the Black Hills of South Dakota. Wilson Bull., vol. 42, pp. 28–31.
PACKARD, FRED MALLERY
1939. Northern sage sparrow on the east slope of the Rockies in Colorado. Auk, vol. 56, pp. 481–482.
1945. The birds of Rocky Mountain National Park, Colorado. Auk, vol. 62, pp. 371–394.
PALMER, RALPH S., and REILLY, E. M., JR.
1956. A concise color standard. Published by A.O.U. Handbook Fund, Albany, N.Y., pp. 1–8.
PALMER, RALPH SIMON
1949. Maine birds. Bull. Mus. Comp. Zool., vol. 102.
1962. Handbook of North American birds, p. 4.
PALMER, ROBERT H.
1923. Notes from Mexico. Murrelet, vol. 4, pp. 12–15.
PALMER, WILLIAM
1899. The avifauna of the Pribilof Islands. The fur-seals and fur-seal islands, pt. 3, pp. 355–431.
PARK, PAUL J.
1936. Banding Harris's sparrow in its winter range; a preliminary report. Proc. Oklahoma Acad. Sci., vol. 16, pp. 29–32.
PARKES, KENNETH CARROLL
1954. Notes on some birds of the Adirondack and Catskill mountains. Ann. Carnegie Mus., vol. 33, pp. 149–178.
1957. The juvenal plumage of the finch genera *Atlapetes* and *Pipilo.* Auk, vol. 74, pp. 499–502.

PARKS, G. HAPGOOD, and PARKS, HAZEL C.
1963a. Some notes on a trip to an evening grosbeak nesting area. Bird-Banding, vol. 34, pp. 22–30.
1963b. Evening grosbeaks died to supply bands for this "jewelry." Bird-Banding, vol. 34, No. 2, pp. 73–86.
1965. Supplementary notes on an evening grosbeak nesting area study. Bird-Banding, vol. 36, pp. 113–115.

PARKS, GEORGE HAPGOOD
1946. Evening grosbeak observations. Maine Audubon Soc. Bull., vol. 2, pp. 71–74.
1947. The evening grosbeak returns to Hartford. Bird-Banding, vol. 18, pp. 57–76.
1948. Evening grosbeaks choose their lipsticks well. Audubon Mag., vol. 50, pp. 110–112.
1950. "Marrying" junco returns again. Bird-Banding, vol. 21, p. 20.
1951. Plumage coloration and age of evening grosbeaks. Bird-Banding, vol. 22, pp. 23–32.

PARMELEE, D. F., and MACDONALD, S. D.
1960. The birds of west-central Ellesmere Island and adjacent areas. Nat. Mus. Canada Bull., vol. 169.

PARMELEE, DAVID F.
1959. The breeding behavior of the painted bunting in southern Oklahoma. Bird-Banding, vol. 30, pp. 1–18.

PARSONS, J. L.
1906. Pine siskins in Ohio. Bird-Lore, vol. 8, p. 211.

PARTIN, J. L.
1933. A year's study of house finch weights. Condor, vol. 35, pp. 60–63.

PAYNTER, RAYMOND ANDREW, JR.
1952. Birds from Popocatépetl and Ixtaccíhuatl, Mexico. Auk, vol. 69, pp. 293–301.
1964. Generic limits of *Zonotrichia*. Condor, vol. 66, pp. 277–281.

PEABODY, P. B.
1901. Nesting habits of Leconte's sparrow. Auk, vol. 18, pp. 129–134.

PEARSE, THEED
1929. Feeding habits of the American crossbill. Murrelet, vol. 10, pp. 65–66.
1935. Sex ratio in birds. Murrelet, vol. 16, p. 17.

PEARSON, HENRY J.
1904. Three summers among the birds of Russian Lapland.

PEARSON, OLIVER P.
1961. Flight speeds of some small birds. Condor, vol. 63, pp. 506–507.

PEARSON, T. G.
1939. Adventures with sparrows and juncos, *in* The book of birds, vol. 2, pp. 280–281.

PEARSON, T. GILBERT, BRIMLEY, CLEMENT S., and BRIMLEY, HERBERT H.
1919. Birds of North Carolina. North Carolina Geol. Econ. Surv., vol. 4.
1942. Birds of North Carolina (rev. ed.).
1959. *In* Wray and Davis, Birds of North Carolina (rev. ed.).

PEARSON, T. GILBERT, BURROUGHS, JOHN, ET AL.
1917. Birds of America, vol. 3.
1936. Birds of America, vol. 3.

PECK, MORTON E.

1911. Summer birds of Willow Creek, Malheur County, Oregon. Condor, vol. 13, pp. 63–69.

PEMBERTON, J. R.

1910. Notes on the rufous-crowned sparrow. Condor, vol. 12, pp. 123–125.

1928. Additions to the known avifauna of the Santa Barbara Islands. Condor, vol. 30, pp. 144–148.

PEMBERTON, JOHN ROY, and CARRIGER, HENRY WARD

1915. A partial list of the summer resident land birds of Monterey County, California. Condor, vol. 17, pp. 189–201.

1916. Snakes as nest robbers. Condor, vol. 18, p. 233.

PENNER, L. R.

1939. *Tamerlania melospizae* n. sp. (Trematoda Eucotylidae) with notes on the genus. Journ. Parasitology, vol. 25, pp. 421–424.

PERRY, EDNA M., and PERRY, WINIFRED A.

1918. Home life of the vesper sparrow and the hermit thrush. Auk, vol. 35, pp. 310–321.

PETERS, HAROLD SEYMOUR

1931. Abert's towhee, a new bird for Texas. Auk, vol. 48, pp. 274–275.

1933. External parasites collected from banded birds. Bird-Banding, vol. 4, pp. 68–75.

1936. A list of external parasites from birds of the eastern part of the United States. Bird-Banding, vol. 7, pp. 9–27.

PETERS, HAROLD SEYMOUR, and BURLEIGH, THOMAS DEARBORN

1951a. The birds of Newfoundland.

1951b. Birds of the St. Pierre and Miquelon Islands. Canadian Field-Nat., vol. 65, pp. 170–172.

PETERS, JAMES L., and GRISCOM, LUDLOW

1938. Geographical variation in the Savannah sparrow. Bull. Mus. Comp. Zool., vol. 80, pp. 445–480.

PETERS, JAMES LEE

1929. An ornithological survey in the Caribbean lowlands of Honduras. Bull. Mus. Comp. Zool., vol. 69, pp. 397–478.

1931. Additional notes on the birds of the Almirante Bay region of Panama. Bull. Mus. Comp. Zool., vol. 71, pp. 293–345.

1942. The Canadian forms of the sharp-tailed sparrow, *Ammospiza caudacuta*. Ann. Carnegie Mus., vol. 29, pp. 201–210.

PETERSON, JAMES G.

1942a. Salt feeding habits of the house finch. Condor, vol. 44, p. 73.

1942b. Social behavior of the Oregon junco. Condor, vol. 44, p. 80.

PETERSON, ROGER TORY

1935. The goldfinch. Bird-Lore, vol. 37, pp. 417–420.

1941. A field guide to western birds.

1947. A field guide to the birds.

1948a. Birds over America, pp. 248–249.

1948b. Arizona junco. Wilson Bull., vol. 60, p. 5.

1960. A field guide to the birds of Texas and adjacent states.

1961. A field guide to western birds.

PETERSON, ROGER TORY, and FISHER, JAMES

1955. Wild America, pp. 220–222, 224.

PETERSON, THEODORE, and PETERSON, MRS. THEODORE

1936. Smith's and McCown's longspur seen in Minnesota. Auk, vol. 53, p. 342.

PETRIDES, GEORGE A.

1942. *Ilex opaca* as a late winter food for birds. Auk, vol. 59, p. 581.

PETTINGILL, OLIN SEWALL, JR.

1936. Impressions of Grand Manan bird life. Wilson Bull., vol. 48, pp. 111–119.

PETTINGILL, OLIN SEWALL, JR., and DANA, EDWARD FOX

1943. Notes on the birds of western North and South Dakota. Auk, vol. 60, pp. 441–444.

PHILIPP, FREDERICK B.

1936. Nesting of the Savannah sparrow in Bottineau County, North Dakota. Auk, vol. 53, p. 222.

PHILIPP, PHILIP BERNARD

1925. Notes on some summer birds of the Magdalen Islands. Canadian Field-Nat., vol. 39, pp. 75–78.

PHILIPP, PHILIP BERNARD, and BOWDISH, BEECHER SCOVILLE

1917. Some summer birds of northern New Brunswick. Auk, vol. 34, pp. 265–275.

1919. Further notes on New Brunswick birds. Auk, vol. 36, pp. 36–45.

PHILLIPS, ALLAN R., MARSHALL, JOE, and MONSON, GALE

1964. The birds of Arizona.

PHILLIPS, ALLAN ROBERT

1933. Further notes on the birds of the Baboquívari Mountains, Arizona. Condor, vol. 35, pp. 228–230.

1943. Critical notes on two southwestern sparrows. Auk, vol. 60, pp. 242–248.

1944. Status of Cassin's sparrow in Arizona. Auk, vol. 61, pp. 409–412.

1947. Records of occurrence of some southwestern birds. Condor, vol. 49, pp. 121–123.

1951a. Complexities of migration: a review. Wilson Bull., vol. 63, pp. 129–136.

1951b. The molts of the rufous-winged sparrow. Wilson Bull., vol. 63, pp. 323–326.

1955. Rufous-winged sparrow, *Aimophila carpalis*, habitat, p. 45. *In* Palmer, ed., Handbook of North American Birds.

1961. Emigraciones y distribución de aves terrestres en México. Rev. Soc. Mexicano Hist. Nat., vol. 22, pp. 295–311.

PHILLIPS, ALLAN ROBERT, and AMADON, DEAN

1952. Some birds of northwestern Sonora, Mexico. Condor, vol. 54, pp. 163–168.

PHILLIPS, ALLAN ROBERT, and DICKERMAN, ROBERT WILLIAM

1957. Notes on the song sparrows of the Mexican plateau. Auk, vol. 74, pp. 376–382.

PHILLIPS, ALLAN ROBERT, and PULICH, WARREN MARK

1948. Nesting birds of the Ajo Mountains region, Arizona. Condor, vol. 50, pp. 271–272.

PHILLIPS, CHARLES L.

1933. The clay-colored sparrow in Florida. Auk, vol. 50, p. 225.

PHILLIPS, HOMER W., and THORNTON, WILMOT A.

1949. The summer resident birds of the Sierra Vieja range in southwestern Texas. Texas Journ. Sci., vol. 1, pp. 101–131.

PHILLIPS, JOHN CHARLES

1911. A year's collecting in the state of Tamaulipas, Mexico. Auk, vol. 28, pp. 67–89.

1929. An attempt to list the extinct and vanishing birds of the Western Hemisphere with some notes on recent status, location of specimens, etc. Verh. Internat. Ornith. Kongr. Kopenhagen, 1926, p. 515.

PHILLIPS, RICHARD STUART

1951. Nest location, cowbird parasitism, and nesting success of the indigo bunting. Wilson Bull., vol. 63, pp. 206–207.

PIERCE, FRED J.

1930. Birds of Buchanan County, Iowa. Wilson Bull., vol. 42, pp. 253–285.

PIERCE, WRIGHT M.

1915. Peculiar nesting site of Anthony towhee. Condor, vol. 17, p. 100.

1916. Notes from the San Bernardino Mountains, California. Condor, vol. 18, p. 34.

1921. Nesting of the Stephens fox sparrow. Condor, vol. 23, pp. 80–85.

PITELKA, FRANK ALOIS

1942. High population of breeding birds within an artificial habitat. Condor, vol. 44, pp. 172–174.

1947. British Columbian records of the clay-colored sparrow. Condor, vol. 49, pp. 128–130.

1950. Additions to the avifaunal record of Santa Cruz Island, California. Condor, vol. 52, pp. 43–46.

1951. Generic placement of the rufous-winged sparrow. Wilson Bull., vol. 63, pp. 47–48.

1959. Numbers, breeding schedule, and territoriality in pectoral sandpipers of northern Alaska. Condor, vol. 61, pp. 233–264.

PITTMAN, JAMES ALLEN, JR.

1960. Bachman's sparrow hiding in a burrow. Auk, vol. 77, p. 80.

PLATH, OTTO EMIL

1919a. Parasitism of nestling birds by fly larvae. Condor, vol. 21, pp. 30–38.

1919b. A muscid larva of the San Francisco Bay region which sucks the blood of nestling birds. Univ. California Publ. Zool., vol. 19, pp. 191–200.

PLESKE, THEODORE

1928. Birds of the Eurasian tundra. Mem. Boston Soc. Nat. Hist., vol. 6, pp. 109–485.

POOLE, EARL LINCOLN

1938. Weights and wing areas in North American birds. Auk, vol. 55, pp. 511–517.

PORTENKO, L. A.

1960. The birds of the U.S.S.R., pt. 4. Acad. Sci. U.S.S.R., vol. 69 (in Russian).

PORTENKO, LEONIDAS

1930. Subdivision of the species *Emberiza rustica* into geographical races. Auk, vol. 47, pp. 205–207.

PORTER, LOUIS H.

1908. Nesting habits of birds at Stamford, Connecticut, as affected by the cold spring of 1907. Auk, vol. 25, pp. 16–21.

PORTER, RICHARD D.

1954. Additional and new bird records for Utah. Condor, vol. 56, pp. ~~362~~–364.

Potter, Julian Kent, and Murray, Joseph James
1956. Winter season: Middle Atlantic coast region. Audubon Field Notes, vol. 10, pp. 240–242.

Potter, L. B.
1943. Bird notes from south-western Saskatchewan. Canadian Field-Nat., vol. 57, pp. 69–72.

Pough, Richard Hooper
1946. Audubun bird guide. Eastern land birds.
1957. Audubon western field guide.

Pratt, Ivan, and Cutress, Charles
1949. *Olssoniella chivosca* n. sp. (Trematoda: Discrocoeliidae) from the western evening grosbeak. Journ. Parasitology, vol. 35, p. 361.

Pray, Russell H.
1950. History of a wintering Harris sparrow at Berkeley, California. Condor, vol. 52, pp. 89–90.

Preble, Edward Alexander
1896. Unpublished notes in files of Fish and Wildlife Service.
1902. A biological investigation of the Hudson Bay region. North Amer. Fauna, No. 22, U.S. Dep. Agric. Biol. Surv. Bull., pp. 120–121.
1908. A biological investigation of the Athabaska-Mackenzie region. North Amer. Fauna, No. 27.

Preble, Edward Alexander, and McAtee, Waldo Lee
1923. Birds and mammals of the Pribilof Islands, Alaska. *In* A biological survey of the Pribilof Islands, Alaska. North Amer. Fauna, No. 46, pp. 128, 245–255.

Preston, J. W.
1887. Nesting habits of the clay-colored sparrow. Ornith. and Ool., vol. 12, pp. 111–112.
1910. Notes on the northwestern crossbill. Condor, vol. 12, pp. 90–93.

Price, Homer F.
1935. The summer birds of northwestern Ohio. Oologist, vol. 52, pp. 26–36.

Price, John B.
1931. Some flocking habits of the crowned sparrows. Condor, vol. 33, pp. 238–242.

Price, William W.
1897. Description of a new pine grosbeak from California. Auk, vol. 14, pp. 182–186.
1899. Some winter birds of the lower Colorado Valley. Bull. Cooper Ornith. Club, vol. 1, pp. 89–93.
1901. *In* Barlow, A list of the land birds of the Placerville-Lake Tahoe state road. Condor, vol. 3, pp. 150–184.

Province of Quebec Society for The Protection of Birds.
1935–1955. Annual Reports.

Pulich, Warren M.
1963. Some recent records of the varied bunting for Texas. Condor, vol. 65, pp. 334–335.

Pulich, Warren M., and Gullion, Gordon W.
1953. Black-and-white warbler, dickcissel and tree sparrow in Nevada. Condor, vol. 55, p. 215.

Putnam, William L.
1955. White-winged crossbill eating teasel seeds. Wilson Bull., vol. 67, p. 215.

QUAINTANCE, CHARLES W.

1938. Content, meaning, and possible origin of male song in the brown towhee. Condor, vol. 40, pp. 97–101.

1941. Voice in the brown towhee. Condor, vol. 43, pp. 152–155.

QUAY, THOMAS L.

1947. Winter birds of upland plant communities. Auk, vol. 64, pp. 382–388.

1957. The Savannah sparrow (*Passerculus sandwinchensis* Gmelin) in winter in the lower Piedmont of North Carolina. Journ. Elisha Mitchell Sci. Soc., vol. 73, No. 2, pp. 378–388.

1958. The foods and feeding habits of the Savannah sparrow in winter. Journ. Elisha Mitchell Sci. Soc., vol. 74, No. 1, pp. 1–6.

QUILLIN ROY W.

1935. New bird records from Texas. Auk, vol. 52, pp. 324–325.

QUILLIN, ROY W., and HOLLEMAN, RIDLEY

1918. The breeding birds of Bexar County, Texas. Condor, vol. 20, pp. 37–44.

RACEY, KENNETH

1926. Notes on the birds observed in the Alta Lake region, B.C. Auk, vol. 43, pp. 319–325.

1948. Birds of the Alta Lake region, British Columbia. Auk, vol. 65, pp. 383–401.

RAGSDALE, GEORGE HENRY

1892. Distribution of the species *Peucaea* in Cooke Co., Texas. Auk, vol. 9, p. 73.

RAINE, WALTER

1892. Bird-nesting in north-west Canada.

RAND, A. L.

1929. Birds on board ship between Nova Scotia and New York City. Auk, vol. 46, pp. 246–247.

1946. List of Yukon birds and those of Canol Road. Nat. Mus. Canada Bull. 105, pp. 1–76.

1948. Birds of southern Alberta. Nat. Mus. Ottawa Bull., vol. 111

RANDALL, PIERCE E.

1940. Seasonal food habits of the marsh hawk in Pennsylvania. Wilson Bull., vol. 52, pp. 165–172.

RAPP, WILLIAM F., JR., RAPP, JANET L. C., BAUMGARTEN, HENRY E., and MOSER, R. ALLYN

1958. Revised check-list of Nebraska birds. Nebraska Ornith. Union, Occas. Pap. 5.

RASMUSSEN, D. IRVIN

1941. Biotic communities of Kaibab Plateau, Arizona. Ecol. Monogr., vol. 11, pp. 229–275.

RAUSCH, ROBERT

1958. The occurrence and distribution of birds on Middleton Island, Alaska. Condor, vol. 60, pp. 227–242.

RAWSON, GEORGE W.

1954. Birds and butterflies or vice versa. Auk, vol. 71, pp. 209–211.

RAY, MILTON SMITH

1903. A list of the land birds of Lake Valley, central Sierra Nevada Mountains, California. Auk, vol. 20, pp. 180–193.

1904. A fortnight on the Farallones. Auk, vol. 21, p. 440.

1906. Summer birds of San Francisco County, California. Condor, vol. 8, pp. 42–44.

1908. From Big Creek to Big Basin. Condor, vol. 10, pp. 219–222.

1910a. From Tahoe to Washoe. Condor, vol. 12, pp. 85–89.

1910b. The discovery of the nest and eggs of the gray-crowned leucosticte. Condor, vol. 12, pp. 145–161.

1911a. Some August notes for Lake Valley. Condor, vol. 13, p. 108.

1911b. Tree-nests of the Point Pinos junco and other notes. Condor, vol. 13, pp. 210–211.

1912a. A journey to the Star Lake country and other notes from the Tahoe region. Condor, vol. 14, pp. 142–147.

1912b. The discovery of the nest and eggs of the California pine grosbeak. Condor, vol. 14, pp. 157–187.

1913. Some further notes on Sierran field-work. Condor, vol. 15, pp. 198–203.

1916. More summer birds for San Francisco County. Condor, vol. 18, pp. 222–227.

1918. Six weeks in the high Sierras in nesting time. Condor, vol. 20, pp. 70–78.

1919. Description of a twenty-year series of eggs of the Sierra junco. Condor, vol. 21, pp. 184–188.

Rechnitzer, Andreas B.

1956. Land birds at sea off southern California. Condor, vol. 58, pp. 388–389.

Reed, Chester A.

1904. North American birds eggs.

Reeks, Esther

1920. House finches eat salt. Bird-Lore, vol. 22, p. 286.

Reid, Russell

1929. Nesting of the pine siskin in North Dakota. Wilson Bull., vol. 41 (n.s., vol. 36), pp. 72–74.

Rett, Egmont Z.

1947. A report on the birds of San Nicolas Island. Condor, vol. 49, pp. 165–168.

1953. Additional notes on the birds of Santa Rosa Island, California. Condor, vol. 55, p. 156.

N.D. Field notes of Ed Andrews and E. Rett. (Typed, Denver Mus. Nat. Hist.)

Rhoads, Samuel N.

1893. The birds observed in British Columbia and Washington during spring and summer, 1892. Proc. Acad. Nat. Sci. Philadelphia, pp. 21–65.

1903. Audubonian. Auk, vol. 20, pp. 377–383.

Richardson, Charles H., Jr.

1904. A list of summer birds of the Piute Mountains, California. Condor, vol. 6, pp. 134–137.

1908. How large a bird can the California shrike kill? Condor, vol. 10, p. 92.

Richardson, Sir John

1831. Fauna Boreali-Americana; or the zoology of the northern parts of British America, pt. 2.

Richmond, Charles W.

1897. The western field sparrow (*Spizella pusilla arenacea* Chadbourne). Auk, vol. 14, pp. 345–347.

Ridgway, Robert

1872. On the occurrence of a near relative of *Aegiothus flavirostris* at Waltham, Massachusetts. Amer. Nat., vol. 6, pp. 433–434.

1873. The birds of Colorado. Bull. Essex Inst., vol. 5, p. 189.

1875. Monograph of the genus *Leucosticte* Swainson; or gray-crowned finches. U.S. Geol. Geogr. Surv. Terr. Bull., ser. 2, No. 2, pp. 51–82.

1876. Ornithology of Guadeloupe Island, based on notes and collections made by Dr. Edward Palmer. U.S. Geol. Geogr. Surv. Terr. Bull. 2, pt. 2, pp. 183–195.

1877. Ornithology. *In* United States geological exploration of the fortieth parallel, vol. 4, pt. 3, pp. 303–669.

1879. On a new species of *Peucaea* from southern Illinois and central Texas. Bull. Nuttall Ornith. Club, vol. 4, pp. 218–222.

1883a. On Leconte's bunting (*Coturniculus lecontei*) and other birds observed in southeastern Illinois. Bull. Nuttall Ornith. Club, vol. 8, p. 58.

1883b. Descriptions of some new birds from Lower California, collected by Mr. L. Belding. Proc. U.S. Nat. Mus., vol. 6, pp. 154–156.

1884. Description of a new snow bunting from Alaska. Proc. U.S. Nat. Mus., vol. 7, pp. 68–70.

1885a. Description of a new cardinal grosbeak from Arizona. Auk, vol. 2, pp. 343–345.

1885b. Some emended names of North American birds. Proc. U.S. Nat. Mus., vol. 8, pp. 354–356.

1886. A nomenclature of colors for naturalists and compendium of useful knowledge for ornithologists.

1887a. A manual of North American birds.

1887b. Description of two new races of *Pyrrhuloxia sinuata* Bonap. Auk, vol. 4, p. 347.

1889. The ornithology of Illinois, vol. 1, pt. 1.

1891. James Bay sharp-tailed sparrow. Proc. U.S. Nat. Mus., vol. 14, p. 483.

1896. A manual of North American birds, ed. 2.

1897. Correct nomenclature of the Texas cardinal. Auk, vol. 14, p. 95.

1898a. Descriptions of supposed new genera, species, and subspecies of American birds. I. Fringillidae. Auk, vol. 15, pp. 223–230.

1898b. New species, etc., of American birds. Auk, vol. 15, pp. 319–324.

1901. Birds of North and Middle America. U.S. Nat. Mus. Bull. 50, pt. 1,

1902. The birds of North and Middle America. U.S. Nat. Mus. Bull. 50, pt. 2.

1912. Color standards and color nomenclature.

Riley, Joseph H.

1911. *Melospiza melodia inexpectata* Riley. Proc. Biol. Soc. Washington, vol. 24, pp. 233–235.

1912. Birds collected or observed on the expedition of the Alpine Club of Canada to Jasper Park, Yellowhead Pass, and Mount Robson region. Canadian Alpine Journ., spec. no., pp. 47–75.

1917. A bird new to the North American fauna. Auk, vol. 34, p. 210.

Riney, Thane A.

1946. Birds aboard ship. Auk, vol. 63, p. 250.

1951. Relationships between birds and deer. Condor, vol. 53, pp. 178–185.

Ripley, S. Dillon

1949. Texas habitat of Botteri's sparrow and gulf coast records of wintering sparrows. Wilson Bull., vol. 61, pp. 112–113.

Ritter, William E., and Benson, Seth B.

1934. "Is the poor bird demented?" Another case of "shadow boxing." Auk, vol. 51, pp. 169–179.

Roadcap, R.

1962. Translocations of white-crowned and golden-crowned sparrows. Western Bird Bander, vol. 37, pp. 55–57.

Robbins, C. S., and Boyer, G. F.

1953a. Audubon Field Notes, vol. 7, p. 111.

1953b. Diked wet meadow. Audubon Field Notes, vol. 7, pp. 354–355.

Robbins, Chandler S.

1949. Wilson's warbler in Maryland in late December. Auk, vol. 66, pp. 207–208.

Robbins, Charles Albert

1932. The advantage of crossed mandibles: A note on the American red crossbill. Auk, vol. 49, pp. 159–165.

Roberts, Thomas Sadler

1879. Notes on some Minnesota birds. Bull. Nuttall Ornith. Club, vol. 4, pp. 152–155.

1932. The birds of Minnesota, vol. 2.

1936. The birds of Minnesota, ed. 2, vol. 2.

1955. A manual for the identification of the birds of Minnesota and neighboring states.

Robertson, Howard

1899. Nesting of Belding's sparrow. Bull. Cooper Ornith. Club, vol. 1, p. 73.

Robertson, John McB.

1930. Roads and birds. Condor, vol. 32, pp. 142–146.

1931. Birds and eucalyptus trees. Condor, vol. 33, pp. 137–139.

Robertson, W. B., Jr.

1961. Florida region. Audubon Field Notes, vol. 15, pp. 3–12.

Rockwell, Robert Blanchard

1908. An annotated list of the birds of Mesa County, Colorado. Condor, vol. 10, pp. 152–180.

1910. Nesting of the gray-headed junco. Condor, vol. 12, pp. 164–165.

Rockwell, Robert Blanchard, and Wetmore, Alexander

1914. A list of the birds from the vicinity of Golden, Colorado. Auk, vol. 31, pp. 309–333.

Rodgers, Thomas Lathan

1937. Behavior of the pine siskin. Condor, vol. 39, pp. 143–149.

Rodgers, Thomas Lathan, and Sibley, Charles G.

1940. Frequency of occurrence of birds on the Berkeley campus, University of California. Condor, vol. 42, pp. 203–206.

Rogers, Charles Henry

1903. Winter birds of Central Park, New York City. Wilson Bull., vol. 44, pp. 91–93.

Rolfe, Eugene S.

1899. Nesting of Nelson's sparrow. Auk, vol. 16, pp. 356–357.

ROOT, OSCAR M.

1944. Song sparrow turning white within a month. Auk, vol. 61, p. 295.

1952. Clay-colored sparrow in Massachusetts. Wilson Bull., vol. 64, pp. 110–111.

1957. The birds of the Andover region. Bull. Massachusetts Audubon Soc., vol. 41, pp. 459–467.

1958. The birds of the Andover region. Bull. Massachusetts Audubon Society, vol. 42, pp. 5–15, 79–87, 119–125.

ROSS, R. DUDLEY

1947. Evening grosbeaks in New Brunswick in late July. Auk, vol. 64, p. 318.

ROWELL, C. H. FRASER, and DAVIES, S. J. J.

1956. Observations on the redwing in Swedish Lapland. Bird Study, vol. 3, pp. 242–248.

ROWLAND, EDWARD GOULD

1925. Notes on swamp sparrows. Bull. Northeastern Bird-Banding Assoc., vol. 1, pp. 40–42.

1928. Abnormal yellow coloration of swamp sparrows. Bull. Northeastern Bird-Banding Association, vol. 4, pp. 53–56.

ROWLEY, JOHN STUART

1939. Breeding birds of Mono County, California. Condor, vol. 41, pp. 247–254.

ROY, FRANK

1958. Resident longspurs in Lucky Lake area. Blue Jay, vol. 16, pp. 56–57.

1959. Further information on resident longspurs in Saskatchewan. Blue Jay, vol. 17, p. 52.

RUSSELL, PHYRNE SQUIER

1951. Florida cardinal, *Richmondena cardinalis floridanus*, as honey-gatherer. Auk, vol. 68, pp. 514–515.

RUSSELL, STEPHEN M.

1964. A distributional study of the birds of British Honduras. Ornith. Monogr. No. 1, pp. 1–195.

RUST, HENRY J.

1915. An annotated list of the birds of Kootenai County, Idaho. Condor, vol. 17, pp. 118–129.

1917. An annotated list of the birds of Fremont County, Idaho, as observed during the summer of 1916. Condor, vol. 19, pp. 29–43.

1919. A favorite nesting haunt of the Merrill song sparrow. Condor, vol. 21, pp. 145–153.

RUTHVEN, ALEXANDER G., THOMPSON, CRYSTAL, and GAIGE, HELEN T.

1928. The Herpetology of Michigan. Michigan Handbook Ser., vol. 3, No. 3, pp. 1–190.

RUTTER, RUSSELL JAMES

1931. Lapland longspurs singing from trees. Canadian Field-Nat., vol. 45, p. 21.

SABINE, WINIFRED S.

1949. Dominance in winter flocks of juncos and tree sparrows. Physiol. Zool. Chicago, vol. 22, pp. 64–85.

1952. Sex displays of the slate-colored junco, *Junco hyemalis*. Auk, vol. 69, pp. 313–314.

1955. The winter society of the Oregon junco: the flock. Condor, vol. 57, pp. 88–111.

1956. Integrating mechanisms of winter flocks of juncos. Condor, vol. 58, pp. 338–341.
1957. Flight behavior of a flock of slate-colored juncos in the late afternoon. Auk, vol. 74, p. 391.
1959. The winter society of the Oregon junco: intolerance, dominance, and the pecking order. Condor, vol. 61, pp. 110–135.

SAGE, JOHN HALL, BISHOP, LOUIS BENNETT, and BLISS, WALTER PARKS
1913. The birds of Connecticut. Connecticut Geol. Nat. Hist. Surv. Bull. 20, pp. 1–370.

SAGE, RUFUS B.
1846. Scenes in the Rocky Mountains, and in Oregon, California, New Mexico, Texas, and the grand prairies.

SALOMONSEN, FINN
1931. On the geographical variation of the snow-bunting (*Plectrophenax nivalis*). Ibis, ser. 13, vol. 1, pp. 57–70.

SALOMONSEN, FINN, and GITZ-JOHANSEN, A.
1950. The birds of Greenland, 3 parts.

SALT, GEORGE WILLIAM
1952. The relation of metabolism to climate and distribution in three finches of the genus *Carpodacus*. Ecol. Monogr., vol. 22, pp. 121–152.
1953. An ecologic analysis of three California avifaunas. Condor, vol. 55, pp. 258–273.
1957a. An analysis of avifaunas in the Teton Mountains and Jackson Hole, Wyoming. Condor, vol. 59, pp. 373–393.
1957b. Observations on fox, Lincoln, and song sparrows at Jackson Hole, Wyoming. Auk, vol. 74, pp. 258–259.

SALT, W. RAY, and WILK, A. L.
1958. The birds of Alberta.

SALT, WALTER RAYMOND
1954. The structure of the cloacal protuberance of the vesper sparrow (*Pooecetes gramineus*) and certain other passerine birds. Auk, vol. 71, pp. 64–73.
1966. A nesting study of *Spizella pallida*. Auk, vol. 83, pp. 274–281.

SAMUELS, EDWARD AUGUSTUS
1883. Our northern and eastern birds, p. 286.

SARGENT, THEODORE DAVID
1959. Winter studies on the tree sparrow, *Spizella arborea*. Bird-Banding, vol. 30, pp. 27–37.

SAUNDERS, ARETAS ANDREWS
1910a. Singing of the female slate-colored fox sparrow. Condor, vol. 12, p. 80.
1910b. Bird notes from southwestern Montana. Condor, vol. 12, pp. 195–204.
1911. A preliminary list of the birds of Gallatin County, Montana. Auk, vol. 28, pp. 26–49.
1912a. Some birds of southwestern Montana. Condor, vol. 14, pp. 22–32.
1912b. Some changes and additions to the list of birds of southwestern Montana. Condor, vol. 14, p. 107.
1912c. A horseback trip across Montana. Condor, vol. 14, pp. 215–220.
1914a. An ecological study of the breeding birds of an area near Choteau, Montana. Auk, vol. 31, pp. 200–210.
1914b. The birds of Teton and northern Lewis and Clark Counties, Montana. Condor, vol. 16, pp. 124–144.

SAUNDERS, ARETAS ANDREWS—Continued

1921. A distributional list of the birds of Montana. Pacific Coast Avifauna, No. 14.

1922a. Flight songs and mating songs. Auk, vol. 39, pp. 172–175.

1922b. The song of the field sparrow. Auk, vol. 39, pp. 386–399.

1923. The summer birds of the Allegany State Park. Roosevelt Wild Life Bull. (Syracuse Univ. Bull., vol. 22), vol. 1, No. 3, pp. 239–354.

1929a. The summer birds of the northern Adirondack Mountains. Roosevelt Wild Life Bull., vol. 5, No. 3, p. 427.

1929b. Bird song. New York State Mus. Handbook, No. 7, pp. 5–202.

1935. A guide to bird songs.

1936a. Ecology of the birds of Quaker Run Valley, Allegany State Park, New York. New York State Mus. Handbook No. 16.

1936b. The relation of field characters to the question of species and subspecies. Auk, vol. 53, pp. 283–294.

1938. Studies of breeding birds in the Allegany State Park. New York State Mus. Bull., No. 318, p. 131.

1947. The season of bird song—the beginning of song in spring. Auk, vol. 64, pp. 97–107.

1948a. The seasons of bird song—the cessation of song after the nesting season. Auk, vol. 65, pp. 19–29.

1948b. The seasons of bird song. Revival of song after the postnuptial molt. Auk, vol. 65, pp. 373–382.

1951a. A guide to field songs, rev. ed.

1951b. The song of the song sparrow. Wilson Bull., vol. 63, pp. 99–109.

1956. Descriptions of newly-hatched passerine birds. Bird-Banding, vol. 27, pp. 121–128.

1959. Forty years of spring migration in southern Connecticut. Wilson Bull., vol. 71, pp. 208–219.

SAUNDERS, W. E.

1902a. The Ipswich sparrow in its summer home. Auk, vol. 19, pp. 267–271.

1902b. Birds of Sable Island, N.S. Ottawa Nat., vol. 16, pp. 15–31.

1907. A migration disaster in western Ontario. Auk, vol. 24, pp. 108–110.

SAUNDERS, WILLIAM E., and DALE, E. M. S.

1933. History and list of birds of Middlesex County, Ontario. Trans. Roy. Canadian Inst., vol. 19, pp. 161–248.

SAVILE, DOUGLAS BARTON OSBORNE

1950. Bird notes from Great Whale River, Que. Canadian Field-Nat., vol. 64, pp. 95–99.

1951. Birds observed at Chesterfield Inlet, Keewatin, in 1950. Canadian Field-Nat., vol. 65, pp. 145–157.

SAXBY, HENRY L.

1874. The birds of Shetland, p. 98.

SAY, THOMAS

1823. *In* Long, Account of an expedition to the Rocky Mountains, vol. 2, p. 40.

SCHAANNING, H. T. L.

1907. Østfinmarkens fuglefauna. Bergens Mus. AArbog, No. 8.

SCHALLER, GEORGE B.

1954. Notes—birds of Talkeetna Mts., Alaska. Unpubl. MS., Univ. Alaska.

SCHANTZ, WILLIAM EDWARD

1937. A nest-building male song sparrow. Auk, vol. 54, pp. 189–191.

SCHMID, FREDERICK C.
1958. Cedar waxwings and fox sparrows feed upon multiflora rose. Wilson Bull., vol. 70, pp. 194–195.

SCHOLANDER, P. F., WALTERS, VLADIMIR, HOCK, RAYMOND, and IRVING, LAURENCE
1950a. Body insulation of some arctic and tropical mammals and birds. Biol. Bull., Woods Hole, vol. 99, pp. 225–236.
1950b. Heat regulation in some arctic and tropical mammals and birds. Biol. Bull., Woods Hole, vol. 99, pp. 237–258.

SCHOLANDER, SUSAN I.
1955. Land birds over the western North Atlantic. Auk, vol. 72, No. 3, pp. 225–239.

SCHOOLCRAFT, HENRY R.
1851. Personal memoirs of a residence of thirty years with the Indian tribes on the American frontiers, p. 166.

SCLATER, WILLIAM LUTLEY
1912. A history of the birds of Colorado.

SCOTT, CARROLL DEWILTON
1920. Domesticating California birds. Condor, vol. 22, p. 189.

SCOTT, WILLIAM EARL DODGE
1885a. Winter mountain notes from southern Arizona. Auk, vol. 2, pp. 172–174.
1885b. Early spring notes from the mountains of southern Arizona. Auk, vol. 2, pp. 348–356.
1886. On the breeding habits of some Arizona birds. Fifth paper. Auk, vol. 3, pp. 81–86.
1887. On the avi-fauna of Pinal County, with remarks on some birds of Pima and Gila counties, Arizona. Auk, vol. 4, pp. 196–205.

SEEBOHM, HENRY
1884. A history of British birds, vol. 2, pp. 96–99.
1885. A history of British birds, plate 19.

SEIBERT, MILTON LEWIS
1942. Occurrence and nesting of some birds in the San Francisco Bay region. Condor, vol. 44, pp. 68–72.

SELOUS, EDMUND
1910. The finches. *In* Kirkman, The British bird book, vol. 1, pp. 83–156.

SEMPLE, J. B., and SUTTON, G. M.
1932. Nesting of Harris's sparrow (*Zonotrichia querula*) at Churchill, Manitoba. Auk, vol. 49, pp. 166–183.

SEMPLE, JOHN B.
1936. The Cape Sable sparrow and hurricanes. Auk, vol. 53, p. 341.

SENNETT, GEORGE BURRITT
1878. Notes on the ornithology of the lower Rio Grande of Texas. U.S. Geol. Geogr. Surv. Bull., vol. 4, No. 1, p. 21.
1879. Further notes on the ornithology of the lower Rio Grande of Texas. U.S. Geol. Geogr. Surv. Bull., vol. 5, No. 3, pp. 371–440.

SERVENTY, D. L.
1939. Migration records at sea. Condor, vol. 41, pp. 257–258.

SETON, ERNEST THOMPSON
1886. The birds of western Manitoba. Auk, vol. 3, pp. 320–329.
1891. The birds of Manitoba. Proc. U.S. Nat. Mus., vol. 13, pp. 457–643.
1908. Bird records from Great Slave Lake region. Auk, vol. 25, pp. 68–74.

SHACKLETON, WALTER, and SHACKLETON, ELIZABETH
1947. Anting by the indigo bunting. Kentucky Warbler, vol. 23, pp. 1–4.

SHADLE, ALBERT RAY
1930. European goldfinch at Buffalo, New York. Auk, vol. 47, pp. 566–567.

SHANK, MAX C.
1958. The natural termination of the refractory period in slate-colored junco and in the white-throated sparrow. Auk, vol. 76, pp. 44–54.

SHARP, CLARENCE SAWYER
1906. Unusual breeding records at Escondido. Condor, vol. 8, p. 75.
1907. The breeding birds of Escondido. Condor, vol. 9, pp. 84–91.

SHARPE, R. BOWDLER
1888. Catalogue of the birds in the British Museum. Vol. 12, pt. 3.

SHARSMITH, CARL
1936. Carnivorous habits of the Belding ground. Yosemite Nat. Notes, vol. 15, pp. 12–14.

SHAUB, BENJAMIN MARTIN
1951a. A study of the behavior and population of pine siskins at Northampton, Mass., February–May, 1947. Bird-Banding, vol. 22, pp. 71–79.
1951b. Young evening grosbeaks, *Hesperiphona vespertina*, at Saranac Lake, New York. Auk, vol. 68, pp. 517–519.
1958. A juvenal evening grosbeak appears in Northampton, Massachusetts, in late October 1957. Bird-Banding, vol. 29, pp. 31–34.

SHAUB, BENJAMIN MARTIN, AND SHAUB, MARY S.
1950–55. Evening grosbeak survey news, 5 vols. (Mimeogr. periodical.)
1953. Adult and young evening grosbeaks at Saranac Lake, New York: summer of 1952. Bird-Banding, vol. 24, pp. 135–141.

SHAUB, MARY S.
1954. Summer appearances of adult and juvenal evening grosbeaks. Bird-Banding, vol. 25, pp. 87–95.
1956. Effect of native foods on evening grosbeak incursions. Bull. Massachusetts Audubon Soc., vol. 40, pp. 481–488.

SHAVER, JESSE MILTON, and ROBERTS, MRS. MARY BARRY
1933. A brief study of the courtship of the eastern cardinal (*Richmondena cardinalis cardinalis* (Linnaeus)). Journ. Tennessee Acad. Sci., vol. 8, No. 2, pp. 116–123.

SHAW, WILLIAM THOMAS
1932. Nesting of the Hepburn rosy finch in Washington State. Condor, vol. 34, p. 258.
1934. Nesting of the Hepburn rosy finch on Mount Baker, Washington. Murrelet, vol. 15, p. 79.
1936. Winter life and nesting studies of Hepburn's rosy finch in Washington State. Auk, vol. 53, pp. 9–16, 133–149.

SHELDON, CHARLES
1909. List of the birds observed on the upper Toklat River near Mt. McKinley, Alaska, 1907–1908. Auk, vol. 26, pp. 66–70.

SHELDON, HARRY HARGRAVE
1907. A bit too previous. Condor, vol. 9, p. 111.
1909. Notes on some birds of Kern County. Condor, vol. 11, pp. 168–172.

SHELTON, ALFRED
1915. Yakutat song sparrow in Oregon. Condor, vol. 17, p. 60.

SHEPARDSON, DURNO IRA
1915. The house finch as a parasite. Condor, vol. 17, pp. 100–101.
1917. Notes from the southern Sierras. Condor, vol. 19, pp. 168–169.

SHEPPARD, JAY M.
1959. Sprague's pipit and Smith's longspur in Ohio. Auk, vol. 76, pp. 362–363.

SHERWOOD, WILLIAM E.
1929. Immature song sparrow in full song. Condor, vol. 31, p. 181.

SHORTT, TERENCE MICHAEL
1951. On the juvenal plumage of North American pipits. Auk, vol. 68, p. 265.

SHOTWELL, R. L.
1930. A study of the lesser migratory grasshopper. U.S. Dep. Agric. Tech. Bull. 190, p. 27.

SIBLEY, CHARLES
1939. Fossil fringillids from Rancho La Brea. Condor, vol. 41, pp. 126–127.
1950. Species formation in the red-eyed towhees of Mexico. Univ. California Publ. Zool., vol. 50, pp. 109–194.
1952. The birds of the south San Francisco Bay region, 44 pp. (mimeo.).
1955. The generic allocation of the green-tailed towhee. Auk, vol. 72, pp. 420–423.
1956. A white-throated golden-crowned sparrow. Condor, vol. 58, pp. 294–295.

SIBLEY, CHARLES G., and PETTINGILL, OLIN SEWALL, JR.
1955. A hybrid longspur from Saskatchewan. Auk, vol. 72, pp. 423–425.

SIBLEY, CHARLES G., and SHORT, LESTER L., JR.
1959. Hybridization in the buntings (*Passerina*) of the Great Plains. Auk, vol. 76, pp. 443–463.

SILLOWAY, PERLEY MILTON
1902. Notes of McCown's longspur in Montana. Osprey, vol. 6, pp. 42–44.
1903. Birds of Fergus County, Montana. Fergus County Free High School, Bull. No. 1.
1904. The song of the dickcissel. Wilson Bull., vol. 16, pp. 52–54.
1907. Stray notes from the Flathead Woods. Condor, vol. 9, pp. 53–54.
1923. Relation of summer birds to the western Adirondack forest. Roosevelt Wild Life Bull., vol. I, No. 4, pp. 397–486.

SIMMONS, GEORGE FINLAY
1914. Notes on the Louisiana clapper rail (*Rallus crepitans saturatus*) in Texas. Auk, vol. 31, pp. 363–384.
1915. On the nesting of certain birds in Texas. Auk, vol. 32, pp. 317–331.
1925. Birds of the Austin region.

SIMPSON, ROGER
1925. Photographing the rufous-crowned sparrow. Condor, vol. 27, pp. 97–98.

SKINNER, M. P.
1920. The pink-sided junco. Condor, vol. 22, pp. 165–168.
1925. The birds of the Yellowstone National Park. Roosevelt Wild Life Bull., vol. 3, pp. 7–192.
1928a. A guide to the winter birds of the North Carolina sandhills.
1928b. Yellowstone's winter birds. Condor, vol. 30, pp. 237–242.
1930. House finches eating watermelon. Condor, vol. 32, p. 301.

SKUTCH, ALEXANDER F.
1961. Helpers among birds. Condor, vol. 63, pp. 198–226.

Slater, William Lutley
1912. History of the birds of Colorado.
Slud, Paul
1964. The birds of Costa Rica. Bull. Amer. Mus. Nat. Hist., vol. 128, pp. 1–430.
Smiley, Daniel, Jr.
1939. A slate-colored junco at least eight years old. Bird-Banding, vol. 10, pp. 161–162.
Smith, Austin Paul
1910. Miscellaneous bird notes from the lower Rio Grande. Condor, vol. 12, pp. 93–103.
1913. Notes and records from Brooks County, Texas. Condor, vol. 15, pp. 182–183.
1915. Birds of the Boston Mountains, Arkansas. Condor, vol. 17, pp. 41–57.
1916. Additions to the avifauna of Kerr County, Texas. Auk, vol. 33, pp. 187–193.
1917. Some birds of the Davis Mountains, Texas. Condor, vol. 19, pp. 161–165.
Smith, Bertrand E.
1949. White-winged crossbills nesting in Maine. Maine Audubon Soc. Bull., vol. 5, pp. 12–13.
Smith, Horace Gardner
1908. Random notes on the distribution of some Colorado birds, with additions to the state avifauna. Auk, vol. 25, pp. 184–191.
Smith, Mrs. Otis H.
1958. Crown markings of golden-crowned sparrows. News from the Bird-Banders, vol. 33, No. 1, p. 2.
Smith, Philbrick
1930. Winter nesting of the California linnet. Condor, vol. 32, p. 121.
Smith, Robert Leo
1959. The songs of the grasshopper sparrow. Wilson Bull., vol. 71, pp. 141–152.
1963. Some ecological notes on the grasshopper sparrow. Wilson Bull., vol. 75, pp. 159–165.
Smith, Ronald W.
1938. Noteworthy records for Nova Scotia. Auk, vol. 55, pp. 548–550.
Smith, Wendell Phillips
1926. A study of the tree sparrow's migration in the Connecticut River valley. Bull. Northeastern Bird-Banding Assoc., vol. 2, pp. 19–22.
1936. An unusual nesting site of the slate-colored junco. Auk, vol. 53, pp. 222–223.
1942. A case of reversed migration. Bird-Banding, vol. 13, p. 182.
Smyth and Bartholomew
1966. The water economy of the black-throated sparrow and the rock wren. Condor, vol. 68, pp. 447–458.
Smyth, Thomas
1930. The dickcissel (*Spiza americana*) in South Carolina. Auk, vol. 47, pp. 421–422.
Snodgrass, Robert Evans
1903. A list of land birds from central Washington. Auk, vol. 20, pp. 202–209.
1904. A list of land birds from central and southeastern Washington. Auk, vol. 21, pp. 223–233.

Snyder, Dana P., and Cassel, J. Frank
1951. A late summer nest of the red crossbill in Colorado. Wilson Bull., vol. 63, pp. 177–180.

Snyder, Dana Paul
1950. Bird communities in the coniferous forest biome. Condor, vol. 52, pp. 17–27.

Snyder, Dorothy E.
1951. Nests of the barn owl, *Tyto a. pratincola*, and the red crossbill, *Loxia curvirostra*, Essex county, Massachusetts. Auk, vol. 68, pp. 377–378.
1954. A nesting study of red crossbills. Wilson Bull., vol. 66, pp. 32–37.

Snyder, L. H., and Brimley, C. S.
1928. The dickcissel in North Carolina. Auk, vol. 45, p. 508.

Snyder, Lester Lynne
1928a. On the bronzed grackle. Canadian Field-Nat., vol. 42, p. 44.
1928b. *In* Dymond, Snyder, and Logler, A faunal investigation of the Lake Nipigon region, Ontario. Trans. Roy. Canadian Inst., vol. 16, pp. 233–291.
1939. A plan of Ontario subdivisions and their names for naturalists. Canadian Field-Nat., vol. 53, pp. 22–24.
1951. Ontario birds.
1957a. Changes in the avifauna of Ontario. *In* Urquhart (ed.), Changes in the fauna of Ontario, pp. 26–42.
1957b. Arctic birds of Canada.

Soper, Joseph Dewey
1928. A faunal investigation of southern Baffin Island (birds). Canada Dep. Mines, Biol. Bull., ser. No. 53, pp. 76–116.
1940. Local distribution of eastern Canadian Arctic birds. Auk, vol. 57, pp. 13–21.
1946. Ornithological results of the Baffin Island expeditions of 1928–1929 and 1930–1931, together with more recent records. Auk, vol. 63, pp. 1–24, 223–239, 418–427.
1949. Birds observed in the Grande Prairie—Peace River region of northwestern Alberta, Canada. Auk, vol. 66, pp. 233–257.

Sowerby, Arthur de Carle
1923. The naturalist in Manchuria, birds, vol. 3, pp. 27–28.

Speirs, Doris Huestis
1949. Evening grosbeaks at Be-Wa-Bic. Jack-Pine Warbler, vol. 27, p. 128.
1950. Some notes on the roosting habits of the evening grosbeak. Wood Duck, vol. 4, No. 2, pp. 1–4.

Speirs, Doris Huestis, and Speirs, John Murray
1947. Birds of the vicinity of North Bay, Ontario. Canadian Field-Nat., vol. 61, pp. 23–38.

Speirs, John Murray
1939. Fluctuations in numbers of birds in the Toronto region. Auk, vol. 56, pp. 411–419.
1950. A March day at Cobble Hill. Wood Duck, vol. 3.
1953. Key dates for birds of the Toronto region 1887–1937, pp. 1–7 (mimeo.).

Speirs, John Murray, and Andoff, R.
1958. Nest attentivity of Lincoln's sparrow determined using thermistor bridge. Canadian Journ. Zool., vol. 36, pp. 843–848.

SPENCER, G. J.
1948. Some records of Mallophaga from British Columbia birds. Proc. Ent. Soc. British Columbia, vol. 44, pp. 3–6.

SPETZMAN, LLOYD A.
1959. Vegetation of the arctic slope of Alaska. Geol. Surv. Professional Paper 302–B.

SPRINGER, PAUL J., and STEWART, ROBERT E.
1948. Tidal marshes, 12th breeding bird census. Audubon Field Notes, vol. 2, pp. 223–226.

SPRUNT, ALEXANDER, JR.
1924. Breeding of MacGillivray's seaside sparrow in South Carolina. Auk, vol. 41, pp. 482–484.
1954. Florida bird life.
1963. Addendum to Florida bird life, pp. 1–24.

SPRUNT, ALEXANDER, JR., and CHAMBERLAIN, E. BURNHAM
1949. South Carolina bird life.

SPURRELL, J. A.
1921. An annotated list of the land birds of Sac County, Iowa. Wilson Bull., vol. 33, p. 126.

SQUIRES, WILLIAM AUSTIN
1917. Some field notes for 1917. Condor, vol. 19, pp. 185–186.
1952. The birds of New Brunswick. Publ. New Brunswick Mus., monogr. ser. No. 4.

STAGER, KENNETH E.
1949. The dickcissel in California. Condor, vol. 51, p. 44.

STANSELL, SIDNEY S.
1909. Birds of central Alberta. Auk, vol. 26, pp. 390–400.

STANWELL-FLETCHER, THEODORA MORRIS COPES
1946. Driftwood valley, p. 176.

STARRETT, WILLIAM CHARLES
1938. Highway casualties in Central Illinois during 1927. Wilson Bull., vol. 50, pp. 193–196.

STEARNS, WINFRED ALDEN
1881. New England bird life, pt. 1, p. 220.

STEELMAN, G. M., and HERDE, K. E.
1937. Supplementary studies of Harris sparrow in its winter range (MS.). Oklahoma A. and M. College, Stillwater, Okla.

STEGEMAN, LEROY C.
1955. Weights of some small birds in central New York. Bird-Banding, vol. 26, pp. 19–27.

STEJNEGER, LEONHARD
1885. Results of ornithological explorations in the Commander Islands and in Kamtschatka. U.S. Nat. Mus. Bull. 29, pp. 262–263.
1887. Notes on the northern palearctic bullfinches. Proc. U.S. Nat. Mus., vol. 10, p. 103.

STEPHENS, FRANK
1885. Notes of an ornithological trip in Arizona and Sonora. Auk, vol. 2, pp. 225–231.
1903. Bird notes from eastern California and western Arizona. Condor, vol. 5, pp. 100–105.

STEPHENS, T. C.
1956. An annotated bibliography of North Dakota ornithology. Occas. Pap. No. 2, Nebraska Ornith. Union.

STEVENS, F.
1878. Notes on a few birds observed in New Mexico and Arizona in 1876. Bull. Nuttall Ornith. Club, vol. 3, pp. 92–94.
STEVENS, O. A.
1931. Goldfinches feeding upon goatsbeard seeds. Wilson Bull., vol. 43, p. 230.
1948. New and unusual North Dakota trapping records. Auk, 65, pp. 136–137.
1950. A migration list from Fargo, North Dakota, 1910–49. Flicker, vol. 22, pp. 90–104.
1957. Fall migration and weather, with special reference to Harris' sparrow. Wilson Bull., vol. 69, pp. 352–359.
STEVENSON, ELMO
1942. Key to the nests of Pacific coast birds. Oregon State Monogr., Studies in Zool., No. 4.
STEVENSON, HENRY M.
1957a. The relative magnitude of the trans-Gulf and circum-Gulf spring migrations. Wilson Bull., vol. 69, pp. 39–77.
1957b. Winter season: Florida region. Audubon Field Notes, vol. 11, pp. 257–263.
1959. Florida region. Audubon Field Notes, vol. 13, pp. 21–25.
STEVENSON, JAMES OSBORNE
1936. Bird notes from the Hualpai Mountains, Arizona. Condor, vol. 38, pp. 244–245.
1942. Birds of the central panhandle of Texas. Condor, vol. 44, pp. 108–115.
STEVENSON, JAMES OSBORNE, and MEITZEN, LOGAN H.
1946. Behavior and food habits of Sennett's white-tailed hawk in Texas. Wilson Bull., vol. 58, pp. 198–205.
STEVENSON, JAMES OSBORNE, and SMITH, TARLETON F.
1938. Additions to the Brewster County, Texas, bird list. Condor, vol. 40, p. 184.
STEWART, PAUL ALVA
1937. A preliminary list of bird weights. Auk, vol. 54, pp. 324–332.
STEWART, ROBERT EARL, and ROBBINS, CHANDLER SEYMOUR
1947. Recent observations on Maryland birds. Auk, vol. 64, pp. 266–274.
1958. Birds of Maryland and the District of Columbia. North Amer. Fauna, No. 62, pp. 1–401.
STILLWELL, JERRY E. and NORMA J.
1955. Notes on the song of lark buntings. Wilson Bull., vol. 67, pp. 138–139.
STIMSON, LOUIS A.
1944. Rediscovery of the Cape Sable sparrow confirmed. Florida Nat., vol. 17, pp. 31–32.
1948. Cape Sable sparrow still in Collier County. Florida Nat., vol. 21, pp. 68–69.
1953. Cape Sable seaside sparrow. Florida Nat., vol. 26, p. 57.
1956. The Cape Sable sparrow: its former and present distribution. Auk, vol. 73, pp. 489–502.
1961. Cape Sable sparrows: fire and range extension. Florida Nat., vol. 34, pp. 139–140.
STOCKARD, CHARLES RUPERT
1905. Nesting habits of birds in Mississippi. Auk, vol. 22, pp. 273–288.

STODDARD, HERBERT L.
1931. The bobwhite quail: its habits, preservation and increase.
1962. Bird casualties at a Leon County, Florida TV tower, 1955–1961. Tall Timbers Res. Sta., Bull. No. 1.

STOKES, ALLEN W.
1950. Breeding behavior of the goldfinch. Wilson Bull., vol. 62, pp. 107–127.

STONE, CLARENCE F.
1933. Shufeldt's junco in Steuben Co., N.Y. Auk, vol. 50, p. 123.

STONE, D. D.
1884. Colorado notes. Ornith. and Ool., vol. 9, pp. 9–10.

STONE, WITMER
1908. The birds of New Jersey. *In* Ann. Rep. New Jersey State Mus., pt. 2.
1909. The birds of New Jersey. Ann. Rep. New Jersey State Mus. 1908, pp. 11–347, 409–419.
1916. Philadelphia to the coast in early days, and the development of western ornithology prior to 1850. Condor, vol. 18, pp. 1–14.
1927. Review: Todd on neotropical goldfinches. Auk, vol. 44, pp. 129–130.
1928a. Dickcissel (*Spiza americana*) in Delaware County, Pennsylvania. Auk, vol. 45, pp. 507–508.
1928b. Dickcissel in New Jersey. Auk, vol. 45, p. 509.
1937. Bird studies at Old Cape May, vol. 2, pp. 521–941.

STONER, DAYTON
1932. Ornithology of the Oneida Lake region: with reference to the late spring and summer seasons. Roosevelt Wild Life Ann., vol. 2, Nos. 3 and 4, pp. 277–764.

STONER, EMERSON A.
1934. Sleeping posture of house finches on the nest at night. Auk, vol. 51, p. 92.
1955. Crown markings in the golden-crowned sparrow. News from the Bird-Banders, vol. 30, pp. 28–29.

STONER, EMERSON A., AUSTIN, E. K., and KRIDLER, E.
1962. An analysis of bird banding reports for the year 1961 within the area of the Western Bird Banding Association. Western Bird-Bander, vol. 37, pp. 16–21.

STONER, EMERSON A., ELMORE, M., AUSTIN, E. K., and MEWALDT, L. RICHARD
1960. An analysis of bird-banding reports for the year 1959 within the area of the Western Bird Banding Association. News from the Bird-Banders, vol. 35, pp. 13–18.

STONER, EMERSON A., ELMORE, M., AUSTIN, E. K., and WESTON, H. G., JR.
1961. An analysis of bird-banding reports for the year 1960 within the area of the Western Bird-Banding Association. Western Bird-Bander, vol. 36, pp. 13–18.

STORER, ROBERT W.
1951. Variation in the painted bunting (*Passerina ciris*) with special reference to wintering populations. Occas. Pap. Mus. Zool., Univ. Michigan, No. 532, pp. 1–12.
1954. A hybrid between the chipping and clay-colored sparrows. Wilson Bull., vol. 66, pp. 143–144.
1955. A preliminary survey of the sparrows of the genus *Aimophila*. Condor, vol. 57, pp. 193–201.

STORER, TRACY IRWIN
1921. American crossbill eating elm aphis. Condor, vol. 23, p. 98.
STRAW, MRS. HERMAN F.
1919. Purple finches. Bird-Lore, vol. 21, pp. 165–166.
STREET, PHILLIPS B.
1954. Birds of the Pocono Mountains, Pennsylvania. Cassinia, vol. 41, pp. 3–76.
STRESEMANN, ERWIN
1963. The nomenclature of plumages and molts. Auk, vol. 80, pp. 1–8.
STRICKLAND, E. H.
1938. An annotated list of the Diptera (flies) of Alberta. Canadian Journ. Res., vol. 16, sect. d, No. 7, p. 219.
STRODE, W. S.
1924. In California. Oologist, vol. 41, pp. 81–82.
STRONG, REUBEN MYRON
1918. The song of Bachman's sparrow. Auk, vol. 35, p. 226.
STUPKA, ARTHUR
1963. Notes on the birds of Great Smoky Mountains National Park.
SUDWORTH, GEORGE B.
1908. Forest trees of the Pacific slope. U.S. Dep. Agric., Forest Service.
SUMNER, E. L., and DIXON, JOSEPH SCATTERGOOD
1953. Birds and mammals of the Sierra Nevada.
SUMNER, E. LOWELL, JR., and COBB, J. L.
1928. Further experiments in removing birds from place of banding. Condor, vol. 30, pp. 317–319.
SUMNER, EUSTACE LOWELL, SR.
1931. Some banded birds recaptured after five to seven and one-half years. Condor, vol. 33, p. 128.
1933. Seasonal behavior of some banded golden-crowned sparrows. Condor, 35, pp. 180–182.
SUTHARD, JAMES
1927. On the usage of snake exuviae as nesting material. Auk, vol. 44, pp. 264–265.
SUTHERS, RODERICK A.
1960. Measurement of some lake-shore territories of the song sparrow. Wilson Bull., vol. 72, pp. 232–237.
SUTTON, GEORGE MIKSCH
1928a. Birds of Pymatuning swamp and Conneaut Lake, Crawford County, Pennsylvania. Ann. Carnegie Mus., vol. 18, pp. 19–239.
1928b. A collection of hawks from Pennsylvania. Wilson Bull., vol. 40, pp. 84–95.
1928c. An introduction to the birds of Pennsylvania.
1931. Notes on birds observed along the west coast of Hudson Bay. Condor, vol. 33, pp. 154–159.
1932. The exploration of Southampton Island, Hudson Bay, part 2, Zoology, sect. 2, The birds of Southampton Island. Mem. Carnegie Mus., vol. 12.
1934. Notes on the birds of the western panhandle of Oklahoma. Ann. Carnegie Mus., vol. 24.
1935. The juvenal plumage and postjuvenal molt in several species of Michigan sparrows. Bull. 3, Cranbrook Inst. Sci., pp. 1–36.
1936a. Birds in the wilderness: Adventures of an ornithologist.

SUTTON, GEORGE MIKSCH—Continued
1936b. The postjuvenal molt of the grasshopper sparrow. Occas. Pap. Mus. Zool. Univ. Michigan, No. 336.
1937. The juvenal plumage and postjuvenal molt of the chipping sparrow. Occas. Pap. Mus. Zool. Univ. Michigan, No. 355, pp. 1–5.
1938b. Some findings of the Semple Oklahoma Expedition. Auk, vol. 55, pp. 501–508.
1941. The juvenal plumage and postjuvenal molt of the vesper sparrow. Occas. Pap. Mus. Zool. Univ. Michigan, No. 445.
1943a. Notes on the behavior of certain captive young fringillines. Occas. Pap. Mus. Zool. Univ. Michigan, No. 474.
1943b. Records from the Tucson region of Arizona. Auk, vol. 60, pp. 345–350.
1949. Meeting the west on Florida's east coast. Florida Nat., vol. 22, pt. 2, pp. 23–33.
1951a. Birds and an ant army in southern Tamaulipas. Condor, vol. 53, pp. 16–18.
1951b. Mexican birds.
1959. The nesting fringillids of the Edwin S. George Reserve, southeastern Michigan (pt. 4). Jack-Pine Warbler, vol. 37, pp. 127–151.
1960. The nesting fringillids of the Edwin S. George Reserve, southeastern Michigan (pts. 6 and 7). Jack-Pine Warbler, vol. 38, pp. 46–65, 125–139.
1964. Ecological check-list of the birds of Oklahoma.

SUTTON, GEORGE MIKSCH, and BURLEIGH, THOMAS DEARBORN
1939. A list of birds observed on the 1938 Semple expedition to northeastern Mexico. Occas. Pap. Mus. Zool. Louisiana State Univ., No. 3, pp. 15–46.
1940a. Birds of Las Vigas, Veracruz. Auk, vol. 57, pp. 234–243.
1940b. Birds of Valles, San Luis Potosí, Mexico. Condor, vol. 42, pp. 259–262.
1941. Some birds recorded in Nuevo León, Mexico. Condor, vol. 43, pp. 158–160.

SUTTON, GEORGE MIKSCH, and PARMELEE, DAVID FREELAND
1954. Nesting of the snow bunting on Baffin Island. Wilson Bull., vol. 66, pp. 159–179.
1955. Summer activities of the Lapland longspur on Baffin Island. Wilson Bull., vol. 67, pp. 110–127.

SUTTON, GEORGE MIKSCH, and PETTINGILL, OLIN SEWALL, JR.
1942. Birds of the Gomez Farias region, southwestern Tamaulipas. Auk, vol. 59, pp. 1–34.
1943. Birds of Linares and Galeana, Nuevo León, Mexico. Occas. Pap. Mus. Zool. Louisiana State Univ., No. 16, pp. 273–291.

SUTTON, GEORGE MIKSCH, PETTINGILL, OLIN SEWALL, JR., and LEA, ROBERT B.
1942. Notes on birds of the Monterrey district of Nuevo León, Mexico. Wilson Bull., vol. 54, pp. 199–203.

SUTTON, GEORGE MIKSCH, and PHILLIPS, ALLAN ROBERT
1942. June bird life of the Papago Indian Reservation, Arizona. Condor, vol. 44, pp. 57–65.

SUTTON, GEORGE MIKSCH, and WILSON, ROWLAND S.
1946. Notes on the winter birds of Attu. Condor, vol. 48, pp. 83–91.

SVERDRUP, OTTO NEUMANN
1904. New land; four years in the Arctic regions, 2 vols.

Swainson, William
1837. On the natural history and classification of birds, vol. 2, p. 288.

Swainson, William, and Richardson, John
1831. Birds. *In* Richardson, Fauna Boreali-Americana, vol. 2.

Swarth, Harry Schelwald
1901. Some rare birds in Los Angeles Co., Cal. Condor, vol. 3, p. 66.
1904. Birds of the Huachuca Mountains, Arizona. Pacific Coast Avifauna, No. 4.
1905a. Summer birds of the Papago Indian Reservation and of the Santa Rita Mountains, Arizona. Condor, vol. 7, pp. 22–28, 47–50.
1905b. *Atratus* versus *megalonyx*. Condor, vol. 7, pp. 171–174.
1908. Some fall migration notes from Arizona. Condor, vol. 10, pp. 107–116.
1911a. Birds and mammals of the 1909 Alexander Alaska expedition. Univ. California Publ. Zool., vol. 7, pp. 9–172.
1911b. Field notes from south-central California. Condor, vol. 13, pp. 160–163.
1912a. The winter range of the Yakutat song sparrow. Condor, vol. 14, p. 73.
1912b. Report on a collection of birds and mammals from Vancouver Island. Univ. California Publ. Zool., vol. 10, pp. 1–124.
1913. A revision of the California forms of *Pipilo maculatus* Swainson, with description of a new subspecies. Condor, vol. 15, pp. 167–175.
1914a. Unusual plumage of the female linnet. Condor, vol. 16, p. 94.
1914b. A distributional list of the birds of Arizona. Pacific Coast Avifauna, No. 10.
1917. Observations on some Fresno County birds. Condor, vol. 19, pp. 129–130.
1918. Notes on some birds from central Arizona. Condor, vol. 20, pp. 20–24.
1920. Revision of the avian genus *Passerella* with special reference to the distribution and migration of the races in California. Univ. California Publ. Zool., vol. 21, pp. 75–224.
1922. Birds and mammals of the Stikine River region of northern British Columbia and southeastern Alaska. Univ. California Publ. Zool., vol. 24, pp. 125–314.
1923. The systematic status of some northwestern song sparrows. Condor, vol. 25, pp. 214–223.
1924a. Birds and mammals of the Skeena River region of northern British Columbia. Univ. California Publ. Zool., vol. 24, pp. 315–394.
1924b. Fall migration notes from the San Francisco Mountain region, Arizona. Condor, vol. 26, pp. 183–190.
1924c. Notes upon certain summer occurrences of the gray flycatcher. Condor, vol. 26, pp. 195–197.
1925. Birds and mammals of the Stikine River region of northern British Columbia and southeastern Alaska. Univ. California Publ. Zool., vol. 24, pp. 125–314.
1926. Report on a collection of birds and mammals from the Atlin region, northern British Columbia. Univ. California Publ. Zool., vol. 30, pp. 51–182.
1928. Occurrence of some Asiatic birds in Alaska. Proc. California Acad. Sci., ser. 4, vol. 17, p. 248.

Swarth, Henry Schelwald—Continued

1929. The faunal areas of southern Arizona: a study in animal distribution. Proc. California Acad. Sci., vol. 18, pp. 267–383.

1930. Nesting of the timberline sparrow. Condor, vol. 32, pp. 255–257.

1934. Birds of Nunivak Island, Alaska. Pacific Coast Avifauna, No. 22, pp. 1–64.

1936a. Savannah sparrow migration routes in the Northwest. Condor, vol. 38, pp. 30–32.

1936b. A list of the birds of the Atlin region, British Columbia. Proc. California Acad. Sci., ser. 4, vol. 23, pp. 35–58.

Swarth, Harry Schelwaldt, and Brooks, Allan

1925. The timberline sparrow: a new species from northwestern Canada. Condor, vol. 27, pp. 67–69.

Swenk, M. H., and Stevens, O. A.

1929. Harris's sparrow and the study of it by trapping. Wilson Bull., vol. 41, pp. 129–177.

Swenk, Myron Harmon

1929. The pine siskin in Nebraska: its seasonal abundance and nesting. Wilson Bull., vol. 41 (N.S. vol. 36), pp. 77–92.

1936. A study of the distribution, migration, and hybridism of the rose-breasted and Rocky Mountain black-headed grosbeaks in the Missouri Valley region. Nebraska Bird Rev., vol. 4, pp. 27–40.

Swenk, Myron Harmon, and Swenk, Jane Bishop

1928. Some impressions of the common winter birds of southern Arizona. Wilson Bull., vol. 40, pp. 17–29.

Swinburne, John

1888a. Breeding of the evening grosbeak (*Coccothraustes vespertina*) in the White Mountains of Arizona. Auk, vol. 5, pp. 113–114.

1888b. Occurrence of the chestnut-collared longspur (*Calcarius ornatus*) and also of Maccown's longspur (*Rhyncophanes maccownii*) in Apache Co., Arizona. Auk, vol. 5, pp. 321–322.

Taber, Richard Douglas

1946. The winter birds of Adak, Alaska. Condor, vol. 48, pp. 272–277.

1947. The dickcissel in Wisconsin. Passenger Pigeon, vol. 9, pp. 39–46.

Taber, Wendell

1952. Ipswich sparrow. Bull. Maine Audubon Soc., vol. 8, No. 2, pp. 39–40.

Taczanowski, Ladislas

1891. Faune Ornithologique de la Sibérie Orientale. Mém. Acad. Imp. Sci. St. Pétersbourg, ser. 7, vol. 39, pt. 1, pp. 680–681.

Taka-Tsukasa, Nobusuke

1928. The cage bird (in Japanese).

Tannehill, Ivan Ray

1945. Hurricanes, their nature and history, particularly those of the West Indies and the southern coasts of the United States.

Tanner, James Taylor

1958. Juncos in the Great Smoky Mountains. Migrant, vol. 29, pp. 61–65.

Tanner, Vasco M., and Hayward, C. Lynn

1934. A biological study of the La Sal Mountains, Utah. Report No. 1 (Ecology). Proc. Utah Acad. Sci., vol. 11, pp. 209–235.

Tashian, Richard E.

1953. The birds of southeastern Guatemala. Condor, vol. 55, pp. 198–210.

Tasker, Ronald Reginald

1955. Chipping sparrow with song of clay-colored sparrow at Toronto. Auk, vol. 72, p. 303.

TATE, RALPH C.

1923. Some birds of the Oklahoma panhandle. Proc. Oklahoma Acad. Sci., vol. 3, pp. 41–51.

1925. The house finch in the Oklahoma panhandle. Condor, vol. 27, p. 176.

TAVERNER, PERCY ALGERNON

1918. Some summer birds of Alert Bay, British Columbia. Condor, vol. 20, pp. 183–186.

1919. The birds of Shoal Lake, Manitoba. Canadian Field-Nat., vol. 33.

1921a. The evening grosbeak in Canada. Canadian Field-Nat., vol. 35, pp. 41–45.

1921b. Swarth on the Fox sparrow. Canadian Field-Nat., vol. 35, pp. 76–78.

1922a. Crossbills eating aphis. Condor, vol. 24, p. 96.

1922b. Birds of eastern Canada, 2d ed. Geol. Surv. Canada Mem. 104.

1926. Birds of western Canada. Victoria Mem. Mus. Bull. 41.

1927. Some recent Canadian records. Auk, vol. 44, pp. 217–228.

1932. A partial study of the Canadian Savannah sparrows, with description of *Passerculus sandwichensis campestris*, subsp. nov., the prairie Savannah sparrow. Proc. Biol. Soc. Washington, vol. 45, pp. 201–206.

1934. Birds of Canada. Nat. Mus. Canada, Dep. Mines Bull. 72, Biol. ser. No. 19.

TAVERNER, PERCY ALGERNON, and SUTTON, GEORGE MIKSCH

1934. The birds of Churchill, Manitoba. Ann. Carnegie Mus., vol. 23, pp. 1–83.

TAVERNER, PERCY ALGERNON, and SWALES, BRADSHAW HALL

1907. The birds of Point Pelee. Wilson Bull., vol. 19, pp. 133–153.

TAYLOR, MRS. H. J.

1920. Habits of a red-breasted sapsucker. Condor, vol. 22, p. 158.

1926. A field trip in the Sierra. Wilson Bull., vol. 38, pp. 201–203.

TAYLOR, WALTER PENN

1912. Field notes on amphibians, reptiles and birds of northern Humboldt County, Nevada, with a discussion of some of the faunal features of the region. Univ. California Publ. Zool., vol. 7, pp. 319–436.

TAYLOR, WALTER PENN, and SHAW, WILLIAM THOMAS

1927. Mammals and birds of Mount Rainier National Park. U.S. Dep. Interior, Nat. Park Service.

TENER, J. S.

1961. Breeding range extensions of two Ellesmere Island birds. Canadian Field-Nat., vol. 75, p. 51.

TEPLOVA, E. N.

1957. Birds of the region of the Pechora-Ilych Reserve (in Russian). Trudy Pechoro-Ilych. Gosud. Zapov., vol. 6, pp. 5–115.

TERRES, J. KENNETH

1939. Grasshopper sparrow caught in spider's web. Auk, vol. 56, p. 342.

TERRILL, L. McI., and SMITH, NAPIER

1930. Birds of the Razades and Basque Island. Provancher Soc. Nat. Hist. of Canada, Ann. Rep., pp. 27–35.

TERRILL, LEWIS McIVER

1952. The clay-colored sparrow in southeastern Ontario. Canadian Field-Nat., vol. 66, pp. 145–147.

1961. Cowbird hosts in southern Quebec. Canadian Field-Nat., vol. 75, pp. 2–11.

THATCHER, DONALD MASON
1954. Upper foothills, ponderosa pine forest. Audubon Field Notes, vol. 8, p. 372.
1955a. Immature lodgepole pine forest. Audubon Field Notes, vol. 9, p. 417.
1955b. Immature Douglas fir forest. Audubon Field Notes, vol. 9, pp. 418–419.
1956. Twentieth breeding-bird census: Upper foothills, ponderosa pine forest. Audubon Field Notes, vol. 10, pp. 421–423.

THAYER, JOHN E.
1909. Some rare birds and sets of eggs from the Cape region of Lower California. Condor, vol. 11, pp. 10–11.
1925. The nesting of the Worthen sparrow in Tamaulipas, Mexico. Condor, vol. 27, p. 34.

THAYER, JOHN ELIOT, and BANGS, OUTRAM
1907. Birds collected by W. W. Brown, Jr., on Cerros, San Benito and Natividad Islands in the spring of 1906, with notes on the biota of the islands. Condor, vol. 9, pp. 77–81.
1908. The present state of the ornis of Guadaloupe Island. Condor, vol. 10, pp. 101–106.

THAYER, MAY R.
1911. A bit of siskin courtship. Bird-Lore, vol. 13, p. 205.
1912. Some nesting habits of the Oregon junco. Bird-Lore, vol. 14, pp. 212–215.

THOBURN, WILBUR WILSON
1899. Report of an expedition in search of the fur seal of Guadalupe Island . . . *In* Treasury Department, Fur seals and fur seal islands of north Pacific Ocean, pt. 3, pp. 275–283.

THOMAS, RUTH H.
1952. Crip, come home.

THOMPSON, C. G.
1960. *In* News from the Bird-Banders, vol. 35, p. 26.

THOMPSON, ERNEST EVAN
1890. The birds of Manitoba. Proc. U.S. Nat. Mus., vol. 13, pp. 457–643.
1891–92. *In* Report of the occurrence of the evening grosbeak . . . in Ontario. Trans. Canadian Inst., vol. 3, p. 114.

THOREAU, HENRY DAVID
1910. Notes on New England birds, pp. 419–420.

THORNE, OAKLEIGH, 2D
1956. Differences between the common house finch and Cassin's purple finch of the genus *Carpodacus*. Thorne Ecol. Res. Sta., Bull. 3.

THORNE, PLATTE MARVIN
1895. List of birds observed in vicinity of Fort Keogh, Montana. Auk, vol. 12, pp. 211–219.

THORNTON, WILMOT A.
1951. Ecological distribution of the birds of the Stockton plateau in northern Terrell County, Texas. Texas Journ. Sci., No. 3, pp. 413–430.

THWAITES, REUBEN G.
1904–05. Original journals of Lewis and Clark. Vol. 2, pp. 19–120.

TINBERGEN, NIKO
1939. The behavior of the snow bunting in spring. Trans. Linn. Soc. New York, vol. 5, pp. 1–94.

TODD, W. E. CLYDE
1922. A new sparrow from southern California. Condor, vol. 24, pp. 126-127.
1924. A new song sparrow from Virginia. Auk, vol. 41, pp. 147–148.
1926. A study of the neotropical finches of the genus *Spinus*. Ann. Carnegie Mus., vol. 17, pp. 11–82.
1938. Two new races of North American birds. Auk, vol. 55, pp. 116–118.
1940. Birds of western Pennsylvania.
1942. Critical remarks on the races of the sharp-tailed sparrow. Ann. Carnegie Mus., vol. 29, pp. 197–199.
1947. Notes on the birds of southern Saskatchewan. Ann. Carnegie Mus., vol. 30, pp. 383–421.
1953. Further taxonomic notes on the white-crowned sparrow. Auk, vol. 70, pp. 370–372.
1963. Birds of the Labrador Peninsula and adjacent areas.

TOMKINS, IVAN REXFORD
1941. Notes on Macgillivray's seaside sparrow. Auk, vol. 58, pp. 38–51.

TOMPA, FRANK S.
1962. Territorial behavior: the main controlling factor of a local song sparrow population. Auk, vol. 79, pp. 687–697.

TOMPKINS, GRACE
1933. Individuality and territoriality as displayed in winter by three passerine species. Condor, vol. 35, pp. 98–106.

TORDOFF, HARRISON B.
1952. Notes on plumages, molts, and age variation of the red crossbill. Condor, vol. 54, pp. 200–203.
1954. Social organization and behavior in a flock of captive, nonbreeding red crossbills. Condor, vol. 56, pp. 346–358.

TORDOFF, HARRISON B., and MENGEL, ROBERT M.
1951. The occurrence and possible significance of the spring molt in Leconte's sparrow. Auk, vol. 68, pp. 519–522.
1956. Studies on birds killed in nocturnal migration. Univ. Kansas Publ. Mus. Nat. Hist., vol. 10.

TORREY, BRADFORD
1885. Birds in the bush, p. 60.

TOUT, WILSON
1902. Ten years without a gun. Proc. Nebraska Ornith. Union, vol. 3, pp. 42–45.
1936. The bird life of Lincoln County. Nebraska Bird Rev., vol. 4, pp. 51–52.

TOWNSEND, CHARLES HASKINS
1887. *In* Healy, Report of the cruise of the revenue steamer *Corwin* in the Arctic Ocean in the year 1885; U.S. Revenue-cutter service.
1923. Birds collected in Lower California. Bull. Amer. Mus. Nat. Hist., vol. 48, pp. 1–26.

TOWNSEND, CHARLES WENDELL
1905. The birds of Essex county, Massachusetts. Mem. Nuttall Ornith. Club, No. 3.
1906. Notes on the birds of Cape Breton Island. Auk, vol. 23, pp. 172–179.
1912a. Notes on the summer birds of the St. John Valley, New Brunswick. Auk, vol. 29, pp. 16–23.
1912b. Bird genealogy. Auk, vol. 29, pp. 285–295.

TOWNSEND, CHARLES WENDELL—Continued

1920. Birds of Essex County, Massachusetts. Mem. Nuttall Ornith. Club, suppl., No. 3, p. 143.

1925. Winter birds seen at the Grand Canyon, Arizona. Condor, vol. 27, p. 177.

1931. A Shufeldt's junco (*Junco oreganus shufeldti*) in Ipswich, Mass. Auk, vol. 48, p. 274.

1933. Shufeldt's junco in the East. Auk, vol. 50, p. 226.

TOWNSEND, CHARLES WENDELL, and ALLEN, GLOVER MORRILL

1907. Birds of Labrador. Proc. Boston Soc. Nat. Hist., vol. 33, pp. 277–428.

TOWNSEND, CHARLES WENDELL, and BENT, ARTHUR CLEVELAND

1910. Additional notes on the birds of Labrador. Auk, vol. 27, pp. 1–18.

TOWNSEND, JOHN KIRK

1837. Description of twelve new species of birds chiefly from the vicinity of the Columbia River. Journ. Acad. Nat. Sci. Philadelphia, vol. 7, pp. 187–192.

TRAUTMAN, MILTON BERNARD

1940. The birds of Buckeye Lake, Ohio. Univ. Michigan Mus. Zool., Misc. Publ. No. 44.

1956. Unusual bird records for Ohio. Auk, vol. 73, pp. 272–276.

TROTTER, SPENCER

1891. Effect of environment in the modification of the bill and tail of birds. Proc. Acad. Nat. Sci. Philadelphia, p. 118.

TUCK, LESLIE M.

1948. Recent observations on Newfoundland birds in the Argentia-Dunville area. Canadian Field-Nat., vol. 62, pp. 103–112.

1952. Dickcissel in Newfoundland. Canadian Field-Nat., vol. 66, p. 68.

TUFTS, HAROLD FREEMAN

1906. Nesting of crossbills in Nova Scotia. Auk, vol. 23, pp. 339–340.

1910. Nesting of the pine grosbeak in Nova Scotia. Warbler, vol. 6, pp. 17–18.

TUFTS, ROBIE W.

1961. The birds of Nova Scotia.

TURNER, LUCIEN M.

1885. Notes on the birds of the Nearer Islands, Alaska. Auk, vol. 2, pp. 154–159.

1886. Contributions to the natural history of Alaska. U.S. Sig. Serv., Arctic ser., No. 2, pt. 5, Birds, p. 169.

TWINING, HOWARD

1940. Foraging behavior and survival in the Sierra Nevada rosy finch. Condor, vol. 42, pp. 64–72.

TWOMEY, ARTHUR CORNELIUS

1942. The birds of the Uinta Basin, Utah. Ann. Carnegie Mus., vol. 28, pp. 341–490.

TYLER, JOHN G.

1910. The Brewer sparrow (*Spizella breweri*) in Fresno County, California. Condor, vol. 12, pp. 193–195.

1913. Some birds of the Fresno District, California. Pacific Coast Avifauna, No. 9.

1923. Observations on the habits of the prairie falcon. Condor, vol. 25, pp. 90–97.

TYLER, WINSOR MARRETT
1916. Evening grosbeaks in Lexington, Mass. Bird-Lore, vol. 18, pp. 107–108.
1922. The season: Boston region. Bird-Lore, vol. 24, p. 153.
1924. The season: Boston region. Bird-Lore, vol. 26, pp. 185–186.

USSHER, R. D.
1935. Fox sparrow wintering at Toronto. Canadian Field-Nat., vol. 49, p. 140.

VACIN, VICTOR
1961. Harris sparrow records, winter 1960–61. Scissortail, vol. 11, No. 1, pp. 21–22.

VAN CLEAVE, HARLEY J.
1942. A reconsideration of *Plagiorynchus formosus* and observations on *Acanthocephala* with atypical *lemnisci*. Trans. American Micr. Soc., vol. 61, pp. 206–210.

VAN CLEAVE, HARLEY J., and WILLIAMS, RALPH B.
1951. *Acanthocephala* from passerine birds in Alaska. Journ. Parasitology, vol. 37, pp. 151–157.

VAN DENBURGH, JOHN
1924. The birds of the Todos Santos Islands. Condor, vol. 26, pp. 67–71.

VAN HOOSE, S. G.
1955. Distributional and breeding records of some birds from Coahuila. Wilson Bull., vol. 67, pp. 302–303.

VAN ROSSEM, ADRIAAN JOSEPH
1911. Winter birds of the Salton Sea region. Condor, vol. 13, pp. 129–137.
1921a. Eastern California occurrences of the golden-crowned sparrow. Condor, vol. 23, p. 136.
1921b. A yellow phase of the Cassin purple finch. Condor, vol. 23, p. 163.
1925. The status of the San Clemente house finch. Condor, vol. 27, pp. 176–177.
1930. Four new birds from north-western Mexico. Trans. San Diego Soc. Nat. Hist., vol. 6, pp. 213–226.
1931. Report on a collection of land birds from Sonora, Mexico. Trans. San Diego Soc. Nat. Hist., vol. 6, pp. 237–304.
1932a. The type of the black-headed grosbeak. Auk, vol. 49, p. 489.
1932b. On the validity of the San Clemente Island Bell's sparrow. Auk, vol. 49, pp. 490–491.
1934a. Notes on some types of North American birds. Trans. San Diego Soc. Nat. Hist., vol. 7, pp. 347–362.
1934b. A northwestern race of the varied bunting. Trans. San Diego Soc. Nat. Hist., vol. 7, pp. 369–370.
1934c. A subspecies of the brown towhee from south-central Texas. Trans. San Diego Soc. Nat. Hist., vol. 7, pp. 371–372.
1935a. A new race of brown towhee from the Inyo region of California. Trans. San Diego Soc. Nat. Hist., vol. 8, pp. 69–71.
1935b. Notes on the forms of *Spizella atrogularis*. Condor, vol. 37, pp. 282–284.
1936a. Birds of the Charleston Mountains, Nevada. Pacific Coast Avifauna, No. 24.
1936b. Notes on birds in relation to the faunal areas of south-central Arizona. Trans. San Diego Soc. Nat. Hist., vol. 8, pp. 121–146.
1943. Description of a race of goldfinch from the Pacific Northwest. Condor, vol. 45, pp. 158–159.

van Rossem, Adriaan Joseph—Continued

1945a. A distributional survey of the birds of Sonora, Mexico. Occas. pap., Mus. Zool. Louisiana State Univ., No. 21.

1945b. Preliminary studies on the black-throated sparrows of Baja California, Mexico. Trans. San Diego Soc. Nat. Hist., vol. 10, pp. 237–244.

1946a. Two new races of birds from the lower Colorado River Valley. Condor, vol. 48, pp. 80–82.

1946b. Two new races of birds from the Harquahala Mountains, Arizona. Auk, vol. 63, pp. 560–563.

1947a. A synopsis of the Savannah sparrows of northwestern Mexico. Condor, vol. 49, pp. 97–107, 173.

1947b. Comment on certain birds of Baja California, including descriptions of three new races. Proc. Biol. Soc. Washington, vol. 60, pp. 51–56.

Van Tyne, Josselyn

1932. Winter returns of the indigo bunting in Guatemala. Bird-Banding, vol. 3, p. 110.

1934. *Pinicola enucleator eschatosus* in Michigan and Ohio. Auk, vol. 51, pp. 529–530.

1935. The Birds of Northern Petén, Guatemala. Univ. Michigan Mus. Zool., Misc. Publ. No. 27.

1936. *Spizella breweri taverneri* in Texas. Auk, vol. 53, p. 92.

1941. Early records of the clay-colored sparrow in Michigan. Auk, vol. 58, pp. 413–414.

1951. A cardinal's, *Richmondena cardinalis*, choice of food for adult and for young. Auk, vol. 68, p. 110.

1953. *In* Bent, Life histories of North American wood warblers. U.S. Nat. Mus. Bull. 203.

Van Tyne, Josselyn, and Berger, Andrew J.

1959. Fundamentals of Ornithology, pp. 287–289.

Van Tyne, Josselyn, and Drury, William Holland, Jr.

1959. The birds of southern Bylot Island, 1954. Occas. Pap. Univ. Michigan Mus. Zool., No. 615.

Van Tyne, Josselyn, and Sutton, George Miksch

1937. The birds of Brewster County, Tex. Univ. Michigan Mus. Zool., Misc. Publ. No. 37.

Vaurie, Charles

1946. Early morning song during middle and late summer. Auk, vol. 63, pp. 163–171.

Vieillot, L. J. P.

1819. *Touit*. *In* Nouveau dictionnaire d'histoire naturelle, vol. 34, pp. 291–293.

Vilks, E. K.

1958. Experimental investigation of the behavior of certain Passerines during the nesting period by means of natural stimuli (in Russian). Trudy Inst. Biol. Akad. Nauk Latviyskoy S.S.R., vol. 6, pp. 177–186.

Visher, Stephen Sargent

1910. Notes on the birds of Pima County, Arizona. Auk, vol. 27, pp. 279–288.

1911. Annotated list of the birds of Harding County, northwestern South Dakota. Auk, vol. 28, pp. 15–16.

1912. A list of the birds of the Pine Ridge Reservation. *In* The biology of south-central South Dakota. Vermilion Bull. Geol. Surv. South Dakota, No. 5, pp. 61–136.

1913. An annotated list of the birds of Sanborn County, southeast-central South Dakota. Auk, vol. 30, pp. 561–573.

1914. A preliminary report on the biology of Harding County, northwestern South Dakota. South Dakota Geol. Surv., Bull. 6.

VOGE, MARIETTA, and DAVIS, BETTY S.

1953. Studies on the cestode genus *Anonchotaenia* (Dilepididae, Paruterininae) and related forms. Univ. California Publ. Zool., vol. 59.

VON BLOEKER, JACK C., JR.

1936. Avian ocean hitch-hikers. Condor, vol. 38, pp. 37–38.

VOOUS, K. H.

1960. Atlas of European birds.

1949. Distributional history of Eurasian bullfinches, genus *Pyrrhula.* Condor, vol. 51, pp. 52–81.

WADA, K.

1933. A captive Cassin's bullfinch (in Japanese). Data on birds and mammals, Dep. Forestry, Tokyo, vol. 9, p. 371.

WAGLER, JOHANN GEORG

1831. Einige Mittheilungen über Thiere Mexicos. Isis von Oken, 1831, pp. 510–535.

WAGNER, HELMUTH OTTO

1955. Bruthelfer unter den Vögeln. Veröff. Überseemus, vol. 2A, pp. 327–330.

WALKER, ALEX

1917. Some birds of central Oregon. Condor, vol. 19, pp. 131–140.

WALKINSHAW, L. H., and STOPHLET, J. J.

1949. Bird observations of Johnson River, Alaska. Condor, vol. 51, pp. 29–34.

WALKINSHAW, LAWRENCE HARVEY

1936. Our evening grosbeak. Bird-Lore, vol. 38, pp. 32–33.

1937. Leconte's sparrow breeding in Michigan and South Dakota. Auk, vol. 54, pp. 309–320.

1938. Life history studies of the eastern goldfinch. Jack-Pine Warbler (Bull. Michigan Audubon Soc.), vol. 16, No. 4, pp. 3–11, 14–15.

1939a. Life history studies of the eastern goldfinch, pt. II, Jack-Pine Warbler (Bull. Michigan Audubon Soc.), vol. 17, No. 1, pp. 3–12.

1939b. Some migration notes of the "Fringillidae" at Battle Creek, Michigan. Jack-Pine Warbler, vol. 17, pp. 107–111.

1939c. Nesting of the field sparrow and survival of the young. Bird-Banding, vol. 10, pp. 107–114, 149–157.

1939d. Notes on the nesting of the clay-colored sparrow. Wilson Bull., vol. 51, pp. 17–21.

1940. Some Michigan notes on the grasshopper sparrow. Jack-Pine Warbler, vol. 18, pp. 50–59.

1943. Snakes destroying birds' eggs and young. Wilson Bull., vol. 55, p. 56.

1944a. Clay-colored sparrow notes. Jack-Pine Warbler, vol. 22, pp. 119–131.

1944b. The eastern chipping sparrow in Michigan. Wilson Bull., vol. 56, pp. 193–205.

1945. Field sparrow, 39–54015. Bird-Banding, vol. 16, pp. 1–14.

1947. Brushy field, woodlots and pond. Audubon Field Notes, vol. 1, pp. 214–216.

WALKINSHAW, LAWRENCE HARVEY—Continued

1948. Nestings of some passerine birds in western Alaska. Condor, vol. 50, pp. 64–70.

1952. Chipping sparrow notes. Bird-Banding, vol. 23, pp. 101–108.

WALLACE, GEORGE JOHN

1942. Returns and survival rate of wintering tree sparrows. Bird-Banding, vol. 13, pp. 81–83.

WARBACH, OSCAR

1958. Bird populations in relation to change in land use. Journ. Wildlife Management, vol. 22, pp. 23–28.

WARBURTON, FREDERICK E.

1952. Nesting of clay-colored sparrow, *Spizella pallida*, in northern Ontario. Auk, vol. 69, pp. 314–316.

WARREN, BENJAMIN HARRY

1890. Report on the birds of Pennsylvania, ed. 2.

WARREN, EDWARD ROYAL

1905. Cassin's sparrow in Colorado. Auk, vol. 22, p. 417.

1906. A collecting trip to southeastern Colorado. Condor, vol. 8, pp. 18–24.

1910a. Some central Colorado bird notes. Condor, vol. 12, pp. 23–39.

1910b. Bird notes from Salida, Chaffee County, Colorado. Auk, vol. 27, pp. 142–151.

1912. Some north-central Colorado bird notes. Condor, vol. 14, pp. 81–104.

1913. Notes on some Mesa County, Colorado, birds. Condor, vol. 15, pp. 110–111.

1915. Some Park County, Colorado, bird notes. Condor, vol. 17, pp. 90–95.

1916. Notes on the birds of the Elk Mountain region, Gunnison County, Colorado. Auk, vol. 33, pp. 292–317.

WATSON, ADAM

1957. Birds in Cumberland Peninsula, Baffin Island. Canadian Field-Nat., vol. 71, pp. 87–109.

WATSON, SERENO

1876. Botanical contributions. On the flora of Guadalupe Island, Lower California. Proc. Amer. Acad. Sci., vol. 11, pp. 105–148.

WAUER, ROLAND H.

1962. A survey of the birds of Death Valley. Condor, vol. 64, pp. 220–233.

1964. Ecological distribution of the birds of the Panamint Mountains, California. Condor, vol. 66, pp. 287–301.

WAYNE, ARTHUR TREZEVANT

1899. Destruction of birds by the great cold wave of February 13 and 14, 1899. Auk, vol. 16, pp. 197–198.

1906. A contribution to the ornithology of South Carolina, chiefly the coast region. Auk, vol. 23, pp. 56–68.

1910. Birds of South Carolina. Contr. Charleston Mus., No. 1.

1917. A list of avian species for which the type locality is South Carolina. Contr. Charleston Mus., No. 3.

1921. Albinism in the sharp-tailed sparrow (*Passerherbulus caudacutus*). Auk, vol. 38, pp. 604–605.

1922a. An albino swamp sparrow (*Melospiza georgiana*). Auk, vol. 39, p. 265.

1922b. The Carolina junco (*Junco hyemalis*) on the coast of South Carolina. Auk, vol. 39, p. 420.

1927. Breeding of Macgillivray's seaside sparrow in South Carolina. Auk, vol. 44, pp. 254–255.

WEAVER, RICHARD LEE

1940. The purple finch invasion of northeastern United States and the Maritime Provinces in 1939. Bird-Banding, vol. 11, pp. 79–105.

1948. Pine siskins in northern Florida. Auk, vol. 65, p. 311.

WEAVER, RICHARD LEE, and WEST, FRANKLIN H.

1943. Notes on the breeding of the pine siskin. Auk, vol. 60, pp. 492–504.

WEBER, WALTER M.

1956. Occurrence of the Aleutian tern and rustic bunting in the Aleutian Islands. Condor, vol. 58, p. 235.

WEBSTER, HAROLD

1944. A survey of the prairie falcon in Colorado. Auk, vol. 61, pp. 609–616.

WEBSTER, JACKSON DAN

1950. Notes on the birds of Wrangell and vicinity, southeastern Alaska. Condor, vol. 52, pp. 32–38.

1954. Censuses numbers 27 and 28. Audubon Field Notes, vol. 8, pp. 376–378.

1958. Further ornithological notes from Zacatecas, Mexico. Wilson Bull., vol. 70, pp. 243–256.

1959. A revision of the Botteri sparrow. Condor, vol. 61, pp. 136–146.

WEBSTER, JACKSON DAN, and ORR, ROBERT THOMAS

1952. Notes on Mexican birds from the states of Durango and Zacatecas. Condor, vol. 54, pp. 309–313.

1954a. Summering birds of Zacatecas, Mexico, with a description of a new race of Worthen sparrow. Condor, vol. 56, pp. 155–160.

1954b. Miscellaneous notes on Mexican birds. Wilson Bull., vol. 66, pp. 267–269.

WEED, CLARENCE M.

1898. The feeding habits of the chipping sparrow. New Hampshire College Agric. Bull. 54, pp. 101–110.

WEISE, CHARLES MARTIN

1956. Nightly unrest in caged migratory sparrows under outdoor conditions. Ecology, vol. 37, pp. 274–287.

WELCH, CECIL M.

1936. Further notes on Montana birds, 1935. Auk, vol. 53, pp. 230–231.

WELLMAN, GORDON BOIT

1920. Dance of the purple finch. Auk, vol. 37, pp. 584–585.

WELLS, PHILIP V.

1958. Indigo buntings in Lazuli bunting habitat in southwestern Utah. Auk, vol. 75, pp. 223–224.

WERNICKE, MALETA MOORE

1948. A fifteen year old rose-breasted grosbeak. Jack-Pine Warbler, vol. 26, pp. 136–138.

WESSEL, B. A.

1904. Ornithologiske meddelelser fra Sydvaranger. Tromsø Mus. Aarshefter, vol. 27, pp. 20–126.

WEST, DAVID A.

1962. Hydridization in grosbeaks (*Pheucticus*) of the Great Plains. Auk, vol. 79, pp. 399–424.

WEST, GEORGE CURTISS

1960. Seasonal variation in the energy balance of the tree sparrow in relation to migration. Auk, vol. 77, pp. 306–329.

WESTMAN, FRANCES

1960. We've been thinking . . . about casualties at the Barrie TV tower. Feder. Ontario Nat. Bull., No. 90, pp. 4–5.

WESTON, FRANCIS MARION

1939. *In* Hyde, The life history of Henslow's sparrow, *Passerherbulus Henslowii* (Audubon). Univ. Michigan Mus. Zool., Misc. Publ. No. 41.

WESTON, HENRY G., JR.

1947. Breeding behavior of the black-headed grosbeak. Condor, vol. 49, pp. 54–73.

WETHERBEE, D. K., and WETHERBEE, N. S.

1961. Artificial incubation of eggs of various bird species and some attributes of neonates. Bird-Banding, vol. 32, pp. 141–159.

WETHERBEE, DAVID KENNETH

1957. Natal plumages and downy pteryloses of passerine birds of North America. Bull. Amer. Mus. Nat. Hist., vol. 113, pp. 345–436.

WETHERBEE, MRS. KENNETH BRACKETT

1934. Some measurements and weights of live birds. Bird-Banding, vol. 5, pp. 55–64.

1935. A singing female song sparrow. Bird-Banding, vol. 6, pp. 32–33.

1937. A study of wintering hoary, common and greater redpolls, and various intermediates or hybrids. Bird-Banding, vol. 7, p. 10.

WETMORE, ALEXANDER

1909. Fall notes from eastern Kansas. Condor, vol. 11, pp. 154–164.

1920. Observations on the habits of birds at Lake Burford, New Mexico. Auk, vol. 37, pp. 221–247, 393–412.

1927. The birds of Porto Rico and the Virgin Islands. *In* Scientific Survey of Porto Rico and the Virgin Islands, New York Acad. Sci., vol. 9, pt. 4, p. 554.

1936a. The number of contour feathers in passeriform and related birds. Auk, vol. 53, pp. 159–169.

1936b. A new race of the song sparrow from the Appalachian region. Smithsonian Misc. Coll., vol. 95.

1944a. The birds of southern Veracruz, Mexico. Proc. U.S. Nat. Mus., vol. 93, pp. 215–340.

1944b. Records of sharp-tailed sparrows from Maryland and Virginia in the National Museum. Auk, vol. 61, pp. 132–133.

1946. The dickcissel in eastern West Virginia. Auk, vol. 63, p. 102.

1956. A check-list of the fossil and prehistoric birds of north America and the West Indies. Smithsonian Misc. Coll., vol. 131.

WETMORE, ALEXANDER, AND LINCOLN, FREDERICK C.

1928. The dickcissel in Maryland. Auk, vol. 45, pp. 508–509.

1932. The sharp-tailed sparrows of Maryland. Auk, vol. 49, p. 231.

WEYDEMEYER, WINTON

1936. Late nesting of six species of Montana birds. Condor, vol. 38, p. 45.

WEYGANDT, CORNELIUS

1930. The Wissahickon Hills; memories of leisure hours out of doors in an old countryside.

WHARTON, WILLIAM P.

1931. Foot disease on birds at Summerville, South Carolina. Bird-Banding, vol. 2, p. 35.

1941. Twelve years of banding at Summerville, South Carolina. Bird-Banding, vol. 12, pp. 137–147.

1953. Recoveries of birds banded at Groton, Massachusetts, 1932–1950. Bird-Banding, vol. 24, pp. 1–7.

Wheelock, Irene Grosvenor
1905. Regurgitative feeding of nestlings. Auk, vol. 22, pp. 54–71.
1912. Birds of California, ed. 3 (ed. 1, 1904).

Wheelwright, H. W.
1871. A spring and summer in Lapland, ed. 2.

Whitaker, Lovie M.
1957a. Lark sparrow oiling its tarsi. Wilson Bull., vol. 69, pp. 179–180.
1957b. A résumé of anting, with particular reference to a captive orchard oriole. Wilson Bull., vol. 69, pp. 195–262.

White, Francis Beach
1937. Local notes on the birds at Concord, New Hampshire.

Whitney, Nathaniel Ruggles, Jr.
1954. Winter bird population study: Open ponderosa pine forest. Audubon Field Notes, vol. 8, pp. 283–284.
1955. Winter bird population study: Open ponderosa pine forest. Audubon Field Notes, vol. 9, p. 305.
1956. Winter bird population study: Open ponderosa pine forest. Audubon Field Notes, vol. 10, p. 300.

Whittle, Charles L.
1922. Miscellaneous bird notes from Montana. Condor, vol. 24, pp. 73–81.
1926. On the nature of the relationship existing among land birds during sustained aerial migration. Auk, vol. 43, pp. 493–500.
1928. Xanthochroism in the purple finch. Bull. Northeastern Bird-Banding Assoc., vol. 4, pp. 25–27.

Whittle, Helen Granger
1928. Color-phases of the purple finch. Bull. Northeastern Bird-Banding Assoc., vol. 4, pp. 102–104.

Widmann, Otto
1896. The peninsula of Missouri as a winter home for birds. Auk, vol. 13, pp. 216–222.
1904. Yosemite Valley birds. Auk, vol. 21, pp. 66–73.
1907. A preliminary catalogue of the birds of Missouri.
1911. List of birds observed in Estes Park, Colorado, from June 10 to July 18, 1910. Auk, vol. 28, p. 316.

Wied-Neuwied, Maximilian Alexander Phillipe
1834. Reise in das innere Nord-America in den jahren 1834, vol. 2.

Wilbur, Sanford R.
1963. A record of the indigo bunting in northwestern California. Condor, vol. 65, pp. 533–534.

Willard, Francis Cottle
1910. Nesting of the western evening grosbeak (*Hesperiphona vespertina montana*). Condor, vol. 12, pp. 60–62.
1912a. A week afield in southern Arizona. Condor, vol. 14, pp. 53–63.
1912b. Breeding of the Scott sparrow. Condor, vol. 14, pp. 195–196.
1913. Late nesting of certain birds in Arizona. Condor, vol. 15, p. 227.
1918. Evidence that many birds remain mated for life. Condor, vol. 20, pp. 167–170.
1923. Some unusual nesting sites of several Arizona birds. Condor, vol. 25, pp. 121–125.

Willett, George
1912. Birds of the Pacific slope of southern California. Pacific Coast Avifauna, No. 7.

WILLETT, GEORGE—Continued

1913. Bird notes from the coast of northern Lower California. Condor, vol. 15, pp. 19–24.

1914. Birds of Sitka and vicinity, southeastern Alaska. Condor, vol. 16, pp. 71–91.

1915. Summer birds of Forrester Island, Alaska. Auk, vol. 32, pp. 295–305.

1919. Bird notes from southeastern Oregon and northeastern California. Condor, vol. 21, pp. 194–207.

1920. Additional notes on the avifauna of Forrester Island, Alaska. Condor, vol. 22, pp. 138–139.

1921a. Distribution of the Townsend fox sparrow. Condor, vol. 23, pp. 36–37.

1921b. Bird notes from southeastern Alaska. Condor, vol. 23, pp. 156–159.

1921c. Ornithological notes from southeastern Alaska. Auk, vol. 38, pp. 127–129.

1928a. Notes on some birds of southeastern Alaska. Auk, vol. 45, pp. 445–449.

1928b. *Melospiza melodia.* Auk, vol. 45, pp. 447–448.

1933. A revised list of the birds of southwestern California. Pacific Coast Avifauna, No. 21.

WILLIAMS, ARTHUR B.

1950. Birds of the Cleveland region. Cleveland Mus. Nat. Hist., Sci. Publ., vol. 10.

WILLIAMS, GEORGE G.

1945. Do birds cross the Gulf of Mexico in the spring? Auk, vol. 62, pp. 98–111.

1950. Weather and spring migration. Auk, vol. 67, pp. 52–65.

WILLIAMS, JOHN J.

1900. Probable causes of bird scarcity in parts of the Sierras, an arraignment of the chipmunk. Condor, vol. 2, pp. 97–101.

WILLIAMS, L. PERCY

1897. Notes on the nesting of the rufous-crowned sparrow. Osprey, vol. 2, pp. 27–28.

WILLIAMS, LAIDLAW

1961. Indigo bunting at Carmel, California. Condor, vol. 63, pp. 341–342.

WILLIAMS, RALPH BENJAMIN

1946. *Ixodes auritulus* on a Savannah sparrow. Auk, vol. 63, p. 590.

WILLIAMS, ROBERT WHITE, JR.

1906. Further notes on the birds of Leon County, Florida. Auk, vol. 23, pp. 153–161.

1929. Additions to the list of the birds of Leon County, Florida, suppl. 5. Auk, vol. 46, p. 122.

WILLIAMSON, FRANCIS S. L.

1957. Ecological distribution of birds in the Napaskiak area of the Kuskokwim River Delta, Alaska. Condor, vol. 59, pp. 317–338.

WILSON, ALEXANDER

1811. American Ornithology, vol. 4, p. 68.

WILSON, ALEXANDER, and BONAPARTE, CHARLES LUCIEN

1832. American ornithology; or the natural history of the birds of the United States, vol. 1.

WILSON, FRANK N.

1931. An uncommon Michigan sparrow. Bird-Lore, vol. 33, pp. 108–110.

WILSON, ROWLAND STEELE

1948. The summer bird life of Attu. Condor, vol. 50, pp. 124–129.

WING, LEONARD W.
1949. Breeding birds of virgin Palouse prairie. Auk, vol. 66, pp. 38–41.
WISNER, ROBERT L.
1952. Land birds at sea. Condor, vol. 54, pp. 62–63.
WITHERBY, H. F., ET AL.
1938–41. The handbook of British birds, 5 vols.
WITHERBY, HARRY FORBES, ED.
1920. A practical handbook of British birds, vol. 1.
WOLFE, LLOYD RAYMOND
1956. Check-list of the birds of Texas.
WOLFSON, ALBERT
1942. Regulation of spring migration in juncos. Condor, vol. 44, pp. 237–263.
1952. The cloacal protuberance—a means for determining breeding condition in live male passerines. Bird-Banding, vol. 23, pp. 159–165.
1960. The role of light and darkness in the regulation of the annual stimulus for spring migration and reproductive cycles. Proc. XII Internat. Ornith. Congr., vol. 2, pp. 758–789.
WOOD, HAROLD BACON
1951. Development of white in tails of juncos, *Junco hyemalis*. Auk, vol. 68, pp. 522–523.
WOOD, MERRILL
1958. Birds of central Pennsylvania. Pennsylvania State Univ. College Agric., Agric. Expt. Sta., Bull. 632.
WOOD, NORMAN ASA
1911. The results of the Mershon Expedition to the Charity Islands, Lake Huron. Wilson Bull., vol. 23, pp. 78–112.
1921. Some southern Michigan bird records. Auk, vol. 38, pp. 590–594.
1923. A preliminary survey of the bird life of North Dakota. Univ. Michigan Mus. Zool., Misc. Publ. No. 10.
1951. The birds of Michigan. Univ. Michigan Mus. Zool., Misc. Publ. No. 75.
WOOD, SHERWIN F., and HERMAN, CARLTON M.
1943. The occurrence of blood parasites in birds from southwestern United States. Journ. Parasitology, vol. 29, pp. 187–196.
WOODBURY, A. M., and COTTAM, C.
1962. Ecological studies of birds in Utah. Univ. Utah Biol. Ser. 12.
WOODBURY, ANGUS M.
1933. The scratching of the spurred towhee. Condor, vol. 35, p. 70.
1941. Bird habitats of the Salt Lake region. Bird-Lore, vol. 43, pp. 253–264.
WOODBURY, ANGUS M., COTTAM, CLARENCE, and SUGDEN, JOHN W.
1949. Annotated check-list of the birds of Utah. Univ. Utah Bull., Biol. Ser., vol. 11.
WOODBURY, ANGUS M., and RUSSELL, H. N., JR.
1945. Birds of the Navajo Country. Univ. Utah Bull., vol. 35, No. 14.
WOODHOUSE, S. W.
1852. Description of a new snow finch of the genus *Struthus*, Boie. Proc. Acad. Nat. Sci. Philadelphia, vol. 6, pp. 202–203.
WOODRUFF, EDWARD SEYMOUR
1908. A preliminary list of the birds of Shannon and Carter counties, Missouri. Auk, vol. 25, pp. 191–214.

WOODS, ROBERT S.

1932. Acquired food habits of some native birds. Condor, vol. 34, pp. 237–240.

WOOLFENDEN, GLEN E.

1956. Comparative breeding behavior of *Ammospiza caudacuta* and *A. maritima*. Univ. Kansas Publ. Mus. Nat. Hist., vol. 10, pp. 45–75.

WORTHINGTON, W. W., and TODD, W. E. CLYDE

1926. The birds of the Choctawhatchee Bay region of Florida. Wilson Bull., vol. 38, pp. 204–229.

WRIGHT, ALBERT HAZEN, and ALLEN, ARTHUR AUGUSTUS

1910. Regular summer crossbills at Ithaca, N.Y. Auk, vol. 27, p. 83.

WRIGHT, HORACE WINSLOW

1911. The birds of the Jefferson region in the White Mountains, New Hampshire, Proc. Inst. Arts Sci., New Hampshire, vol. 5.

WRIGHT, HOWARD, and SNYDER, G. K.

1913. Birds observed in the summer of 1912 among the Santa Barbara Islands. Condor, vol. 15, pp. 86–92.

WRIGHT, MABEL OSGOOD

1907. The indigo bunting. Bird-Lore, vol. 9, pp. 179–182.

WYMAN, L. E., and BURNELL, E. F.

1925. Field book of birds of the southwestern United States.

WYNNE-EDWARDS, VERO COPNER

1952. Zoology of the Baird expedition (1950): 1. The birds observed in central and south-east Baffin Island. Auk, vol. 69, pp. 353–391.

1956. Birds observed at Goose Bay and elsewhere in Labrador. Canadian Field-Nat., vol. 70, pp. 76–77.

WYTHE, MARGARET WILHELMINA

1917. Sierra junco breeding at Berkeley. Condor, vol. 19, p. 185.

YAMASHINA, YOSHIMARO

1933. A natural history of Japanese birds (in Japanese), vol. 1.

YOUNG, HOWARD

1963. Breeding success of the cowbird. Wilson Bull., vol. 75, pp. 115–122.

YOUNGWORTH, WILLIAM

1930. Prairie birds seek the shade. Wilson Bull., vol. 42, p. 55.

1932. Another hybrid between the indigo and lazuli buntings. Wilson Bull., vol. 44, p. 239.

1933. Spring migration dates from Sioux City, Iowa. Iowa Bird Life, vol. 3, pp. 38–39.

1935. The lazuli bunting in northeastern South Dakota. Wilson Bull., vol. 47.

1953. From the observer's note book. Iowa Bird Life, vol. 23, pp. 68–71.

1955a. The saga of a cardinal nest. Iowa Bird Life, vol. 25, pp. 58–59.

1955b. Another grosbeak food. Iowa Bird Life, vol. 25, p. 59.

1957. The bouncy goldfinch. Iowa Bird Life, vol. 27, p. 101.

1958. The blue grosbeak in western Iowa, a summary. Iowa Bird Life, vol. 28, pp. 57–59.

1959a. The Harris sparrow in the Missouri Valley. South Dakota Bird Notes, vol. 11, No. 4, pp. 64–67.

1959b. Hail to the crabgrass! Iowa Bird Life, vol. 29, p. 106.

ZIMMER, JOHN T.

1913. Birds of the Thomas County Forest Reserve. Proc. Nebraska Ornith. Union, vol. 5, pp. 51–104.

ZIMMERMAN, DALE A.
1954. Bird mortality on Michigan highways. Jack-Pine Warbler, vol. 32, pp. 60–66.
1957. Notes on Tamaulipan birds. Wilson Bull., vol. 69, pp. 273–277.

Index

(Page numbers of principal entries are in *italics*)

B

E

I

J

K

L

N

O

P

T

U

V

A CATALOGUE OF SELECTED DOVER BOOKS IN ALL FIELDS OF INTEREST

A CATALOGUE OF SELECTED DOVER BOOKS IN ALL FIELDS OF INTEREST

America's Old Masters, James T. Flexner. Four men emerged unexpectedly from provincial 18th century America to leadership in European art: Benjamin West, J. S. Copley, C. R. Peale, Gilbert Stuart. Brilliant coverage of lives and contributions. Revised, 1967 edition. 69 plates. 365pp. of text.
21806-6 Paperbound $3.00

First Flowers of Our Wilderness: American Painting, The Colonial Period, James T. Flexner. Painters, and regional painting traditions from earliest Colonial times up to the emergence of Copley, West and Peale Sr., Foster, Gustavus Hesselius, Feke, John Smibert and many anonymous painters in the primitive manner. Engaging presentation, with 162 illustrations. xxii + 368pp.
22180-6 Paperbound $3.50

The Light of Distant Skies: American Painting, 1760-1835, James T. Flexner. The great generation of early American painters goes to Europe to learn and to teach: West, Copley, Gilbert Stuart and others. Allston, Trumbull, Morse; also contemporary American painters—primitives, derivatives, academics—who remained in America. 102 illustrations. xiii + 306pp. 22179-2 Paperbound $3.50

A History of the Rise and Progress of the Arts of Design in the United States, William Dunlap. Much the richest mine of information on early American painters, sculptors, architects, engravers, miniaturists, etc. The only source of information for scores of artists, the major primary source for many others. Unabridged reprint of rare original 1834 edition, with new introduction by James T. Flexner, and 394 new illustrations. Edited by Rita Weiss. 6⅝ x 9⅝.
21695-0, 21696-9, 21697-7 Three volumes, Paperbound $13.50

Epochs of Chinese and Japanese Art, Ernest F. Fenollosa. From primitive Chinese art to the 20th century, thorough history, explanation of every important art period and form, including Japanese woodcuts; main stress on China and Japan, but Tibet, Korea also included. Still unexcelled for its detailed, rich coverage of cultural background, aesthetic elements, diffusion studies, particularly of the historical period. 2nd, 1913 edition. 242 illustrations. lii + 439pp. of text.
20364-6, 20365-4 Two volumes, Paperbound $6.00

The Gentle Art of Making Enemies, James A. M. Whistler. Greatest wit of his day deflates Oscar Wilde, Ruskin, Swinburne; strikes back at inane critics, exhibitions, art journalism; aesthetics of impressionist revolution in most striking form. Highly readable classic by great painter. Reproduction of edition designed by Whistler. Introduction by Alfred Werner. xxxvi + 334pp.
21875-9 Paperbound $3.00

VISUAL ILLUSIONS: THEIR CAUSES, CHARACTERISTICS, AND APPLICATIONS, Matthew Luckiesh. Thorough description and discussion of optical illusion, geometric and perspective, particularly; size and shape distortions, illusions of color, of motion; natural illusions; use of illusion in art and magic, industry, etc. Most useful today with op art, also for classical art. Scores of effects illustrated. Introduction by William H. Ittleson. 100 illustrations. xxi + 252pp.
21530-X Paperbound $2.00

A HANDBOOK OF ANATOMY FOR ART STUDENTS, Arthur Thomson. Thorough, virtually exhaustive coverage of skeletal structure, musculature, etc. Full text, supplemented by anatomical diagrams and drawings and by photographs of undraped figures. Unique in its comparison of male and female forms, pointing out differences of contour, texture, form. 211 figures, 40 drawings, 86 photographs. xx + 459pp. 5⅜ x 8⅜. 21163-0 Paperbound $3.50

150 MASTERPIECES OF DRAWING, Selected by Anthony Toney. Full page reproductions of drawings from the early 16th to the end of the 18th century, all beautifully reproduced: Rembrandt, Michelangelo, Dürer, Fragonard, Urs, Graf, Wouwerman, many others. First-rate browsing book, model book for artists. xviii + 150pp. 8⅜ x 11¼. 21032-4 Paperbound $2.50

THE LATER WORK OF AUBREY BEARDSLEY, Aubrey Beardsley. Exotic, erotic, ironic masterpieces in full maturity: Comedy Ballet, Venus and Tannhauser, Pierrot, Lysistrata, Rape of the Lock, Savoy material, Ali Baba, Volpone, etc. This material revolutionized the art world, and is still powerful, fresh, brilliant. With *The Early Work,* all Beardsley's finest work. 174 plates, 2 in color. xiv + 176pp. 8⅛ x 11.
21817-1 Paperbound $3.00

DRAWINGS OF REMBRANDT, Rembrandt van Rijn. Complete reproduction of fabulously rare edition by Lippmann and Hofstede de Groot, completely reedited, updated, improved by Prof. Seymour Slive, Fogg Museum. Portraits, Biblical sketches, landscapes, Oriental types, nudes, episodes from classical mythology—All Rembrandt's fertile genius. Also selection of drawings by his pupils and followers. "Stunning volumes," *Saturday Review.* 550 illustrations. lxxviii + 552pp. 9⅛ x 12¼. 21485-0, 21486-9 Two volumes, Paperbound $10.00

THE DISASTERS OF WAR, Francisco Goya. One of the masterpieces of Western civilization—83 etchings that record Goya's shattering, bitter reaction to the Napoleonic war that swept through Spain after the insurrection of 1808 and to war in general. Reprint of the first edition, with three additional plates from Boston's Museum of Fine Arts. All plates facsimile size. Introduction by Philip Hofer, Fogg Museum. v + 97pp. 9⅜ x 8¼. 21872-4 Paperbound $2.00

GRAPHIC WORKS OF ODILON REDON. Largest collection of Redon's graphic works ever assembled: 172 lithographs, 28 etchings and engravings, 9 drawings. These include some of his most famous works. All the plates from *Odilon Redon: oeuvre graphique complet,* plus additional plates. New introduction and caption translations by Alfred Werner. 209 illustrations. xxvii + 209pp. 9⅛ x 12¼.
21966-8 Paperbound $4.50

DESIGN BY ACCIDENT; A BOOK OF "ACCIDENTAL EFFECTS" FOR ARTISTS AND DESIGNERS, James F. O'Brien. Create your own unique, striking, imaginative effects by "controlled accident" interaction of materials: paints and lacquers, oil and water based paints, splatter, crackling materials, shatter, similar items. Everything you do will be different; first book on this limitless art, so useful to both fine artist and commercial artist. Full instructions. 192 plates showing "accidents," 8 in color. viii + 215pp. 8⅜ x 11¼. 21942-9 Paperbound $3.50

THE BOOK OF SIGNS, Rudolf Koch. Famed German type designer draws 493 beautiful symbols: religious, mystical, alchemical, imperial, property marks, runes, etc. Remarkable fusion of traditional and modern. Good for suggestions of timelessness, smartness, modernity. Text. vi + 104pp. 6⅛ x 9¼.
20162-7 Paperbound $1.25

HISTORY OF INDIAN AND INDONESIAN ART, Ananda K. Coomaraswamy. An unabridged republication of one of the finest books by a great scholar in Eastern art. Rich in descriptive material, history, social backgrounds; Sunga reliefs, Rajput paintings, Gupta temples, Burmese frescoes, textiles, jewelry, sculpture, etc. 400 photos. viii + 423pp. 6⅜ x 9¾. 21436-2 Paperbound $5.00

PRIMITIVE ART, Franz Boas. America's foremost anthropologist surveys textiles, ceramics, woodcarving, basketry, metalwork, etc.; patterns, technology, creation of symbols, style origins. All areas of world, but very full on Northwest Coast Indians. More than 350 illustrations of baskets, boxes, totem poles, weapons, etc. 378 pp.
20025-6 Paperbound $3.00

THE GENTLEMAN AND CABINET MAKER'S DIRECTOR, Thomas Chippendale. Full reprint (third edition, 1762) of most influential furniture book of all time, by master cabinetmaker. 200 plates, illustrating chairs, sofas, mirrors, tables, cabinets, plus 24 photographs of surviving pieces. Biographical introduction by N. Bienenstock. vi + 249pp. 9⅞ x 12¾. 21601-2 Paperbound $4.00

AMERICAN ANTIQUE FURNITURE, Edgar G. Miller, Jr. The basic coverage of all American furniture before 1840. Individual chapters cover type of furniture—clocks, tables, sideboards, etc.—chronologically, with inexhaustible wealth of data. More than 2100 photographs, all identified, commented on. Essential to all early American collectors. Introduction by H. E. Keyes. vi + 1106pp. 7⅞ x 10¾.
21599-7, 21600-4 Two volumes, Paperbound $11.00

PENNSYLVANIA DUTCH AMERICAN FOLK ART, Henry J. Kauffman. 279 photos, 28 drawings of tulipware, Fraktur script, painted tinware, toys, flowered furniture, quilts, samplers, hex signs, house interiors, etc. Full descriptive text. Excellent for tourist, rewarding for designer, collector. Map. 146pp. 7⅞ x 10¾.
21205-X Paperbound $2.50

EARLY NEW ENGLAND GRAVESTONE RUBBINGS, Edmund V. Gillon, Jr. 43 photographs, 226 carefully reproduced rubbings show heavily symbolic, sometimes macabre early gravestones, up to early 19th century. Remarkable early American primitive art, occasionally strikingly beautiful; always powerful. Text. xxvi + 207pp. 8⅜ x 11¼. 21380-3 Paperbound $3.50

ALPHABETS AND ORNAMENTS, Ernst Lehner. Well-known pictorial source for decorative alphabets, script examples, cartouches, frames, decorative title pages, calligraphic initials, borders, similar material. 14th to 19th century, mostly European. Useful in almost any graphic arts designing, varied styles. 750 illustrations. 256pp. 7 x 10. 21905-4 Paperbound $4.00

PAINTING: A CREATIVE APPROACH, Norman Colquhoun. For the beginner simple guide provides an instructive approach to painting: major stumbling blocks for beginner; overcoming them, technical points; paints and pigments; oil painting; watercolor and other media and color. New section on "plastic" paints. Glossary. Formerly *Paint Your Own Pictures*. 221pp. 22000-1 Paperbound $1.75

THE ENJOYMENT AND USE OF COLOR, Walter Sargent. Explanation of the relations between colors themselves and between colors in nature and art, including hundreds of little-known facts about color values, intensities, effects of high and low illumination, complementary colors. Many practical hints for painters, references to great masters. 7 color plates, 29 illustrations. x + 274pp.
20944-X Paperbound $2.75

THE NOTEBOOKS OF LEONARDO DA VINCI, compiled and edited by Jean Paul Richter. 1566 extracts from original manuscripts reveal the full range of Leonardo's versatile genius: all his writings on painting, sculpture, architecture, anatomy, astronomy, geography, topography, physiology, mining, music, etc., in both Italian and English, with 186 plates of manuscript pages and more than 500 additional drawings. Includes studies for the Last Supper, the lost Sforza monument, and other works. Total of xlvii + 866pp. 7⅞ x 10¾.
22572-0, 22573-9 Two volumes, Paperbound $10.00

MONTGOMERY WARD CATALOGUE OF 1895. Tea gowns, yards of flannel and pillow-case lace, stereoscopes, books of gospel hymns, the New Improved Singer Sewing Machine, side saddles, milk skimmers, straight-edged razors, high-button shoes, spittoons, and on and on . . . listing some 25,000 items, practically all illustrated. Essential to the shoppers of the 1890's, it is our truest record of the spirit of the period. Unaltered reprint of Issue No. 57, Spring and Summer 1895. Introduction by Boris Emmet. Innumerable illustrations. xiii + 624pp. 8½ x 11⅝.
22377-9 Paperbound $6.95

THE CRYSTAL PALACE EXHIBITION ILLUSTRATED CATALOGUE (LONDON, 1851). One of the wonders of the modern world—the Crystal Palace Exhibition in which all the nations of the civilized world exhibited their achievements in the arts and sciences—presented in an equally important illustrated catalogue. More than 1700 items pictured with accompanying text—ceramics, textiles, cast-iron work, carpets, pianos, sleds, razors, wall-papers, billiard tables, beehives, silverware and hundreds of other artifacts—represent the focal point of Victorian culture in the Western World. Probably the largest collection of Victorian decorative art ever assembled—indispensable for antiquarians and designers. Unabridged republication of the Art-Journal Catalogue of the Great Exhibition of 1851, with all terminal essays. New introduction by John Gloag, F.S.A. xxxiv + 426pp. 9 x 12.
22503-8 Paperbound $5.00

A History of Costume, Carl Köhler. Definitive history, based on surviving pieces of clothing primarily, and paintings, statues, etc. secondarily. Highly readable text, supplemented by 594 illustrations of costumes of the ancient Mediterranean peoples, Greece and Rome, the Teutonic prehistoric period; costumes of the Middle Ages, Renaissance, Baroque, 18th and 19th centuries. Clear, measured patterns are provided for many clothing articles. Approach is practical throughout. Enlarged by Emma von Sichart. 464pp. 21030-8 Paperbound $3.50

Oriental Rugs, Antique and Modern, Walter A. Hawley. A complete and authoritative treatise on the Oriental rug—where they are made, by whom and how, designs and symbols, characteristics in detail of the six major groups, how to distinguish them and how to buy them. Detailed technical data is provided on periods, weaves, warps, wefts, textures, sides, ends and knots, although no technical background is required for an understanding. 11 color plates, 80 halftones, 4 maps. vi + 320pp. 6⅛ x 9⅛. 22366-3 Paperbound $5.00

Ten Books on Architecture, Vitruvius. By any standards the most important book on architecture ever written. Early Roman discussion of aesthetics of building, construction methods, orders, sites, and every other aspect of architecture has inspired, instructed architecture for about 2,000 years. Stands behind Palladio, Michelangelo, Bramante, Wren, countless others. Definitive Morris H. Morgan translation. 68 illustrations. xii + 331pp. 20645-9 Paperbound $3.00

The Four Books of Architecture, Andrea Palladio. Translated into every major Western European language in the two centuries following its publication in 1570, this has been one of the most influential books in the history of architecture. Complete reprint of the 1738 Isaac Ware edition. New introduction by Adolf Placzek, Columbia Univ. 216 plates. xxii + 110pp. of text. 9½ x 12¾. 21308-0 Clothbound $12.50

Sticks and Stones: A Study of American Architecture and Civilization, Lewis Mumford.One of the great classics of American cultural history. American architecture from the medieval-inspired earliest forms to the early 20th century; evolution of structure and style, and reciprocal influences on environment. 21 photographic illustrations. 238pp. 20202-X Paperbound $2.00

The American Builder's Companion, Asher Benjamin. The most widely used early 19th century architectural style and source book, for colonial up into Greek Revival periods. Extensive development of geometry of carpentering, construction of sashes, frames, doors, stairs; plans and elevations of domestic and other buildings. Hundreds of thousands of houses were built according to this book, now invaluable to historians, architects, restorers, etc. 1827 edition. 59 plates. 114pp. 7⅞ x 10¾. 22236-5 Paperbound $3.50

Dutch Houses in the Hudson Valley Before 1776, Helen Wilkinson Reynolds. The standard survey of the Dutch colonial house and outbuildings, with constructional features, decoration, and local history associated with individual homesteads. Introduction by Franklin D. Roosevelt. Map. 150 illustrations. 469pp. 6⅝ x 9¼. 21469-9 Paperbound $5.00

THE ARCHITECTURE OF COUNTRY HOUSES, Andrew J. Downing. Together with Vaux's *Villas and Cottages* this is the basic book for Hudson River Gothic architecture of the middle Victorian period. Full, sound discussions of general aspects of housing, architecture, style, decoration, furnishing, together with scores of detailed house plans, illustrations of specific buildings, accompanied by full text. Perhaps the most influential single American architectural book. 1850 edition. Introduction by J. Stewart Johnson. 321 figures, 34 architectural designs. xvi + 560pp.
22003-6 Paperbound $4.00

LOST EXAMPLES OF COLONIAL ARCHITECTURE, John Mead Howells. Full-page photographs of buildings that have disappeared or been so altered as to be denatured, including many designed by major early American architects. 245 plates. xvii + 248pp. 7⅞ x 10¾. 21143-6 Paperbound $3.50

DOMESTIC ARCHITECTURE OF THE AMERICAN COLONIES AND OF THE EARLY REPUBLIC, Fiske Kimball. Foremost architect and restorer of Williamsburg and Monticello covers nearly 200 homes between 1620-1825. Architectural details, construction, style features, special fixtures, floor plans, etc. Generally considered finest work in its area. 219 illustrations of houses, doorways, windows, capital mantels. xx + 314pp. 7⅞ x 10¾. 21743-4 Paperbound $4.00

EARLY AMERICAN ROOMS: 1650-1858, edited by Russell Hawes Kettell. Tour of 12 rooms, each representative of a different era in American history and each furnished, decorated, designed and occupied in the style of the era. 72 plans and elevations, 8-page color section, etc., show fabrics, wall papers, arrangements, etc. Full descriptive text. xvii + 200pp. of text. 8⅜ x 11¼.
21633-0 Paperbound $5.00

THE FITZWILLIAM VIRGINAL BOOK, edited by J. Fuller Maitland and W. B. Squire. Full modern printing of famous early 17th-century ms. volume of 300 works by Morley, Byrd, Bull, Gibbons, etc. For piano or other modern keyboard instrument; easy to read format. xxxvi + 938pp. 8⅜ x 11.
21068-5, 21069-3 Two volumes, Paperbound $10.00

KEYBOARD MUSIC, Johann Sebastian Bach. Bach Gesellschaft edition. A rich selection of Bach's masterpieces for the harpsichord: the six English Suites, six French Suites, the six Partitas (Clavierübung part I), the Goldberg Variations (Clavierübung part IV), the fifteen Two-Part Inventions and the fifteen Three-Part Sinfonias. Clearly reproduced on large sheets with ample margins; eminently playable. vi + 312pp. 8⅛ x 11. 22360-4 Paperbound $5.00

THE MUSIC OF BACH: AN INTRODUCTION, Charles Sanford Terry. A fine, nontechnical introduction to Bach's music, both instrumental and vocal. Covers organ music, chamber music, passion music, other types. Analyzes themes, developments, innovations. x + 114pp. 21075-8 Paperbound $1.50

BEETHOVEN AND HIS NINE SYMPHONIES, Sir George Grove. Noted British musicologist provides best history, analysis, commentary on symphonies. Very thorough, rigorously accurate; necessary to both advanced student and amateur music lover. 436 musical passages. vii + 407 pp. 20334-4 Paperbound $2.75

JOHANN SEBASTIAN BACH, Philipp Spitta. One of the great classics of musicology, this definitive analysis of Bach's music (and life) has never been surpassed. Lucid, nontechnical analyses of hundreds of pieces (30 pages devoted to St. Matthew Passion, 26 to B Minor Mass). Also includes major analysis of 18th-century music. 450 musical examples. 40-page musical supplement. Total of xx + 1799pp.
(EUK) 22278-0, 22279-9 Two volumes, Clothbound $17.50

MOZART AND HIS PIANO CONCERTOS, Cuthbert Girdlestone. The only full-length study of an important area of Mozart's creativity. Provides detailed analyses of all 23 concertos, traces inspirational sources. 417 musical examples. Second edition. 509pp. 21271-8 Paperbound $3.50

THE PERFECT WAGNERITE: A COMMENTARY ON THE NIBLUNG'S RING, George Bernard Shaw. Brilliant and still relevant criticism in remarkable essays on Wagner's Ring cycle, Shaw's ideas on political and social ideology behind the plots, role of Leitmotifs, vocal requisites, etc. Prefaces. xxi + 136pp.
(USO) 21707-8 Paperbound $1.50

DON GIOVANNI, W. A. Mozart. Complete libretto, modern English translation; biographies of composer and librettist; accounts of early performances and critical reaction. Lavishly illustrated. All the material you need to understand and appreciate this great work. Dover Opera Guide and Libretto Series; translated and introduced by Ellen Bleiler. 92 illustrations. 209pp.
21134-7 Paperbound $2.00

BASIC ELECTRICITY, U. S. Bureau of Naval Personel. Originally a training course, best non-technical coverage of basic theory of electricity and its applications. Fundamental concepts, batteries, circuits, conductors and wiring techniques, AC and DC, inductance and capacitance, generators, motors, transformers, magnetic amplifiers, synchros, servomechanisms, etc. Also covers blue-prints, electrical diagrams, etc. Many questions, with answers. 349 illustrations. x + 448pp. 6½ x 9¼.
20973-3 Paperbound $3.50

REPRODUCTION OF SOUND, Edgar Villchur. Thorough coverage for laymen of high fidelity systems, reproducing systems in general, needles, amplifiers, preamps, loudspeakers, feedback, explaining physical background. "A rare talent for making technicalities vividly comprehensible," R. Darrell, *High Fidelity*. 69 figures. iv + 92pp. 21515-6 Paperbound $1.25

HEAR ME TALKIN' TO YA: THE STORY OF JAZZ AS TOLD BY THE MEN WHO MADE IT, Nat Shapiro and Nat Hentoff. Louis Armstrong, Fats Waller, Jo Jones, Clarence Williams, Billy Holiday, Duke Ellington, Jelly Roll Morton and dozens of other jazz greats tell how it was in Chicago's South Side, New Orleans, depression Harlem and the modern West Coast as jazz was born and grew. xvi + 429pp.
21726-4 Paperbound $3.00

FABLES OF AESOP, translated by Sir Roger L'Estrange. A reproduction of the very rare 1931 Paris edition; a selection of the most interesting fables, together with 50 imaginative drawings by Alexander Calder. v + 128pp. 6½x9¼.
21780-9 Paperbound $1.50

AGAINST THE GRAIN (A REBOURS), Joris K. Huysmans. Filled with weird images, evidences of a bizarre imagination, exotic experiments with hallucinatory drugs, rich tastes and smells and the diversions of its sybarite hero Duc Jean des Esseintes, this classic novel pushed 19th-century literary decadence to its limits. Full unabridged edition. Do not confuse this with abridged editions generally sold. Introduction by Havelock Ellis. xlix + 206pp. 22190-3 Paperbound $2.00

VARIORUM SHAKESPEARE: HAMLET. Edited by Horace H. Furness; a landmark of American scholarship. Exhaustive footnotes and appendices treat all doubtful words and phrases, as well as suggested critical emendations throughout the play's history. First volume contains editor's own text, collated with all Quartos and Folios. Second volume contains full first Quarto, translations of Shakespeare's sources (Belleforest, and Saxo Grammaticus), Der Bestrafte Brudermord, and many essays on critical and historical points of interest by major authorities of past and present. Includes details of staging and costuming over the years. By far the best edition available for serious students of Shakespeare. Total of xx + 905pp.
21004-9, 21005-7, 2 volumes, Paperbound $7.00

A LIFE OF WILLIAM SHAKESPEARE, Sir Sidney Lee. This is the standard life of Shakespeare, summarizing everything known about Shakespeare and his plays. Incredibly rich in material, broad in coverage, clear and judicious, it has served thousands as the best introduction to Shakespeare. 1931 edition. 9 plates. xxix + 792pp. (USO) 21967-4 Paperbound $3.75

MASTERS OF THE DRAMA, John Gassner. Most comprehensive history of the drama in print, covering every tradition from Greeks to modern Europe and America, including India, Far East, etc. Covers more than 800 dramatists, 2000 plays, with biographical material, plot summaries, theatre history, criticism, etc. "Best of its kind in English," *New Republic*. 77 illustrations. xxii + 890pp.
20100-7 Clothbound $8.50

THE EVOLUTION OF THE ENGLISH LANGUAGE, George McKnight. The growth of English, from the 14th century to the present. Unusual, non-technical account presents basic information in very interesting form: sound shifts, change in grammar and syntax, vocabulary growth, similar topics. Abundantly illustrated with quotations. Formerly *Modern English in the Making*. xii + 590pp.
21932-1 Paperbound $3.50

AN ETYMOLOGICAL DICTIONARY OF MODERN ENGLISH, Ernest Weekley. Fullest, richest work of its sort, by foremost British lexicographer. Detailed word histories, including many colloquial and archaic words; extensive quotations. Do not confuse this with the Concise Etymological Dictionary, which is much abridged. Total of xxvii + 830pp. 6½ x 9¼.
21873-2, 21874-0 Two volumes, Paperbound $7.90

FLATLAND: A ROMANCE OF MANY DIMENSIONS, E. A. Abbott. Classic of science-fiction explores ramifications of life in a two-dimensional world, and what happens when a three-dimensional being intrudes. Amusing reading, but also useful as introduction to thought about hyperspace. Introduction by Banesh Hoffmann. 16 illustrations. xx + 103pp. 20001-9 Paperbound $1.00

POEMS OF ANNE BRADSTREET, edited with an introduction by Robert Hutchinson. A new selection of poems by America's first poet and perhaps the first significant woman poet in the English language. 48 poems display her development in works of considerable variety—love poems, domestic poems, religious meditations, formal elegies, "quaternions," etc. Notes, bibliography. viii + 222pp.
22160-1 Paperbound $2.50

THREE GOTHIC NOVELS: THE CASTLE OF OTRANTO BY HORACE WALPOLE; VATHEK BY WILLIAM BECKFORD; THE VAMPYRE BY JOHN POLIDORI, WITH FRAGMENT OF A NOVEL BY LORD BYRON, edited by E. F. Bleiler. The first Gothic novel, by Walpole; the finest Oriental tale in English, by Beckford; powerful Romantic supernatural story in versions by Polidori and Byron. All extremely important in history of literature; all still exciting, packed with supernatural thrills, ghosts, haunted castles, magic, etc. xl + 291pp.
21232-7 Paperbound $2.50

THE BEST TALES OF HOFFMANN, E. T. A. Hoffmann. 10 of Hoffmann's most important stories, in modern re-editings of standard translations: Nutcracker and the King of Mice, Signor Formica, Automata, The Sandman, Rath Krespel, The Golden Flowerpot, Master Martin the Cooper, The Mines of Falun, The King's Betrothed, A New Year's Eve Adventure. 7 illustrations by Hoffmann. Edited by E. F. Bleiler. xxxix + 419pp. 21793-0 Paperbound $3.00

GHOST AND HORROR STORIES OF AMBROSE BIERCE, Ambrose Bierce. 23 strikingly modern stories of the horrors latent in the human mind: The Eyes of the Panther, The Damned Thing, An Occurrence at Owl Creek Bridge, An Inhabitant of Carcosa, etc., plus the dream-essay, Visions of the Night. Edited by E. F. Bleiler. xxii + 199pp. 20767-6 Paperbound $1.50

BEST GHOST STORIES OF J. S. LEFANU, J. Sheridan LeFanu. Finest stories by Victorian master often considered greatest supernatural writer of all. Carmilla, Green Tea, The Haunted Baronet, The Familiar, and 12 others. Most never before available in the U. S. A. Edited by E. F. Bleiler. 8 illustrations from Victorian publications. xvii + 467pp. 20415-4 Paperbound $3.00

MATHEMATICAL FOUNDATIONS OF INFORMATION THEORY, A. I. Khinchin. Comprehensive introduction to work of Shannon, McMillan, Feinstein and Khinchin, placing these investigations on a rigorous mathematical basis. Covers entropy concept in probability theory, uniqueness theorem, Shannon's inequality, ergodic sources, the E property, martingale concept, noise, Feinstein's fundamental lemma, Shanon's first and second theorems. Translated by R. A. Silverman and M. D. Friedman. iii + 120pp. 60434-9 Paperbound $2.00

SEVEN SCIENCE FICTION NOVELS, H. G. Wells. The standard collection of the great novels. Complete, unabridged. *First Men in the Moon, Island of Dr. Moreau, War of the Worlds, Food of the Gods, Invisible Man, Time Machine, In the Days of the Comet.* Not only science fiction fans, but every educated person owes it to himself to read these novels. 1015pp. (USO) 20264-X Clothbound $6.00

LAST AND FIRST MEN AND STAR MAKER, TWO SCIENCE FICTION NOVELS, Olaf Stapledon. Greatest future histories in science fiction. In the first, human intelligence is the "hero," through strange paths of evolution, interplanetary invasions, incredible technologies, near extinctions and reemergences. Star Maker describes the quest of a band of star rovers for intelligence itself, through time and space: weird inhuman civilizations, crustacean minds, symbiotic worlds, etc. Complete, unabridged. v + 438pp. (USO) 21962-3 Paperbound $2.50

THREE PROPHETIC NOVELS, H. G. WELLS. Stages of a consistently planned future for mankind. *When the Sleeper Wakes,* and *A Story of the Days to Come,* anticipate *Brave New World* and *1984,* in the 21st Century; *The Time Machine,* only complete version in print, shows farther future and the end of mankind. All show Wells's greatest gifts as storyteller and novelist. Edited by E. F. Bleiler. x + 335pp. (USO) 20605-X Paperbound $2.50

THE DEVIL'S DICTIONARY, Ambrose Bierce. America's own Oscar Wilde—Ambrose Bierce—offers his barbed iconoclastic wisdom in over 1,000 definitions hailed by H. L. Mencken as "some of the most gorgeous witticisms in the English language." 145pp. 20487-1 Paperbound $1.25

MAX AND MORITZ, Wilhelm Busch. Great children's classic, father of comic strip, of two bad boys, Max and Moritz. Also Ker and Plunk (Plisch und Plumm), Cat and Mouse, Deceitful Henry, Ice-Peter, The Boy and the Pipe, and five other pieces. Original German, with English translation. Edited by H. Arthur Klein; translations by various hands and H. Arthur Klein. vi + 216pp.
20181-3 Paperbound $2.00

PIGS IS PIGS AND OTHER FAVORITES, Ellis Parker Butler. The title story is one of the best humor short stories, as Mike Flannery obfuscates biology and English. Also included, That Pup of Murchison's, The Great American Pie Company, and Perkins of Portland. 14 illustrations. v + 109pp. 21532-6 Paperbound $1.25

THE PETERKIN PAPERS, Lucretia P. Hale. It takes genius to be as stupidly mad as the Peterkins, as they decide to become wise, celebrate the "Fourth," keep a cow, and otherwise strain the resources of the Lady from Philadelphia. Basic book of American humor. 153 illustrations. 219pp. 20794-3 Paperbound $1.50

PERRAULT'S FAIRY TALES, translated by A. E. Johnson and S. R. Littlewood, with 34 full-page illustrations by Gustave Doré. All the original Perrault stories—Cinderella, Sleeping Beauty, Bluebeard, Little Red Riding Hood, Puss in Boots, Tom Thumb, etc.—with their witty verse morals and the magnificent illustrations of Doré. One of the five or six great books of European fairy tales. viii + 117pp. 8⅛ x 11. 22311-6 Paperbound $2.00

OLD HUNGARIAN FAIRY TALES, Baroness Orczy. Favorites translated and adapted by author of the *Scarlet Pimpernel.* Eight fairy tales include "The Suitors of Princess Fire-Fly," "The Twin Hunchbacks," "Mr. Cuttlefish's Love Story," and "The Enchanted Cat." This little volume of magic and adventure will captivate children as it has for generations. 90 drawings by Montagu Barstow. 96pp.
22293-4 Paperbound $1.95

THE RED FAIRY BOOK, Andrew Lang. Lang's color fairy books have long been children's favorites. This volume includes Rapunzel, Jack and the Bean-stalk and 35 other stories, familiar and unfamiliar. 4 plates, 93 illustrations x + 367pp.
21673-X Paperbound $2.50

THE BLUE FAIRY BOOK, Andrew Lang. Lang's tales come from all countries and all times. Here are 37 tales from Grimm, the Arabian Nights, Greek Mythology, and other fascinating sources. 8 plates, 130 illustrations. xi + 390pp.
21437-0 Paperbound $2.50

HOUSEHOLD STORIES BY THE BROTHERS GRIMM. Classic English-language edition of the well-known tales — Rumpelstiltskin, Snow White, Hansel and Gretel, The Twelve Brothers, Faithful John, Rapunzel, Tom Thumb (52 stories in all). Translated into simple, straightforward English by Lucy Crane. Ornamented with headpieces, vignettes, elaborate decorative initials and a dozen full-page illustrations by Walter Crane. x + 269pp. 21080-4 Paperbound **$2.00**

THE MERRY ADVENTURES OF ROBIN HOOD, Howard Pyle. The finest modern versions of the traditional ballads and tales about the great English outlaw. Howard Pyle's complete prose version, with every word, every illustration of the first edition. Do not confuse this facsimile of the original (1883) with modern editions that change text or illustrations. 23 plates plus many page decorations. xxii + 296pp.
22043-5 Paperbound $2.50

THE STORY OF KING ARTHUR AND HIS KNIGHTS, Howard Pyle. The finest children's version of the life of King Arthur; brilliantly retold by Pyle, with 48 of his most imaginative illustrations. xviii + 313pp. $6\frac{1}{8}$ x $9\frac{1}{4}$.
21445-1 Paperbound $2.50

THE WONDERFUL WIZARD OF OZ, L. Frank Baum. America's finest children's book in facsimile of first edition with all Denslow illustrations in full color. The edition a child should have. Introduction by Martin Gardner. 23 color plates, scores of drawings. iv + 267pp. 20691-2 Paperbound $2.50

THE MARVELOUS LAND OF OZ, L. Frank Baum. The second Oz book, every bit as imaginative as the Wizard. The hero is a boy named Tip, but the Scarecrow and the Tin Woodman are back, as is the Oz magic. 16 color plates, 120 drawings by John R. Neill. 287pp. 20692-0 Paperbound $2.50

THE MAGICAL MONARCH OF MO, L. Frank Baum. Remarkable adventures in a land even stranger than Oz. The best of Baum's books not in the Oz series. 15 color plates and dozens of drawings by Frank Verbeck. xviii + 237pp.
21892-9 Paperbound $2.25

THE BAD CHILD'S BOOK OF BEASTS, MORE BEASTS FOR WORSE CHILDREN, A MORAL ALPHABET, Hilaire Belloc. Three complete humor classics in one volume. Be kind to the frog, and do not call him names . . . and 28 other whimsical animals. Familiar favorites and some not so well known. Illustrated by Basil Blackwell. 156pp. (USO) 20749-8 Paperbound $1.50

EAST O' THE SUN AND WEST O' THE MOON, George W. Dasent. Considered the best of all translations of these Norwegian folk tales, this collection has been enjoyed by generations of children (and folklorists too). Includes True and Untrue, Why the Sea is Salt, East O' the Sun and West O' the Moon, Why the Bear is Stumpy-Tailed, Boots and the Troll, The Cock and the Hen, Rich Peter the Pedlar, and 52 more. The only edition with all 59 tales. 77 illustrations by Erik Werenskiold and Theodor Kittelsen. xv + 418pp. 22521-6 Paperbound $3.50

GOOPS AND HOW TO BE THEM, Gelett Burgess. Classic of tongue-in-cheek humor, masquerading as etiquette book. 87 verses, twice as many cartoons, show mischievous Goops as they demonstrate to children virtues of table manners, neatness, courtesy, etc. Favorite for generations. viii + 88pp. 6½ x 9¼. 22233-0 Paperbound $1.25

ALICE'S ADVENTURES UNDER GROUND, Lewis Carroll. The first version, quite different from the final *Alice in Wonderland,* printed out by Carroll himself with his own illustrations. Complete facsimile of the "million dollar" manuscript Carroll gave to Alice Liddell in 1864. Introduction by Martin Gardner. viii + 96pp. Title and dedication pages in color. 21482-6 Paperbound $1.25

THE BROWNIES, THEIR BOOK, Palmer Cox. Small as mice, cunning as foxes, exuberant and full of mischief, the Brownies go to the zoo, toy shop, seashore, circus, etc., in 24 verse adventures and 266 illustrations. Long a favorite, since their first appearance in St. Nicholas Magazine. xi + 144pp. 6⅝ x 9¼. 21265-3 Paperbound $1.75

SONGS OF CHILDHOOD, Walter De La Mare. Published (under the pseudonym Walter Ramal) when De La Mare was only 29, this charming collection has long been a favorite children's book. A facsimile of the first edition in paper, the 47 poems capture the simplicity of the nursery rhyme and the ballad, including such lyrics as I Met Eve, Tartary, The Silver Penny. vii + 106pp. (USO) 21972-0 Paperbound $1.25

THE COMPLETE NONSENSE OF EDWARD LEAR, Edward Lear. The finest 19th-century humorist-cartoonist in full: all nonsense limericks, zany alphabets, Owl and Pussycat, songs, nonsense botany, and more than 500 illustrations by Lear himself. Edited by Holbrook Jackson. xxix + 287pp. (USO) 20167-8 Paperbound $2.00

BILLY WHISKERS: THE AUTOBIOGRAPHY OF A GOAT, Frances Trego Montgomery. A favorite of children since the early 20th century, here are the escapades of that rambunctious, irresistible and mischievous goat—Billy Whiskers. Much in the spirit of *Peck's Bad Boy,* this is a book that children never tire of reading or hearing. All the original familiar illustrations by W. H. Fry are included: 6 color plates, 18 black and white drawings. 159pp. 22345-0 Paperbound $2.00

MOTHER GOOSE MELODIES. Faithful republication of the fabulously rare Munroe and Francis "copyright 1833" Boston edition—the most important Mother Goose collection, usually referred to as the "original." Familiar rhymes plus many rare ones, with wonderful old woodcut illustrations. Edited by E. F. Bleiler. 128pp. 4½ x 6⅜. 22577-1 Paperbound $1.00

TWO LITTLE SAVAGES; BEING THE ADVENTURES OF TWO BOYS WHO LIVED AS INDIANS AND WHAT THEY LEARNED, Ernest Thompson Seton. Great classic of nature and boyhood provides a vast range of woodlore in most palatable form, a genuinely entertaining story. Two farm boys build a teepee in woods and live in it for a month, working out Indian solutions to living problems, star lore, birds and animals, plants, etc. 293 illustrations. vii + 286pp.
20985-7 Paperbound $2.50

PETER PIPER'S PRACTICAL PRINCIPLES OF PLAIN & PERFECT PRONUNCIATION. Alliterative jingles and tongue-twisters of surprising charm, that made their first appearance in America about 1830. Republished in full with the spirited woodcut illustrations from this earliest American edition. 32pp. 4½ x 6⅜.
22560-7 Paperbound $1.00

SCIENCE EXPERIMENTS AND AMUSEMENTS FOR CHILDREN, Charles Vivian. 73 easy experiments, requiring only materials found at home or easily available, such as candles, coins, steel wool, etc.; illustrate basic phenomena like vacuum, simple chemical reaction, etc. All safe. Modern, well-planned. Formerly *Science Games for Children.* 102 photos, numerous drawings. 96pp. 6⅛ x 9¼.
21856-2 Paperbound $1.25

AN INTRODUCTION TO CHESS MOVES AND TACTICS SIMPLY EXPLAINED, Leonard Barden. Informal intermediate introduction, quite strong in explaining reasons for moves. Covers basic material, tactics, important openings, traps, positional play in middle game, end game. Attempts to isolate patterns and recurrent configurations. Formerly *Chess.* 58 figures. 102pp. (USO) 21210-6 Paperbound $1.25

LASKER'S MANUAL OF CHESS, Dr. Emanuel Lasker. Lasker was not only one of the five great World Champions, he was also one of the ablest expositors, theorists, and analysts. In many ways, his Manual, permeated with his philosophy of battle, filled with keen insights, is one of the greatest works ever written on chess. Filled with analyzed games by the great players. A single-volume library that will profit almost any chess player, beginner or master. 308 diagrams. xli x 349pp.
20640-8 Paperbound $2.75

THE MASTER BOOK OF MATHEMATICAL RECREATIONS, Fred Schuh. In opinion of many the finest work ever prepared on mathematical puzzles, stunts, recreations; exhaustively thorough explanations of mathematics involved, analysis of effects, citation of puzzles and games. Mathematics involved is elementary. Translated bv F. Göbel. 194 figures. xxiv + 430pp. 22134-2 Paperbound $3.50

MATHEMATICS, MAGIC AND MYSTERY, Martin Gardner. Puzzle editor for Scientific American explains mathematics behind various mystifying tricks: card tricks, stage "mind reading," coin and match tricks, counting out games, geometric dissections, etc. Probability sets, theory of numbers clearly explained. Also provides more than 400 tricks, guaranteed to work, that you can do. 135 illustrations. xii + 176pp.
20335-2 Paperbound $1.75

MATHEMATICAL PUZZLES FOR BEGINNERS AND ENTHUSIASTS, Geoffrey Mott-Smith. 189 puzzles from easy to difficult—involving arithmetic, logic, algebra, properties of digits, probability, etc.—for enjoyment and mental stimulus. Explanation of mathematical principles behind the puzzles. 135 illustrations. viii + 248pp.
20198-8 Paperbound $1.75

PAPER FOLDING FOR BEGINNERS, William D. Murray and Francis J. Rigney. Easiest book on the market, clearest instructions on making interesting, beautiful origami. Sail boats, cups, roosters, frogs that move legs, bonbon boxes, standing birds, etc. 40 projects; more than 275 diagrams and photographs. 94pp.
20713-7 Paperbound $1.00

TRICKS AND GAMES ON THE POOL TABLE, Fred Herrmann. 79 tricks and games—some solitaires, some for two or more players, some competitive games—to entertain you between formal games. Mystifying shots and throws, unusual caroms, tricks involving such props as cork, coins, a hat, etc. Formerly *Fun on the Pool Table.* 77 figures. 95pp. 21814-7 Paperbound $1.00

HAND SHADOWS TO BE THROWN UPON THE WALL: A SERIES OF NOVEL AND AMUSING FIGURES FORMED BY THE HAND, Henry Bursill. Delightful picturebook from great-grandfather's day shows how to make 18 different hand shadows: a bird that flies, duck that quacks, dog that wags his tail, camel, goose, deer, boy, turtle, etc. Only book of its sort. vi + 33pp. 6½ x 9¼. 21779-5 Paperbound $1.00

WHITTLING AND WOODCARVING, E. J. Tangerman. 18th printing of best book on market. "If you can cut a potato you can carve" toys and puzzles, chains, chessmen, caricatures, masks, frames, woodcut blocks, surface patterns, much more. Information on tools, woods, techniques. Also goes into serious wood sculpture from Middle Ages to present, East and West. 464 photos, figures. x + 293pp.
20965-2 Paperbound $2.00

HISTORY OF PHILOSOPHY, Julián Marias. Possibly the clearest, most easily followed, best planned, most useful one-volume history of philosophy on the market; neither skimpy nor overfull. Full details on system of every major philosopher and dozens of less important thinkers from pre-Socratics up to Existentialism and later. Strong on many European figures usually omitted. Has gone through dozens of editions in Europe. 1966 edition, translated by Stanley Appelbaum and Clarence Strowbridge. xviii + 505pp. 21739-6 Paperbound $3.50

YOGA: A SCIENTIFIC EVALUATION, Kovoor T. Behanan. Scientific but non-technical study of physiological results of yoga exercises; done under auspices of Yale U. Relations to Indian thought, to psychoanalysis, etc. 16 photos. xxiii + 270pp.
20505-3 Paperbound $2.50

Prices subject to change without notice.
Available at your book dealer or write for free catalogue to Dept. GI, Dover Publications, Inc., 180 Varick St., N. Y., N. Y. 10014. Dover publishes more than 150 books each year on science, elementary and advanced mathematics, biology, music, art, literary history, social sciences and other areas.